CLASSICAL INFLUENCES ON WESTERN THOUGHT
A.D. 1650–1870

CLASSICAL
INFLUENCES ON
WESTERN
THOUGHT

A.D. 1650–1870

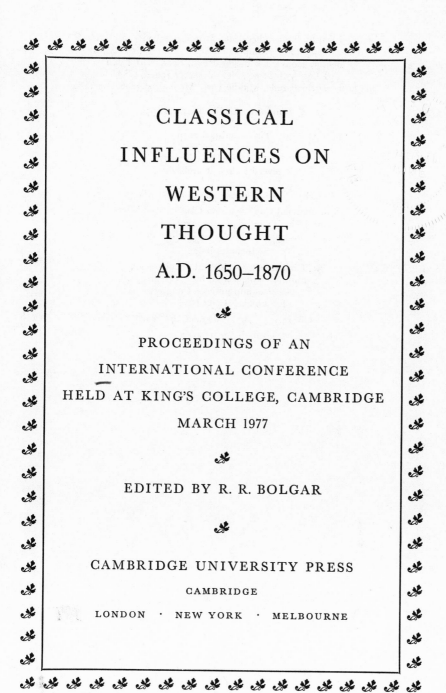

PROCEEDINGS OF AN
INTERNATIONAL CONFERENCE
HELD AT KING'S COLLEGE, CAMBRIDGE
MARCH 1977

EDITED BY R. R. BOLGAR

CAMBRIDGE UNIVERSITY PRESS

CAMBRIDGE

LONDON · NEW YORK · MELBOURNE

Published by the Syndics of the Cambridge University Press
The Pitt Building, Trumpington Street, Cambridge CB2 1RP
Bentley House, 200 Euston Road, London NW1 2DB
32 East 57th Street, New York, NY 10022, USA
296 Beaconsfield Parade, Middle Park, Melbourne 3206, Australia

© Cambridge University Press 1979

First published 1979

Printed in Great Britain at the
University Press, Cambridge

Library of Congress Cataloguing in Publication Data

International Conference on Classical Influences,
3rd, King's College, Cambridge, Eng., 1977.
Classical influences on Western thought A.D. 1650–1870

Includes index

1. Civilization, Occidental – Congresses.
2. Europe – Intellectual life – Congresses.
3. Classical antiquities – Congresses.
I.   Bolgar, R. R. II. Title.

CB245.I57   1977   809′.02   77–91078
ISBN 0 521 21964 7

PREFACE:
THE KING'S COLLEGE CONFERENCE

This volume represents the Proceedings of the Third International Conference on Classical Influences organised at the Research Centre of King's College, Cambridge, by Dr. R. R. Bolgar and myself, with generous help from the College in funds and facilities. The first took place on 8–12 April 1969, when twenty-seven scholars spoke, some for half-an-hour, some for ten minutes. The subject was *Classical Influences on European Culture, A.D. 500–1500*, and the Proceedings, edited by Dr Bolgar and handsomely printed by the Cambridge University Press, were published in 1971. The second took place on 7–11 April 1974, when twenty-eight scholars spoke, fifteen minutes instead of ten being allowed for the shorter papers. The title made the object of the conference more explicit: *Classical Influences on European Culture, A.D. 1500–1700: What Needs to be Done?* The Proceedings were published in the same way, in 1976.

The present Conference was held on 27–31 March 1977. The form was as before: there were no complimentary introductions and no formal discussion. Though anyone interested was invited to attend the sessions, and satisfactory numbers did, the conditions were sufficiently intimate for discussion to take place easily between interested individuals over coffee or wine after the papers. On this occasion however it seemed appropriate to have fewer speakers and to allow them more time. Four of the twenty spoke for an hour after dinner, the rest for half-an-hour. Professor Owen generously agreed at short notice to speak on Aristotle, Professor G. Patzig having withdrawn. Dr Bolgar read a paper himself besides contributing the final summing-up which has been a feature of these conferences and the basis of his Introductions to the Proceedings.

The starting-date of 1650 was chosen, despite the overlap, because, as things turned out, hardly anyone at the previous Conference had touched on the second half of the seventeenth century. It also seemed appropriate to give rather more of a lead as to subject when inviting speakers, and to limit to certain aspects a field which would otherwise have been too vast. Literature and art were therefore deliberately excluded for this occasion.

As before, we had the help of a Committee consisting of Cambridge scholars – Dr C. P. Courtney and Professors M. I. Finley, L. W Forster, E. J. Kenney, U. Limentani and G. E. L. Owen – to whom we are very grateful. Again also we had invaluable advice from Professor J. B. Trapp, now Director of the Warburg Institute, who attended the Conference as a guest of honour, as did also Professor A. Dihle of Heidelberg and Sir Isaiah Berlin. Dr J. J. Hall again kindly arranged an exhibition at the University Library of books relevant to the Conference, and Mr Michael Roberts, Mrs E. L. Brown and Mrs H. M. Clark helped greatly with the organisation within the College.

We are only too well aware that even the collective knowledge of our Committee, greatly reinforced by Professor Finley, could not hope to avoid overlooking scholars who had a strong claim to be invited – not that we would have wished to exclude any of those we were fortunate enough to obtain. As it was, we had to lament the unavoidable withdrawal of Professors H. Dieckmann, A. Momigliano, G. Oestreich and G. Patzig, and Bodley's Librarian R. Shackleton; also of Mr Stuart Hampshire, who was to have been a guest of honour.

Once more we must emphasise that we made only a very sketchy attempt to cover the whole field though several speakers responded to suggestions that they should deal with topics we should have been sorry to omit. In general scholars were given their head to deal with what they were interested in within the framework of the Conference.

L. P. WILKINSON

EDITOR'S NOTE

It will be obvious that the subjects discussed at this Conference relate for the most part to the history of ideas. They are concerned almost exclusively with social, political, philosophical and educational issues. When this more restricted scope was chosen – restricted when compared with the two earlier conferences – it was hoped that the material we have here would be supplemented at a later date by the proceedings of another conference that would deal specifically with literature and art. The series would then have extended over the whole period from the fall of the Roman Empire to the beginning of modern times.

As was the case with the proceedings of the two previous conferences, the papers do not follow here the order in which they were delivered, but are arranged in groups according to subject; and it must be pointed out once again that this arrangement is often crude and arbitrary, since some speakers covered a wide range of subjects. We can see from the Introduction that parts of their papers would have fitted more appropriately under another heading than the one under which they are placed.

Less attention was paid on this occasion to the gaps in our knowledge about the influence of the classical tradition, but the item 'research opportunities' has been included in the Index to call attention to such references as were made.

Authors were asked to correct their contributions, and most of them have added substantial notes. One major disappointment must however be recorded. Professor G. E. L. Owen, who read papers on Plato and Aristotle in the nineteenth century, was unfortunately unable owing to illness to prepare these for publication.

Finally, the editor would like to take this opportunity to offer his thanks to the Provost and Fellows of King's College; to the Syndics and Staff of the Cambridge University Press; to Dr Elisabeth Bond-Pablé for her help in checking the German texts; and to Mrs H. M. Clark, Administrative Secretary of the King's College Research Centre, without whose help with correspondence this volume would never have seen the light.

CONTENTS

CONTENTS

CONTRIBUTORS

Dr R. R. BOLGAR is Fellow of King's College and Reader in the History of the Classical Tradition at the University of Cambridge. He is author of *The Classical Heritage and its Beneficiaries* (1954); and editor of *Classical Influences on European Culture*, A.D. *500–1500* (1971) and *Classical Influences on European Culture*, A.D. *1500–1700* (1976).

Professor H. COING, Dr. jur., Dr. mult.h.c., is Director of the Max-Planck-Institut für europäische Rechtsgeschichte, Frankfurt.

Professor GUSTAVO COSTA is Professor of Italian at the University of California at Berkeley. He is author of *La leggenda del secolo d'oro nella letteratura italiana* (1972) and *Le antichità germaniche nella cultura italiana da Machiavelli a Vico* (1977).

Professor Dr MANFRED FUHRMANN is Professor of Latin Philology at the University of Konstanz. He is author of *Einführung in die antike Dichtungstheorie* (1973) and *Alte Sprachen in der Krise – Analysen und Programme* (1976).

Professor Dr THOMAS GELZER is Professor of Classical Greek Literature at the University of Bern. He is author of *Der epirrhematische Agon bei Aristophanes* (1960) and *Aristophanes der Komiker* (1971); and editor of Musaeus, *Hero und Leander* (1975).

Professor UVO HÖLSCHER is Professor of Classical Philology at the University of Munich. He is author of *Untersuchungen zur Form der Odyssee* (1939), *Empedokles und Hölderlin* (1965), *Die Chance des Unbehagens – zur Situation der klassischen Studien* (1965) and *Der Sinn von Sein in der älteren griechischen Philosophie* (1976); editor and translator of Parmenides, *Vom Wesen des Seienden* (1969); and editor of Karl Reinhardt, *Die Ilias und ihr Dichter* (1961).

Dr E. D. JAMES is Fellow of St John's College and Lecturer in French at the University of Cambridge. He is author of *Pierre Nicole, Jansenist and Humanist: A Study of his Thought* (1972).

Professor R. A. LEIGH, C.B.E., Litt.D., F.B.A., is Professor of French at the University of Cambridge. His major work is the *Correspondance de Jean-Jacques Rousseau* of which thirty-one volumes have been published.

Dr NICOLE LORAUX is Maître-assistant in Greek History at the École des Hautes Études en Sciences Sociales, Paris. She is author of *Athènes imaginaire: Histoire de l'oraison funèbre athénienne et de sa fonction dans la 'cité classique'* (to be published 1978).

xi

Professor Dr JÜRGEN MITTELSTRASS is Professor of Philosophy at the University of Konstanz. He is author of *Die Rettung der Phänomena* (1962), *Neuzeit und Aufklärung* (1970), *Das praktische Fundament der Wissenschaft und die Aufgabe der Philosophie* (1972) and *Die Möglichkeit der Wissenschaften* (1974); and editor of *Methodologische Probleme einer normativ-kritischen Gesellschaftstheorie* (1975).

Dr H. O. PAPPÉ is sometime Reader in the History of Social Thought at the University of Sussex. He is author of *Methodische Strömungen in der eherechtsgeschichtlichen Forschung* (1934), *John Stuart Mill and the Harriet Taylor Myth* (1960) and *Sismondis Weggenossen* (1963); and editor of Sismondi's *Statistique du Département du Léman* (1971).

Mr S. G. PEMBROKE is former Fellow of King's College, Cambridge and Lecturer in Greek at Bedford College, London.

Professor MEYER REINHOLD is Professor of Classical Studies at the University of Missouri, Columbia. He is author of *The Classick Pages: Classical Reading of Eighteenth Century Americans* (1975) and, with N. Lewis, of *Roman Civilization* (1951–5).

Professor KLAUS SCHALLER is Professor of Philosophy and History of Education at the Ruhr University of Bochum. He is author of *Pädagogik: eine Geschichte der Bildung und Erziehung* (2 vols.+, 1970, 1973), *Kritische Erziehungswissenschaft und kommunikative Didaktik* (3rd ed., 1976), *Einführung in die kritische Erziehungswissenschaft* (1974), *Pädagogik der Kommunikation* (2nd ed., 1977), etc. and editor of several works by J. A. Comenius.

Professor JEAN SEZNEC is Emeritus Fellow of All Souls College and Emeritus Professor of French Literature at the University of Oxford. He is author of *La survivance des dieux antiques* (1940) and *Essais sur Diderot et l'antiquité* (1957).

Professor PETER G. STEIN, F.B.A. is Regius Professor of Civil Law in the University of Cambridge and Fellow of Queens' College.

Professor CESARE VASOLI is Professor Ordinarius of the History of Philosophy at the University of Florence. He is the author of *Guglielmo d'Occam* (1953), *Due studi per Alano di Lilla* (1961), *La filosofia medievale* (1961), *La dialettica e la retorica dell'Umanesimo* (1968), *Umanesimo e Rinascimento* (1969), *Profezia e Ragione* (1974) and *I miti e gli astri* (1977); and editor of *Magia e scienza nella civiltà umanistica* (1976).

Professor PIERRE VIDAL-NAQUET is Directeur d'Études in Greek History at the École des Hautes Études en Sciences Sociales, Paris. He is author of *Clisthène l'Athénien* (with P. Lévêque, 1964), *Le bordereau d'ensemencement dans l'Égypte ptolémaïque* (1967), *Mythe et tragédie* (with J.-P. Vernant, 1972), *Torture, Cancer of Democracy* (1963) and *The French Student Uprising* (with Alain Schnapp, 1971).

Professor J. H. WHITFIELD is Serena Professor Emeritus at the University of Birmingham. His recent books include *A Short History of Italian Literature* and editions, with introductions, of Castiglione, *The Book of the Courtier* and Guarini, *Il pastor fido* (ed. with introduction 1976).

Mr L. P. WILKINSON is Fellow of King's College, Cambridge and was until 1974 Brereton Reader in Classics and Orator in the University of Cambridge. He is the author of *Horace and his Lyric Poetry* (1945), *Letters of Cicero* (1949), *Ovid Recalled* (1955), *Golden Latin Artistry* (1962), *The Georgics of Virgil* (1969) and *The Roman Experience* (1974).

INTRODUCTION

R. R. BOLGAR

The period 1650–1870 completed the work of the Renaissance and saw the first beginnings of that Age of Organisation in which we live. For the historian of classical influences it figures as a time of transition. In some fields, in which ancient knowledge had not yet been fully assimilated, classical studies continued to follow patterns that the humanists had established. In other fields, new patterns emerged.

We still find practical men in this period – lawyers, scientists, philosophers – pondering the implications of ancient discoveries. But at the same time, we see the institutions and experience of Greece and Rome and maxims from their authors cited to provide support for current political theories and political movements. We see the records of Greek and Roman culture ransacked for the evidence that was needed to develop new branches of learning. And we see the Romantics, who were prepared to find something of unique value in every society and every age, turning with special interest to classical antiquity. The information that the classical literatures could provide had not much practical value by the nineteenth century, so they did not look for useful facts as the men of the Renaissance had done. They looked instead for something that was at once more vague and more profound. They searched for flashes of insight that could illuminate the deeply rooted problems of human life.

The papers delivered at our Conference have been arranged in groups that correspond roughly to these developments. Part 1 of this book covers therefore what might be termed the epilogue to the Renaissance. It discusses some areas of learning in which the influence of classical learning made itself felt along what were by then traditional lines.

To say that the humanists desired simply to know all that the ancients had known and to match with their own creations all that the ancients had created is to credit them with a more limited ambition than was properly theirs. The Renaissance was an Age of Opportunity that stimulated men's energies and inclined them to regard what they had learnt as a starting-point for new advances. This positive, forward-looking attitude affected all areas of knowledge from agriculture to metaphysics. It did not however affect

I

them all in quite the same way, so that there are certain distinctions one must bear in mind.

In subjects where a close acquaintance with the facts that were known in antiquity was sufficient to place an ardent humanist on a level with the ancients – in history, the natural sciences, mathematics or medicine – the successful assimilation of classical learning was generally followed by attempts to collect further appropriate data. In these cases, the wish to extend the existing stock of knowledge often led to the introduction of new methods for discovering, interpreting and retrieving information, with the result that the discipline in question was radically transformed. The theoretical framework that had served its needs in antiquity, could not then accommodate the growing mass of fresh material; and the process begun by the studies of the humanists ended generally with the formation of a new theoretical basis for each branch of knowledge.

In other fields, where the humanists aimed to match the creative triumphs of the past, modern elements showed even more obviously. Imitations of classical models, whether in technology, literature or art, were intended for contemporary use and had for the most part to be constructed out of contemporary materials. Only in literature could man employ an ancient medium, if he chose to write in Latin; and even there we see Petrarch – and who admired the ancients more than he did? – presenting contemporary situations under the veil of pastoral allegory in the *Bucolicum carmen* he modelled on Virgil. Moreover, the artistic conventions and technological devices that imitation produced did not remain unaltered. Such conventions and devices are always subject to change and improvement, and over the years they grew progressively more remote from their classical models. The products of vernacular literature show this tendency with particular force.

Finally, some mention must be made of philosophy, which in any study of influences seems always to stand on its own. It is a subject that at certain times followed the pattern we observe in the case of the sciences and developed through a steady accumulation of knowledge. The recovery of Aristotle's writings in the twelfth and thirteenth centuries was followed by the enlargement of the Aristotelian tradition at the hands of the Scholastics. But at other times the subject has been fertile in new departures. Philosophers have been eager to break with their immediate predecessors and have harked back to other long-neglected systems of thought. Descartes is an obvious example. Philosophy is a subject where we have to consider two different types of development, the one cumulative, the other sporadic.

Furthermore, we have to remember that philosophical ideas have an exceptionally wide range of influence. Ancient medicine left its mark primarily on medical thought. Ancient buildings, ancient treatises on architecture left their mark on architectural practice. But the notions formulated by the Greek philosophers were transmitted through philosophy to literature and some of them were familiar to every educated man by the sixteenth century. The influence of philosophy can be traced in love poetry, history, medicine, science, education and religious belief.

By 1650 the heritage of classical learning constituted an important, if not the most important, part of Europe's intellectual assets, but there were areas where the knowledge of the ancients still had something to offer. The work of the Renaissance was not complete, and the Conference discussed four instances of its continuing importance: in law, in the physical sciences, and in Neoplatonist and sceptical philosophy.

The study of classical influences during the Renaissance has come to centre very properly on the contribution made by Greece and Rome to the development of human knowledge and the various arts and skills; but this emphasis on development gives rise to difficulties when one comes to discuss the subject of law. 'Iuris prudentia est divinarum atque humanarum rerum notitia, iusti atque iniusti scientia', the *Digest* tells us,[1] but the philosophic generality of this statement is misleading. The advancement of legal knowledge at the time it derived most sustenance from Roman law did not follow the simple pattern one traces in the sciences. It did not depend on the gathering of information concerning some particular aspect of life, the discovery of relationships between available facts or the tracing of the uniformities that governed these relationships. In the field of law, development meant progress in the application of legal enactments to particular cases of a type to which they had not been applied earlier, and the appearance of new enactments to govern areas that had previously remained outside legal control.

It is true that even in Roman times jurists had tried to rationalise judicial decisions and legal enactments where these had touched on

[1] I. 1.10, §2.

closely related topics, and in doing so had appealed to general principles of justice. It is true also that the laws enacted by sovereign states and the pronouncements of responsible judges had generally taken such principles into account. But all the same it would not be correct to say either that individual laws derived from these principles, or that the principles could be inferred from the laws. The legal tradition of Europe was not a science, but a collection of practical rules for resolving a particular type of problem.

Eventually however, as Professsor Coing tells us, law was rationalised, and over the greatest part of Europe the fortunes of the legal heritage of antiquity provide us with a paradigm of how classical influences functioned. The span of time we have to cover here is exceptionally long, since the beginnings of a serious interest in Roman law date back to the eleventh century. By 1650 the legal system of nearly every country in Europe was based on Roman models, England being the most notable exception. But borrowed law does not fit any better than borrowed clothes. The classical *Corpus iuris* had to be reinterpreted to suit social conditions which were very different from those that had prevailed in Rome, and which did not any way remain static during the long period we have to consider. It was also largely supplemented by local regulations, by the enactments of a long series of modern sovereigns, and, in areas that the ancients had neglected (such as the control of commercial transactions), by fresh laws derived by analogy from those in kindred fields.

Given the nature of law, the presence of these heterogeneous elements resulted in discrepancies, which led to further efforts at interpretation. Progress was slow. The law's delays extended to its own ordering. But finally at the end of the seventeenth century interpretation was systematised in the sense that general principles were established. These became the basis for a criticism of existing laws, and paved the way for further rationalisation. After another hundred years we have the great codes, which, harmonising Roman and national laws, provided Europe with a number of coherent legal systems.

A development similar in character to the one examined by Professor Coing – similar at least in the context of classical influences – meets us in Professor Mittelstrass' masterly account of how men came to adopt a mechanistic view of the universe. Once again the story begins with the humanists' interest in classical

4

learning, with their exploration of Archimedean statics, the optics of Euclid and the pseudo-Ptolemy, and Ptolemy's own effort to 'save the appearances'. Mathematical interpretations of physical phenomena had found little favour during the Middle Ages, when they were regarded as arbitrary constructs unrelated to the actual nature of the universe. But in the fifteenth and sixteenth centuries, after Regiomontanus, Maurolico and others[1] were prompted by humanist enthusiasm and helped by humanist learning to make a more detailed and accurate study of the Greek mathematicians, attitudes changed. The hypotheses of Kepler that provided a relatively simple picture of planetary movements proved a turning-point. Mathematical explanations came into general use, and eventually, thanks to the genius of Newton, their use was crowned by the emergence of a new theory of the universe.

Up to this point the pattern of influences traced by Professor Mittelstrass corresponds (when viewed in broad terms) to the one traced by Professor Coing. But now he carries his story one stage further. What had started life as a mathematical theory is shown to have influenced the popular view of the universe, Newton's success tempting men to believe that all phenomena would one day be explained by mathematical means, so that the eighteenth century came to look upon the world as a machine whose future would be determined by its past – a belief that had important moral, psychological and even aesthetic consequences.

This reference to the wider impact of Newton's ideas paves the way neatly for the next two papers. Professor Vasoli and Professor Schaller take up the history of Neoplatonism at a point when its teachings were already familiar to educated Europe, and the lines of Neoplatonic influence that they describe lie well outside of the philosophical field.

Neoplatonism was the most protean of the systems of thought that antiquity bequeathed to the western world, and in particular it had close connections with magic and the occult. Already in the fourth century A.D. its exponents had stressed the value of ritual and magical practices. The works of the pseudo-Dionysius, one of the main avenues by which Neoplatonism reached the mediaeval west, recommended utilising physical objects to invoke divine or demonic assistance, for such objects derived occult power from the sympathy that binds the universe. It is not surprising therefore that both in the

[1] Paul Lawrence Rose, *The Renaissance of Mathematics* (London, 1976).

Middle Ages and the Renaissance we find Neoplatonists practising alchemy and astrology and holding cabbalistic and gnostic doctrines.

Professor Vasoli examines the influence of Neoplatonist and occultist ideas in the scientific field. He draws attention to the unexpected fact that many of the men responsible for the scientific revolution of the sixteenth and seventeenth centuries, men like Copernicus and Kepler, had a marked interest in occult ideas. He had touched on this topic in his recent book, *Profezia e Ragione*,[1] but here he co-ordinates the evidence and adds the telling example of Newton. The coincidence of scientific creativity and occultist preoccupations is undoubtedly striking, even though the nature of the connections between them remains obscure. Should we be content with the simple assumption that the lively curiosity and temperamental disinclination to accept conventional ideas, which made these men pioneers in their chosen field of mathematics, also led them quite independently to explore the exciting mysteries of the occult? Or are we to suppose that there was some element in occultist studies or in the occultist picture of the universe that encouraged a preoccupation with the observable and measurable aspects of the physical world? The problem is evidently one that calls for further research.

Professor Schaller is also concerned with the influence of Neoplatonism, since he takes Comenius as his subject. This Moravian chiliast and polymath is known to us nowadays principally as a writer on education, who considered that a knowledge of things was more important than a knowledge of words. 'Scire', he tells us, 'est rem ingenio tenere: idque gradu trino. 1. Quod sit. 2. Per quid sit. 3. Ad quid adhibenda sit.'[2] This made him popular with practical men. William Petty, who at the close of the Civil War outlined a detailed programme for setting up workshop schools (*ergastula literaria*) and colleges where tradesmen could learn their crafts (*gymnasia mechanica*), recommended a course of elementary instruction that was plainly modelled on Comenius. Boys were to begin with the observation of 'all sensible objects and actions, whether they be natural or artificial, which the educators must on all occasions expound to them'.[3]

---

[1] Cesare Vasoli, *Profezia e Ragione* (Napoli, 1974), pp. 448–76.

[2] *Korrespondence J. A. Komenského a vrasetnikû jeho. Nová sbirka*, ed. J. Kvačala (Prag, 1897), p. 306, cited in J. A. Comenius, *Janua rerum*, ed. K. Schaller (Munich, 1968).

[3] William Petty, *The Advice of W.P. to Mr. Samuel Hartlib for the Advancement of Particular Parts of Learning* (n.p., 1647/8).

But if we think of Comenius primarily as an educational innovator, it is likely that he saw himself as a man whose special task was the organisation of knowledge. During his schooldays at Herborn he was taught by the encyclopaedist J. H. Alsted, and we hear of him planning at the early age of twenty-four a survey of universal knowledge of which only fragments have survived, and soon after this he formulated his pansophic ideal, which he then tried to realise in a long series of works including his monumental *Consultatio catholica*.[1]

He regarded the physical universe as a reflection of God's Being. The ideas in the divine mind find expression in the world around us insofar as the spiritual can find expression in the material[2] and can do so because there is a harmony in the universe that is dependent on number. Our task as Christians is to prepare the world for Christ's millennial coming which is promised in the Revelation of John, and so it is important for us to form a clear idea of the nature of our physical surroundings. He believed that once men's knowledge of the world (and therefore of God) was placed on a sound footing, the salvation of mankind would be at hand. These beliefs, which have obvious Neoplatonist associations, came to him from J. V. Andreae, the populariser or (as some claim) the inventor of Rosicrucianism.[3]

Comenius had little sympathy for those lines of thought that were doing most in his day to promote the advancement of science.[4] But the value he set on an accurate observation of the physical world, his number-mysticism and his respect for systematised knowledge go some way perhaps towards explaining why the Neoplatonist tradition should have attracted the champions of the new scientific revolution.

The remaining paper in this Part examines the influence of Scepticism which made a marked impact on European thought after Sextus Empiricus was translated in the second half of the sixteenth century. Dr James focusses his attention on religious belief and takes as his examples Pascal, Bayle and Hume.

Oddly enough, it is the two last-named, who came later in time,

---

[1] J. A. Comenius, *De rerum humanarum emendatione consultatio catholica*, in *Opera omnia*.
[2] *Ibid*. I. 443 (*Mundus materialis* I).
[3] Jaromír Červenka, *Die Naturphilosophie des Johann Amos Comenius* (Prag, 1970), p. 46; Frances A. Yates, *The Rosicrucian Enlightenment* (London, 1972), chs. 4 and 5.
[4] This can be inferred from his bombastic and superficial attack on Descartes: *Cartesius cum sua naturali philosophia a mechanicis eversus* (Amsterdam, 1659), ed. J. Reber (Giessen, 1896). Červenka (*Comenius*, p. 80) informs us that Comenius wrote a later essay on Descartes which was more judicious, but gives no details of this.

who followed the pattern common in the Renaissance and used what they learnt from antiquity to develop their own sceptical attitudes. Bayle in his *Dictionnaire* does in many cases present us with opposing views that he makes no effort to reconcile; and if on the key issue of religious faith he does seem to incline to traditional solutions, the reader is still left feeling that Bayle was like E. M. Forster and did not 'believe in Belief'.[1]

Hume similarly sets opinion against opinion, theist against atheist in his *Dialogues concerning Natural Religion*. Having done this, he does not in true Pyrrhonist fashion abandon all speculation as valueless. Dr James sees him trying instead to discover a modicum of common ground between the rival camps. But the natural religion that he advocates is not one whose demands will upset the unperturbedness of its votaries. Hume may have arrived at a modified scepticism, but he belongs clearly to the Pyrrhonist tradition.

It is quite otherwise with Pascal. Although he is the earliest in time of the three thinkers Dr James examines, he is the one who stands furthest from the humanists in the use he makes of classical knowledge. He does not resort to Pyrrhonist arguments to develop a Pyrrhonist attitude, but employs them simply to support the dogmatic Christianity to which he is committed. His approach foreshadows that of the eighteenth-century writers we shall be considering in Part II, who did not turn to the classical heritage for information or guidance as their predecessors had done, but used appeals to antiquity propaganda-fashion to justify contemporary political or cultural programmes.

The five papers we have been considering all show the heritage of antiquity in an active rôle. Without Justinian's *Corpus iuris*, without Archimedes and Diophantus, without the Neoplatonists and the Pyrrhonists, European culture would not have developed along the lines we know today. The Renaissance can be defined as the epoch when the past was creative. What followed is less impressive. By 1650 there was not much more that the classical heritage could immediately contribute to the progress of European civilisation, or at any rate there was not much that it could contribute in the old straightforward manner that had been favoured by the humanists. But it had transformed the intellectual life of Europe, and its reputation stood high. If a man could cite an ancient example or an ancient opinion in

[1] E. M. Forster, 'What I believe', *Two Cheers for Democracy* (first pub. 1951; Penguin Books, Harmondsworth, 1965), p. 75.

support of his views, they acquired an air of respectability. Secular writers formed the habit of appealing to classical precedents as religious writers appealed to the Bible; and this happened most obviously in the field of political thought.

The political causes that the eighteenth century took most seriously were nationalism and middle-class liberties. Nationalism had been a powerful force since the Renaissance in unified countries like France and England, but now it was beginning to show its teeth in disunited Italy and Germany. At the same time, there was a growing opposition to the arbitrary privileges of the nobles and the church, wherever an increasingly prosperous middle class found itself face to face with a weakened aristocracy; and in cases where a country's rulers were foreign or the creatures of a foreign power, these two strands of feeling, the nationalistic and the radical, reinforced each other. France was preparing for 1789 so its propagandists emphasised republican sentiments; but the American colonists who saw themselves as liberal-minded republicans opposing an autocracy also saw themselves, since they were conscious of their remoteness from Great Britain, as a potentially independent nation opposing the rule of an alien government.

Nationalism and political radicalism had their roots in the climate of opinion that Renaissance humanism had created centuries earlier. They were indebted to the classical past, but their current representatives no longer depended on that past for their ideas. With a few exceptions that Professor Reinhold mentions, they consulted classical writers merely to confirm what they already believed or in order to impress others with the respectability of their notions. These men were not out to learn from antiquity.

Professor Fuhrmann's paper sets the scene admirably for Part II. He writes about literature, but the literary movements he discusses reflected nationalist ambitions. He begins with the notorious *Querelle des Anciens et des Modernes*. The programme of the *Modernes* was an expression of French self-confidence. It proclaimed that France had now enough by way of cultural resources to dispense with her Greek and Latin models. The main point that Professor Fuhrmann makes in this part of his argument – and it is important in view of what happens later – is that Perrault and Fontenelle did not reject the classical tradition. For all their rodomontade, they had no intention of jettisoning what previous generations had learnt from antiquity. All they were concerned to reject was the need for further imitation

9

of a rigid sort. In spite of the *Querelle*, the literary tradition of eighteenth-century France remained classical, or to be more precise it remained Latin, in character.

The next event the paper discusses is the revolt of German writers in the latter half of the century against the francophilia that marked the age of Frederick II. National pride was at stake in this attempt to shake off the Latin-based classicism of France; but the rebels, though energetically creative, were not quite ready to stand on their own. They needed not so much a model to imitate as a model to revere, to give them confidence; and when we turn to tracing their attempts to find this model, we come across a fascinating example of how different strands of cultural development can meet and intertwine.

A growing interest in classical archaeology and classical art was one of the pleasant features of the eighteenth century. Great collectors like the Comte de Caylus and Cardinal Albani were imitated by an army of lesser amateurs. The Greek items in these collections – ironically enough they were for the most part inferior works of a late period - fired the imagination of an eccentric who happened to have a rare gift for communicating his enthusiasms. This man, Winckelmann, exhorted his contemporaries to imitate the artistic and literary achievements of the Greeks at the very moment when they were looking round for a new ideal. His *History of Art among the Ancients* appeared in 1764. Twenty years earlier its recommendations would have fallen on deaf ears, and even at this point their influence would have been much less, had they not received support from developments that had made themselves felt in quite another field of study.

As soon as civilisation arrives at a certain degree of complexity, it seems to give rise to longings for a simple life. Dreams of a golden age of hardy, undemanding contentment haunted the Graeco-Roman world from Alexander onwards. This dream had faded when men came in contact with the harsh reality of primitive conditions during the Middle Ages, but we meet it again in the sixteenth century. If Spenser had doubts about the merits of Meliboee's pastoral semi-paradise,[1] Montaigne genuinely admired his cannibals, and the cult of the noble savage flourished with an increasing vigour during the seventeenth century until it produced the idealised picture of primitive community that we find in Fénelon's *Télémaque*.

---

[1] *The Fairie Queene*, book VI, cantos 9–11.

It was appropriate that this idealisation should have appeared in a book modelled on the *Odyssey*, for Homer was to be the poet who benefited most from the primitivist cult. At the time of the *Querelle* his epics had been the weak link in the armour of the *Anciens*. The humanists nurtured on Virgil and on the altruistic principles of a Christian society had considered them crude, had even labelled them as vulgar, and had found the Homeric heroes morally distasteful; but such was their respect for ancient opinion that most of them continued to rank Homer in theory as the greatest of epic writers. The *Modernes* naturally enough took advantage of this equivocal valuation. They damned Homer with faint praise, taught the world to sneer at him as the child of a primitive age, excellent in his day, but not a poet whose work a sophisticated reader could be expected to enjoy. Their criticisms merely made explicit what most people (other than Chapman) had felt since Pilatus gave the first pages of his clumsy translation to Petrarch. Their importance for the future lay in the reaction they provoked. Mme Dacier, the translator and principal champion of Homer, admitted the primitive character of his work; but then she went on to claim – impressed perhaps by the success of *Télémaque* – that this was precisely the feature that made the epics valuable.

During the next fifty years Homer was thought of as the voice of the primitive world. Vico, who held that unsophisticated people had a better chance than the sophisticated of producing poetry that was sublime (in the pseudo-Longinian sense of the word),[1] described the Homeric epics as 'civil histories of ancient Greek customs'.[2] The Aberdonian Blackwell made a detailed study of Homer's background to see why his society was able to produce so great a genius,[3] and Blackwell's disciples came out with the theory that only primitive societies could foster true genius.[4]

All this happened at the very time when Jean-Jacques Rousseau, driven by his private devils, embarked on his denunciations of civilised society, and it affected the reception of Winckelmann's book. Winckelmann maintained that the Greeks had been a race gifted with exceptional genius. His contemporaries maintained that Homer had been an exceptional genius because he was the product

---

[1] See below, pp. 257–8.
[2] Leon Pompa, *Vico: A Study of the New Science* (Cambridge, 1975), p. 137.
[3] Thomas Blackwell, *An Enquiry into the Life and Writings of Homer* (London, 1735).
[4] Notably, the Scottish primitivists: Dr K. Simonsuuri discusses this aspect of Blackwell's influence in a book she hopes to publish in the near future.

of a primitive culture. Inevitably, the two ideas became linked. Not only Homer, but Greek culture in general – and certainly the Greek culture of the fifth century B.C. and earlier – came to be regarded as typical of an unspoilt, and therefore by Rousseau's criteria highly desirable, state of human society.

The linking of Winckelmann's artistic ideals with primitivism proved decisive for Germany. The Germans had long glorified the simplicity, morality and courage of their ancestors whom Tacitus had depicted in his *Germania*.[1] Proud of their kinship with the warriors of Arminius, they flattered themselves that they still possessed the characteristic virtues of a primitive tribe; and the notion – however questionable – that the Greek world too had been at a primitive stage during its period of greatest achievement, attracted them to the Greeks. Initially, Winckelmann, Lessing and Goethe (during the first half of his career) were satisfied with recommending that German artists and poets should be guided by the ideals that the Greeks had realised. But then Humboldt and Friedrich Schlegel went one decisive step further. They proclaimed the existence of a natural identity between Germans and Greeks. The countrymen of Goethe were the divinely appointed heirs of the countrymen of Homer.

The last part of Professor Fuhrmann's paper is devoted to the efforts Goethe and Schiller made to define what the artistic ideals of the Greeks had been, and how they could be realised in the modern world. Discussion of it must therefore be postponed to a later stage. It does not belong to the simple story of the eighteenth century when writers used classical authorities to justify whatever purposes they happened to have at heart.

These purposes were generally political. In Italy, the pattern was one of revolt against an established order. During the Renaissance, men all over the peninsula had paid honour to the ancient Romans whom they considered their ancestors. But since that time the cult of Rome had been adopted by tyrannical governments. It had narrowed to a cult of imperial power, and by the eighteenth century it was one of the main buttresses of papal authority. Professor Whitfield relates in vivid detail how the Italians in their divided and oppressed country ransacked the ancient historians for evidence that would enable them to discredit Livy's heroes and would exalt the virtues of the Italian peoples whom Rome had conquered.

---

[1] Frank L. Borchardt, *German Antiquity in Renaissance Myth* (Baltimore and London, 1971), *passim*.

Generally speaking, nationalism provided the impulse behind this phase of Italian scholarship; but radical attitudes also had some influence. The only Romans to win any praise from their freedom-loving descendants were men like Caius Gracchus who had championed the rights of the common people. The Roman ruling class was seen as the oppressor both at home and abroad.

The malcontents of Italy could look to the Samnites and the Volsci for inspiration. For the malcontents of France such a course would have had no meaning. Their resentments were social, not national in origin, and what they required were models for a just society. They turned to Livy's early republic and to Sparta.

The republic was an obvious choice. As Professor Leigh points out, the Romans had already managed to elevate its virtues into a myth; and readers of Lucan were bound to see it as the polar opposite of tyranny. Reasons for admiring Sparta were less evident, though here again an historical myth fostered by Plato and Xenophon was not without influence. But however favourably one interprets its rather sparse records, the fact that Sparta was a rigid, militaristic state ruling over a subject population cannot be easily ignored. The admiration it evoked suggests therefore that the men who made the French Revolution were not exclusively committed to the pursuit of Equality and Liberty.

What had Sparta and the early Roman republic, Lycurgus and Cincinnatus in common? Discipline, surely, and hardihood, and a love of simplicity. We are back in short with Fénelon's tough utopia and the day-dreams of Rousseau. Some at least of France's revolutionaries aimed at more than just the downfall of tyranny. Some aimed – and Robespierre perhaps aimed primarily – at the downfall of luxury and sophistication.

We are often told that the final result of 1789 was to make the world safe for capitalist enterprise; and in that case, the soldiers of Sparta and the yeoman farmers of early Rome were strange models for the age to follow. The interest of Professor Vidal-Naquet and Dr Loraux's joint paper lies in its analysis of how these models were jettisoned, and how their place was taken by Athens.

Eighteenth-century attitudes to the democratic freedoms and commercial prosperity of Athens do not suggest a very conscious hankering after a 'bourgeois' type of society. Though Blackwell and others were busy relating Homer's achievements to the social conditions of the Homeric age, the relationships between Athenian literature and the Athenian way of life in the fifth and fourth centuries B.C. was left largely unexplored. Athens was rarely discussed, and when she was, she appeared for the most part to her disadvantage as the city responsible for the judicial murder of Socrates.[1]

The one detailed account of Athens came in the Abbé Barthélemy's *Le voyage du jeune Anacharsis en Grèce*. It was published in 1788, and its startling popularity must have done something to counterbalance the neglect of the Athenian scene by graver authors. But for all its careful antiquarian detail, it painted a society that called to mind the frivolous Paris of Barthélemy's own day, and we may follow Professor Leigh in feeling it to be significant that the hero of the book preferred Sparta to Athens and elected in the end to return to his own wild Scythia.

If the precursors of the Revolution paid little attention to Athens (her only serious champion, De Pauw, was a German and lived, it seems, outside of France), the men actually involved in the revolutionary upheaval were unanimous in condemning her. Equality was the beloved ideal of the age; and it did not seem proper to slur over the fact that Athens had been a slave state, though the Jacobins managed to forget the helots when they gave so much praise to Sparta. Condorcet, hiding in holes and corners from his future executioners, insisted that Greek institutions were based on slavery, and Volney reminded his readers that four out of every five Athenians were slaves.

In the second half of their paper Professor Vidal-Naquet and Dr Loraux trace how the revolutionary picture of ancient Greece was gradually transformed during the nineteenth century. They show how Sparta came to be regarded as the home, not of liberty, but of discipline, and as such passed from being the ideal of the radicals to being the ideal of reactionaries like Joseph de Maistre and Charles Nisard, while Athens, the democratic, artistic, trading city came just as gradually into favour. Lévesque still located his golden age in the days of Solon. Constant, who had nothing but praise for the expansion of human energies made possible by the Athenians' participation in political decision-making, was still troubled by the existence of slavery and by the subordination of the individual to the ancient state. But by the days of the Second Empire, the transformation was

---

[1] William Thomas Conroy Jr, 'Diderot's *Essai sur Sénèque*', *Studies on Voltaire and the Eighteenth Century* (Voltaire Foundation, vol. CXXXI, Banbury, 1975), p. 21.

complete; and Victor Duruy could paint his picture of a moderate democracy, devoted to freedom, art and commerce, the Athens that the nineteenth century saw as the prototype of its own achievements.

The American Revolution preceded the French, and the reason for discussing Professor Reinhold's paper after the ones dealing with France lies in the nature of the Founding Fathers' classical interests. Committed by events to republicanism and democracy, they bolstered their sense of the rightness of their cause by references to Greek and Roman heroes. They too venerated the Spartans and saw themselves as modern Cincinnati. But unlike the French, they went a step further. They sought for useful information.

Professor Reinhold calls our attention to two interesting features of the American experience. The legislators who talked so freely about Greece and Rome had not for the most part much direct knowledge of the Greek and Roman authors. They relied on undistinguished translations and summaries which were often sadly superficial. Without saying it in so many words, Professor Reinhold contrives to suggest that this lack of scholarship may have been due to the inevitable backwardness of a colonial culture; but was Europe in a much better state? There is evidence to suggest that knowledge of Latin and Greek in the eighteenth century fell below the level reached in the seventeenth and regained with pedantic effort in the nineteenth, while translations and books on classical subjects appeared in great numbers and provided the reading public with an easy avenue to learning.[1]

The other feature to which our attention is drawn, and which distinguishes the American attitude to the classics from the French, offers more interest. The Founding Fathers, faced with the task of framing a constitution, did not just examine contemporary precedents. They searched the ancient historians for information about republics and federal leagues, which, they hoped, would help them to make wise decisions; and in the end, they did not use the classical material they had painstakingly collected, but preferred more modern constitutional arrangements. What they did differed significantly from the habit we have noted among contemporary politicians of citing classical examples to support their policies. It differed also from the way the humanists had used classical information, for the Founding Fathers not only reviewed material that historians like Polybius had recorded, but they also drew conclusions

---

[1] *Ibid.* pp. 19–20.

from this material which the ancients had not drawn. They fitted into a new and fruitful tradition.

Montesquieu had shown how one could use the facts of ancient history in conjunction with facts from other sources, treating them as a valid, but not specifically privileged, part of human knowledge. But the really important advance in this period was made in connection with the group of subjects we now call anthropology and ethnography. It was here that men came to discover from a study of the ancient world facts that were of a kind antiquity had not dreamt of. Discussion of Professor Fuhrmann's paper earlier brought up the question of the interest that was taken in primitive societies and its relation to eighteenth-century ideas on Homer; but Vico, coming to the subject through his attempts to solve problems connected with the Homeric poems, was the first to make primitive society the object of serious study.

Vico's originality and the fruitful lines of inquiry that he initiated lend a certain importance to the development of his thought. Professor Costa shows us that the starting-point of Vico's interest in the primitive were some routine lectures he was giving on rhetoric. He became an enthusiastic admirer of the famous treatise *On the Sublime*, which persuaded him that great poetry was always characterised by powerful emotion. Vico's wife was an uneducated and tempestuous woman; and personal experience had left him convinced that women and children and other unsophisticated persons had stronger emotions than the sophisticated and were better able to give expression to them. A poet who lived in an unsophisticated age was more likely to attain to sublimity than one like Virgil who knew the court of Augustus.

As he pursued his inquiries further he came to the conclusion that the epics as we have them are a compilation from the untutored works of earlier bards and therefore truly an expression of the general culture of the primitive epoch when they were composed.

Once they were formulated, these ideas quickly gained converts. Blackwell who wrote on Homeric society mentions Vico, and Adam Smith is unlikely to have missed reading Blackwell's work since they moved in the same circles. Smith's theory that legal rules in any particular society are governed by an estimate of what an impartial observer from that society would approve recalls Blackwell's insistence on the formative rôle of social forces and Vico's concept of the changing principles that have determined the history of Law;[1] and when Professor Stein adds that Smith regarded Homer 'almost as a text of social anthropology', it becomes clear that Smith had his place in that line of development which leads us from Fénelon's romantic idealisation of the primitive to the serious beginnings of a new science.

Since Smith's interest in his *Theory of Moral Sentiments* was centred on the origins of law, he drew his evidence from several periods of ancient history, citing Thucydides, the Attic orators, Cicero, Livy and Plutarch as well as Homer. Discussing the first three of his four stages of men's social evolution, when they kept themselves alive as hunters, shepherds and farmers, he uses both classical and non-classical sources. His method resembles that of the American federalists. The ancient world is no longer privileged as it was in the Renaissance, and its authors are no longer asked to provide general conclusions. It has become one source of information among many.

A technique similar to Adam Smith's was followed by Adam Ferguson and John Millar, whom Dr Pembroke evidently classes as professional anthropologists, and to whom one might add the eccentric Lord Kames, another of Blackwell's friends. They all combined classical evidence with the reports of more recent travellers. Dr Pembroke reminds us that a precedent can be found for this in Thucydides, who used contemporary information about barbarian tribes to help him to reconstruct what conditions had been like in early Greece; but the two cases are not quite parallel. Thucydides had no interest in primitive habits as such, and the facts he established by his comparative method had none of the precision that marks the conclusions of the eighteenth-century anthropologists. At best he can be seen as having provided a hint, but they moved far beyond the position he had reached.

John Millar's *The Origin of Ranks* appeared in 1773, and the next important contribution to anthropological knowledge, Bachofen's *Das Mutterrecht*, followed in 1861. Dr Pembroke calls attention to this long gap, but refrains from offering an explanation. Had analysis progressed as far as it could on the basis of unsystematic records so that nothing more could be achieved until some new scientific evidence became available? But speculation did not cease even though ordered analysis had come to a stop. It was during the long period between Millar and Bachofen that Charles Fourier formu-

[1] Pompa, *Vico*, pp. 121–2.

lated his theories about the primitive utopia which had existed, in his opinion, before the introduction of property. It was then that Comte coined the term 'sociology', and Creuzer wrote his *Symbolik*, which, though admittedly fantastical, did attempt to picture the intellectual world of primitive man.

With Part IV we reach the nineteenth century, and this intellectually crowded period has some general features we need to keep in mind. The educational reforms that occurred round about 1800 – promoted by state action in France and Germany, but coming informally and piecemeal in England – resulted in more efficient teaching and a more accurate knowledge of Greek and Latin on the part of the educated public; and a large number of men were brought by their schooling to adopt the basic assumptions and categories that had guided Greek and Roman thinking without being properly aware of how their minds had been moulded.

Meanwhile, in another respect, the impact of the classical world upon the modern appeared to diminish. The practice of appealing to idealised examples from the past (Greece, Sparta, early Rome) to recommend political or cultural programmes fell out of favour, discredited by the failure of the Revolution's more doctrinaire ideas, and made stale by repetition.

Nevertheless, some men continued to hope that an understanding of the past would one day yield insights that would guide mankind towards a better future, so that the influence of antiquity operated during this period in two distinct ways. On the one hand, there was the general impress left by ancient ideas – an impress often unrealised – that affected those who had received a classical training. On the other hand, there was the striking, but often vague and unfathomable inspiration that some minds seemed to draw from their classical reading, and that had a creative power we cannot disregard.

Mention must be made at this point of two papers which were given during the Conference by Professor G. E. L. Owen, but which illness has prevented him from preparing for publication. They dealt with the nineteenth-century editions of Plato and Aristotle; and their loss is particularly regrettable since they shed a useful light on the character of the classical learning of the time, which was not without its defects.

During the Middle Ages and the Renaissance serious students of ancient literature had contributed generally both to the advancement of scholarship and the spread of classical ideas. How one studied, how one used the fruits of one's study, were inseparable. With the seventeenth century this situation gradually altered. Scholarship continued to flourish. It continued to attract many of the best minds of Europe. Texts were emended. Difficulties of interpretation were resolved. But thanks in part to the increased specialisation of classical learning, and in part to the changing character of the influence that learning could hope to exert now that it had nothing strikingly new to offer (since the improved texts and interpretations rarely altered the broad impression left by an ancient author on his readers), the interests pursued by professional scholars became increasingly remote from the general development of the classical tradition.

Professor Owen's paper showed us nineteenth-century professional scholarship at work; and what he had to say illustrated the point made in the last paragraph. With the exception of Jowett, none of the Platonic or Aristotelian scholars he mentioned made a serious contribution to philosophical thought or even to the intellectual life of their generation; and Jowett was heavily attacked for being an inaccurate scholar. There was, it is true, a revival of Platonism in France in the middle years of the century, which was not without effect on the literature of the time, but the man who did most to promote it, Victor Cousin, can hardly rank as a classical scholar. He was what Jowett could have become – an educationist, an administrator, a politician.[1]

If we want to assess what influence classical writers had in the nineteenth century, we must pass over men like Immanuel Bekker and Karl Friedrich Hermann who did not write on general subjects or take part in political activity, and turn to some whose main interests lay outside the classical field.

The group of thinkers known as the utilitarians were committed to publicising their ideas and applying them, when opportunity offered, in the public service. They read Plato and Aristotle as part of a general study of philosophical problems. Professor Pappé assembles a substantial amount of biographical material bearing on their knowledge of the ancient writers. On the subject of Bentham, there is not much to be said. He disliked Plato, but knew and used Aristotle's logical works. The Mills on the other hand had both received a

[1] R. R. Bolgar, 'Victor Cousin and nineteenth-century education', *Cambridge Journal*, II. 6 (March 1949).

thorough classical training. Which of us could hope to rival John Stuart Mill's boyhood acquaintance with Greek literature? And both the father and the son had a marked admiration for Plato.

The question one wants answered is what effect the Mills' classical training and their admiration for the author of the *Republic* had on their ideas; and it is obvious that a good deal of research will need to be done before an answer can be produced. Professor Pappé furnishes us with some useful indicators. It is evident that the utilitarians shared some of the views of their Greek mentors. They placed a high value on logical thought and an even higher value on Socrates' readiness to question accepted beliefs. It is interesting to be told that John Stuart Mill felt himself, beyond any modern he knew of except his father and perhaps even beyond him, a pupil of Plato; and he thought that it was his familiarity with Plato's dialectic that made him capable of appreciating Bentham. Notably too the Utilitarians believed in justice as a basic principle of social order. James Mill called for an identity of interest between governors and governed and claimed that Plato's purpose had been to discover what means would lead to this identity, while Bentham and John Stuart Mill both emphasised the need for benevolence, holding that one's best road to happiness was to promote the happiness of others.

The similarities between the teaching of Plato and the teachings of the utilitarians are striking; but a quick consideration is enough to show that they have a imprecise and general character. The world in which the Founding Fathers of the United States had looked for models of federalism in the history of the Greek leagues was gone for ever. What distinguished the nineteenth century from the eighteenth – and does so most forcibly in the fields of political and social thought – was the realisation that change is not only inevitable, but also inevitably slow; that the conditions a would-be reformer finds around him must be taken into account when he makes his plans; and that theoretically attractive utopias derived from the past have little value. All a man can hope to do is to prepare his next step forward.

The line that divides the mental world of the eighteenth century from the mental world of the nineteenth comes in fact between Bentham and the Mills and between Thomas Arnold and his son, Matthew. In each case, the first-named still belonged to the age of Turgot and Condorcet, while the others faced a less tractable universe. They had to come to terms with an economic order – and consequently with a social order – for which antiquity offered no parallels.

The classical literatures were still the main subject of study in schools and universities, but in the new conditions of the nineteenth century, their influence was likely to be (in most cases) subliminal rather than overt. Class feeling provides us with a pertinent example of how that influence worked. Class divisions certainly existed in antiquity and were, just as certainly, different from their modern counterparts. The Athenian *demos* and the *populus Romanus* had no exact equivalents in a mid-nineteenth-century England that possessed no slaves (except for wage-slaves) and possessed a whole range of classes between the aristocracy and the labouring poor, classes whose rôles could be defined in economic terms. The only characteristic that the ancient and the Victorian system had in common was the age-old distinction between potential rulers and those destined to be ruled. What past and present could share was the assumption that certain social categories were fitted for the work of governing while others needed to be governed. Formative years spent reading Greek and Latin authors made men like the Mills and the Arnolds take this assumption for granted and made it easy for them to believe that England's future prosperity depended on the formation of a capable élite.

Sometimes however even in the nineteenth century the classical heritage was put to a more personal and more creative use. If we look back to the last part of Professor Fuhrmann's paper, we shall see that the Hellenism of the *Goethezeit* did not remain a mere offshoot of nationalism; nor indeed could it be reduced to the cult of noble simplicity and serene greatness that Winckelmann's idealism had advocated.

What developed under the guidance of Goethe and Schiller was not merely a desire to recreate the spontaneity and harmony of the Greek genius as they conceived it to have been, but also a determination to achieve this revival in a higher form that would be suited to the subtler self-awareness of an age of scientific knowledge and romantic feeling.

Professor Gelzer analyses the history of Goethe's attempt to transcend the eighteenth-century concept of Hellenism. The Goethe who wrote *Iphigenie* looked for salvation through the unremitting pursuit of an ideal. He thought that if he adopted what he took to be the Greek view of life, he could solve the problems that harassed him and his contemporaries. Experience however proved this hope ill-founded. And the Goethe who wrote *Faust II* put his trust in *Bildung*, the enlargement of man's intellectual horizons; and he had realised that such an enlargement could not come from the contemplation of a single culture however excellent. Goethe in his old age accepted the Romantic view of the universe as a place of numerous possibilities which different cultures had explored in different ways. The Hellenic world no longer appeared to him uniquely privileged. He saw it as one source of enlightenment among many, though it remained for him a source of great importance.

Moreover – and this was perhaps an even more important change – he realised that neither the Greek nor any other past culture could offer the present a ready-made solution for its problems. All they could offer were hints that had to be creatively exploited. He thought that the answer to the enigma of human existence lay somewhere in that no-man's-land where beauty, goodness and knowledge meet. The Greeks had won a glimpse of it, and so at other times had the people of other cultures, and it was only through an understanding of their recorded experience that man could hope to advance.

The paper on the Arnolds has been placed after the two we have just discussed, though Thomas, like Bentham, still stood in the shadow of the eighteenth century. It has been placed there because Matthew, a more important figure than his father, was one of Goethe's disciples. Like Goethe, he stressed the supreme value of a wide culture, an infinitely extended *Bildung*. Like Goethe, he had come under the spell of Romanticism. And like Goethe, he was passionately attached to ancient Greece.

But it is impossible to give a satisfactory summary account of Matthew. Protean, he changes shape and slips through our fingers. Admiring Goethe, he was in many ways Goethe's opposite. Where the great German had moved from a belief in the serene, the controlled and the harmonious to an appreciation of diversity, Arnold began as a Keatsian Romantic and moved (in theory at least) to advocating a beauty that was 'particular, precise and firm'. Where Goethe saw *Bildung* as providing materials for creative activity, Matthew gave 'culture' a different rôle. It was to guarantee the sharpness of the tools (sensibility, logic, the power to relate ideas) that make creation possible.

It is true that when we attempt to assess the importance of Hellenism in Matthew's thought, there is a central principle that can serve us as a life-line. This is the famous statement that poetry is or should be 'a criticism of life', which can be interpreted to mean that poetry should offer an ordered view of the universe embodying a truer, fuller set of values than the mean ones we habitually follow, and therefore constituting a 'criticism' of the latter. This notion owes something to Aristotle, and the ordered view Matthew recommends is the one we find in the best Greek writers. Here is a firm commitment, but alas, it still lacks precision. Matthew does not spell out in detail the nature of the Greek view of life and the Greek values. Apart from his three essays about Homer, he did not write much about ancient Greece. He looked for moral inspiration elsewhere, in writers who by his own admission were inferior to the Greeks, in Joubert, in Spinoza, in Marcus Aurelius. And most of all he looked for examples of the absence of the values he cherished. So much of his writing is negative. It consists of attacks on 'humdrum people, slaves to routine, enemies to light'.[1]

Matthew is elusive. But he undoubtedly belongs to that nineteenth-century group of experimenters who tried to bring in the Old World to redress the balance of the New. With Nietzsche we come to an experimenter of a different sort. Here was a man who turned not to the Greeks, but to a particular Greek; and he did not aim to produce an amalgam of Greek and modern ideas, or Greek, oriental and mediaeval ideas as Goethe had done. He just allowed his own thought to develop, with a remarkable insight and an almost insane energy, the hints that had been left by his ancient predecessor.

Professor Hölscher tells us that Nietzsche's interest in Heraclitus dated from that early period in his life when he was still a disciple of Schopenhauer. A youthful essay, composed as a supplement to *Die Geburt der Tragödie*, gives prominence to those very characteristics of the Presocratic sage that will meet us again in the works that follow *Also sprach Zarathustra*. Nietzsche notes here the pride and isolation of Heraclitus; the latter's belief that Becoming is the only form of existence; and that further important belief which makes the struggles that necessarily characterise the world of Becoming their own justification. At this early stage in Nietzsche's career, the Heraclitean conceptions are merely placed on record as a possible view of the universe. They are to remain in the background during

[1] Matthew Arnold, 'Heinrich Heine', *Essays in Criticism* (1865).

his sceptical middle period; but when he transcends his scepticism, they win his full consent. His later philosophy is built upon them as Scholasticism was built on Aristotle. Nietzsche is the one nineteenth-century thinker who makes us suspect that in Greece, as in Africa, there may always turn out to be something new.

In *Culture and Anarchy* Matthew Arnold quotes Montesquieu to the effect that 'the first motive which ought to impel us to study is the desire to augment the excellence of our nature and to render an intelligent being yet more intelligent'.[1] The problem of how to augment the excellence of our nature also troubled John Stuart Mill as we can see from his final essays, though he would have described what was needed in less flattering terms; and it certainly troubled Nietzsche, who had perhaps a clearer idea than either Arnold or Mill of the universe that the thought of his age was revealing. But the man who envisaged most lucidly how one should proceed towards self-improvement was Ernest Renan. Where others formulated ideals or relied on intuition to carve them a road to their goal, Renan came forward with a method.

Renan put his trust in philology, and to understand what he meant by this, we must, as Professor Seznec's elegant paper demonstrates, establish first what he did not mean. He saw no merit in the classical teaching common in his day whose aim was a stylistic imitation of the ancients; and he mocked the kind of scholarship that quibbles over meaningless trivialities. It was true that a scholar's work had to rest on accurate attention to detail, and what appeared to be trivial was not to be neglected merely for that reason. But detail had always to relate to a larger purpose.

A Göttingen professor, Friedrich Gottlieb Welcker, who was in the habit of praising the literary and artistic achievements of the Greeks, had spoken contemptuously of oriental studies and had deplored the reading of Greek authors outside the Golden Age. Renan rose to their defence, and we find him arguing that the literatures of the east and Greek writings of the second rank often have more to tell us about the history of the human mind than the greatest masterpieces.

'L'histoire de l'esprit humain' was in Renan's view the proper concern of a serious philologist, and the phrase he used distinguishes him from the aged Goethe or his own contemporary, Matthew Arnold. He thought in terms of an ordered history instead of a vague *Bildung* or 'a commerce with the best that men have thought or

---

[1] Matthew Arnold, *Culture and Anarchy*, ed. J. Dover Wilson (Cambridge, 1971), p. 44.

read'. And seeing his goal plainly, he knew how to set about reaching it.

The eighteenth century had believed that the world could be made perfect (or at any rate vastly improved) by the application of reason to its problems. The nineteenth had learnt that this simple recipe would not work. The French Revolution had demonstrated that rational arrangements could not be readily imposed on an irrational society. The rapid spread of human knowledge had revealed a complexity in the universe that no-one had previously suspected; and the study of biology, the broadening of historical perspectives and the exploration of new cultures, all contributed to a picture of life that was dominated by variety and change. To discover how to guide one's life, how the world should be guided, was a much harder assignment in the 1850s and 1860s than it had been a hundred years earlier.

Since the men of this time lacked the techniques that might have helped them to analyse the conditions they saw around them, they trusted to the techniques they did know and assumed that the nature of the world could be discovered from its history, from a careful analysis of the records of the past. Renan aimed to put this analysis on a firm footing. Its scope was to embrace all cultures and all ages, but naturally some portions of this vast field seemed likely to yield more than others. The classical civilisations, and Greece in particular, promised a great deal. The Greeks had been unequalled in the vigour of their speculations, the beauty of their art and their response to a great variety of experiences. Towards the end of his life Renan joined Matthew Arnold in holding that Greece was our best guide after all; but where he was concerned it was to be a Greece reconstituted through a careful use of all the resources of scholarship.

Our investigations end with Renan. The period we have been examining has shown us the close of the transformations wrought by humanism. By the eighteenth century, European culture was capable of making swift progress without help from the classical past. The past however was still familiar. It dominated education and was unlikely to be disregarded. During the next hundred years, we see it attacked. Its heroes are denigrated, but at the same time myths derived from its history are offered as ideals, and its records are searched for evidence that helps the development of old and new branches of knowledge. Finally, against a background of classically oriented thinking produced by the education of the period, we see individuals coming to hope that insights derived from classical learning, in company perhaps with insights from other cultures, might provide a clue to the purpose of life.

Renan was the organiser of this hope. He suggested procedures by which it could be realised.

We know now that his planning met with no success. What he proposed was too difficult. Success in the ordering of human experience in a form that would yield intellectually useful results depended on man's ability to co-ordinate achievements in a great number of fields. It depended in the last analysis on the imposition by common consent of a programme that would guarantee that each stage of research would be completed as required. Besides, even if the records had been fully understood, the experience sifted, the lessons drawn, we should have been enlightened at best about man's character and deep purposes. The whole enterprise might have taught us to live more wisely, but it would have had nothing to offer by way of material prosperity or power. So, before long, the historical approach to the problems of life was pushed into the background by the development of techniques – economic, sociological, psychological – for controlling the present. And the twentieth century entered upon a road that led far from the dreams of the nineteenth.

PART I

THE EPILOGUE TO
THE RENAISSANCE

1

ROMAN LAW AND THE NATIONAL LEGAL SYSTEMS

H. COING

I

1. About the year 1650 the so-called 'reception' of Roman–Canon law on the continent of Europe had come to an end. With one great exception – England – all the countries that had belonged in the Middle Ages to the church of Rome had adopted the rules of Roman–Canon law as their *ius commune*. From Italy in the south to the Sweden of the Vasa monarchy, from Portugal in the west to Poland and Hungary in the east, Roman law had been accepted as the basis of legal education and was considered as an authority by judges and administrators. It is to an Englishman, Arthur Duck, that we are indebted for a description of the influence Roman law had gained in the different kingdoms of Europe. Duck's book, *De usu ac auctoritate iuris civilis Romanorum in dominiis principum Christianorum*, a defence of Roman law written under the Commonwealth, appeared in 1653 and is one of the first treatises on comparative law in the legal history of Europe.

2. We should begin perhaps by making clear the position that Roman law held as a source of law in these different countries. In defining this position, it is important first of all to remember that in the seventeenth century, Europe had not yet discovered all the consequences that the theory of sovereignty can have for the theory of the sources of law. To the political idea of sovereignty there corresponds in law the concept of a completely centralised and unified legal system. According to the doctrine developed in the nineteenth century by John Austin, all legal rules are to be traced to the will of the sovereign. They are to be understood as orders that he gives to his subjects. The ideal realisation of this concept would be a system of codified law where the codes were made by the sovereign (be it king or parliament), and where judges were strictly bound to the letter of the existing codes. Now, if such a system has ever existed in reality, it certainly did not exist in seventeenth-century Europe.

What we find at that time is a pluralistic system of legal sources. Lawyers were trained to look for rules not only in statutes but also in the traditions of their profession, and used whatever they found to solve their problems.

It is this attitude – on the whole, a rather mediaeval attitude to law – that made the so-called reception of Roman law possible. Practically no state adopted Roman law by a legislative act. It is true that in the Holy Roman Empire the authority of Roman law had for a long time been connected with the idea that the mediaeval emperors were the direct successors of Rome's Constantine and Justinian, so that it seemed natural to adopt the codes these had created. But in the majority of European countries, and especially in the kingdoms that grew most obviously in power during the sixteenth and seventeenth centuries, the Holy Roman emperors had never exercised political authority. In these states, the only basis for the authority of Roman law was the idea of reason. Roman law was applied because it seemed to express what reason dictated for the solution of legal problems. Even in Germany, it was only at the beginning of our period, in the middle of the seventeenth century, that people became aware that Roman law had not been introduced by the emperors, but had developed through what they called the *usus fori*, the practice of the courts.

Since it formed part of a body of law which consisted of very different elements, the authority of Roman law was in no way absolute. It had in fact a subsidiary character. A lawyer who needed to solve some practical problem would look first at local statutes and customs. These existed in nearly every town and county. They varied from place to place, and their number was legion. Secondly, he would apply the rules laid down in ordinances and statutes given by the sovereign for his dominions. These too were often local in their scope and governed just one single province or one city or county. It was only when a lawyer failed to find a rule to suit his problem in these sources, that he turned as a last resort to Roman law. Nevertheless, it would be misleading to assume that Roman law was of small importance because it had only this subsidiary authority. The local laws we have mentioned applied to only a small number of the social problems of the time; and, what was perhaps more important, statutes, customs and ordinances were not considered to be a complete and autonomous system which could be understood by itself and so extended by *ratiocinatio* to cases not covered by express rules.

Instead, they were considered as isolated rules that had to be explained and construed in the light of the concepts of Roman law, and this led in practice to a reversal of the hierarchy of the sources. Roman law offered an enormous mass of legal rules, not casuistry only, but also principles and broad conceptions. Even where immediate solutions could not be discovered in the classical sources, a lawyer could find there arguments and points of view that could help him solve his problems. Consequently, the influence of Roman law was much greater in practice than its position within the contemporary system of sources of law suggests.

3. The influence of Roman law rested on a mass of legal literature which had developed since the Middle Ages. This literature was written in Latin and so could be understood by lawyers in all the countries of Europe. German law-courts used not only the works of Italian jurists, but also, for example, the commentaries of the Frenchman, Argentré, on the *coutume* of Brittany, and I have found in Portugal in the former library of a Portuguese judge, whose manuscript notes show that he used the book for his own practice, a copy of Carpzov, a German lawyer of the middle of the seventeenth century who wrote on criminal law. In this legal literature, lawyers found what was called the *communis opinio doctorum*, that is the rules which a majority of leading lawyers had developed for resolving particular legal problems.

Based as it was on this large body of learned commentary, the Roman law of this period cannot be regarded as a fixed and final set of rules that allowed no variation or development. It must be understood rather to have been a living tradition, capable of adapting itself to new developments and of assimilating new methods of construction and interpretation.

II

This leads to the question of what we must understand under the term 'Roman law' in the seventeenth and eighteenth centuries. The expression 'a living tradition' calls for further comment.

1. The basis of Roman law, as we see it understood and applied in the period we have to consider here, was always the *Corpus iuris* of Justinian. It is important to remember however that this *Corpus* is a

body of law of a very specific type. It cannot be compared to a modern code. It is in fact a vast collection of legal materials, comprising thousands of items from the law books of classical Rome, hundreds upon hundreds of specific decisions in *responsa* and imperial *constitutiones*, as well as particular statutes promulgated by the emperors. There are items that go back to the last years of the Roman Republic. Many go back to the time of the Principate. There are imperial constitutions from the late Empire and regulations laid down by Justinian. Even the Middle Ages made some additions, the most important of which are the *libri feudorum*, feudal laws that derive from north Italian statutes and customs. The materials that make up the *Corpus iuris* belong to periods widely separated in time and very different in their constitutional and social structure.

It is not surprising therefore that out of this great mass of material different epochs selected different sections to serve their particular purposes. The nineteenth-century pandectists for example were interested mostly in the law concerning contracts, delicts and real property as this is set out in the fragments of the Roman jurists; and they completely disregarded administrative law and the Justinian Code's rules concerning the different orders of Roman society, matters which seventeenth-century lawyers on the other hand still found deeply interesting. So we have our first point. The existence of a living tradition meant a selective use of the legal materials that the *Corpus iuris* offered.

Secondly, it meant that the Roman sources were used as a kind of broad framework into which new topics were introduced that antiquity had not properly explored. Let me illustrate this by two examples. During the fifteenth and sixteenth centuries, Italian lawyers linked Roman and commercial law. Their procedure was as follows. First they stated the positive rules that had developed in commercial law. Then they fitted these rules into a Roman framework and finally reinterpreted them in the light of Roman sources. The seventeenth century saw a similar process occur with respect to international law, both private and public. Making free use of rules found in the *Corpus iuris* and adding rules found in ancient philosophy or ancient historians, the great internationalists of the seventeenth century developed what has become the historical basis for our international law. This method was used by Hugo Grotius and to an even greater extent by the first great British international lawyers, Albericus Gentilis and Richard Zouche. Thus Roman law was a living tradition also in the sense that it could be extended to cover completely new subjects.

2. The instrument which made such selections and extensions possible was the *interpretation* of Roman law. The methods of interpretation changed. During the period of the 'reception' the Scholastic method had prevailed. Mediaeval lawyers, lacking an historical sense, used to identify their own world with the Roman. But they used their ancient sources mainly to provide arguments for the solution of legal problems, and not to provide rules that would be strictly applied. Then in the sixteenth century juridical humanism began to use methods that had been developed in philology. That resulted in a new understanding of the legal texts of the ancients as they were now related to their historical background, but it also led to the discovery that Roman law had been affected by the social changes of antiquity, and that the ancient world had been very different from the contemporary one. The difficulties involved in applying the legal system of the sixth century A.D. to the problems of the sixteenth and seventeenth centuries became increasingly apparent. But although they differed widely, the results of both these methods – the mediaeval and the humanistic – were used by lawyers in the middle of the seventeenth century when our period begins.

At the end of that century however there was a decisive change, and the systematic method of interpretation began its ascendancy. The great work in which this new method was applied to the ancient texts in a systematic and convincing way was *Les lois civiles dans leurs ordres naturels* written by the French judge Domat in 1692.

This work has three main characteristics.

(a) It develops *principles* and rules out of Roman casuistry. The text consists of principles and rules formulated by the author, and the Roman sources appear only in footnotes.

(b) The principles and rules are formulated in French and not in Latin.

(c) All the rules and principles are placed within the framework of a system that the author himself developed, and the order in which they are arranged is completely different from the one in the Roman sources. This systematic method suited the spirit of the Age of Reason.

Domat's book proved a great success, not only in France but also in other European countries. The English translations went through

33

three editions before 1750; and during the eighteenth century the new method conquered the universities. Instruction at their law courses was given in the systematic way that Domat had pioneered, and on the basis of textbooks that followed his method. The old technique of explaining text after text, which had been characteristic of the Middle Ages, was abandoned.

The heyday of this approach to Roman law was reached when the German pandectists wrote their great system of Roman law in which they merged the results of Roman legal science with the systematic outlook of the eighteenth century natural law movement, and it was in that systematic form that Roman law survived and dominated this period.

III

But the days of its dominance were numbered. We see already in the eighteenth century the rise of two movements that progressively diminished the rise of Roman law. These were the ascendancy of national law and the development of the natural law of the Enlightenment.

1. National law means in this context the local statutes and customs and the contemporary state legislation of the different European countries. In France, for example, national law or *le droit français* was composed out of the *coutumes* (e.g. *les coutumes d'Orléans*) and the *grandes ordonnances* (especially those given by Louis XIV). Similarly in the Savoyard *diritto patrio* we find the local statutes and the *constitutiones* of the dukes.

These examples show that 'national law' did not mean in the eighteenth century a unified national legal system as it did in the nineteenth. It was used to describe the law formed by state legislation in the period of absolutism. The more usual name for it was *ius patrium* or *ius modernum*.

This *ius modernum* gained in strength as the political system of enlightened despotism developed, and the new state bureaucracy became increasingly influential. We can use the curricula drawn up for legal education as an indicator for this evolution. For a long time, the *ius modernum* was a topic treated within the framework of the Roman law course. The regulations of the Strasbourg Law School for example laid down in 1603 that the professor who lectured on the *Codex* had first to set out the Roman rules on procedure and then in the appropriate place he had to add the possibly different rules used by the city court or by the *Reichskammergericht* of the Holy Roman Empire. At the end of the century on the other hand special courses on the *ius modernum* made their appearance. Swedish law schools for example added courses on Swedish law to their introductory courses on the *Institutes* of Justinian. The most important advance in this respect was made however by the French reform of legal teaching in 1679 when courses on *le droit français* were introduced into the curriculum – courses in which there was a fusion of Roman and French national law – a fusion which became the basis of the *Code Napoléon*; and similar changes can be observed during the eighteenth century in other European states.

2. The natural law movement of the Enlightenment had its historical origins in the renaissance of Stoic philosophy during the sixteenth century, as we can see from the writings of Grotius. Later deductive reasoning became important from axioms such as liberty, equality or property whose legal validity was assumed, and the rule of law was regarded as the instrument of their realisation. Two schools of thought emerged. One, based on Locke's political writings, proclaimed the rule of law. The other, founded by Pufendorf and Thomasius and popular on the continent, advocated the system of enlightened despotism.

The principles developed by these schools quickly became an instrument for criticising the existing law, which meant for the most part Roman law. Examples of this kind of criticism can be found in the writings of Thomasius at Halle. Its objects were mainly the historical or non-rational elements in Roman law, its so-called 'subtleties', its shortcomings in respect of contemporary needs, and last but not least, the great uncertainties that attended the application of Roman law to modern times. On the whole, we are confronted here with the same sort of criticism that Bentham was to direct against the English common law.

This criticism had for its logical result a demand for new legislation and especially for codification. For the eighteenth century a code meant in practice that 'standing rule to live by' of which Locke had spoken. The idea was to compile a book in which citizens could see their rights and duties, and the limits placed on their liberty by the establishment of a government. The first great codes appeared at the end of the eighteenth century: the Prussian *Allgemeines Landrecht*

(1794), the Austrian *Allgemeines bürgerliches Gesetzbuch* (1811) and most important of all, the Napoleonic codes, especially the *Code civil* (1804).

The later history of this codification movement contains a certain element of irony. On the one hand, the codes were the product of the natural law movement, which was based on the idea of there being one legal system for all rational beings. On the other hand, the codes were the work of national legislation, and so they meant the end of the *ius commune*, the breakdown of the continental common law. Codification meant in practice the nationalisation of the legal system. Once again, legal education is a good indicator. Curricula were now devoted to the national codes, and Roman law survived only as a kind of historical introduction to national legislation. Legal science, which had for centuries formed a spiritual unit, was now divided up into provinces, that were rather strictly separated along national lines.

Codification also meant the end of the formal authority of Roman law in most European states. This statement must however be qualified. Roman law did live on in the codes themselves, since these took their systematic and conceptual framework from it and also many principles and rules, especially in the fields of contract, succession and testamentary dispositions. But though its material influence lasted, its formal authority disappeared.

IV

The outcome of these developments was that nineteenth-century Europe presents us with a picture of many national legal systems functioning side by side, as we see them still today. Roman law remained – historical studies apart – only as an element of general juridical culture and as one of the elements out of which the new codes had been made.

A special situation existed in Germany however. During the nineteenth century, she did not have a unified legal system. In the Austrian monarchy, the great codes of the eighteenth century were in force. Where Prussia was concerned, the Prussian Code had authority only in its eastern provinces. In the Rhenish territories, which the monarchy had gained at the Treaty of Paris, the French Code remained in force, and in central Germany a broad strip of territory was still governed by Roman law. Thus Germany was practically the only country in Europe where Roman law still had authority, and what appears more important, it was Roman law that gained predominance in German legal science. It is characteristic that the Law School of the University of Berlin, which was founded in 1810 and became Germany's model university during the nineteenth century, based its law teaching on Roman, and not on Prussian, law. It had no course on Prussian law during the first decade of its existence, and when that subject did make its appearance in the curriculum, the fundamental courses were still all devoted to Roman law.

The Berlin course became the model for legal instruction in all the other German universities, and after 1850, under the guidance of its Minister of Justice, Thun-Hohenstein, Austria adopted the same system. It is no wonder then that the German Civil Code, which came into force at the end of the century, has probably been the one most influenced by Roman law.

With this development, Roman law came once again to exercise a decisive influence in Germany, and its success there gave it a momentum that affected the whole of Europe. The German school of pandectists became one of Europe's most important centres of legal science during the second half of the nineteenth century. The details of its history have not yet been fully explored; and there are many questions that require further research. But I think one can state without undue exaggeration that this school of pandectists exercised a great influence on Italian, Scandinavian, and even on English legal science and jurisprudence. I shall mention only the fact that John Austin came in touch with the school during the time he studied in Bonn.

2

'PHAENOMENA BENE FUNDATA': FROM 'SAVING THE APPEARANCES' TO THE MECHANISATION OF THE WORLD-PICTURE

JÜRGEN MITTELSTRASS

1. In a letter to de Volder written in 1705 Leibniz calls the rainbow 'a real or well-founded phenomenon (*phaenomenon reale seu bene fundatum*) which, if we proceed methodically, does not disappoint our expectations'.[1] Apart from their aesthetic qualities, rainbows are reckoned among those phenomena whose explanation, with regard to the applicability of optical laws to empirical phenomena, plays an important rôle in the history of optics. Now, on this occasion as well as on other occasions where he uses the expression 'phaenomenon bene fundatum', Leibniz is not particularly interested in rainbows or in optical laws. Rather, he points out that phenomena in a physical sense are always to be conceived as parts of an already structured experience, common or scientific. The world of phenomena, the 'univeral system of the phenomena', as Leibniz says,[2] is not given 'as such', but is itself the result of perceptual and conceptual constructions performed by the subject of experience. In philosophy, in this context, one speaks about Kant's 'Copernican revolution'. Such a revolution already exists to some extent in Leibniz, representing the *epistemological* conclusion from a *methodological* development.

The methodological development refers to the organisation of rational physics, i.e. to the establishment of Galilean kinematics together with its transformation into dynamics, achieved by the *genius loci*, Isaac Newton, who also succeeded in giving the first

---

[1] *Die philosophischen Schriften von G. W. Leibniz*, ed. C. I. Gerhardt (7 vols., Berlin, 1875–90) vol. II, p. 276; cf. letter of 6 December 1715 to A. Conti, *Der Briefwechsel von Gottfried Wilhelm Leibniz mit Mathematikern*, ed. C. I. Gerhardt (Berlin, 1899): 'La matière même n'est pas une substance, mais seulement *substantiatum*, un Phénomène bien fondé, et qui ne trompe point quand on y procède en raisonnant suivant les lois idéales de l'Arithmétique, de la Géométrie et de la Dynamique etc.'.

[2] *Discours de métaphysique*, § 14, in *Philosophische Schriften*, vol. IV, p. 439.

comprehensive axiomatisation of classical mechanics. Leibniz, too, has his place in this physical history. First, with regard to his endeavours towards a foundation of mechanics in an axiomatic structure, applying the (Hobbesian) notion of *conatus* and his theory of differentials in the solution of dynamic problems; secondly, for instance, with regard to a planetary theory, where he provides a physical explanation of planetary motion on the basis of Kepler's analysis of the elliptical orbit into a circulation and a radial motion, combining the mechanics of *conatus* and inertial motion with the concept of a fluid vortex.[1] What Leibniz calls a transition from geometry to physics through a 'science of motion that unites matter with forms and theory with practice',[2] means simply the attempt to explain mechanically all the phenomena of the empirical world. From a methodological point of view the programme of rational physics, which dominates science and philosophy in the seventeenth and eighteenth centuries, is defined by this attempt: to place the foundation of physics on the three fundamental quantities of length, time and mass (or force). In the words of the critical Cartesian Christiaan Huygens, in the true philosophy 'one conceives the causes of all natural effects in terms of mechanical motions (*par des raisons de mécanique*). This, in my opinion, we must necessarily do, or else renounce all hopes of ever comprehending anything in Physics'.[3]

The systematical insight that the world of (physical) phenomena is the result of perceptual and conceptual constructions performed by the subject of experience (only then reaching the status of a *phaenomenon bene fundatum*) leads, as you know, to the so-called mechanisation of the world-picture (E. J. Dijksterhuis), promoted, among other things, by the common desire for satisfaction of our imagination which may be metaphysically, but is not methodologically, oriented. Within this development, the concept of nature is put on a par with mechanical laws which are valid in technical practice. The transition to this concept of nature is marked by the disintegration of the

---

[1] Cf. E. J. Aiton, *The Vortex Theory of Planetary Motions* (London and New York, 1972); E. J. Aiton and Jürgen Mittelstrass, 'Leibniz: physics, logic, metaphysics', *Dictionary of Scientific Biography*, ed. C. C. Gillispie (14 vols., New York, 1970–6), vol. VIII (1973), pp. 151f.

[2] *Pacidius Philalethi*, in *Opuscules et fragments inédits de Leibniz*, ed. L. Couturat (Paris, 1903; reprinted Hildesheim, 1966), p. 596.

[3] *Treatise of Light*, trans. S. P. Thompson (London, 1912; reprinted Dover, 1962), p. 3 (*Œuvres complètes de Christiaan Huygens* (22 vols., Société hollandaise des sciences, La Haye, 1888–1950), vol. XIX, p. 461).

metaphor 'nature acts' (in Boyle).[1] Its place is taken by metaphors from the world of machines: man as a jointed doll (in Descartes),[2] his home a *machina mundi* (already in Copernicus)[3] or *machina caelestis* (in Kepler),[4] itself compared with a clockwork creature (*instar horologii*), in contrast to a divine creature (*instar divini animalis*) as seen by tradition.[5] The mechanistic world-view proves to be the *cosmological* side of the *methodological* restriction to mechanical explanatory models.

2. A methodological restriction to mechanical explanations already characterises Galilean mechanics. In the historiography of science it has led to the convention of linking Galilean mechanics both with the overcoming of Aristotelian physics and the foundation of modern physics. Such a characterisation, however, is still too general. Particularly, it also permits us to link the genesis of the 'new science' (*nuova scienza*), as Galilean physics is forthwith called, with earlier, mediaeval developments. A 'Galilean revolution' could then only be described with respect to a rather long process.

Now, what matters is to represent and to judge systematical insights (in this case insights underlying classical mechanics) both against the (naïve) myth of 'beginnings without history' and the (sophisticated) myth of 'history the leveller'. Accepting the first myth, one would not be aware of the fact that science, too, is part of man's historical practice, a fact which rules out the possibijo ʎʇı putting oneself outside of developments; accepting the second, one would overlook the fact that systematical knowledge does not depend (for reasons mentioned in the first case) on the validity of statements about developments. At best, historical processes refer to steps of *rational development*. Such development, in the first instance, has the status of a *supposition*. A methodically reflective historiography uses such a supposition, because efforts towards reconstructions – particularly when they are dealing with scientific and therefore *theoretical* orientations – cannot start at all without an assumption about the

---

[1] 'A free inquiry into the vulgarly received notion of nature', *The Works of the Honourable Robert Boyle*, ed. T. Birch, 2nd ed. (6 vols., London, 1772), vol. v, p. 219.

[2] *Le monde* (*Traité de l'homme*), in *Œuvres de Descartes*, ed. C. Adam and P. Tannery (12 vols., Paris, 1897–1910), vol. xi, p. 120.

[3] *De revolutionibus orbium caelestium libri sex*, in *Gesamtausgabe*, vol. ii, ed. F. Zeller and C. Zeller (München, 1949), p. 5.

[4] Letter of 10 February 1605 to Herwart von Hohenburg, *Gesammelte Werke*, ed. W. v. Dyck and M. Caspar and F. Hammer (München, 1937ff.), vol. xv, p. 146.

[5] *Ibid.*

rationality of developments. If in the following I draw attention to elements of Greek science in classical mechanics, founded in Galilean physics, it is not my intention to point to the historical relativity of the Galilean achievements, but to show on which systematical, particularly methodological, insights Galileo was able to rely. Those insights are part of non-Aristotelian, Greek axiomatic science.

First, let me deal with the opposition between Aristotelian and Galilean physics. This opposition can be illustrated by indicating two concepts of experience differing basically from each other. Experience in its Aristotelian sense is defined as conceptual ('universal') knowledge based on concrete distinctions in the field of phenomena; the principles and propositions of physics are theoretical accounts of these distinctions, or, to put it in another way, explicit generalisations of the conceptual knowledge inherent in everyday experience:

It falls to experience to provide the principles of any subject. In astronomy, for instance, it was astronomical experience that provided the principles of the science, for it was only when the phenomena were adequately grasped that the proofs in astronomy were discovered. And the same is true of any art or science whatever.[1]

We have learned from Professor Owen's excellent article on Τιθέναι τὰ φαινόμενα[2] that φαινόμενα in Aristotle are not only (indeed, are seldom) empirical data, i.e. observed facts, but are also ἔνδοξα (common conceptions on the subject) and λεγόμενα (a conceptual structure revealed by language).[3] Hence, already in Aristotle the world of phenomena has a conceptual structure. Only this structure is not a *theoretical* structure, in the sense that it already includes as its methodological core a recourse to measurements of length, time and mass.

This, however, is the case in classical mechanics, its concept of experience being therefore distinguished from the Aristotelian concept by its dependence on a *technical practice*, based upon a *theory of measurement*. Whereas in Aristotelian physics, because of the genetic relationship between experiential and theoretical knowledge, propositions of everyday experience and propositions of physics never contradict each other (the genetic relationship being therefore

[1] *An. pr.* A30.46a17–22.
[2] *Aristote et les problèmes de méthode. Communications présentées au Symposium Aristotelicum tenu à Louvain du 24 août au 1er septembre 1960* (Louvain and Paris, 1961), pp. 83–103.
[3] *Ibid.* pp. 85ff.

an analytic one as well), the propositions of classical mechanics (for instance in the case of free fall or inertial motion) often in fact contradict everyday experience. I.e. phenomena 'explained' by those propositions are not in the first instance provided by everyday experience at all. They are rather produced in experiments, and serve, among other things, to *correct* everyday experience. In experiment as a technically produced and technically controlled experience, hypotheses (formed in the case of Galilean mechanics by means of an axiomatic part) are controlled by inserting the results of measurement into the formulae of the theory. Phenomena, in this sense, are 'well-founded' if passive sensibility, i.e. 'phenomenal' experience, has been replaced by an attempt to control instrumentally the conditions of sensibility. Both Aristotelian and Galilean physics represent *empirical* science: the former because it can be understood as a generalisation ('objectivisation') of the knowledge of everyday experience (basic knowledge of concrete distinctions and demonstrated knowledge being in principle one and the same); the latter because it submits its propositions to objective, technically controlled experiences (basic knowledge of concrete distinctions and demonstrated knowledge diverging in this case). The Aristotelian and the Galilean concepts of experience stand for two different concepts of *empirical knowledge*. The Aristotelian concept has as its goal a stabilisation of everyday experience, the Galilean concept an instrumental domination of nature.

3. The constituent element of the Galilean concept of empirical knowledge, within the framework of the foundation of empirical physics in its modern sense, is the distinction between strictly empirical parts, and theoretical parts (or 'axioms', from the point of view of its logical structure). Galilean mechanics consists of an *axiomatic theory*, which is subsequently as it were linked through its logical conclusions with *existential assumptions*, and is thus extended into an empirical, 'experimental' part. According to Galileo, the physicist 'wants to recognize in the concrete the effect which he has proved in the abstract'.[1] As far as propositions of an axiomatic theory

---

[1] *Dialogue Concerning the Two Chief World Systems – Ptolemaic and Copernican*, trans. Stillman Drake (Berkeley and Los Angeles, 1967), p. 207 (*Le opere di Galileo Galilei* (20 vols., Edizione Nazionale, Florence, 1890–1909), vol. vii, p. 234). For Galileo's axiomatic theory, cf. J. Mittelstrass, *Neuzeit und Aufklärung. Studien zur Entstehung der neuzeitlichen Wissenschaft und Philosophie* (Berlin and New York, 1970), pp. 207ff.; also 'The Galilean revolution', *Studies in History and Philosophy of Science*, ii (1972), 297–328.

are concerned, the validity of these propositions is untouched by this extension. If the properties of uniformly accelerated motion, deduced in the framework of pure kinematics, are not realised in freely falling and accelerated bodies, Galileo writes, 'our proofs lose none of their force and conclusiveness as they are only supposed to be valid for our own hypotheses. They are no more affected than are the propositions of Archimedes on spirals by the fact that no bodies can be found in nature which carry out a spiral motion'.[1] Already when he is working on *De motu*, Galileo recalls a demand, which he has obviously found in the *Book on Balance* attributed to Euclid, 'that heavy and light are to be handled mathematically', i.e. geometrically and axiomatically.[2] In the elaboration of this programme, Galilean mechanics obtains its *Euclidean structure*, the characteristic form of classical mechanics up to Newton.

This form belongs to mechanics, and does not do so superficially (despite certain textbook traditions), nor is the recourse to statics accidental. Archimedean statics is given as a mathematical theory, supplementing in its axiomatic structure the axioms and postulates of Euclidean geometry by adding only seven propositions.[3] In this form, Archimedean statics is not only the most advanced example of pre-Galilean physics, it also makes clear how physics as a theoretical science (even in the modern sense of theoretical physics) is possible. Besides, we are dealing here with a physical theory which, in a strict sense, has no *empirical* parts. The method employed in this theory is to infer *physical* equilibrium from considerations about *geometrical* equilibrium. Here only the homogeneity of the physical body, i.e. its constant density, is being presupposed. If one disregards for the time being the problem that determining the homogeneity of physical bodies as to their masses involves applying the theorem of the lever – which then, in order to avoid a vicious circle, must have been established independently of the claim of homogeneity – Archimedean statics renders experiments unnecessary. What could be proved

[1] Letter of 5 June 1637 to P. Carcavy, *Opere*, vol. XVII, p. 90.
[2] 'De gravi et levi tractationem mathematicam esse, testatur fragmentum Euclidis', *Opere*, vol. I, p. 414; cf. R. S. Westfall, *Force in Newton's Physics. The Science of Dynamics in the Seventeenth Century* (London and New York, 1971), pp. 12ff.
[3] *De planorum aequilibriis*, in *Opera omnia cum commentariis Eutocii*, ed. J. L. Heiberg, 2nd ed. (3 vols., Leipzig, 1910–15), vol. II, pp. 124ff.; or *The Works of Archimedes*, ed. in modern notation with introductory chs. by T. L. Heath (Cambridge, 1912), pp. 189f.; or M. Clagett, *The Science of Mechanics in the Middle Ages* (Madison and London, 1959), p. 31. For a discussion of the axiomatic character of Archimedean statics (briefly discussed in the following) cf. Mittelstrass, *Neuzeit und Aufklärung*, pp. 243ff.

experimentally is the real homogeneity of physical bodies but, again, this homogeneity is nothing other than the condition on which certain statements about physical bodies are made. That homogeneous bodies have all the properties stated by the propositions of his statics, Archimedes knows *a priori*.

No doubt it was the example of Archimedean statics in its Euclidean structure which served as the standard for the theoretical part of Galileo's mechanics. Since 1269 the works of Archimedes were almost entirely available in the Latin translation from the Greek by William of Moerbeke. They were known, for instance, in fourteenth-century Paris; in sixteenth-century Italy we have an Archimedes renaissance which manifests itself not least through intensive translating activities (F. Commandino, L. Gaurico, N. Tartaglia and others).[1] As Professor of Mathematics at Pisa (1589–92) and Padua (1592–1610), Galileo lectured particularly on Euclid, Ptolemy and Archimedes, whom he called *suprahumanus* and *divinissimus*. His criticism of Aristotelian physics in *De motu* refers first of all to its non-mathematical character.[2]

The foundation of an axiomatic kinematics is only one side of Galilean physics, the other side being its empirical part, which is not contained in Archimedean statics for methodological reasons. This, however, implies that the discovery of the possibility of exact physics, represented by Archimedean statics, is not yet identical with the discovery of physics in its modern, general sense. To achieve this, what was needed was precisely the extension of a mathematical theory of physics into empirical parts, or rather into the correlation between theory and experience, which Galileo also cleared up from the theoretical point of view. The structure of Archimedean statics, however, explains in what sense classical mechanics up to Newton could be rendered as an *extended Euclidean geometry*.

4. This conception has nothing to do with the misunderstanding, often connected with speaking about the mechanisation of the world-picture, according to which the physical world ('nature') has itself a mathematical structure. Here a *method* is confounded with *properties of its object*. Such a confusion is often ascribed to

---

[1] See M. Clagett, *Archimedes in the Middle Ages*, vol. I: *The Arabo-Latin Tradition* (Madison, 1964), pp. 1ff. ('The impact of Archimedes on medieval science'); also G. Sarton, *The Appreciation of Ancient and Medieval Science during the Renaissance (1450–1600)* (Philadelphia, 1955), pp. 140ff.; and W. R. Shea, *Galileo's Intellectual Revolution* (London, 1972), pp. 1ff.

[2] *De motu*, in *Opere*, vol. I, pp. 302f.

Galileo,[1] with reference to the famous remark about the book of nature written in mathematical language,[2] but I dare say it in fact makes its début originally in Descartes. According to Descartes, nature is defined by the property of extension, a circumstance which 'explains' why the *instrumental* Galilean physics, which presupposes a theory of measurement, is valid in our world, and not the *phenomenal* Aristotelian physics, which does not presuppose such a theory. Descartes knows that in Galilean physics statements about nature rest upon the measurement of geometrical quantities. Those quantities determine what a 'physical entity' is. From this Descartes concludes that nature itself is adequately determined by the geometrical property of extension; the description of a method is identified with a statement about the structure of its object. In a third step this identification is then described as if the reduction of physical statements to statements about the measurement of physical quantities follows from the identification of these statements with statements about the structure of the physical object. In other words, *methodology of physics* once again becomes *metaphysics of nature* – and this, as Descartes erroneously assumed, for methodological reasons.

There are earlier examples in the development of post-Greek science of this unclear relationship between methodology of science and metaphysics of nature; for instance, in the theory of light of the Franciscan friar and Chancellor of the University of Oxford, Robert Grosseteste. Light (*lux*) is the fundamental physical substance, created together with prime matter by God, propagating itself into a sphere and thus giving rise to spatial dimensions and all physical bodies, forming the initially formless matter.[3] Here, too, we are dealing with the speculative aspect of an endeavour which can likewise be explained methodologically: in Grosseteste geometrical laws of rays and optical experiments form the basis of a scientific explanation of the physical world, i.e. optics is conceived as the basis of science. This, again, is important in our context insofar as the history of optics helped to keep alive the Greek idea of non-empirical science (Grosseteste is fully conversant, for instance, with Euclid's

---

[1] Cf. A. C. Crombie, *Robert Grosseteste and the Origins of Experimental Science 1100–1700* (Oxford, 1962), p. 310.

[2] *Il Saggiatore*, in *Opere*, vol. VI, p. 232; cf. letter of January 1641 to Fortunio Liceti, *Opere*, vol. XVIII, p. 295.

[3] *De luce seu de inchoatione formarum*; *De motu corporali et luce*. Cf. A. C. Crombie's outstanding presentation of Robert Grosseteste's physical theories in *Robert Grosseteste*, pp. 91ff.; also his article on Grosseteste in *Dictionary of Scientific Biography*, vol. v, pp. 548–54.

Optica and *Catoptrica*, the *Optica* attributed to Ptolemy, and pertinent writings of Avicenna, Alkindi and Averroes).[1] At the same time, with respect to the investigation of the refraction of light, it comes close to experimental physics (even in Ptolemy). Optics, besides statics, is that physical discipline which stays nearest to mathematics: most parts of optics are nothing but geometrical theory. The favourite object of investigation in physical optics in mediaeval times, however, was the rainbow (R. Bacon, Dietrich of Freiberg, Grosseteste, Witelo).

5. As constituent parts of this development, which clings side by side with Aristotelian physics to Greek forms of non-empirical science in proposing geometrical theories of statics and optics, there are, furthermore, some *methodological* considerations. These are, above all, concerned with the relationship between *a priori* and *a posteriori* elements within the structure of knowledge, linked up systematically with problems of the *Second Analytics*. The original meaning of the *a priori–a posteriori* distinction, which has gradually emerged since the twelfth century within the context of arguments *ex prioribus* and arguments *ex posterioribus*, was a *proof-theoretical* one. According to Thomas Aquinas, Albert of Saxony and others, *a priori* arguments serve to identify a proof which proceeds from causes to effects (or, in the logical mode, from premises to conclusions), *a posteriori* arguments serve to identify proofs which derive causes from effects (or premises from conclusions).

This meaning of *demonstratio a priori* and *demonstratio a posteriori* has been connected with the Aristotelian distinction between 'prior according to nature' and 'prior according to knowledge'[2] and, furthermore, with the distinction between giving the reasons for the fact (*demonstratio propter quid*) and giving the fact (*demonstratio quia*). In Grosseteste these distinctions already approach a conception of empirical science.[3] But it is in Paduan Aristotelianism and Galilean

---

[1] Cf. Crombie, *Robert Grosseteste*, pp. 116f.

[2] *An. post.* A2.71b33–72a5.

[3] Cf. Crombie, *Robert Grosseteste*, pp. 290f. Crombie summarises his investigations into the history of methodology with respect to the rise of modern empirical science as follows: 'The history of the theory of experimental science from Grosseteste to Newton is in fact a set of variations on Aristotle's theme, that the purpose of scientific inquiry was to discover true premises for demonstrated knowledge of observations, bringing in the new instrument of experiment and transposing into the key of mathematics' (*ibid.* p. 318). In a recent article, A. C. Crombie discusses the important influence of the Aristotelian distinction between *demonstratio propter quid* and *demonstratio quia* in the earlier writings of Galileo ('Sources of Galileo's early natural philosophy', *Reason,*

physics that the proof-theoretical *a priori* in fact becomes part of a methodology of the empirical sciences (in which '*a posteriori*' is used eventually in the sense of 'empirical'.) Leibniz, for instance, defines *demonstratio a priori* as *independens ab experimento*.[1]

6. Even more important than the history of statics and optics, with regard to the elaboration of scientific explanations of the physical world, is Greek astronomy. Astronomy provides a further example of axiomatic science, determined, moreover, by a research programme which was to play an important rôle in the genesis of modern science and the mechanisation of the world-picture linked to it: σῴζειν τὰ φαινόμενα – *to save the appearances*. This programme is passed on (erroneously as Platonic) in Simplicius' commentary on *De caelo*, relying on information from Eudemus' *History of Astronomy* which through Sosigenes, the teacher of Alexander of Aphrodisias, was passed on to Simplicius.[2] The phenomena, i.e. the motions of the planets, are 'saved' if one succeeds in reducing the apparent irregularities of the planetary motions to both uniform and circular motions.[3] Uniformity (i.e. constant angular velocity) and circularity, therefore, are the main principles of Greek astronomy which, in contrast to empirically oriented Babylonian astronomy, was established in the form of an axiomatic procedure. The distinction between a real (or true) motion and an apparent one, the identification of the real (or true) motion with one which is both uniform and circular, and the interpretation of the apparent motion, i.e. the irregularities, as being the real (or true) motion just as it appears to an observer on

Experiment and Mysticism in the Scientific Revolution, ed. R. Bonelli and W. R. Shea (New York, 1975), pp. 157–305). For a detailed discussion of the interrelated distinctions between *demonstratio propter quid* and *demonstratio quia*, *prior according to nature* and *prior according to knowledge*, as well as *demonstratio a priori* and *demonstratio a posteriori*, see J. Mittelstrass, 'Changing concepts of the *a priori*', *Part Four of the Proceedings of the Fifth International Congress of Logic, Methodology and Philosophy of Science* (University of Western Ontario Series in the Philosophy of Science, XII, Dordrecht and Boston, 1977), pp. 113–28.
[1] *Primae veritates*, in *Opuscules*, p. 518.
[2] Simplicius, *In Aristotelis de Caelo commentaria*, ed. J. L. Heiberg (*Comm. in Arist. Graeca*, vol. VII, Berlin, 1894), p. 488, 16–24. Cf. Duhem's classic investigation into the history of that programme: P. Duhem, Σῴζειν τὰ φαινόμενα. *Essai sur la notion de théorie physique de Platon à Galilée* (Paris, 1908; first pub. in *Annales de philosophie chrétienne* (1908); English trans. E. Doland and C. Maschler, *To Save the Phenomena. An Essay on the Idea of Physical Theory from Plato to Galileo* (Chicago and London, 1969)); also J. Mittelstrass, *Die Rettung der Phänomene. Ursprung und Geschichte eines antiken Forschungsprinzips* (Berlin, 1962), pp. 140ff. (also an attempt to prove that Eudoxus, not Plato, was the author of that programme).
[3] Simplicius, *In Aristotelis physicorum libros quattuor priores commentaria*, ed. H. Diels (*Comm. in Arist. Graeca*, vols. IX–X, Berlin, 1882–95), p. 292, 17–18.

the earth – these are the constituent parts of a σώζειν τὰ φαινόμενα, which has guided the elaboration of qualitative kinematical models in astronomy since Eudoxus.

These models are *kinematical* models, since bodies are considered only insofar as they move, forces behind the motions thus not being taken into account. And these models are *qualitative*, since they do not essentially use numerical aids: Eudoxus' system, for instance, used the concept of circular motion, but nothing is said about the magnitude of any radius; and it also used the concept of constant rotation, but lacked any account of velocities, apart from the distinction between diurnal and annual rotation. This situation does not change before Hipparchus, in whom, characteristically, Babylonian influences are once more evident (e.g. in the use of arithmetical methods) and who has at his disposal the trigonometric methods which are indispensable for quantitative considerations in astronomy.

In the framework of a qualitative astronomy, which had become increasingly quantitative since Hipparchus, and which was pre-occupied with the establishment of kinematical (geometrical) models, Greek science for the first time succeeded even before the formation of Archimedean statics in getting a firm footing in one part of the physical world, with the mathematical description of exact regularities. The possibility of science in its modern sense, specified by classical mechanics, turns out to be a discovery of astronomy, i.e. a gift of heaven. Within the development of pre-modern science, it is true, progress also continues to be a matter of astronomy, in the sense that (a) 'to save the appearances' was taken to be exclusively an astronomical programme, and (b) within astronomy 'to save the appearances' meant only mathematical, i.e. kinematical, theories in contrast to physical theories. The distinction, discussed for instance by writers like Poseidonius, Proclus, Ptolemy and Simplicius,[1] had become necessary with the success of Aristotelian physics. According to this distinction, *physical* theories like the Aristotelian theory of elements 'explained' the nature of the physical world; *mathematical* theories like the Ptolemaic astronomy, using eccentric circles, deferents, equants and epicycles, simply 'saved the appearances'. The geometrical equivalence of eccentric and epicyclic systems, already demonstrated in ancient times (Apollonius, Hipparchus),[2]

---

[1] Cf. Simplicius, *In Aristotelis physicorum libros*, pp. 290f.

[2] Cf. Claudius Ptolemaeus, *Syntaxis mathematica* III. 3, in *Opera quae extant omnia*, ed. J. L. Heiberg *et al.* (3 vols., Leipzig, 1898–1952), vol. I, pp. 216ff.; or *Handbuch der Astronomie*, trans. K. Manitius, 2nd ed. (2 vols., Leipzig, 1963), vol. I, pp. 148ff.

emphasises the 'hypothetical' character of mathematical astronomy. Aristotelian physics, however, which gave rise to the distinction between physical and mathematical theories, cannot be described by a principle like 'saving the appearances'. According to the Aristotelian concept of experience, there are no irregularities, at least not 'under the moon', which call for some theoretical device like a kinematical model in astronomy.

7. In Graeco-Arabic scientific learning the idea of an axiomatic–deductive structure of science was passed on to mediaeval science and philosophy. The σῴζειν τὰ φαινόμενα of the commentators of Aristotle becomes the *salvare apparentias* of the Latin tradition. The mediaeval continuation of the controversy about the distinction between physical and mathematical theories starts with a translation of Alpetragius' *Liber astronomiae* by Michael Scot (1217). Taking up the endeavours of Averroes (whose commentaries on Aristotle are available in Latin translations by 1230), Alpetragius had presented a modified Aristotelian system (without eccentrics and epicycles) explicitly, as Grosseteste remarks, in order to save the appearances.[1] Grosseteste, again, who also translates parts of Simplicius' commentary on *De caelo* (including Simplicius' account of saving the appearances), classifies the system of Alpetragius as Aristotelian, but he, however, uses the Ptolemaic model[2] – and is followed, for instance, by Albertus Magnus.[3] In 1271 William of Moerbeke translated Simplicius' commentary, inducing Thomas Aquinas, whose philological adviser William of Moerbeke was, to write his own commen-

[1] 'Alpetragius nuper adinvenit modum, et explanavit quomodo possibile est salvare processus et stationes et retrogradationes planetarum et reflexiones et inflexiones et cetera apparentia per modum Aristotelis, et absque excentrico et epiciclo', *Compotus venerabilis patris Domini et Sancti Roberti Grosse Capitis Lincolniensis Episcopi factus ad correctionem communis kalendarii nostri*, ed. R. Steele (*Opera hactenus inedita Rogeri Baconi*, vol. vi, Oxford, 1926), p. 217. Michael Scot's translation of Alpetragius' *Liber astronomiae* is available in print: al-Biṭrûjî, *De motibus celorum. Critical Edition of the Latin Translation of Michael Scot*, ed. F. J. Carmody (Berkeley and Los Angeles, 1952).

[2] Cf. L. Baur, *Die Philosophie des Robert Grosseteste, Bischofs von Lincoln (Beiträge zur Geschichte der Philosophie des Mittelalters*, vol. xviii, 4–6, Münster, 1917), pp. 41ff.; also F. J. Carmody in his edition of Alpetragius' *De motibus celorum*, p. 35. For Grosseteste's account of the distinction between the mathematical and the physical astronomer, emphasised by Simplicius, see Grosseteste, *Commentarius in VIII libros physicorum Aristotelis*, ed. R. C. Dales (Boulder, 1963), pp. 36f.

[3] See *Metaphysica*, lib. xi, tract. 2, cap. 22–4, in *Opera Omnia*, ed. B. Geyer, vol. xvi. 2 (1964), pp. 510–14 (also taking up Aristotle's version of saving the appearances in *Met.* Λ 8.1074a1 (cap. 23, pp. 512f.)). Cf. Crombie, *Robert Grosseteste*, pp. 189ff.; and W. A. Wallace, article on Albertus Magnus, *Dictionary of Scientific Biography*, vol. i, p. 101.

tary on *De caelo*.[1] In this commentary one reads about mathematical astronomy:

[The astronomers'] assumptions are not necessarily true: although these assumptions appear to save the appearances, one ought not to affirm that they are true; for the appearances concerning the stars might also be saved in some other way of which men have not as yet thought.[2]

Thomas, no doubt, expresses a general conviction within the tradition of Aristotelianism. For example, Averroes writes in his commentary on *De caelo*:

We find nothing in the mathematical sciences that would lead us to believe that eccentrics and epicycles exist. For astronomers propose the existence of these orbits as if they were principles and then deduce conclusions from them which are exactly what the senses can ascertain. In no way do they demonstrate by such results that the assumptions they have employed as principles are, conversely, necessities.[3]

Again, in his commentary on Aristotle's *Metaphysics*:

The epicycle and the eccentric are impossible. We must, therefore, apply ourselves to a new investigation concerning that genuine astronomy whose foundations are principles of physics...Actually, in our time astronomy is nonexistent; what we have is something that fits calculation but does not agree with what is.[4]

Roger Bacon expresses himself no less clearly:

Mathematical physicists, those who follow the ways of nature, try, no doubt, as do pure mathematicians, who do not know physics, to save the appearances. But they try at the same time to save the order and the principles of physics, whereas pure mathematicians destroy them. It seems, therefore, that we had better imitate the physicists in our assumptions.[5]

Astronomy which follows the programme of saving the appearances appears thence like a mathematical extension, hardly ever (and in these cases usually with reference to the unqualified proposal of Alpetragius) compatible with the programme of Aristotelian physics.

[1] *Expositio in libros Aristotelis de Caelo et Mundo*, in *Opera omnia* (12 vols., Rome, 1882–1948), vol. III. Cf. M. Grabmann, *Guglielmo di Moerbeke O.P. Il traduttore delle opere di Aristotele* (*Miscellanea Historiae Pontificiae*, vol. XI (*I Papi del Duecento e l'Aristotelismo* II), Roma, 1946). For a general account of how *De caelo* and the commentary of Simplicius were introduced into the Latin world cf. D. J. Allan, 'Medieval versions of Aristotle, *De caelo*, and of the commentary of Simplicius', *Medieval and Renaissance Studies*, ed. R. Hunt and R. Klibansky, vol. I (London, 1941–3), pp. 82–120.

[2] Lib. II, cap. 12, lect. 17, pp. 186bf.; cf. *Sum. theol.* I, qu. 32, art. 1, ad 2: 'Alio modo inducitur ratio quae non sufficienter probet radicem, sed quae radici iam positae ostendat congruere consequentes effectus; sicut in astrologia ponitur ratio excentricorum et epicyclorum ex hoc quod hac positione facta salvari possunt apparentia sensibilia circa motus caelestes; non tamen ratio haec est sufficienter probans, quia forte etiam alia positione facta salvari possent'.

[3] Quoted from Duhem, *To Save the Phenomena* (English trans.), p. 30.
[4] *Ibid.* p. 31.   [5] *Ibid.* pp. 38f.

In this sense, for instance, Nicholas of Cusa still draws attention to the point that 'Alpetragius takes Aristotle's side, rejecting the views of Ptolemy and others about eccentric circles and epicycles and assuming all spheres to be concentric, thereby saving the appearances.'[1] Naturally, estimations of this kind are also relevant within the development of astronomy. Copernicus, as the historian knows, becomes their most prominent victim. In this context, Agostino Nifo's remark in his commentary on *De caelo* (1553) sounds like a reminder of the old orthodoxy in the face of a (mathematical) astronomy which passes beyond its Aristotelian boundaries: 'those men are mistaken who, taking a natural phaenomenon which might follow from many causes, conclude in favour of one cause. For these appearances can be saved...possibly by others which have not yet been discovered.'[2]

8. It was the astronomer Johannes Kepler who was the first to realise that only with a new *physical hypothesis* could the controversy between mathematical and physical theories, lasting for more than a millennium, be brought to an end. According to Kepler, astronomy has two goals: to save the appearances and to explain the structure of the universe.[3] His formulation of a mutual attraction between two bodies, its size depending on their separation,[4] already points out the direction in which Galileo's kinematics is to be extended by Newton's dynamics. That extension too, from a methodological point of view, follows the programme of saving the appearances. Galileo, for instance, always recalls the distinction between pure astronomers,

---

[1] *Reparatio calendarii*, in *Nikolaus von Kues. Werke* (new ed. of the Strasbourg printing of 1488), ed. P. Wilpert (2 vols., Berlin, 1967), vol. II, p. 370.

[2] *De Coelo et Mundo Commentarii*, II (Venetiis, 1553), fol. 90vb (quoted from Crombie, *Robert Grosseteste*, pp. 298ff.). Stillman Drake has drawn attention to the fact that in Nifo's time ancient commentaries on Aristotle's *Physics* and *De caelo* were printed and reprinted in increasing quantity, particularly after 1508 when Nifo's commentary on the *Physics* was published (*Galileo Studies. Personality, Tradition, and Revolution* (Ann Arbor, 1970), pp. 37f.).

[3] *Epitome astronomiae Copernicanae*, in *Gesammelte Werke*, vol. VII, p. 257: 'Cum Astronomia duos fines habeat, salvare apparentias, et contemplari genuinam formam aedificii mundani'; cf. Kepler's comment on a letter of Michael Mästlin of 21 September 1616, *Gesammelte Werke*, vol. XVII, pp. 188f.

[4] The attraction (force) acts towards a point such that the ratio of the distances of the two bodies from this point is the inverse of the ratio of their masses: $d_1:d_2 = m_2:m_1$. Cf. J. Kepler, *Astronomia nova*, in *Gesammelte Werke*, vol. III, p. 25: 'If two stones were placed anywhere in the world near to each other, but outside the reach of force of a third cognate body, then they would come together, like two magnetic bodies, at an intermediate point, each approaching the other in proportion to the other's mass.'

who are dealing with the requirement that appearances be saved, and philosophical astronomers, who 'seek to investigate the true constitution of the universe',[1] the method of this investigation consisting in the establishment of kinematical models combined with dynamical considerations, i.e. in the application of a modified principle of saving the appearances. Descartes explicitly points to the similarity of such a procedure to the methods of the astronomers.[2] In other words, the history of the separation of mathematical and physical astronomy proves to be the methodological background of the Galilean revolution which in physics results in the establishment of classical mechanics. The mechanisation of the Aristotelian world-picture signifies the victory of the mathematical astronomer over the Aristotelian physicist.

In Newton's dynamical (mechanical) foundation of the kinematical (geometrical) conception of the heliocentric hypothesis, this victory is accomplished. By traditional standards, a change of rôles takes place: the geocentric hypothesis is valid now only kinematically (it can be transformed into the heliocentric hypothesis); the heliocentric hypothesis is valid also dynamically. The subsumption of the Keplerian laws of planetary motion under laws valid in a terrestrial *technical* practice, for instance in the practice covered by ballistics,

[1] *Istoria e dimostrazioni intorno alle macchie solari e loro accidenti* (Roma, 1613), in *Opere*, vol. v, p. 102: 'posti [*sc.* eccentrics, deferents, equants, epicycles] da i puri astronomi per facilitar i lor calcoli, ma non già da ritenersi per tali da gli astronomi filosofi, li quali, oltre alla cura del salvar in qualunque modo l'apparenze, cercano d'investigare, come problema massimo et ammirando, la vera costituzione dell'universo'; cf. *Dialogo sopra i due massimi sistemi del mondo*, III, in *Opere*, vol. vII, p. 369; *Il Saggiatore*, XI, in *Opere*, vol. vI, p. 242. Undoubtedly, Galileo, since the writing of *De motu*, was quite familiar with the commentaries on Aristotle, among them those of Simplicius from whom he may have learned (or learned again) about the ancient research programme in astronomy. Cf. Stillman Drake and I. E. Drabkin, *Mechanics in Sixteenth-Century Italy. Selections from Tartaglia, Benedetti, Guido Ubaldo, and Galileo* (Madison and London, 1969), p. 55 (Introduction). In his *Discorso delle comete* Galileo explicitly recalls the fact that one of the principal reasons which caused both Tycho and Copernicus 'to depart from the Ptolemaic system was the impossibility of saving the appearances by means of motions which are absolutely circular and perfectly equable in their own circles and around their own centers' (*Opere*, vol. vI, pp. 88f.; *The Controversy on the Comets of 1618*, trans. Stillman Drake and C. D. O'Malley (Philadelphia, 1960), p. 50).

[2] *La dioptrique. Discours I*, in *Œuvres*, vol. vI, p. 83: 'il n'est pas besoin que i'entreprene de dire au vray quelle est sa nature [*sc.* of light], & ie croy qu'il suffira que ie me serue de deus ou trois comparaisons, qui aydent a la conceuoir en la façon qui me semble la plus commode, pour expliquer toutes celles de ses propriétés que l'expérience nous fait connoistre, & pour deduire en suite toutes les autres qui ne peuuent pas si aysement estre remarquées; imitant en cecy les Astronomes, qui, bien que leurs suppositions soyent presque toutes fausses ou incertaines, toutefois, a cause qu'elles se rapportent a diuerses obseruations qu'ils ont faites, ne laissent pas d'en tirer plusieurs consequences tres vrayes & tres assurées'.

3-2

fulfils Huygens' demand 'to conceive the causes of all natural effects in terms of mechanical motions'. Newton's theory of universal gravitation becomes the paradigm of an explanation of physical phenomena by means of mechanical models, i.e. of saving the appearances in its new sense. From his 'principle of gravity', Newton writes in an intended preface for the 1704 edition of the *Opticks* that he derived

all the (Phaenomena of nature) motions of the heavenly bodies & the flux & reflux of ye sea, shewing by mathematical demonstrations that this force alone was sufficient to produce all those Phaenomena, & deriving from it [a priori] some new motions wch Astronomers had not then observed.[1]

The fact, however, that the use of mechanical models to explain astronomical matters places celestial physics in the foreground, accounts for the concept of the mechanisation of the world-picture, beyond both common and metaphysical imagination.

9. In a Newtonian world heavy masses move within absolute time through absolute space, entirely determined by laws stated in Newton's celestial physics. This conception passes into the organic, psychic and social universe. Already in Newton one comes across the remark that 'if natural Philosophy in all its Parts, by pursuing this Method, shall at length be perfected, the Bounds of Moral Philosophy will be also enlarged'.[2] This is meant literally, and is understood in that way. The expressions 'experimental physics of the soul' (*la physique expérimentale de l'âme*, used by d'Alembert in order to characterise Locke's merits)[3] and 'social physics' (*physique sociale*, in the terminology of A. Comte) are coined. Such an unusual physics is elaborated in a mechanistic psychology which is to supply the basis of moral philosophy. No-one else has formulated this goal as clearly as Condorcet:

The sole foundation for belief in the natural sciences is this idea, that the general laws directing the phenomena in the universe, known or unknown, are necessary

[1] Quoted from J. E. McGuire, 'Newton's "Principles of Philosophy": an intended preface for the 1704 *Opticks* and a related draft fragment', *The British Journal for the History of Science*, v (1970–1), 186. McGuire puts in parentheses what he calls 'interpolations and cancellations' in the manuscript.

[2] *Opticks, or a Treatise of the Reflections, Inflections and Colours of Light*, 4th ed. (London, 1730), p. 381.

[3] 'Discours préliminaire de l'Encyclopédie', *Encyclopédie, ou Dictionnaire raisonné des sciences, des arts et des métiers*, ed. D. Diderot and J. le Rond d'Alembert, vol. 1 (Paris, 1751), p. xxvii.

and constant. Why should this principle be any less true for the development of the intellectual and moral faculties of man than for the other operations of nature?[1]

Determinism and materialism, being the epistemological heirs of Newtonian mechanics, dominate the philosophical programme not only among the French encyclopaedists (Condillac, Diderot, Helvétius, d'Holbach, Lamettrie), but also in England. For instance, Joseph Priestley enriches David Hartley's work, which he edited in 1775 under the title *Hartley's Theory of the Human Mind on the Principles of Association of Ideas*, with a rigorously materialistic conception; William Godwin, on the other hand, with deterministic elements.[2] Laplace, the author of a celestial mechanics in five volumes (*Traité de la mécanique céleste*, 1799–1825) and co-founder of the so-called Kant–Laplace theory, invents his demon, which assuming an entirely mechanistic causality, is able to realise from a given state of the world every past state as well as every future state. The idea of a *definitely determined* world, supported by a mechanistic world-view, dominates the way of thinking in these times; even Leibniz, with respect to a logical explanation of his concept of pre-established harmony,[3] is one of its supporters. He fails in his attempts to redefine the foundations of mechanistic explanations by his theory of monads; the so-called *vis-viva* controversy between 'Leibnizians' (among them Joh. Bernoulli, W. J. 'sGravesande, Chr. Wolff) and 'Cartesians' (among them the Abbé de Catelan, S. Clarke, P. J. S. Mazière) remains an episode which has also suffered from several misunderstandings.[4]

The same happens with Kant's distinction between 'causality according to the laws of nature' and 'causality of freedom'.[5] Kant himself had originally (in his *Inquiry Concerning the Clarity of the*

---

[1] *Sketch for a Historical Picture of the Progress of the Human Mind*, trans. J. Barraclough, with an introduction by S. Hampshire (London, 1955), p. 173.
[2] *Enquiry Concerning Political Justice, and its Influence on Morals and Happiness*, 3rd ed. (2 vols., London, 1798).
[3] From a logical point of view, the assumption that every monad represents ('mirrors') the universe is to be understood as the possibility of extending the description of one monad by adding any statements about other monads, representing thereby statements about any objects as statements about one and the same object. Cf. *Discours de métaphysique*, § 14, *Philosophische Schriften*, vol. IV, p. 440.
[4] Cf. R. Dugas, *La mécanique au XVIIe siècle* (Neuchâtel, 1954), pp. 477ff.; T. L. Hankins, 'Eighteenth-century attempts to resolve the vis viva controversy', *Isis*, LVI (1965), 281–97; L. L. Laudan, 'The vis viva controversy. A post-mortem', *Isis*, LIX (1968), 131–43.
[5] *Kritik der reinen Vernunft* B 472ff.

Principles of Natural Theology and Ethics, 1763) held the idea of mechanism, in a quite orthodox manner:

The true method of metaphysics is basically the same as that introduced by Newton into natural science and which had such useful consequences in that field. It is said there that the rules, according to which certain natural phenomena occur, should be sought by means of certain experience and, if need be, with the help of geometry. Although the first principle is not perceived in the bodies, nevertheless it is certain that they operate according to this law. Involved natural occurences are explained, when it is clearly shown how they are contained under these well proved rules. It is exactly the same in metaphysics.[1]

It was almost twenty years before the *Critique of Pure Reason* supplied a critical foundation of mechanistic explanations (in the framework of a theory of instrumental experience) which Leibniz, in a methodologically insufficient way, tried to give within a metaphysical terminology, and which Kant himself had formerly looked upon as the task of a new monadology (*Monadologia physica,* 1756). Here it becomes clear in what sense phenomena have to be taken as parts of scientific experience already structured in itself, precisely as *phaenomena bene fundata.* In a similar sense Johann Heinrich Lambert, under the title of a 'Phenomenology', had already outlined a *scientia apparentiae* as an *optica transcendentalis.*[2] The principle of saving the appearances again serves as *tertium comparationis.* Lambert explicitly speaks in this connection about the 'method which was used by astronomers long ago',[3] or the astronomical rule which is also used in experimental physics (*Versuchskunst*).[4] Epistemology keeps alive the relation between a Greek research principle and mechanistic explanations.

10. With electrodynamics and thermodynamics (with respect to its statistical models of description and explanation), mechanistic

---

[1] *Kant. Selected Pre-critical Writings and Correspondence with Beck,* trans. with introduction by G. K. Kerferd and D. E. Walford, with a contribution by P. G. Lucas (Manchester and New York, 1968), pp. 17f.

[2] *Über die Methode die Metaphysik, Theologie und Moral richtiger zu beweisen,* ed. K. Bopp (Berlin, 1918), § 88, p. 28; cf. *Neues Organon oder Gedanken über die Erforschung und Bezeichnung des Wahren und dessen Unterscheidung von Irrthum und Schein* (2 vols., Leipzig, 1764; reprinted in *Philosophische Schriften,* ed. H.-W. Arndt, vols. I–II (Hildesheim, 1965)), p. 220 (*Phänomenologie oder Lehre von dem Schein,* 1. Hauptstück § 4), p. 273 (2. Hauptstück § 91).

[3] *Anlage zur Architectonic, oder Theorie des Einfachen und des Ersten in der philosophischen und mathematischen Erkenntniß,* vol. I (Riga, 1771; reprinted in *Philosophische Schriften,* vol. III (Hildesheim, 1965)), p. 39 (1. Hauptstück § 43); cf. letter of 1770 to I. Kant, *Joh. Heinrich Lamberts deutscher gelehrter Briefwechsel,* ed. J. Bernoulli (Berlin, 1782; reprinted in *Philosophische Schriften,* vol. IX (Hildesheim, 1968)), p. 363.

[4] *Neues Organon,* vol. II, p. 273.

explanations, from a methodological point of view, lose their exclusivity; and as a consequence of this change within physics the mechanistic world-view loses its scientific legitimation. The mechanistic world-view, in the words of Ernst Mach, becomes a 'mechanical mythology':[1]

The view that makes mechanics the basis of the remaining branches of physics, and explains all physical phenomena by mechanical ideas, is in our judgement a prejudice...The mechanical theory of nature is, undoubtedly, in an historical view, both intelligible and pardonable; and it may also, for a time, have been of much value. But, upon the whole, it is an artificial conception.[2]

Again:

The French encyclopaedists of the eighteenth century imagined they were not far from a final explanation of the world by physical and mechanical principles; Laplace even conceived a mind competent to foretell the progress of nature for all eternity, if but the masses, their positions, and initial velocities were given. In the eighteenth century, this joyful overestimation of the scope of the new physico-mechanical ideas is pardonable. Indeed, it is a refreshing, noble, and elevating spectacle; and we can deeply sympathise with this expression of intellectual joy, so unique in history.[3]

The transition to other modes of explanation in the eighteenth century is prepared for by the analytical systems of Euler[4] and Lagrange.[5] In these systems, equation-systems of motions replace axioms of motions, and thereby they also replace the Euclidean structure of mechanics. An *analytic* concept of science supersedes the former *synthetic* concept of science which also holds true of Newtonian mechanics.

Peculiarly enough, this change is already indicated in Newton, namely in his methodological remarks in the second and third editions of the *Principia* (1713, 1726) as well as in the *Queries* added to the *Opticks* in the Latin edition (1706) and in the English edition (1718). Here, the methodological programme (as a supplement to the foundation of classical mechanics within the *Principia*, and not agreeing with that foundation) reads: 'to derive two or three general Principles of Motion from Phaenomena, and afterwards to tell us

[1] *The Science of Mechanics. A Critical and Historical Account of its Development*, trans. J. McCormack, 4th ed. (Chicago and London, 1919), p. 464.
[2] *Ibid.* pp. 495f. [3] *Ibid.* pp. 463f.
[4] *Mechanica sive motus scientia analytice exposita* (2 vols., Petersburg, 1736); *Theoria motus corporum solidorum seu rigidorum* (Rostock and Greifswald, 1765).
[5] *Mécanique analytique* (Paris, 1788; 3rd ed. (2 vols., Paris, 1853-5)).

how the Properties and Actions of all corporeal Things follow from those manifest Principles'.[1] Propositions of physics are considered as 'deduced from Phaenomena and made general by Induction'.[2] More than 150 years later, when mechanistic explanations had long been supplemented by other means of explaining physical facts, James Clerk Maxwell, in 1876, still corroborates Newton's methodological programme:

> In forming dynamical theories of the physical sciences, it has been a too frequent practice to invent a particular dynamical hypothesis and then by means of the equations of motion to deduce certain results...The true method of physical reasoning is to begin with the phenomena and to deduce the forces from them by a direct application of the equations of motion.[3]

To save the appearances no longer seems to be necessary, at all events not in the sense that phenomena are to be rated as *founded* only with respect to a structured scientific experience. The idea of a purely *empirical* basis for explanation (for the present still mechanistic) appears on the scene. Whereas the structure of mechanistic explanations (for instance in the *Principia*) is *Euclidean*, i.e. *synthetic*, and the epistemology appertaining to it *rationalistic*, the methodology of empirical sciences, not least through the reception of Newton in the eighteenth century, becomes *inductive*, and the epistemology appertaining to it, *empiricist*. But this is another story.

The core of our story is this. Greek science had not only achieved the discovery of the possibility of exact science (in the form of axiomatic astronomy, statics, optics, and partly also acoustics) but had also set up a *principle of research*. This principle later led in physics towards the organisation of non-Aristotelian, *mechanistic* explanations, and by doing so to the temporary identification of physics with mechanics. The mechanistic world-picture is a result of this development. Even more, the analytic and the empiricist turning-point in the methodology of empirical sciences, so far as it is represented by Newton's remarks, can also be understood as a turning-point with a Greek background; or, somewhat dramatised, as a return to Anaxagoras. Socrates' disappointment, which stands in the *Phaedo* as a biographical construction at the beginning of the

---

[1] *Opticks* (1730), p. 377.
[2] Letter of 28 March 1713 to R. Cotes, *Correspondence of Sir Isaac Newton and Professor Cotes, including Letters of other Eminent Men*, ed. J. Edleston (London, 1850), p. 155.
'On the proof of the equations of motion of a connected system', *Proceedings of the Cambridge Philosophical Society*, vol. II (1876), in *The Scientific Papers of James Clerk Maxwell*, ed. W. D. Niven (2 vols., Cambridge, 1890), vol. II, p. 309.

Greek idea of a synthetic *theoria*, is being revoked: ὄψις ἀδήλων τὰ φαινόμενα[1] – the appearances themselves supply the explanation of the invisible. So it appears.

[1] Anaxagoras, *Die Fragmente der Vorsokratiker*, ed. H. Diels and W. Kranz, 12th ed. (3 vols., Dublin and Zurich, 1966), or 6th ed. (1951), 46 B 21a. Democritus approved of this statement (55 A 111). Cf. H. Diller, 'ΟΨΙΣ ΑΔΗΛΩΝ ΤΑ ΦΑΙΝΟΜΕΝΑ', *Hermes*, LXVII (1932), 14–42; O. Regenbogen, 'Eine Forschungsmethode antiker Naturwissenschaft' (*Quellen und Studien zur Geschichte der Mathematik* B 1.2 (1930)), in O. Regenbogen, *Kleine Schriften* (München, 1961), pp. 141–94. In its origin, the principle of seeking in the appearances the explanation of the invisible was related particularly to medicine.

3

L'INFLUENCE DE LA TRADITION HERMÉTIQUE ET CABALISTIQUE

CESARE VASOLI

Le sujet de cet exposé est d'une grande actualité; il fait partie de ceux qui, au cours des dernières décennies, ont joui d'une fortune d'autant plus significative qu'elle était liée à des attitudes et à des prises de position qui sous-entendaient des choix historiographiques et méthodologiques bien définis. Déjà les travaux de la première équipe du 'Warburg Institute' datant des années 1920–40,[1] exploraient avec une extrême clarté l'histoire des images astrologiques et de la symbologie magique dans la culture occidentale et préparèrent le terrain pour une évaluation vraiment neuve de phénomènes et de situations intellectuelles que les historiens de la philosophie et de la science avaient souvent négligés dans leur vision synthétique de la civilisation de la Renaissance. Mais c'est surtout à partir des enquêtes sur la tradition hermétique et sur la cabale de la Renaissance, menées par Eugenio Garin,[2] mademoiselle Frances A. Yates,[3]

---

[1] E. Panofski et F. Saxl, *Dürers 'Melencolia I'. Eine Quellen- und typengeschichtliche Untersuchung* (Studien der Bibliothek Warburg, 2, Leipzig, 1923); F. Saxl, *Antike Götter in der Spätrenaissance. Ein Freskenzyklus und ein 'Discorso' des Jacopo Zucchi* (Studien der Bibliothek Warburg, 8, Leipzig et Berlin, 1937); A. Warburg, *Die Erneuerung der heidnischen Antike. Kulturwissenschaftliche Beiträge zur Geschichte der europäischen Renaissance* (Leipzig et Berlin, 1932); F. Saxl, *La fede astrologica di Agostino Chigi. Interpretazione dei dipinti di Baldassarre Peruzzi nella sala di Galatea della Farnesina* (La Farnesina, 1, Roma, 1934); W. Gundel, *Dekane und Dekansternbilder. Ein Beitrag zur Geschichte der Sternbilde der Kulturvölker* (Studien der Bibliothek Warburg, 19, Gluckstadt et Hamburg, 1936); J. Seznec, *La survivance des dieux antiques* (Studies of the Warburg Institute, 11, London, 1940); F. Saxl, *Lectures* (London, 1957), part. pp. 58–124, 174–9; R. Klibanski, E. Panofski et F. Saxl, *Saturn and Melancholy. Studies in the History of Natural Philosophy, Religion and Art* (Edinburgh, 1958), 2e éd. (New York, 1964).

[2] E. Garin, 'Magia e astrologia nella cultura del Rinascimento' et 'Considerazioni sulla magia', *Medioevo e Rinascimento. Studi e ricerche* (Bari, 1954), pp. 170–91; *idem, La cultura filosofica del Rinascimento italiano* (Firenze, 1961), part. pp. 143–65; *idem, L'età nuova. Ricerche di storia della cultura dal XII al XVI secolo* (Napoli, 1969), part. pp. 387–447; *idem, Rinascite e rivoluzioni. Movimenti culturali dal XIV al XVII secolo* (Bari, 1975), pp. 255–82; *idem, Lo zodiaco della vita. La polemica sull'astrologia dal Trecento al Cinquecento* (Bari, 1976).

[3] F. A. Yates, *The French Academies of the Sixteenth Century* (Studies of the Warburg Institute, 15, London, 1947); *idem, Giordano Bruno and the Hermetic Tradition* (London, 1964); *idem, The Art of Memory* (London, 1966); *idem*, 'The hermetic tradition in Renaissance Science', *Art, Science and History in the Renaissance*, éd. C. S. Singleton (Baltimore, Mass., 1968), pp. 155–274; *idem, Theatre of the World* (London, 1964).

C. VASOLI

Daniel P. Walker,[1] Gershom G. Scholem[2] et François Secret[3] et par les études toujours plus raffinées autour d'un complexe de doctrines, croyances ésotériques et opérations techniques fondées sur la grande reprise de l'alchimie et de la magie astrologique, que de tels problèmes se sont imposés à l'attention des savants et ont entraîné ainsi une littérature abondante et controversée. Pour me limiter à des textes connus de tous et non seulement des spécialistes, je vais me contenter de citer les travaux si importants, faits, au cours des années cinquante et soixante, par Pagel,[4] Debus,[5]

[1] D. P. Walker, 'Orpheus the theologian and Renaissance Platonists', *Journal of the Warburg and Courtauld Institutes* (1953), 100–19; *idem*, 'The *prisca theologia* in France', *ibid.* (1954), 204–59; *idem*, 'The astral body in Renaissance medicine', *ibid.* (1958), 119–33; *idem*, *Spiritual and Demonic Magic from Ficino to Campanella* (Studies of the Warburg Institute, 22, London, 1958); *idem*, *The Ancient Theology. Studies in Christian Platonism from the Fifteenth to the Eighteenth Century* (London, 1972); *idem*, 'Francis Bacon and *Spiritus*', *Science, Medicine and Society in the Renaissance. Essays to honor W. Pagel*, éd. A. G. Debus (New York, 1972), t. II, pp. 122–30. Mais v. aussi E. Wind, *Pagan Mysteries in the Renaissance* (London, 1958).

[2] G. G. Scholem, 'Zur Geschichte der Anfänge der christlichen Kabbala', *Essays presented to L. Baeck* (London, 1954); *idem*, *Die jüdische Mystik in ihren Hauptströmungen* (Zürich, 1957); *idem*, *Ursprung und Anfänge der Kabbala* (Berlin, 1962).

[3] F. Secret, 'L'astrologie et les kabbalistes chrétiens à la Renaissance', *La Tour Saint-Jacques*, IV (1956), 45–56; *idem*, 'L'interpretazione della Kabbala nel Rinascimento', *Convivium* (1956), 511–14; *idem*, 'Pico della Mirandola e le origini della Cabbala cristiana', *Convivium* (1957), 31–47; *idem*, *Les Kabbalistes chrétiens de la Renaissance* (Paris, 1964); *idem*, *Le Zôhar chez les Kabbalistes chrétiens de la Renaissance* (Paris et La Haye, 1964).

[4] W. Pagel, *J. B. Van Helmont. Einführung in die philosophische Medizin des Barock* (Berlin, 1930); *idem*, 'J. B. Van Helmont, *De tempore*, and biological time', *Osiris* (1949), 346–417; *idem*, 'Giordano Bruno, the philosophy of circles and the circular movement of the blood', *Journal of the History of Medicine* (1951), 116–24; *idem*, 'The position of Harvey and Van Helmont in the history of European thought', *ibid.* (1958), 186–99; *idem*, *Paracelsus. An Introduction to Philosophical Medicine in the Era of the Renaissance* (Basel et New York, 1958); *idem*, 'Paracelsus and Neoplatonic and Gnostic tradition', *Ambix* (1960), 125ss.; *idem*, 'The prime matter of Paracelsus', *ibid.* (1961), 119ss.; *idem*, *Die medizinische Weltbild des Paracelsus. Seine Zusammenhänge mit Neuplatonismus und Gnosis* (Wiesbaden, 1962); *idem* et P. M. Rattansi, 'Vesalius and Paracelsus', *Medical History* (1964), 309–28; *idem*, *William Harvey's Biological Ideas. Selected Aspects* (Basel et New York, 1967); *idem*, 'The spectre of Van Helmont and the idea of continuity in the history of chemistry', *Changing Perspectives of the History of Sciences. Essays in Honour of J. Needham*, éd. M. Teich et R. Young (London, 1973), pp. 100–9.

[5] A. G. Debus, 'Robert Fludd and the circulation of the blood', *Journal of the History of Medicine and Allied Sciences* (1961), 374–93; *idem*, 'Paracelsian doctrines in English medicine', *Chemistry in the Service of Medicine*, éd. F. N. L. Poynter (London, 1963), pp. 1–26; *idem*, 'The Paracelsian Aerial Niter', *Isis* (1964), 43–61; *idem*, *The English Paracelsians* (London, 1965); *idem*, 'The significance of the history of early chemistry', *Cahiers d'histoire mondiale* (1965), 39–58; *idem*, 'The sun in the universe of Robert Fludd', *Le soleil à la Renaissance. Sciences et mythes* (Bruxelles, 1965), pp. 259–77; *idem*, *Alchemy and Chemistry in the Seventeenth Century. Papers read by A. G. Debus and R. P. Multhauf* (Los Angeles, 1966); *idem*, 'Philosophical chemistry and the scientific revolution', *Actes du XIe Congrès International d'Histoire des Sciences*, vol. IV (Wrocław, Varsovie, Cracovie, 1968), pp. 26–30; *idem*, 'Renaissance chemistry and the work of Robert Fludd', *Ambix* (1967), 42–59; *idem*, *The Chemical Dream of the Renaissance* (Cambridge, 1968); *idem*,

McGuire,[1] Rattansi[2] et Jacob,[3] qui sont les documents brillants d'une recherche qui s'étend désormais à tous les aspects de la vie intellectuelle depuis les milieux philosophiques et scientifiques aux milieux religieux et politiques. Et si ensuite on reflète sur les réactions que les études de la tradition hermético-cabalistique ont provoquées dans le délicat domaine de l'histoire de la science, et aussi sur les débats qui ont accueilli l'emblématique essai de mademoiselle Yates sur la 'mythologie' des Rose-croix,[4] on devra reconnaître que nous nous trouvons réellement en face d'un point de référence obligatoire avec lequel devront régler leurs comptes, à un moment ou à l'autre, tous ceux qui se penchent sur la difficile et controversée histoire intellectuelle du XVIIe siècle. Ce n'est pas par hasard si de tels sujets ont fourni, il y a quelques années, l'occasion d'une dispute serrée entre Mary

'Mathematics and nature in the chemical texts of the Renaissance', *Ambix* (1968), 1–28; *idem*, 'Edward Jorden and the fermentation of the metals: an iatrochemical study of terrestrial phenomena', *Toward a History of Geology*, éd. C. J. Schneer (Cambridge, Mass., 1969), pp. 100–21; *idem*, 'Harvey and Fludd. The irrational factor in the rational sciences of the seventeenth century', *Journal of the History of Biology* (1970), 81–105; *idem, Science and Education in the Seventeenth Century. The Webster–Ward Debate* (London et New York, 1970); *idem*, 'Guintherius, Libavius and Sennert: the chemical compromise in English modern medicine', *Science, Medicine and Society in the Renaissance*, t. I, pp. 151–66; *idem*, 'The medico-chemical world of the Paracelsians', *Changing Perspectives of the History of Sciences*, pp. 85–99; *idem*, 'The chemical debate of the seventeenth century: the reaction to Robert Fludd and Jean Baptiste van Helmont', *Reason, Experiment and Mysticism in the Scientific Revolution*, éd. M. L. Righini Bonelli et W. R. Shea (New York, 1975), pp. 19–47.

[1] J. E. McGuire et P. M. Rattansi, 'Newton and the pipes of Pan', *Notes and Records of the Royal Society* (1966), 108–41; J. E. McGuire, 'Body and void in Newton's *De mundi systemate*', *Archive for History of Exact Sciences* (1966), 206–48; *idem*, 'Transmutation and immutability: Newton's doctrine of physical qualities', *Ambix* (1967), 84–6; *idem*, 'Force, active principles, and Newton's invisible realm', *Ambix* (1968), 154–208; *idem*, 'Atoms and the "analogy of nature"', *Studies in History and Philosophy of Science* (1970), 1–58; *idem*, 'Newton and the demonic furies: some current problems and approaches in the history of science', *History of Science* (1973), 21–41.

[2] P. M. Rattansi, 'Paracelsus and the Puritan revolution', *Ambix* (1963), 124–32; *idem*, 'The Helmontian–Galenist controversy in Restoration England', *Ambix* (1964), 1–23; *idem*, 'Alchemy and natural magic in Raleigh's "History of the World"', *ibid.* (1966), 122–38; *idem*, 'Politics and natural philosophy in Civil War England', *Actes du XI Congrès International d'Histoire des Sciences*, t. II, pp. 162–6; *idem*, 'The intellectual origins of the Royal Society', *Notes and Records of the Royal Society* (1968), 129–43; *idem*, 'The Comenian natural philosophy in England', *Studia comeniana et historica* (1971), 9–20; *idem*, 'The sacral interpretation of science in the seventeenth century', *Science and Society 1600–1900*, éd. P. Mathias (Cambridge, 1972), pp. 1–32; *idem*, 'Newton's alchemical studies', *Science, Medicine and Society in the Renaissance*, t. II, pp. 167–82.

[3] M. C. Jacob, 'Bentley, Newton and providence', *Journal of the History of Ideas* (1969), 307–18; *idem*, 'John Toland and the Newtonian ideology', *Journal of the Warburg and Courtauld Institutes* (1969), 307–31; *idem*, 'Early Newtonianism', *History of Science* (1974), 142–6.

[4] F. A. Yates, *The Rosicrucian Enlightenment* (London, 1972).

Hesse et Rattansi,[1] d'où sont sorties des opinions, je ne dirais pas antagonistes, mais certes très éloignées les unes des autres à propos du sujet capital qu'est l'interprétation de l'idée de 'raison' aux origines de la science moderne. Non seulement, plus récente encore est la publication des actes d'un congrès d'historiens de la science,[2] consacré à l'analyse du lien entre 'raison, expériences et mysticisme' pendant la révolution scientifique. Des travaux différents précisent les motifs essentiels d'un contraste qui semble avoir désormais dépassé les limites de la recherche historiographique pour assumer une signification épistémologique et idéologique évidente. Il ne manque même pas les références explicites aux discussions épistémo-logiques de nos jours, et en particulier à la querelle qui oppose Sir Karl Popper et ses disciples à Thomas Kuhn et Paul Feyerabend[3] et qui est centrée sur les concepts de 'science normale' et de 'révolution scientifique'. De telle sorte que les discussions sur le sens et l'incidence des traditions ésotériques dans la culture du siècle de la science est en train d'investir quelques questions fondamentales, relatives au 'status' du savoir scientifique dans la culture moderne et à son rapport avec la présence persistante de conceptions et modes de pensée irréductibles à ses règles, étrangères à ses fondements rationnels et à l'inflexible cohérence de ses méthodes.

Ces simples considérations sont suffisantes pour souligner la complexité d'un problème de nature historiographique, qui est d'autant plus difficile à traiter que l'acquisition de données indiscu-tables cède le pas au heurt entre critères de jugement, préoccupés surtout de se mesurer à des paramètres philosophiques et scienti-fiques même trop actuels. Il est démontré que ce danger est réel par la tendance qu'ont les parties adverses à résoudre, d'une part, dans le concept toujours plus compréhensif et général de 'tradition hermétique' des idées, attitudes et programmes souvent différents les uns des autres,[4] et d'autre part, à accentuer le caractère de rupture de la nouvelle science en en soulignant la discontinuité face à toutes les

---

[1] M. Hesse, 'Reason and evaluation in the history of science', *Changing Perspectives of the History of Sciences*, pp. 127–47; P. M. Rattansi, 'Some evaluation of reason in sixteenth and seventeenth century natural philosophy', *ibid.* pp. 148–66.

[2] P. Rossi, 'Hermeticism, rationality and the scientific revolution', *Reason, Experiment and Mysticism in the Scientific Revolution*, ed. Righini Bonelli et Shea, pp. 247–73, part. pp. 264ss.

[3] I. Lakatos et A. Musgrave, édd., *Criticism and the Growth of Knowledge*, 3e éd. (Cambridge, 1974); T. Kuhn, *The Structure of Scientific Revolution*, 2e éd. (Chicago, 1970); K. Popper, *Objective Knowledge: An Evolutionary Approach* (Oxford, 1972); P. Feyerabend, *Against Method* (London, 1972).

[4] E. Garin, 'Divagazioni ermetiche', *Rivista critica di storia della Filosofia* (1976), 462–6.

tendances et traditions du passé. Je ne nierai pas que de telles prises de positions polémiques ont servi ou servent encore à corriger des déformations voyantes de la réalité historique imposées par des analyses trop limitées ou tendancieuses ; je reconnais qu'elles peuvent servir à empêcher l'impact trop brutal de certains résultats de la recherche historiographique sur les problèmes embrouillés de l'épistémologie de nos jours. Je retiens également qu'elles sont une juste admonition pour celui qui essaie toujours de constituer des perspectives privilégiées mais inévitablement réductrices. Je ne crois pas, toutefois, à leur utilité pour celui qui veut vraiment essayer de reconstituer, avec le moins de lacunes possible, le cours effectif du processus historique, sans renoncer à reconnaître la nature complexe et contradictoire de son développement, les éléments contrastants et dialectiques qui le conditionnent ainsi que le lien continu et inévitable entre passé et futur, nouveauté et tradition, qui est propre à tout grand événement culturel. Et comme je suis convaincu que le devoir de l'historien consiste, avant tout, à fixer au moins quelques points de référence qui permettent de s'orienter dans l'entremêlement des faits, je voudrais maintenant laisser de côté les divergences d'opinion des spécialistes pour essayer de trouver un critère capable de rendre compte de la présence singulière, dans les mêmes milieux et même chez la même personne, de conceptions scientifiques révolutionnaires et de croyances ésotériques, d'enthousiasmes millénaristes et d'aspirations utopistes, qui culminent dans le double rêve d'une unité totale du savoir et de l'acquisition de pouvoir et de capacités exceptionnelles de suprématie sur le monde.

A mon avis le premier élément à souligner est le fait que la révolution scientifique (soit que l'on indique par ce terme un critère de périodicité dont le centre est justement le siècle dont nous parlons, soit qu'on se serve de ce concept pour signifier au contraire un changement radical et irréversible de la connaissance humaine, de ses méthodes et de ses instruments), n'est nullement un événement isolé mais, au contraire, le résultat d'une transformation beaucoup plus vaste et profonde qui bouleversa toutes les formes de la vie historique, depuis les structures économiques et sociales aux idées philosophiques et religieuses, des techniques de la politique aux formes les plus élaborées d'une organisation de la culture. Or, au cours de ce procès de longue haleine (mais dont l'épicentre se situe au XVIIe siècle), il me semble que l'on peut reconnaître au moins deux caractères singulièrement décisifs : l'exigence sociale d'élaborer des instruments théoriques et pratiques capables d'assurer un contrôle toujours plus étendu de la réalité naturelle et en même temps la formation de nouveaux types et groupes d'intellectuels qui participent naturellement à l'évolution de la société du XVIIe siècle, mais sont liés aux institutions par un rapport très différent de celui du 'clerc' traditionnel. Ces intellectuels essaient et essaieront toujours davantage d'être les porteurs de conceptions politiques, philosophiques et scientifiques innovatrices dont le sens est certes très différent selon les milieux et les conditions historiques particulières. Mais, au cours des premières décennies du siècle, et même plus avant, ils entretiennent des rapports complexes, si non ambigus soit avec les traditions scientifiques des Écoles où ils se sont formés, soit avec les conceptions religieuses qui indépendamment des différentes confessions constituent encore le tissu idéologique profond de toutes les sociétés européennes. Du reste – et je me permets d'attirer votre attention sur cet autre point – un des aspects principaux de la transformation culturelle est justement constitué par la crise des idées et par celle des institutions religieuses qui ne se limite pas seulement au conflit central entre la discipline catholique durcie dans des formes de défense à outrance de la Contre-Réforme et la foi réformée, ou aux batailles de tous les théologiens contre les embûches 'diaboliques' des libertins. Bien plus, même le XVIIe siècle, après la maturité du XVIe, voit la diffusion croissante d'expériences religieuses irréductibles aux doctrines magistrales, la survivance des espoirs millénaristes, l'attrait des croyances magiques et théurgiques ou du moins la suggestion constante de mythes non-chrétiens, rachetés toutefois par la foi en une révélation commune 'très ancienne' à la source du pouvoir et des destinées humaines. Ces suggestions sont particulièrement fortes chez les intellectuels qui sont les plus exposés aux contre-coups des grandes crises de l'époque, parmi les hommes qui mirent d'une manière encore incertaine et irrationnelle à un renouveau radical du savoir et, encore, parmi ceux qui essaient de les assumer comme instruments possibles de défense de l'ordre ancien et les structures consacrées de l'ordre cosmique et civil.

Il me semble prouvé par de nombreuses recherches qui soulignent leur incidence sur des événements et des personnalités emblématiques qui appartiennent justement aux plus lointaines expériences religieuses et intellectuelles, que c'est le meilleur point de vue pour juger la fortune, au XVIIe siècle, de l'hermétisme et de la cabale – et en général de croyances de type magique. Je ne vais pas citer ici des noms et des faits connus de tous (comme l'utilisation en un sens anti-trinitaire des doctrines hermétiques par Servet et ses disciples ou, au contraire, leur exaltation par le pieux 'magicien' anglican Robert Fludd, le théologien luthérien J. V. Andreae ou par un remarquable représentant de la culture jésuite au cœur du XVIIe siècle comme le très célèbre Père Athanasius Kircher). Mais ce propos ne change guère en ce qui concerne les sujets cabalistiques qui opèrent dans des milieux et des directions très divergentes, parfois en relation avec la reprise de grandes aspirations visionnaires. Ces sujets sont employés le plus souvent comme support de la diffusion de conceptions, à leur façon, radicales, ou comme soutien pour la recherche d'instruments et de méthodes pour la construction de la 'grande science', unique et totale. Il s'agit là, sans aucun doute, d'attitudes propres au monde restreint d'hommes de culture, d'intellectuels qui, en tout cas, s'adressent uniquement à leurs semblables, même si parfois leurs discours laissent transparaître l'inquiétude de leur conscience à l'égard de la diffusion populaire des croyances magiques, des pratiques de la sorcellerie et de la survivance de cultes démoniaques qui n'est pas le dernier motif de la longue obsession 'du diable' qui bouleverse encore tant d'hommes d'église et de toge. Et pourtant, même sans donner des accents trop romanesques à ces événements, il est de fait que les doctrines hermétiques et de la cabale, comme les croyances magiques et alchimiques, fournissent, dans plusieurs cas, les motifs théoriques pour avancer des conceptions du monde incompatibles avec celles du vieux savoir 'officiel' ou pour justifier de nouveaux moyens et des techniques pour s'approcher de la recherche naturelle. De telles doctrines entourent d'une *aura* prodigieuse et d'un prestige encore efficace la figure du philosophe-magicien ou du savant-magicien, quand elles ne servent pas à opposer une sorte de nouveau charisme à l'ancien *clericus* ou *magister*. Ainsi, la fortune de l'hermétisme et de la cabale, née de la rencontre de la culture occidentale et de la sagesse mythique de l'Orient et avec le rappel de la *prisca theologia*, peut se transformer en aspiration à la possession de pouvoirs cosmiques exceptionnels mis au service d'un renouvellement radical du monde humain.

Il est clair que je ne veux dire par là que ces aspirations appartiennent au domaine de la science ou en constituent les conditions nécessaires. Après ces précisions, on devra toutefois reconnaître, qu'encore pendant une bonne partie du XVIIe siècle, les limites entre science, idées métaphysiques et expériences religieuses sont souvent assez faibles et qu'il est difficile de tracer une ligne précise de démarcation qui sépare, par exemple, l'intérêt pour les techniques et la croissante admiration pour les prodiges des arts mécaniques, de l'attrait pour la magie, ou distingue d'une manière irrévocable la recherche des médecins hermétiques paracelsiens des disciples de l'art alchimique. On ne peut honnêtement nier que les débuts du 'désenchantement du monde' dont on a tant parlé depuis l'époque de Max Weber ont été beaucoup plus incertains, problématiques et contradictoires qu'on ne veut parfois l'admettre. Ils furent le résultat d'une situation de conflits dans laquelle agissaient ensemble des exigences rationnelles et des motivations psychologiques encore au niveau de l'idéologie, la pression objective des nécessités sociales et les stimulations dérivant d'un changement toujours plus accentué des mêmes fondements de la recherche intellectuelle. Sans aucun doute, le point d'abordage final de ce processus, qui culmine dans la révolution scientifique, consiste justement dans la critique de chaque type d'opération magique, dans le refus de toute forme de savoir mystérieux, dans la dissolution historiographique des mythes hermétiques, dans la reconnaissance critique du caractère d'exégèse mystique propre de la cabale et dans le renoncement au grand rêve alchimique qui avait nourri, pendant tant de siècles, le désir d'une domination totale du genre humain sur les derniers éléments cosmiques. La science se forma avec des caractères théoriques spécifiques, fondés sur des méthodes rationnelles de la pensée mathématique, sur la connaissance expérimentale (irréductible à la nature mystique de l'*experimentum* alchimique), sur la clarté de son discours, en contraste avec la longue tradition du mystère ésotérique. Et pourtant, qui procède à la reconstitution de cet événement ainsi qu'à celle d'autres événements décisifs pour l'histoire de la civilisation moderne, est dans l'obligation de ne pas faire de généralisations hâtives et de ne pas croire que la vérité de l'épilogue a été présente depuis les origines et que les raisons qui constituent la science, désormais bien définie dans son domaine théorique, sont les mêmes qui en ont sollicité la naissance. En toute franchise, je n'arrive à trouver ni motif de scandale, ni aucun danger de contamination de la raison scientifique dans la reconnaissance d'une donnée de fait objective des sympathies occultes ou des tentations ésotériques encore cultivées par de nombreux hommes de science en plein XVIIe siècle. De même la constatation de longues et persistantes recherches sur les frontières de l'obscur domaine alchimique de la part de grands savants, ou la survivance de lointaines ou récentes vocations cabalistiques ou lulléennes tendues vers la recherche des racines de l'*arbor scientiarum*, ne constitue pas, certes, un démenti des valeurs inséparables de l'*ordre méthodique* du XVIIe siècle.

Quand, par exemple, on rappelle des sujets ou des phrases hermétiques que Copernic avance pour renforcer ou parafer un discours conduit selon les canons de l'astronomie mathématique;[1] quand on cite les indubitables références néo-platoniciennes ou pythagoriciennes de Kepler,[2] on n'entend vraiment pas nier la valeur rationnelle du *De revolutionibus orbium* ou de l'*Harmonice mundi* pour les transformer en autant de chapitres d'une théosophie hermétique. Je considère, au contraire, que l'on veut seulement rappeler des éléments très utiles, du moins du point de vue de la recherche historique, pour comprendre comme s'est effectivement formée une nouvelle mentalité et est née une attitude différente à l'égard d'une antique façon de concevoir la science avec des conséquences inexplicables en dehors de certaines suggestions ou tensions culturelles. Je ne crois pas que le fait de souligner certaines pages inquiétantes des *Olympica* cartésiens[3] ou rappeler la singulière 'recherche' des Rose-croix suivie également par le jeune Descartes[4] puisse vraiment servir à celui qui veut jouer la vieille carte de l'interprétation 'spiritualiste' de son message philosophique ou de sa méthode scientifique; je pense, au contraire, qu'elle peut servir à identifier certaines racines profondes d'une conception du savoir moins neutre et simplement fonctionnelle que la présentent les amateurs actuels d'un rationalisme très suspect. Mais le chercheur aura toujours le devoir de préciser et de distinguer, de savoir en somme reconstituer avec la plus grande précision possible, les différentes phases, et les moments distincts dans lesquels s'articule le long processus de décantation de la nouvelle science avec son lent

---

[1] Nicolaus Copernicus, *De revolutionibus orbium caelestium liber primus*, éd. A. Birkenmajer (Varsovie, 1953), p. 38.

[2] Johannes Kepler, *Harmonice mundi libri*, dans *Gesammelte Werke*, t. VI (München, 1940), pp. 365ss.

[3] R. Descartes, *Œuvres*, éd. C. Adam et P. Tannery (12 vols. Paris, 1897–1910), t. X, pp. 180–8.

[4] A. Baillet, *La vie de Monsieur Descartes* (Paris, 1691), pp. 87–92, 106–8. Pour les rapports entre Descartes et Johann Faulhaber, l'auteur du *Mysterium arithmeticum sive cabalistica et philosophica inventio... illuminatissimis laudatissimisque fratribus R.C. dicata* (Ulm, 1615), v. *ibid.* p. 68; et cf. Yates, *The Rosicrucian Enlightenment*, pp. 113–16. Pour la discussion de la 'thèse des Rose-croix' cf. H. Gouhier, *Les premières pensées de Descartes. Contribution à l'histoire de l'anti-renaissance* (Paris, 1958).

cheminement, ses reculs, ses sauts de qualité effectifs et le dépasse-
ment de formes de la pensée qui sont trop anciennes pour être
rapidement liquidées ou dissoutes. Et c'est pour cela qu'il ne faudra
pas oublier, toujours pour garder notre exemple, que la révolution
astronomique ne se résoud pas dans les cosmologies hermétiques,
pourtant pleines d'attraits, qui soutiennent l'héliosophie néoplatoni-
cienne pas plus qu'on ne peut comprendre la méthode galiléenne en
la reportant *in toto* aux précédents platoniciens ou aristotéliciens que
lui ont attribué des historiens de grand prestige.

Ceci ne porte toutefois pas préjudice à l'existence d'un autre
problème historique réel qui concerne l'inspiration ou la motivation
du même mouvement scientifique à l'intérieur de la société, et ses
rapports avec les conflits intellectuels, les crises religieuses, les
grandes batailles politiques et même si l'on veut avec les espérances
utopistes et les mythes dont ils se nourrissaient. Que l'on accepte ou
que l'on repousse les conclusions théoriques de Kuhn[1] (auxquelles je
n'adhère pas), la recherche historique ne peut en effet ignorer que
l'affirmation des idées scientifiques passe *aussi* à travers leur succès
social et leur pouvoir de se transformer en forces institutionnelles
opérant dans des conditions économico-sociales précises. C'est
pourquoi celui qui ne considère pas que les origines de la Royal
Society, une des institutions scientifiques modernes de la plus grande
importance, dépendent exclusivement des enthousiasmes millénaristes et utopiques de Hartlib, de Dury et de Comenius[2] ainsi que de
leur influence, d'ailleurs indiscutable, sur un groupe important
d'intellectuels anglais, ne peut éluder les problèmes qui sont posés par
la continuité de certains intérêts et surtout, par le contexte politique
et religieux dans lesquels ils se développèrent, en se transformant à
la rigueur, de mythes, en principes d'une organisation concrète et
collective de la recherche ou en poursuite d'une science humanitaire

---

[1] T. Kuhn, *The Copernican Revolution. Planetary Astronomy in the Development of Western
Thought* (Cambridge, Mass., 1957); idem, *The Structure of Scientific Revolution*.

[2] G. H. Turnbull, *Hartlib, Dury and Comenius* (London, 1947; réimprimé 1968); R. H.
Syfret, 'The origin of the Royal Society', *Notes and Records of the Royal Society* (1948),
117ss.; H. Hertly, éd., *The Royal Society, its Origins and Founders* (London, 1960); C. Hill,
Intellectual Origins of the English Revolution (Oxford, 1965); H. R. Trevor-Roper, 'Three
foreigners: the philosophers of Puritan revolution', *Religion, the Reformation and Social
Change* (London, 1967); M. Purver, *The Royal Society: Concepts and Creation* (London,
1967); P. M. Rattansi, 'The intellectual origins of the Royal Society'; D. Čapková,
'The Comenian group in England and Comenius' idea of universal reform', *Acta
comeniana* (1969), 25–34; C. Webster, *Samuel Hartlib and the Advancement of Learning*
(Cambridge, 1970); idem, 'Samuel Hartlib and great reform', *Acta comeniana*
(1970).

et bénéfique.[1] Il se peut que le fait de montrer ces aspects d'un événement capital pour l'histoire de la pensée ou de l'activité scientifique moderne ne serve pas à nous éclairer sur les critères méthodologiques et sur la logique interne de la nouvelle science. Il sera toutefois toujours nécessaire pour comprendre quels furent ses buts et ses projets à l'intérieur de la culture anglaise de la fin du XVIIe siècle dans laquelle, par exemple, l'alchimiste, astrologue et 'franc-maçon' Elias Ashmole,[2] encore lié si étroitement à la tradition hermétique, vivait avec Robert Boyle[3] et les autres hommes de science de la Society et alors que la tradition de Paracelse et des Rose-croix était encore si étendue et si forte. Sans parler des questions suscitées par les travaux très sérieux qui ont déjà reconstitué en partie le chemin complexe et tortueux qui conduit de l'alchimie hermétique aux premières affirmations de l'iatrochimie et aux origines mêmes de la 'chimie sceptique'.[4]

Et justement, parce que nous sommes à Cambridge, il est impossible d'éviter un sujet qui depuis des années a été à l'origine de tant de polémiques, a divisé les historiens et les a induits à proposer des hypothèses et des solutions les plus contrastantes. Qui m'écoute a déjà compris que je veux parler ici des intérêts, des lectures, des écrits et des expériences d'alchimie de Newton et aussi, car ces deux sujets me paraissent difficilement séparables, de ses profondes préoccupations théologiques et exégétiques ainsi que de ses rapports avec les platoniciens de Cambridge et leur méditation, si liée à l'antique matrice de Ficin. Il est clair que je ne peux pas rappeler ici les résultats désormais acquis d'une abondante littérature qui compte parmi ses auteurs R. J. Forbes,[5] F. Sherwood Taylor,[6]

---

[1] A propos des influences 'millénaristes' v. L. Trengove, 'Newton's theological views', *Annals of Science* (1966), 277–94; D. Kubrin, 'Newton and cyclical cosmos: providence and the mechanical philosophy', *Journal of History of Ideas* (1967), 325–46; W. M. Lamont, *Godly Rule* (London, 1969); B. Capp, '"Godly Rule" and English millenarianism', *Past and Present* (1971), no. 52; C. Hill, *Antichrist in Seventeenth Century England* (London, 1971); B. Capp, 'The millennium and eschatology in England', *Past and Present* (1972), no. 57; *idem, The Fifth Monarchy Men* (London, 1972); M. C. Jacob et W. A. Lockwood, 'Political millenarianism and Burnet's sacred theology', *Science Studies* (1972), 265–79; M. C. Jacob, 'Millenarianism and science in the late seventeenth century', *Journal of History of Ideas* (1976), 335–41. Mais v. aussi F. Manuel, *Isaac Newton Historian* (Cambridge, 1963); *idem, The Religion of Isaac Newton* (Oxford, 1974).
[2] C. H. Josten, *Elias Ashmole* (Oxford, 1965); Yates, *The Rosicrucian Enlightenment*, pp. 193–205; 209–10.
[3] J. R. Jacob, 'The ideological origins of Robert Boyle's natural philosophy', *Journal of European Studies* (1972), 1–21.   [4] V. part. les travaux de Debus cités à la p. 62, n. 5.
[5] R. J. Forbes, 'Was Newton an alchemist?', *Chymia* (1949), 27–36.
[6] F. Sherwood Taylor, 'An alchemical work of Isaac Newton', *Ambix* (1965), 59–84.

Marie Boas Hall, A. R. Hall,[1] B. J. T. Dobbs[2] ainsi que mademoiselle Yates[3] et Rattansi.[4] Je ne possède ni la préparation scientifique, ni une connaissance de ces textes de Newton qui me permette de formuler un jugement personnel sur un problème historique si controversé. Mais en lecteur attentif de ces travaux, je crois pouvoir affirmer que peu de cas sont aussi clairs pour celui qui veut se rendre compte du rapport étroit et des interférences entre les raisons scientifiques et les exigences, projets et buts de genre très divers qui se vérifiaient souvent dans l'histoire intellectuelle des plus grands hommes de science de l'époque. Il me semble, en ce sens, que ce qu'a écrit récemment Richard Westfall,[5] d'une manière si éloignée de toute extrapolation anti-historique comme de toute tentative de réduction, est un bon abord pour prendre connaissance de documents si révélateurs pour l'histoire d'un esprit. Il est bien vrai qu'on pourrait partir des manuscrits d'alchimie de Newton pour en faire un disciple de la 'lumière' hermétique, lui dont les travaux d'optique et de mécanique céleste doivent être réinterprétés d'une manière ésotérique ou rendus objet d'analyses psycho-analytiques souvent les plus aventureuses. Il n'est pourtant pas permis, pour éviter ces dangers, de considérer ces textes et ces documents comme des témoignages de peu de valeur, comme une survivance bizarre ou comme des concessions à la mentalité de l'époque, et donc négligeables dans la reconstitution de l'esprit de Newton, de la genèse de ses doctrines philosophiques et scientifiques et de ses rapports avec la situation culturelle 'réelle'. On court autrement le risque de retomber dans ce type d'historiographie, autant limité que peu explicatif, qui néglige encore aujourd'hui d'étudier une partie importante de l'œuvre de Leibniz et tend à n'en présenter que les côtés modernes, dans la direction de la nouvelle logique formelle, comme si elle craignait presque de se mesurer avec les intérêts lulléens et vaguement cabalistiques du jeune secrétaire de la

---

[1] M. Boas et A. R. Hall, 'Newton's chemical experiments', *Archives internationales d'histoire des sciences* (1958), 113–52. Mais v. aussi D. Geoghegan, 'Some indications of Newton's attitude toward alchemy', *Ambix* (1957), 102–6.

[2] B. J. T. Dobbs, *The Foundation of Newton's Alchemy. The Hunting of the Greene Lyon* (Cambridge, 1976). Mais v. aussi F. Manuel, *A Portrait of Isaac Newton* (Cambridge, Mass., 1968), pp. 169–90.

[3] Yates, *The Rosicrucian Enlightenment*, pp. 200–5.

[4] Rattansi, 'Newton's alchemical studies'.

[5] R. S. Westfall, 'Newton and the hermetic tradition', *Science, Medicine and Society in the Renaissance*, éd. Debus, t. II, pp. 183–98; *idem*, 'The role of alchemy in Newton's career', *Reason, Experiment and Mysticism in the Scientific Revolution*, éd. Righini Bonelli et Shea, pp. 189–232.

mystérieuse societé alchimiste de Nuremberg,[1] admirateur d'Andreae et de Coménius.

D'autre part – et ceci est le dernier sujet sur lequel je voudrais attirer votre attention – il faudrait également considérer un autre aspect de la culture du XVIIe siècle qui me semble difficile à expliquer sans avoir recours à l'influence de la tradition ésotérique et en particulier au filon cabalistique: je veux parler de la vocation encyclopédique, de la ferme croyance en l'unité du savoir qui se traduisait par l'image de la *catena scientiarum* ou de l'*arbor scientiarum* correspondant parfaitement à la structure 'harmonieuse' et hiérarchique du cosmos. À ce propos l'accord entre les hommes de science, les disciples de l'hermétisme et de la cabale, les théologiens des différentes confessions et les derniers adeptes de l'*ars magna* de Lulle est parfaitement symptomatique. Il ne serait pas difficile de démontrer comment des adversaires acharnés comme l'étaient Fludd et P. Mersenne étaient d'accord, fondamentalement, sur l'idée de l'*harmonia mundi* et de la communication cyclique de toutes les sciences, ni de citer un célèbre passage de Descartes sur l'admirable 'chaîne' des sciences[2] ou même des phrases très semblables de savants qui furent critiques à son ègard ou adversaires comme Coménius ou Juan Caramuel Lobkowitz.[3] Mais le fait le plus intéressant est que ces *loci communes*, si répandus à différents niveaux dans la culture du XVIIe siècle, n'expriment pas seulement une conviction radicale et profonde, mais donnent lieu à un intense travail encyclopédique, à des tentatives aussi impressionnantes que complexes pour redonner une vision totale du savoir, mise en crise par les progrès de la science nouvelle et par la dissolution des vieux 'fondements' traditionnels. Ainsi, le XVIIe siècle, défini souvent comme 'siècle de la méthode', pourrait être à juste titre appelé le 'siècle de l'encyclopédie'. Car cette époque s'ouvre par les tentatives encyclopédiques d'Alsted et de ses collègues et disciples de Herborn et se termine par les projets 'pansophistes' de Leibniz. Et sa vrai conclusion idéale se trouve – peut-être – dans le célèbre discours, prononcé dans une loge franc-maçonnique parisienne, en 1737, par le fameux chevalier Ramsay pour engager ses confrères 'à fournir des matériaux d'un *Dictionnaire universel*

---

[1] G. M. Ross, 'Leibniz and the Nuremberg Alchemical Society', *Studia leibnitiana* (1974), 222–48.

[2] *Cogitationes privatae*, dans *Œuvres*, t. x, p. 213.

[3] D. Pastine, *Juan Caramuel: probabilismo ed enciclopedia* (Firenze, 1975), pp. 153–220.

des Arts libéraux et des sciences utiles, la théologie et la politique seules exceptées...'.[1]

Entre ces deux extrêmes, entre l'œuvre d'un théologien protestant, enclin toutefois aux idées millénaristes, aux idées astrologiques et aux sujets hermétiques paracelsiens et les discours d'un personnage, jugé de manière tres diverse, mais qui était l'héritier direct de nombreuses traditions ésotériques du 'grand siècle' se trouvent les documents de l'encyclopédisme du XVIIe siècle, les nombreux *sintagma, artes universales, digesta sapientiae, arbores scientiarum,* etc. dont est si riche la littérature philosophique et également théologique. Il s'agit presque toujours d'œuvres ou de projets dans lesquels on rencontre des souvenirs cabalistiques et lulléens plus ou moins marqués, qui sont souvent à l'origine des spéculations sur la possibilité de 'langages universels' ou de recherches à la limite entre l'analyse mathématique de techniques combinatoires et la survivance d'un idéal pansophiste souvent marqué d'inquiétantes traces magiques. Le fait que ces travaux furent conduits surtout par des hommes d'église ou de religion qui appartiennent à tout l'arc des dénominations ecclésiastiques (nous avons Andreae le luthérien, Alsted le calviniste, le 'Frère bohème' Coménius, Caramuel Lobkowitz, théologien contre-réformiste, sceptique et probabiliste, les jésuites Kircher et Izquierdo, ainsi qu'Yves de Paris et Léon de Saint-Jean, personnalités si marquantes de l'histoire religieuse française) est une autre circonstance significative pour juger le rôle de cet encyclopédisme dans les grands débats du siècle, face à la diffusion croissante de la propagande libertine et à l'infiltration de l'athéisme. Mais je crois surtout que l'encyclopédisme du XVIIe siècle était un des éléments de fonds de sa culture et, sans doute, celui qui exprimait le mieux la difficulté du passage entre 'l'ancien' et 'le nouveau', entre les rêves pansophistes pleins d'attente religieuse et de grandes espérances utopistes et la connaissance désenchantée d'un nouvel univers 'artificiel', fait d'expériences, de techniques et d'instruments dans lequel on devait trouver un principe d'ordre et de discipline rationnelle et au moins un critère d'orientation moins incertain et moins provisoire des anciennes topiques. Des hommes de sévère formation rationnelle n'étaient pas étrangers à ces exigences et étaient con-

[1] F. Venturi, *Le origini dell'Enciclopedia*, 2e éd. (Torino, 1964), pp. 16–26; P. Chevallier, *Les ducs sous l'Acacia ou les premiers pas de la Franc-Maçonnerie française* (Paris, 1964), pp. 133ss.; R. Le Forestier, *La Franc-Maçonnerie templière et occultiste* (Paris et Louvain, 1970). Pour le texte v. J. Palou, *La Franc-Maçonnerie* (Paris, 1964), pp. 317–24.

vaincus que l'on pouvait reconstruire un système achevé du savoir, structuré selon la rigueur des axiomes d'Euclide.

On dira – et c'est exact – que cette sorte de *background* culturel est très différent de la naissance de la 'vraie' mentalité scientifique et qu'il représente plutôt la survivance extrême de modes de pensée désormais condamnés. On peut également comprendre la réserve et la défiance envers une représentation de la réalité qui adhère souvent plus au fondement rhétorique des *artes memoriae* qu'à la clarté des processus rationnels et se fie au goût baroque des temples, musées ou théâtres universels du savoir. De telles conceptions eurent leur part, non secondaire, dans l'histoire des idées, pendant une longue période qui ne fut pas aussi limpide et rationnelle que ne nous la présentent de nombreuses synthèses historiques. La révolution scientifique ne fut pas non plus une barrière très nette et irréversible en face des idées, mythes et traditions dont on peut vérifier la continuité au-delà des limites préétablies de l'"âge de la Raison'. Que de telles survivances aient été 'regressives', que la vitalité des mythes hermétiques au-delà de la réfutation critique de Casaubon ait été (comme l'a souligné mademoiselle Yates) 'réactionnaire',[1] et que les persistances des doctrines cabalistiques, après avoir été rendues à leur effective nature exégétique, aient constitué désormais une sorte d'épave culturelle, est un autre fait sur lequel on pourra et l'on devra discuter, seulement après avoir constaté leur influence réelle. Autrement l'histoire d'une époque, si décisive pour toutes les formes de notre civilisation, continuera à être partielle ou déformée, et obéira plus aux exigences idéologiques de nos jours qu'aux canons de l'intelligence et de la critique du passé.

[1] Yates, *Giordano Bruno and the Hermetic Tradition.*

'EMENDATIO OMNIUM' – A PEDAGOGIC OR A POLITICAL PROGRAMME?

K. SCHALLER

Rerum humanarum emendatio is the title of the programme for the reform of mankind that J. A. Comenius (1592–1670) drew up in his maturity. It is a programme that has not been carried out yet and perhaps never will be, which explains why people do not regard it as urgent. Many of us do not even feel that there is much need for reform.

But those who envisage the end of the historical process have always taken a different view. They have been impatient. They have tried to bring the promised end nearer and have been prepared to use violence for the purpose. And in Comenius' day there were many such. There were men who had worked out the year in which the fall of Antichrist would occur, and Christ's millennial reign of peace would dawn. Comenius shared their chiliastic hopes. He was one of their great spokesmen. He felt that it was essential to put things in order without delay. Everything that could be done had to be done for the Lord's coming, so that the Lord would come.

This is what Comenius had in mind. But with such all-embracing plans of improvement, the difficulty is to know where to begin. Can one succeed by educating mankind, or is direct political action required? This was Comenius' dilemma. We are now going to examine that episode in his life which imposed on him the task of a *reformatio mundi*, and we shall see how he tried to solve its problems. The drama of his career will be presented here in three acts.

ACT I: COMENIUS AS THE AUTHOR OF THE 'DIDACTICA MAGNA' AND THE EARLY PANSOPHICAL BLUEPRINTS

It would take us too long to trace the early development of Comenius' ideas,[1] and we must begin with the immense success of his textbook,

---

[1] For the present state of research on Comenius see K. Schaller, *Comenius* (*Erträge der Forschung* 19, Veröffentlichungen der Comenius-Forschungsstelle der Ruhr-Universität Bochum, no. 5, Darmstadt, 1973). For a summary of the writings see the bibliographies in Josef Brambora, 'Komenský́s literarische Tätigkeit in Form von Medallions dargestellt',

Janua linguarum reserata (Leszno, 1631), which convinced him of the value of his Christian pansophy and was responsible for his becoming known in England. Samuel Hartlib, an east European exile, who had lived in London since 1630, had circulated the work among his English friends; and when he learnt from a couple of students, Daniel Erastus and Samuel Benedict (*duo de nostris*[1] that Comenius had given some Czech lectures in 1634 on the subject of *janua rerum*, he wrote asking for information.[2] Comenius responded by sending him *In janua rerum sive totius pansophiae seminarium introitus, praecognita*, which was a preliminary sketch of his philosophy, and he followed this, since Hartlib now produced a further set of questions, with a new work, the *Praeludia pansophiae*. Hartlib was so impressed by this that he allowed Joachim Hübner to have it printed in Oxford in 1637, much to the dismay of Comenius, who refused permission for a second edition. Instead he revised the *Praeludia* and produced an improved version, the *Pansophiae prodromus* (London, 1639).

As we shall see later, the *Pansophiae prodromus* met with such interest in England that it overshadowed Comenius' other works and caused them to be judged in the light of the expectations aroused by its doctrines. This was particularly evident in the case of the *Didactica magna*. Hartlib received a copy of this work, which had appeared originally in Czech, and he passed it to Hübner who had developed a great enthusiasm for pansophy, having an eye, evidently, to its effect *in politicis*.[3] Hübner, who had expected the *Didactica* to be an introduction to pansophy, was bitterly disappointed, and in November 1639 he sent some harsh comments to Comenius.[4] He did

and Hildburg Bethke, 'Bibliographie der deutschsprachigen Comenius-Literatur 1870–1970', both in H.-J. Heydorn, *J. A. Comenius, Geschichte und Aktualität 1670–1970*, vol. II (Glashütten in the Taunus, 1971). The most important editions of Comenius' individual works are given in the notes that follow. The latest biographies are: Milada Blekastad, *Comenius, Versuch eines Umrisses von Leben, Werk und Schicksal des J. A. Komenský* (Oslo and Prague, 1969); J. E. Sadler, *J. A. Comenius and the Concept of Universal Education* (London, 1966).

[1] *Continuatio admonitionis...*, § 47, in *Ausgewählte Werke*, ed. with introduction by Klaus Schaller (3 vols., Hildesheim and New York, 1976–7) (hereafter *A.W.*), vol. II. 1, p. 5.
[2] Blekastad, *Comenius*, p. 225. The *Praecognita* mentioned later and the *Janua rerum* (1643; first published Leiden, 1681 were edited by G. H. Turnbull, *J. A. Komenský, Dva spisy vševědné: Two Pansophical Works* (Prag, 1951). *Pansophiae praeludia* revised as *Pansophiae prodromus* can be found in *Veškeré spisy*, ed. Jan Kvačala (Brno, 1914) (hereafter *V.S.*), vol. I, pp. 305–88.
[3] Hübner to Bisterfeld (?), London, 1638, in J. Kvačala, *Pädagogische Reform des Comenius*, vol. I (Mon. Germ. Paed., XXVI, Berlin, 1903), no. 86, p. 105.
[4] Hübner to Comenius, November 1639, in J. Kvačala, *Korrespondence J. A. Komenskýs*, vol. I (Prag, 1898), LXII, pp. 73–82.

not desire, we read, to be classed with 'that pedagogical or rather, that didactic, sect'. As for Comenius' system: 'although a great many people believe it to be the best guarantee for a better era, I have no doubt that it will bring about the worst possible and the most futile things for our age, that it is a great evil for learning and the church'.

Hübner's criticism of the *Didactica*, which he did not consider to be in a fit state as yet for publication, concentrated particularly on the fact that Comenius had concerned himself only with the general principles of teaching. He had not considered individual school subjects, and even his general principles lacked a solid foundation. 'What more unnatural and outrageous way of proving one's point is there', Hübner asks, 'than supporting one's reasoning by parables and laying down laws for schools, based on the world of the birds and plants?' The confusion could not have been worse if Comenius had got his notes muddled:

Imagine what laughter you would cause with this...among the followers of Jungius, Tassius, Descartes and others...I only want to show you briefly that there is little use preceding your Pansophy with your Didactica. Your Didactica fails to prove sufficiently that it must necessarily be linked to your Pansophy.

This criticism proved to be of great importance. Hübner's reading of the *Didactica* had been superficial, and his strictures suggest that the interest he took in the ideas of its author was limited to their political usefulness; but his advice that the *ars didactica* should be linked closely to the pansophical system was adopted by Comenius and colours the account the latter was to give of his educational ideas in the *Pampaedia*,[1] the central section of his main pansophical work, the seven-part *De rerum humanarum emendatione consultatio catholica*.[2]

Pansophy for Comenius was primarily an important element in the new educational programme that he hoped to base on the principle: 'In scholis omnes *omnia* docendos esse';[3] and that educational programme in its turn had aims beyond the nurturing of man's inner self. It was connected in his mind with the revival of the kingdom of Bohemia after the return of the Moravian Brethren to their own country. At the time he wrote the *Pansophiae prodromus*, Comenius' conception of his system was still predominantly static.

---

[1] The first Latin–German ed. is by D. Tschiževskij, H. Geissler, and K. Schaller (Heidelberg, 1960).
[2] Complete ed. (Prag, 1966).
[3] *Didactica magna* x.1, in *V.S.*, vol. IV, p. 123.

Its theoretical framework was Neoplatonism;[1] and its dynamic element, its practical relevance and its political impetus were not yet clearly revealed. There was nothing to indicate that the *mundus artificialis* (the world of human activity) was to become the pivot of the universal pansophical process. All this was to be changed by Comenius' visit to England.

Wisdom, according to the *Pansophiae prodromus*, is the goal of scholarly education.[2] Pansophy, the type of wisdom Comenius anticipates, was to reflect a picture of the universe teeming with life: 'I. Universae eruditionis breviarium solidum. II. Intellectus humani fax lucida. III. Veritatis rerum norma stabilis. IV. Negotiorum vitae tabulatura certa. V. Ad deum ipsum scala beata.'[3] It was to be of use to scholars, to schoolchildren, to all Christians. Having attained this universal wisdom we would know our life here to be 'merely' a preparation for life everlasting.[4] In the *Didactica magna* three dwelling places of man are mentioned: the womb, earth and heaven. The first two prepare man for life in the third. Thus the world is nothing but 'our nursery garden, our store room, our school', and there is something beyond this (*plus ultra*), to which we are to be promoted on leaving the classroom of this school, namely the eternal academy.[5] This theory of education promised paradise in the form of a regenerated church.

Comenius' early works were the fruits of a lively contact with his co-religionists and were generally written in their language, Czech. His writings gave expression to their sufferings, their anxieties and also their hopes, and became a comfort and a guide to those whose interests he had at heart:

I declare above all that it was never my intention to write, let alone to publish, in Latin. From my earliest childhood I was filled with the desire only to serve my nation and to write a few books in my mother tongue...It was outward circumstances that induced me to try other means...[6]

The outward circumstances were various, but it was first and foremost the dwindling hope of a return to his native country which opened new horizons for Comenius. The ideas which were to have

---

[1] K. Schaller, *Die Pädagogik des J. A. Comenius und die Anfänge des pädagogischen Realismus im 17. Jh.*, 2nd ed. (Heidelberg, 1967), pp. 35ff.
[2] *Pansophiae prodromus*, § 7, in *V.S.*, vol. I, p. 331.
[3] *Ibid.* § 39, in *V.S.*, vol. I, pp. 335f.
[4] *Didactica magna* III, in *V.S.*, vol. IV, p. 63. For the translation of the Czech original see *Böhmische Didaktik*, trans. and ed. K. Schaller (Paderborn, 1970).
[5] *Didactica magna* III. 3, in *V.S.*, vol. IV, p. 67.
[6] Comenius to Montanus, 10 December 1661; in *A.W.*, vol. II. 1, p. 46.

been of use to his fatherland now had to be made available to other nations so that a basic reformation could be set in motion. Originally Comenius also wanted to write the *Pansophia* in Czech, but Rafael Leszczinski intervened, no doubt pointing out the reasons we have just mentioned. He prompted what was probably the most important decision in Comenius' life, that he would no longer offer consolation only to his own people, but would proclaim his teaching to the whole world.[1] Comenius, the pansophist, speaks Latin.

The consequences of this decision were considerable. His writings had frequently to be defended before his own congregation. Worse than this, however, was the fact that in the form in which they were presented, they were no longer firmly rooted in society. Comenius had gone into exile in a far more drastic sense than when he and the Bohemian Brethren had been forced to leave their native country. Pansophy now became an abstract product of academic contemplation, which was certainly not what its author had intended. These theoretical concepts could only become relevant for life (in the sense of a guide-line rather than of mere instrumental application) if people could be found who would accept them as the expression of their own future. This was to happen in England where all available materials on pansophy had already been eagerly collected.

ACT II: COMENIUS IN ENGLAND AND THE ORTHODOX SOLUTION TO THE TASK OF 'EMENDATIO': THE PANSOPHICAL EDUCATIONAL THEORY

Pansophy, which was in danger of becoming lost in philosophical speculations, and the didactic writings, which gave mankind a goal in the world to come, were to be set on their feet again in England.

In his book *Religion, the Reformation and Social Change* H. R. Trevor-Roper puts forward a thesis to explain this important process.[2] After eleven years' obstruction, the Long Parliament met in London in November 1640. Outraged men, members of the English gentry and the country party had united to oppose the royal court. They

---

[1] Blekastad, *Comenius*, p. 210.

[2] H. R. Trevor-Roper, *Religion, the Reformation and Social Change* (London, 1967). German trans. (Frankfurt and Berlin, 1970), pp. 221–69. The chapter 'Three foreigners: the philosophers of the Puritan Revolution' refers to G. H. Turnbull, *Hartlib, Dury and Comenius. Gleanings from Hartlib's Papers* (London, 1947). Cf. also C. Webster, 'Macaria, Samuel Hartlib and the Great Reformation', and J. Simon, 'The Comenian educational reformers 1640–60 and the Royal Society of London', *Acta Comeniana*, II (1971), 147ff. and 165ff. respectively.

demanded two things, the decentralisation and the laicisation of the
church, judicature and education. For the gentry themselves higher
education was the most important qualification for gaining positions
in keeping with their rank and, at a lower level, there was a great
need for a uniform, decentralised system of primary schooling. This
was the model for the new society, whose philosophers – the only
philosophers of the English Revolution – were to be three foreigners,
Hartlib, Dury and Comenius.

This revolution could not successfully be set in motion from above.
Archbishop Laud had been forced to recognise this after attempting
to improve the foundations of the church by beginning at the top.
A reform which failed to use the support of the laity's new social
power could not reach its goals. The country party announced that
society had to be changed by the vigour of the laity and their
learning. Paradoxically, the 'philosophy' of these people, enemies of
the court, was the philosophy of that uncompromising royalist,
Francis Bacon. Admittedly the country party had to adapt this
philosophy in a number of ways. Included in their 'country
Baconism' were chiliastic calculations (calculations of the day of the
apocalypse – in 1639 the fall of Antichrist was expected), messianic
hopes and a mystic philosemitism.

The early contacts between Comenius and Hartlib have already
been mentioned. The group, consisting of Hartlib, Dury and a
number of other central Europeans, mainly refugees, became the
connecting link within the English country party. These spiritual
leaders were supported by all the party's prominent members, in
particular by John Williams, Bishop of Lincoln and Dean of
Westminster, and by Elizabeth, the sister of Charles I and 'Queen of
Bohemia'. The earliest and most faithful patron of Hartlib, Dury and
Comenius was John Pym, and as the days of Laud and Strafford
drew to a close, the resolute men of the parliamentary opposition
paid ever more attention to the prophets of the new revelation and
the reform of society.

What were the concrete political conceptions of the Long Parliament? The Advent sermons held before Parliament are an important
source of information here. Both Pym and his much admired heroine,
Queen Elizabeth, cultivated the art of using the pulpit to good
advantage, and so a few days after 17 November 1640, the words of
the preacher John Gauden appeared to state what the influential
members of Parliament had instructed him to say. Gauden's sermon

was entitled 'The love of truth and peace'. Towards the end of it, the preacher drew the attention of Parliament to the noble efforts of two great men who had been publicly active in working for truth and peace, Comenius and Duraeus. As he pointed out, they were both famed for their knowledge, their devoutness and their sincerity and were without doubt well known to many of the honourable, well-educated and pious congregation through the reputation of their works. Who, asked Gauden, had done more for truth than Comenius and for peace than Dury? Unfortunately, he added, they were like two fine plants, withering and doomed to infertility since they lacked general encouragement. He then begged his audience to consider whether it was not due to the honour and the name of the state and the church to invite these men to unfold their noble and excellent plans, for these to be weighed carefully so that every possible public support and encouragement might be bestowed on them and that such happy tasks might be tackled and completed as might benefit the advancement of truth and peace.

Eventually Hartlib was charged with issuing an invitation to Comenius and Dury on behalf of the English Parliament.

For some time, however, the legal proceedings taken against Strafford cast a shadow over the social and political prospects of Parliament. It was not until after Strafford's execution on 12 May 1641 that there was a fresh opportunity for making plans to reform the church and the state and that Pym, having taken over power, was able to dismiss his armed forces. Pym, in the House of Commons, and John Williams, in the House of Lords, were now indisputably in control, though of all the leaders of the country party Williams was the only one to hold high political office.

In the summer of 1641, the plan to invite Comenius and Dury to London was taken up again, as the right time for completing the programme of reform had come. Comenius arrived in London on 21 September 1641. He stayed with Hartlib, and his plans for the new golden age were awaited with interest. He soon met Williams and Pym, and the three (Hartlib, Dury, Comenius) began to prepare their plans for a new society. In the same year *A Description of the Famous Kingdom of Macaria*, a model for this new society, was published by Hartlib; Dury completed a supplement to this work and, shortly after his arrival in England, Comenius wrote three papers, the *Via lucis*, which was not published until 1668, and two shorter ones, *De iis quae ad universalem et fundamentalem ecclesiae reformationem spectare videntur consultationis brevissima delineatio* and *Ad excitanda publice veritatis et pacis hoc est communis salutis ope Dei studia elaborandorum operum catalogus.*[1] In this latter he quotes Gauden's Advent appeal for truth and peace. In his *Brevissima delineatio* Comenius exclaims on 1 October 1641, 'Praesuppono convenire nos in eo: Ultimum mundi seculum Christo et Ecclesiae victoriosum appropinquare.'[2] He envisages an age of divine inspiration when the earth will be filled with the wisdom of God as the waters cover the sea, an age of peace: 'And they shall beat their swords into plowshares and their spears into pruninghooks; nation shall not lift up sword against nation, neither shall they learn war any more' (Isaiah II. 4).

It is clear that by September 1641 Comenius was on firm ground once again and no longer indulged in speculations above the heads of his readers. He was expressing the thoughts and expectations of the oppressed on earth, their hopes for a better future. As the letter 'Ad amicos Lesnae in Polonia agentes', which he wrote on 8/18 October 1641, reveals,[3] Comenius was, at this time, living in a kind of ecstasy in London.

Comenius' writings reflect most clearly the contact which had been re-established with social reality, the fact that he had overcome the problems of his 'emigration'. What had so far been regarded at the most as a further development of an idea now proved to be a new outlook acquired from the political activities of the English country party. In England Comenius' homeless pansophy became a political programme for the improvement of man's condition (*rerum humanarum emendatio*).

In a letter written to Louis de Geer on 8/18 April 1645 Comenius for the first time expresses the results of this newly discovered sense of pansophy:

The thesis I am now working on is called 'General advice on improving the human condition, addressed to the human race, in particular to all men of learning in Europe'. The *Pansophia* has become a seventh of this book, likewise the *Pampaedia*, i.e. the book on the general culture of the mind (*cultura animorum*) etc.[4]

The truth of pansophy cannot be deduced, but its practical sense has to be demonstrated in the concrete circumstances of this world. (A demonstration of this nature was also to be aided by the *perpetuum*

[1] *Didactica opera omnia ab anno 1627 ad 1657 continuata* (Amsterdam, 1657; reprinted Prague, 1957) (hereafter *O.O.*), vol. XIV, pp. 117–36.

[2] *O.O.*, vol. XIV, p. 129; cf. Comenius, *Continuatio admonitionis*, § 51, in *A.W.*, vol. II. 1, p. 7.

[3] *O.O.*, vol. XIV, pp. 111–16.

[4] Comenius to L. de Geer, in A. Patera, *J. A. Komenského korespondence* (Prag, 1892), p. 97.

mobile.)[1] A brief comparison of the *Via lucis*, written in England in 1641–2, and the *Didactica magna* reveals this most distinctly. This work was not printed until 1668 and the letter of dedication to the Royal Society in London was likewise dated 'Idibus Aprilis 1668'. (It is not possible to discuss here how Comenius regarded the relation of the Royal Society to the three philosophers of the Revolution and to their plans for a college of scholars.) The dedication, of course, refers to the title of the original, then largely completed, work of improvement, 'Prima parte operis nostri toto genere novum est scopus universalis, *Emendatio rerum humanarum omnium, in omnibus, omnino*'.[2] The foremost aim of schools in this world is to praise God by providing his image, man, with the best possible education: 'Tres hae subcoelestes scholae...sunt pro praesenti vita, quam sub coelo vivimus: non pro illa futura...'[3] School is no longer a preparation (in the strict sense of the word) for life in the world hereafter. It does not need to be this, because once we are there God himself will teach us, not in the form of shadows or images, but through direct contemplation of his countenance.[4] The new practical and political context of Comenius' pansophical pedagogy is apparent, not only in this later dedication, but in the text itself. 'Ex ipsa itaque Creatoris intentione mundus nihil est nisi aeternitatis praeludium ("Didactica magna": praeparatorium), h.e. schola inferior, in quam mittimur, antequam ad coelestem Academiam promoveamur.'[5] 'The matter is so vital that all hopes of a better reformation of the world...depend on the instructing of the young...Either the goal of universal reform will be attained by this or all other efforts will be in vain.'[6] Chapter xx inquires into the kind of world that can be hoped for from this concept of school and we are told that the three books of God (nature, the human spirit and the holy scriptures) 'huic vitae dati sunt, non futurae, ubi Deus non per typos et specula docebit, sed semetipsum immediate, facie ad faciem videndum dabit.[7] Thereafter, 'pax universalis orbis terrarum' will reign.[8] Thus this work, which was written in England, can already be regarded as a *Consultatio catholica* in embryo.

As has already been mentioned, this was in September and October 1641. All of a sudden came bad news from Ireland: the

---

[1] Cf. *A.W.*, vol. III.
[2] *O.O.*, vol. XIV, p. 286 (§ 5).
[3] *O.O.*, vol. XIV, p. 288 (§ 19).
[4] *Ibid.*
[5] *Via lucis* I. 8; in *O.O.*, vol. XIV, p. 294.
[6] *Ibid.* XVII. 3f.; in *O.O.*, vol. XIV, p. 345.
[7] *Ibid.* XX. 3, in *O.O.*, vol. XIV, p. 357.
[8] *Ibid.* XX. 13; in *O.O.*, vol. XIV, p. 359.

4-2

Irish Catholics were in revolt. The king, temporarily in residence in Scotland, received the news with gratification. In the summer the king's unwillingness to accept the new social order had already cast a shadow over everyone's rejoicing. There was discord in the country, in church and Parliament, particularly between the Lords and the Commons, and between Williams and Pym. After the king's return from Scotland, Pym could feel his power tottering, moved further to the left and, in his *Grand Remonstrance*, proclaimed a head-on attack on the crown.[1] There was no longer any hope of constructive reforms. These were only possible within an effectively functioning constitution, a *monarchia mixta* of king and Parliament. The social reform which depended on this constitution had to be postponed.

On 21 June 1642, Comenius sailed from London. He left the patrons of pansophical studies a pamphlet entitled *Studii pansophiae in Anglia fautoribus*.[2] Later political events in England and the numerous attempts to encourage Comenius to return there at certain critical stages can be passed over here. What needs to be noted are the consequences which the events we have described had on Comenius' work.

The fact that Comenius' pansophy had become linked to the supporters of reform, the country party and its prominent advocates, had given it practical and political relevance. But now the supporting structure of his concept collapsed beneath him. He did not participate in the move to the left, being prevented from doing so by his principle of peace. Thus, apart from his numerous contacts, he was, once again, dependent on his own resources and his work. In March 1642 he was again without a home. Between 4 and 14 March he wrote to Hotton: 'My work flourishes best in peace and seclusion and today I still regret having been drawn into the light of publicity.'[3] In his *Autobiography* he says: 'What is expected of me is a new, firm, eternally unshakeable system of things, not a patchwork, even if it were wonderfully joined together.'[4] This was not, however, a complete withdrawal. It did not result in his entirely abandoning the practical and political intentions of his work of reform. The most perfect stage of wisdom was for him still the *chresis*, the implementation, the final accomplishment of God's desire for peace in this world. His social and political commitment remained, as is proved

[1] Trevor-Roper, *Religion*, p. 253. [2] *O.O.*, vol. xiv, pp. 137–40.
[3] Comenius to Hotton, in Patera, *J. A. Komenského korespondence*, p. 50.
[4] Comenius, *Continuatio admonitionis*, § 57, in *A.W.*, vol. ii. 1, p. 11.

by the essay *Gentis felicitas*. The theme of *renuntiatio mundi*, the renouncement of the world, which emerged early in his writing, did not annihilate his striving for an *emendatio mundi*.[1] Instead of being rooted in a direct political impetus his *emendatio* was from now on based on a strangely orthodox foundation. When Comenius decided to make a political appeal as, for instance, in *Panegyricus Carolo Gustavo* (1655), it was influenced by some direct political commitment and was not contained within the pansophical vision of his *Consultatio catholica*. This, however, is not the place to discuss these activities.

Instead we are going to concentrate on the political activities rooted in the *Consultatio catholica*, for instance when Comenius recommends in the *Panorthosia* a *collegium lucis*, a *consistorium sanctitatis* and a *dicasterium pacis*; or when he demands the foundation of a supreme world council, *orbis concilium*. What do we mean when we talk of the 'orthodox foundation' of this political activity? Orthodox is not used in a particular religious sense, but with regard to Comenius' increasingly strictly developed panorthotic theory. As was the case before his stay in England, this moves within the categories of a Neoplatonic philosophy, but with one remarkable change. The structure of the universe is no longer pictured as something static, but as something dynamic and genetic. Whereas the older Neoplatonists were primarily interested in the descent (*emanatio*) of all things from one origin, God, Comenius is mainly concerned with the (uni-versal) return of all things to the One, with the ascent (*epistrophe*). The descent passes through the *mundus idealis*, *mundus intelligibilis* and *mundus materialis*, whilst the stages of the ascent are *mundus moralis*, *mundus spiritualis* and *mundus aeternus*. This ascent does not happen automatically. It is man's task to advance it. Between the descent and the ascent is the *mundus artificialis*, the world of human activity. It has its roots in that web of ideas in which Comenius attempted to gather together reality, and which he called pansophy. The determination with which man works to achieve the perfection of the whole clears the way for the *mundus possibilis*, that supporting pillar of the entire pansophical system. Seen in this light the political activities ascribed to the *Panorthosia* are orthodox.

What was achieved by this admirably complete work of reform,

---

[1] Cf. Franz Hofmann, 'Die Dialektik von "emendatio", "renuntiatio" und "revelatio" im politischen Denken Komenskýs', in *Gesellschaft, Menschenbildung, pädagogische Wissenschaft* (Halle, 1971). Also Schaller, *Comenius*, pp. 102–5.

the *Consultatio catholica* and its centrepiece, the system of education? Nothing! Comenius ignored the lesson he should have learnt from the failure of the reforms in England, namely that for the realisation of his work of reform, certain concrete political and social conditions were required. These had been gambled away in England and were not to return again in his time. Thus the drama of his life now entered its third act; and the curtain rises for us with a study of his *Clamores Eliae*.

ACT III: THE 'CLAMORES ELIAE' – PANSOPHICAL POLITICS

The manuscript of Comenius' *Clamores Eliae* was not found until 1885 in the archives of the Brethren's meeting place in Leszno. For a long time it was considered undecipherable. The notes had been written in a hurry by hand, and annotations had been made mainly in Czech and Latin, but also in German, Hebrew and Greek. It was read for the first time in 1975 by Julie Nováková.[1]

How does Comenius approach the programme of reform in this work? First we need to recall the rôle of education in Comenius' previously known writings. Since its inclusion as the fourth part (*Pampaedia*) in his main work, the *Consultatio catholica*, that is to say since Comenius' visit to England, it had certainly had a political function. Let us look briefly at its main ideas. Man has been appointed to complete the work of creation begun by God. In order to be able to accomplish this, he has first to be trained to recognise the basic possibilities of his existence by means of *educatio*, education. The movement implied here has two phases: man has to be led away from his position 'offside', *jinudost* as it is called in the *Centrum securitatis*,[2] where he is unable to see his tasks, away from the 'labyrinth of the world',[3] and has to be returned to the centre of creation where he can accomplish his task in the fundamental order of things as revealed by God.

Even in his earliest works, written before he went into exile, Comenius' concept of education was always embedded in an irenic,

---

[1] Veröffentlichungen der Comenius-Forschungsstelle der Ruhr-Universität, Bochum, no. 8 (1977). See also K. Schaller, *Die Pädagogik der 'Mahnrufe des Elias'* (Kastellaun, forthcoming 1978).

[2] According to the German edition by A. Macher (1737), ed. K. Schaller (Heidelberg, 1964).

[3] Czech text in *V.S.*, vol xv; German trans. by Zd. Baudnik (1908); latest ed. Comenius, *Labyrinth der Welt und Paradies des Herzens*, ed. Jiři Všetečka und Klaus Schaller (Veröffentlichungen der Comenius-Forschungsstelle, no. 6, Bochum, 1972).

political context. But its educational and political significance became completely transparent only in the *Consultatio catholica*. In the same way that man acts as mediator between God and the world, the fourth and middle part of his seven-part work deals with man's reinstatement (*restitutio*) by means of education. A universal school reform (*panscholia*), a universal book reform (*pambiblia*) and a universal reform of teaching and learning (*pandidascalia*) are the instruments to lead man back into the whole as disclosed to him by Pansophy. With these he can assume his rôle as mediator, in accordance with God's intentions. Comenius' concept of education is used to support the orthodox, political programme of the *Panorthosia*.

As a source of information about the key rôle of education in Comenius' scheme of universal reform, the *Clamores Eliae* are disappointing at first sight. This is not because of their form, though they appear to be no more than a collection of notes or perhaps a collection of sayings. Nor is it caused by the author's insistence on finding biblical proof for every statement. The disappointment we feel derives rather from the lack of interest shown in the *Clamores* in educational matters. The place of education in Comenius' system, which had been so clearly and convincingly outlined in the *Consultatio catholica*, is not evident here at all. This however is the very point on which a commentator should focus his attention.

Let me begin by stating my thesis. The *Clamores Eliae* were directly connected with Comenius' great plan for reform. This is proved by the many references and annotations which indicate that some of the notes were intended for inclusion in the *Panorthosia*, the *Pampaedia* or elsewhere. This close connection between the *Clamores* and the *Consultatio catholica* makes one ask why Comenius should have chosen to launch his programme afresh in this new and different form. The explanation that the *Clamores Eliae*, like the pamphlet *Angelus pacis*,[1] was perhaps intended as a direct appeal to the holders of political power and composed perhaps on the occasion of Comenius' appearance in the City Hall in Amsterdam or at an ecumenical council, is not wholly convincing. One is driven to look for some other, more general motive.

Since his schooldays Comenius had been a chiliast. He had seen it as his immediate task to remove the obstacles that were preventing the establishment of Christ's thousand-year kingdom on earth. But

---

[1] In German in *A.W.*, vol III (1977).

he was an old man now. It must have been plain to him that he had not many years of life left; and the great books in which he had set out his blueprint for reform, the *Pansophia*, *Panaugia*, *Pampaedia*, cannot have seemed to him to be taking effect sufficiently fast. It was natural for him to be impatient, to feel that so much delay in man's preparations for the coming of a new age could not be tolerated. It was natural for him to feel that book-learning in which he had taught his contemporaries to place their trust was a clumsy tool; that even his scholarly pansophy, with its theoretical and practical approach, was not truly efficient. They were means to which people could have access only after a long process of education. An academic approach to reform was bound to be a closed world to all but scholars, until universal schooling succeeded in making its contents apparent to everyone.

Given this background, it is not surprising to find that in the *Clamores* Comenius abandons learned plans in favour of a direct appeal to his contemporaries, and that he brings in the biblical character, Elias. One Elias was not enough. That is his message. Many were needed – politicians, theologians, philosophers as well as ordinary men and women – through whom God could speak and reveal his will. We know that Comenius had always been impressed by popular revelations, which he had collected and edited under the titles, *Lux in tenebris* and *Lux e tenebris*.[1] In 1667, in the *Angelus pacis*, he had still grouped the *Lux e tenebris* with the *Christianismus reconciliabilis* and the *Consultatio catholica*, and had referred to them as the 'threefold dawning' of the new age. The reference recurs in the *Clamores*, but here the revelations take on a more propagandist rôle. Comenius calls on men to make the most of their opportunities and also to call others – the whole world – to the work of reform. He wants deeds instead of words, action instead of theory.

This realisation, with its negative consequences for education, provides an informative comment on the relationship between education and politics, a relationship which, for us today, is essential to educational and social thinking. Comenius sees this quite differently from the Swiss educator, Pestalozzi (1746–1827), and in order to contrast the two approaches I am now going to sketch the latter's point of view. In a work on which attention has been particularly focussed during the last few years, Pestalozzi clarified his attitude to the French Revolution and to his 'Yes or no' statement on

---

[1] *Lux in tenebris* (1657); *Lux e tenebris* (1665).

it.[1] It is true that he said 'no' to a degeneration of the Revolution that he had both feared and seen confirmed in the September blood-bath, but this by no means revoked his positive assessment of its aims, of the 'right and necessity of the Revolution'. However, the Revolution did not, in his view, succeed in freeing itself entirely from the power-structure of the pre-revolutionary society. It merely reversed the structure of power. 'The despotism you are supposed to be fighting', he tells the people, 'is essentially nothing but an uncurbed licence in the claims of the few to the goods and blood of the many. And the prevailing attitude of the people is now daily approaching an uncurbed licence in the claims of the many to the goods and blood of the few.'[2] And as regards the quantitative situation resulting from the reversal of the structure of power, Pestalozzi can claim Cabinet stupidity to be preferable to the stupidity of the masses. Revolution as a political upheaval was doomed to failure because the people supporting it could not break out of the patterns imposed on them by the previous tyranny. They could only become despots again themselves. It was this realisation that resulted in his programme of initiating the education of mankind *before* preparing a political revolution. Only new men could produce new conditions. 'The dream of making something of man by means of politics before he really is anything, this dream has vanished for ever for me. My only politics are now to make something of man and to make as much of him as is ever possible.'[3] This is what Pestalozzi wrote in 1807, having come to change the opinion he had held in his youth and early middle age.

This was the very view of education and politics to which Comenius had subscribed for the greatest part of his life. The reformation of mankind by means of education was to prepare the way for a new society. But unlike Pestalozzi he was forced in his old age to recognise that this was too lengthy a process and might never produce the right results. Bad conditions were likely to worsen if one hesitated too long. He was aware that schemes he had himself proposed had been marred by the unfavourable conditions of his day and had even been made to serve corrupt ends. The academies he

[1] J. H. Pestalozzi, *Ja oder Nein? Äusserungen über die bürgerliche Stimmung der europeischen Menschheit in den oberen und unteren Stenden von einem freyen Mann* (1793), in *Sämtliche Werke*, ed. A. Buchenau, K. Spranger and A. Stettbacher, vol. x. Cf. Adalbert Rang, *Der politische Pestalozzi* (Frankfurt, 1967). For discussion: *Der politische Pestalozzi. Mit Beiträgen von Leonhard Froese und anderen* (Weinheim and Basel, 1972).
[2] Pestalozzi, *Ja oder Nein*, in *Sämtliche Werke*, vol. x, pp. 158f.
[3] Pestalozzi to Usteri, 1807, in *Sämtliche Briefe*, ed. W. F. Fales and E. Dejung (Zurich, 1961), vol. v, p. 251.

had once praised so highly had became 'the schools of the devil'. He saw that anyone who stops to think about education fails to take the action which is demanded by the present and which forms the future. For Comenius in his old age politics came before education.

His was a view of politics that cannot be described in terms of the present-day structures of political behaviour; for it does not rely on the existing balance of power and cannot be reduced to the relations between the great powers of this world. Comenius' politics related to situations where people were trying to work out terms that would make a new and better future possible He sent his message to Breda[1] where attempts were being made to end the naval war between England and the Netherlands. He analysed the contradictions between the principles of the Peace of Westphalia and the way in which the pope interpreted the treaty.[2] These, he thought, were the points where men like Elias would need to act.

Comenius realised that the determination he expected them to show involved taking sides. And we find here one of his first attempts to provide a theoretical justification for an arbitrary approach to decision-making. For this purpose he employs several different kinds of proof. He produces biblical references. In the *Clamores Eliae* these develop at times into an endless string of quotations. He arrives logically at certain theoretical conclusions and expounds their practical consequences. He cites instances of contemporary (as distinct from biblical or historical) divine revelation through mystics like Drabík and Poniatowska whose pronouncements he had cited in *Lux e tenebris*. And finally he appeals to pansophy. But pansophy has a different function from the one it had in the large work of that name. It now shows in the form of the *perpetuum mobile* what the power issuing from God can accomplish as a whole. It keeps everything in motion in harmony with a life-giving order of being.

The *Clamores Eliae* shows the final synthesis of Comenius' ideas. It is neither politics nor education alone that is the proper instrument of the *emendatio omnium*, but politics and education together. What is important is not the orthodox panorthotic tradition of a laborious diffusion of knowledge. It is not a spontaneous, and in the long run futile, political activism. It is a kind of political action that leaves the powerful no peace, but forces them to use their power for the redemption of all: *omnes, omnia, omnino*.

[1] *Angelus pacis*; in German in *A.W.*, vol III; in Latin in *O.O.*, vol. XIII, pp. 177–211.

[2] *Orbis terrarum syllogismus practicus*, in *O.O.*, vol. XIII, pp. 157–74; in German in *A.W.* vol. III.

5

SCEPTICISM AND RELIGIOUS BELIEF: PASCAL, BAYLE, HUME*

E. D. JAMES

In sixteenth-century France, philosophical scepticism was intimately connected with religious fideism, and the scholarly Latin translations of the *Outlines of Pyrrhonism* of Sextus Empiricus which appeared in the second half of the sixteenth century gave the sceptical fideist arguments a special fillip.[1] The most influential fideist work based on Sextus was of course the so-called *Apologie de Raimond Sebond*, an *essai* of Montaigne's which provided an arsenal of arguments for the seventeenth-century apologist Blaise Pascal.

The sceptical or Pyrrhonist method of argument as presented by Sextus was to set against any judgement or appearance another judgement or appearance which conflicted with it. The method was claimed to be therapeutic inasmuch as it was designed to turn men's minds away from dogmatism, fanaticism and the conflicts that result therefrom, and to encourage men instead to yield undogmatically to the guidance of nature and custom and to instinctive feelings.[2] The ultimate aim of Pyrrhonism, which in fact it shared with dogmatic philosophies, was to achieve *ataraxia* or unperturbedness.[3] But to Pascal, unperturbedness in the face of the apparent contradictoriness and absurdity of the human condition appeared baffling and exasperating. For him Pyrrhonism was to be a means of perturbing the unperturbed, of creating a sense of existential anguish from which he could then offer a dogmatic deliverance.[4]

---

* Works included in the Bibliographical notes at the end of this chapter are referred to by short titles when cited in the footnotes.

[1] See R. H. Popkin, *The History of Skepticism from Erasmus to Descartes*, revised ed. (New York: Harper Torchbooks, 1968). The *Outlines of Pyrrhonism* or *Purrhoneioi Hupotuposeis* was published in 1562 in a Latin translation by H. Estienne, which was re-published in 1569 by Gentien Hervet together with the latter's Latin translation of the *Adversus Mathematicos* of Sextus.

[2] *Outlines of Pyrrhonism*, vol. i, ch. xxxiv.

[3] *Outlines of Pyrrhonism*, vol. i, ch. iv.

[4] La. 427, Br. 194 ('Cette négligence où il s'agit d'eux-mêmes, de leur éternité, de leur tout, m'irrite plus qu'elle ne m'attendrit; elle m'étonne et m'épouvante: c'est un monstre pour moi.'); La. 130, Br. 420; La. 131, Br. 434. It should be noted that the Pyrrhonists to whom Pascal alludes are in fact fideists and really reduce themselves to one, namely Montaigne.

Pascal in his *Pensées* presents Pyrrhonism now as a philosophy of negation, now as a metaphilosophy surveying the inconclusiveness of philosophical dispute and pointing towards, or providing an opening for, a view of life and a way of life of a different order.[1] This second view of Pyrrhonism is closer to the truth, though Pyrrhonism might be said to turn us away from philosophical conflict towards not a higher reality but a lower reality – a reality which is experienced rather than excogitated. The Pyrrhonist asserted that we should surrender ourselves, or that he surrendered himself, to the world of appearances, since there could be no certainty of what might lie behind appearances.[2] Now, Pascal undoubtedly thought that certainty lay only in a world beyond appearances, but he perceived an analogy between the principles of belief and conduct which prevail in that world of appearances and the principles of belief and conduct appropriate to an ideal world which alone was truly real. For truth and ultimate reality are reached or apprehended by a kind of instinct or intuition which is like the promptings of nature, and perhaps indistinguishable from nature to the eye of those who lack faith, but which is supernatural nevertheless.[3] Hence, the Pyrrhonist argument which turns us aside from reasoning and towards nature and instinct is seen by Pascal as a providential aid which prepares the heart for the gift of divine grace.

It is notable that Pascal speaks of the *ambiguïté ambiguë* which characterises Pyrrhonist arguments, of a certain *obscurité douteuse*;[4] and here he is plainly describing the character of his own arguments, for there is a hint of hidden certainty in this, a suggestion of the *Dieu caché* which is quite contrary to the tendency of a true Pyrrhonism. Pyrrhonism is opposed precisely to claims that signs of hidden truths can safely be discerned in the phenomena. Pascal maintains an appearance of hesitation and suspension of judgement, yet speaks of a certain clarity. Pyrrhonist argument in his own interpretation is characterised by 'a certain doubtful obscurity of which our doubts cannot remove all the clarity nor our natural lights dissipate all the darkness'.[5] There is, then, clarity and darkness. And significantly Pascal adds: 'The slightest things are of this nature. God is the beginning and the end.'[6] So that it appears that, for Pascal, the peculiar difficulties in achieving certainty which are brought to our

---

[1] E.g. La. 33, Br. 374; La. 688, Br. 323; La. 691, Br. 432 – and see above, p. 93, n. 4 and below, n. 4. [2] *Outlines of Pyrrhonism*, vol. 1, ch. x.
[3] La. 155 and 110, Br. 281 and 282. [4] La. 109, Br. 392 *in fin.*
[5] *Ibid.* [6] *Ibid.*

notice by the Pyrrhonists reflect God's plan to reveal himself to some and to conceal himself from others.

There is something naïve about this confident belief that the very confusions and contradictions in human thinking fall into a pattern which is a sign that there is a hidden God in whom such contradictions are resolved. The French Protestant fideist, or apparent fideist, Pierre Bayle, writing later, at the turn of the seventeenth century, is less inclined to rationalise confusion and disorder or to claim to find in it a definite divine plan. Bayle is a tougher-minded Pyrrhonist – where he *is* a Pyrrhonist – and he is closer to the original sources. Faith in his account appears much more precarious than in Pascal's. Indeed, whereas in Pascal Pyrrhonism is a weapon employed against secular philosophical dogmatisms in the interests of a higher religious dogmatism, in Bayle Pyrrhonism is also employed against certain forms of religious dogmatism itself – ostensibly in the interests of Christian humility.[1]

In the article 'Pyrrhon' in Bayle's *Dictionnaire historique et critique*, Pyrrhonism is defined as the art of disputation concerning all things without coming to any other conclusion than to suspend one's judgement. And two views which Christians have taken of it are indicated: Pyrrhonism is detested by theologians because of its advocacy of suspense of judgement, for theology requires certainty; but Pyrrhonism can have its uses in obliging man, out of a sense of his darkness, to implore aid from on high and to submit to the authority of faith.[2]

Bayle's account of the nature of the grounds of religious belief is only equivocally Pyrrhonist. He traces the source of religious belief to a variety of factors represented as conventional, natural or instinctive – such as upbringing or education, conscience, or an instinctive sense of the divine.[3] And with this appeal to conscience and to the

---

[1] See *Éclaircissement sur les Pyrrhoniens*, § v (annexed to *Dictionnaire*); in *Dictionary*, ed. Popkin, pp. 430–1. 'Le mérite de la Foi devient plus grand, à proportion que la Vérité révélée qui en est l'objet surpasse toutes les forces de notre esprit; car à mesure que l'incompréhensibilité de cet objet s'augmente par le grand nombre de Maximes de la Lumière naturelle qui le combattent, il nous faut sacrifier à l' autorité de Dieu une plus forte répugnance de la Raison, et par conséquent nous nous montrons plus soumis à Dieu, et nous lui donnons de plus grandes marques de notre respect, que si la chose était médiocrement difficile à croire.'

[2] 'Pyrrhon', *in corp.*; in *Dictionary*, ed. Popkin, p. 194.

[3] *Dictionnaire*, art. 'Spinoza', Rem. M; in *Dictionary*, ed. Popkin, pp. 298–9. 'Je crois qu'on peut dire qu'il y a des gens qui ont la religion dans le cœur, et non pas dans l'esprit... dès qu'ils ne disputent plus et qu'ils ne font qu'écouter les preuves de sentiment, les instincts de la conscience, le poids de l'éducation, etc., ils sont persuadés d'une religion.'

sense of the divine he leans towards dogmatism – as he does else-where, in his claim that a pagan philosopher could not reasonably deny that there is something supernatural about the chain of events narrated in the Scriptures.[1] Equally dogmatic is his assertion that our concept of rational order provides of itself a strong argument for monotheism as against polytheism.[2]

But although, when summarised, Bayle's views often sound almost indistinguishable from those of Pascal, the Pyrrhonian doubts which Bayle in fact wants to set aside are never really overcome. Whereas for Pascal the evil in the world simply reflects its fallen condition, for Bayle it presents grave difficulties for monotheism. For Pascal, merely conventional, natural or instinctive belief mimics super-natural inspiration and may be a means to it. For Bayle, the fact that natural, instinctive and conventional beliefs mimic divinely inspired beliefs means that doubts whether there is such a thing as divine inspiration, or at any rate doubts whether one has received it, will recur. The belief of the Christian assailed by doubts will indeed be supported by various feelings, habits and instinctive tendencies, but the question of the validity of that belief is not thereby finally settled.[3]

It is largely through the medium of the work of such modern thinkers that ancient scepticism exerts an influence on David Hume in the eighteenth century. The distinction which, in section XII of the *Enquiry Concerning Human Understanding*, he seems to be making between Pyrrhonian and Academic scepticism is not very close to the historical difference between the two, even allowing for the fact that the nature of that historical difference is not perfectly clear. Pyrrhonian scepticism is said in the *Enquiry* to be so extreme as to paralyse and prevent action, did not nature assert itself in spite of sceptical doubts. Here as elsewhere in Hume the account of Pyrrhonism is Pascalian rather than historical, for submission to the force or guidance of nature was part of the Pyrrhonian doctrine, not a phenomenon which furnishes a practical objection to Pyrrhonism.

[1] *Dictionnaire*, art. 'Simonide de Ceos', Rem. F; in *Dictionary*, ed. Popkin, p. 280.
[2] *2e Éclaircissement sur les manichéens, ad fin.* (annexed to the *Dictionnaire*); cf. *Dictionary*, ed. Popkin, p. 418.
[3] In his *Réponse aux questions d'un provincial*, Bayle speaks of 'ces personnes qui, se sentant incapables de satisfaire aux difficultés, tomberaient dans l'incrédulité si elles ne faisaient que suivre par une certaine route les suggestions de leur esprit; mais la conscience, les preuves directes, le péril d'offenser Dieu, le grand intérêt du salut les soutiennent contre les objections les plus embrouillées; et ainsi, nonobstant les doutes qui se pourraient élever de temps en temps, ils se tiennent à l'affirmative' (quoted by Élisabeth Labrousse in *Pierre Bayle*, vol. II, *Hétérodoxie et rigorisme*, p. 316).

Historically, the Pyrrhonists were not such a 'fantastical sect' a Hume (and legend) hold them to be. And as for Academic scepticism, this, historically, is associated on the one hand with the claim that nothing can be known with certainty, and on the other hand with an epistemological probabilism which permits assent to what experience makes plausible. The 'mitigated' or Academical scepticism which Hume professes, however, soon turns out to be a cautious critical (rather than sceptical) approach to philosophical questions, confining itself within the bounds of common life. This sounds as if it owed more to Locke than to the Greeks, although Locke himself wavers, and sometimes argues for a probabilist theory of knowledge analogous to that of the Academic sceptics.[1] Locke was much indebted to thinkers such as Descartes, Gassendi and Pascal, all of whom were strongly influenced by scepticism.

The most characteristic expression of Hume's view of Pyrrhonism is to be found in a well-known passage in the first section of Book I, Part IV of the *Treatise of Human Nature*:

Should it ...be asked me...whether I be really one of those sceptics, who hold that all is uncertain, and that our judgement is not in *any* thing possessed of *any* measures of truth and falsehood; I should reply, that this question is entirely superfluous, and that neither I, nor any other person was ever sincerely and constantly of that opinion. Nature, by an absolute and uncontrollable necessity, has determined us to judge as well as to breathe and feel...belief is more properly an act of the sensitive, than of the cogitative part of our natures.[2]

This emphasis on the allegedly sensitive rather than cogitative character of belief, which is analogous to Bayle's emphasis on the mostly instinctive or non-reflective character of belief, leads Hume to argue that the more abstruse the contentions of the disputant, as in metaphysical argument, the less lively is the conviction that they create. Pyrrhonian dispute has a rarefied character, whereas our judgements are prompted or determined by what appeals directly or easily to the mind or the imagination. This claim is essential to Hume's view of natural religion.

The question what that view is, precisely, is posed quite clearly by the first and last paragraphs of the final section of Hume's *Natural*

---

[1] Hume, *Enquiry Concerning Human Understanding*, section XII, parts II and III; in *Enquiries*, ed. Selby-Bigge and Nidditch, pp. 160–2. Locke, *An Essay Concerning Human Understanding*, IV, xi, 3 and IV, xvi, 6. On the difference between the Pyrrhonian and Academic scepticisms, see C. L. Stough, *Greek Skepticism*, pp. 50–66.

[2] Hume, *Treatise*, ed. Selby-Bigge, p. 183.

History of Religion. The last paragraph, concerning the variety and contradictions of religious beliefs and practices, reads as follows:

The whole is a riddle, an aenigma, an inexplicable mystery. Doubt, uncertainty, suspense of judgement appear the only result of our most accurate scrutiny, concerning this subject. But such is the frailty of human reason, and such the irresistible contagion of opinion, that even this deliberate doubt could scarcely be upheld; did we not enlarge our view, and opposing one species of superstition to another, set them a quarrelling; while we ourselves, during their fury and contention, happily make our escape into the calm, though obscure regions of philosophy.[1]

The beginning of this is Pyrrhonist in terminology and spirit, but the conclusion, in favour of philosophy, is not obviously so. The philosophical view of which Hume speaks is certainly one of doubt concerning religious cults as they have grown up, but a positive religious conviction is expressed in the first paragraph of the final section:

A purpose, an intention, a design is evident in every thing; and when our comprehension is so far enlarged as to contemplate the first rise of this visible system, we must adopt with the strongest conviction, the idea of some intelligent cause or author. The uniform maxims, too, which prevail through the whole frame of the universe, naturally, if not necessarily, lead us to conceive this intelligence as single and undivided, where the prejudices of education oppose not so reasonable a theory. Even the contrarieties of nature, by discovering themselves every where, become proofs of some consistent plan, and establish one single purpose or intention, however inexplicable and incomprehensible.[2]

This latter argument echoes dogmatic affirmations of Bayle and Pascal and can hardly be described as Pyrrhonist,[3] but there are Pyrrhonist features in the arguments when taken together. The mystery mongers are left to quarrel among themselves, and the seeker turns to what impresses itself inescapably upon the mind. Of course

[1] *Hume on Religon (Natural History),* ed. Colver and Price, p. 95.
[2] *Ibid.* p. 92.
[3] The notion that the *contrariétés* in things are the expression of a divine plan is essential to the Pascalian apologetic: 'Ce qui y [= en ce monde] paraît ne marque ni une exclusion totale ni une présence manifeste de divinité, mais la présence d'un Dieu qui se cache. Tout porte ce caractère' (La. 449, Br. 556). 'On n'entend rien aux ouvrages de Dieu si on ne prend pour principe qu'il a voulu aveugler les uns et éclaircir les autres' (La. 232, Br. 566). Hume, however, would not have approved of Pascal's claim that the key to the understanding of the human condition is the concept of original sin. But neither would Pascal have approved of Hume's leaning towards the argument from design. Pascal did not think that most people perceive a design in nature (La. 3, Br. 244). Whether he would have held that monotheism is unlike polytheism in being a rational belief, as Bayle did (see above, p. 96, n. 2) is not clear, but it seems likely. At any rate, Hume, in the *Natural History,* seems to share Bayle's view on this.

there is a gap between the philosophical theism which supposedly impresses itself upon the mind and the natural promptings to which the Pyrrhonists advised us to yield undogmatically, but there is a formal analogy with Pyrrhonism in the contrast drawn between mysterious and sophisticated theological doctrine and the simplicity and directness of the apprehension of intention in nature. The analogy no doubt seemed stronger to Hume than to a modern mind, which might well feel that the argument from design is too complex to be reduced to a simple and direct apprehension of an intention. In fact, some readers, perhaps many or most, would say that a sceptical view of the argument from design is taken by Hume himself in the *Dialogues Concerning Natural Religion,* a work of later date – at least in its final form.

In the *Dialogues* there are three interlocutors: first, Demea, who argues *a priori* for a First Cause of the universe; second, Cleanthes, who argues empirically for a Great Designer; and third, Philo, a sceptic, who reduces Demea's *a priori* arguments to arguments for religious scepticism, and who sharply restricts the character and conclusions of Cleanthes' arguments for or from design. In the first Part of the *Dialogues,* the sceptic Philo gives his rather Baylian or Pascalian account of scepticism:

All sceptics pretend, that if reason be considered in an abstract view, it furnishes invincible arguments against itself, and that we could never retain any conviction or assurance, on any subject, were not the sceptical reasonings so refined and subtile, that they are not able to counterpoize the more solid and more natural arguments, derived from the senses and experience.[1]

And another more clearly Humean passage of Philo's in the same Part reads:

So long as we confine our speculations to trade, or morals, or politics or criticism, we make appeals, every moment, to common sense and experience, which strengthen our philosophical conclusions, and remove (at least in part) the

[1] *Hume on Religion (Dialogues),* Part I, ed. Colver and Price, p. 152. Bayle draws a distinction between sceptical reasoning and everyday experience in the article 'Pyrrhon' (*Dictionary,* ed. Popkin, p. 194). He writes in several places of the self-contradictions of the reason, e.g. in art. 'Bunel', Rem. E (*Dictionary,* ed. Popkin, p. 42), but he concludes rather to the need for revelation than to the need to fall back on ordinary experience. It was Pascal who made the very Humean assertion: 'La nature soutient la raison impuissante' (La. 131, Br. 434).

There is another source of Hume's *Dialogues* which deserves at least mention, namely the *De natura deorum* of Cicero, with which there are parallels in the structure and in the characterisation (see J. V. Price, 'Sceptics in Cicero and Hume', *Journal of the History of Ideas,* xxv (1964), 97–106). But the influence of seventeenth-century and eighteenth-century thinkers goes much deeper.

suspicion, which we so justly entertain with regard to every reasoning, that is very subtle and refined. But in theological reasonings, we have not this advantage; while at the same time we are employed upon objects, which we must be sensible, are too large for our grasp, and of all others, require most to be familiarized to our apprehension.[1]

What is noticeable about this passage is its unsceptical elements. The appeals to commonsense and experience which fit well enough with a Pyrrhonist view are not made as alternatives to a philosophical view, but are made in support of it. The Pyrrhonian distinction between philosophical arguments and the direct experiences of ordinary life is broken down, even if the scepticism about theological argument is maintained. In Cleanthes, the experimental theist, however, one theological argument, the argument from design, is claimed to have the force of ordinary direct experience. He exhorts Philo in Part III to

Consider, anatomize the eye: survey its structure and contrivance; and tell me, from your own feeling, if the idea of a contriver does not immediately flow in upon you with a force like that of sensation. The most obvious conclusion surely is in favour of design; and it requires time, reflection and study to summon up those frivolous, though abstruse objections, which can support infidelity.[2]

And although this is the position of an experimental theist, it is essentially the view which Philo the erstwhile sceptic finally admits to holding. It may well be that for Philo the concept of a contriver of the universe was never itself an idea of the abstruse theological kind to which scepticism is the only appropriate response.

If that is so, what is the aim or function of the sceptical arguments advanced by Philo in the body of the work? They are not intended to undermine the claim that there is a principle of order in the universe, but to enjoin modesty on those who would make confident claims as to the nature of that principle. None of the interlocutors believes in the existence of a pure atheism. Anyone who does not believe in a personal God is for them an atheist, but such atheism plainly does not necessarily exclude belief in the existence of a principle of order in things. Consequently, having set the theist and atheist side by side in quasi-Pyrrhonian fashion, Philo is finally able to claim that there is nothing to choose between their arguments, the whole dispute being verbal or a matter of degree. (Not the same thing, one would have thought.)

I am in fact inclined to think that there is some inconsistency in

[1] *Dialogues*, Part I, ed. Colver and Price, p. 152.   [2] *Ibid.* Part III, pp. 176–7.

Philo's assertions, for although he claims in Part XII of the *Dialogues* to believe firmly in the existence of 'a first intelligent Author' who is the contriver of the order of the world,[1] he has previously argued that that contriver or contriving principle might be animal or vegetative.[2] He argues finally that animal, vegetable and intelligent are analogous notions here,[3] and sums up his thesis as follows:

The theist allows, that the original Intelligence is very different from human reason: The atheist allows, that the original principle of order bears some remote analogy to it. Will you quarrel, gentlemen, about the degrees, and enter into a controversy, which admits not of any precise meaning, nor consequently of any determination.[4]

Now, I cannot say that I am convinced by this claim that there is nothing to choose between this theist and this atheist, but what I want to point out is that instead of setting one view against another in order to achieve stalemate in the true Pyrrhonian manner, Philo sets the one beside the other to reveal an analogy of doctrine.

And Philo's position with regard to the theist and the atheist is very much that of Hume himself with respect to the sceptic and the dogmatist, as he formulates it in a note to the twelfth Part of the *Dialogues*. For Hume asserts, rather incautiously, and no doubt influenced by Pascal and Descartes, that:

No philosophical dogmatist denies, that there are difficulties both with regard to the senses and to all science, and that these difficulties are in a regular, logical method, absolutely insolveable. No sceptic denies, that we lie under an absolute necessity, notwithstanding these difficulties, of thinking and believing, and reasoning with regard to all kind of subjects, and even of frequently asserting with confidence and security.[5]

Hence, dogmatism and scepticism are assimilated to one another, and a positive view of things is held to be common to both.

Now, to return to Philo's parallel of the theist and the atheist, it is important to observe that the analogy of doctrine which Philo seeks to reveal is claimed to be based on something directly felt, rather in the way that the natural promptings of which the Pyrrhonists speak are directly felt. But the directly felt belief in a principle of design to

[1] *Ibid.* Part XII, p. 245.   [2] *Ibid.* Part VII, pp. 202–3.
[3] *Ibid.* Part XII, p. 249.   [4] *Ibid.* p. 249.
[5] *Ibid.* p. 250. Cf. Pascal, *Pensées*, La. 131, Br. 434 *init.*, and Descartes, *Discours de la méthode*, Part IV: 'J'avais dès longtemps remarqué que pour les mœurs, il est besoin quelquefois de suivre des opinions qu'on sait fort incertaines, tout de même que si elles étaient indubitables, ainsi qu'il a été dit ci-dessus' (i.e. in the third Part of the *Discours* on 'la morale par provision').

which Philo alludes is not merely a prompting to which one yields in Pyrrhonian fashion. It is a conception in which one firmly believes. One could say that this is a dogmatism advanced under the colour of Pyrrhonism, but one could also say that it is a dogmatism advanced in the guise of empirically discovered truth; and the concern with the empirical, with the world of experience, is something which underlies ancient Pyrrhonism also.

Unlike Pascal and Bayle, Hume argues only for natural religion, and therefore need not deal in mysteries as they do. The principle of order which is directly apprehended in nature might, for all Hume says, itself be natural. In Hume, the ostensible outcome of Pyrrhonist analysis is not an intuitive religious faith but the conviction that there exists in the universe an empirically apprehensible principle of order whose nature is nevertheless not precisely determinable.[1] Now, no doubt Hume's empirical outlook is closer to the spirit of Pyrrhonism than are the equivocally transcendental intuitions of a Pascal or a Bayle, but his mode of argument still resembles the conjuring trick by which they use the techniques of Pyrrhonism to support dogmatic conclusions. Nevertheless, the concern with the common ground of competing philosophies which Pascal, Bayle and Hume display is of importance. It is not for nothing that nature has such a prominent rôle in the philosophies of sceptics, dogmatists, fideists and empiricists alike.

BIBLIOGRAPHICAL NOTES

Sextus Empiricus can conveniently be read in the following editions:
Sextus Empiricus, with an English trans. by the Rev. R. G. Bury (4 vols., The Loeb Classical Library, London, 1933–49).
Scepticism, Man, and God, Selections from the Major Writings of Sextus Empiricus, ed. with introduction, notes and bibliography by Philip P. Hallie, trans. from the original Greek by Sanford G. Etheridge (Middletown, Connecticut: Wesleyan University Press, 1964).
Œuvres choisies de Sextus Empiricus (*Contre les physiciens; Contre les moralistes; Hypotyposes pyrrhoniennes*), trans. Jean Grenier and Geneviève Gordon (Paris: Aubier, 1948).

[1] In fact, Philo concludes by saying (*Dialogues*, Part XII, ed. Colver and Price, p. 261): 'But believe me, *Cleanthes*, the most natural sentiment, which a well disposed mind will feel on this occasion, is a longing desire and expectation, that heaven would be pleased to dissipate, at least alleviate, this profound ignorance, by affording some more particular revelation to mankind, and making discoveries of the nature, attributes, and operations of the divine object of our faith.' It is not clear that this is entirely ironic. What Philo/Hume is wistfully asking for is some degree of precise information as to the nature of 'the cause or causes of order in the universe'. Nevertheless, one cannot fail to note that even the 'regenerate' Philo seems a pretty uncertain monotheist – or even theist *tout court*.

All of these works have interesting introductions.
Standard works on Greek scepticism include:
V. Brochard, *Les sceptiques grecs* (Paris, 1887).
L. Robin, *Pyrrhon et le scepticisme grec* (Paris, 1944).
C. L. Stough, *Greek Skepticism* (Berkeley and Los Angeles, 1969).
See also:
A. A. Long, *Hellenistic Philosophy*, London, 1974.
Pascal's *Pensées* may be read in the editions of L. Lafuma published by Éditions du Seuil, Paris:
Pensées (1962), with preface by André Dodin ('Livre de vie')
Œuvres complètes (1963), with preface by Henri Gouhier ('L'intégrale') or in the little edition of L. Brunschvicg published by Hachette. References are given in the footnotes to the editions of both Lafuma (La.) and Brunschvicg (Br.)
    A brief survey of the relations between Greek scepticism and the ideas of Montaigne and Pascal is to be found in the conclusion to Robin, *Pyrrhon*. The question is treated more or less briefly in the standard works on Pascal, e.g.:
J. H. Broome, *Pascal* (London, 1965).

Pierre Bayle's *Dictionary* can be read in the following editions:
Dictionnaire historique et critique, 4th ed., revised, corrected and enlarged (4 vols., Amsterdam, 1730).
Dictionnaire historique et critique, new ed., ed. A. J. Q. Beuchot (16 vols., Paris, 1820).
Historical and Critical Dictionary, selections trans. with an introduction by R. H. Popkin, with the assistance of C. Brush (The Library of Liberal Arts, Indianapolis, 1965).
The standard work on Pierre Bayle is:
É. Labrousse, *Pierre Bayle* (2 vols., The Hague, 1963–4).
See also:
C. B. Brush, *Montaigne and Bayle* (*Variations on the Theme of Skepticism*) (The Hague, 1966).
R. H. Popkin, 'Bayle's place in 17th-century scepticism', in *Pierre Bayle, le philosophe de Rotterdam, études et documents*, ed. Paul Dibon (Amsterdam and Paris, 1959).

David Hume may be read in the following editions:
A Treatise of Human Nature, ed. L. A. Selby-Bigge (Oxford: The Clarendon Press, 1888, and reprints).
Enquiries Concerning Human Understanding and Concerning the Principles of Morals, ed. L. A. Selby-Bigge, 3rd ed. with text revised and notes by P. H. Nidditch (Oxford: The Clarendon Press, 1975).
Dialogues Concerning Natural Religion, ed. Norman Kemp Smith (Edinburgh, 1935; 2nd ed., 1947).
The Natural History of Religion, ed. H. Chadwick and with an introduction by H. E. Root (London, 1956).
Hume on Religion (*The Natural History of Religion* and *Dialogues Concerning Natural Religion*), ed. A. W. Colver and J. V. Price (Oxford: The Clarendon Press, 1976).
Two relevant studies are:

John Laird, *Hume's Philosophy of Human Nature* (London, 1932; reprinted U.S.A.: Archon Books, 1967).

Antony Flew, *Hume's Philosophy of Belief* (London, 1961, and re-impressions).

Further bibliographies may be found in this last volume and in:

Hume (*Modern Studies in Philosophy: A Collection of Critical Essays*), ed. V. C. Chappel (London: Macmillan, 1968).

PART II

ANTIQUITY
AS MYTH

6

DIE 'QUERELLE
DES ANCIENS ET DES MODERNES',
DER NATIONALISMUS UND DIE
DEUTSCHE KLASSIK

MANFRED FUHRMANN

I. ANTIK–MODERN

Die *Querelle des Anciens et des Modernes* hat das Geschichtsbild der Renaissance zur Voraussetzung; sie ist der Disput über dessen Richtigkeit. Sie übernimmt daher vom Geschichtsbild der Renaissance den universalen Zuschnitt: es geht hier wie dort um den ganzen Menschen, um alle Bereiche menschlicher Tätigkeit, um die Künste und Wissenschaften, um die Philosophie, die Technik, die Politik und die Moral, kurz, um die gesamte Kultur. Die *Querelle* übernimmt weiterhin vom Geschichtsbild der Renaissance den Bezugspunkt einer fernen Vergangenheit, der Antike: es geht hier wie dort darum, am Vor- und Gegenbild der Antike den eigenen Standort zu bestimmen. Das Denken der Renaissance operierte freilich mit einem Dreiphasenschema, und es genügte ihm, die Überlegenheit der eigenen Zeit über die soeben beendete Phase, das Mittelalter, zu behaupten – über die Antike wagte es sich nicht zu erheben. Die *Querelle* hingegen dachte polar oder antithetisch; das Mittelalter war ihr entrückt, und sie beschränkte ihre Aufmerksamkeit im wesentlichen auf die beiden Gipfel des überkommenen Geschichtsbildes, auf die Antike und die Gegenwart. Hierbei begnügte sie sich nicht damit, ehrfurchtsvoll zum früheren Gipfel, zur Antike, aufzublicken; dieses Erbstück der Renaissance war vielmehr kontrovers: die *Anciens* behaupteten nach wie vor, dass der frühere Gipfel höher sei, die *Modernes* hingegen beanspruchten für die eigene Gegenwart den Primat.

König Ludwig XIV. war von einer Operation genesen; Charles Perrault verlas, um dieses Ereignis zu feiern, am 27. Januar 1687 in der Akademie zu Paris sein Gedicht 'Le siècle de Louis le Grand'. Das Datum wird mit Recht so oft genannt. Zwar waren die Motive von Perraults Gedicht durchaus nicht originell – seit zwei Jahrhunderten schon hatte man immer wieder im Namen einer überlegenen Gegenwart gegen den Kult der Antike protestiert.[1] Einzelne beriefen sich hierbei auf den Fortschritt des Wissens und der Wahrheit – so z. B. Giordano Bruno und Francis Bacon. Andere behaupteten, die poetischen Leistungen ihrer Zeit seien allem Bisherigen überlegen – so die Anhänger eines Góngora oder eines Marino. Wieder andere argumentierten systematisch und universal, d. h. sie suchten in allen oder möglichst vielen Bereichen menschlicher Tätigkeit den Vorrang der Gegenwart zu erweisen. So schon im Jahre 1460 der Florentiner Benedetto Accolti in seinem *De praestantia virorum sui aevi dialogus*; so während der Blüte des Barocks, im Jahre 1620, Alessandro Tassoni in seinem *Paragone degl'ingegni antichi e moderni*. Aber es hatte sich bei alledem nur um einzelne Stimmen gehandelt, die an der von der Renaissance behaupteten Vorbildlichkeit der Antike nicht zu rütteln vermochten. Perraults Gedicht hingegen war ein Funke, der einen mächtigen Brand entfachte; der Streit um den Rang der Antike wurde seither mit schwankenden, aber nicht mehr allzu ungleichen Kräften und vor den Augen der europäischen Öffentlichkeit geführt.

Das Gedicht Perraults geht aufs Ganze: es sucht wie die Schriften eines Accolti oder Tassoni die Antike in allen Bereichen der Kultur zu entthronen.[2] Geschickt stellt es das stärkste Argument, die unleugbaren Fortschritte in den Naturwissenschaften, an die Spitze. Dann folgen die Künste, von denen sich die Überlegenheit der Gegenwart teils mit grösserem Recht (wie im Falle der Musik), teils mit geringerem Recht (wie im Falle der Plastik) dartun liess; am Schluss findet sich wieder eine – jedenfalls für die Zeitgenossen – unanfechtbare Position: die innen- und aussenpolitischen Erfolge Ludwigs XIV., das Prestige seiner Herrschaft. Perraults Gedicht macht kein Hehl aus seiner panegyrischen Bestimmung: es feiert das Zeitalter Ludwigs als den Höhepunkt der nationalen Kultur Frankreichs; es bekräftigt den französischen Hegemonieanspruch in Europa. Schon der Anfang lässt diese frankozentrische Tendenz

---

[1] Zum Folgenden s. A. Buck, *Die 'Querelle des Anciens et des Modernes' im italienischen Selbstverständnis der Renaissance und des Barocks* (Sitzungsberichte der wissenschaftlichen Gesellschaft Frankfurt/M., XI. 1, Wiesbaden, 1973); W. Krauss, 'Der Streit der Altertumsfreunde mit den Anhängern der Moderne und die Entstehung des geschichtlichen Weltbildes', in *Antike und Moderne in der Literaturdiskussion des 18. Jahrhunderts*, hrsg. von W. Krauss und H. Kortum (Berlin, 1966), S. ixff.; G. Finsler, *Homer in der Neuzeit* (Leipzig und Berlin, 1912), S. 48ff.

[2] Zum Folgenden s. Kortum, *Antike und Moderne*, S. lxiff.

deutlich hervortreten – es heisst dort nach einigen einleitenden Versen, die von der bedingten Grösse der Antike handeln:[1]

> Et l'on peut comparer, sans crainte d'être injuste,
> Le siècle de Louis au beau siècle d'Auguste.

Dieselbe Tendenz kehrt innerhalb des Gedichts allenthalben wieder: Homer hätte, wäre er in unserem Jahrhundert, und zwar in Frankreich, geboren, die Fehler, die seine Werke entstellen, vermeiden können; den antiken Dichtern wird eine lange Liste von literarischen Grössen der Moderne gegenübergestellt, die durchweg französische Namen enthält; in der Malerei gilt dem Verfasser Le Brun, in der Musik Lully als Kulminationspunkt der Entwicklung; der Abschnitt über die Plastik nennt nur Franzosen, der Abschnitt über den Gartenbau preist die Wunder von Versailles. Diese nationale Tendenz hat indes, so aufdringlich sie ist, das überkommene Epochenschema nicht gesprengt und nicht beseitigt; *antiquité* und (*notre*) *siècle* – so lautet auch bei Perrault die zumindest vordergründig dominierende Antithese. Mit dieser Diktion beanspruchte der Autor, jedenfalls *expressis verbis*, nur die diachrone Überlegenheit Frankreichs; er hütete sich hingegen, zugleich so etwas wie eine synchrone Überlegenheit, den Vorrang seines Landes vor den übrigen europäischen Ländern, zu beanspruchen. Der Charakter des Epochenvergleichs blieb somit trotz der nationalen Färbung gewahrt; Perraults Preisgedicht suchte keinerlei Exklusivität, kein Privileg Frankreichs geltend zu machen - es hielt die Türen zu den europäischen Nachbarn offen.

Diese Tonart setzte sich während der ganzen Debatte, die Perraults Gedicht entfesselte, während der eigentlichen *Querelle des Anciens et des Modernes*, fort. Die Titel der Streitschriften hoben, sofern sie überhaupt etwas von dem Inhalt verrieten, den Epochendualismus hervor: *Digression sur les anciens et les modernes* (von Fontenelle), *Parallèle des anciens et des modernes* (von Perrault), *Histoire poétique de la guerre nouvellement déclarée entre les anciens et les modernes* (von Callières). Die Schriften selbst pflegten mit einer weniger neutralen Diktion aufzuwarten: man sprach nicht nur von *modernes* und *notre siècle*, sondern auch von *Français* und *notre nation*; man exemplifizierte fast nur mit französischen Geistesgrössen, und auch, wenn man schlicht *nous* sagte, dachte man im allgemeinen *nous, les Français*.

---

[1] Zitiert nach H. Rigault, *Histoire de la Querelle des Anciens et des Modernes* (Paris, 1859), S. 150.

So verfährt z. B. die erwähnte Abhandlung von Fontenelle, die *Digression sur les anciens et les modernes* (1688), ein vortreffliches Paradigma für den Standpunkt der *Modernes*, das während des ganzen 18. Jahrhunderts in ganz Europa immer wieder Leser fand. Fontenelle verwendet meistens die Ausdrücke *modernes* und *siècle*; einmal jedoch lässt er die Katze aus dem Sack: 'Nous voilà donc tous parfaitement égaux', schreibt er, 'anciens et modernes, Grecs, Latins et Français', und gegen Ende der Schrift werden den poetischen Leistungen der Antike einzig und allein Titel zeitgenössischer französischer Werke gegenübergestellt: 'Les meilleurs ouvrages de Sophocle, d'Euripide, d'Aristophane, ne tiendront guère devant *Cinna*, *Ariane*, *Andromaque*, *Le Misanthrope*' (von Pierre Corneille, Thomas Corneille, Racine, Molière).[1]

Die eigentliche *Querelle des Anciens et des Modernes* endete nach etwa zehnjähriger Dauer im Jahre 1697; damals erschien der vierte und letzte Band von Perraults grossangelegtem Dialog *Parallèle des anciens et des modernes*. Eines der wichtigsten Ergebnisse des Streites bestand offenbar darin, dass es sich als schwierig erwiesen hatte, für die Künste in gleichem Masse den Primat der Gegenwart zu beanspruchen wie für die Wissenschaften, und beide Bereiche – sowohl die Künste als auch die Wissenschaften – in dieselbe Perspektive stetiger Vervollkommnung zu rücken.[2] Denn selbst Perrault sah sich genötigt, immerhin zwei Künsten, der Beredsamkeit und der Dichtung, eine besondere Stellung zuzubilligen.[3] 'Nous conclurons', schreibt er am Schluss des *Parallèle*, '... que dans tous les arts et dans toutes les sciences, à la réserve de l'éloquence et de la poésie, les modernes sont de beaucoup supérieurs aux anciens, comme je croy l'avoir prouvé suffisamment, et qu'à l'égard de l'éloquence et

---

[1] *Entretiens sur la pluralité des mondes – Digression sur les anciens et les modernes*, hrsg. von R. Shackleton (Oxford, 1955), S. 163 und 174; s. ferner S. 169: 'il faut pouvoir digérer que l'on compare Démosthène et Cicéron à un homme qui aura un nom français, et peut-être bas'.

[2] Hierzu H. R. Jauss, 'Ästhetische Normen und geschichtliche Reflexion in der "Querelle des Anciens et des Modernes"', Einleitung zum Facsimiledruck des *Parallèle* von Ch. Perrault (München, 1964), bes. S. 21ff., 46f., 63f.

[3] Schon Accolti und Tassoni hatten nicht alles über einen Kamm geschoren, sondern den Vergleich von Antike und Gegenwart nach den einzelnen Künsten und Wissenschaften gegliedert und den Leistungsstand einer jeden Disziplin gesondert beurteilt. Und Fontenelle hatte in seiner *Digression* die Künste, den Bereich der *imagination*, von den Wissenschaften und der Philosophie, dem Bereich des *raisonnement*, abgehoben. Er hatte dann zwar geglaubt, beides demselben Gesetz des Fortschritts unterstellen zu können (*Digression*, S. 166 und 171f.) – hierbei war indes offen geblieben, wie sich der stetige Fortschritt bei den Künsten vollziehe.

de la poésie, quoy-qu'il n'y ait aucune raison d'en juger autrement, il faut pour le bien de la paix ne rien décider sur cet article.'[1]

Dieser Schluss des *Parallèle* war wohl mehr als eine Floskel – jedenfalls hat die folgende Zeit, das 18. Jahrhundert, so geurteilt.[2] Die Kontinuität des Antike–Moderne-Vergleichs blieb nämlich gewahrt, und man knüpfte immer wieder an die grosse Debatte des ausgehenden 17. Jahrhunderts an. Hierbei fehlte es zwar nicht an radikalen Modernisten vom Schlage eines Terrasson, die nach wie vor erklärten, dass sich der Fortschritt auf alle Bereiche der Kultur erstrecke; ferner destillierte sich die Richtung eines Turgot und Condorcet heraus, die vornehmlich auf eine progressistische Geschichtsauffassung, auf perfektionistische politisch–soziale Modelle zielte. Im ganzen aber hatte man zu differenzieren gelernt, und die vorherrschende Tendenz lief darauf hinaus, dass zumindest die Dichtung von der Gewissheit oder dem Wunschbilde des Fortschritts ausgenommen werden müsse. So hat sich der nächste grosse französische Streit, der vom Jahre 1713 an zwischen Madame Dacier und La Motte als Protagonisten ausgetragen wurde, die *Querelle d'Homère*, auf das umstrittene Teilgebiet, auf die Dichtung, und auf Homer als dessen wichtigsten Exponenten beschränkt. Vor allem aber bekannten sich in den folgenden Jahrzehnten gewichtige Einzelstimmen zur Trennung, ja zum Antagonismus, zur gegenläufigen Entwicklung von Dichtung und Wissenschaft, von Dichtung und Zivilisation – so Marivaux, Dubos und Voltaire, ferner, nach der Jahrhundertmitte, Diderot und Marmontel.

Die *Modernes* der grossen *Querelle* zielten, so wurde gesagt, mit der von ihnen gepriesenen Gegenwart zuallererst auf den Höhepunkt, den die nationale Kultur Frankreichs erreicht hatte; sie waren jedoch klug genug, zumindest äusserlich an der epochalen Nomenklatur, an der Antithese antik–modern festzuhalten und hiermit das kulturkritische Schema als für ganz Europa verbindlich hinzustellen. Der Funke sprang denn auch sofort nach England über und entfachte dort eine der *Querelle* analoge Auseinandersetzung – mit Temple und Wotton als den Hauptbeteiligten und mit Bentleys *Dissertation upon the Epistles of Phalaris* als deren wichtigstem wissenschaftlichem Ertrag. Auch in Deutschland wurde die *Querelle* rasch bekannt.[3]

---

[1] *Parallèle*, S. 445 = Bd. IV, S. 292f. des Originals (Paris, 1688–97).

[2] Zum Folgenden vgl. Krauss, 'Der Streit der Altertumsfreunde', S. xxxvff.; zur *Querelle d'Homère* s. Finsler, *Homer in der Neuzeit*, S. 212ff.

[3] Zum Folgenden s. F. Martini, 'Modern, die Moderne', in *Reallexikon der deutschen Literaturgeschichte*, hrsg. von W. Kohlschmidt und W. Mohr, Bd. II (Berlin, 1965), S. 393f.

Dort rief sie freilich keine selbständigen Streitschriften hervor; man machte sich lediglich mit ihrem Inhalt vertraut und neigte bald mehr der einen, bald mehr der anderen Seite zu. Immerhin war der Epochenvergleich während des ganzen 18. Jahrhunderts ein konstitutives Element auch des deutschen Kulturbewusstseins; er war Hintergrund und Voraussetzung vielfältiger Betrachtungen über die neuzeitliche Zivilisation, zumal über Kunst und Literatur der Gegenwart. Zunächst, während des Übergangs vom Barock zur Aufklärung, überwogen die Stimmen, die sich auf die Seite der 'Modernen' schlugen; hierbei vermischte sich der neue Fortschrittsglaube mit christlicher Abneigung gegen die heidnischen Mythen und machten sich zugleich erste patriotische Ansprüche auf eine eigene nationale Literatur bemerkbar. So z. B. beim jungen Gottsched in einer Ode vom Jahre 1724:[1]

> Umsonst erhebt man dich, berufnes Altertum!
> Umsonst ist man bemüht, die graue Welt zu preisen.

In reiferen Jahren hat sich Gottsched freilich stärker zur Musterhaftigkeit der Alten bekannt; so versah er die von ihm herausgegebene Übersetzung der *Digression* Fontenelles mit kritischen Anmerkungen.[2] Vor der Jahrhundertmitte plädierte man öfters für jene differenzierte Auffassung, die auch im zeitgenössischen Frankreich – zumal durch den Einfluss von Dubos – vorherrschte: in den Naturwissenschaften sei die Gegenwart der Antike, in der Dichtung und Beredsamkeit die Antike der Gegenwart überlegen. So etwa von Haller in seinem *Sermo academicus ostendens quantum antiqui eruditione et industria antecellant modernis* (vom Jahre 1734); so auch der junge Lessing in seinem Gedicht 'An den Herrn M...' (vom Jahre 1748):[3]

> Das Alter wird uns stets mit dem Homer beschämen,
> Und unsrer Zeiten Ruhm muss Newton auf sich nehmen.

2. GRIECHISCH–MODERN

Im Jahre 1755 erschienen Winckelmanns *Gedanken über die Nachahmung der griechischen Werke in der Malerei und Bildhauerkunst*. Schon der Titel deutet auf die beiden Postulate, um die es in dieser Programmschrift geht: es geht – einmal – um Nachahmung, also um

---

[1] Zitiert nach Krauss, 'Der Streit der Altertumsfreunde', S. lvi.
[2] S. G. Waniek, *Gottsched und die deutsche Literatur seiner Zeit* (Leipzig, 1897), S. 61.
[3] *Werke*, hrsg. von H. G. Göpfert, Bd. 1 (Darmstadt, 1970), S. 159ff.; vgl. 182ff. S. hierzu V. Riedel, *Lessing und die römische Literatur* (Weimar, 1976), S. 29f.

Vorbildlichkeit, indes – zum anderen – nicht um die Vorbildlichkeit der Antike schlechthin, sondern um die Vorbildlichkeit der Griechen. Mit dem ersten Postulat ergreift Winckelmann gegen die 'Modernen' Partei; er verwirft implizite den freundlichen Kompromiss, zu dem die *Querelle* während der ersten Hälfte des 18. Jahrhunderts verebbt war: 'Der einzige Weg für uns, gross, ja, wenn es möglich ist, unnachahmlich zu werden, ist die Nachahmung der Alten.' Das zweite Postulat, die These von der exemplarischen Bedeutung der Griechen, enthält in dieser Schärfe und Unbedingtheit etwas Neues: 'Eine Bildsäule von einer alten römischen Hand wird sich gegen ein griechisches Urbild allemal verhalten, wie Virgils Dido, in ihrem Gefolge mit der Diana unter ihren Oreaden verglichen, sich gegen Homers Nausicaa verhält, welche jener nachzuahmen gesuchet hat.'[1]

Das zweite Postulat (dem sich diese Skizze zunächst zuwendet) richtet sich gegen Rom, gegen das nicht ur- und vorbildliche, sondern seinerseits schon abbildliche Rom; es richtet sich ferner gegen alles, was von Rom abgeleitet ist, gegen die romanische Kultur, gegen Frankreich, gegen Barock und Rokoko.

Die Franzosen des absolutistischen Zeitalters hatten, wenn sie von der Antike sprachen, im wesentlichen Rom gemeint:[2] der Staat und die Geschichte, die Kultur und die Schriftsteller der Römer waren der Fixsternhimmel, an dem sich, wie die italienische Renaissance, so auch das klassische Frankreich zuallererst orientierte, und Griechisches wurde meist nur in der mehr oder minder starken Umprägung aufgenommen, die die vermittelnden Römer ihm hatten angedeihen lassen. Die Franzosen des absolutistischen Zeitalters hatten überdies, wenn sie von der Antike sprachen, ein bestimmtes Rom, das Imperium der Kaiserzeit, gemeint: Perraults Vergleich des *siècle de Louis* mit dem *siècle d'Auguste* war ein Topos der Epoche. Dieses romanozentrische Antikebild herrschte bis zum Auftreten Winckelmanns auch in Deutschland: Gottscheds *Critische Dichtkunst* nennt in einem Katalog vorbildlicher 'Poeten von gutem Geschmacke' Terenz, Virgil, Ovid und Horaz, ferner Italiener, Franzosen, Holländer und Deutsche – jedoch keinen einzigen Griechen.[3]

---

[1] 'Der einzige Weg': 'Gedanken über die Nachahmung der griechischen Werke in der Malerei und Bildhauerkunst', in *Kleine Schriften – Vorreden – Entwürfe*, hrsg. von W. Rehm (Berlin, 1968), S. 29. 'Eine Bildsäule': *ibid.* S. 30.
[2] Zum Folgenden s. W. Rehm, 'Römisch-französischer Barockheroismus und seine Umgestaltung in Deutschland', in *Götterstille und Göttertrauer* (Bern, 1951), S. 14ff.
[3] *Versuch einer critischen Dichtkunst*, 4te Aufl. (Leipzig, 1751), S. 130f. Vgl. H. Rüdiger, *Wesen und Wandlung des Humanismus*, 2te Aufl. (Hildesheim, 1966), S. 160f.

Zwei Wege standen dem zu Gebote, der sich von dem Antikebild der französischen Klassik distanzieren wollte: er konnte das republikanische Rom gegen das kaiserzeitliche Rom, oder er konnte die griechische Kultur gegen die gesamte römische Kultur ausspielen. Beide Wege sind während der ersten Hälfte des 18. Jahrhunderts eingeschlagen worden. Der eine, der zum republikanischen Rom führte, war nicht zuletzt politisch bedingt; er wurde vor allem in England und Frankreich begangen.[1] Den anderen, den zu den Griechen führenden Weg hingegen wählten diejenigen, die nicht so sehr am absolutistischen Herrschaftssystem wie an der gesamten Zivilisation ihres Zeitalters litten: wer immer die *simplicité*, die *simplicity*, die Einfalt Homers und der Griechen schlechthin auf den Schild erhob – einzelne Franzosen wie schon Fénelon, Engländer wie Blackwell,[2] und seit Winckelmanns Programmschrift mit erstaunlicher Radikalität die meisten Deutschen.

Nicht alle Deutschen. Lessing z. B. hat sich in seinen frühen Schriften nur mit römischen Autoren befasst; wenn bei ihm später, etwa im *Laokoon* und in der *Hamburgischen Dramaturgie*, die Griechen überwogen, so beabsichtigte er hiermit keine grundsätzliche Abkehr von Rom.[3] Auch Schiller hat sich trotz seines Bekenntnisses zu den Griechen vom heroischen Pathos der römischen Dichtung angezogen gefühlt; das wichtigste Zeugnis seiner Neigung zu Rom ist seine Übersetzung des zweiten und vierten Buches der *Äneis*.[4] Derlei Ausnahmen ändern indes wenig am Gesamtbild: Winckelmanns Propaganda für die Griechen hat in Deutschland Epoche gemacht – so sehr, dass nunmehr der Antike–Moderne-Vergleich nicht selten ausdrücklich als Vergleich der Gegenwart mit den Griechen vorgeführt wurde, und auch, wenn man die überkommene Formulierung beibehielt und weiterhin vom Altertum, von den Alten sprach, dachte man gewöhnlich zuallererst an die Griechen.

So viel zu Winckelmanns zweitem Postulat, zu seinem Rückgriff auf die griechischen Ursprünge, zu seiner Abkehr von Rom. Auch mit dem ersten Postulat hat Winckelmann – jedenfalls in Deutschland – Epoche gemacht. Die seit langem schwebenden Waagschalen neigten sich durch sein Wirken wieder den Alten (d. h. nunmehr: den

---

[1] Vgl. K. Borinski, *Die Antike in Poetik und Kunsttheorie* (Leipzig, 1914–24), Bd. II, S. 110f.
[2] Fénelon: s. Finsler, *Homer in der Neuzeit*, S. 221ff.; Blackwell: *ibid.* S. 332ff. und M. Fuhrmann, 'Friedrich August Wolf', *Deutsche Vierteljahrsschrift für Literaturwissenschaft und Geistesgeschichte*, XXXIII (1959), S. 211ff.
[3] Vgl. Riedel, *Lessing*, S. 210f.
[4] S. W. Rehm, *Griechentum und Goethezeit*, 4te Aufl. (Bern und München, 1968), S. 194.

Griechen) zu – eine Entwicklung, die nicht nur das Gebiet ergriff, dem sein Wirken gegolten hatte, die bildenden Künste, sondern das Ganze der Kultur.

Dieser Erfolg war zunächst dadurch bedingt, dass die grundsätzliche Antithese der französischen *Querelle* auch während der zweiten Jahrhunderthälfte als massgebliches Schema der geistigen Standortbestimmung diente.[1] Im Jahre 1779 veröffentlichte der Popularphilosoph Garve eine *Betrachtung einiger Verschiedenheiten in den Werken der ältesten und neuern Schriftsteller* – eine Abhandlung, die der absichtslosen Simplizität von einst das ausgeklügelte Verfahren neuerer Dichter gegenüberstellte. Im Jahre 1790 kam der Philosoph Bouterwek in seinem *Fragment vom griechischen und modernen Genius* zu Resultaten, die für die Gegenwart noch ungünstiger ausfielen: während die Griechen echte Poeten waren, hat sich der Mensch der Gegenwart dem Räsonnement und Raffinement, dem Witz, dem Frappanten und Interessanten ergeben. Im Jahre 1796 erschienen Herders *Siebente* und *Achte Sammlung der Briefe zur Beförderung der Humanität*, ein geschlossenes Ganzes, das von Hinweisen auf die französische *Querelle* umrahmt ist[2] und als eine Art Anti-Perrault zu beweisen sucht, dass sich die Literaturen der verschiedenen Völker und Zeiten nicht miteinander vergleichen lassen. Goethe zeichnete im Jahre 1813 in der Skizze *Shakespeare und kein Ende* ein Schema auf, das die Differenzen zwischen dem Antiken und dem Modernen verdeutlichen sollte;[3] im Jahre 1818 wollte er in dem Essay *Antik und Modern* die beiden Kategorien als überhistorische Archetypen, als zwei grundverschiedene Weisen künstlerischen Produzierens aufgefasst wissen – dort fällt das berühmte Wort 'Jeder sei auf seine Art ein Grieche! Aber er sei's.'[4]

Die ungebrochene Wirkung der französischen *Querelle* erklärt freilich nur den universalen Zuschnitt der kulturkritischen Erörterungen, die zumal gegen Ende des 18. Jahrhunderts eine üppige

---

[1] Zum Folgenden vgl. Martini, 'Modern, die Moderne', S. 394ff. S. ferner H. D. Weber, *Friedrich Schlegels 'Transzendentalpoesie'* (Theorie und Geschichte der Literatur und der schönen Künste, xii, München, 1973), S. 108ff.

[2] S. Nr. 81: 'Ihnen ist der berühmte Streit bekannt', usw. und Nr. 107: 'Sehr leer war daher der Streit', usw. Herder hat die *Querelle* noch öfters erwähnt; s. *Hodegetische Abendvorträge* (1799), in *Sämtliche Werke*, hrsg. von B. Suphan (Berlin, 1877–1913), Bd. xxx, S. 516f.; *Adrastea I* (1801), in *ibid.* Bd. xxiii, S. 72f. Vgl. J. G. Sulzer, *Allgemeine Theorie der schönen Künste*, 2te Aufl. (Leipzig, 1792), Bd. ii, S. 647ff.

[3] *Gedenkausgabe der Werke, Briefe und Gespräche*, hrsg. von E. Beutler, 2te Aufl. (Zürich und Stuttgart, 1961–6), Bd. xiv, S. 755ff.; das Schema auf S. 760.

[4] *Gedenkausgabe der Werke*, Bd. xiii, S. 841ff.; 'Jeder sei auf seine Art': S. 846.

Blüte erlebten; sie erklärt jedoch nicht die veränderte Wertung, das Mass an Bewunderung, das man für die Griechen aufbrachte, und das Mass an Geringschätzung, dem die Gegenwart anheimfiel. Hierin machte sich ein Zeitbewusstsein geltend, das den Fortschrittsglauben der Aufklärung bezweifelte und schliesslich verwarf, ja ihn gewissermassen auf den Kopf stellte und in die Perspektive des Verfalls rückte. Der wichtigste und erfolgreichste Repräsentant dieses Zeitbewusstseins war Rousseau. Seine beiden *Discours* der Jahre 1750 und 1755 verkündeten die Lehre vom glücklichen naturhaften Urzustand des Menschen;[1] der erste *Discours* rügte vor allem die Künstlichkeit der Kultur, der zweite behauptete, dass zwei einander bedingende ökonomische Ursachen, das Eigentum und die Arbeitsteilung, den Menschen um seine ursprüngliche Freiheit, um den Status einer vollen Existenz gebracht hätten.

Winckelmanns Griechenglaube und Rousseaus Glaube an einen glücklichen Urzustand ergänzten einander;[2] sie liessen sich zu jener umfassenden Kulturkritik verbinden, für die das überlieferte Schema der *Querelle* als Rahmen diente. Erst beides zusammen ergab die Lebensanschauung der deutschen Klassik: Rousseau bestimmte die Richtung des Denkens; Winckelmann stellte für das neue Humanitätsideal ein historisches oder richtiger quasi-historisches Modell bereit. Ein wichtiger Beitrag Rousseaus bestand in der Lehre von der Arbeitsteilung, der fortschreitenden Spezialisierung. Diese Theorie gab die Möglichkeit an die Hand, die 'Modernen' mit den eigenen Waffen zu schlagen: man konnte die mannigfaltigen Fortschritte, die in der Neuzeit erzielt worden waren, anerkennen und gleichwohl behaupten, dass der Mensch das Menschsein immer gründlicher verfehle. So zumal Schiller im *6. Briefe über die ästhetische Erziehung*: der Grieche besass Ganzheit; jedes Individuum entfaltete den Reichtum seiner natürlichen Anlagen zu einer Totalität harmonischer Kräfte und repräsentierte so die gesamte Menschheit; der moderne Mensch hingegen musste seine Erfolge mit dem Verlust der Totalität, mit der einseitigen Ausbildung einzelner Anlagen, kurz, mit Beschränktheit, Zerrissenheit, Verkrüppelung bezahlen.[3]

---

[1] *Discours sur les sciences et les arts, Discours sur l'origine de l'inégalité parmi les hommes*, oder *Schriften zur Kulturkritik*, französisch-deutsch, hrsg. von K. Weigand, 2te Aufl. (Philosophische Bibliothek, CCXLIII, Hamburg, 1971).

[2] Wie schon Diderot und Goethe erkannten; s. H. Hatfield, *Aesthetic Paganism in German Literature* (Cambridge, Mass., 1964), S. 21.

[3] Vgl. M. Fuhrmann, 'Selbstbestimmung und Fremdbestimmung', in *Alte Sprachen in der Krise?* (Stuttgart, 1976), S. 21ff.

Schiller ist indes bei dieser für die Moderne so ungünstigen Antithese nicht stehen geblieben;[1] gerade er hat einen überaus folgenreichen Schritt getan: er hat das Zweiphasenschema der *Querelle* um eine dritte Phase, um die Dimension der Zukunft erweitert. Seine Lehre, wie er sie am Nachdrücklichsten in der Abhandlung *Über naive und sentimentalische Dichtung* dargestellt hat, fand über die rückwärts gewandte Sicht sowohl Winckelmanns als auch Rousseaus hinaus: der naturhaft-naive Zustand der Griechen sei unwiederbringlich verloren; der moderne, sentimentalische Mensch habe indes die Aufgabe, das Verlorene durch bewusste Wahl und bewusstes Ringen auf einer höheren, nicht mehr physischen, sondern moralischen Stufe wiederherzustellen. Diese Lehre enthielt bei aller Kritik eine deutliche Rechtfertigung der Gegenwart: sie bestritt, dass die Gegenwart der Antike überlegen sei, und räumte ihr zugleich die Chance ein, sich über die Antike zu erheben.

Die Problematik der *Querelle*, die während der zweiten Hälfte des 18. Jahrhunderts in der hier skizzierten Weise abgewandelt wurde, behielt bei alledem den Charakter eines Epochenvergleichs bei, d. h. es ging nach wie vor um die Frage, wie man die diachronen Unterschiede innerhalb der gesamten europäischen Kultur beurteilen solle; es ging hingegen nicht um das synchrone Verhältnis einzelner europäischer Nationen. So stand es jedenfalls bei einem Teil der deutschen Autoren, insbesondere bei Schiller und Goethe. Und wenn der Epochenvergleich bei den Franzosen des 17. Jahrhunderts eine unverkennbare nationale Färbung gezeigt hatte, so lässt sich hiervon bei den beiden Hauptrepräsentanten der Weimarer Klassik nichts feststellen: Schiller und Goethe meinten offenbar die Modernen oder Neueren, wenn sie von den Modernen oder Neueren sprachen – sie meinten keine bestimmte Nation, etwa die Deutschen.

Schillers Besprechung der goetheschen *Iphigenie* vergleicht das moderne Stück mit der Fassung des Euripides. Sie bemerkt zum Monolog Orests im dritten Akt:

Hätte die neuere Bühne auch nur dieses einzige Bruchstück aufzuweisen, so könnte sie damit über die alte triumphieren. Hier hat das Genie eines Dichters, der die Vergleichung mit keinem alten Tragiker fürchten darf, durch den Fortschritt der sittlichen Kultur und den milderen Geist unserer Zeiten unterstützt, die feinste,

---

[1] Zum Folgenden s. H. R. Jauss, 'Schlegels und Schillers Replik auf die "Querelle des Anciens et des Modernes"', in *Literaturgeschichte als Provokation* (Frankfurt/M., 1970), S. 67ff., bes. 95ff.

edelste Blüte moralischer Verfeinerung mit der schönsten Blüte der Dichtkunst zu vereinigen gewusst.[1]

Die *Briefe über die ästhetische Erziehung* mit der grossen Anklage der modernen Kultur bedienen sich derselben, einzig den Unterschied der Epochen hervorhebenden Diktion. 'Die Zeitumstände, das Jahrhundert, das Zeitalter': so heisst es alsbald im '2. Brief', und die vergleichende Analyse von Antike und Moderne – im '6. Brief' – beginnt mit dem Satz: 'Aber bei einiger Aufmerksamkeit auf den Zeitcharakter muss uns der Kontrast in Verwunderung setzen, der zwischen der heutigen Form der Menschheit und zwischen der ehemaligen, besonders der griechischen, angetroffen wird.'[2] So geht es fort durch die ganze Schrift; das Wort deutsch oder ein anderer Name einer europäischen Nation kommt nirgends vor.

Als drittes Beispiel diene die Abhandlung *Über naive und sentimentalische Dichtung*. Sie setzt mit dem Gegensatz von künstlichen Verhältnissen und einfältiger Natur (worunter Schiller die Kinder, das Landvolk, das ferne Altertum subsumiert) ein und leitet daraus das die Zukunft einbeziehende Dreiphasenmodell ab: 'Sie [d. h. die Kinder, usw.] sind, was wir waren; sie sind, was wir wieder werden sollen.' Im weiteren Gang der Argumentation bringt Schiller den üblichen Epochenkontrast: 'die alten Griechen – wir Neuern'; er operiert sodann mit der Antithese 'alte und moderne Dichter'. Die Beispiele entnimmt er der gesamten europäischen Tradition, z. B. bei der Erörterung der These, dass dem Genie stets etwas Naives, Kindliches eigne (er nennt dort Sophokles, Archimed, Hippokrates und 'aus neuern Zeiten' Ariost, Dante, Tasso, Raphael, Dürer, Cervantes, Shakespeare, Fielding und Sterne), ferner bei der Behandlung der drei Formen sentimentalischer Dichtung, der Satire, Elegie und Idylle. Eine Bemerkung über die Franzosen enthält Tadel und Lob zugleich: die Franzosen, meint Schiller, hätten es in der Unnatur, aber auch in der Reflexion darüber am weitesten gebracht.[3]

Für Goethes 'weltbürgerliche' Betrachtungsweise (so hiess ja das übernationale Ideal der Zeit) mögen zwei Beispiele genügen – ihnen

---

[1] 'Über die Iphigenie auf Tauris', in *Ausgewählte Werke* (Darmstadt, 1954–9), Bd. VIII, S. 478ff.; 'Hätte die neuere Bühne': S. 503f.; s. ferner S. 505: 'Was für ein glücklicher Gedanke', usw.

[2] *Ausgewählte Werke*, Bd. V, S. 272f.

[3] *Ibid.* S. 377ff.; 'Sie sind, was wir waren': S. 379; 'die alten Griechen': S. 395ff.; 'alte und moderne Dichter': S. 402ff.; Beispiele aus der europäischen Tradition: S. 390 u. ö.; Bemerkung über die Franzosen: S. 398.

liessen sich leicht weitere programmatische Äusserungen, etwa die erwähnte Skizze *Antik und Modern,* zur Seite stellen. In der 'Einleitung zu den *Propyläen*', einer von Goethe gegründeten Zeitschrift, macht der Kontrast der Epochen den roten Faden aus: den Griechen, heisst es sogleich am Anfang, war eine Vollkommenheit, die wir wünschen und nie erreichen, natürlich; wir hingegen vermögen die griechische Bildung nur als Stückwerk vorübergehend zu verwirklichen. Dann freilich scheint Goethe auf eine Art nationaler Sendung zu zielen: 'Welche neuere Nation', schreibt er, 'verdankt nicht den Griechen ihre Kunstbildung? und, in gewissen Fächern, welche mehr als die deutsche?' Ein späteres Aperçu zeigt indes, dass diese Äusserung eher einen negativen Sinn hat: 'Dem deutschen Künstler, sowie überhaupt jedem neuen und nordischen, ist es schwer, ja beinahe unmöglich, von dem Formlosen zur Gestalt überzugehen' – mit anderen Worten: die mangelnde Formkraft des deutschen Künstlers bedarf in besonderem Masse der Anleitung durch die Griechen.[1]

Ein überaus eindrucksvolles Zeugnis für die Denkart Goethes sind die *Skizzen zu einer Schilderung Winckelmanns,* Goethes Beitrag zu dem Sammelband *Winckelmann und sein Jahrhundert.*[2] Diese Skizzen enthalten zumal in den ersten fünf Kapiteln – sie tragen die Überschriften 'Eintritt', 'Antikes', 'Heidnisches', 'Freundschaft' und 'Schönheit' – mancherlei kategoriale Bestimmungen. Der Begriff deutsch indes findet sich nicht darunter, was um so mehr ins Auge fällt, als die Zeitgenossen, z. B. Herder, mit grossem Nachdruck den Deutschen Winckelmann gepriesen hatten. Goethe hält sich vielmehr ganz und gar an den traditionellen Epochenvergleich; er verwendet die Antithese antik–modern, und zwar in der Bedeutung, die Winckelmann ihr verliehen hatte: 'antik' steht für 'griechisch'. Die Alten, schreibt Goethe, wobei er sich dem geschichtsphilosophischen Konzept Schillers verpflichtet zeigt, suchten die gleichmässige Vereinigung sämtlicher Eigenschaften und waren bestrebt, mit aller Kraft auf die Gegenwart zu wirken; die Neueren hingegen kranken an ihrer Partikularität und an ihrem Hang zur Transzendenz. Sie können indes, glaubt Goethe, ihr Stigma überwinden, wie es zum ersten Male von Winckelmann überwunden worden sei – Winckel-

---

[1] 'Einleitung zu den *Propyläen*', in *Gedenkausgabe der Werke,* Bd. XIII, S. 135ff.; Vollkommenheit der Griechen, 'Welche neuere Nation': S. 137; 'Dem deutschen Künstler': S. 147.
[2] *Gedenkausgabe der Werke,* Bd. XIII, S. 407ff. Zum Folgenden vgl. M. Fuhrmann, 'Winckelmann, ein deutsches Symbol', *Neue Rundschau,* LXXXIII (1972), S. 271ff.

mann, eine 'antike Natur',[1] ist Paradigma und Sinnbild für die Wiederherstellbarkeit menschlicher Existenz schlechthin.

3. GRIECHISCH–DEUTSCH

Unter allen europäischen Nationen sei es ohne Widerrede die deutsche, die sich am meisten bestrebe, den französischen Geschmack nachzuahmen; bei ihr habe sich auch die französische Sprache am allgemeinsten verbreitet. So urteilte ein französischer Beobachter der deutschen Szene, Le Guay de Prémontval, in seiner Abhandlung *Contre la gallicomanie ou le faux goût français* (1759). Unter den Gründen, die Prémontval für die deutsche Gallikomanie anführt, ist wohl der triftigste der Hinweis auf die grosse Anzahl von Höfen und Souveränen, die den deutschen Staatskörper teilten: gerade sie hätten mächtig zur Verbreitung der französischen Kultur beigetragen. Viele Deutsche, fährt Prémontval fort, läsen nur französische Bücher, so dass sie ihre eigenen Schriftsteller nicht mehr verstehen könnten – er wundere sich daher nicht über den Verdruss und Unwillen, mit dem mehrere Gelehrte Deutschlands dem ausschweifenden Geschmack an der französischen Literatur begegneten.[2]

Die Höfe, die Adligen sprachen und lebten französisch, und das gebildete Bürgertum las zumindest französisch: sowohl der Absolutismus als auch die Aufklärung waren über den Rhein nach Deutschland gekommen. Für deutsche Gelehrte und Literaten, wie sie sich im Laufe des 18. Jahrhunderts mit wachsendem Können und wachsendem Selbstbewusstsein regten, ergaben sich aus diesen Verhältnissen überaus ungünstige Wettbewerbsbedingungen, und so bemächtigte sich ihrer in der Tat nicht selten Verdruss und Unwillen über die Franzosen und die deutsche Französelei. Die Franzosen, meint z. B. Winckelmann in seinen Briefen, seien Esel, Tröpfe, Ignoranten, sie seien gar nicht gemacht, etwas Ernstliches zu treiben; 'alle Franzosen', berichtet er einem Freunde aus Rom, 'sind hier lächerlich als eine elende Nation, und ich kann mich rühmen, dass ich mit keinem von der verachtungswürdigsten Art zweifüssiger Kreaturen eine Gemeinschaft habe'. Und derselbe Winckelmann bedenkt folgerichtig auch die französische Mode der Höfe mit seinem

---

[1] *Gedenkausgabe der Werke*, Bd. XIII, S. 418.
[2] Zitiert nach J. G. Herder, *Briefe zur Beförderung der Humanität*, hrsg. von H. Stolpe (Berlin und Weimar, 1971), Bd. II, S. 155ff. (*Neunte Sammlung*, Nr. 110). Zum Folgenden vgl. H. A. Korff, *Voltaire im literarischen Deutschland des 18. Jahrhunderts* (Beiträge zur neueren Literaturgeschichte, X/XI, Heidelberg, 1917), bes. Bd. I, S. 380ff.

Ressentiment: 'ich weiss', schreibt er jenem Freunde, 'dass Du mit der französischen Seuche ein wenig angesteckt bist, welches Übel an deutschen Höfen, wo ein französischer Harlequin mehr als ein wahrer Deutscher gilt, nicht leicht zu heilen ist'.[1] Nicht lange vor seinem Tode, im Jahre 1765, erfuhr Winckelmann am eigenen Leibe, wie ein deutscher Fürst, sein Landesherr Friedrich II. von Preussen, die deutschen Gelehrten einschätzte. Er hatte sich um die vakante Stelle des königlichen Bibliothekars beworben und, von seinem Berliner Mittelsmann hierzu ermuntert, ein Gehalt von zweitausend Talern gefordert. Der König bot ihm die Hälfte, wozu er bemerkt haben soll: 'Für einen Deutschen sind tausend Taler genug.'[2]

Der Konkurrenzkampf der deutschen Intellektuellen erzeugte ein Klischee vom französischen Nationalcharakter, dem man in der Publizistik jener Zeit allerorten begegnet – selbst so verschiedene Naturen wie Lessing und Herder stimmen in ihrem Urteil über 'die Franzosen' genau überein.[3] Die Franzosen, heisst es, sind korrekt, höflich, auf Konventionen und einstudierte Umgangsformen versessen; sie kultivieren den Spott, den Witz, die Pointe; sie tragen Eitelkeit und Arroganz zur Schau; sie vernünfteln und ergehen sich in Sophistereien; sie vernachlässigen über dem Aussen, dem Schein, der Schale das Innen, das Wesen, den Kern – sie sind unnatürlich, kraftlos, gefühlskalt und wahrer Empfindungen nicht fähig. Diesem Bilde mag manche Beobachtung zugrundeliegen: der französelnde Kulturbetrieb an den deutschen Fürstenhöfen hatte gewiss seit der Jahrhundertmitte ein recht epigonenhaftes Aussehen. Die Gegenwartserfahrung wurde nun aber in die Vergangenheit zurückprojiziert; zumal Herder unterwarf nahezu alles, was in der deutschen Geschichte von Frankreich, von den Romanen, von Rom ausgegangen war, einer herben Kritik – sie läuft darauf hinaus, dass die Deutschen durch diese Einflüsse sich selbst entfremdet worden seien.[4]

[1] Esel, Tröpfe, usw.: *Briefe*, hrsg. von W. Rehm (Berlin, 1952–7), Bd. I, S. 235ff. und 329; 'alle Franzosen...ich weiss': *ibid.* S. 267; s. ferner Bd. III, S. 119. Vgl. Lessing, *Hamburgische Dramaturgie*, hrsg. von O. Mann, 2te Aufl. (Stuttgart, 1963), S. 392 (101.–4. Stück).

[2] S. C. Justi, *Winckelmann und seine Zeitgenossen*, 5te Aufl. (Köln, 1965), Bd. II, Buch 2, Kap. 4: 'Ruf nach Berlin'.

[3] Das Folgende nach Lessing, *Hamburgische Dramaturgie*, S. 58, 62, 79, 120ff., 128f., 269, 394 (14., 15., 19., 30., 32., 68., 101.–4. Stück) und Herder, *Journal meiner Reise*, in *Sämtliche Werke*, Bd. IV, S. 413ff.

[4] S. J. G. Herder, *Über die neuere deutsche Literatur*, hrsg. von A. Gillies (Oxford, 1969), S. 70ff. (3, 1); *Auch eine Philosophie der Geschichte zur Bildung der Menschheit* Abschnitt 3 (Theorie, I, Frankfurt-am-Main, 1967), S. 108ff.; *Briefe zur Beförderung der Humanität*, Bd. II, S. 152ff. (*Neunte Sammlung*, Nr. 110).

Offensichtlich bedurften die rückständigen Deutschen, um vor ihren westlichen und südlichen Nachbarn bestehen zu können, einer historischen Legitimation, einer Art geistigen Stammbaums. Hierin lag für sie gewiss ein wichtiger Antrieb, sich nicht nur von der römischen Antike ab- und der griechischen Antike zuzuwenden, sondern auch so etwas wie eine griechisch–deutsche Wesensverwandtschaft zu behaupten. Diese These hob nun wirklich das überkommene Epochenschema antik (oder griechisch) – modern auf; sie ersetzte es durch eine überhistorische Perspektive, mit der die Deutschen zwar nicht schlankweg den Vorrang vor den übrigen Europäern, wohl aber eine besondere Qualifikation, ein bestimmtes Charisma, kurz, etwas Exklusives beanspruchten.

Die Transformation des Epochenvergleichs in den Parallelismus zweier Völker ging schrittweise vonstatten. Man stellte z. B. Betrachtungen über das Verhältnis der deutschen Sprache zur griechischen an; Klopstock etwa meinte, das Deutsche könne besser als das Englische, Französische oder Italienische die Fülle der griechischen Periode wiedergeben.[1] Grösseres Gewicht kommt wohl der Tatsache zu, dass man sich daran gewöhnte, bedeutende deutsche Schriftsteller als 'Griechen' zu bezeichnen. Derartige Identifikationen zeitgenössischer Persönlichkeiten mit einem überzeitlichen Wesensbild mussten auf diese Persönlichkeiten zurückwirken und sie ebenfalls als Verkörperungen eines überzeitlichen Wesens erscheinen lassen – man brauchte dann nur noch einen kleinen Schritt weiterzugehen und von der Person auf die Nation, der sie angehörte, zu schliessen, und das Denkbild von der Wesensnähe des griechischen und deutschen Nationalcharakters war vollendet.

Die Entwicklung hat offenbar auch hier mit Winckelmann begonnen. Dieser schrieb selbst einem Freunde, dass er in Rom als der grösste Grieche gelte.[2] Herder nahm alsbald das Stichwort auf, um es auf mancherlei Weise zu variieren. Das früheste Zeugnis preist Winckelmann 'als einen würdigen Griechen..., der aus der Asche seines Volkes aufgelebt ist, um unser Jahrhundert zu erleuchten', als 'den Griechen unserer Zeit'. Wie ersichtlich, geht es hier vor allem um die epochale, weniger um die nationale Figur Winckelmann; immerhin deutet der wie Phönix aus der Asche seines Volkes

---

[1] *Von der Nachahmung des griechischen Silbenmasses im Deutschen* (1756), in *Sämtliche Werke* (Leipzig, 1856/7), Bd. x, S. 4. S. ferner F. A. Wolf, *Darstellung der Altertumswissenschaft*, in *Kleine Schriften*, hrsg. von G. Bernhardy (Halle, 1869), Bd. II, S. 865 u. ö.

[2] *Briefe*, Bd. I, S. 328.

Aufgelebte patriotischen Stolz an. So nachdrücklicher Herders nächste Äusserung; sie bezeichnet Winckelmann als den 'edlen Griechen unsres Vaterlandes', verbindet freilich dieses Lob mit gemessenem Tadel – Winckelmann, dem allzusehr auf die Griechen Fixierten, sei das Grösste entgangen: 'wie die Kette der Mitteilung Zeiten und Völker verknüpft habe', 'wie ein Volk das andre bildete'. Weitere Verlautbarungen erheben Winckelmann in die Höhen der Transzendenz. In dem 'Lobgesang auf meinen Landsmann Winckelmann' apostrophiert Herder seinen Helden mit den Worten:

> Noch tast' ich schwere Träume! Du
> webst schon als Griechengott in hoher, stiller Ruh
> der zweiten Jugend.

Ähnlich spricht Herder im *Denkmal Johann Winckelmanns* vom Geist des Gepriesenen als einem 'griechischen Dämon', und er wünscht, dass jemand dessen Theorie zur Tat mache, einen 'neuen Raffael und Angelo der Deutschen, der uns griechische Menschen und griechiche Kunst schaffe'.[1]

Goethe, der Winckelmann eine 'antike Natur' nannte, wurde selbst von seinen Zeitgenossen als Reinkarnation griechischen Geistes gedeutet. So Schiller in seinem berühmten Geburtstagsbrief vom Jahre 1794. Wenn Goethe als ein Grieche geboren wäre, schreibt Schiller, so hätte er mit viel geringerer Mühe sein Künstlertum vollenden können; Schiller fährt fort:

nun, da Sie ein Deutscher geboren sind, da Ihr griechischer Geist in diese nordische Schöpfung geworfen wurde, so blieb Ihnen keine andere Wahl, als entweder selbst zum nordischen Künstler zu werden, oder Ihrer Imagination das, was ihr die Wirklichkeit vorenthielt, durch Nachhilfe der Denkkraft zu ersetzen und so gleichsam von innen heraus und auf einem rationalen Wege ein Griechenland zu gebären.[2]

Wie ersichtlich, zielt Schiller eher auf einen Gegensatz als auf eine besondere Nähe des Deutschen zum Griechischen; es geht um die ungünstigen physischen Bedingungen des Genies Goethe, die im Sinne der überkommenen Klimatheorie gedeutet werden – Goethe selbst argumentierte vier Jahre später, in der 'Einleitung zu den *Propyläen*', ähnlich, wenn er von den Schwierigkeiten des deutschen, ja überhaupt jedes neuen und nordischen Künstlers sprach. Wie

---

[1] 'Als einen würdigen Griechen...': *Sämtliche Werke*, Bd. III, S. 186f.; 'edlen Griechen', usw.: *ibid.* Bd. II, S. 119ff.; 'Noch tast' ich': *ibid.* Bd. XXIX, S. 301; 'griechischer Dämon', usw.: *ibid.* Bd. VIII, S. 482f.

[2] Schiller an Goethe, 23. August 1794, in Goethe, *Gedenkausgabe der Werke*, Bd. XX, S. 14.

Schiller, so meinte auch der Philologe Friedrich August Wolf, in Goethe sei griechisches Wesen wiedergekehrt; er feierte ihn als jemanden, in dem 'sich der das Leben verschönernde wohltätige Geist des Altertums eine zweite Wohnung genommen' habe.[1] Derlei Identifikationen waren damals offenbar – jedenfalls in bestimmten, für das Altertum aufgeschlossenen Kreisen – gängige Münze; ein Student erklärte z. B. von Wolf: 'Wenn ich mit ihm spreche, glaube ich immer einen Griechen reden zu hören, so ganz auf griechische Weise allseitig ausgebildet ist sein Geist. Und sein Charakter selbst ist ganz antik, leicht kindlich, gemütlich und zugleich tief, so wie unseres Winckelmanns.'[2] Doch patriotische Töne hat man hierbei wohl im allgemeinen nicht angeschlagen – eine Ausnahme sind die folgenden Verse des Homerübersetzers Voss:[3]

> Auch, Lessing, deins [nämlich dein Lied], der deutsche Art
> mit Griechheit, unerkannt, gepaart.

So war die Atmosphäre beschaffen, als Wilhelm von Humboldt – während der produktivsten Phase der deutschen Klassik – den letzten Schritt vollzog, als er auch in die deutsche Seite des Vergleichs ein Abstraktum einbrachte und die Verwandtschaft zweier Wesenheiten, des griechischen und deutschen Nationalcharakters, verkündete.[4] Das früheste Zeugnis scheint ein Brief des Jahres 1795 zu enthalten; Humboldt äussert dort Schiller gegenüber die Absicht, seine 'Grille von der Ähnlichkeit der Griechen und Deutschen ins Licht zu setzen'.[5] Er ist dieser 'Grille', wie Briefe an Goethe beweisen, auch weiterhin nachgegangen; die ausführlichsten Bemerkungen über sie finden sich in der *Geschichte des Verfalls und Untergangs der griechischen Freistaaten*, die im Jahre 1807 in Rom entstand. Humboldt stellt dort fest, dass man lange nicht rein und sorgfältig zwischen griechischem und römischem Geist geschieden habe; er fährt fort:

Die Deutschen besitzen das unstreitige Verdienst, die griechische Bildung zuerst treu aufgefasst und tief gefühlt zu haben...Andere Nationen sind hierin nie gleich glücklich gewesen...Deutsche knüpft...ein ungleich festeres und engeres Band

---

[1] *Kleine Schriften*, Bd. ii, S. 808.
[2] S. M. Lenz, *Geschichte der Friedrich-Wilhelms-Universität zu Berlin* (Halle, 1910–18), Bd. i, S. 352.
[3] 'Allegro', in *Sämtliche Gedichte* (Königsberg, 1802), Bd. vi, S. 203.
[4] Zum Folgenden s. C. Menze, *Wilhelm von Humboldts Lehre und Bild vom Menschen* (Ratingen, 1965), S. 154ff.
[5] *Briefwechsel zwischen Schiller und Wilhelm von Humboldt*, hrsg. von A. Leitzmann, 3te Aufl. (Stuttgart, 1900), S. 143; = *Schillers Werke, Nationalausgabe*, Bd. xxxv (*Briefe an Schiller, 1794–95*), hrsg. von G. Schulz (Weimar, 1964), S. 349 (22. September 1795).

an die Griechen, als an irgendeine andere, auch bei weitem näher liegende Zeit oder Nation.

Bald darauf heisst es, dass 'Deutschland (fremde Leser' – setzt Humboldt hier hinzu – 'mögen der wehmütigen Seite dieser Vergleichung die ehrenvolle verzeihen) in Sprache, Vielseitigkeit der Bestrebungen, Einfachheit des Sinnes, in der föderalistischen Verfassung und seinen neuesten Schicksalen eine unleugbare Ähnlichkeit mit Griechenland' zeige.[1] Mit den neuesten Schicksalen ist offensichtlich die napoleonische Besetzung gemeint; der Anspruch auf Ähnlichkeit mit den Griechen sucht also die politisch militärische Niederlage auf kulturellem Gebiet zu kompensieren. Humboldt ist sich bewusst, dass dieser Anspruch vom Ausland für Anmassung gehalten werden könnte; beschwichtigend fügt er den Hinweis auf den hohen Preis ein, den die Deutschen für ihren Ehrentitel bezahlen müssen.[2]

Während Schiller an seiner Abhandlung *Über naive und sentimentalische Dichtung* schrieb, und Humboldt sich zum ersten Male zu seiner 'Grille' bekannte, in demselben Jahre 1795 verfasste Friedrich Schlegel die Schrift *Über das Studium der griechischen Poesie*, eine Schrift, die auf eigentümliche Weise beides vereinigt: das Dreiphasenmodell Schillers und die 'Grille' Humboldts. Er geht darin von der traditionellen Problematik der *Querelle* aus; er wolle versuchen, schreibt er, 'den langen Streit der einseitigen Freunde der alten und der neuen Dichter zu schlichten'.[3] Seine Lehre läuft auf die Erwartung hinaus, dass sich die Bildung, welche die Griechen in zeitlichen Grenzen verwirklicht hätten, auf höherer Stufe und ohne zeitliche Grenzen nochmals verwirklichen lasse – hierin

---

[1] Briefe an Goethe: *Goethes Briefwechsel mit Wilhelm und Alexander von Humboldt*, hrsg. von L. Geiger, S. 124 (30. Mai 1800) und 173 (25. Februar 1804). 'Die Deutschen', usw.: *Werke in fünf Bänden*, hrsg. von A. Flitner und K. Giel (Stuttgart, 1960–4), Bd. II, S. 87; 'Deutschland', usw.: Bd. II, S. 88f.; vgl. *ibid.* S. 121f: S. ferner *Das achtzehnte Jahrhundert*, Bd. I, S. 385f.

[2] Spätere Äusserungen Humboldts schwächen die Thesen der Schrift über die *Griechischen Freistaaten* etwas ab. So heisst es in einem Bruchstück des Jahres 1814 (*Werke*, Bd. I, S. 554), kein Volk habe die Griechen und Römer so verstanden und aufgefasst wie die Deutschen – Humboldt scheint auf die ersten Erfolge der jungen Altertumswissenschaft zu zielen, gibt aber damit die These eines spezifischen Verhältnisses zu den Griechen preis. Das Alterswerk über den Sprachbau hebt einen gewichtigen Unterschied der beiden Sprachen hervor (Bd. III, S. 470): das Griechische, meint Humboldt, zeichne sich durch klare und feste Objektivität, das Deutsche hingegen durch seine tiefer geschöpfte Subjektivität aus – hier wirkt offenbar die auch von Humboldt oft beschriebene Differenz der Epochen, der Antike und der Moderne, auf das Urteil ein.

[3] *Kritische Schriften*, hrsg. von W. Rasch (Darmstadt, 1971), S. 114.

entspricht sie den Spekulationen Schillers.[1] Am Schluss aber heisst es, gerade die Deutschen seien berufen, die erwünschte dritte Phase der Rückkehr zum Objektiven und Schönen einzuleiten: 'In Deutschland', schreibt Schlegel, 'und nur in Deutschland hat die Ästhetik und das Studium der Griechen eine Höhe erreicht, welche die gänzliche Umbildung der Dichtkunst und des Geschmacks notwendig zur Folge haben muss' – zur Begründung beruft er sich, hierin Humboldt sekundierend, auf die Griechennähe der Deutschen, insbesondere eines Goethe.[2] Neu ist – im Verhältnis zu Humboldt – der Wechsel auf die Zukunft, eine Konsequenz des Dreiphasenmodells: Schlegel prophezeit, dass gerade Deutschland die von ihm erwartete Selbsterlösung des Menschen durch die Kunst vollziehen werde.[3]

Herders Winckelmannpreis stellte das Paradigma für einen deutschen Griechen bereit; Humboldts 'Grille' zog sowohl hieraus als auch aus der literarischen Blüte, wie sie sich in Deutschland entfaltet hatte, allgemeine Konsequenzen – dieses Fazit ergibt sich wohl im wesentlichen für die deutsche Sonderentwicklung des europäischen Epochenschemas antik–modern zur nationalen Parallele griechisch–deutsch. Das Denkbild widersprach im Grunde den Überzeugungen Herders wie Humboldts: der Einsicht in die Vielfalt und Unvergleichbarkeit alles Geschichtlichen, dem Konzept individueller und somit unnachahmbarer Nationalcharaktere. Während sich die Erscheinung bei Herder in engen Grenzen hielt, gaben Humboldt und erst recht Schlegel in einem nicht unbedenklichen Masse einen deutschen Exklusivanspruch, ein deutsches Sendungsbewusstsein zu erkennen, das aus übergeschichtlichen Wesenheiten abgeleitet war; hier begann sich – wohl durch deutsche Kompensationsbedürfnisse bedingt – ein nationaler Mythos zu entfalten.

[1] S. hierüber Jauss, 'Schlegels und Schillers Replik', bes. S. 75ff.

[2] *Kritische Schriften*, S. 228ff.

[3] Humboldt hat sich, vielleicht von Schlegel beeinflusst, einmal zu einer ähnlichen Perspektive bekannt (*Wilhelm von Humboldts Briefe an Johann Gottfried Schweighäuser*, hrsg. von A. Leitzmann (Jenaer Germanistische Forschungen, xxv, Jena, 1934, S. 42)): 'Zugleich kann ich nicht leugnen', schrieb er im Jahre 1807 über seine *Geschichte der griechischen Freistaaten*, 'dass ich dem armen zerrütteten Deutschland ein Monument setzen möchte, weil, meiner langgehegten Überzeugung nach, griechischer Geist, auf deutschen geimpft, erst das gibt, worin die Menschheit ohne Stillstand fortschreiten kann.' S. ferner Humboldt an Wolf, in *Gesammelte Werke*, hsrg. von C. Brandes (Berlin, 1841–52), Bd. v, S. 194f.: 'die Verbindung der Eigentümlichkeit der Alten und Neuern ...könnte man gleichsam die Endabsicht des deutschen Charakters nennen', usw.

SCHLUSSBEMERKUNG

Man könnte fortfahren und etwa Hölderlins Glauben an die Wiederkunft der Griechengötter in Deutschland erwähnen. Man könnte sich ausserdem mit weiteren Transformationen des Begriffspaares antik–modern befassen, mit der Dichotomie griechisch–romantisch, wie sie Jean Paul in der *Vorschule der Ästhetik* verwendet, und mit der analogen Dichotomie klassisch–romantisch, die lange Zeit als Schlüssel für die Deutung der Goethezeit gedient hat. Das Bisherige mag genügen – eine Skizze, der es nicht darum ging, die Vielfalt der Reflexionen über die Nachahmung der Alten, zumal der Griechen, und über die Grenzen dieser Nachahmung zu beschreiben, die vielmehr lediglich gewisse Rahmenbedingungen und Leitbegriffe zum Vorschein bringen wollte.

Die Skizze hat Folgendes ergeben. Es ist einerseits richtig, dass – wie gemeinhin angenommen wird – die deutschen Schriftsteller seit Winckelmann mit der römisch und romanisch vermittelten Antikerezeption brachen und sich ziemlich einseitig den Griechen zuwandten. Hiermit wurde das erste Glied des Epochenschemas antik–modern abgewandelt, jedenfalls der Sache nach, d. h. man pflegte auch dann die Griechen zu meinen, wenn man weiterhin von den 'Alten', usw., sprach. Andererseits aber ist nicht richtig, was vielerorts behauptet und nirgends dementiert wird: dass sich die deutsche Klassik auf monolithische Formeln wie griechisch–deutsche Verwandtschaft, griechisch–deutsche Begegnung, usw., bringen lasse. Das Selbstverständnis der deutschen Klassiker war durchaus nicht so einseitig auf eine derartige nationale Perspektive fixiert. Die Terminologie der Quellen gibt vielmehr zwei Hauptrichtungen, zwei Traditionsstränge zu erkennen. Die Repräsentanten des einen Traditionsstranges, zuallererst Schiller und Goethe, halten an der überkommenen Problematik fest; sie argumentieren also bei ihren Versuchen, die eigenen Leistungen und Möglichkeiten am Gegenbild der Griechen abzuschätzen, als 'Moderne', d. h. als aufgeklärte Europäer des späten 18. und beginnenden 19. Jahrhunderts, nicht als Deutsche. Die Repräsentanten des anderen Traditionsstranges – etwa Wilhelm von Humboldt und Friedrich Schlegel – haben hingegen in der Tat begonnen, die überkommene Opposition auf eine national gefärbte Perspektive, auf die Opposition griechisch–deutsch einzuengen und so für die Deutschen einen besonderen Rang zu beanspruchen. Allerdings handelt es sich hierbei nicht – wie bei Schiller und Goethe – um zusammenhängende theoretische Reflexionen, sondern um Aperçus, um, wie Humboldt sich ausdrückt, eine 'Grille'.

Die deutsche Rezeption der Goethezeit, zumal ihr Sprachrohr, die deutsche Germanistik, hat diese Zweisträngigkeit ignoriert; sie hat ignoriert, dass die Hauptrepräsentanten der Weimarer Klassik europäisch, nicht national gedacht haben, und statt dessen einseitig die national gefärbte Perspektive, die Opposition griechisch–deutsch, hervorgehoben. Diese nationalistische Verzerrung der historischen Wirklichkeit beruht wohl vornehmlich auf zwei Ursachen:

1. Die deutsche Klassik wurde als Erscheinung von grösster Originalität betrachtet; man deutete sie weithin nach dem Bilde, das schon Herder auf die Gründerfigur Winckelmann anwandte: als Phönix aus der Asche. So pflegte man die Bedeutung ihres europäischen Hintergrundes, zumal die enorme Beisteuer der französischen und englischen Aufklärung, zu unterschätzen.

2. Die Aussagen der deutschen Klassiker selbst wurden parteiisch interpretiert, ja unter Missachtung des eindeutigen Wortlauts verfälscht – im Sinne einer nationalistischen Einstellung, die so sehr Allgemeingut geworden war, dass der einzelne Interpret sie nicht mehr zu durchschauen vermochte. Die wichtigste Darstellung des hier behandelten Themas ist noch stets Walter Rehms Werk *Griechentum und Goethezeit*, das im Jahre 1936 die erste, im Jahre 1968 wenig verändert die vierte Auflage erlebt hat. Es pflegt um seines Leitmotivs, der deutsch–griechischen Begegnung willen drei Dinge miteinander zu vermengen: einmal das *Querelle*-Problem, die Frage des Ranges der Epochen, zum anderen das *imitatio*-Problem, die Frage nach der Nachahmbarkeit der Griechen, und schliesslich das sich in einem idealen Bild von den Griechen spiegelnde deutsche Nationalbewusstsein.

Überdies ist die Goethezeit selbst ein einmaliger Ablauf, ein Prozess von grosser Dynamik gewesen – ein vielstimmiges öffentliches Gespräch über vielerlei Themen, das von sehr verschiedenartigen Individuen auf immer neue Weise geführt wurde, eine Periode einer reichen literarischen Produktion und mannigfaltiger Entwürfe eines Humanitätsideals; diese Zeit ging, wie schon Heine erkannte, mit Goethes Tod zu Ende. Die nationalistische Rezeption der Goethezeit aber – die wissenschaftliche und populäre Schriftstellerei, die Schule bis zum Zeitalter der Weltkriege – wollte dieses

Ende nicht wahrhaben: sie suchte gleichsam stillzustellen und ins Überzeitliche zu erheben, was ein einmaliger Ablauf gewesen war. Als Beispiel kann abermals das Buch von Rehm dienen: es beginnt – nach einer Einleitung – mit einem Kapitel über Winckelmann und endet mit einem Kapitel über Hölderlin; aller weiteren Entwicklungen wird mit keinem Worte gedacht. Man kann hiermit Eliza Butlers Werk *The Tyranny of Greece over Germany* vergleichen, das dem Jahre 1935 entstammt. Auch Butler beginnt mit Winckelmann; sie lässt jedoch auf das Hölderlinkapitel eine ausführliche Behandlung Heines sowie einen Ausblick folgen, der bis zu George reicht. Der Unterschied des Aufbaus zeigt die unterschiedlichen Absichten: während Butler eine – wenn auch in vieler Hinsicht anfechtbare – historische Darstellung gibt, die sich bis zur Gegenwart der Autorin erstreckt und deren Perspektive offen erkennen lässt, sucht Rehm als zeitloser Autor eine Reihe von zeitentrückten Bildern vorzuführen, die ein ebenso zeitentrückter Leser andächtig in sich aufnehmen soll.

Wer derlei Kritik an der deutschen Rezeption der deutschen Klassik, an der Mythisierung dieser Epoche übt, rennt heutzutage überall offene Türen ein. Hiermit ist freilich nicht gesagt, dass die Spuren der Vergangenheit bereits beseitigt, die einstigen Unzulänglichkeiten behoben seien, jedenfalls nicht im Bereich der wissenschaftlichen Literatur. Auf der deutschen Klassik scheint – wegen des Missbrauchs, der mit ihr getrieben wurde – jedenfalls in Westdeutschland noch stets ein Bann zu liegen; die gegenwärtige westdeutsche Germanistik weicht ihr im allgemeinen aus und wendet sich teils früheren Epochen, dem Barock, dem Humanismus, usw., teils der Gegenwart zu. Meines Erachtens besteht kein Anlass, diesen Bann aufrechtzuerhalten; die deutsche Klassik ist nach Leistung und Selbsteinschätzung nicht nur eine deutsche, sondern durchaus auch eine europäische Angelegenheit.[1]

[1] S. hierzu W. H. Bruford, *Germany in the Eighteenth Century – The Social Background of the Literary Revival* (Cambridge, 1965), S. 304ff.

7

THE INTERMITTENT BEAT OF
CLASSICISM

J. H. WHITFIELD

There is in Dante a notable puzzle. At the bottom of hell he lumps together Brutus and Cassius, who betrayed the empire, and Judas Iscariot, who betrayed the church. And in the next Canto, the first of *Purgatorio*, he meets the compeer of Brutus and Cassius, Cato. Cato is not only the relentless opponent of Caesar's ambition, he is a suicide whom we might expect to find along with Pier della Vigna. Dante greets him with deep respect, as one

> degno di tanta reverenza in vista,
> che piú non dee a padre alcun figliuolo;[1]

and makes him, surprisingly, guardian either of the first circle or, as it might seem, of the whole of purgatory. We cannot ignore, still less dismiss, this contradiction; though we may understand it as inevitable. If we turn back to the beginning of the poem, where Virgil shows Dante his peers (that circle to whose company Dante will be himself elected), we find three Latins after Homer:

> l'altro è Orazio satiro che vene;
> Ovidio è il terzo, e l'ultimo Lucano.[2]

I mean that Dante takes uncritically, as a single undifferentiated whole, the great exemplars of Latin poetry. He cannot repudiate the Christian overtones which a long tradition had found in Cato, already abundantly testified to by Dante in the *Convivio*.[3]

Now we saw, on our last meeting, that Machiavelli had advanced on the road to criticism of his authorities.[4] He read Livy and Tacitus, and he rejected the period of the one for the sake of the other. But we should not applaud too quickly, or too much, this victory for a critical sense. For there is a contradiction in Machiavelli, but it is latent, and he, shall we say, did not suspect it. It is embedded in the *Discourses on Livy*, where he discusses why men fight less hard for

---

[1] *Purgatorio* I.32. [2] *Inferno* IV.89.
[3] E.g. *Convivio* IV.xxviii: 'E quale uomo terreno piú degno fu di significare Iddio, che Catone? Certo nullo.'
[4] 'Livy > Tacitus', *Classical Influences on European Culture, A.D. 1400–1700*, ed. R. R. Bolgar (Cambridge, 1976), pp. 281ff.

liberty now than they did of old against the Romans.[1] It is a page where the critics' eyes have been fastened on what seems an anti-Christian bias in Machiavelli, but the real nub comes a moment later when he says, 'ancora che io creda piú tosto essere cagione di questo, che lo Imperio romano con le sue arme e sua grandezza spense tutte le republiche e tutti e' viveri civili'.[2] Do not be misled by the word 'Imperio', because he has spoken of the Veii and the Etruscans, and will conclude in a moment with the wonderful example of the Samnites. It is the rise of Rome which he here equates with the downfall of liberty (others' liberty). If we were to keep this potent reflection in our mind when we read the early chapters of the *Discourses*, especially where he proclaims the perfect nature of the Roman constitution, we should realise that Machiavelli is as uncritical as Dante. He looks always with Livy's eyes at the progressive prosperity of a virtuous race. Although himself a Florentine, he is never tempted to adopt an Etruscan point of view – still less a Samnite one. He never suspects, as did the authors of the Universal History in the English eighteenth century, the partiality of Livy.

Hardly had Machiavelli been restored in Italy to his own name, with the publication of his works in Florence in 1782, than a genuine Machiavellian stepped into the gap which I have opened between the viewpoint of Rome, who conquered, and that of those who were destroyed. I say that he was a Machiavellian with some confidence, for if you write a preface of two pages, and put in it two quotations from Machiavelli, one acknowledged, one concealed, then I think there is no doubt (if there are no other quotations in your preface) where your admiration lies. First then: 'Se con troppa fiducia ho deliberato entrare per una via non ancora da alcuno aperta'; and secondly (that wish common to many Italians in the opening years of the nineteenth century): 'perché "questa provincia pare nata per risuscitare le cose morte"'.[3] The writer was Giuseppe Micali, and his book – whose origins go back to 1790 – appeared in four volumes in 1810, as *L'Italia avanti il dominio dei Romani*. I do not think Micali saw the contradiction which I have suggested to you as undercutting, if we let it grow, all Machiavelli's account of Rome: for what perfection can there be in a state which destroys the general liberties of Italy, as the first stage of destroying its own? Nevertheless, while

[1] *Discorsi*, in *Opere*, ed Feltrinelli (Milan, 1961–), II.ii.   [2] *Ibid.* 283.
[3] For the first, see Machiavelli, *Discorsi* I, Proemio, p. 123; for the second, in *Arte della guerra*, ed. Feltrinelli (Milan, 1961), book VII, p. 519.

approving Machiavelli, Micali is necessarily committed to dis-approving Livy.

Naturally there had been hints, like the one which I have cited from Machiavelli, coming at times from others less committed to the heritage of Rome than were the Italians. We have Saint-Évremond saying 'A proprement parler, les Romains étoient des voisins fâcheux & violens, qui vouloient chasser les justes possesseurs de leurs maisons, & labourer, la force à la main, les champs des autres.' That was a casual remark, in a work whose title was *Réflexions sur les divers génies du peuple romain*.[1] This is to be, instead, a looking from the other side. It may be that the impetus came from a chapter in Carlo Denina's *Delle Rivoluzioni d'Italia* (1769), where he argues against the attempts of both Machiavelli and Montesquieu to show why it had been Rome which had emerged as victor. Their error, or their prejudice, had been to presuppose that this was due to its institutions: 'e per certi suoi ordini propri e particolari'.[2] But the fact was that they had these in common with other peoples in Italy. And as for their military disciplines, where did they learn them? 'Is it not clear that not the Romans only, but all the peoples of Latium, all the Samnites, the Sabines, the Etruscans had more or less the same *ordini* for warfare...?'[3] True, the Roman writers give the impression that their confederates learnt from Rome:

But it is easy to recognise the vanity and falsity of such a boast. And as it cannot in any way be claimed that the Latins learned anything from the Romans, so it is a thing openly declared by the testimony of the Romans themselves, that they learnt from the Samnites especially, and from other peoples, the art of war.[4]

And in the margin Denina produced no less a witness than Caesar to this process: 'Maiores nostri...arma atque tela militaria a Samniti-bus sumpserunt, &...quod ubique apud socios aut hostes idoneum videbatur, cum summo studio domi exequebantur.'[5] Their begin-nings violent, ignoble, ignominious, even in the accounts of their own writers; and if, says Denina, we had the other side of the coin, the history of Rome written by their antagonists, we should find worse things related. And they spent over four hundred years before they could move away from the immediate vicinity of Rome itself.

I shall leave you, if you are curious to find Denina's retort to the

[1] In *Œuvres* (Amsterdam, 1739), vol. II, p. 11.
[2] Carlo Denina, *Delle rivoluzioni d'Italia* (Torino, 1769), vol. I, book II, ch. i, 'Riflessioni generali sopra le cause della grandezza Romana', p. 64.
[3] *Ibid.* p. 65.   [4] *Ibid.*
[5] *Ibid.* For Caesar, see his speech, in *De coniuratione Catilinae*, 1513 Giunta, 19v.

panegyrics of Machiavelli and Montesquieu, to read his chapter (II, i). But if he defined the area for Micali you will see that he revealed the difficulty of passing to the other side of the looking-glass. As Micali says, in those four hundred years the Romans were too barbaric to write annals, and in their victories they suppressed all those of their victims. *Rebus sic stantibus*, it is easier to rewrite, with transferred sympathies and contrapuntal emphasis, the process of their disappearance, than to reconstruct the surface of their prosperity. But as evidence that this existed, there is first the length of the struggle to prove its quality; and there are such details as the survival of Oscan (language or plays), or the Roman habit of sending their sons to learn, especially in matters of religion, from the Etruscans. And then it is possible, by stroking the cat against the fur, to find the admissions which had no interest from the viewpoint of Rome, and so were not picked out by Machiavelli. Livy had said it at the outset: 'Tanta opibus Etruria erat ut jam non terras solum, sed mare etiam per totam Italiae longitudinem ab Alpibus ad fretum Siculum fama sui nominis implesset.'[1] And to show that it was common knowledge, Virgil attested it in the *Georgics*:

> Hanc olim veteres vitam coluere Sabini,
> Hanc Remus et frater, sic fortis Etruria crevit.[2]

The next step is to discover (what Denina had hinted) that the institutions of Rome were borrowed from their neighbours. Here Romulus, that hero of the early pages of Machiavelli's *Discorsi*, fades from the page, his prudence disappearing as Rome imitates Etruria and Latium, not only for its basic constitution, but even in the outward signs of its magistratures.

In each city of Italy... there was then the model of the basic constitution of Rome, which took from its neighbours not only the essential forms of government, but even the outward signs of its magistrature, as the curule chair, the fasces and the axes. Finally, the high reputation and the authority at once acquired by the ministers of religion in matters of state must convince us that the *ordini* established were not those of Romulus.[3]

Dispense with Romulus (and Numa), you will soon find that you can dismiss much else of the legendary beginnings of Rome (and in this Micali anticipates Salvatore Betti who in 1839 will label it all as

---

[1] Giuseppe Micali, *L'Italia avanti il dominio dei Romani* (Firenze, 1810), vol. I, p. 114, n. 1, quoting Livy I.ii.

[2] *Ibid.* p. 116, n. 3; 'In Thuscorum jure pene omnis Italia fuerat' (Cato, in Serv. XI.567); 'Nam constat Thuscos usque ad mare Siculum omnia possedisse' (*Georgics* II.533).

[3] *Ibid.* vol. III, pp. 14–15.

legend).[1] And if you side with the peoples of Italy against Rome, you can proclaim them native, and not imports from the eastern Mediterranean. Nor are the tell-tale admissions lacking. As with Juvenal,

> Et quidquid Graecia mendax
> audet in historiis,[2]

or with Quintilian, 'Graecis historiis plerumque poeticae similis est licentia.'[3] Away with all that stuff about Aeneas, whose coming to Italy is as fabulous as that of Hercules. It is arrogance that makes the Grecians claim that they gave birth to the Romans, or to any others of the aboriginals of Italy, and all the poetry of the *Aeneid* is reduced to a vain opinion in the form of a 'bel romanzo storico'.[4] And so we come, less to the picture of the Italy that was, in those four hundred years, than to the odium that Rome incurs in its destruction. Sometimes you can find the evidence in Livy as in that triumphant (if you go with the victors), or that melancholy (if you are with the vanquished) footnote, when the Aequi renew the struggle they had lost, and are obliterated, 'quorum pleraque diruta atque incensa, nomenque Aequorum prope ad internecionem deletum'.[5] And sometimes you will find it by looking to other accounts than Livy – as where Dionysius of Halicarnassus tells that while Servilius was fighting the Volsci his colleague Appius decapitated three hundred hostages in Rome.[6] Livy, says Micali, was ashamed for his Romans, and did not register 'questo tratto di insana ferocia'. The same Dionysius shows that where Livy acclaims the Roman reasonableness in making war, they were unscrupulous in their ambition.[7] A fact that Bossuet, for all his admiration, will also note: 'L'ambition ne permettoit pas à la justice de régner dans leurs Conseils.'[8] And

---

[1] *Ibid.* vol. III, p. 63: 'Que' miracoli di valore, d'intrepidità, di coraggio d'un Orazio Coclite, d'un Muzio Scevola e di Clelia, che, conforme disse Floro [i.x], noi rigetteremmo come favole se non fossero descritti nella storia, debbono pur una volta considerarsi quai speciosi racconti, immaginati o abbelliti almeno da' primi annalisti, a fin di colorire sotto l'apparenza d'eroismo un fatto umiliante.' And what Florus said, 'quae nisi in annalibus forent, hodie fabulae viderentur'.

[2] *Ibid.* vol. I, p. 46 n., quoting Juvenal x.174.

[3] *Ibid.* quoting Quintilian II.4.

[4] *Ibid.* vol. I, p. 150.

[5] *Ibid.* vol. I, p. 338, no. 1, quoting Livy IX.xlv.

[6] *Ibid.* vol. III, p. 75, quoting Dionysius VI.xxx.

[7] *Ibid.* vol. IV, p. 19, quoting Dionysius, *Excerpta* 2328–32. To which we might add Florus II.ii, on the First Punic War, where the pretext was to help an ally, 're autem sollicitante praeda'.

[8] *Ibid.* vol. IV, p. 47, n. 2. For Bossuet, see *Discours sur l'histoire universelle* (Amsterdam, 1722), vol. I, pp. 414–15.

Florus will underline in his description of the fate of the Samnites, who took seventy years in being crushed, and left in their defeat the legacy of general dominion for Rome, the same consequences which Livy expresses for the Aequi. For Rome annihilates Samnium, 'ita subegit ac domuit, ita ruinas ipsas urbium diruit, ut hodie Samnium in ipso Samnio requiratur'.[1] And here we may guess the reasons behind the protraction of the threat from Hannibal over so many years. The Roman writers call him names, *Dirum Hannibalem* (Horace), but they exaggerate his cruelty and his avarice, while Micali looks to Polybius for a clearer glimpse of his character.[2] If he survived in Italy, it is obviously because the enemies of Rome found him a welcome fellow-combatant. And did they not think of summoning Mithridates to their aid? So that Racine, alluding in his tragedy to this idea of the time of the *Bellum sociale*, makes Mithridates say:

> Et de près, inspirant les haines les plus fortes,
> Tes plus grands ennemis, Rome, sont à tes portes.[3]

Once again, the chorus for the Social War comes from Florus: 'Nec Annibalis, nec Pyrrhi, fuit tanta devastatio.'[4] While for the hate of which Racine wrote we can find the testimony of Velleius Paterculus, where the Samnite general Pontius, evading Pompey and Sylla, turns from Palestrina towards Rome with the idea of eradicating the scourge: 'Adesse Romanis ultimum diem: eruendam delendamque urbem: nunquam defuturos raptores Italicae libertatis lupos, nisi silva, in quam refugere solerent, esset excisa.'[5]

It would be easy to multiply the testimony on this record of destruction, drawn by Micali from a range of authors. There is, for instance, Petronius on Crotona: 'Videbitis, inquit, oppidum, tanquam in pestilentia campos, in quibus nihil aliud est, nisi cadavera quae lacerantur, aut corvi qui lacerant.'[6] But I had better remind you that, in his eagerness to damn the Romans, Micali this time caught a crab, since the passage does not mean what he thought it so plainly said. But there is Pausanias on Metapontum, reduced to walls and a theatre;[7] or Strabo on the desolation of southern Italy, where

---

[1] *Ibid.* vol. IV, p. 97, quoting Florus I.xvi.
[2] *Ibid.* vol. IV, p. 197, n. 4, quoting Polybius IX.xxii.
[3] *Ibid.* vol. IV, p. 298, quoting Racine, *Mithridate* III.i.
[4] *Ibid.* n. 3, quoting Florus III.xix.
[5] *Ibid.* vol. IV, p. 314, n. 1, quoting Velleius Paterculus II.xxvii.
[6] *Ibid.* vol. IV, p. 215, n. 1, quoting the *Satyricon* 116. But here it is all a question of legacy-leavers and legacy-hunters.
[7] *Ibid.* quoting Pausanias V.xix.

you could scarcely trace the vestiges of its former state;[1] or we may come back to Livy for that transformation of the Italian scene, where once free men lived, and now only slaves till the soil: 'Aut innumerabilem multitudinem liberorum capitum in eis fuisse locis, quae nunc, vix seminario exiguo militum relicto, servitia Romana ab solitudine vindicant.'[2]

I should like to refer you to those splendid words of Valla on Livy, which I quoted last time, and which are full of examples.[3] It will be plain to you that whereas Valla and Machiavelli hero-worshipped Livy, this is a reading which concentrates on the ferocity and the malevolence of Rome, and offers only non-examples. Let me sum it up in one dire anecdote. You will find this, not in Livy, but hidden in an unlikely place, in Seneca *On clemency*, where Sylla is weighed against Dionysius, and found more tyrannical:

Quis tamen unquam tyrannus tam avide humanum sanguinem bibit, quam ille, qui septem millia civium Romanorum contrucidari jussit? Et cum in vicino, ad aedem Bellonae sedens, exaudisset conclamationem tot millium sub gladio gementium, exterrito senatu: Hoc agamus, inquit, P.C., seditiosi pauculi meo jussu occiduntur.[4]

When we read from this side of the looking-glass our blood will run cold as we think of those lines which seemed the word of God to Dante, promising universal and endless power to both the empire and the church:

> tu regere imperio populos Romane memento,
> hae tibi erunt artes, pacique imponere morem,
> parcere subiectis, et debellare superbos.[5]

If you have come across that *mot* of Thierry about Napoleon ('Nous avons vu César'), it will seem more than obvious to you that an author who publishes in Florence in 1810 a work of this nature, where the Romans figure as the wreckers of Italy, and not its saviours, will be classed with the opposition. This was the deduction about Micali, though nothing, as it happened, was further from his intention. The urge had come to him soon after 1790, when he was travelling with Melchiorre Delfico in southern Italy, and he had been writing his book for twenty years. There is never any flicker of a glance towards the tumultuous history that had been played out in that time. But

---

[1] *Ibid.* vol. IV, p. 218, quoting Strabo VI.
[2] Micali quotes this capital text from Livy VI.xii twice (vol. I, p. 133, vol. IV, p. 337).
[3] 'Livy > Tacitus', p. 282.
[4] Micali, *L'Italia*, vol. IV, p. 315, n. 2, quoting Seneca, *De clementia* I.xii.
[5] *Aeneid* VI.851.

Micali's readers, and he had many during the nineteenth century, read him with contemporary eyes, and saw, as did Sismondi, the danger of putting 'la haine des Romains à la place de l'amour des Italiens' and thus emphasising, not a unifying symbol, but something which, long destroyed, could not be the basis of a *risorgimento*.[1] Nevertheless, Micali's history of the *vinti*, and his discovery of Roman history as only so far written by the conquerors, points forward on the one side through Niebuhr to Mommsen, and on the other to Manzoni and Verga, with their romantic concentration of interest on those who succumbed. Those who in this century have recommended the replacement of Roman history by that of Italy underline the importance of Micali's own discovery.

Where Micali trod with eyes blinkered to the present, others were aware of the implications of what they said, and saw. Thus in 1797, in a work which he published as an exile in London, Vittorio Barzoni half rewrote the history of *I Romani nella Grecia*, and half envisaged the rising Bonaparte in terms of Flamininus.[2] Here there is the assertion (admitted to the high official record only a century later) that 'no foreign army ever comes into a country solely to set it free', related to the unhappy fate of the Greeks, who, blinded by their desire to escape from one domination, did not realise that the liberty they would be given by Rome could only be masked slavery. Here the anti-Romanism is both conscious and explicit (allied as it is to anti-Bonapartism); and the heart of the matter lies still, as with Micali, in the repudiation of all sense of the providential mission of Rome. And once again that noble Virgilian pattern which I have contrasted sadly with Sylla's 'clemency' is shattered: 'La loro massima di perdonare ai vinti e di debellare i superbi eseguivano calpestando i primi, e mettendo tutto ad opra onde soverchiare i secondi'.[3] As for the Romans, we are back to that Augustinian view of them; they are thieves who suck the riches of all the world into their treasury, while their ambition makes the limits of the world itself those of their patrimony.

Taken all together, and under the control of the senate, they formed the most fierce and imposing spectacle; taken separately, and in the play of their fierce brutality, they were the dregs of the human race. Such were those famous Latin

[1] Piero Treves, *L'idea di Roma e la cultura italiana del secolo XIX* (Milano and Napoli, 1962), p. 30.
[2] For Barzoni, see Piero Treves, *Lo studio dell'antichità classica nell'Ottocento* (Milano and Napoli, 1962), p. 103. [3] *Ibid.* p. 144.

heroes, who with rapacious and blood-covered hands set up the trophy of their immortal glory.[1]

And the homage which posterity has paid to them? It is that which human weakness has always given to splendid vices and illustrious crimes, to the luminous misdeeds which ennobled 'gli esecrandi eccessi dei Romani'.[2]

This vision was shared, and anticipated, by Alessandro Verri. In the periodical *Il Caffè* in 1764 he had reduced the exemplary history of Rome to a catalogue of massacres, part of the 'chronology of human crimes'.[3] This judgement he maintained in a sketch of Roman history as part of a popular *History of Italy* which he did not publish; and it tinges his *Notti romane* (1792): 'Conchiude la mente mia ch'eglino furono grandi piú che buoni, illustri piú che felici, per istituto oppressori, per fortuna mirabili, per indole distruttori, generosi nelle malvagità, eroi nelle ingiustizie, magnanimi nella atrocità.'[4] With this debit to the Roman account, Verri moderated the high opinion he had had of Rome, and considered the world was granted repose when a people who had coveted it all, and disturbed it all, was at last overcome by time. But that is the end of volume I. At the end of volume II, although it is not out of sight, it merges into a different picture, the providentiality of the successor to that ancient universality of Rome: the Rome whose swords were the *flagello del mondo* becomes that other Rome which brings the world redemption: 'Sí: l'imperio vostro nasce da feroci masnadieri: questo incomincia da una benefica umiltà.'[5] I would not say, as has been said, that this brings Verri entirely into line with the official version of that sequence. But it approximates, at least, to that utterance of Leo Magnus which will be quoted by Angelo Mai in 1837 in his panegyric on the Christian Empire of Rome:

Civitas sacerdotalis et regia, per sacram beati Petri sedem caput orbis effecta, latius praesides religione divina, quam dominatione terrena: minus enim est quod tibi bellicus labor subdidit, quam quod pax christiana subiecit.[6]

For obvious reasons, I do not dwell on that official underwriting of the classical world as the prerequisite of the papal one. Indeed, it is natural that we should see it in reverse, as with that scornful remark of D'Azeglio: 'L'antiquaria era ed è uno de' pochi studi possibili sotto

[1] *Ibid.* p. 145.   [2] *Ibid.*
[3] Treves, *L'idea di Roma*, p. 55.
[4] *Ibid.* p. 57; or *Le notti romane* (Milano, 1825), vol. I, book III, ch. vi, p. 254.
[5] *Le notti romane*, vol. II, book VI, ch. vi, p. 221.
[6] Treves, *Studio*, p. 389.

il governo de' preti.'[1] Or with that twin remark of Cesare Balbo, equally, or more, notorious: 'Il piú gran letamajo di corruzione che sia stato mai, fu il nostro Impero romano (quell'impero cosí stoltamente desiderato e fin santificato da tanti).'[2] What we need, in fact, is that key witness from the opposition, the classical and non-official Pietro Giordani. We remember him, if at all, as the friend of Leopardi, accused unfairly by Monaldo of aiding Giacomo on the path to unbelief. For the rest, he has sunk as a rhetorician who left no durable work of his own. But his ideas were enlightened, and are not without their sting today. In a world where all formal education was based on Latin, he was against the torment of teaching it to boys:

Believe me, the Latin language is a most useless and harmful torment for boys; believe me, the age to learn it is not childhood, but youth; believe me that in Italy it is known now only by very few precisely because of the attempt to teach it to everybody.[3]

With this broom he meant to sweep away the whole apparatus of the Jesuit brand of classical instruction, whose aim had been directed away from the understanding of the classical texts, and towards the skills of composition and of speech in the Latin tongue. Giordani condemns the practice of teaching people to write in Latin, or to translate into Latin:

I count it a foolish and harmful (and in many a malicious) pedantry to insist on composition or translation into Latin, which is a putting of your brain into reverse. And by God all these compositors and translators into Latin are the ones who least understand the true value of the Latin classics...The important thing is to understand them well, the classics: and this today is very rare, and especially rare in those who teach.[4]

For of course the irony, or the logic, of it is that the *virtuosi* in the skills of composition (or in the monstrosity of turning Horace's odes into Virgilian hexameters, and vice versa) are those who understand the classics least, because they seek in them only the *loci communes* which they can imitate.

Since old traditions die hard, and I was myself brought up in a not entirely different way, where my skills did not develop, but my interest died, and my understanding was never born, I had better leave you to make your own way (if you need to) towards Giordani's ideas on the scope and practice of a classical education. What we

---

[1] Timpanaro, *La filologia di Giacomo Leopardi* (Firenze, 1955), p. 98, n. 2, or Massimo D'Azeglio, *I miei ricordi* (Salani, 1928), ch. x, p. 144.

[2] Treves, *L'idea di Roma*, p. 83.   [3] Treves, *Studio*, p. 421.

[4] S. Timpanaro, *Classicismo e illuminismo nell'Ottocento italiano* (Pisa, 1965), p. 53.

want from him is the indication of an author: one whom we have
seen at the beginning as part and parcel of the one and indivisible
Roman legacy, and who now reappears, in all his tender impiety, as
the great poet of the opposition: Lucan. It is interesting that
Giordani, whose fate it is to be dismissed as a rhetorician, dismissed
Cicero ('Egli è tutto eloquenza: egli è la stessa eloquenza. E la
eloquenza in Cicerone (ma in lui solo) è una veste che tiene luogo di
persona'),[1] and fought against those who condemned Lucan for his
vicious style. There are in Lucan excesses, especially in the matter of
shedding blood, which lead on directly to the damnablest bits of
Chapelain's unfortunate *La Pucelle* (I am thinking especially of that
egregious episode of the soldier scaling the wall, only to find his
hands chopped off, and then his head, so that he clings to the vantage-
point with teeth and hands, while his lifeless trunk plops in the
moat).[2] But Giordani resolutely ignored all this, challenged Lucan's
detractors to a test, in which they would not be able to say offhand
whether a line came from Lucretius, Virgil, Ovid, Lucan or Statius,
and having put him back into the pool, brought him out in prominence as the most vitally relevant of all. Let us also take a dip, in
which I shall not expect you to be wrong in your guessing, for if we
have followed Giordani on that path to understanding of an author,
instead of learning how to write pastiche, what Lucan has to say is
unmistakable:

> Quis enim laesos impune putaret
> esse deos? Servat multos fortuna nocentes,
> et tantum miseris irasci numina possunt.[3]

This is the great anti-establishment poem, the consolation prize, in
which what is triumphant is wrong, and what fails is right.

> Victrix causa deis placuit, sed victa Catoni.[4]

[1] Treves, *Studio*, p. 442.
[2] Lucan III. 610ff.; which Chapelain caps in *La pucelle* (1656), XI.454:
> Geoffroy saist le mur, d'une main triomphante,
> Tout prest à le franchir, si Morton survenu,
> Au fort de son ardeur, n'eust son cours retenu.
> Morton leve le bras, & d'une lourde hache,
> Du robuste poignet une main luy detache;
> De l'autre il se racroche, & voit Morton soudain,
> Avec le mesme fer, luy trancher l'autre main.
> Les dents, tout luy manquant, dans les pierres il plante;
> Mais perd la teste encor, sous la hache tranchante;
> Le tronc, en sang, retourne au François indigné;
> Luy, des mains & des dents, garde le mur gaigné.
[3] Lucan III.447. [4] *Ibid.* I.128.

The landscape of the beginning, with that desolation of the Civil War, is the same as that of Micali, and the upshot is the death of liberty:

> fugiens civile nefas redituraque nunquam
> Libertas ultra Tigrim Rhenumque recessit
> ac, totiens nobis iugulo quaesita, vagatur,
> Germanum Scythicumque bonum, nec respicit ultra
> Ausoniam.[1]

On which the comment of Giordani is notable:

So it seemed to me really sacred, and to be preferred to any other, this poem which took as its matter not the foundation or the conquest of a kingdom, not some curious or rare navigation, not the gods of a people or an age, but the funeral of Liberty, universally and eternally divine, which even if it could be driven into exile from the world, could not lose its right to reign there.[2]

Let us read together, my friends, says Giordani, 'questa nobilissima Farsalia!' It was an invitation made at the right time, and it finds deep echoes in the most significant authors at the end of the eighteenth and the beginning of the nineteenth centuries. Even Monti, with whose ambivalence we must somehow reckon, encouraged Francesco Cassi (cousin of his son-in-law, Perticari) to his translation of Lucan, which ensured a wide popularity for the *Pharsalia* through the century. But more significant are the traces which Lucan leaves in the trio, Alfieri, Foscolo and Leopardi. In Alfieri the last epigraph to the *Misogallo* (if that is the right word for a line which is not a quotation, and which follows the final sonnet and the words 'The End') is: 'Tenea 'l Ciel dai ribaldi, Alfier dai buoni';[3] which is a refashioning of Lucan on Cato, Fortune and the gods. Foscolo in 1789, defending Monti against the Jacobins (who could not forget he was the author of the *Bassvilliana*) appealed first to the anti-Caesarian tone of Lucan (a warning for those who doubted whether Foscolo knew Lucan).[4] And in the *Sepolcri*, as Professor Aquilecchia has shown, one of the famous passages,

> e quando
> Il tempo con sue fredde ale vi spazza
> Fin le rovine,[5]

should not be thought of without reference to that visit of Caesar to the site that once was Troy, where 'etiam periere ruinae',[6] and

---

[1] *Ibid.* VII.432.
[2] Treves, *Studio*, p. 452; and for the reading together, p. 459.
[3] Alfieri, *Il Misogallo* (Londra, 1800), p. 173.   [4] Treves, *Studio*, p. 412.
[5] Giovanni Aquilecchia, *Schede d'italianistica* (Einaudi, 1976), Scheda tredicesima, p. 277 'Foscolo e Lucano'.   [6] Lucan IX.969.

where a heap of shapeless stones is all that remains of the altar of Jove. Nor can we think of the Foscolian theme of the *sacro vate* without remembering

> O sacer et magnus vatum labor, omnia fato
> eripis et populis donas mortalibus aevum.[1]

And finally, though Leopardi may have been too fastidious to care for the defects in Lucan's poem and therefore to quote him much, yet in *Bruto minore*, which meant so much to him, he speaks in terms that Lucan would have owned:

> Dunque degli empi
> siedi, Giove, a tutela?[2]

And again, when the moon looks calmly on the fraternal slaughter of Philippi, might we not marry these passages of Leopardi to that one in the *Pharsalia* which proclaims the indifference of the heavens to the earlier slaughter of Pharsalia:

> Sunt nobis nulla profecto
> numina: cum caeco rapiantur saecula casu,
> mentimur regnare Jovem. Spectabit ab alto
> aethere Thessalicas, teneat cum fulmina, clades?[3]

Of all the Italian names I have mentioned, only one (and him I have not really mentioned, but he hovered in the margin when I cited Giordani's remarks about Cicero) appears in the pages of that thin book, Pfeiffer's *History of Classical Scholarship 1300–1850*. This is because Pfeiffer, though he records Petrarch's enthusiasm for the 'sweetness and sonority' of the Latin authors, is not at all concerned with the variations in the pattern of their rating. But where he puts in Angelo Mai as the sole Italian representative of classical scholarship during this period, he picked a losing candidate even on his own terms. Mai, as Timpanaro has shown, was a good finder, and a bad keeper.[4] He published the palimpsest Cicero *De republica*, but he was less than scholarly in his use of it (and it, as Giordani remarked, was less than it might have been). Looming up alongside Mai, and left unnumbered on the page by Pfeiffer, there is the great name of Leopardi. Now it is not in my competence – and I say this for the benefit of any Regius Professor of Greek who reviews our proceedings – to touch on matters of Greek scholarship. But it is imperative for anyone who reviews Pfeiffer to examine Sebastiano Timpanaro's

---

[1] *Ibid.* IX.980. [2] *Bruto minore* v.26, in Leopardi, *Canti*.
[3] Lucan VII.445.
[4] Timpanaro, *La filologia di Giacomo Leopardi*, pp. 44 etc.

book *La filologia di Giacomo Leopardi*. No-one who does so will make the elementary mistake of including Angelo Mai in his account of classical philology and leaving out Leopardi. But what we can do, and with the more pleasure in that it links us with the close of my last paper to you, is to look at Leopardi on Tiberius. The reference back is to my closing quotations from Bouhours and Fénelon,[1] to be connected with my beginning here with Saint-Évremond.[2] For in his *Réflexions sur les divers génies du peuple romain* he also dismisses the idea of Augustus choosing Tiberius as a successor who would by comparison flatter his predecessor:

C'est ce qui a trompé Tacite, à mon avis, dans ce rafinement malicieux qu'il donne à Auguste. Il savoit que le naturel de Tibère ne lui étoit pas inconnu; & pour ne pas croire qu'un grand Empereur pût aller dans une chose si importante contre son propre sentiment, il a mis du dessein & du mystère, où il n'y a eu, si je ne me trompe, que de la facilité.[3]

As we have seen with Micali reading Livy, it is an important part of the fortune of an author, whether one reads with him, or against him. And here Leopardi makes a vital contribution. You will find it in the *Zibaldone*, and it concerns Tiberius, though the author queried is here Suetonius rather than Tacitus. What the classical biographer has done is to attribute to dissimulation the benignity and humility which Tiberius shows in his diffident approach to assuming power. As Saint-Évremond did in his remarks on Augustus, Leopardi dismisses the refinements of policy by a psychological approach.

I see in it nothing feigned, or artificial. Tiberius was, unlike Caesar, timid by nature. Unlike both Caesar, who from his youth rose continually, accustoming his mind and character successively to ever greater heights, and Augustus, who also from his youth found himself at the head of affairs, Tiberius, born to private station, and having lived out his youth and mature age suspect to Augustus and his relatives, and even in no little danger (he spent eight years in retreat at Rhodes to escape or lessen this), had neither the mind or character formed to power when fortune put it in his hands. So in the beginning he was modest, even timid and humble, even when he had freed himself from all fear, as Suetonius says expressly (c. xxvi). Nor in this was there any dissimulation, I can see nothing else in it than a man accustomed to fear and to avoid offence, who when he is brought to dominance still keeps the habit of these fears and this avoidance. He lost it with time and with the sustained experience of his power, and of the subjection, even the abjection, of others. This is no unmasking; it is a change in character and nature, through change of circumstance.[4]

---

[1] 'Livy > Tacitus', p. 292.   [2] See above, p. 133.
[3] *Réflexions sur les divers génies du peuple romain*, p. 107.
[4] Leopardi, *Zibaldone* 4194.

It is Piero Treves, in his invaluable anthology, who makes the point that this psychological approach – which I have taken back to the French writers of the seventeenth century – is lacking in the classical world, but has been followed in our time in the criticism of Tacitus and Suetonius.[1]

Leopardi wrote his entry on Tiberius in Bologna in 1826; but since the *Zibaldone* was not published till 1898 he did not influence Salvatore Betti (1792–1882) on the road to scepticism. It could have been Micali who persuaded him, in 1839, to dismiss the story, rather the legend, of Romulus;[2] while later, in 1864, he defended Tiberius against 'le tante favole della piazza raccolte al solito, nuovo Teopompo, da Svetonio e provvedutone l'amico Tacito'.[3] He foresees the need to write the history of the Roman emperors without the compulsion of Tacitus' account. But if he leaves that for others, for Mommsen and his wake, he did apply his acumen to another author who had seemed gospel before. This was in *Intorno a Sallustio* (1854). Here we might put into reverse what Machiavelli quoted from Sallust: 'omnia mala exempla a bonis initiis orta sunt'. For now in the case of Sallust 'omnes bonae sententiae a malis initiis ortae sunt'. I mean that Betti considers first the character of Sallust and deduces that all his noble maxims are a show of empty rhetoric, and that we cannot trust his evidence: 'Quamvis iurato metuam tibi credere testi'.[4] The case is against Sallust's version of the Jugurthine war, with his gravamen of the corruption of the patrician class of Rome. Here he can quote the *Catilina* to show from Sallust himself that the degeneracy came after Sulla, and that before him ambition more than avarice was the ruling passion ('Sed primo magis ambitio, quam avaritia, animos hominum exercebat...Sed postquam L. Sylla...rapere omnes, trahere...').[5] Then he defends Scaurus against the imputations of Sallust, finds reverence for him in Cicero, finds him an example of rectitude in Valerius Maximus, with praise from Horace and Juvenal (who puts Scaurus with Cato and Fabricius), and offers us the choice between these witnesses and Sallust. And then, the *coup de grâce*, he looks at the celebrated *mot* of Jugurtha himself, retreating from Rome: 'Urbem venalem et mature perituram si emptorem invenerit.'[6] With what righteous indignation has it not echoed down the centuries! But who overheard it? And did

---

[1] Treves, *Studio*, p. 501.
[2] *Ibid.* p. 544.
[3] *Ibid.* pp. 545–6.
[4] *Ibid.* p. 559.
[5] *Ibid.* p. 565, quoting Sallust, *Catilina* II. iy.
[6] *Ibid.* p. 581.

not all the circumstances belie it? Had he not tried in vain himself to buy it, according to Sallust, and failed in his attempt? Was he not fleeing from that failure, to meet the force of Roman arms? And look how Sallust embellishes the unlikely tale, with that *saepe tacitus respiciens*, and smudges it with a *fertur*, to show that it could have no basis.[1] We shall find the same scepticism, more hilariously executed, in Manzoni against Tacitus; but here let us note Betti's reproaches against Sallust:

While I admire his great powers as a writer I cannot not regret that in imitating Cato he did not imitate him also by having on his lips what was in his mind and heart: as did particularly that supreme austere Roman, whose words on the sacred page of literature were never belied by his life.[2]

I would ask you to reserve our position with regard to Cato, for his reputation is also up for demolition by Manzoni. But I think we should look first to one whose works have often seemed suspect on the surface, or different from the reality of his feelings. This is Vincenzo Monti. We may think, *sbrigativamente*, that he was well dismissed by De Sanctis, when he said that classicism 'muore rumorosamente ne' sonanti versi del Monti'; or by that contemptuous phrase of the Austrian monarch, that he had praised all in turn. Or we may feel that any rescue operation must be limited to him as a cultural force, and that his only real poetry (as it has been said) is in the translation of the *Iliad*. Certainly, we are unlikely to repeat the claim made in 1832 that he was the sun of the *Bassvilliana* which flooded the horizon of Italy with a light which will last for ever, or as long as the names of Homer, Virgil, Dante.[3] And I think we may view with some distaste the fact that Monti is sufficiently backward-looking to view mythology as the staple for poetry. Witness his defence of Parini's tortured periphrasis for almond-flour: 'if you don't know mythology, and the metamorphosis of Rhodope, you will never guess – but in that case, don't read poetry!' ('chi non la sa non legga poeti, molto meno s'ardisca di giudicarli!').[4] But against this, an obscurantism destined to perish, we may note with sympathy that he never indulged in the sterile exercise of composing verses in the Latin tongue, agreeing tacitly here with Giordani. And we may sympathise with him in his predicaments, or at the least, in one of them. He fled from papal Rome, and from his fame as the author of the *Bassvilliana*,

[1] *Ibid.* p. 582.   [2] *Ibid.* 559.
[3] Vincenzo Monti, *Opere inedite e rare* (6 vols., Milano, 1832), vol. I, p. xxix.
[4] *Ibid.* vol. III, p. 279.

to the new republican north of Italy. 'Sognai', he said, 'd'essere venuto alle nozze d'una bella e casta vergine, e mi sono svegliato fra le braccia d'una laida meretrice.'[1] He expressed this dilemma in the best of his three plays, *Caio Gracco*, which was conceived in 1778, and completed in 1800.

Before I come to *Caio Gracco* I would like to offer you two prophets, neither I think much recognised. The first is Emanuele Duni, whose book *Origine, e progressi del cittadino e del governo di Roma* was published at Rome in 1763–4 (almost coeval with the *Contrat social* of 1762). While the official line is that of Dante (the providentiality of both the Romes, the lesser miracle, attested to by Virgil, Livy, Cicero, leading to the major one – see once again that ending to the *Notti romane* of Alessandro Verri), Emanuele Duni is concerned with the sociology of Rome: not its virtues as a unifying power, but the flaws of its social structure. There are two passages, one from each of his two volumes, which I wish to quote:

> The Roman plebs were born in servitude to the patricians: they lived for long in this wretched state; then by means of ripening opportunity and contingencies their coarse minds awakened, they began to reflect on the pure law of humanity which recognises no reasons for inequality between man and man, they became conscious of their true condition uniform to all, and of the injustice which they suffered, so naturally they sought all means to shake off the yoke, or rather to reach that same status in which they saw their Patricians, as men of their own nature.[2]

These are the basic principles on which 1789 will call. The passage from the second volume draws the prophetic consequence:

> All these considerations show us that for lack of civil means the plebs will have recourse to the last resort of rebellion, as happens also in absolute monarchies, in which the subjects cannot enjoy true civil liberty, as something which depends only on the arbitrary will of the monarch, so that when they find themselves oppressed by tyranny, with no other way of saving their natural liberty, they turn to nature's means, that is to say, they defend themselves by violence.[3]

It is at this point that I should insert Monti's *Caio Gracco*, since its context and content is the conflict between this basic desire for justice, and the violence resulting from its absence, from which justice cannot come. But for the sake of keeping my prophets together, where they belong by time, let me give you first the resolution of the dilemma, the clearest prophecy of Napoleon. The

---

[1] *Ibid.* vol. I, p. xxxii.
[2] Emanuele Duni, *Origine, e progressi del cittadino e del governo di Roma* (2 vols., Roma, 1763–4), vol. I, p. 180.   [3] *Ibid.* vol. II, p. 213.

author is a French one, but I am using the Italian translation of 1766, close, as you see, to Duni. This is the Abbé de Mably, in his *Osservazioni sopra i Romani*, and he is applying to the present the lesson of the failure of ancient states to stop the progress to domination of the Roman people:

Should there arise presently some Power in Europe whose forces are superior to those of any particular State, and who exceeds them all in the goodness of its military discipline and its experience in war; and if this Power conduct itself always with the same principles, without letting itself be dazzled by its successes, or cast down by adversities...then one will see very soon the disappearance of those leagues, confederations, alliances, by which each State preserves its independence. Note carefully: our modern policies are the work of two passions, the one of which is fear, which inspires anxiety over some People which wishes to dominate; the other is the hope of resisting it, since it does not have the qualities or the means to subjugate everybody. Destroy this hope by means of wisdom and courage, nothing will remain but fear, and then Europe will not be long in losing its liberty.[1]

In Emanuele Duni the line is drawn which leads to the French Revolution; in the Abbé de Mably there is the mechanism for the succeeding phase, for the hegemony of Napoleon. And to return to that disillusioned phrase of Monti, the tragedy of *Caio Gracco* lies in between the two. It could have sprung from a reading of the *Origine, e progressi del cittadino e del governo di Roma*, for its theme is the struggle of the Roman plebs against their oppression by the patrician class. In this struggle Caio Gracco is the great protagonist, but he is also the idealist, who acts only by, and for, the law. As such he is doomed from the start:

> DRUSO Console, bada: temerario e fiero
> E bollente è quel cor.
> OPIMIO   Ma generoso,
> Ma leal. Sua virtú mi fa sicuro
> Di sua caduta.[2]

Here, out of the classical world, there opens up the path to the romantic hero: the Conte di Carmagnola and Adelchi are both waiting in the wings. Nor will you miss the connection back with that rise to prominence of Lucan. Or, if you have, Caio will make it clear for you, where he confronts the leader of the Senate, Opimio:

> CAIO Per te il Senato è tutto, il popol nulla.
> Ben io ti dico, che mia patria è quella
> Che nel popolo sta. Piace agli Dei

---

[1] Abate de Mably, *Osservazioni sopra i Romani* (2 vols., Venezia, 1766), vol. II, p. xxiv.
[2] Monti, *Caio Gracco*, in *Tragedie* (Firenze, 1816), II.i.141–2.

Del Senato la causa? A Gracco piace
La causa della plebe.[1]

I offered Monti before as an encourager to Cassi to translate the
Pharsalia, but here he is its customer. And though it is not explicit in
what Caio says, yet it is immediately obvious from the source that the
victrix causa is that of the Senate, and the *victa* that of Caio Gracco.
And this carries with it Lucan's judgement on the gods. It comes in
the scene between the mother of the Gracchi and the wife of Caio:

> CORNELIA   Alto è il periglio
> Del tuo consorte, ma piú alto, credi,
> Il suo coraggio; e vi son numi in cielo.
> LICINIA Sí, ma non giusti.[2]

et tantum miseris irasci numina possunt.[3]

I have omitted so far the mechanism of Caio's defeat. Its principal
author is Fulvio, who is on his side but who sees the need to meet
violence with violence; and who is also tainted by the fact that he has
an adulterous passion for Caio's sister who is married to Aemilianus
Scipio. And Janus-like, the accusation that he makes against
Emiliano (whom he has already killed) looks backward to that
non-exemplary view of Roman history, which began for us with
Micali, and forward to the dismissal of the classical world as exemplary in any way by Manzoni. You serve my cause with crimes, says
Caio. And you forget, says Fulvio, those of the proud Scipio whom
I have killed. And here there is rehearsed that siege of Numantia,
with four hundred boys sent back to their parents with stumps
instead of hands, and the indiscriminate slaughter at Carthage.[4]
Caio appeals to justice, Fulvio leaps forward into violence. But we
are concerned with more than their fate. If we looked again at the
Abbé de Mably we should find him quoting approvingly out of Livy
those Roman habits of magnanimity: 'Plus pene parcendo victis
quam vincendo imperium auxisse.'[5] When we last met the proud
lines out of Virgil, which chime with Livy, it was in the context of
Sulla and the seven thousand throats he cut. Here they re-echo,

---

[1] *Ibid.* II.iv.150.
[2] *Ibid.* v.v.220.
[3] Lucan III.449.
[4] *Caio Gracco* II.viii.157.
[5] *Osservazioni sopra i Romani,* vol. II, p. 168. To this optimistic quotation from Livy xxx the
Abbé de Mably adds another: 'Qui beneficio quam metu obligare homines malit
exterasque gentes fide a societate junctas habere, quam tristi subjectas servitio' (Livy
XXVI).

coupled with this episode of the four hundred boy hostages, and the sack of Carthage:

> Erano barbare genti, eran nemiche;
> Ma disarmate, imbelli e lagrimanti
> E chiedenti mercede: e la romana
> Virtú comanda perdonare ai vinti,
> Debellar i superbi.[1]

When we think of all those noble pictures of the *Continence of Scipio* we realise that we have turned the corner into a different world.

It is easy, indeed natural, to dismiss Monti as one who bends before every wind. But there is one obstacle to this satisfactory assumption of moral superiority. This is his translation of Persius (1803), and his account of his own attitude not only to Persius, but also to Horace and Juvenal, which will be found in the long note to *Satire* v. Now his Persius is an episode normally passed over quickly, as either a chore or an aberration. But it appears very differently in Monti's words:

We love, we esteem ourselves in the books that please us most, and we reveal unintentionally in this the secrets of our heart. A literary judgement, especially where a moral element is present, is very often only a gratuitously imprudent manifestation of something which lurks within us.[2]

And what is Monti's literary judgement on the satirists? It is the austerity of Persius, and the non-austerity of Horace. 'L'uno in somma è il catechismo della virtú, l'altro è l'apostolo della mollezza e il breviario de' cortigiani.'[3] On these terms he chooses Persius; and we may note that he hereby distances himself from Metastasio, whose translations include *Satires* from Horace, and none from Persius. It is not that Monti makes the mistake of equating Persius artistically with either Horace or Juvenal: but they wrote in their maturity, and Persius in his youth. And he adds a reflection on Juvenal which may make us pause with regard to himself and his panegyrics for Napoleon: 'Poetry, alas, has often divinised tyranny. Juvenal has expiated this crime: he has paid the debt contracted against right by Virgil and Horace.'[4] And what of that contracted by Monti? Then there is the stylistic appreciation of Persius, which comes strangely from the mellifluous Monti, with his acreage of presentable verse. It is the sharpness and the swiftness of Persius which he recommends to

---

[1] *Caio Gracco* II.viii.158.
[2] Vincenzo Monti, *Satire di A. Persio Flacco* (Firenze, 1826), p. 117.
[3] *Ibid.* p. 107. [4] *Ibid.* p. 116.

us, not like Horace, 'ma piú acre, piú rapido, piú unito': and for its characterisation he finds a comparison surprising at this date. In the rapidity of his touch Persius is like Caravaggio. But his justification lies *in the sacred and eternal rights of virtue against vice*:

> Quin damus id superis, de magna quod dare lance
> non possit magni Messalae lippa propago?
> Compositum jus, fasque animi, sanctosque recessus
> mentis, et incoctum generoso pectus honesto.[1]

When I seek the canons of taste, I go to Horace: when I need spleen against the crimes of mankind, I visit Juvenal: when I strive to live in honesty, I stay with Persius; and old as I now am, with infinite pleasure mingled with shame, I drink the dictates of reason on the lips of this *verecondo e santissimo giovanetto*.[2]

I would recommend to you (especially if perhaps you have been disappointed with the celebrated translation of the *Iliad*) the muscular version of Persius; and most particularly the dozen pages of the note to *Satire* v, which gives us a different view of Monti from what we are led elsewhere to expect.

We began with the total non-criticism of Dante, and we end, symmetrically, with the total criticism of Manzoni. Dante began what Treves calls the *inveramento cattolico del retaggio pagano*,[3] and Manzoni destroys it. His demolition is in the notes he wrote to his copy of Rollin's *Histoire romaine*,[4] where the heroes whom we know – such as Cato, Scipio – meet exemplary dismissal; and where our author Lucan finds an equally irrefutable reproof. If you find the *Promessi sposi* long and prosy, I would suggest you pick up the notes to Rollin, where you will find Manzoni always acute enough to correct Rollin on points of interpretation, and unflagging in rebutting the praise which Rollin lavishes on the protagonists of Rome: as the vaunted stoicism of Cato, caught in the act of striking a slave so hard in the mouth that his hand is covered with blood; or the same Cato, refusing to enlist slaves in his force because this would interfere with the rights of their proprietors. And Scipio:

'Je ne dois pas omettre ici un nouveau trait de la générosité et du désintéressement de Scipion...' says Rollin.

'Un nouveau trait de la générosité, après celui qui se trouve au bout de la page antécédente, est incroyable...' answers Manzoni.[5]

And the page he is referring to takes us back to Fulvio in *Caio Gracco*, and those four hundred boys with their hands chopped off. The

---

[1] *Ibid.* p. 90 (Persius II.71).   [2] *Ibid.* p. 119.
[3] Treves, *Studio*, p. 388 (on Angelo Mai's *Ragionamento* of 1837 for the Anniversary of the Foundation of Rome).
[4] Published in full in Treves, *Studio*, pp. 596–651.   [5] *Ibid.* p. 625.

demolition of the *reportage* of Sallust that we saw accomplished by Salvatore Betti Manzoni does hilariously for Tacitus, when Rollin's successor Crevier takes as literally true the speech which Tacitus had written for Calgacus:

en ces termes me paraît trop décidé; car, quoiqu'on doive croire que le discours aura été dans le moniteur breton, tel qu'il avait été prononcé (antiqua simplicitate) et que Tacite l'aura traduit fidèlement, il est toujours constant que le même Tacite dit: in hunc modum locutus fertur.[1]

And in case I should have confused you as to priorities, let me say that Manzoni's notes date from *c.* 1802. As for Lucan, he had presumed to regret the waste of Roman blood at Pharsalia, when it might have been employed more reasonably in vengeance for Crassus, in the conquest of the world. Manzoni makes the calculation that, combined, the Roman armies might have taken on three hundred thousand barbarians, 'on aurait une bataille de 300 m. hommes au lieu d'une de 70 m.: que ce serait plus philosophique! et encore pour achever la conquête de l'univers, ce qui l'est au dernier point!'[2] And he caps this with the next reflection on Rollin, who noted the clemency of Caesar when victory was assured, and he 'ordonna à ses soldats d'épargner le citoyen et de ne tuer que l'étranger'. 'Quel Romain que ce Rollin!' comments Manzoni, 'voyez comme il a bien compris que de ne tuer que l'étranger, c'est de la clémence.'[3]

In the intransigently Christian view of Dante, all the Roman virtues were projected into the divine preparation of Christian Rome; in the intransigently Christian view of Manzoni, they are all cancelled as having no connection with that sole superiority of any man over others, which consists in doing them some service. There is a lot which I leave reluctantly unquoted in these notes of Manzoni to his Rollin. But if I have half a minute left before the bell expunges me I should like to devote it to a not irrelevant suggestion. Virgil in a famous passage in the *Georgics* writes:

Me vero primum dulces ante omnia Musae
quarum sacra fero ingenti perculsus amore
accipiant, caelique vias et sidera monstrent,
defectus solis varios, lunaeque labores.[4]

I have often been puzzled by what seemed to me a lack of logic, a *non sequitur*, in that passage from the realm of poetry to the dry pheno-

---

[1] *Ibid.* p. 611.
[2] *Ibid.* p. 641.
[3] *Ibid.*
[4] Virgil, *Georgics* ii.475.

mena of astronomy. Then I realised that the conquest of culture as the appanage of the muses, just as real a conquest as that of space in Alberti's *De pictura*, is the work of the Renascence; whose principle is not the imitation of antiquity as so often, and so foolishly, advertised, but – what is very different – the absorption of antiquity. So that if Petrarch were to rewrite this passage from the *Georgics* he would throw out the labours of the moon, which never, I believe, interested him at all, and put in Virgil, Livy, Cicero. Europe lived long enough on this splendid legacy from the past as the main staple of its culture; and again we might take a line from Lucan to suggest the endless continuation of this process:

saecula Romanos numquam tacitura labores.[1]

In all the diverse efforts, which I have tried to illustrate, to dismiss the Roman world, or to reduce it to an ordinary, fallible and unheroic level, there is one constant that I have not so far pointed out: it is this uniform concern with the classical world. Even in the death throes of what is only one conception, or one content, of culture, we can sense the strength of the fixation which had held all Europe for so long.

[1] Lucan viii.622.

8

JEAN-JACQUES ROUSSEAU AND THE MYTH OF ANTIQUITY IN THE EIGHTEENTH CENTURY*

R. A. LEIGH

I

Anyone who has the slightest familiarity with the atmosphere of Revolutionary France must have been struck by a singular, if superficial, paradox. On the one hand, those early years of revolutionary fervour are characterised by a millennial, even a messianic, sense of a new beginning, of which the most spectacular, though not the most permanent symbol is the introduction of a new calendar, and the inauguration of a new era. The year 1 heralded a new epoch for mankind in the now certain march towards Utopia: whilst the poetic rhapsody of the Revolutionary calendar seemed an earnest of the spontaneous and unsullied idealism of the new republic.

On the other hand, the fervour of those times was also characterised by awareness of a return to an ancient tradition, of which the French revolutionaries clearly believed they were the legitimate heirs: a return, that is to say, to the civic virtues of classical antiquity. In the speeches, the painting and sculpture, the decorative and applied arts, the fashions, the coiffure, even the bookbinding of the

---

* *Bibliographical note.* Mme Denise Leduc-Fayette has written a scholarly and interesting book on this subject (*J.-J. Rousseau et le mythe de l'antiquité*, Paris, 1974), which deals with many of the matters raised here, but at far greater length than was possible in a brief discussion. However, I have not drawn on it as heavily as I had hoped to do, since I agree neither with her view of the rôle of the myth in Rousseau's thought nor with her interpretation of Rousseau's political theory.

There is a large and growing literature on the influence of classical writers on Rousseau (which, of course, is not the subject of this paper). A useful bibliography will be found in Mme Leduc-Fayette's book.

The following sigla are used in my notes:

Pléiade: Jean-Jacques Rousseau, *Œuvres complètes*, ed. Bernard Gagnebin and Marcel Raymond (Paris: Gallimard, 1959–). (Four volumes have so far appeared.)

Leigh: Jean-Jacques Rousseau, *Correspondance complète*, ed. R. A. Leigh (Geneva–Oxford, 1965–). (Thirty-one volumes have so far appeared.)

I should add that, except for the restoration of one or two minor cuts, and the addition of the notes (which are, of course, illustrative rather than exhaustive), this paper is printed exactly as given at the colloquium.

time, and for many years afterwards, we see and hear little but *les anciens*. No-one thought then of echoing the irreverent jibe of Molière: 'Les anciens sont les anciens et nous sommes les gens de maintenant.' Such a pert witticism would have seemed almost sacrilegious. And so we are not at all surprised to discover that the hall in which the Convention met, and in which Fabre d'Eglantine, to almost universal acclaim, unveiled his new calendar, was itself a silent tribute to the republican ideals of Greece and Rome. A bust of Brutus occupied a conspicuous position, and the walls were adorned with portraits of Lycurgus, Solon, Cincinnatus and other worthies. Right to the end of his career, the great Robespierre, both in the Jacobin Club and in the Convention, saw himself (or chose to project himself) as the spokesman of the cult. In a long and important speech, delivered on 5 February 1794, he asked: 'What is the fundamental principle of democratic or popular government, that is, the essential mainspring that supports and drives it forward?' and he answered: 'It is virtue; and I mean that public virtue which performed such miracles in Greece and Rome.'[1] More significantly still perhaps, on 26 July 1794, on the eve of his overthrow, he exclaimed, in defence of his policies: 'If I must conceal these truths, then bring me the hemlock!'[2] Today, it would be difficult to think of a member of a democratic legislature risking such a bald allusion: but it was fully intelligible to Robespierre's audience, and needed neither context nor elaboration.[3]

Here surely is a phenomenon worthy of investigation: but since our terms of reference are to explore rather than to exhaust our topics (an exhortation which I gladly obey) I shall confine myself to suggesting one or two lines of approach.

As we all know, education in eighteenth-century France, as elsewhere, meant a classical education, with the emphasis on Latin

---

[1] 'Or, quel est le principe fondamental du gouvernement démocratique ou populaire, c'est-à-dire le ressort essentiel qui le soutient et le fait mouvoir? C'est la vertu; je parle de la vertu publique qui opéra tant de prodiges dans la Grèce et dans Rome, et qui doit en produire de bien plus étonnans dans la France républicaine; de cette vertu qui n'est autre chose que l'amour de la patrie et de ses lois...' (*Œuvres de Maximilien Robespierre* (Nancy, 1930–), vol. x, p. 352). The rest of the speech contains some illustrations from ancient history.

[2] 'S'il faut que je dissimule ces vérités, qu'on m'apporte la ciguë!' (*ibid.* p. 566). Cf. a cancelled passage (p. 567, n. 1): 'qu'ils me préparent la ciguë...'.

[3] It would be easy to add similar instances. Perhaps one more will suffice. Mirabeau, defending himself at a critical and stormy meeting of the Jacobin Club held on 28 February 1791, declared: 'Je resterai parmi vous jusqu'à l'ostracisme' (Louis Barthou, *Mirabeau* (Paris, 1913), p. 284).

rather than on Greek. But classical authors were not studied and taught exclusively, or even largely, on purely aesthetic or general cultural grounds. Classical authors were studied with didactic and ethical preoccupations in mind. The history and literature of Greece and Rome were regarded as a vast treasure-house of moral precepts, of exalted characters and exemplary attitudes.

This was particularly true in eighteenth-century France, where the régime, though not reaching anything like the depths of depravity we have witnessed elsewhere in our time, was arbitrary, corrupt and unjust; and so gave an additional dimension to moral approaches to the study of ancient literature, history and institutions. This further dimension, already implicit in the school-room, was extended by what is apt to seem nowadays an odd quirk of cultural history. In Paris, and to a certain extent in the provinces, the minds of the educated, and even of the uneducated, were conditioned by the unrivalled, and indeed almost unchallenged, sway of neo-classical aesthetics, particularly in the theatre. For more than a century, any serious play with the slightest pretension to literary merit made use of a Greco-Latin décor and exploited scenes and situations from ancient history: a convention only partly undermined from about 1760 onwards. Roman politics, Roman history, Roman heroism, Roman-style *sententiae*, were more familiar to the average French playgoer than contemporary affairs, the discussion of which was effectively inhibited by lack of information and of freedom of expression. The ancient world provided an alternative to the present, an alternative which afforded a welcome amount of intellectual elbow-room.[1] And so it was that, for moral exemplars and heroic prototypes, the mind of an educated eighteenth-century Frenchman turned naturally to Greece and Rome. Just one instance among many: when in the 1760s Paoli raised the standard of national independence in Corsica, and became the idol of every European liberal, a future member of the Convention, who was eventually to vote for the death of Louis XVI, but was then chafing in the humiliating obscurity of a petty Italian court, referred to the liberator of Corsica as 'cet homme antique de nos temps modernes'.[2]

---

[1] The custodians of orthodoxy were occasionally awakened by too strident a use of this subterfuge, even if the royal censors slumbered on; as in the case of *Bélisaire* (1767), a mediocre and comparatively inoffensive tale by Marmontel, which discussed sensitive contemporary political and theological issues in an antique setting.

[2] Alexandre Deleyre, letter to Rousseau of 21 April 1766, in Leigh, vol. XXIX, p. 129, no. 5166, para. 4.

By this time the myth of antiquity was firmly established, and provided an effective frame of reference to which anyone could appeal. But what exactly was the myth of antiquity? The answer to this question takes us back, of course, to antiquity itself: for it is common knowledge that by the end of the first century, and no doubt earlier, the ancient world had invented a myth about itself. In its most conspicuous form, the myth can be observed in the works of Plutarch, Livy and Tacitus, in Sallust, and in a number of quite minor writers once widely read (Aulus Gellius, Valerius Maximus, Dio Cassius).

Briefly, it consisted in the belief that in the early days of the Roman and Greek republics, men were brave, hardy, upright, self-sacrificing, frugal, austere, brimming over with the domestic virtues and above all imbued with zeal for the common good. A convenient stage in the development of the myth can be observed in Plutarch's *Life of Lycurgus*, where of course he was writing some eight or nine hundred years after the event; or in the work of Livy, who again was writing several hundred years after most of the stirring deeds and interesting speeches which he records verbatim. Nor is it, of course, without significance that Plutarch and Livy were writing at a time when the greatness of Greece was irretrievably lost and the liberties of Rome irretrievably compromised. In eighteenth-century France, this myth of antiquity about itself, now raised to the second degree, constituted an imposing tapestry or pageant representing the glory and grandeur of the human spirit; a pageant peopled with the exhortatory but somewhat reproachful figures of Regulus, Scaevola, Scipio, Brutus, Solon, Aristides, and so on. But the greatest heroes of the myth in eighteenth-century France were Socrates and Cato: Socrates, the prototype of the Sage, done to death by a stupid and corrupt society; Cato, the quintessence of virtue and patriotism, the model of the 'antique Roman'. In a century which was swinging steadily away from Christianity, Socrates and Cato became the two principal saints in the free-thinker's calendar. Their bibliography and iconography in this period are both extensive and revealing.[1]

Perhaps I ought to say a word at this point about the power of mythical thinking, thinking in terms of myth. Myths embody perennial human aspirations which are, of course, perennially

---

[1] It is not always clear, however, which of the two Catos is meant: cf. Claude Pichois and R. Pintard, *Jean-Jacques entre Socrate et Caton* (Paris, 1972), p. 85.

frustrated: and it is from this antinomy that they derive their strength and their efficacy. Behind the façade of the myth of classical antiquity, there lies a more far-reaching series of myths, all of which tell of a time buried deep in the remote past of humanity, and which, in their different ways, all express the revulsion of men from the contingencies, the cares and the corrupt compromises of a degrading present, their recoil from all those 'black ingrainéd spots which will not leave their tinct'. The classical Golden Age, the biblical garden of Eden, the various kinds of noble savage, the South Sea paradise – all convey man's longing to escape into a world where everyone is healthy, happy, innocent and free. The quasi-historical myth of classical antiquity had the great merit of giving some of these aspirations a local habitation and a name, a spurious realism and a precise identity. No-one in modern times could believe literally in Prometheus punished by the gods for benefiting humanity: everyone could believe quite literally the secular version of Socrates, a real person, punished by society for attempting to enlighten it.

I lack both time and competence to deal with the evolution of this powerful fiction from the time of its resuscitation in the Renaissance to the eighteenth century, with which I am principally concerned. The story was no doubt somewhat different in different countries. In England, it was perhaps a tradition rather than a cult. But even in this country, we find Horatio declaring himself, on the verge of a sympathetic suicide, to be 'more an antique Roman than a Dane': and Shakespeare's Brutus, we learn, if it were a question of the general good, could set honour in one eye and death in the other, and look on them both indifferently, for he loved the name of honour more than he feared death. It is also true that Addison's *Cato* at the beginning of the eighteenth century struck a topical note in the context of the political squabbles of the day, and descanted on antique virtues to such effect that it roused its first audiences to a frenzy. And as late as the 1730s, Voltaire could inform his fellow-countrymen that 'English Members of Parliament like to compare themselves as often as possible to the ancient Romans.'[1] But in England the myth had less momentum than in France, perhaps because it was thought there was less of a contrast between Roman and British liberty. In France, however, the grandeur of the Roman soul and the virtues of the Roman republic became the stock in trade

---

[1] 'les membres du Parlement d'Angleterre aiment à se comparer aux anciens Romains autant qu'ils le peuvent' (*Letters philosophiques* (1734), lettre VIII).

of a wide spectrum of reformers and enthusiasts.[1] Robespierre's words in 1794 echo the strange but significant analyses of Montesquieu's *Esprit des Lois* nearly half a century earlier. For Montesquieu, the 'mainspring' (*ressort*) of the ancient republics is 'virtue' as against the 'terror' of despotism and the 'honour' of monarchy. 'Virtue' in Montesquieu was a chord of great resonance, striking mainly the note of integrity, but arousing also the pseudo-historical harmonics of justice, equality and frugality, and above all love of one's country, willingness to sacrifice private interest to the common good. Whatever Montesquieu's intentions may have been, for most of his readers his model republic wore a political and social halo borrowed from antiquity which set it apart from all other forms of political association.

II

In the life and work of J.-J. Rousseau, however, the myth enters a new phase. I say 'life and work' because in his case it is characteristically difficult to separate the two: he was not only a propagandist for the myth but also a part of it. Merging with his own personal legend, it becomes a myth raised as it were to the third power, and he himself becomes a leading figure in it. Two factors contributed to bring this about: the cultural context of the city in which he grew up, and the special character of his mission as a writer.

First of all, it must be remembered that Rousseau was not a Frenchman. He was not even a Swiss, as we might think of him today: that would be a gross anachronism. He was very much a citizen of the free and independent republic of Geneva, and he always went out of his way to call himself precisely that until in 1762 his native city blotted her copy-book by condemning his two great works, *Émile* and the *Contrat social*, to be lacerated and burnt by the common hangman.

---

[1] It is tempting to connect with this phenomenon the considerable interest shown in the laws and institutions of antiquity, some of it discreetly tendentious: e.g.

'*Par quelles causes et par quels degrés les loix de Lycurgue se sont altérées chez les Lacédémoniens, jusqu'à ce qu'elles aient été anéanties*... par M. Mathion de la Cour le fils. 100 pages in 8⁰ imprimées...avec permission tacite' (manuscript *Journal* of Joseph d'Hémery, inspector of the book-trade; Paris, Bibliothèque nationale, MS. fr. 22164, fol. 110r, 27 August 1767); or again: '*La République Romaine où plan général de l'ancien gouvernement de Rome ou l'on developpe les differens Ressorts de ce gouvernement, l'Influence qu'y avoit la Religion; la Souveraineté du peuple Et la maniere dont il l'exerçoit; qu'elle étoit l'autorité du senat et celle des Magistrats, l'administration de la Justice, les prérogatives du Citoyen romain et les différen te conditions des sujets de ce vaste Empire*. 6 vol. in 12⁰ imprimés...avec approbation et privilege' (*ibid.* fol. 54r, 25 September 1766, and fol. 106, 6 August 1767).

The importance of Rousseau's origin and allegiance can hardly be over-estimated. Geneva was a city-state, far smaller of course then in both population and extent than it is today. For most of the eighteenth century, the population of Geneva was under 20,000 and its territory (to be doubled by the Congress of Vienna) not only covered less than half its present area but was split up by potentially dangerous enclaves. It was much smaller, then, than Athens, Sparta or early republican Rome; but being, like them, a city-state, it tended to see its political and social problems in similar terms. By the beginning of the eighteenth century, Geneva had become the scene of what was to be a long and obstinate struggle for power. The government of the city was as peculiar as its political structure. Out of a total population of just under 20,000, only 1,600 (males of course) had any semblance of political rights. These were the *Citoyens* and *Bourgeois*, whom I shall call Citizens for short. The rest, *Habitants* or *Natifs* (the *Natifs* were the children of *Habitants* born in the city), not only had no say in the government, but they were also socially and economically oppressed, for they were not allowed to exercise the more lucrative or prestigious trades or professions: those were all reserved for the Citizens. The 1,600 citizens in theory made up the sovereign body: but the authority of this assembly had become quite illusory. All effective power was concentrated in the hands of a narrow oligarchy, a council of twenty-five, in principle elective, but in reality self-perpetuating, and recruited exclusively from a group of wealthy families connected by inter-marriage, many of them bankers or merchants with far-ranging international interests. The history of eighteenth-century Geneva is the history of the struggle for power between the 1,600 citizens and the oligarchic Petit Conseil. It was a stormy history; and it is pertinent to recall that eighteenth-century Geneva had as many, if not more, revolutions and changes of régime than nineteenth-century France, and was often precariously poised on the brink of civil war. If the theatre was small, passions were intense, sometimes ferocious: and much may be learnt from the struggle. As a historian of this university has sagely remarked: 'It is neither uninteresting nor uninstructive to see men imitating on a small stage the warfare of the great world and striving to attain their petty ambitions with as much fury and as little scruple as if contending for empires.'[1]

[1] D. A. Winstanley, *The University of Cambridge in the Eighteenth Century* (Cambridge, 1958), p. 2.

The intense political ferment in eighteenth-century Geneva was one of the factors, then, which made the intellectual climate there very different from that of eighteenth-century France. Another difference was that the cultural level in Geneva was unusually high. The city had both a college and a university in which Latin played a conspicuous part. The Citizens were not only litigious and belligerent in defence of their rights, like Burke's Americans 'snuffing the approach of tyranny in every tainted breeze', they were also intelligent, highly articulate and unusually literate. When one considers the extraordinary stream of scientists, scholars, jurists, doctors and theologians, many of them with international reputations, produced by eighteenth-century Geneva, one can readily understand why the Citizens tended to think of their republic as a modern Athens, though in their struggle against the oligarchy, they cast themselves rather in the rôle of the Roman plebs bursting the shackles fastened on them by the patricians. So many aspects of life in eighteenth-century Geneva, in fact, invited a parallel with early republican Rome – not just the fact of being a city-state, not just republican patriotism, austerity and virtue, partly underpinned by calvinism; but also a certain amount of social detail. Geneva, for instance, had its sumptuary laws, only just beginning to slide into abeyance, and an active 'censorship' in the Roman sense, that is to say a close supervision of morals and even of manners, actively monitored by a vigilant Consistory. Geneva had its Senate and its patricians, its Syndics were thought of as Tribunes. So the citizens of Geneva, in their struggle for power, seized on the parallel with the ancients, resorted to the vocabulary of justice, integrity, patriotism, liberty and equality, which they derived from Plutarch and the Roman historians, and harped on the antique virtues which had made their city great. They unfortunately forgot about the *Habitants* and the *Natifs*, who formed the majority of the population. These, of course, listened to the debate with growing interest, took the terminology literally, and finally, to the dismay of the Citizens, who found themselves attacked in the rear with their own weapons, pressed for inclusion in the democratic scheme of things.

In Geneva, then, the myth of antiquity was particularly potent. Foreign observers, too, saw its citizens as the heirs of Greece and Rome, sometimes ironically, sometimes not. For instance, in March 1766, when French troops were poised to enter the city in order to bolster up the oligarchy threatened by the civic resistance of the

Citizens, a minor French *littérateur* wrote to a French diplomatic agent in the city: 'I suppose that all these Genevan squabbles must resemble quite closely those of ancient, very ancient Rome...'[1]

That was how outsiders saw the Genevans, and more to the point that was how the Genevans saw themselves.[2] A little later in the year, one of the leaders of the Genevan Citizens, J.-F. Deluc, appealed to the famous Bernese scientist, Haller, to use his influence on their behalf. Haller had expressed democratic sentiments in his youth, but, unknown to Deluc, had since become a diehard conservative. Their correspondence (which is unpublished) is instructive, for it is conducted to an interesting extent in terms of ancient history.[3]

---

[1] 'Je m'imagine que tous ces demeslés de Genève ne ressemblent point mal à ceux de l'ancienne, très-ancienne Rome, quand les nobles, qui partout ont été insolens, vouloient à leur plaisir pouvoir donner cent coups d'étrivières au peuple qui ne payoit pas ses dettes' (A.-L. Thomas to Pierre de Taulès, in Leigh, vol. xxix, p. 161, no. 5178, note *s*).

Unlike Taulès, a careerist who came down heavily, not to say brutally, on the side of authority against the turbulent Genevans, Thomas was saturated with the myth of antiquity. In his *Discours de réception à l'Académie française* (delivered on 22 January 1767) he made great play with the wisdom of Socrates and the heroism of Roman soldiers.

[2] Even the theologians of Geneva, who might have been expected to exhibit considerable reservations about pagan virtues, were impressed by the parallel between Geneva and the ancient republics. We find Jacob Vernet, the principal pillar of orthodoxy in mid-eighteenth-century Geneva, writing 'm'intéressant comme je le fais aux Républiques modernes qui ont quelque rapport avec celles de l'ancienne Grèce', and illustrating his points with a great array of allusions and quotations from Tacitus, Livy and others (*Lettres critiques d'un voyageur anglois* (1763; reprinted several times), lettre xii).

The laymen were even more enthusiastic. An anonymous citizen writes in 1770: 'J'en reviens toûjours aux loix des Grecs & des Romains' (*Lettre d'un Genevois à Monsieur Burlamaqui sur l'éducation* (Berlin, 1770), p. 19).

[3] Deluc attempts to persuade Haller that, contrary to the propaganda of the oligarchy, the people are to be trusted to make correct decisions (by 'people', he means, of course, the Citizens). To prove his point he turns naturally to Roman history and speaks of:

cette verité reconnue depuis plus de 20 siècles par Valerius PUBLICOLA, l'un des plus vertueux consuls & des plus vrais Héros de la République Romaine...La Republique est composée de deux ordres, de Patriciens & de Plébéiens. Il est question de décider auquel de ces deux Ordres il est plus sur de confier la garde & le dépôt de la liberté. Je soutiens, ajouta ce grand homme, qu'elle sera plus en sureté entre les mains du Peuple qui ne demande que de n'etre pas oprimé, que dans celles des Nobles qui tous ont une violente passion de dominer.

Deluc follows this up by contrasting the deceitfulness of Tarquin and his ambassador (a tilt at France) with the candour and probity of the Roman people, and illustrates the wisdom of the citizens of Athens in their treatment of Aristides and Themistocles. Haller, not to be outdone, points out in his reply that the Roman republic was not a democracy, and that in the Greek city-states there were many instances of unjust decisions made by the people. He also added somewhat tartly, in a reference to the French troops massing on the frontiers of Geneva: 'Pour faire les Romains il faloit en avoir les légions'. Deluc replies that one must distinguish between the vast Roman Empire, built up on slavery, and the tiny republic of Geneva. The abuses of Athenian democracy provide no parallel. In Geneva, the Citizens have to earn their living, and cannot sit in constant session as did the Athenians, who were idlers supported by the

I regret I have no time to illustrate this in detail, but their exchanges are a remarkable example of the power of the myth of antiquity and of its application to contemporary political problems. Nor was the myth a mere decorative element in the struggle. When France intervened, she was taken aback by the vehemence and tenacity of the opposition of these neo-Romans, which did so much to take the sting out of Haller's sarcastic quip: 'Pour faire les Romains, il faloit en avoir les légions.'

At this critical moment in the history of the republic, Rousseau, then in England, wrote to one of the Citizens praising their conduct: 'I seem to see the Roman Senate, seated solemnly in the forum, awaiting death at the hands of the Gauls.'[1]

III

J.-J. Rousseau grew up in this atmosphere of political strife, democratic propaganda and veneration for the virtues of classical antiquity. His father, who belonged to the opposition, discharged the obligations of a brief and somewhat intermittent paternal vocation by instilling patriotic feelings into the boy, and by introducing him, whilst still a child, first to Plutarch, and then to Livy. The effect on Rousseau, as on his French contemporary Vauvenargues, was electrifying: 'constantly thinking of Rome and Athens, living with their great men,...my feelings were set on fire... I imagined I was a Greek or a Roman; I became the character whose life I was reading.'[2] As a young man, seeing the Pont du Gard for the first time, he exclaims: 'Why wasn't I born a Roman?'[3] And twenty-five years later, towards the end of his career, we find him writing: 'When you read ancient history, you think you are in a different universe, living among a different species of being.'[4]

The reasons for this exceptional degree of fervour must no doubt be sought partly in Rousseau's personality, in his powerful imagina-

labour of slaves. The worst features of Athenian democracy would therefore be automatically avoided in Geneva. And so on. (Letters between J.-F. Deluc and Baron Albrecht von Haller, MSS. Haller xxv, Burgerbibliothek, Berne.)

[1] 'Je crois voir le Sénat de Rome assis gravement dans la place publique, attendant la mort de la main des Gaulois' (Rousseau to F.-H. d'Ivernois, 31 January 1767: in Leigh, vol. xxxii (forthcoming)).

[2] *Confessions* I, in *Pléiade*, vol. I, p. 9.

[3] *Ibid.* vi, in *Pléiade*, vol. I, p. 256.

[4] 'Quand on lit l'histoire ancienne, on se croit transporté dans un autre univers et parmi d'autres êtres' (*Considérations sur le gouvernement de Pologne*, in *Pléiade*, vol. III, p. 956).

tion and in his exceptional sensibility. But he also stands apart from his contemporaries in another important respect. Unlike them, he had little formal education, and no schooling. Some Latin, of course, he must have learnt as a boy; otherwise the ten-year-old semi-orphan, farmed out to a country parson to get a grounding in the three R's, would hardly have sat up in bed one night shrieking 'carnifex! carnifex!' for hours on end, when unjustly punished for a trifling misdemeanour.[1] But he had only the rudiments. He did not really become familiar with any Latin author in the original until much later, when as a young man of twenty-five or so he taught himself the language as part of a curriculum of self-improvement, and embarked on a course of reading which took him through Virgil and the other usual poets. Indeed, his enthusiasm for the Ancients may perhaps be partly explained by his very lack of a formal education. In his case, the delights of discovery were completely free from all association with irksome constraint, lack-lustre pedagogues, repetitive exercises, disagreeable sanctions, and dusty schoolrooms. At all events, he taught himself enough Latin to select for his works telling and significant epigraphs: 'Barbarus hic ego sum, quia non intelligor illis' (from Ovid's *Tristia*, used for both the *First Discourse* and for the *Dialogues*); the *Inégalité* has an incisive summary of his argument, taken from his Latin Aristotle: 'Non in depravatis, sed in his quae bene secundum naturam se habent, considerandum est quid sit naturale'; and *Émile* has this apt sentence from Seneca: 'Sanabilibus aegrotamus malis: ipsaque nos in rectum genitos natura, si emendari velimus, juvat' (*De ira* II.13). And we must not forget his famous motto, adapted from Juvenal, which resounded so challengingly throughout eighteenth-century Europe: 'Vitam impendere vero.'

It is, of course, no part of my intention in this paper to try to assess the influence of classical literature and philosophy on Rousseau's mind and personality.[2] For my present purpose, it is enough to recall a few obvious instances of the influence of the myth of antiquity in his work: the oddly protracted study of Roman institutions and voting methods in the *Contrat social*; the sketches for an unfinished tragedy on the rape of Lucretia; the masses of notes and extracts he made from Plutarch's *Moralia* – those are just a few examples. The most remarkable, perhaps, is the idealisation of Rome in the *First*

---

[1] *Confessions* I, in *Pléiade*, vol. I, p. 20.

[2] Much attention has been given to this subject: for a bibliography, see Mme Leduc-Fayette's book, cited above p. 155, note.

Discourse, and that of Sparta towards the end of the *Lettre à D'Alembert*.

This reminds me of one point I should like to make in greater detail, though it involves an apparent digression. In September 1766, a German countess wrote to Rousseau[1] in order to consult him on a moral problem which I suspect was more personal than appears at first sight. A young man of her acquaintance, whom she significantly calls CASSIUS, inspired by patriotic fervour and the example of the ancients, has undertaken to liberate his country (some petty German principality, unnamed) from oppression. So far, so good. Unfortunately, in order to achieve his aims, he has thought it necessary to sever all ties with his wife and family on the grounds that a conflict or duty or feeling might arise which would deflect him from his purpose; claiming, into the bargain, that such conduct is justified by the example and precept of classical antiquity. The countess asks: does Rousseau think this is right?

No, most emphatically, he doesn't: 'Don't all virtuous feelings hang together? Can any one of them be destroyed without weakening them all? "I thought for a long time", says he 'that I could combine affection and duty." What need is there of combination, when the affection itself is a duty?...How dare any man who deliberately decides to give up being a son, or a husband, or a father, usurp the title of citizen? How dare he usurp the title of human being?'[2] And Rousseau then proceeds to back up this judgement from antiquity itself.

In quoting this remarkable letter, I must confess to an *arrière-pensée*. There is nowadays a tendency in some quarters to denounce Rousseau as an intellectual and temperamental ancestor of twentieth-century totalitarianism. I believe this to be a grave error. Evidence for the claim is based primarily on his *Contrat social*, but it is sometimes also sought in his admiration for Sparta.[3] Both in the idealisation and in the reality, it is said, Sparta was a close approximation to

---

[1] Leigh, vol. xxx, no. 5426 (hitherto unpublished).

[2] 'Tous les sentimens vertueux ne s'étayent-ils point les uns les autres? et peut-on en détruire un sans les affoiblir tous? "J'ai cru longtemps" dit-il "combiner mes affections avec mes devoirs." Il n'y a point là de combinaison à faire quand ces affections elles-mêmes sont des devoirs...Tout homme qui se fait une expresse loi de n'être plus ni fils, ni mari, ni père, ose-t-il usurper le nom de citoyen? ose-t-il usurper le nom d'homme?' (Leigh, vol. xxx, no. 5450). This letter has been known since 1782, but the addressee has been wrongly identified. She is Caroline Frederica zu Salm-Grumbach, wife of Karl Friedrich, Graf von Wartensleben, diplomatic representative of Holland in the Rhineland (see Leigh, vol. xxx, no. 5426, explanatory notes).

[3] See, for instance, Mme Leduc-Fayette's book, pp. 89–90, p. 96, etc.

the totalitarian state, in which the dehumanised citizens were completely subordinated to collective activities and purposes, leaving no room for individual autonomy. The letter I have quoted today is a pointer to the fact that, however great his admiration for certain qualities, real or imagined, of Spartan society, Rousseau never believed that the obliteration of the individual, or his absorption in a collective soul, was the price to be paid for the creation of a just and free society – the sole object of his political thought.

By the time his early works had appeared, say by 1758, Rousseau had already acquired a public image which made of him a latter-day Roman, and assimilated him to the category of the heroes he so greatly admired. As early as 1753, he had become a by-word in Paris for unimpeachable integrity, candour, dedicated poverty and civic virtue. He had attacked contemporary society root and branch; and in order to project himself as a living confutation of it and of all its values he had adopted an ostentatiously austere mode of existence, acting out his philosophy in real life. So much so that certain court circles recommended that he should be deported as a bad example. Detractors called him Diogenes; admirers, Socrates. When in 1762 he left France in order to avoid arrest after the condemnation of *Émile*, the parallel with the Greek sage became almost obligatory. In fact, the authorities felt it necessary to hold up the production of a tenth-rate tragedy on the death of Socrates,[1] because they feared that Paris audiences would pounce on the opportunity to demonstrate their sympathy for Rousseau. Even the level-headed David Hume wrote to a friend (before his famous quarrel with Rousseau, of course), 'I think Rousseau in many things very much resembles Socrates: the Philosopher of Geneva seems only to have more genius than he of Athens, who never wrote anything.'[2]

Rousseau retained this public image right up to and including the Revolutionary period, in spite of the strenuous efforts made by Voltaire, the Genevan oligarchy and the *philosophes* (whom he had antagonised) to smash it to smithereens. Three factors combined to destroy it in the end. First of all, in the complete change of political climate which came with the Restoration in 1815, he was identified

---

[1] *La mort de Socrate*, by Billardon de Sauvigny: first produced in May 1763, but accepted earlier.

[2] David Hume to Hugh Blair, in Leigh, vol. xxviii, no. 4938 (December 1765). Somewhat earlier, Diderot had called Rousseau 'le censeur des lettres, le Caton, le Brutus de notre âge...' ('Essai sur la peinture', in *Œuvres*, ed. J. Assezat and M. Tourneux (20 vols., Paris, 1875–7), vol. x, pp. 483–4.

with the Revolution of which he had been one of the patron saints, and with whose excesses he was unjustly associated. Secondly, there was the time-bomb of the spurious *Memoirs of Madame d'Épinay*, which blackened Rousseau's character by a number of skilful fictions interwoven with a small amount of verifiable truth. Lastly, there was of course the *Confessions*, which set new standards of frankness and insight, but also revealed a very different personality from the public image he had acquired during his lifetime, and which he himself had helped to foster. The destruction of that image is, however, another story. What I have tried to illustrate today, in the brief time available, and, I fear, without much nuance, is the power of the myth of antiquity in the eighteenth century, its dynamism and momentum, and its creative vitality. That power is no more. In our day, both of the twin pillars on which our civilisation has for so long rested, the classical and the biblical, have crumbled away. It will be interesting to see if our civilisation goes with them.

9

LA FORMATION DE L'ATHÈNES BOURGEOISE: ESSAI D'HISTORIOGRAPHIE 1750–1850

NICOLE LORAUX ET PIERRE VIDAL-NAQUET

Pour Geoffrey Lloyd

Dans un article récent, Zvi Yavetz a posé cette question: 'Why Rome?'[1] Autrement dit: pourquoi l'histoire ancienne s'est-elle constituée en discipline scientifique en Allemagne à travers la *Römische Geschichte* de B. G. Niebuhr, dont les deux premiers volumes paraissent en 1811–12? Le fait peut surprendre, estime Yavetz, car c'est la Grèce qui, suivant une formule bien connue, exerçait alors sa 'tyrannie' sur l'esprit allemand.[2] Selon l'historien israélien, la réponse est à chercher dans le modèle que représentait, pour l'interprétation de l'histoire romaine, le conflit entre seigneurs et paysans prussiens à l'aube du XIXe siècle, conflit arbitré, après Iéna (1806), par l'intervention réformiste de l'État (Stein, Hardenberg, Scharnhorst, Gneisenau...). Niebuhr n'a-t-il pas été un proche collaborateur de Stein, après avoir débuté dans la fonction publique au service du roi de Danemark?

Le problème posé est tout à fait réel, mais il faut, croyons-nous, aller beaucoup plus loin.[3] Certes, l'intégration de la révolte paysanne par l'état prussien réformé fournit un schème pour interpréter l'opposition du patriciat et de la plèbe et pour comprendre les crises du IIe et du Ier siècles avant notre ère, mais il n'y a pas que Rome et la Prusse; la formation de Niebuhr a été, très largement, une réaction à l'immense 'événement' qui ouvre l'histoire contemporaine, à la Révolution française. Si la 'question agraire' s'est réveillée en Allemagne, c'est en partie parce que, en 1789, les paysans français l'avaient posée, et partiellement résolue, avec l'énergie que l'on sait. Niebuhr a été un observateur attentif de cet ébranlement, violem-

---

[1] Z. Yavetz, 'Why Rome? *Zeitgeist* and ancient historians in early 19th century Germany', *American Journal of Philology*, XCVII (1976), 276–96.
[2] Cf. E. M. Butler, *The Tyranny of Greece over Germany* (Cambridge, 1935).
[3] Avec l'aide notamment de la monographie de S. Rytkönen, *Barthold Georg Niebuhr als Politiker und Historiker* (Helsinki, 1968); ce livre semble avoir échappé à l'attention de Z. Yavetz.

ment hostile aux Montagnards de l'an II, mais rallié, de loin, à la république de Thermidor, conçue comme devant répandre une 'Aufklärung généralisée', envisageant même de venir étudier à l'École Normale de l'an III, où professera Volney.[1]

Quelques années avant la grande œuvre de Niebuhr, un autre savant allemand, A. H. L. Heeren, dans un manuel publié en 1799 et qui devait, en diverses langues, connaître un succès fort durable, avait dit les choses avec une très grande netteté :

Les événements de notre temps ont répandu sur l'histoire ancienne une lumière et un intérêt qu'elle n'avait ni ne pouvait avoir auparavant... et si, par hasard, on trouvait dans plusieurs parties de mon ouvrage, particulièrement dans l'histoire de la république romaine, quelques rapports avec les événements survenus pendant les dix ans qui ont précédé la publication de l'ouvrage, je crois n'avoir pas besoin d'excuse pour cela.[2]

Que les conflits politiques de l'antiquité puissent appuyer et éclairer le monde moderne, et s'éclairer de celui-ci, on avait pu le pressentir avant la Révolution. Ainsi Diderot, en 1772 :

Ce fut au milieu des orages continus de la Grèce que cette contrée se peupla de peintres, de sculpteurs, et de poètes. Ce fut dans les temps où cette bête fauve qu'on appelait le peuple romain, ou se dévorait elle-même, ou s'occupait à dévorer les nations, que les historiens écrivirent et que les poètes chantèrent.

Et si, de nos jours, 'l'esprit du commerce est sans contredit l'esprit dominant du siècle...', à travers lui, c'est bien la lutte politique et 'la passion des conquêtes' qui continue.[3]

En Allemagne comme en France, le rapport au monde romain introduisait à une réflexion sur l'État, que celui-ci fût la république ou l'empire. Par le biais de la cité grecque, c'est plutôt le problème de l'action politique, de sa place dans la société, qui est posé. Aussi nous demanderons-nous, dans cet exposé sur la France et sur Athènes, comment, et, si cela peut se faire, pourquoi, Athènes est devenue pour les professeurs français et pour nombre de leurs élèves le modèle de la société libérale et bourgeoise, et même, à la limite, d'une 'société civile' détachée de la société politique mais ayant tout de même une histoire, ayant connu un commencement, un apogée, un déclin ?

---

[1] Rytkönen, *Niebuhr*, p. 34.

[2] A. H. L. Heeren, *Handbuch der Geschichte der Staate des Alterthums mit besonderer Rücksicht auf ihre Verfassungen, ihren Handel und ihre Colonien* (Göttingen, 1799), pp. vii–viii; nous citons et corrigeons quelque peu la traduction de A. L. Thurot (Paris, 1827), pp. x–xi.

[3] Diderot, 'Pensées détachées ou Fragments politiques échappés au portefeuille d'un philosophe', *Œuvres complètes*, t. x (Paris, 1971), pp. 81–3; rappelons que Diderot avait publié, en 1743, une traduction de l'*Histoire de Grèce* en trois tomes de Temple Stanyan.

Le terme de l'évolution ne pose pas de sérieux problèmes. En 1851, Victor Duruy, alors professeur au lycée Saint-Louis, publie la première édition de son *Histoire grecque*. Là, tout est présent de cette vision d'Athènes qui fut plus tard, avec les transitions nécessaires, celle de Glotz et de tant d'autres. 'On sent moins,' écrit-il, 'à Athènes qu'à Sparte, le lien qui unit les institutions civiles aux institutions politiques...La propriété n'est pas absorbée à Athènes par l'État...Le mariage a plus de vraie dignité qu'à Sparte...La famille conserve ici tout son mystère.'[1] Liberté, commerce, propriété, famille: les éléments d'une Athènes bourgeoise sont rassemblés pour la joie des petits et des grands. Mais le point de départ? Un siècle avant Duruy, dans le fameux 'Tableau philosophique des progrès successifs de l'esprit humain' que Turgot, alors âgé de vingt-trois ans, présente à la Sorbonne comme sa harangue de prieur, on apprend que si 'la barbarie égalise tous les hommes', le progrès est fondé, lui, sur l'inégalité des nations. Athènes, face à Sparte, n'en est pas moins 'le modèle des nations', et ce sont 'le commerce et les arts' qui, plus tard, rendront Alexandrie rivale d'Athènes. 'L'univers connu, si j'ose ainsi parler, l'univers commerçant...'[2] Mais Turgot, nous le verrons, reprend ici des thèmes plus anciens que lui, et ces thèmes ne résument pas, à beaucoup près, le XVIIIe siècle dans son rapport au monde grec.

Entre Turgot et ses prédécesseurs, d'une part, et Duruy et ses successeurs, de l'autre, comment marquer les étapes? Comment, sur quels critères, choisir nos témoins? Au milieu du XIXe siècle, l'histoire ancienne est devenue, en France, la chose des professeurs. Cela fut vrai plus tôt en Allemagne, plus tard en Angleterre, et, si George Grote n'est pas un professeur de formation et de vocation, il n'en sera pas moins un des fondateurs, contre Oxford et Cambridge, de l'Université de Londres. Mais entre Turgot et Duruy? Les professionnels de l'étude du monde grec existent déjà à la fin du XVIIIe siècle. Un D'Ansse de Villoison, un Jean Schweighaeuser, éditeurs et piocheurs de textes, règnent sur leur domaine à la façon dont M. Louis Robert règne sur le sien. A. J. Letronne naît en 1787, et dès qu'il prend la parole, en 1814, c'est comme un professionnel, et comme notre contemporain. Mais il s'en faut de beaucoup que le

---

[1] V. Duruy, *Histoire grecque* (Paris, 1851), p. 103.
[2] Turgot, *Œuvres*, t. I, éd. G. Schelle (Paris, 1913), pp. 214–34; nous citons les pp. 217, 225–6; la place de ce discours et de celui prononcé par Turgot sur le rôle du christianisme dans l'histoire est fortement soulignée, après d'autres, par F. E. Manuel, *The Prophets of Paris* (Cambridge, Mass., 1962), p. 13.

triomphe des professeurs soit acquis, même en 1820. Entre Paul-Louis Courier (1772–1825), colonel d'artillerie, et son beau-père Clavier (1762–1817), traducteur de Pausanias et professeur au Collège de France, qui marquera davantage les études grecques?

D'Ansse de Villoison (1750–1805) décide au moment de la Révolution de 'ne pas se mêler des affaires de la République', et, bien sûr, il le dit en grec: τῷ σοφῷ οὐ πολιτευτέον. Dans une lettre du 17 juin 1792, il allègue 'les longues et immenses recherches' que demande la composition de son grand ouvrage, une 'histoire comparée de la Grèce dans les temps anciens et modernes', pour justifier sa retraite, mais la maxime ne lui porta pas chance, car, perdu dans sa documentation, il n'écrira jamais l'histoire qu'il rêvait d'écrire.[1]

Mais, inversement, J. Schweighaeuser (1742–1830) qui, de Strasbourg, salua la Révolution avec enthousiasme et fut un patriote ardent (malgré certaines difficultés en l'an II), publiera à Leipzig, de 1789 à 1795, sa grande édition de Polybe, en ajoutant dans une lettre à un Représentant cette remarque: 'Je suis fâché et presque honteux d'offrir aux républicains français un ouvrage imprimé dans le pays des esclaves.'[2] Effectivement, entre la Révolution et la Contre-Révolution, Polybe pouvait, à bon droit, demeurer neutre.

Aussi avons-nous choisi nos témoins principaux en dehors de cet univers strictement professionnel. Dans le monde des spécialistes, nous avons décidé de donner la parole à ceux qui n'étaient pas uniquement des spécialistes du monde antique. Ainsi Pierre-Charles Lévesque (1736–1812), avant de consacrer sa vie à Thucydide et au monde gréco-romain, se préoccupa de la Chine, de voyages imaginaires, et écrivit une *Histoire de Russie* où l'on pouvait lire ceci: 'L'histoire de quelques petites Républiques dont la domination occupait à peine un point imperceptible du globe [il s'agit, bien sûr, d'Athènes et de Sparte] a fait longtemps un des principaux objets de nos études: le nom même du plus vaste empire du monde n'était pas connu de nos pères.'[3] Nos témoins occupent en fait toute la gamme

---

[1] Cf. C. Joret, *D'Ansse de Villoison et l'hellénisme en France pendant le dernier tiers du XVIIIe siècle* (Paris, 1910), pp. 331–2.

[2] Cf. C. Rabany, *Les Schweighaeuser, biographie d'une famille de savants alsaciens d'après leur correspondance inédite* (Paris, 1884), p. 18.

[3] P.-C. Lévesque, *Histoire de Russie*, vol. 1 (Paris, 1782), p. 71. Cette phrase disparut lorsque Lévesque réédita son œuvre pour la seconde fois en 1800, puis en 1812; on lit alors: 'La Russie était peu connue de nos pères; ils ignoraient même assez communément le nom de cet empire, le plus vaste du monde...' (t. 1, p. 91 de la réédition de Paris, 1812).

qui va de l'écrivain et de l'homme politique engagés dans un combat essentiellement idéologique: Benjamin Constant, Chateaubriand, Joseph de Maistre, à un philosophe acteur et victime de la Révolution comme Condorcet, à un amateur étrangement audacieux comme Cornelius De Pauw ou à un célèbre orientaliste, Volney, 'idéologue' au sens qu'avait ce mot à la fin du siècle, membre de l'Assemblée constituante et professeur d'histoire à l'École Normale de l'an III. C'est donc à ces hommes, et non à de grands savants comme Nicolas Fréret (1688–1749)[1] ou comme Sainte-Croix (1746–1809), à ces hommes qui furent à la fois des citoyens d'Athènes et des hommes de la Révolution, de l'Empire et de l'Europe, que nous demanderons comment Athènes est devenue le fruit suprême de l'histoire bourgeoise. Et ce groupement, qui nous paraissait à nous-mêmes quelque peu artificiel, a pris peu à peu, au fur et à mesure que l'enquête progressait, une certaine consistance. Nous les avions traités comme un ensemble, et ils constituent effectivement un ensemble, se répondant les uns aux autres, partageant la même culture de base. C'est avec surprise, par exemple, que nous avons constaté le rôle central d'un personnage comme Cornelius De Pauw (1739–99), à peu près inconnu des historiens de l'histoire grecque,[2] mais qui fut lu et médité par Lévesque, par Constant, par Joseph de Maistre et tant d'autres.

Au centre de la période historique que nous jalonnerons, il y a, bien sûr, cet énorme ébranlement social et intellectuel que fut la Révolution française. Dans un travail précédent, l'un d'entre nous avait tenté[3] de définir le rôle que joua la Grèce dans la conscience politique de la Révolution, et, plus précisément, au centre de ce centre que fut l'an II. Notre objectif est aujourd'hui tout à fait différent. Il ne s'agit pas d'analyser un phénomène d'identification sociale, celui, soit dit pour faire bref, des Montagnards avec une Sparte mythique, phénomène qui relève, à la limite, du millénarisme, mais de comprendre la fonction d'un certain nombre d'œuvres, et celles-ci se situent immédiatement avant et après la crise majeure: dans les années 1786–88 et 1795–1800. L'an III, par exemple, est un

[1] Cf. Renée Simon, 'Nicolas Fréret, académicien', Studies on Voltaire, t. XVII (Genève, 1961).

[2] V. cependant E. Egger, L'hellénisme en France (Paris, 1869), t. II, p. 275; E. Rawson, The Spartan Tradition in European Thought (Oxford, 1966), p. 260.

[3] P. Vidal-Naquet, 'Tradition de la démocratie grecque', publié en guise de préface à la traduction (par Monique Alexandre) de M. I. Finley, Démocratie antique et démocratie moderne (Paris, 1976).

grand moment de publications et de republications.[1] C'est à l'époque de la Convention thermidorienne et du Directoire que les Idéologues, ces créateurs du laïcisme contemporain, et leurs adversaires mesureront leur proximité et leur éloignement par rapport à Athènes. Dès lors, et pour longtemps, les jeux seront faits.

Mais avant d'en venir aux environs de la Révolution, osons émettre quelques formules générales sur l'époque des Lumières prise dans son ensemble, face à l'antiquité grecque. Nous disons bien: prise dans son ensemble, car il serait trop simple de s'en tenir à cette redécouverte de 'l'antique' qui triomphe à la fin du siècle, aussi bien dans la rhétorique que dans l'architecture et l'ensemble des arts plastiques. Encore moins peut-il être question de réduire le XVIIIe siècle français à ce qui, en lui, annonce l'historicisme du XIXe siècle, aux très rares disciples ou émules de Vico ou de Herder. S'en tenir là reviendrait à juger une époque avec les catégories de l'époque suivante, attitude qui, en l'espèce, a été justement dénoncée par Cassirer: 'Cette idée si courante que le XVIIIe siècle est un siècle typiquement "an-historique" est elle-même une idée sans aucun fondement historique, rien de plus qu'un mot d'ordre lancé par le romantisme, une devise pour partir en campagne contre la philosophie des Lumières.'[2]

Partons de quelques formules empruntées à un Mémoire de l'Académie des Inscriptions et Belles-Lettres présenté en 1760 par Jean-Pierre de Bougainville (1722–63), frère de l'explorateur et membre de la compagnie:

Il est certain que l'histoire de la Grèce, se peuplant et se policcant par degrés, est moins le spectacle des destinées d'une nation qu'une perspective où le genre humain se peint en raccourci dans différents états. C'est à la fois un cours abrégé, mais complet, d'Histoire, de Morale et de Politique, puisqu'elle a le mérite de rassembler dans un assez court espace tous les traits épars dans les annales des siècles divers, de faire connaître l'homme sous tous les points de vue possibles, sauvage, errant, civilisé, religieux, guerrier, commerçant; de fournir des modèles de toutes les lois, en un mot, une théorie complète, prouvée par les faits, de la formation des sociétés, de la naissance, de la propagation et du progrès des arts, de toutes les révolutions de toutes les variétés auxquelles l'humanité peut être assujettie, de toutes les formes qui peuvent la modifier. Pour un observateur

[1] Sont publiés alors, outre les *Leçons d'histoire* de Volney, l'*Origine de tous les cultes* de Dupuis, le *Tableau historique* de Condorcet. C'est aussi le moment où furent republiés ou rassemblés des textes comme la *Richesse des Nations* d'Adam Smith, les œuvres de C. De Pauw, de Condillac, de Mably.

[2] E. Cassirer, *La philosophie des Lumières*, trad. P. Quillet (Paris, 1966), p. 207.

attentif...la Grèce est en petit l'univers, et l'histoire de la Grèce un excellent précis de l'histoire universelle.[1]

Rien de plus banal, dira-t-on. Notons tout de suite la métaphore spatiale. Le 'court espace' dont il est question n'est pas seulement une allusion à la place que tient la Grèce sur une carte. Qu'un 'espace' résume un temps est, au XVIIIe siècle, dans l'ordre des choses.[2] Espace et temps, présent et passé lointain, monde sauvage et monde des vieilles civilisations, projets utopiques et utopies incarnées, sur les débris du *Discours sur l'Histoire universelle* toutes les combinaisons sont possibles dans un espace-temps incroyablement élargi.

Pour comprendre ce qu'a été la Grèce des philosophes,[3] il faut voir, bien sûr, que le passé lointain sert de machine de guerre contre la société chrétienne,[4] celle d'hier et celle d'aujourd'hui, contre le mythe judéo-chrétien qui la sous-tend; mais il faut comprendre surtout que toutes les associations sont possibles, y compris les plus contradictoires. Tous les temps et tous les espaces sont bons pour donner place aux fantasmes, pour y chercher la liberté ou la sécurité. Temps primitifs et espaces immobiles, terres nouvellement conquises et socialisées de l'Amérique anglo-saxonne, monde russe, monde chinois, monde de l'Inde, continent africain. Tout peut être combiné: le repos et le mouvement, la liberté et le despotisme éclairé. Voltaire peut, s'agissant de la Grèce, choisir Athènes contre Sparte, mais être

[1] J.-P. de Bougainville, 'Vues générales sur les antiquités grecques du premier âge, et sur les premières histoires de la nation grecque...', *Mémoires de littérature tirés des registres de l'Académie royale des Inscriptions et Belles-Lettres*, t. xxix (1764), pp. 27–86; nous citons les pages 32–3. On appréciera le progrès parallèle à l'intérieur des deux triades: sauvage, errant, civilisé; religieux, guerrier, commerçant.

[2] Sur l'espace des 'philosophes', v. la thèse de P. Broc, *La géographie des philosophes* (Lille, 1972), et, pour la fin du siècle, S. Moravia, 'Philosophie et géographie à la fin du XVIIIe siècle', *Studies on Voltaire*, t. lvii (Genève, 1967), pp. 937–1011.

[3] Il s'en faut de beaucoup que nous disposions pour cette étude de tous les travaux qui seraient nécessaires. Le seul ouvrage d'ensemble où le problème soit sérieusement abordé est celui de Peter Gay, *The Enlightenment. An Interpretation*, t. i, *The Rise of Modern Paganism* (London, 1966); sur le mirage spartiate, v. les deux chapitres que consacre au XVIIIe siècle Rawson, *The Spartan Tradition*, pp. 220–67; sur Voltaire, D. H. Jory, 'Voltaire and the Greeks', *Studies on Voltaire*, t. cliii (Genève, 1976), pp. 1169–87; sur Rousseau, D. Leduc-Fayette, *Jean-Jacques Rousseau et le mythe de l'antiquité* (Paris, 1974); sur Diderot, J. Seznec, *Essais sur Diderot et l'antiquité* (Oxford, 1957); sur Montesquieu, un article admirable, seule étude peut-être à répondre exactement aux questions que nous nous posions: G. Cambiano, 'Montesquieu e le antiche repubbliche greche', *Rivista di filosofia*, lxv, 2–3 (avril–septembre 1974), 93–144. Naturellement, nous avons beaucoup appris en lisant les *Contributi* de A. Momigliano; signalons tout spécialement son dernier article sur notre sujet, 'Eighteenth century prelude to Mr. Gibbon', *Gibbon et Rome à la lumière de l'historiographie moderne*, éd. P. Ducrey (Lausanne, 1977), pp. 57–70.

[4] C'est le thème essentiel de Gay, *The Enlightenment*.

aussi le propagateur du mirage chinois.[1] Une étude détaillée devrait associer Grèce et Amérique, Grèce et monde sauvage, Grèce et Hollande, Grèce et Suisse. Parce qu'au terme du siècle il y a la 'révolution bourgeoise', on est tenté de croire que le mouvement des idées n'a retenu en Grèce que ce qui allait dans le sens du mouvement du siècle, après qu'il eut été accompli. Mais rien ne serait plus inexact. Au moins autant qu'à incarner la raison conquérante, la Grèce a servi de support au rêve d'une histoire immobile[2] ou atteignant la perfection. Telle fut Athènes elle-même pour Winckelmann, telle fut Sparte dont le Législateur institue d'un seul coup la société bonne, mythe sur lequel la Révolution aura un effect multiplicateur. Comme dans les modernes controverses sur l'économie grecque,[3] la Grèce voit s'affronter à son propos 'primitivistes' et 'modernistes', sans parler de ceux pour qui elle est précisément le lieu du passage et qu'incarne assez bien J.-P. de Bougainville. Le premier thème, esquissé dès 1724 par le R.P. Lafitau,[4] prend un nouveau visage dans le dernier quart du siècle. Face au monde moderne, le monde primitif apparaît comme le lieu du symbole, de l'allégorie, du secret à déchiffrer. Ainsi Court de Gébelin, dans les neuf volumes de son *Monde primitif*, parus de 1773 à 1782, un des rares ouvrages français à avoir subi l'influence de Vico, est à la recherche de la langue unique, expression immédiate du symbolisme naturel, qui est le secret de ce monde.[5] C'est par le monde grec que se termine la quête: 'Enfin nous voilà parvenus jusqu'à toi, aimable Grèce',[6] le monde grec dont la langue est à certains égards un dialecte du celtique. Nos ancêtres les Grecs...Et son disciple, l'astronome Bailly, qui sera le premier maire de Paris, est à la recherche, par delà les Brahmanes

[1] Cf. Rawson, *The Spartan Tradition*, pp. 255–7, et, sur Voltaire et la Chine, la synthèse fondamentale de B. Guy, 'The French image of China before and after Voltaire', *Studies on Voltaire*, t. xxi (Genève, 1963): sur Voltaire, pp. 214–84; en dernier lieu, S. Pitou, 'Voltaire, Linguet and China', *Studies on Voltaire*, t. xcviii (Genève, 1972), pp. 61–8.

[2] Sur ce thème, cf. J. Ehrard, *L'idée de nature en France dans la première moitié du XVIIIe siècle* (Paris et Chambéry, 1963), t. ii, pp. 768–86.

[3] Cf. E. Will, 'Trois-quarts de siècle de recherches sur l'économie grecque antique', *Annales E. S. C.*, ix (1954), 7–22.

[4] Cf. P. Vidal-Naquet, 'Les jeunes: le cru, l'enfant grec et le cuit', *Faire de l'histoire*, édd. J. Le Goff et P. Nora, t. iii (Paris, 1974), pp. 137–68; Edna Lemay, 'Histoire de l'antiquité et découverte du Nouveau Monde chez deux auteurs du XVIIIe siècle', *Studies on Voltaire*, t. cli (Genève, 1976), pp. 1313–28.

[5] V. sur Court de Gébelin, outre les travaux de son disciple immédiat, Rabaut Saint-Étienne, *Œuvres* (2 t., Paris, 1826), t. i, pp. 355–90; F. Baldensperger, *Mélanges E. Huguet* (Paris, 1940), pp. 315–30; F. E. Manuel, *The Eighteenth Century Confronts the Gods* (Cambridge, Mass., 1959), pp. 250–8; G. Genette, *Mimologiques* (Paris, 1976), pp. 119–48.   [6] Court de Gébelin, *Monde primitif*, t. ix, p. i.

chers à Voltaire, de ce peuple primitif dont les Atlantes de Platon furent un rameau, et dont la grandeur explique l'existence même du monde antique.[1] Au delà de la période révolutionnaire, la postérité de ce symbolisme primitiviste sera, de Dupuis à Creuzer, immense.

Insistons cependant sur le thème inverse, celui de la modernité. Modernité, autant dire 'commerce', car c'est le négoce qui permet de séparer Athènes de Sparte et de la rapprocher d'Amsterdam, Londres ou Paris. Il ne fait d'abord qu'une apparition très discrète dans le livre, inspiré du modèle néerlandais, que publie en 1711 le célèbre Huet, évêque d'Avranches. Athènes y est vue, à l'aide des *Revenus* de Xénophon, comme 'une ville fort marchande et pourvue de toutes sortes de commodités pour le trafic';[2] mais l'opposition, sur ce plan, entre Athènes et Lacédémone, n'entraîne aucune conséquence majeure ni pour les représentations du monde antique, ni pour les choix du monde moderne.

En 1734 cependant, paraît anonymement l'*Essai politique sur le commerce* de J.-F. Melon, qui fut le secrétaire de Law. Le livre a sa préhistoire, qui est principalement anglaise et le rattache à la *Fable des abeilles* de Mandeville où est développée l'idée que moralité et efficacité économique sont deux choses différentes.[3] Il a sa postérité: la controverse, essentiellement française, sur l'avantage du luxe pour le développement économique.[4] Athènes joue son rôle dans cette partition:

L'austère Lacédémone n'a été ni plus conquérante, ni mieux gouvernée, ni n'a produit de plus grands hommes que la voluptueuse Athènes. Parmi les hommes illustres de Plutarque, il y a quatre Lacédémoniens et sept Athéniens, sans compter Socrate et Platon oubliés. Les lois somptuaires de Lycurgue ne méritent pas plus d'attention que ses autres lois qui révoltent tant la pudeur.[5]

[1] J. S. Bailly, *Histoire de l'astronomie ancienne* (Paris, 1776); *Lettres sur l'origine des sciences et sur celle des peuples de l'Asie* (Londres, 1777); *Lettres sur l'Atlantide de Platon et sur l'ancienne histoire de l'Asie* (Londres et Paris, 1779).

[2] P. D. Huet, *Histoire du commerce et de la navigation des anciens* (Paris, 1711), p. 75. L'année suivante, Huet publiera le *Grand trésor historique et politique du florissant commerce des hollandais*.

[3] V., en dernier lieu, L. Dumont, *Homo aequalis, Genèse et épanouissement de l'idéologie économique* (Paris, 1977), pp. 83–104.

[4] La bibliographie est considérable: cf. surtout, Ehrard, *L'idée de nature*, t. II, pp. 378–81 et 595–8; Rose de Labriolle, 'Le pour et le contre et son temps, II', *Studies on Voltaire*, t. XXXV (Genève, 1965), pp. 531–7; E. Ross, 'Mandeville, Melon and Voltaire: the origins of the luxury controversy in France', *Studies on Voltaire*, t. CLV (Genève, 1976), pp. 1897–912; Cambiano, 'Montesquieu e le antiche repubbliche greche', pp. 131–44; sur Melon, cf. la dissertation de F. Megnet, *Jean-François Melon, 1675 bis 1738, Ein origineller Vertreter der vorphysiokratischen Ökonomen Frankreichs* (Winterthur, 1955).

[5] J.-F. Melon, *Essai politique sur le commerce* (s.l., s.d. [1734]), p. 139.

Athènes et le luxe, le thème sera désormais banal, et Rousseau en fait un des arguments de sa critique.[1]

Mais il ne s'agit pas que du luxe, car à propos, sinon d'Athènes et de Sparte, du moins de Rome et de Carthage, Melon pose un couple d'oppositions dont le destin devait être durable, celui de l'esprit de conquête et de l'esprit de commerce. 'L'esprit de conquête et l'esprit de commerce s'excluent mutuellement dans une Nation'; si Rome qui, jusqu'à l'empire, 'a plutôt été un camp qu'une ville', si les Romains 'qui n'avaient qu'un commerce de nécessité', ont vaincu les Carthaginois, c'est que 'l'esprit de commerce et de conservation était, pour ainsi dire, dans son enfance'.[2] Le XVIIIe siècle, siècle du commerce et de l'industrie, doit pousser l'esprit de commerce et d'entreprise jusqu'au bout, par exemple en faisant des expériences chirurgicales sur les condamnés à mort, ou en infligeant aux criminels 'ces travaux pénibles qui abrègent la vie', moyennant quoi, il peut espérer la paix perpétuelle: 'Enfin l'esprit de paix a éclairé notre Europe.'[3]

L'opposition entre l'esprit de conquête et l'esprit de commerce sera connue de Montesquieu,[4] mais, dans l'*Esprit des lois* (1748), il hésite à attribuer l'esprit de commerce à Athènes; la démocratie jouait contre le commerce:

Athènes...plus attentive à étendre son empire maritime qu'à en jouir, avec un tel gouvernement politique, que le bas peuple se distribuait les revenus publics, tandis que les riches étaient dans l'oppression, ne fit point ce grand commerce que lui promettaient le travail de ses mines, la multitude de ses esclaves, le nombre de ses gens de mer, son autorité sur les villes grecques, et, plus que tout cela, les belles institutions de Solon.

Mais, dans la même page, il dit aussi, s'appuyant sur le témoignage du 'Vieil Oligarque' qu'il prend pour l'auteur de *L'Anabase*: 'Vous diriez que Xénophon a voulu parler de l'Angleterre.'[5] D'autres résistent aussi à cette identification, en particulier David Hume, qui y céda d'abord, mais conclut qu'en définitive, 'le taux d'intérêt de l'argent, les grands profits que donnait le commerce, sont une

---

[1] Cf. par exemple, 'Sur la réponse qui a été faite à son discours [sur les Sciences et les Arts], *Œuvres complètes*, éd. Bernard Gagnebin et Marcel Raymond, t. III (Paris, 1966), pp. 49–53.

[2] Melon, *Essai politique*, pp. 96–8.

[3] *Ibid.* pp. 107, 113, 115–16; cf., en général, M. Foucault, *Surveiller et punir* (Paris, 1975).

[4] Cf. par exemple, dans 'Mes pensées', no. 1228, *Œuvres*, t. I (Pléiade, Paris, 1949), pp. 1306–7.

[5] *Esprit des lois*, book XX, ch. VII, *Œuvres*, t. II (Pléiade, Paris, 1951), p. 611; cf. Cambiano, 'Montesquieu e le antiche repubbliche greche', pp. 133–5.

indication infaillible comme quoi l'industrie et le commerce étaient encore dans l'enfance', ce qui revenait, très consciemment, à généraliser les arguments de Thucydide dans l'"Archéologie'.[1]

Mais ces voix restent isolées, et le thème d'Athènes cité du commerce va triompher. Sir William Young publie en 1777 à Londres une histoire d'Athènes qui devait être rééditée deux fois, en 1786 et en 1804.[2] Le titre de la seconde édition définit la cité comme '*a free and commercial state*', et, de toute l'argumentation de Montesquieu, Sir William Young, qui joua un rôle important dans l'administration coloniale britannique, ne retient que la comparaison avec l'Angleterre. Athènes y incarne, grâce à son commerce, l'état le mieux calculé pour le bonheur général: 'The free state of Athens, in the high perfection of its establishment, was the state the best calculated for general happiness.'[3] C'est déjà, bien sûr, le thème de la philosophie utilitariste. Mais comment concilier 'l'esprit de commerce' et le patriotisme, autre sentiment qui grandit à la fin du siècle et dont la Grèce ancienne, et notamment Athènes presque au même titre que Sparte, fournissait tout de même le modèle? Quand le marquis de Chastellux, qui fut un des théoriciens du gouvernement représentatif,[4] voyage en Amérique au début des années quatre-vingts, il fait d'un négociant de Philadelphie ce portrait:

C'est un négociant très riche; c'est par conséquent un homme de tous les pays, car le commerce a partout le même caractère. Il est libre dans les monarchies, il est

[1] Cf. 'On the populousness of ancient nations' (1752), D. Hume, *Essays, Literary, Moral and Political* (London, 1894), pp. 245 et (à propos de Thucydide) 248; on comparera avec les indications beaucoup plus optimistes données dans le traité antérieur 'On commerce' (*ibid.* pp. 149–58); sur l'originalité de D. Hume, cf. M. I. Finley, *The Ancient Economy* (London, 1973), pp. 21–2.

[2] La première édition est ainsi intitulée: *The Spirit of Athens. Being a political and philosophical investigation of the history of that republic*; la seconde édition s'appelle: *The History of Athens politically and philosophically considered with the view to an investigation of the immediate causes of elevation and of decline, operative in a free and commercial state*; la troisième, post-révolutionnaire, s'appelle: *The History of Athens, including a commentary on the principles, policy and practice of republican government, and on the causes of elevation and decline, which operate in every free and commercial state*; seule la seconde édition nous a été accessible, mais notre ami Simon Pembroke a bien voulu comparer systématiquement la première et la seconde et n'a relevé, à l'exception du titre, aucune différence significative quant à l'importance du thème commercial.

[3] *The History of Athens*, p. 63; cf. pour la référence à Montesquieu, p. xi.

[4] Chastellux, *De la félicité publique ou considérations sur le sort de l'homme dans les différentes époques de l'histoire* (Amsterdam, 1772). Nous citons ce livre à la fois parce que, contre Rousseau, il se fait le théoricien du gouvernement représentatif en des termes qui annoncent Constant: 'Pour moi, je pense qu'il n'y aura de liberté solide et durable, et surtout de félicité que parmi les peuples chez lesquels tout se fera par représentation' (p. 43), et parce qu'il contient un exemple relativement rare de critique adressée à Athènes et à Sparte, ce qui annonce Volney (cf. pp. 22–49).

égoïste dans les Républiques; étranger ou, si l'on veut, citoyen dans tout l'univers, il exclut également les vertus et les préjugés qui s'opposent à son intérêt.[1]

Arrêtons-nous maintenant quelque peu aux années qui précèdent immédiatement la Révolution. Deux livres paraissent, en 1787-8, dont le caractère est très opposé et dont le destin devait être très différent. L'un est connu, voire illustre; ce sont les six volumes du *Voyage du Jeune Anacharsis en Grèce*, de l'abbé Barthélemy, monument d'érudition qui sera réimprimé tout au long du XIXe siècle, portrait d'une Athènes à la mode de Paris ou de Chanteloup – ce domaine tourangeau du duc de Choiseul où Barthélemy écrivit sa grande œuvre et dont il ne reste plus aujourd'hui qu'une pagode de fantaisie. Que ces Athéniens sont donc parisiens, disent à l'envi tous les commentateurs, qui ne savent s'il faut s'en émerveiller ou s'en indigner.[2] On a peu fait attention au fait que ce voyageur est un Scythe, qu'il préfère, tout comme Rollin, Rousseau ou Mably, Sparte à Athènes, et la Scythie à la Grèce. Ce 'bon sauvage', instruit pourtant par Platon et Aristote, choisit en dernière analyse de rentrer chez lui.

Les *Recherches philosophiques sur les Grecs*, de Cornelius De Pauw, qui paraissent à Berlin en 1787 et à Paris en 1788, bien que réimprimées en l'an III avec l'ensemble de l'œuvre de leur auteur et traduites en anglais, n'ont jamais, croyons-nous, fait l'objet d'une étude.[3]

Petit-neveu des frères De Witt dont l'assassinat, en 1672, désespéra Spinoza, oncle d'Anacharsis Cloots, 'l'orateur du genre humain', dont l'exécution, pendant la Terreur montagnarde, le désespéra, lui, C. De Pauw (1720–99) est un Allemand de Clèves en Rhénanie, qui

---

[1] *Voyages de M. le marquis de Chastellux dans l'Amérique septentrionale dans les années 1780, 1781 et 1782* (2 t., Paris, 1784).

[2] On s'émerveilla d'abord, on s'indigna ensuite, après la Révolution. Sur l'œuvre de l'abbé Barthélemy, publiée à Paris à la fin de 1788, voir la thèse de M. Badolle, *L'Abbé Jean-Jacques Barthélemy (1716-1795) et l'hellénisme en France dans la seconde moitié du XVIIIe siècle* (Paris, 1927); sur la réaction après la Révolution, cf. R. Canat, *L'hellénisme des Romantiques*, t. I (Paris, 1951), pp. 115ss.; typique est la lettre de P.-L. Courier à Chlewaski (27 février 1799): 'Je crois que tous les livres de ce genre, moitié histoire, moitié roman, où les mœurs modernes se trouvent mêlées avec les anciennes, font tort aux unes et aux autres, donnent de tout des idées très fausses et choquent également le goût et l'érudition' (*Œuvres*, t. II, p. 662).

[3] Sur De Pauw, quelques indications dans C. Becdelièvre, *Biographie liégeoise*, t. II (1835), no. 1799, pp. 531–6, qu'on s'est parfois contenté de recopier (cf. Michaud, *Biographie universelle*, 2e éd., vol. XXXII (Paris, 1861), pp. 321–2); v. aussi G. Avenel, *Anacharsis Cloots* (Paris, 1865) et, sur son œuvre, les informations données ci-dessus p. 173, n. 2 et ci-dessous p. 181, n. 2, et p. 184, n. 2. Notre attention a été attirée sur De Pauw par un mémoire de maîtrise consacré à Barthélemy et soutenu en 1976 par Alain Chauvet. Nous citons De Pauw d'après la réédition de l'an III.

servit d'ambassadeur à la ville de Liège. Ses *Recherches* grecques s'insèrent en réalité dans un ensemble beaucoup plus vaste. 'Ce polygraphe protestant prend le contre-pied des jésuites en tout.'[1] En 1768, à Berlin, il publie des *Recherches philosophiques sur les Américains ou Mémoires intéressants pour servir à l'histoire de l'espèce humaine*; c'est, de loin, la plus connue de ses œuvres.[2] Face au mythe du bon sauvage ou de l'utopie qui avait souvent trouvé à s'incarner dans l'Amérique précolombienne,[3] il s'agit de présenter l'Amérique indienne comme un vaste pourrissoir, où rien, ni les hommes ni les plantes, ne peuvent germer correctement. Quelques années plus tard, en 1773, il publie d'autres *Recherches philosophiques*, sur les Égyptiens et les Chinois. Le but était double: séparer le destin de l'Égypte qui avait fasciné – à tort selon De Pauw – les intellectuels depuis l'époque grecque, de celui de la Chine. N'avait-on pas écrit – et encore, en 1759, le grand linguiste J. de Guignes – que la Chine, ce mirage des intellectuels du siècle des Lumières, était une colonie égyptienne?[4] Une fois cette séparation accomplie, il fallait aussi montrer que la Chine dont rêvaient les intellectuels n'était, au témoignage de ceux qui avaient été à Canton, précisément qu'un mirage.

Peu avant de mourir, C. De Pauw détruisit le manuscrit d'un troisième ouvrage, sur la Germanie; il n'est guère douteux qu'il ne s'y employât à démolir les représentations idéalisées que la noblesse française se donnait de ses ancêtres 'francs'.

Entre ces destructions, la construction grecque, ou plutôt athénienne. Car la Grèce, ce n'est ni les Lacédémoniens 'qui ne contribuèrent jamais aux progrès d'aucune science, ni aux développements d'aucun art', ni les Étoliens que l'on comparait aux bêtes féroces, ni les Thessaliens ('chez eux l'agriculture était un métier déshonorant'), ni les Arcadiens, ces bons sauvages de l'Antiquité qui n'existent pas politiquement avant Épaminondas,[5] la Grèce c'est, avant tout, Athènes. Une Athènes démocratique, certes, cité de la

---

[1] Broc, *La géographie des philosophes*, p. 457. Ce 'protestant' fut du reste ordonné sous-diacre et fut chanoine de Xanten.

[2] Elle est notamment commentée par M. Duchet, *Anthropologie et histoire au Siècle des Lumières* (Paris, 1972); v. à l'index.

[3] V. sur ces thèmes au XVIIIe siècle, outre l'ouvrage de P. Broc, H. Baudet, *Paradise on Earth: Some Thoughts on European Images of Non-European Man*, trad. E. Wentholt (New Haven et London, 1965), pp. 37–55.

[4] J. de Guignes, *Mémoire dans lequel on prouve que les Chinois sont une colonie égyptienne* (Paris, 1758); la thèse avait déjà été soutenue par P. D. Huet dans son *Histoire du commerce*. Cet ouvrage provoqua toute une polémique dont les références importent peu ici (t. i, pp. 166–7).

[5] C. De Pauw, *Œuvres* (Paris, an III [1795]), t. vi, pp. i–iv.

parole politique: 'La politique ne s'y cachait pas sous des voiles et des nuages.'[1] Étrange Athènes tout de même, où le commerce, qui fait toute la vie de la cité, est vu à travers la pastorale, puisque De Pauw insiste sur le penchant des Athéniens pour la vie champêtre. La ville même d'Athènes ne comportait pas d'édifices somptueux. De Pauw s'appuie sur la description célèbre du Pseudo-Dicéarque[2] ('La route est agréable, dans un paysage bien cultivé, d'aspect accueillant. Mais la ville est aride et manque d'eau; elle est mal tracée, à la manière archaïque'),[3] pour démontrer la modestie toute démo-cratique d'Athènes: 'Ils craignaient avec raison de choquer les principes essentiels d'un gouvernement populaire et l'égalité qui en formait la loi.'[4] Tout, et même les *Jardins* des philosophes, est intégré à cette pastorale.

Mais cette Athènes champêtre est aussi, depuis Solon, le pays des arts mécaniques, d'un 'immense commerce d'industrie', facilité par 'le nombre prodigieux des manufactures', autant dire Londres, ou Amsterdam.[5] Tout cela est rendu possible par l'esclavage dont l'importance est admise sans réticence aucune. De Pauw admet même le chiffre de 400,000 esclaves du 'recensement' de Démétrios de Phalère, donné par Athénée dans un texte aussi célèbre que controversé.[6]

Il ne faut pas croire que De Pauw accepte pour autant sans critique toutes les données de la tradition. Son Athènes est une démocratie historique qui ne commence nullement avec Thésée comme le veut la rhétorique classique, hellénistique et moderne. La période la plus ancienne de l'"histoire' d'Athènes, les premières dates du 'marbre de Paros', par exemple, qui mentionne 'l'arrivée de Cérès à Éleusis', est rejetée comme entièrement légendaire, ce en quoi De Pauw se montre très largement en avance sur son temps. La constitution de Solon est définie comme mixte, non comme démo-cratique. La démocratie n'est réellement fondée que par Aristide, lorsque 'le dernier des Athéniens devint un Roi'. Il n'est pas vrai de dire avec Rousseau que 'des dieux seuls peuvent vivre dans une démocratie'.[7] Commentant l'*Économique* du Pseudo-Aristote, il écrit

---

[1] *Ibid.* p. ix.
[2] De Pauw, *Œuvres*, t. VI, p. 16.
[3] Nous citons la traduction de R. Martin, *L'urbanisme dans la Grèce antique* (Paris, 1956), p. 26.
[4] De Pauw, *Œuvres*, t. VI, pp. 20ss. [5] *Ibid.* pp. 64–5, 156.
[6] Athénée VI, 272 c; De Pauw, *Œuvres*, t. VI, p. 156 et t. VII, pp. 305 ss.
[7] De Pauw, *Œuvres*, t. VII, pp. 153–5, 201, 215–16; sur la démocratie, il s'appuie sur Plutarque, *Aristide* 22. 1.

que, 'l'auteur de ce livre singulier intitulé *Les Économiques* n'y dit pas un seul mot de l'économie, mais il y développe différentes opérations faites par des satrapes de Perse, des rois de Carie...',[1] observations que bien des commentateurs modernes de ce traité de stratagématique fiscale et d'ordre familial auraient intérêt à méditer.[2]

A la veille de l'insurrection de 1789, les principaux cadres d'une Athènes bourgeoise avaient donc été mis en place: ensemble que l'on peut estimer cohérent, mais qui nous paraît aujourd'hui caractérisé par un manque de distance critique du présent par rapport au passé. La critique et la distance seront creusées par la Révolution.

Pendant la 'tourmente', on le sait, Athènes recula au profit de Sparte, qui n'avait du reste cessé de dominer dans l'enseignement des collèges comme dans un large secteur de la critique politique. 'Sparte brille comme un éclair dans des ténèbres immenses', dit Robespierre le 18 floréal an II (7 mai 1794). Sparte fut l'instrument idéologique au moyen duquel les dirigeants montagnards ont pensé la société française comme transparente, c'est-à-dire imaginairement unifiée. La 'fête révolutionnaire', un des aspects les plus conscients de l'imitation de l'antiquité, se veut événement niant l'événement, annulant le temps au profit de la commémoration, incarnant dans l'espace le rêve du législateur.[3]

Ouvrons ici une parenthèse: quittons provisoirement les réseaux de signes qui font l'objet de notre étude pour aborder ce qu'il est convenu d'appeler – par un abus de langage – la réalité sociale, et posons cette question: l'identification à l'antiquité, caractéristique de la forme la plus radicale de la Révolution,[4] a-t-elle eu des conséquences sur le système scolaire, notamment sur l'enseignement des langues anciennes, instrument normal de l'accès à cette antiquité que l'on révérait?

Le problème vaut qu'on le pose, car il s'agit d'un phénomène sérieux engageant tout l'imaginaire d'un groupe d'hommes. Au

---

[1] *Ibid.* p. 358.

[2] Nous pensons par exemple à B. A. Van Groningen, préfacier de l'édition des Belles-Lettres (Paris, 1968).

[3] Cf. Mona Ozouf, *La fête révolutionnaire, 1789–1799* (Paris, 1976); un rapport de Talleyrand qu'on trouvera reproduit en C. Hippeau, *L'instruction publique en France pendant la Révolution*, t. i, *Discours et rapports* (Paris, 1881), p. 169, montre que Barthélemy et De Pauw ont été parmi les auteurs auxquels on a demandé une inspiration pour l'organisation des fêtes révolutionnaires.

[4] Rappelons simplement ici le livre le plus important, H. T. Parker, *The Cult of Antiquity and the French Revolutionaries* (Chicago, 1937).

témoignage du prince de Ligne, à l'occasion d'une de leurs rencontres, le Grand Frédéric 'fit un petit tour à Rome et à Sparte: il aimait à s'y promener'.[1] Les puritains anglais du XVIIe siècle n'allaient pas faire 'un petit tour' dans l'Israël ancien, ils *étaient* largement des personnages de la Bible, ce qui ne signifiait pas du tout – bien au contraire – que, hors quelques exceptions, ils éprouvassent le besoin d'apprendre l'hébreu. Les révolutionnaires français – les législateurs du moins – savaient, en général, assez bien le latin et fort peu le grec. Les plus 'spartiates' d'entre eux n'éprouvaient probablement pas le besoin d'apprendre le grec à leurs enfants. Ils étaient eux-mêmes des exemples vivants.

Aussi bien, un coup d'œil rapide sur les sources et sur les travaux consacrés à cette question[2] le montre-t-il très bien: les révolutionnaires français ne se sont nullement passionnés pour l'apprentissage des langues et de l'histoire classiques.

Ainsi Mirabeau, qui, il est vrai, n'est ni spartiate ni romain, et peut-être à cause de cela, se justifie: 'Je suis loin de vouloir proscrire l'étude des langues mortes; je voudrais surtout qu'on pût faire renaître de ses cendres cette belle langue grecque...mais je crois nécessaire d'ordonner que tout enseignement public se fasse désormais en français.'[3] L'enseignement du latin n'était-il pas lié aux vétustes collèges? Tout au plus le mathématicien montagnard Gilbert Romme entend-il associer l'étude du latin à 'l'amour énergique des Romains pour la liberté dans les temps héroïques de la République', ce latin au sujet duquel Condorcet avait été très réservé, 'puisque tous les préjugés doivent aujourd'hui disparaître'.[4] Le célèbre plan éducatif de Le Peletier, qui concerne les enfants de cinq à douze ans, ne dit rien, et pour cause, des langues anciennes;[5] et pourtant Fourcroy, rappelant l'exemple de Le Peletier, déclarait, le 30 juillet 1793: 'Il n'avait de guides que dans les législateurs anciens. Il regardait, avec les sages de la Grèce, les fils des citoyens comme les

---

[1] Prince de Ligne, *Mémoires et mélanges historiques et littéraires*, t. 1 (Paris, 1827), p. 25.

[2] Bon chapitre de synthèse, dans le livre de S. Moravia, *Il tramonto dell'illuminismo. Filosofia e politica nella società francese (1770–1810)* (Bari, 1968), pp. 315–444; nous avons utilisé les ouvrages de F. Ponteil, *Histoire de l'enseignement 1789–1965* (Paris, 1966); E. Allain, *L'œuvre scolaire de la Révolution* (Paris, 1891); les recueils de C. Hippeau, *L'instruction publique en France pendant la Révolution*, t. 1 et 11, *Débats législatifs* (Paris, 1883), et de J. Guillaume, *Procès verbaux du Comité d'instruction publique de l'Assemblée législative* (Paris, 1889), et *de la Convention nationale* (6 t., Paris, 1891–1917).

[3] Hippeau, *L'instruction publique en France pendant la Révolution*, t. 1, p. 11.

[4] *Ibid.* pp. 205–9 et 306–7.

[5] *Ibid.* pp. 342–86; le texte fut présenté par Robespierre le 13 juillet 1793.

enfants de la République.' Mais lui-même propose simplement ceci:
'Vous pouvez imiter Athènes, où les écoles étaient ouvertes au lever
du soleil et fermées à son coucher.'[1]

En pleine exaltation de l'an II, le 15 brumaire (5 novembre 1793),
on entendit même Marie-Joseph Chénier faire ces remarques
critiques, exceptionnelles il est vrai:

Il faut étudier les hommes et les mœurs, les temps et les lieux, la nature immuable
dans les principes mais toujours variée dans les résultats, et peut-être alors sera-t-on
moins empressé de nous présenter des romans politiques, facilement échafaudés
d'après la *République* de Platon ou d'après les romans historiques composés sur
Lacédémone.[2]

Mais l'"idéologue' Chénier, auteur, pourtant, d'un *Caius Gracchus* au
goût du jour, joué en 1792, avait, il est vrai, une connaissance directe
de la culture grecque.

En fait, c'est avec les temps thermidoriens que le problème se pose
sérieusement, bien que l'École Normale de l'an III ne comporte pas
de chaire de langues anciennes. Les 'Écoles centrales', fondées alors
dans chaque département, font, pour leur part, une place à ces
langues.[3] Un professeur de grammaire générale à l'École centrale du
Lot écrit même à son ministre que 'la langue grecque doit enfin
occuper dans l'instruction publique la place distinguée que sa
supériorité sur toutes les langues connues aurait dû lui assurer...'.[4]
Mais l'accent pédagogique, très novateur, est mis sur les sciences, sur
l'économie politique. 'Lisez la *Richesse des nations*, l'ouvrage peut-être
le plus utile aux peuples de l'Europe', déclarait Lakanal le 16
décembre 1794 (26 brumaire an III).[5] Le principe est que l'enseignement du latin (et du grec) doit se faire en deux ans, ce qui entraîne
les plaintes que l'on imagine.[6] C'est Bonaparte, après 'Brumaire',
puis l'Empereur qui rétablira progressivement la supériorité absolue
du latin, aux dépens, notamment, des mathématiques, et lui
(re)donnera le rôle de sélection sociale qui fut longtemps le sien.[7]
Rome, il est vrai, avait 'remplacé Sparte', mais entre le culte

[1] *Ibid.* pp. 387–97.
[2] *Ibid.* t. II, p. 99.
[3] V., outre les ouvrages cités ci-dessus, le bel article de L. C. Pearce Williams, 'Science,
education and the French Revolution', *Isis*, XLIV (1953), 311–30.
[4] Rouziès, *Tableau analytique des études de l'École centrale du département du Lot* (Paris, an VII),
p. 13.
[5] Hippeau *L'instruction publique en France pendant la Révolution*, t. I, p. 432.
[6] Allain, *L'Œuvre scolaire de la Révolution*, pp. 116–19.
[7] Cf. A. Prost, *Histoire de l'enseignement en France, 1800–1967* (Paris, 1968), pp. 52–6.

révolutionnaire et la pratique des lycées impériaux, le clivage est à peu près total.

Proscrit, le girondin Condorcet, dernier grand représentant des encyclopédistes, donnait aux thèmes en honneur en l'an II un contrepoint minoritaire, mais qui deviendra peu à peu le thème majeur des bourgeois libéraux (dont beaucoup acceptaient alors de mourir pour la liberté). Le 13 germinal an III, sur le rapport de l''idéologue' Daunou, la Convention décidait de faire l'acquisition de 3,000 exemplaires de l'ouvrage posthume de Condorcet, *Esquisse d'un tableau historique des progrès de l'esprit humain* (le titre même dit la dette de l'auteur envers Turgot), et d'en organiser la distribution en commençant par la totalité de ses membres survivants.[1] Nous avons là le texte fondamental par lequel l'idéologie du progrès élaborée au XVIIIe siècle fut transmise par les Thermidoriens au XIXe siècle.[2] Ni Bonald, ni Joseph de Maistre, ni Chateaubriand ne s'y tromperont.[3]

Comment se situe la Grèce dans ce *Tableau*?[4] S'il est vrai que 'la perfectibilité de l'homme est réellement indéfinie', il en résulte que jamais la marche du progrès 'ne sera rétrograde'.[5] Après les clans, l'apparition de l'agriculture et celle de l'écriture, la quatrième époque de l'histoire de l'humanité est symbolisée par 'le progrès de l'esprit humain dans la Grèce jusqu'au temps de la division des sciences, vers le siècle d'Alexandre'.[6] La neuvième, rappelons-le, va 'depuis Descartes jusqu'à la formation de la République française'. La dixième est réservée au futur.

L'attitude de Condorcet envers la Grèce est exempte de tout simplisme. Il écrit ceci, qui va loin:

Presque toutes les institutions des Grecs supposent l'existence de l'esclavage et la possibilité de réunir dans une place publique l'universalité des citoyens; et pour

---

[1] On trouvera le rapport de Daunou en Condorcet, *Œuvres*, éd. A. Condorcet O'Connor, t. VI (Paris, 1847), pp. 3–5.

[2] Bon chapitre sur Condorcet dans Manuel, *The Prophets of Paris*, pp. 53–102; on dispose en outre d'un ensemble très riche sur Condorcet avec le numéro spécial que lui ont consacré les *Cahiers de Fontenay*, V, *Philosophie* (décembre 1976).

[3] 'Apocalypse du nouvel Évangile', dit Bonald, cité par Manuel, *The Prophets of Paris*, p. 61; sur J. de Maistre, cf. ci-dessous p. 199; sur Chateaubriand, v. J. Dagen, 'L'*Essai sur les révolutions* ou les mémoires d'outre-histoire', *Annales publiées par la Faculté des Lettres de Toulouse, Littératures*, XIV (1967), 19–42.

[4] Que nous citons d'après l'édition de Paris, 1829, simplement parce que c'est celle que nous avons sous la main.

[5] *Esquisse*, pp. 7–8.

[6] *Ibid.* pp. 60–79; cf. aussi les fragments reproduits pp. 291–382.

bien juger de leurs effets, surtout pour prévoir ceux qu'elles produisent dans les grandes nations modernes, il ne faut pas perdre un instant de vue ces deux différences si importantes.[1]

Certes, et Condorcet dira aussi ailleurs[2] que l'imprimerie rend la démocratie directe et l'éloquence à la Démosthène inutiles et la représentation possible. Mais, en dernière analyse, ce qui est important, c'est que Condorcet crée en quelque sorte Athènes comme modèle historique lointain. 'On trouverait à peine dans les républiques modernes, et même dans les plans tracés par les philosophes, une institution dont les républiques grecques n'aient offert le modèle ou donné l'exemple.'[3] Condorcet emploie ici le pluriel, mais le modèle est bien Athènes: 'A l'exception d'Athènes, pendant quelque temps, il n'y avait peut-être aucune cité où la généralité des citoyens jouît de la plénitude de ses droits.'[4] La chute des rois, à l'aube de l'histoire grecque, marque le début des révolutions.

C'est à cette même révolution que le genre humain doit ses lumières et *devra* sa liberté. Elle a plus influé sur le sort des nations actuelles de l'Europe que des événements bien plus rapprochés de nous dont nos ancêtres ont été les acteurs et leur pays le théâtre; elle forme en quelque sorte la première page de *notre* histoire.[5]

Si Condorcet admire Léonidas, sans croire toutefois qu'il soit mort pour obéir aux lois de Lacédémone, il écrit que 'la bataille de Salamine est un de ces événements si rares dans l'histoire, où le hasard d'un jour décide pour une longue suite de siècles des destinées du genre humain'.[6] L'histoire est progrès, mais la Grèce anticipe: Démocrite et Pythagore annoncent à leur façon Descartes et Newton.[7] Dans ce rapport double à la Grèce, de distance et d'immédiateté, Condorcet n'est pas très éloigné de Hegel, et ce rapprochement suggère qu'un tournant essentiel a été pris. Car ce discours, Chateaubriand le prolonge, Benjamin Constant le critique, Joseph de Maistre l'inverse et le rend tragique.

Athènes proche et lointaine. Et pourtant un Thermidorien typique, Volney, eut le courage d'exprimer, avec une énergie sans pareille, l'idée que le proche était largement illusoire et que le lointain était

---

[1] *Ibid.* p. 76.
[2] Dans son 'projet de décret sur l'Instruction publique', présenté à la Législative, dans Hippeau, *L'instruction publique en France pendant la Révolution*, t. i, pp. 208–9.
[3] *Esquisse*, p. 75.   [4] *Ibid.* p. 366.
[5] *Ibid.* p. 292. Les mots mis en italiques le sont par nous.
[6] *Ibid.* pp. 380–1.
[7] *Ibid.* p. 65: 'Au milieu de la nuit de ces systèmes, nous voyons même briller deux idées heureuses qui reparaîtront encore dans des siècles plus éclairés.'

réel. Le compromis d'où naît Athènes bourgeoise est ainsi dénoncé dès l'origine.

La chance de Volney (1757–1820) est d'être, certes, un homme qui sait le grec et le latin, qui a lu, et parfois de fort près, Hérodote, mais d'être aussi un orientaliste, et même un orientaliste qui a connu l'Orient.[1] Homme des Lumières, Volney (son pseudonyme se décompose ainsi: *Vol*taire+Fer*ney*) publie en 1787 son *Voyage en Syrie et en Égypte*, avec cette épigraphe qui en résume génialement l'esprit: 'J'ai pensé que le genre des voyages appartenait à l'histoire et non aux romans.'[2] Grande date que ce voyage, car ce que Volney découvre, ce n'est pas l'Orient des *Origines*, ni même la terre du despotisme abstrait qui avait inspiré de façon ambiguë tant de contemporains de Louis XIV ou de Louis XV, c'est très exactement ce que nous appelons aujourd'hui le monde 'sous-développé', le tiers-monde.[3] Il s'agit en effet de décrire un monde malade et, à l'étonnement des commentateurs, le chapitre premier, qui donne une classification des habitants, introduit 'sans raison apparente, un développement sur la maladie'. L'Orient n'est ni exotique ni pittoresque, il est dégradé,[4] parce qu'il a choisi la mauvaise direction historique. Et quand nous lisons la célèbre description d'Alexandrie, c'est bien le tiers-monde, ses foules et son écrasante misère, qui nous saute au visage:

Ce marché mal fourni de dattes et de petits pains ronds et plats; et cette foule immonde de chiens errants dans les rues et ces espèces de fantômes ambulants qui, sous une draperie d'une seule pièce, ne montrent d'humain que deux yeux de femme...ces rues étroites et sans pavé, ces maisons basses et dont les jours rares sont masqués de treillage, ce peuple maigre et noirâtre, qui marche nu-pieds, et n'a pour tout vêtement qu'une chemise bleue, ceinte d'un cuir ou d'un mouchoir rouge.[5]

Et, certes, on peut juger simple l'explication de cette dégradation puisque Volney ne fait guère appel qu'au despotisme turc. En fait,

[1] Sur Volney, le livre essentiel est celui de J. Gaulmier, *L'idéologue Volney (1757–1820)* (Beyrouth, 1951); son auteur l'a lui-même résumé dans *Un grand témoin de la Révolution et de l'empire, Volney* (Paris, 1959); pour l'encadrement intellectuel, cf. le livre déjà cité de Moravia, *Il tramonto dell'illuminismo*.

[2] Nous citons le *Voyage* d'après l'édition critique de J. Gaulmier (Paris et La Haye, 1959); les autres œuvres de Volney d'après ses *Œuvres complètes* (Paris, 1838).

[3] Ce point ne nous paraît pas suffisamment souligné dans les pages consacrées à Volney de l'étude déjà citée de Moravia, 'Philosophie et géographie à la fin du XVIIIe siècle'; l'*Itinéraire* de Chateaubriand sera largement un dialogue avec Volney, cf. J. Gaulmier, 'Chateaubriand et Volney', *Annales de Bretagne*, LXXV (1968), 570–8.

[4] Cf. J. Gaulmier dans son édition, pp. 8–9.

[5] Volney, *Voyage*, p. 26.

Volney se fait ici le porte-parole inspiré d'un Occident qui, lui, a choisi la bonne direction, et les débuts de la Révolution le confirment pleinement dans cette voie. En 1791, il publie *Les Ruines*, ce 'Discours sur l'histoire universelle laïque'.[1] *Les Ruines*, ce sont les traces des 'révolutions du passé', c'est aussi l'appel à un Législateur à l'échelle de l'univers, à un peuple législateur. Et le 'génie' des ruines de s'écrier:

Qu'il se montre un *chef* vertueux, qu'un *peuple puissant* et *juste* paraisse, et la terre l'élève au pouvoir suprême: la terre attend un *peuple législateur*; elle le désire et l'appelle, et mon cœur l'entend...Et tournant la tête du côté de l'Occident: Oui, continua-t-il, déjà un bruit sourd frappe mon oreille: un cri de *liberté*, prononcé sur des rives lointaines, a retenti sur l'ancien continent.[2]

Ce peuple, c'est bien entendu le peuple français, lequel peuple, avec Bonaparte, envahira bientôt l'Égypte, avec l'œuvre de Volney (qui n'avait pas voulu cela) pour guide. Volney lui-même, orientaliste, proposa d'écrire l'arabe et l'hébreu en caractères latins.[3] Disciple pourtant de l'abbé Raynal, et comme lui adversaire de principe de l'entreprise coloniale, il n'en joua pas moins son rôle dans la conquête occidentale, précisément dans la mesure où il fut un des philosophes de l'histoire de l'Occident.[4]

La Révolution française ne s'engagera pas immédiatement sur le grand chemin de la rationalité bourgeoise. En l'an III, après avoir connu la prison et donné ses célèbres leçons à l'École Normale, Volney s'embarque pour l'Amérique. Le *Tableau du climat et du sol des États-Unis* qu'il publiera bien après son retour, en 1803, et qui ne se montre pas enthousiaste pour cette autre branche de l'aventure occidentale, annonce la disparition des derniers Indiens. 'Dans cent ans, dans deux cents ans, il n'existera peut-être plus un seul de ces peuples',[5] et il est grand temps de les étudier, de classer leurs mœurs

---

[1] Gaulmier, *L'idéologue Volney*, p. 220. Gaulmier cite, p. 221, une lettre de Volney du 26 décembre 1814, dénonçant 'le roman juif de Bossuet tant prôné'; v. aussi, sur *Les Ruines*, Moravia, *Il tramonto dell'illuminismo*, pp. 163–8.

[2] Volney, *Œuvres*, p. 30.

[3] Sur la place de Volney dans l'histoire de l'orientalisme, cf. M. Rodinson, 'The western image and western studies of Islam', *The Legacy of Islam*, édd. J. Schacht et C. E. Bosworth, 2e éd. (Oxford, 1974), pp. 9–62, part. p. 42. Sur ses tentatives pour écrire l'arabe et l'hébreu en caractères latins, v. Gaulmier, *L'idéologue Volney*, pp. 543–7.

[4] Volney visita aussi un autre pays qui, 'par sa constitution physique, par les mœurs et le caractère de ses habitants, diffère totalement du reste de la France' et participe 'de l'état sauvage et d'une civilisation commencée': la Corse; cf. son 'précis de l'état de la Corse', qui fut publié dans le *Moniteur* des 20 et 21 mars 1793, et *Œuvres*, p. 738.

[5] *Œuvres*, p. 728; toute une partie du livre est une polémique contre Chateaubriand; cf. Gaulmier, 'Chateaubriand et Volney'.

et leurs langues. Comment ne pas le faire à l'aide du passé de la Grèce? C'est l''Archéologie' de Thucydide, citée dans la nouvelle traduction de P.-Ch. Lévesque,[1] qui permet de comprendre et la Grèce et les Iroquois. 'Ce fragment me semble si bien adapté à mon sujet, que je crois faire une chose agréable au lecteur en le lui soumettant ici, afin qu'il fasse lui-même la comparaison.'[2] Mais Volney va beaucoup plus loin que Thucydide, au risque de rendre incompréhensible le phénomène que fut l'existence même de l'historien athénien, car ce qui vaut pour Homère vaut aussi pour les contemporains de Périclès, et pas seulement pour les Étoliens, dont la barbarie avait frappé et Thucydide et Cornelius De Pauw, mais pour les Athéniens eux-mêmes:

Je suis surtout frappé de l'analogie que je remarque chaque jour entre les sauvages de l'Amérique du nord et les anciens peuples si vantés de la Grèce et de l'Italie. Je retrouve dans les Grecs d'Homère, surtout dans ceux de son *Iliade*, les usages, les discours, les mœurs des *Iroquois*, des *Delawares*, des *Miâmis*. Les tragédies de Sophocle et d'Euripide me peignent presque littéralement les opinions des *hommes rouges* sur la nécessité, sur la fatalité, sur la misère de la condition humaine et sur la dureté du destin aveugle.[3]

Paradoxalement pourtant, Volney admet, l'espace d'un instant, parce que Thucydide, dans l''Archéologie', a parlé du destin particulier de l'Attique, que celle-ci a connu des 'causes occasionnelles de civilisation'.[4]

En l'an III, dans ses leçons de l'École Normale,[5] Volney s'était livré à une critique radicale de l'imitation de l'antiquité, conçue comme un des phénomènes majeurs de la Révolution, et de l'historicisme auquel le mouvement des Idéologues n'avait certes pas été étranger. La page est célèbre, mais il n'est pas inutile de la citer de nouveau. Volney y rappelle

Qu'à Athènes, ce sanctuaire de toutes les libertés, il y avait quatre têtes esclaves contre une tête libre; qu'il n'y avait pas une maison où le régime despotique de nos colonies d'Amérique ne fût exercé par ces prétendus démocrates; que sur environ quatre millions d'âmes qui durent peupler l'ancienne Grèce, plus de trois millions étaient esclaves; que l'inégalité politique et civile des hommes était le dogme des peuples, des législateurs; qu'il était consacré par Lycurgue, par Solon, professé par Aristote, par le divin Platon, par les généraux et les ambassadeurs d'Athènes, de

---

[1] Cf. ci-dessous p. 206.   [2] *Œuvres*, p. 725.

[3] *Ibid.* p. 724–5.

[4] *Ibid.* p. 725, s'appuyant sur Thucydide I. 2, 5–6; mais Volney, lorsqu'il cite en cette même page la fameuse évocation d'une Sparte ruinée (Thucydide I. 10, 2), supprime le parallèle avec Athènes.

[5] Sur l'École Normale, Moravia, *Il tramonto dell'illuminismo*, pp. 380–91.

Sparte et de Rome qui, dans Polybe, dans Tite-Live, dans Thucydide, parlent comme les ambassadeurs d'Attila et de Tchinguizkan (Gengis Khan).[1]

Et Volney ajoute: 'Oui, plus j'ai étudié l'antiquité et ses gouvernements si vantés, plus j'ai conçu que celui des Mamlouks d'Égypte et du dey d'Alger ne différaient point essentiellement de ceux de Sparte et de Rome; et qu'il ne manque, à ces Grecs et à ces Romains tant prônés, que le nom de Huns et de Vandales pour nous en retracer tous les caractères.' La 'seule guerre juste et honorable fut la guerre contre Xerxès'. A peine est-elle terminée qu'Athènes inaugure ses 'insolentes vexations'. Les chefs-d'œuvre de l'art attique furent la 'première cause' de la ruine d'Athènes, 'parce qu'étant le fruit d'un système d'extorsions et de rapines, ils provoquèrent à la fois le ressentiment et la défection de ses alliés, la jalousie et la cupidité de ses ennemis, et parce que ces masses de pierre, quoique bien comparties, sont partout un emploi stérile du travail et un absorbement ruineux de la richesse'.[2] Une idéologie bourgeoise de la production est ici au travail et rejoint la lecture de Thucydide que Pierre-Charles Lévesque achevait alors de traduire.

On a pu se demander, à propos d'Edward Gibbon, si l'historien de la décadence de l'Empire romain vivait son aventure intellectuelle en continuité ou en rupture avec la tradition historiographique des classiques.[3] Dans le cas de Volney, il n'y a pas matière à hésitation; à aucun titre il n'est un contemporain de Thucydide.

Donc, la rupture est acquise. Encore faut-il en répéter le geste plus d'une fois, encore faut-il creuser l'écart avant de s'y installer. Après Thermidor, il faut tout revoir, tout récrire, tout comprendre à nouveaux frais. Dans cette entreprise de reconstruction du discours, la Grèce a sa place. Elle l'a encore, ou elle l'a déjà – la Grèce révolutionnaire encore, la Grèce des libéraux déjà. Le temps viendra avec Pierre-Charles Lévesque, avec Benjamin Constant, de constituer la cité grecque (et la démocratie athénienne) en objet d'étude. Pour l'heure, le plus pressé est de s'aider de l'antiquité pour comprendre ce présent déjà passé qu'est la Révolution française. Tel est

[1] On pourrait comparer avec ce qu'écrivait J. de Lolme, théoricien genevois du régime représentatif, dans sa *Constitution de l'Angleterre* (1778), nouvelle éd. (Genève, 1793), t. II, p. 22, n. 1: 'A Athènes même, qui est la seule des républiques anciennes où il paraisse qu'il y ait eu de la liberté, on voit les magistrats procéder, à peu près comme on fait aujourd'hui chez les Turcs.'

[2] Volney, *Œuvres*, pp. 592-3.

[3] On notera les réponses opposées de Sir Ronald Syme et d'Arnaldo Momigliano dans *Gibbon et Rome*, éd. Ducrey, pp. 47-56 et 57-72.

le projet de l'*Essai historique sur les révolutions* de Chateaubriand, publié à Londres en 1797.[1]

Curieux ouvrage en vérité. Livre d'un émigré mais 'dédié à tous les partis'. Livre d'histoire mais hanté par l'intemporelle loi qui 'nous précipitera de révolution en révolution jusqu'au dernier siècle' (Ière partie, ch. LXX, p. 314), et qui tente d'amarrer à l'antiquité un présent sorti du cours du temps – le présent de la France, celui aussi de Chateaubriand, tiraillé entre les 'perfections imaginaires' de novateurs trop audacieux et le retard obscurantiste de ceux qui 'veulent rester les hommes du quatorzième siècle dans l'année 1796'.[2] Essai politique mais qui s'achève dans la nuit, chez les sauvages de l'Amérique: 'plus de villes,...plus de présidents, de républiques, de rois' mais une révolution tout intérieure (IIe partie, ch. LVII, p. 573). On ne se hâtera pas pour autant de crier à l'incohérence de ce 'livre étrange et désordonné';[3] ce serait tomber dans le piège que Chateaubriand lui-même tend au lecteur lorsque, en 1826, profitant de la réédition de l'*Essai*, il feint de prendre ses distances vis-à-vis d'un texte de jeunesse.[4]

Qu'est-ce qu'une révolution? Réponse: 'une conversion totale du gouvernement d'un peuple, soit du monarchique au républicain ou du républicain au monarchique' (Introduction, pp. 10–11). Nanti de cette définition, Chateaubriand compte douze révolutions, dont cinq antiques, au nombre desquelles 'l'établissement des républiques en Grèce' – la première – et 'leur sujétion sous Philippe et Alexandre' – la seconde. Autant dire, si l''on peut fixer à la retraite d'Hippias l'époque des beaux jours de la Grèce et la fin de la révolution républicaine' (I, ch. XII, p. 52), que, pour la Grèce, à l'origine il y eut la révolution. Aussi Chateaubriand se gardera-t-il

---

[1] *Essai historique, politique et moral sur les révolutions anciennes et modernes considérées dans leurs rapports avec la Révolution française* (Londres, 1797). Nous utiliserons ici l'édition de Lefèvre (*Œuvres complètes*, t. 1 (Paris, 1830)), plus aisément consultable que l'édition originale; toutefois, attentifs à la mise en garde de J. Mourot sur la nécessité de recourir à l'édition de 1797 (J. Mourot, *Études sur les premières œuvres de Chateaubriand* (Paris, 1962), pp. 37–179, et tout spécialement p. 88), nous avons systématiquement vérifié que les textes cités ne présentaient pas de modification appréciable par rapport à l'édition originale.

[2] Introduction, p. 3. 'Le mal, le grand mal, c'est que nous ne sommes point de notre siècle', etc.

[3] Sainte-Beuve, *Chateaubriand et son groupe littéraire*, 2e éd. (Paris, 1889), t. I, pp. 145 et 152.

[4] Le ton est donné par la Préface, p. xxii ('livre détestable et parfaitement ridicule'); les notes de 1826 se chargeront d'en asséner la preuve – parfaitement ambiguë; sur ces notes destinées à 'garder le beau rôle' et à 'faire office de paratonnerre' contre l'originalité d'un texte, que Chateaubriand cherche à rattacher au *Génie du Christianisme* v. Mourot, *Études*, p. 94 et Dagen, 'L'*Essai sur les révolutions* ou les mémoires d'outre-histoire', p. 20.

bien de mener son exposé au-delà de cette révolution originaire, comme si, entre 510 av. J.-C. et 1789, le temps s'était arrêté. Dans 'l'espace à deux moments' de cette histoire,[1] on verra peut-être le signe de ce que Chateaubriand doit beaucoup au climat intellectuel de la Révolution;[2] on y verra surtout le lieu privilégié du projet comparatif qui anime l'*Essai*.

Car la seule, la vraie question se formule ainsi: 'Parmi ces révolutions, en est-il quelques-unes qui, par l'esprit, les mœurs et les lumières du temps, puissent se comparer à la révolution actuelle de France?' (Introduction, p. 9). Reste à admettre le postulat que 'rien n'est nouveau sous le soleil' et que l'histoire se répète, parfois à la lettre (Préface, p. xxiii; I, ch. LIX, p. 257; II, ch. LVI, p. 559), et l'on obtient un livre où la Révolution française sert de 'foyer commun' (Introduction, p. 10) et l'histoire grecque de miroir. Une histoire grecque qui n'est jamais étudiée pour elle-même – les faits 'étrangers dans leurs causes et dans leurs effets à ceux de la révolution française' ont été écartés (Introduction, p. 12) – et que Chateaubriand ne constitue pas comme telle puisqu'il doit largement son information à l'abbé Barthélemy:[3] mais dans ce domaine les scrupules ne l'embarrassent guère et, si son érudition n'est pas aussi fantaisiste que le prétendait Renan,[4] 'rares sont les passages qui relèvent d'une véritable méthode historique'.[5]

---

[1] Nous empruntons cette expression à J. Dagen, 'L'*Essai sur les révolutions*', p. 22.

[2] On évoquera l'exclamation de Saint-Just: 'Le monde est vide depuis les Romains' (*Œuvres complètes*, éd. C. Vellay (Paris, 1908), t. II, p. 331). Sur la surprenante absence du Moyen Age dans l'*Essai*, v. F. Engel-Janosi, 'Chateaubriand as a historical writer', *Four Studies in French Romantic Historical Writing*, The Johns Hopkins University Studies in Historical and Political Science, LXXI, 2 (1955), 31–56 (et tout spécialement p. 35).

[3] Les protestations de sérieux de Chateaubriand (v. Introduction, p. 5, n. 2 et I, ch. LXX, p. 313) n'ont guère impressionné M. Badolle (*L'Abbé Jean-Jacques Barthélemy*, pp. 366–70), pour qui Chateaubriand a pillé le *jeune Anacharsis*; même conviction chez Mourot, *Études*, pp. 66, 87–8 et 91. Position beaucoup plus nuancée chez F. Letessier, 'Une source de Chateaubriand: *Le voyage du jeune Anacharsis*', *Revue d'histoire littéraire de la France*, LIX (1959), 180–203 (dossier de la question).

[4] 'Le sens esthétique si éminent dont il était doué ne reposait pas sur une solide instruction' (*L'avenir de la science* (Paris, 1890), p. 295); dans la note 133 (*ibid.*), Renan va même jusqu'à accuser Chateaubriand d'avoir, par une fausse lecture du mot λιλαιομένη (*Odyssée*, I, 15), 'tapissé de lilas' la grotte de Calypso. Pour n'avoir pas vérifié le bien-fondé de cette assertion dans le passage du *Génie du Christianisme* (II, ch. V, p. 1; t. II de l'éd. originale (Paris, 1802), p. 219) auquel Renan fait une allusion fort imprécise, C. R. Hart (*Chateaubriand and Homer* (Baltimore et Paris, 1928), p. 101) perpétue cette légende que la critique littéraire s'est, peu de temps après, employée à détruire: v. la démonstration dans les articles 'Renan et Chateaubriand' de G. Moulinier (*Journal des Débats*, 15 mai 1935), M. Duchemin (*Chateaubriand. Essais de critique et d'histoire littéraire* (Paris, 1938), pp. 455–61) et R. Lebègue (*Revue d'histoire littéraire de la France*, LIX (1959), 39–49).

[5] De l'aveu même de F. Letessier ('Une source de Chateaubriand', p. 203).

Il s'ensuit, on le devine, une série d'audacieuses assimilations, parfois limpides (les 'Montagnards' du temps de Pisistrate et les Montagnards de la Convention;[1] les élégies de Tyrtée et la Marseillaise – I, ch. XXIII, pp. 102–5; les lois de Dracon et les décrets de Robespierre – I, ch. V, p. 35), souvent déroutantes (Mégaclès et Tallien – I, ch. VIII, p. 44; Pythagore et Bernardin de Saint-Pierre – I, ch. XLI, p. 195);[2] et surtout, donnant à l'ouvrage sa charpente, l'identification des guerres médiques et des guerres révolutionnaires: 'A l'hymne de Castor, à celle des Marseillais, les républicains s'avancent à la mort. Des prodiges s'achèvent au cri de *Vive la liberté!* et la Grèce et la France comptent Marathon, Salamine, Platées, Fleurus, Wissembourg, Lodi.'[3] Où est la Grèce? Où est la France? Leur histoire s'écrit dans le même intemporel présent et il suffit d'une phrase pour que s'abolisse le temps polyphonique de l'histoire: 490 av. J.-C. = 1793 (I, ch. LXV, p. 277).

Dans cet aplatissement de la temporalité on peut voir 'le comble du ridicule', comme l'auteur de l'*Essai* lui-même y invite lorsque, devenu Chateaubriand, il revient trente ans après sur cet écrit de jeunesse,[4] et, depuis Montlosier, la critique ne s'en est pas privée.[5] On peut également accuser Chateaubriand d'avoir méconnu 'cette grande et première vérité qui devait faire la base de son œuvre:... que la Révolution française n'a aucun rapport avec les autres révolutions de la terre;... [qu'] en dimension, en esprit, en résultat, tout y a été différent'.[6] Mais Chateaubriand n'était pas si naïf et

---

[1] I, ch. VII, pp. 41–2; on notera que, dans son compte rendu de l'*Essai*, Montlosier, l'un des premiers lecteurs de Chateaubriand, donne ce chapitre comme exemple 'de l'esprit et du ton de cet ouvrage' (*Journal de France et d'Angleterre*, fascicule du 22 avril 1797, p. 318). Sur cette revue, publiée par Montlosier à Londres entre le 6 janvier et le 29 juillet 1797, et sur le compte rendu de l'*Essai*, v. P. Christophorov, *Sur les pas de Chateaubriand en exil* (Paris, 1960), pp. 203–5 et 216; A. Andrewes nous a procuré une photocopie de cet article, introuvable en dehors de la Bibliothèque Bodléienne d'Oxford, et nous l'en remercions très chaleureusement.

[2] On pourrait ajouter: les Sept Sages et les encyclopédistes (I, ch. XXIV, p. 112), les archers scythes et les Suisses des Rois de France (I, ch. XLIX, p. 216), etc.

[3] I, ch. XXV, p. 126. V. la note de la p. 258 (I, ch. LX), où Chateaubriand annonce que, 'parlant désormais de la Perse et de l'Allemagne ensemble', il se contentera d'indiquer par un simple tiret 'le changement d'un empire à l'autre' et, entre les pages 276 et 277, le tableau des forces en présence des deux côtés.

[4] I, ch. VI, p. 38; voir aussi pp. 33, 42, 45, 58, 267, 271, 301, etc.

[5] Montlosier, *Journal de France et d'Angleterre*, p. 317, parle de rapprochements 'piquants', 'minutieux, puérils, inexacts, forcés'; la critique moderne renchérit (par exemple, Canat, *L'hellénisme des Romantiques*, t. I, p. 53); voir toutefois, sur les rapprochements comme clé de l'œuvre, les remarques de Sainte-Beuve, *Chateaubriand et son groupe littéraire*, p. 152, et Dagen, 'L'*Essai sur les révolutions*', p. 21.

[6] Montlosier, *Journal de France et d'Angleterre*.

savait consacrer un chapitre entier (I, ch. LXVIII) à la 'différence générale entre notre siècle et celui où s'opéra la Révolution Républicaine de la Grèce', chapitre où l'on apprend que 'la dissemblance des temps se fait sentir dans toute sa force' (p. 303) et qu''il faut s'attendre que l'effet des mouvements actuels de la France surpasse infiniment celui des troubles de la Grèce' (p. 301). Ainsi l'auteur de l'*Essai* se paie le luxe tout aristocratique de risquer de 'battre en ruine [son] propre système' (note de 1826, p. 301); il ne renonce pas pour autant à son projet comparatif, et c'est là pour nous l'essentiel.

Il est donc permis de voir dans ce projet plus qu'un simple ridicule; d'y entrevoir même ce que Chateaubriand, ancien ministre et personnalité ministrable, n'aimait point trop en 1826 à retrouver sous sa plume de 1797, comme si, à comparer Tyrtée et la Marseillaise, il pactisait de fait avec le processus révolutionnaire: la compréhension de la Révolution française avec ses propres catégories; bref, la reconnaissance de l'imitation comme principe théorique de la Révolution. Chateaubriand l'a superbement écrit, dans un des quatre chapitres qu'il consacre aux Jacobins: 'Un trait distinctif de notre révolution, c'est qu'il faut admettre la voie spéculative et les doctrines abstraites pour infiniment dans ses causes. Elle a été produite en partie par des gens de lettres qui, plus habitants de Rome et d'Athènes que de leur pays, ont cherché à ramener dans l'Europe les mœurs antiques' (I, ch. XVII, p. 70).

Ainsi, faire de l'imitation le centre de l'*Essai*, c'est tenter de réfléchir sur l'identification du moderne à l'antique, pour mieux en dénoncer les dangers. Trois protagonistes – Sparte, Athènes et les Français – l'histoire universelle pour théâtre, le drame vaut la peine d'être à nouveau mis en scène. Parce qu''une race d'hommes, se levant tout à coup, se [mit] dans son vertige à sonner l'heure de Sparte et d'Athènes' (I, ch. LXX, p. 318), le meneur de jeu négligera les 'annales des autres petites villes', 'trop peu connues pour intéresser' (I, ch. IV, p. 32).

Ici commence la stratégie de Chateaubriand qui prend la Révolution au piège de ses propres désirs, c'est-à-dire de son imaginaire, ou de son réel, car à l'émigré l'exil a appris que 'nous n'apercevons jamais la réalité des choses, mais leurs images réfléchies faussement par nos propres désirs' (II, ch. LVI, p. 569). La France a voulu être Sparte (I, ch. XIII–XVI, pp. 54–7, 60, 67)? Il faut, coûte que coûte, dénoncer la non-conformité de la 'copie'. Oui, la révolution a été pure à Sparte 'qui fut assez heureuse pour posséder dans le même homme le révolutionnaire et le législateur' (I, ch. IV, p. 33). Mais, parce qu'ils ressemblent à s'y méprendre aux Athéniens,[1] les Français n'ont jamais imité réellement qu'Athènes, en une imitation involontaire autant que dépourvue de génie: 'Autant le siècle de Solon' – encore et toujours lui! – 'surpasse le nôtre en morale, autant les factieux de l'Attique furent supérieurs en talent à ceux de la France' (I, ch. VIII, p. 43).

Ainsi Chateaubriand use d'Athènes comme d'une autre France, une France antique pour mettre à distance la France actuelle. Une France antique qui a 'réellement possédé ce que la France prétend avoir de nos jours: la constitution la plus démocratique qui ait jamais existé chez aucun peuple' (I, ch. VI, pp. 37–8). Mieux encore: Athènes sert à prouver qu'en France la république est impossible puisqu'il n'existe pas de vraie démocratie sans esclavage (I, ch. LVIII, p. 302). Certes, en 1826, Chateaubriand s'accusera d'avoir méconnu le fossé qui sépare démocratie antique et république représentative mais, pour nous, l'essentiel est qu'en 1797 et pour les besoins de l'identification, l'*Essai sur les révolutions* ait fait de l'esclavage le fondement du système athénien.[2]

La France n'est donc pas Athènes, mais Athènes est la France, une France plus conséquente avec elle-même. A ce retournement des identifications, Athènes gagne une position dominante, dans l'*Essai* ('Placés à Athènes comme au centre, nous suivrons les rayons de la révolution qui en partent...')[3] comme dans le discours sur la Grèce antique. Dès que sa figure pâlit, au IVe siècle – ou dès que la comparaison devient difficile – l'*Essai* se mue en une collection hétéroclite de rapprochements toujours plus étranges, révélant ainsi au grand jour son caractère de rhapsodie mal jointe. Inversement,

---

[1] V. I, ch. V, p. 34 ('les Athéniens semblables aux Français sous tant de rapports'), I, ch. XLIX, p. 217, et surtout I, ch. XVIII (caractère des Athéniens et des Français), chapitre dont Chateaubriand reprendra la péroraison presque mot pour mot dans *Le Génie du Christianisme* (III, ch. III, 5, pp. 97–8 de l'édition originale).

[2] A cet égard, la critique adressée à Chateaubriand par Montlosier (*Journal de France et d'Angleterre*, pp. 317–18) est intéressante: Chateaubriand n'aurait pas vu la différence entre une société ancienne, où l'esclavage 'épurait' l'atmosphère du gouvernement politique parce que 'tous ces hommes connus aujourd'hui sous le nom de sans-culottes étaient dans la servitude' et la Révolution française qui a 'mis en mouvement une classe de barbares et de sauvages que les sociétés modernes renferment dans leur sein'.

[3] I, ch. XXVII, p. 131; v. encore I, ch. LXVIII, pp. 300–1 (Athènes ou le nez de Cléopâtre). Montlosier avait bien vu la chose ('On rit de voir comparer les événements de l'Attique ...à ceux de la France' (*Journal de France et d'Angleterre*, p. 317)). Sur la construction de l'*Essai* autour d'Athènes, cf. Dagen, 'L'*Essai sur les révolutions*', p. 32.

l'*Essai* a peut-être contribué à faire d'Athènes une sorte d'*analogon* de la Grèce tout entière, ainsi qu'on peut s'en assurer à lire les chapitres où guerres médiques et guerres révolutionnaires s'entremêlent étroitement.[1]

Tout cela ne va pas sans ambiguïté. Certes, admettant des 'biens' à côté des 'maux' dans l'examen qu'il fait de l''influence de la Révolution républicaine sur les Grecs' (i, chs. xxv–xxvi), Chateaubriand feint de ne parler que de la Grèce. Mais à chaque ligne la France perce derrière Athènes, au point que le lecteur s'interroge: les Français eux aussi ne viennent-ils pas de vivre 'le siècle des merveilles' (p. 127)? Pour eux, il est vrai, les maux se sont mêlés aux biens, et la liberté des guerres révolutionnaires aux exactions de la conquête;[2] mais, par l'intermédiaire de la Grèce, c'est bien la France révolutionnaire qu'admire Chateaubriand,[3] ses victoires, sa 'valeur indomptable', sa 'constance dans l'adversité' et, en une inconséquence significative, il va même jusqu'à créditer les Jacobins de la cohérence qu'il cherche pourtant à leur refuser.[4] Sans le vouloir peut-être, sans le savoir peut-être, il retrouve ainsi la démarche d'un autre 'émigré'(?), le Vieil Oligarque qui, au Ve siècle av. J.-C., créditait la démocratie athénienne d'une politique rationnelle et systématique. On ne s'étonnera pas, dès lors, que les émigrés, 'compagnons d'infortune' de Chateaubriand, aient accordé à l'*Essai* un accueil assez froid.[5]

Et pourtant l'*Essai* leur réservait, nous réserve une ultime surprise: décidément installé dans l'ambiguïté au point de contredire ses propres contradictions, Chateaubriand n'hésite pas, après avoir identifié démocrates athéniens et républicains français, à comparer les Trente à la Convention, les Trois Mille aux Jacobins et les démocrates de Thrasybule aux royalistes émigrés (ii, chs. iv–viii, pp. 339–52). Nous en retiendrons pour finir que – ces inconséquences

[1] i, ch. xxvi, p. 129 où, par deux fois, 'les Grecs' désignent les Athéniens; i, ch. lxii, p· 268. Sans doute y verra-t-on l'effet direct de l'équivalence, implicite dans l'*Essai*, entre 'les Français' et 'Paris'; mais cela suppose aussi qu'Athènes soit pensée comme une sorte de capitale de la Grèce.

[2] Athènes est au contraire sauvée par une coupure chronologique qui met les 'biens' du côté de 'la guerre médique' (c'est-à-dire pour Chateaubriand, de 504 à la paix d'Artaxerxès) et les 'maux' dans la 'fureur de conquête' impérialiste.

[3] Comme l'a bien vu P. Barberis qui parle de 'fascination' ('Chateaubriand et le préromantisme', *Colloque de Rennes (Bicentenaire de la naissance de Chateaubriand)*, *Annales de Bretagne*, lxxv (1968), 547–58; citation p. 552).

[4] Voir les chs. xiii à xvii et surtout les pp. 59, 66 (et la note de 1826), 68, 69 (n. 1) et 70 (conclusion).

[5] Sur l'accueil fait à l'*Essai*, voir Christophorov, *Sur les pas de Chateaubriand*, pp. 201–10.

mêmes l'indiquent – Athènes est devenue le *topos* de la réflexion sur la France: une réserve – inépuisable – de lieux communs.

En cette même année 1797 étaient publiées, fictivement à Londres, en réalité à Bâle, les *Considérations sur la France* de Joseph de Maistre, chef-d'œuvre de la littérature réactionnaire sur la Révolution française.[1]

Le premier classique de ce type d'ouvrage avait été, en 1790, les *Reflections on the Revolution in France* de Burke.[2] Le thème grec n'en est pas absent, mais Burke se contente, en fidèle héritier de la tradition scolaire, de déplorer le déclin de l'Aréopage, et le danger que représente le fait de gouverner avec des décrets (*pséphismata*). Avec Louis de Bonald, dont la *Théorie du pouvoir politique* paraît en 1796 à Constance et est aussitôt saisie sur le territoire français par ordre du Directoire, avec Joseph de Maistre, il s'agit de tout autre chose.

Dans son étude récente sur ce 'matérialiste mystique', M. Robert Triomphe a pu consacrer plus de cent pages à Joseph de Maistre et l'hellénisme, montrant comment 'la Grèce, la menteuse Grèce, qui a tout osé dans l'histoire', a obsédé le théoricien de la contre-révolution qui, comme tant d'autres après lui, s'appuya sur Platon contre la pratique athénienne.[3]

Notre propos n'est pas ici d'explorer à nouveau cet ensemble, mais simplement de noter ce qu'apportent de neuf, dans un discours traditionnel, le texte des *Considérations*, celui, antérieur mais que Maistre ne publia pas lui-même, de l'*Étude sur la souveraineté* de 1794–96,[4] et les *Fragments sur la France*, contemporains des *Considérations*.[5] Trois points nous paraissent essentiels. Le premier est la critique, partiellement renouvelée de Platon, de la législation écrite, à moins, bien sûr, ce qui ne va pas sans difficulté, qu'elle n'ait été

---

[1] Il y a en fait sur la date de l'édition originale une querelle dont nous ne savons pas si elle est définitivement tranchée, certains auteurs et certains catalogues soutenant l'existence d'une ou deux éditions lausannoises en 1796. Robert Triomphe, dans sa grande monographie, *Joseph de Maistre. Étude sur la vie et sur la doctrine d'un matérialiste mystique* (Genève, 1968), ne tranche pas la question puisqu'il adopte la date la plus ancienne dans la chronologie (p. 602) et la plus récente dans le cours du texte (pp. 170–4). Nous avons, pour notre part, suivi les conclusions de l'édition de R. Johannet et F. Vermale (Paris, 1936), d'après laquelle nous citons les *Considérations*.

[2] Nous citons l'édition des *Reflections* procurée par C. C. O'Brien (Penguin books, Harmondsworth, 1969), pp. 326–7.

[3] Triomphe, *Joseph de Maistre*, pp. 375–485; le texte de Juvénal, *Satires* x. 174–5, 'quidquid Graecia mendax audet in historia', est cité dans les *Soirées de Saint-Pétersbourg*, dans *Œuvres complètes*, t. IV (Lyon, 1884), p. 81.

[4] Reproduit dans *Œuvres complètes*, t. I (Lyon, 1884), pp. 309–554.

[5] *Ibid.* pp. 187–220.

dictée par Dieu même, ce que fut à la limite toute bonne législation, toute vraie législation, celle de Moïse, celle de Charlemagne, mais aussi celle de Numa, celle de Lycurgue, sur lequel Joseph de Maistre revient de façon obsédante.[1] Ni l'attitude envers le concept de législateur, ni l'attitude envers la Grèce ne sont tout à fait semblables à celles de Bonald. Ce dernier n'admet, à la limite, qu'une seule constitution, celle dictée par le Dieu des Juifs et des Chrétiens. Il oppose catégoriquement Lycurgue à Moïse, et l'apocalypse divine à la 'trompette prophétique' sonnée par Condorcet.[2] La société précède l'homme et, 'dans la Grèce, [nous voyons] le pouvoir général de la société devenir le pouvoir particulier de chaque membre de l'association, c'est-à-dire la société devenue l'homme',[3] ce qui est tout simplement l'inverse de la vision libérale de la Grèce. Celle-ci est tout entière l'ennemie, 'le Grec [peut être comparé] à un Roi de théâtre qui, la pièce finie, a déposé le sceptre et le diadème, et qui, revenu à son premier état, mêle à des habitudes de valet le langage emphatique de son rôle'.[4] Lacédémone est, entre toutes, haïssable: 'Sparte, à laquelle de prétendus amis de l'humanité veulent sans cesse nous ramener, Sparte n'était qu'une école de guerriers farouches.'[5]

Joseph de Maistre est, en réalité, beaucoup plus proche, à sa façon, de la tradition des Lumières. Il est symbolique que, parvenant à Lausanne, il ait tenu à faire le pèlerinage de la maison de Gibbon.[6]

Le Législateur est inspiré par Dieu, mais le Législateur existe, la meilleure législation étant, bien entendu, orale: 'Plus on écrit et plus l'institution est faible; voilà pourquoi l'institution la plus vigoureuse de l'Antiquité profane fut celle de Lacédémone, où l'on n'écrivit rien.'[7]

Il en résulte, et c'est notre second point, que, comme Rousseau, Mably ou Robespierre, Joseph de Maistre choisit Sparte contre Athènes. Contre la grande cité, Maistre s'est nourri de l'œuvre de Mitford, historien tory de la Grèce, et de Sir William Young, qui

---

[1] Sur Lycurgue, cf. *Étude sur la souveraineté*, pp. 333–41, 346 (avec Moïse, Servius, Numa, Charlemagne, Saint Louis), 361–2; *Considérations*, pp. 50, 68 (avec Numa, Moïse, Mahomet), 77, et dans les *Fragments*, p. 205.

[2] *Théorie du pouvoir politique et religieux dans la société civile démontrée par le raisonnement et par l'histoire* ([Constance], 1796), t. II, pp. 94 et 482.

[3] *Ibid.* t. I, p. 140.

[4] *Ibid.* p. 143.   [5] *Ibid.* p. 141.

[6] Johannet et Vermale, *Considérations*, p. xviii.

[7] *Considérations*, p. 77; l'idée vient pour une part du *Phèdre* de Platon que Maistre citera plus tard, en 1814, cf. *Œuvres complètes*. t. I, p. 255.

peignait une démocratie commerçante.[1] Par delà les critiques classiques sur la versatilité des foules démocratiques qui un jour acclament Miltiade et un autre le condamnent,[2] ce que représente Athènes, c'est l'idée de délibération, or, 'ce qu'il y a de sûr, c'est que la constitution civile des peuples n'est jamais le résultat d'une délibération'.[3] Solon, cette exception à la règle selon laquelle 'les plus grands législateurs ont été des souverains', créa une institution qui fut, elle, 'la plus fragile de l'Antiquité'.[4]

Joseph de Maistre inaugure donc l'usage réactionnaire moderne du mirage spartiate qui s'est prolongé jusqu'à l'Allemagne nazie et au-delà. En quelques années, par un bond singulier, Sparte a glissé des Montagnards au plus violent des 'réacteurs'. Maistre n'écrit pas contre les Montagnards qui sont le passé, mais contre les Thermidoriens, Benjamin Constant par exemple. Les *Considérations* sont une riposte à sa brochure 'Sur la force du gouvernement actuel et la nécessité de s'y rallier'.[5]

En troisième lieu, le rapport de Maistre à la philosophie des Lumières n'est pas sans rappeler celui du marquis de Sade à cette même philosophie. L'état de nature, chez Sade, est pur désir. Chez Maistre, à la limite, il n'y a pas d'état de nature, puisque l'homme est toujours un être sociable et que les sauvages sont 'déchus' ou 'non parvenus' à la sociabilité. Quant à l'"enfant sauvage', thème alors à la mode, c'est un 'conte'.[6] Mais la violence est en nous. 'Nous naissons tous despotes.' Il n'y a pas plus de 'bons sauvages' que de 'peuple de Dieux'. Pour réfuter le mythe américain, Maistre s'appuie sur Cornelius De Pauw: 'Je ne vois pas qu'on ait répondu à l'ingénieux auteur des *Recherches philosophiques sur les Américains.*'[7]

Mais ce pessimisme entraîne une vision proprement tragique de l'histoire. Chose très neuve, Maistre utilise la tragédie grecque, en concurrence avec Shakespeare, comme moteur de sa philosophie de l'histoire. C'est par le sacrifice sanglant que l'humanité achète le droit tà l'existence et Joseph de Maistre cite, en grec, l'*Oreste* d'Euripide (1639–42): 'La beauté d'Hélène, dit Apollon, ne fut qu'un instrument dont les dieux se servirent pour mettre aux prises

---

[1] Lecture de Mitford et de Young, cf. Triomphe, *Joseph de Maistre*, p. 381. Sur l'*History of Greece* de Mitford (London, 1784–1810), cf. A. Momigliano, *Studies in Historiography* (London, 1966), pp. 57–62.
[2] *Étude sur la souveraineté*, p. 486.
[3] *Ibid.* p. 346. [4] *Ibid.* p. 347; *Considérations*, p. 78.
[5] Cf. Johannet et Vermale, *Considérations*, pp. xxii–xxiii.
[6] *Étude sur la souveraineté*, pp. 321–2. [7] *Ibid.* pp. 380, 449, 453.

les Grecs et les Troyens et faire couler le sang afin d'*étancher* sur la terre l'iniquité des hommes devenus trop nombreux.'[1] Et peu importe ici qu''iniquité' rende très mal le grec ὕβρισμα (outrage). Il en découle ce que personne, en France, n'avait osé dire avant Maistre, et ce que personne n'osera répéter après lui, que 'le point rayonnant pour les Grecs fut l'époque terrible de la Guerre du Péloponnèse'.[2]

Telle est la machine de guerre que J. de Maistre a dressée contre Condorcet, 'ce philosophe si cher à la révolution, qui employa sa vie à préparer le malheur de la génération présente, léguant bénignement la perfection à nos neveux'.[3]

Ce n'était pas là, certes, l'idéologie majoritaire de la bourgeoisie libérale, cette idéologie qu'un historien patenté va dégager pour nous.

Donc, quittant Londres, Bâle et l'émigration, nous revenons en France. C'est en effet dans la France post-thermidorienne, puis napoléonienne, où le savoir, pris en charge par des institutions prestigieuses, s'est déjà réorganisé après la 'tourmente', que se constitue réellement l'objet historique nommé Grèce et, sur cet objet, un discours articulé, auquel s'attache le nom de Pierre-Charles Lévesque.

Discours de spécialiste, certes, produit au sein de l'Institut dont il est en l'an IV, avec Volney, un des membres fondateurs.[4] Mais la Classe des Sciences morales et politiques, où il s'élabore entre 1795 et 1803,[5] n'a rien d'une tour d'ivoire; grâce aux Idéologues qui y siègent en force, elle vit d'une intense activité: on y disserte sur les institutions de Sparte et d'Athènes mais on s'y empoigne aussi sur le procès de formation du langage, sur le sens et la valeur de l'histoire.

---

[1] *Considérations*, p. 44.

[2] *Considérations*, p. 42. Par un sophisme remarquable, Maistre ajoute aussitôt: 'Le siècle d'Auguste *suivit* immédiatement la guerre civile et les proscriptions'; cf. aussi, p. 42: 'l'extrême carnage s'allie souvent avec l'extrême population, comme on l'a vu surtout dans les anciennes républiques grecques'.

[3] *Ibid.* p. 43.

[4] Cf. Gaulmier, *L'idéologue Volney*, p. 380 (Volney était alors en Amérique).

[5] 1795: date de la création de l'Institut, après la vacance de la période révolutionnaire; 1803: date de la dissolution de la Classe des Sciences morales et politiques par Napoléon, hostile aux Idéologues et qui préfère de beaucoup rétablir l'ancienne Académie des Inscriptions sous le nom de 'Classe d'histoire et de littérature ancienne' (sur l'histoire de l'Académie des Inscriptions de 1789 à 1832, voir l'Avertissement à la *Table générale et méthodique des mémoires de l'Académie des Inscriptions et Belles-Lettres* par E. de Rozière et E. Châtel (Paris, 1856), pp. xi–xvi). Sur les Idéologues à l'Institut, v. Moravia, *Il tramonto dell'illuminismo*, pp. 425 et 439.

Aux attaques que le fougueux Louis-Sébastien Mercier[1] lance contre l'histoire ancienne ('Ce que nous faisons est aussi de l'histoire; faisons cette histoire-là sans modèle, il y aura plus de chances pour qu'elle soit bonne'),[2] Lévesque répond en professionnel de l'histoire mais sans mésestimer le choc de l'événement: 'Les témoins de notre révolution doivent être dans une disposition favorable pour écrire l'histoire des siècles passés. Ils ont tant vu de renversements, tant de grandes calamités...'[3] Vive l'histoire ancienne, donc. Pourvu toutefois qu'elle s'enracine dans le présent de tous. Besoin évident, dont prend acte le pouvoir napoléonien: ainsi, dans le *Rapport* qu'en 1808 il fit devant l'empereur *sur les progrès de l'histoire et de la littérature ancienne depuis 1789*, Bon-Joseph Dacier, secrétaire perpétuel de l'Académie des Inscriptions,[4] conclura à la nécessité de mettre textes anciens et savoir historico-philologique 'à la portée de tout le monde'. Nul mieux que Lévesque, présent en la circonstance aux côtés de Dacier, n'a tenté de réaliser ce programme, dans sa traduction de Thucydide publiée en 1795 à l'usage d'un large public, dans son *Histoire critique de la République romaine* parue en 1807, dans ses *Études d'histoire ancienne* de 1811, destinées à 'une classe nombreuse de lecteurs'.[5]

C'est de ces *Études* que nous nous occuperons ici, et il n'est pas indifférent à nos yeux que, pour l'essentiel, elles reprennent, en y élaguant largement l'érudition, des Mémoires présentés par Lévesque dans la Classe des Sciences morales et politiques de l'Institut entre 1796 et 1801.[6] Il est tout aussi important pour notre propos de

---

[1] Sur Louis-Sébastien Mercier avant 1789, v. L. Béclard, *Sébastien Mercier, sa vie, son œuvre, son temps d'après des documents inédits* (Paris, 1903), et surtout pp. 153–88, à propos de l'*Essai sur l'art dramatique* (1773), où Mercier dénonçait avec fougue l'imitation des anciens et plaidait pour un 'théâtre neuf relatif à la nation devant laquelle on parle'; sur Mercier à l'Institut et sur ses rapports mouvementés avec les Idéologues, cf. Moravia, *Il tramonto dell'illuminismo*, pp. 97, 423, 425, 435–8.

[2] Daunou, qui résume cette 'Appréciation de l'histoire ancienne' dans la *Notice des travaux de la Classe des Sciences morales et politiques de l'Institut (nivôse–ventôse an X)* (Paris, s.d.), pp. 15–16, observe que les affirmations de Mercier n'ont pas 'empêché la Classe de s'occuper, durant ce trimestre, surtout de sciences historiques'.

[3] *Notice des travaux...pendant le dernier trimestre de l'an X* (Paris, s.d.), p. 3: 'Mémoire sur l'histoire, comme science et comme art', par le citoyen Lévesque.

[4] Sur Bon-Joseph Dacier, secrétaire perpétuel de l'Académie des Inscriptions 'avec laquelle il s'était pour ainsi dire identifié', v. la notice de la *Biographie générale Michaud* (Paris, 1885). Le *Rapport* a été publié à Paris en 1810; nous renvoyons à sa réédition dans le *Tableau historique de l'érudition française* (Paris, 1862), p. 74.

[5] V. ses déclarations dans les préfaces respectives de *Histoire de Thucydide, fils d'Olorus* (Paris, 1795) (t. I, p. iii), *Histoire critique de la République romaine* (Paris, 1807) (p. i), *Études d'histoire ancienne et de celle de la Grèce* (Paris, 1811) t. I (pp. x et xv).

[6] 'Considérations sur les trois poètes tragiques de la Grèce', 'Mémoire sur Aristophane', *Mémoires de l'Institut national des Sciences et Arts, Classe des Sciences morales et politiques*, t. I

rappeler que la vie de Lévesque ne se confond pas totalement avec celle d'un professeur d'histoire grecque – il le fut, au Collège de France, dès 1791,[1] mais lorsque, en 1789, Lévesque entre à l'Académie des Inscriptions et Belles-Lettres, cet honneur s'adressait tout autant à l'historien de la Russie ou du Moyen Age français qu'au traducteur de Thucydide. Dans la vie de Lévesque, né en 1736, il y a donc d'abord eu la Russie, où il enseigna à l'École des Cadets de Saint-Pétersbourg[2] entre 1773 et 1780; de ce séjour il tirera profit, publiant dès 1781 une *Histoire de Russie*, suivie en 1783 d'une *Histoire des différents peuples soumis à la domination des Russes* – après 'l'histoire civile et politique', 'l'histoire naturelle de l'homme', comme il l'écrit lui-même.[3] Mais, de Saint-Pétersbourg, il avait déjà fait publier en 1775 et 1779, à Amsterdam, un *Homme moral* et un *Homme pensant*, essais où la réflexion sur les progrès de l'humanité lui permet de formuler les grandes lignes de sa pensée, libérale avec mesure.[4] En 1788, il s'essaie à l'histoire de France avec un ouvrage sur *La France sous les cinq premiers Valois* et, après une prudente retraite sous la Terreur, produit en 1795 sa traduction de Thucydide. Puis ce sont les nombreux 'Mémoires' présentés devant l'Institut, et, pour finir,

(Paris, 1798), pp. 305–44 et 345–73 (= *Études*, t. v, pp. 48–80); Mémoires 'sur Hésiode', 'sur Homère', 'sur les mœurs et usages des Grecs du temps d'Homère', présentés en 1796 et 1797, *Mémoires*, t. II, pp. 1–21, 22–37, 38–67 (= *Études*, t. IV, pp. 454–85 et 486–507; II, pp. 131–75); et surtout Mémoires 'sur la Constitution de la République de Sparte' et sur celle de 'la République d'Athènes', prononcés de 1799 à 1801, publiés dans *Mémoires*, t. III (Paris, 1801), pp. 347–81 et t. IV (Paris, 1803), pp. 113–277 et repris dans les *Études*, t. II, pp. 282–330 (Sparte) et t. IV, pp. 257–387 (Athènes). La confrontation systématique des 'Mémoires' et des *Études* prouve que, de 1799–1800 à 1811, Lévesque n'a apporté que peu de modifications à ses développements sur Sparte et Athènes: quelques transformations du style, le retrait de quelques allusions trop précises à l'époque révolutionnaire, la disparition des discussions critiques (en particulier, la polémique avec De Pauw, jugé trop ami de la démocratie athénienne (*Mémoires*, t. IV, pp. 181, 203–11, 264, 265–6) disparaît dans les *Études*).

[1] Sur la vie de P.-C. Lévesque, v. la 'Notice historique sur la vie et les ouvrages de M. Lévesque' par B.-J. Dacier, *Histoire et Mémoires de l'Institut royal de France* (Paris, 1821), t. V, pp. 162–78. A notre connaissance, aucune étude n'a jusqu'à présent été consacrée à P.-C. Lévesque, historien de la Grèce. Sur la vie de Lévesque et sur son activité d'historien de la Russie, voir A. Mazon, 'P.-C. Lévesque, humaniste, historien et moraliste', *Revue des études slaves*, XLII (1963), 7–66.

[2] Lévesque a été 'recruté' par Diderot pour Catherine: v. l'examen du contrat dans Mazon, 'P.-Ch. Lévesque', pp. 18–23.

[3] Préface de l'*Histoire des différents peuples*, p. iii.

[4] *L'homme moral ou l'homme considéré tant dans l'état de pure nature que dans la société* (Amsterdam, 1775); *L'homme pensant ou essai sur l'histoire de l'esprit humain* (Amsterdam, 1779). A en juger par les nombreuses rééditions-pirates dont ils furent l'objet, ces deux ouvrages ont eu un certain succès. Lévesque lui-même reprendra ces essais sous la forme de Mémoires: 'Considérations sur l'homme observé dans la vie sauvage, dans la vie pastorale, et dans la vie policée', 'Considérations sur les obstacles que les anciens ont apportés aux progrès de la saine philosophie' (1796), *Mémoires*, t. I.

deux ouvrages consacrés à l'histoire de l'antiquité: en 1807, l'*Histoire critique de la République romaine*, en 1811 les *Études*, qui précèdent d'un an sa mort.

Nul hiatus entre toutes ces recherches. Lorsque l'auteur des *Études d'histoire ancienne* revendique le droit de parler 'comme un Français fier de sa patrie, comme un Européen orgueilleux des progrès de l'Europe moderne et de ne pas [se] condamner à l'humble adoration de l'antique Grèce',[1] on reconnaît les préoccupations qui, trente ans plus tôt, avaient conduit Lévesque à expliquer à ses compatriotes que la Russie fait partie de l'Europe. Combattant le mythe de la Moscovie 'désert peuplé de quelques animaux sauvages dont [Pierre le Grand aurait] su faire des hommes',[2] Lévesque ouvrait une nouvelle ère dans l'historiographie de la Russie;[3] mieux: il manifestait avec éclat cet acharnement à détruire tous les mirages qui caractérise l'ensemble de son œuvre: mirage de Pierre le Grand, mirage de la 'démocratie' franque ou de la république romaine, mirage spartiate, il n'en est aucun qui ait échappé à ses attaques.[4]

'Histoire morale' pour dénoncer la république romaine et son 'fanatisme de liberté',[5] 'histoire comme science et comme art' pour traiter de la Russie, de la Grèce ancienne et de la France de jadis. Car telle est bien la triade qui domine l'œuvre de Lévesque. Entre la Russie du XVIe siècle et la Grèce antique, les affinités sont, à l'en croire, multiples,[6] et l'historien ne s'en étonne pas, mais, concluant

---

[1] *Études*, t. I, Préface, p. xii.

[2] *Histoire de Russie*, t. I, p. 73.

[3] Sur la qualité de son *Histoire de Russie*, qui devait rester longtemps 'la seule entreprise de ce genre menée par un Français', v. M. Cadot, *L'histoire de la Russie dans la vie intellectuelle française (1839–1856)* (Paris, 1967), pp. 382 (citation) et 542, ainsi que Mazon, 'P.-Ch. Lévesque', pp. 41–3.

[4] Mirage de Pierre le Grand: voir les remarques de A. Lortholary, *Le mirage russe en France au XVIIIe siècle* (Paris, 1948), nn. 155, p. 303, et 222, p. 306; Lévesque critique implicitement le mythe orchestré par Voltaire: v. encore Mazon, 'P.-Ch. Lévesque', pp. 38–40 et 43. Mirage de la 'démocratie' franque, cher à l'abbé de Mably: v. l'Introduction à *La France sous les cinq premiers Valois*, pp. 45–6 et le 'Mémoire sur le gouvernement de la France sous les deux premières dynasties', *Mémoires*, t. v (1804), pp. 244 et 279; nous citerons encore la p. 315: 'Renonçons à l'illusion de vouloir trouver, chez des peuples ignorants et barbares, un bon gouvernement.' Mirage de la république romaine, ou plus exactement illusion des Français qui ont imité Rome, et, 'par la folle prétention de devenir des citoyens romains, sont devenus de mauvais citoyens': v. *Histoire critique*, Préface, p. xxxvii. Mirage spartiate: v. ci-dessous, pp. 206–7. On ajoutera que, dès *L'homme pensant* (p. 3), Lévesque affirmait sa méfiance vis-à-vis des constructions de l'imaginaire.

[5] C'est l'aspect essentiel de l'ouvrage (voir Préface, p. xxxiv), mais il en est d'autres: sur Lévesque précurseur de Niebuhr, v. Rytkönen, *Niebuhr*, p. 57.

[6] Comparaison de la Russie avec la Grèce: *Histoire de Russie*, t. III, pp. 81–3, 88, 93, etc.; sur le 'classicisme' de l'*Histoire*, v. C. Wilberger, dans 'French scholarship on Russian

de la parenté des langues slave et grecque à celle des peuples, il affirme que les Grecs sont venus du Nord.[1] C'est au contraire par le Midi que la France tient de la Grèce, ou que la langue française révèle son origine hellénique: et Lévesque d'évoquer 'l'antique colonie fondée à Marseille par les Phocéens'.[2]

La Russie, la Grèce, la France: entre l'itinéraire scientifique et les investissements théorico-affectifs d'un historien, qui pourra jamais faire le départ?

La Grèce de P.-C. Lévesque est une construction composite où l'héritage d'Isocrate et de Plutarque, c'est-à-dire de l'abbé Barthélemy,[3] coexiste, non sans quelques contradictions éclatantes, avec la lecture de Thucydide: ainsi la même page des *Études* présente tour à tour Périclès comme le démagogue qui changea la démocratie de Thésée et de Solon en un 'régime tumultuaire', et comme l'homme d'état irremplaçable dont la mort livra les Athéniens aux 'charlatans effrontés et misérables tels que Cléon'.[4] Toutefois Lévesque en général choisit: il choisit Thucydide, 'celui de tous les historiens anciens qui mérite le plus de confiance',[5] ou, mieux encore, celui qui, face à l'état libéral qui s'esquisse, 'doit être le plus étudié dans les pays où tous les citoyens peuvent avoir un jour quelque part au gouvernement'. Et notre historien d'ajouter: 'Un membre très éclairé du Parlement d'Angleterre disait qu'il ne pouvait s'agiter dans les Chambres aucune question sur laquelle on ne trouvât des lumières dans Thucydide.'[6] C'est donc un Thucydide à l'usage de la

literature', *Eighteenth Century*, v (1971–2), 503–26 et tout spécialement 515–18. Comparaison de la Grèce avec la Russie: 'Mémoire sur les mœurs et usages des Grecs du temps d'Homère', *Mémoires*, t. II, pp. 46, 52–3, 56, 65; 'Mémoire sur Hésiode' (où Lévesque compare les mythes de Pandore et des races avec un livre sacré des Kalmouks, dont il a lu une traduction russe).

[1] V. les deux excursus, 'sur l'identité primitive de la langue grecque avec l'une des plus anciennes langues du Nord', 'sur l'origine septentrionale...prouvée par...les rites religieux', aux t. II et III de la traduction de Thucydide, pp. 315–63 et 278–322, ainsi que *Études*, t. II, pp. 77–89.

[2] Préface aux *Études*, p. iii; on retrouve la même idée, deux ans après, dans l'*Essai sur les révolutions*, t. I, ch. XXXVIII, pp. 186–7. L'ouvrage de Egger, *L'hellénisme en France...*, véhicule le même historicisme, qui fait une large place à 'l'introduction de l'hellénisme en France par Marseille' (t. I, pp. 24–39) après avoir longuement évoqué l'affinité du génie gaulois et de l'esprit grec (comparaison entre l'oraison funèbre athénienne et la poésie militaire des Gaulois: t. I, pp. 11–14).

[3] Voir *Études*, t. II, pp. 238–67 (rois mythiques d'Athènes et 'démocratie de Thésée') et 280 (les Athéniens dès l'origine 'amoureux de la démocratie pure'). Sur Lévesque critique de Barthélémy, v. cependant les remarques de Malte-Brun ('Éloge de feu M. Lévesque', *Histoire de Russie*, 4e éd. (Paris, 1812), p. xxii).

[4] *Études*, III, p. 25.

[5] *Études*, Préface, p. xx.

[6] *Histoire de Thucydide*, t. I, Préface, p. xxvii.

bonne bourgeoisie que prône Lévesque. Un Thucydide dont le retour, en pleine période thermidorienne, marque la rupture définitive avec la Grèce imaginaire des législateurs chère aux révolutionnaires.[1] Mais, sur ce Thucydide où tout un chacun peut lire désormais 'l'action politique des peuples envers les peuples',[2] la Révolution française jette une lumière nouvelle. L'historien de *la Guerre du Péloponnèse* mentionne-t-il la présence d'esclaves ou l'intervention active des femmes aux côtés du *dèmos* de Corcyre en lutte contre les *oligoi*? Lévesque reprend la parole pour insister sur l'alliance naturelle du peuple et des esclaves ou pour expliquer la conduite des femmes, 'toujours plus violentes que les hommes dans les mouvements séditieux';[3] Thucydide disait très exactement le contraire, affirmant que 'les femmes dominaient leur naturel pour affronter le tumulte (III. 74)'; mais, à l'évidence, l'efficacité passe pour Lévesque avant la fidélité au texte, et ses lecteurs l'entendent, qui se rappellent que la société des 'Femmes révolutionnaires' fut le soutien très pugnace des Enragés.[4]

Entre la Grèce et l'historien s'est donc interposée la Révolution, et lorsque, d'après Hérodote cette fois, Lévesque raconte comment Pisistrate exilé usa des services d'une fausse Athéna pour rentrer dans Athènes, on ne s'étonnera pas que l'historien moderne fasse de cette 'bouquetière' déguisée en 'Sagesse' un personnage déjà allégorique pour les Athéniens, préfiguration grecque de toutes les 'déesses Raison' des fêtes révolutionnaires.[5] Ainsi l'histoire récente de la France éclaire celle de la Grèce. Ou, plus exactement, celle d'Athènes. Car, pour éclairer l'histoire de Sparte, Lévesque remonte plus haut dans l'histoire de France, au temps, qu'il connaît bien pour l'avoir étudié, de 'l'odieuse aristocratie qui affligeait la France sous la première et la seconde races, lorsqu'une caste peu nombreuse et privilégiée s'attribuait à elle seule le nom de peuple français'.[6]

---

[1] Disparition du législateur: *Études*, t. II, pp. 102 et 366–7. L'un de nous a déjà souligné l'importance de la traduction de Thucydide en 1795 (Vidal-Naquet, 'Tradition de la démocratie grecque', p. 34).

[2] *Histoire de Thucydide*, Préface, p. xxvii.

[3] *Études*, t. III, pp. 54–5 (commentaire de Thucydide III. 73–4).

[4] Cf. G. Lefebvre, *La Révolution française*, 6e éd. (Paris, 1968), p. 361, et Paule-Marie Duhet, *Les femmes et la Révolution, 1789–1794* (Paris, 1971), pp. 129–31 et 135–60.

[5] *Études*, t. II, pp. 375–6. On n'oubliera pas que Pisistrate est le chef des 'Montagnards': la préfiguration est complète.

[6] *Études*, t. II, pp. 306–7. Inversement, étudiant 'la France sous les deux premières dynasties', Lévesque se réfère à Sparte (*La France sous les cinq premiers Valois*, pp. 46 et 86; *Mémoires*, t. IV, pp. 254 et 258): l'existence de la 'servitude de la plèbe' permet de comparer Francs et *Homoioi*, serfs et hilotes.

Ennemis du travail, du commerce et de l'industrie, tout entiers consacrés au métier des armes, 'ignorants, féroces et grossiers', tels sont les Spartiates, 'ces hommes que l'on peut justement appeler les nobles' – et, cette fois-ci, point n'est besoin de remonter jusqu'aux Mérovingiens pour comprendre l'allusion.[1] S'étonnera-t-on dès lors qu'entre Sparte et Athènes Lévesque choisisse Athènes et la 'vérité des faits' contre Sparte et 'les idées consacrées sur l'excellence de la constitution lacédémonienne'?[2] 'On admire Lacédémone guerrière . . .mais on aime sa rivale',[3] écrit-il sans détour. Encore l'admiration n'est-elle pas accordée sans réticence: auteur d'un *Essai sur l'histoire de l'esprit humain* qui, dès 1779, critiquait 'l'estime exclusive accordée aux guerriers',[4] Lévesque peut-il admirer un 'couvent guerrier' que les réformes de Lycurgue ont immobilisé au stade de 'l'ignorance et de la barbarie'?[5] Peut-il admirer l'éducation spartiate qu'en 1775 il condamnait dans *L'homme moral* et dont les Jacobins ont voulu faire un modèle? Si la loi de la société civile est la conservation de la propriété – et, pour notre auteur, les enfants sont une propriété – comment admettre la 'tyrannie' d'un état républicain qui ôte à la famille l'éducation des enfants?[6] Il n'est jusqu'à l'ordre du récit qui ne se conforme aux sympathies athéniennes de l'historien: sans doute n'est-il pas indifférent que les siècles obscurs de la Grèce soient évoqués dans le chapitre consacré à Lacédémone, ou que l'histoire de Sparte soit explicitement destinée à meubler les silences de l'histoire athénienne.[7] Inversement, l'histoire d'Athènes éclaire l'histoire générale de la Grèce jusqu'à Alexandre; mieux: elle concerne l'humanité entière, que Lévesque convoque avant d'entamer le récit, funeste pour Athènes, de la guerre du Péloponnèse.[8]

Respect de la propriété, respect de la vie privée, épanouissement

---

[1] Sur Sparte, voir *Études*, t. II, pp. 286, 295, 303–8, 322–4, 328, et les notes explicatives de Lévesque à l'*épitaphios* de Périclès (*ad* Thucydide II. 37, 2; 29, 1; 40, 2).

[2] *Études*, t. II, pp. 291–2; v. encore pp. 293–4 (les Spartiates 'sauvages de la Grèce; l'âge d'or de Sparte n'est que ténèbres').

[3] *Études*, t. II, pp. 237–8; v. aussi p. 461.

[4] *L'homme pensant*, ch. XVII, pp. 74–6: 'Il faut plaindre les peuples chez qui le guerrier l'emporte sur tous les autres citoyens uniquement parce qu'il est guerrier.'

[5] *Études*, t. II, pp. 318 et 324.

[6] *L'homme moral*, p. 163. A cette conception l'on opposera la déclaration de Danton, lors du débat sur le projet d'enseignement de Le Peletier: 'Je suis père; mais mon fils ne m'appartient pas: il est à la République' (cité par Ponteil, *Histoire de l'enseignement en France*, p. 68).

[7] *Études*, t. II, pp. 283 et 281.

[8] *Études*, t. I, Préface, p. ix; t. II, pp. 237–8; t. III, p. 2 ('On se représente l'humanité tout entière intéressée à la conservation de ce peuple qui honore l'humanité').

du commerce, du travail et de l'industrie,[1] telles sont les principales caractéristiques de l'Athènes de Lévesque. Tiendrions-nous cette fois-ci le paradigme même de l'Athènes bourgeoise, construction de l'imaginaire libéral offerte à tous les développements de l'histoire? L'affirmer serait aller trop vite en besogne, oubliant que la démocratie est à ce modèle de liberté civile quelque chose comme une pièce rapportée, tout au plus un mal inévitable: à n'en pas douter, Lévesque aime dans Athènes la cité industrieuse beaucoup plus que la *polis* démocratique... Ce n'est pas que notre historien chérisse les adversaires du régime athénien: 'l'oligarchie féroce' des Trente lui rappelle trop la Terreur pour lui inspirer une quelconque sympathie.[2] Mais, parmi les chefs démocrates de l'époque classique, seul Thrasybule mérite le titre d'"ami de la liberté' parce qu'il était 'non moins ami de l'humanité, de la justice et de l'ordre': Lévesque a lu Xénophon et sait gré à Thrasybule victorieux d'avoir plaidé contre toute agitation révolutionnaire au sein de la démocratie restaurée.[3] La grande époque de la démocratie, il est vrai, reste celle de Solon, et c'est à propos de Solon que Lévesque exalte la liberté civile ou le respect de la propriété. Il faudrait citer tout entière la page où l'historien commente le refus opposé par le législateur à toute revendication de partage des terres; contentons-nous d'en retenir que, 'attenter à la propriété ce serait attenter au principe même de l'association' et que, de l'"égalité forcée', rien de bon ne peut sortir, à moins qu'on n'emploie 'pour la maintenir l'action des plus violents ressorts; action qui contrarierait encore le but social, puisque l'un des objets qui ont donné naissance aux sociétés a été le désir légitime des associés de jouir, à l'appui les uns des autres, du plus grand repos'.[4]

Et la démocratie athénienne, qu'en advient-il? Qu'advient-il de ce que nous, historiens du XXe siècle, nommons 'démocratie athénienne' et qui, depuis Grote et quelques autres, commence à Clisthène? Son cas est clair: elle n'est qu'une corruption de la

---

[1] La propriété: *Études*, t. II, p. 363 (à propos de Solon; cf. *L'homme moral*, p. 70, et les *Observations et discussions sur quelques parties des ouvrages de l'abbé de Mably* (Paris, 1787), pp. 77–8). La vie privée: *Études*, t. II, pp. 360–1 (à propos de Solon). Le commerce: *ibid.* t. II, p. 320 ('Comme les nations pauvres par nature, ils faisaient du commerce'); *e contrario*, sur les Spartiates, v. l'*Éloge historique de l'abbé de Mably* (Paris, 1787), p. 59. Le travail et l'industrie: *Études*, t. II, pp. 364–5 (toujours à propos de Solon).
[2] *Histoire de Thucydide*, t. I, Préface, p. vi; *Études*, t. III, p. 180. Même thème dans la 3ème édition (1804) de l'ouvrage de Young (voir ci-dessus p. 179, n. 2).
[3] *Études*, t. III, p. 186, que l'on rapprochera de Xénophon, *Helléniques* II. 4, 42.
[4] *Études*, t. III, p. 363.

démocratie solonienne, marquée par l'excès et vouée aux malheurs qui ne manquent jamais de s'abattre sur les 'régimes trop populaires'.[1] Périclès en est le symbole, et la postérité est invitée à toujours le blâmer 'd'avoir détruit la force du gouvernement'.[2] Résumons-nous: entre Solon et Thrasybule, un régime tumultuaire; entre 1789 et Thermidor, la Révolution...Le rapprochement parle de lui-même, et tout indique que la démocratie athénienne pâtit d'être appréciée à l'aune des derniers 'troubles de la France'. Certes, l'historien ne procède jamais ouvertement à cette identification; mais, lorsqu'il se contente de comparer – tout au contraire – les Trente et les Montagnards, que l'on ne s'y trompe pas: l'oligarchie des Trente n'est pour lui que l'envers, violent mais inévitable, de la démocratie. Encore une fois, l'histoire de la France permet de lire celle d'Athènes.

Et cependant, le dernier mot est à la distance. Concluant la longue étude qu'il consacre à la 'constitution de la république d'Athènes', Lévesque affirme qu'Athènes est loin, très loin dans le temps:

Parce qu'Athènes a brillé du plus grand éclat dans les lettres et les arts, écrit-il, on aime à croire que tout fut bien dans cette république, constitution, législation, formes des tribunaux. J'avoue qu'en ces parties, elle nous a laissé de beaux modèles à suivre; mais je pense aussi qu'en tout cela, nous l'emportons sur elle et sur toutes les républiques de la Grèce...Nous avons à la fois leur expérience et celle des Romains, et celle des longs siècles où nous avons vécu.[3]

'Nous avons vécu'...La Révolution est passée, Athènes s'est éloignée. Le temps de l'histoire est en place.

Le propos de Benjamin Constant (1767–1830), contemporain de Saint-Just et de Napoléon, n'est pas de créer un discours historique qui fasse des Grecs les ancêtres des Français libéraux, mais de trouver le lieu idéologique du libéralisme moderne, et, pour cela, de creuser la distance nécessaire entre un modèle capable d'inspirer à la fois Saint-Just et Joseph de Maistre et le régime qu'il croit possible et souhaitable. Il ne s'agit ni de définir une anticipation, comme l'avait

---

[1] *Études*, t. III, p. 143 (la démocratie responsable de la défaite de Sicile); t. IV, pp. 258-62 (Clisthène; on notera que les *Études* sont, au sujet de Clisthène, en retrait par rapport au premier Mémoire: on comparera *Mémoires*, t. IV, p. 121 et *Études*, passage cité); t. IV, p. 375 (la justice populaire).

[2] *Études*, t. III, p. 25.

[3] *Études*, t. IV, p. 387. Cette péroraison, où réapparaissent les thèmes de la 'querelle des Anciens et des Modernes', reprend sans changement appréciable celle des Mémoires présentés à l'Institut.

fait Condorcet, ni de proclamer de façon provocante la rupture, comme l'avait fait Volney, mais de définir la distance correcte. Et, pour cela, il ne suffit pas d'utiliser Athènes contre Sparte, bien que Constant ait eu recours très abondamment à cet usage déjà ancien.[1]

Constant a ceci de particulier parmi les idéologues de la bourgeoisie libérale, qu'il a non seulement la culture gréco-latine du collège, mais une éducation universitaire acquise à Erlangen et à Édimbourg. Il a personnellement connu Gibbon et traduit, en 1787, une partie de l'histoire grecque de l'Écossais John Gillies. On peut juger le détail symbolique, car, sans être le moins du monde un démocrate, Gillies n'était pas le réactionnaire passionné que fut Mitford, inspirateur de Joseph de Maistre.[2] Cette connaissance, il la renouvellera en 1803, et à bien d'autres reprises, à Gœttingen, et il sera l'un des rares Français à avoir une connaissance directe de la jeune science allemande, tant par la lecture de Wolf et de Creuzer que par les entretiens qu'il eut avec W. Schlegel, rencontré dans l'entourage de Madame de Staël. Il note dans son journal, le 14 septembre 1804: 'Jamais, sur les antiquités, je ne serai aussi érudit que les érudits. Pour le devenir, il faudrait sacrifier le temps nécessaire à la pensée.'[3] Peut-être fut-ce la chance de Constant de ne pas être devenu, en dépit d'immenses lectures, un érudit.[4] Mais il est bien vrai qu'il pensa là où d'autres répétèrent.

Constant est typiquement, comme Volney, un Thermidorien, mais, contrairement à Volney, il ne sera ni sénateur, ni comte de l'Empire, ni pair de France de la Restauration. Dans une lettre du 25 mai 1795, il écrit: 'La propriété et les talents, ces deux raisons raisonnables d'inégalité parmi les hommes, vont reprendre leurs

---

[1] Nous ne connaissons aucun travail de synthèse sur B. Constant et le monde antique. On trouvera cependant quelques pages dans Canat, *L'hellénisme des Romantiques*, t. I, pp. 44ss.; v. aussi, du même auteur, sa thèse latine: *Quae de Graecis Mme de Stael scripserit* (Paris, 1904). Le dernier ouvrage d'ensemble, Paul Bastid, *Benjamin Constant et sa doctrine* (2 t., Paris, 1965), est, de ce point de vue, très décevant. Sur l'attitude générale de Constant, nous avons lu avec profit B. C. Fink, 'Benjamin Constant and the Enlightenment', *Studies in Eighteenth Century Culture*, éd. H. S. Pagliaro, t. III (London, 1973), pp. 67–81; R. Mortier, 'Constant et les Lumières', *Europe*, no. 467 (mars 1968), 5–18; P. Thompson, 'Constant et les vertus révolutionnaires', *ibid.*, 49–62.

[2] Cf. Momigliano, *Studies in Historiography*, p. 49.

[3] *Journal*, dans *Œuvres*, éd. A. Roulin (Pléiade, Paris, 1964), p. 359.

[4] Sur la formation de Constant et ses rapports avec la science allemande, v. le vieux livre de G. Rudler, *La jeunesse de Benjamin Constant* (Paris, 1909), et, tout récemment, P. Deguise, *Benjamin Constant méconnu* (Genève, 1966) (porte surtout sur le *De la Religion*). Nous ne nous intéresserons ici qu'à la dimension politique des rapports de Constant avec la Grèce, laissant entièrement de côté ses travaux sur les religions antiques qui l'ont pourtant occupé jusqu'à sa mort.

droits.'[1] Et c'est bien d'*inégalité*, en même temps que de liberté, qu'il sera question tout au long de son œuvre. Contrairement toutefois à Volney, il partage entièrement, au début de son activité, la vision traditionnelle, rhétorique, de l'antiquité. Les brochures et discours qu'il publie, entre janvier 1796 et l'été 1797,[2] en témoignent. A ceux qui rêvent d'une Restauration, il prédit une Vendée républicaine et d'héroïques insurgés: 'La vérité serait leur religion, l'histoire leur légende, les grands hommes de l'Antiquité leurs saints, la liberté leur autre vie. Ils n'espéreraient pas ressusciter dans trois jours, mais il combattraient et mourraient libres.'[3] Réfutant ceux qui identifient monarchie et vertu, il déclare: 'La *monarchie* romaine fut fondée par des brigands et la monarchie romaine ne subjugua pas le quart de l'Italie. La république romaine fut fondée par les plus austères et les plus vertueux des hommes.'[4] Et déjà apparaît un thème qui, modulé, restera présent toute sa vie: 'Les Républiques anciennes avaient des hommes illustres à la fois dans tous les genres. Miltiade, Aristide, Xénophon cultivaient les lettres, commandaient dans les camps, entraînaient à la tribune; déjà ces glorieux exemples se renouvellent parmi nous.'[5] Pour qu'une nouvelle – et originale – problématique apparaisse dans l'œuvre publiée de Constant, il faut attendre le célèbre pamphlet *De l'esprit de conquête et de l'usurpation*, qui sort des presses en Allemagne en janvier 1814. Entre-temps, Benjamin Constant avait été, en 1802, chassé du tribunat.

En fait, l'acquisition récente par la Bibliothèque Nationale de sept manuscrits d'œuvres de Constant, achevées en 1810[6] mais rédigées principalement entre 1806 et 1810, a montré que, dès ce moment, la conception que se fait Constant des rapports entre l'hellénisme et la monde moderne est définitivement fixée. Les deux textes principaux

---

[1] Lettre citée par P. Bastid, *Benjamin Constant*, t. i, p. 109.
[2] *De la force du gouvernement actuel de la France et de la nécessité de s'y rallier* (1796); *Des réactions politiques* suivi de *Des effets de la terreur* (1797); *Discours prononcés au cercle constitutionnel pour la plantation de l'arbre de la liberté* (30 fructidor an V); tous textes que l'on trouvera rassemblés dans *Gli Scritti politici giovanili di Benjamin Constant*, éd. C. Cordié (Côme, 1944); v. aussi Bastid, *Benjamin Constant*, t. i, pp. 118–28, et Moravia, *Il tramonto dell'illuminismo*, pp. 247–9; l'étude la plus complète sur cette période de la vie de Constant est cependant: B. Jasinski, *L'engagement de Benjamin Constant. Amour et politique (1794–1796)* (Paris, 1971).
[3] *De la force*, dans *Gli Scritti politici*, p. 45.
[4] *Des effets de la terreur, ibid.* p. 114.
[5] *Discours, ibid.* p. 229.
[6] Nouvelles Acquisitions françaises (NAF), 14358–64; sur l'importance de ces manuscrits, cf. par exemple, Fink, 'Benjamin Constant and the Enlightenment', et la préface et les notes d'O. Pozzo di Borgo à son édition des *Écrits et Discours politiques de Benjamin Constant* (Paris, 1964).

que contiennent les manuscrits, les *Principes de politique applicables à tous les gouvernements* et les *Fragments d'un ouvrage abandonné sur la possibilité d'une constitution républicaine dans un grand pays* – cela même que J. de Maistre déclarait à jamais impossible[1] – étaient la source d'où dérivait, textuellement, ou presque textuellement, tout ce que Constant a publié depuis sur ce problème, qu'il s'agisse de l'*Esprit de conquête*, dont des chapitres entiers proviennent des manuscrits de la Bibliothèque Nationale ou de la célèbre conférence de 1819, *De la liberté des anciens comparée à celle des modernes*.[2]

Tout comme son contemporain Hegel, Constant parle de la cité grecque comme d'une totalité harmonieuse.[3] Encore en 1829, à la fin de sa vie, il republiera dans les *Mélanges de littérature et de politique* un texte où il écrivait: 'Il y a des époques harmonieuses où l'homme paraît jouir de la plénitude de ses facultés', et d'évoquer Socrate soldat à Potidée, Eschyle à Salamine et même Sophocle archonte, ce qu'il ne fut pas; et il en tire argument pour justifier la mobilité sociale qu'a connue et favorisée la Révolution française. Des garçons d'écurie devinrent généraux. 'En dépit des prédictions sinistres, précisément parce que chacun n'a pas fait uniquement son métier, tous les métiers ont été faits.'[4]

A la limite, Benjamin Constant ne conteste pas que la liberté d'un citoyen athénien est plus grande que celle d'un moderne, même s'il est anglais ou suisse. Il s'exprime ainsi dans un texte inédit: 'Il ne faut donc pas dire: les Athéniens étaient plus libres que nous, donc le genre humain perd en liberté. Les Athéniens étaient une petite partie des habitants de la Grèce; la Grèce une petite partie de l'Europe et le reste du monde était barbare, et l'immense majorité des habitants de la Grèce elle-même était composée d'esclaves.'[5] Nous sommes séparés de la Grèce par trois révolutions qui ont constitué un indéniable progrès, celle qui a mis fin à l'esclavage, celle qui a détruit

---

[1] *Considérations*, p. 49.

[2] On la trouvera dans le *Cours de politique constitutionnelle*, éd. E. Laboulaye, t. II (Paris, 1861), pp. 539–60.

[3] Cf. D. Janicaud, *Hegel et le destin de la Grèce* (Paris, 1975), 'La constitution de l'idéal de la belle totalité', pp. 27–48.

[4] *Mélanges de littérature et de politique* (Paris, 1829), pp. 469–72; formules analogues, par exemple, dans un article de la *Minerve française*, LI (1818), repris dans B. Constant, *Recueil d'articles. Le Mercure, la Minerve et la Renommée*, publié par E. Harpaz (Genève, 1972), p. 494.

[5] *De la perfectibilité de l'espèce humaine*, NAF, 14362, fol. 76r; à quoi l'on peut opposer ce qu'il dit en 1819: 'L'individu était encore bien plus asservi à la suprématie du corps social à Athènes, qu'il ne l'est de nos jours dans aucun État libre de l'Europe' (*De la liberté*, dans *Cours de politique constitutionnelle*, éd. Laboulaye, p. 547).

la féodalité et celle qui a mis un terme aux privilèges de la noblesse.[1] Tout cela dérive, bien évidemment, en droite ligne de Condorcet, y compris la reconnaissance de l'importance de l'esclavage, sur laquelle Constant se prononcera de façon lapidaire en 1819 : 'Sans la population esclave d'Athènes, vingt mille Athéniens n'auraient pas pu délibérer chaque jour sur la place publique.'[2]

Alors, où se situe, à nos yeux, l'originalité de Constant? Elle s'exprime, croyons-nous, dans la triple opposition qu'il établit entre la guerre et le commerce, entre la participation et la représentation, entre le plaisir d'action et le plaisir de réflexion. C'est cet ensemble qu'il faut maintenant considérer.

Comprenons-le bien: la signification de cette συστοιχία est double, et même un peu plus compliquée encore. L'ensemble: guerre, participation, plaisir d'action, caractérise certes le monde antique pris en bloc, et l'ensemble: commerce, représentation, plaisir de réflexion, le monde moderne, mais le premier groupe définit aussi cette période de l'histoire qui commence en 1789 et s'achèvera à la chute de Napoléon, et qui a été marquée par l'imitation moderne des républiques antiques.[3]

Au sein du monde antique, cette même opposition existait dans une certaine mesure et caractérisait le couple Athènes–Sparte. Toute l'ambiguïté de Constant est là, car il a emprunté, singulièrement à C. De Pauw, la description d'une Athènes moderne, d'une Athènes commerçante: 'L'on jouissait à Athènes d'une liberté individuelle beaucoup plus grande qu'à Sparte, parce qu'Athènes était à la fois guerrière et commerçante.'[4] Les Athéniens connaissaient l'usage de la lettre de change et, en somme, leur cité était, dans certains limites, une cité moderne: 'Il est assez singulier que ce soit précisément Athènes que nos modernes réformateurs ont évité de prendre pour modèle: c'est qu'Athènes nous ressemblait trop'; et d'évoquer en bloc, pour convaincre son lecteur 'du caractère tout à fait moderne des Athéniens', Xénophon et Isocrate.[5] A cette modernité s'oppose le couvent guerrier et égalitaire de Sparte, cher aux philosophes anciens et modernes (Platon, Mably). Mais, même à Athènes, le commerce ne régnait pas sans partage, puisque, après Hume, Constant fait cette

---

[1] *Ibid.* fol. 76r. Les Grecs de l'antiquité ont vécu après la chute de la théocratie.
[2] *De la liberté*, dans *Cours de politique constitutionnelle*, éd. Laboulaye, p. 545.
[3] Les chapitres VI–VIII du pamphlet *De l'usurpation* (*Œuvres*, pp. 1010–23) reprennent et résument plusieurs chapitres des *Principes de politique*, livre XVI, NAF, 14360, fols. 2–27.
[4] *Principes de politique*, fol. 10. De Pauw est cité à ce propos plusieurs fois en référence.
[5] *De l'usurpation*, dans *Œuvres*, p. 1011, reprenant NAF, 14360, fols. 10–11.

constatation: 'A Athènes,...la république la plus commerçante de l'Antiquité, l'intérêt maritime était d'environ 60%, tandis que l'intérêt ordinaire n'était que de 12%, tant l'idée d'une navigation lointaine impliquait celle de danger.'[1] Il y eut dans l'antiquité des peuples commerçants et l'embryon d'une lutte entre l'esprit de conquête et l'esprit de commerce – puisque Constant reprend à son compte cette opposition que nous avons vu naître chez Jean-François Melon[2] – mais le mode normal d'acquisition de la richesse était la guerre: 'Nous sommes arrivés à l'époque du commerce, époque qui doit nécessairement remplacer celle de la guerre, comme celle de la guerre a dû nécessairement la précéder.' De l'une à l'autre, il y a progrès: 'L'une est l'impulsion sauvage, l'autre le calcul civilisé.' L'une influe sur l'autre: 'Le commerce a modifié jusqu'à la nature de la guerre.'[3] Carthage fut vaincue. La moderne Carthage l'emporte, c'est l'Angleterre: 'Si la lutte s'établissait maintenant entre Rome et Carthage, Carthage aurait pour elle les vœux de l'univers. Elle aurait pour alliés les mœurs actuelles et le génie du monde.'[4] C'est le triomphe de ce qu'Auguste Comte appellera l'esprit positif.

Le commerce est l'univers du différé, et c'est pourquoi il est associé à la représentation, non à la participation. Si évidente que soit à nos yeux – en un sens depuis Rousseau – l'opposition entre démocraties directes et régimes représentatifs, entre l'antiquité et le monde moderne, si nombreux qu'aient été les prédécesseurs de Constant, outre ceux qu'il cite lui-même,[5] il s'en faut de beaucoup que le débat soit alors considéré comme clos. Nous verrons à ce

---

[1] *Principes de politique*, fol. 7.

[2] Nous n'avons pas trouvé la preuve que Constant avait lu Melon. Il s'appuie principale-ment sur l'œuvre de son ancien collègue du tribunat Charles Ganilh, *Essai politique sur le revenu public des peuples de l'antiquité, du Moyen Age, des siècles modernes* (2 t., Paris, 1806), qui utilise, lui aussi, ces concepts (cf. t. i, pp. 47–9) et cite également (NAF, 14360, fols. 9–10) l'*Essai sur l'histoire de l'espèce humaine* de C. A. Walkenaer (Paris, 1798), qui consacre, pp. 251–368, toute une section de son œuvre aux conséquences de 'l'intro-duction des manufactures et du commerce', sans qu'on puisse voir avec clarté à quel moment de l'histoire se situe cette introduction.

[3] *Esprit de conquête*, dans *Œuvres*, pp. 959–60, reprenant NAF, 14360, fol. 9.

[4] *Esprit de conquête, ibid.* p. 960 et NAF, 14360, fol. 10; la victoire anglaise n'est donc pour rien dans cette remarque.

[5] Nous pensons particulièrement, parce qu'il s'agit d'apologistes du système représentatif, au marquis de Chastellux, *De la félicité publique*; cf. p. 43, où il écrit, contre Rousseau: 'Pour moi, je pense qu'il n'y aura de liberté solide et durable, et surtout de félicité que parmi les peuples chez lesquels tout se fera par représentation.' Nous pensons aussi à un autre citoyen de Genève, J. de Lolme, sur lequel H. Pappé a attiré notre attention; v. sa *Constitution de l'Angleterre*, t. ii, pp. 14ss.

propos errer un professionnel comme Victor Duruy.[1] Constant a réfléchi, à partir de Rousseau, mais ses maîtres immédiats ont surtout été Condorcet et Sismondi. Dans son *Histoire des républiques italiennes du Moyen Age*, celui-ci écrivait:

Dans les Républiques de l'Antiquité, il n'existait aucune liberté civile; le citoyen s'était reconnu esclave de la nation dont il faisait partie; il s'abandonnait en entier aux décisions du souverain, sans contester au législateur le droit de contrôler toutes ses actions, de contraindre en tout sa volonté; mais d'autre part, il était lui-même à son tour ce souverain et ce législateur.[2]

L'inexistence de la société civile a pour corollaire le haut degré de participation politique. Mais qu'est-ce aujourd'hui que la liberté, si ce n'est d'abord 'la jouissance paisible de l'indépendance indivi-duelle'?[3] Le système représentatif moderne a pour but de faciliter cette jouissance paisible, étant entendu que le plaisir politique, plaisir d'action chez les anciens, ne sera plus qu'un plaisir par procuration. 'L'immense majorité, toujours exclue du pouvoir, n'attache nécessairement qu'un intérêt très passager à son existence publique.'[4] Benjamin Constant ne cherche pas à dorer la pilule:

La liberté politique offrant moins de jouissance qu'autrefois, et les désordres qu'elle peut entraîner étant plus insupportables, il n'en faut conserver que ce qui est absolument nécessaire. Prétendre aujourd'hui consoler les hommes par la liberté politique de la perte de la liberté civile, c'est marcher en sens inverse du génie actuel de l'espèce humaine.[5]

Et ailleurs: les modernes 'ne sont appelés tout au plus à l'exercice de la souveraineté que par la représentation, c'est-à-dire d'une manière fictive',[6] et il est si vrai qu'il y a chez Constant, comme chez Hegel, une nostalgie de la belle totalité,[7] qu'il écrit ceci:

Les anciens avaient sur toutes choses une conviction entière; nous n'avons presque sur rien qu'une conviction molle et flottante, sur l'incomplet de laquelle nous cherchons en vain à nous étourdir. Le mot illusion ne se trouve dans aucune langue ancienne, parce que le mot ne se crée que lorsque la chose n'existe plus.[8]

Voilà l'antiquité devenue la chose et le monde moderne le royaume des mots.

---

[1] Cf. ci-dessous p. 222.
[2] Sismondi, *Histoire*..., t. IV (Zurich, 1808), p. 369; le texte est cité dans NAF, 14364, fol. 79 et *De l'usurpation*, dans *Œuvres*, p. 1011 (avec une légère erreur de pagination).
[3] *Ibid*. p. 1010.   [4] *Ibid*. p. 1013.
[5] NAF, 14360, fol. 18.
[6] *De l'usurpation*, dans *Œuvres*, p. 1012.
[7] Ce que Thompson, 'Constant et les vertus révolutionnaires', p. 55, appelle 'une forme de sa mauvaise foi d'homme moderne'.
[8] *Œuvres*, p. 1013 et NAF, 14360, fol. 12: 'Le mot illusion est un mot dont l'*équivalent* ne se trouve dans aucune langue ancienne.'

La jouissance existe dans le monde moderne, mais ce n'est plus le plaisir immédiat de la participation. Chez nous,

Le plaisir immédiat est moins vif: il ne se compose d'aucune des jouissances du pouvoir; c'est un plaisir de réflexion: celui des anciens était un plaisir d'action. Il est clair que le premier était moins attrayant; on ne saurait exiger des hommes autant de sacrifices pour l'obtenir et le conserver.[1]

Renonçons certes à tout bouleversement, puisque la révolution est finie. Renonçons à l'ambition législatrice: 'Plus de Lycurgues, plus de Numas.'[2] Mais dans cette voie de la France bourgeoise Constant ne s'engage pas sans un discret regard en arrière – vers la cité grecque et ses 'modernes imitateurs' de l'an II. Il y a 'la sécurité des jouissances privées',[3] certes, mais il y a aussi le rêve:

Je ne me réunirai point aux détracteurs des républiques. Celles de l'Antiquité, où les facultés de l'homme se développaient dans un champ si vaste, tellement fortes de leurs propres forces, avec un tel sentiment d'énergie et de dignité, remplissent toutes les âmes qui ont quelque valeur d'une émotion d'un genre profond et particulier. Les vieux éléments d'une nature antérieure pour ainsi dire à la nôtre, semblent se réveiller en nous à ces souvenirs.[4]

Pour être bourgeois, on n'en est pas moins nostalgique.

Au terme de notre parcours, Victor Duruy et son *Histoire grecque*, publiée en 1851[5] et destinée à d'innombrables rééditions.

Autant dire que, passant sur un demi-siècle d'histoire de France et d'historiographie de la Grèce antique, nous achevons bien loin de Thermidor ce qui fut une traversée de l'idéologie thermidorienne. Dans ce saut final, rien que de délibéré. Parce que l'histoire vit de décentrement. Parce que, surtout, les formations imaginaires ne s'imposent pas en un jour: en l'occurrence, c'est au milieu du XIXe siècle que l'Athènes bourgeoise des Thermidoriens trouve, dans l'œuvre historique de Duruy, sa figure efficace de modèle. C'en est alors fini de son histoire; commence son destin universitaire[6] – et rien ne ressemble plus à une page de Duruy qu'une page de Glotz.[7]

---

[1] *Ibid.* p. 1012.

[2] *Ibid.* p. 1014; on lit dans NAF, 14360, fol. 16: 'Plus de Lycurgue, plus de Numa, *plus de Mahomet.*'

[3] *De la liberté*, dans *Cours de politique constitutionnelle*, éd. Laboulaye, p. 548.

[4] *De l'usurpation*, dans *Œuvres*, pp. 993-4, partiellement repris (la dernière phrase) de NAF, 14360, fol. 2.

[5] La seconde édition paraîtra en 1862, avec de substantielles additions et des corrections significatives: de 1851 à 1862, Duruy a lu Grote et l'Empire s'est installé.

[6] Rappelons qu'à la Bibliothèque Nationale l'*Histoire grecque* de Duruy faisait encore partie des 'Usuels' l'année dernière!

[7] A titre d'exemple, on comparera les pages de Glotz sur l'"œuvre d'entraide et de préservation sociales' de Périclès (*La cité grecque*, 2e éd. (Paris, 1968), pp. 142-3) avec

Entre-temps, il est vrai, la Grèce 'réelle', celle de l'Insurrection de 1821, avait partiellement relayé dans les esprits la Grèce imaginaire dont nous avons traité. Des hommes comme Chateaubriand et Constant n'avaient pas été étrangers à cette transformation du philhellénisme. Mais il s'agit, ici, de l'Université.

D'autres ont dit avant nous l'influence déterminante exercée par Duruy sur l'enseignement de l'histoire en France,[1] influence immédiate et spectaculaire qui devait inciter la maison d'édition Hachette à lui confier la direction d'une collection d'*Histoire univer-selle*. Fait capital: bien avant que le ministre Victor Duruy ne '[mobilise] la science pour la mettre à la portée du plus grand nombre',[2] le professeur Victor Duruy a cru à la force de la vulgarisa-tion.[3] L'Université suivra, mais avec du retard (et, à l'issue de ce parcours, nous ne nous en étonnons pas trop).

Auteur de manuels à succès, Duruy est en 1851 professeur au lycée Saint-Louis; il appartient à cette génération, formée par Michelet, qu'anime un 'souffle libéral' et qui 'cherche avec sympathie les destinées des peuples... sans pour cela agiter follement le drapeau de la démocratie'.[4] Mais parce que ce spécialiste de l'antiquité (et tout par-ticulièrement de Rome, la grande affaire de sa vie) croit que l'histoire ancienne a son mot à dire dans les enjeux politiques les plus actuels,[5] il ne nous est pas indifférent que l'orientation pro-athénienne de son *Histoire* ait pu, au milieu du XIXe siècle, soulever encore l'indignation.

celles que Duruy consacre aux 'mesures de Périclès pour assurer le bien-être du peuple' (*Histoire grecque* (Paris, 1851), pp. 284–5; sauf exception, nous citerons systématique-ment cette première édition).

[1] Cf. G. Monod, 'Victor Duruy', *Revue internationale de l'enseignement*, xxviii (1894), 481–9, et E. Lavisse, *Un ministre, Victor Duruy* (Paris, 1895), pp. 164–5; v., plus récemment, les remarques de P. Gerbod, *La condition universitaire en France au XIXe siècle* (Paris, 1965), p. 442, sur la 'révolution pédagogique' opérée par la parution du premier tome de l'*Histoire des Romains* en 1843.

[2] Circulaire du 1er octobre 1864, citée par J. Rohr, *Victor Duruy, ministre de Napoléon III. Essai sur la politique de l'Instruction publique au temps de l'empire libéral* (Paris, 1967), p. 112. Rappelons que, ministre de l'Instruction publique entre 1863 et 1869, Duruy, tout en introduisant une distinction tranchée entre la recherche (avec la création de l'École des Hautes Études) et l'enseignement, chercha tout particulièrement à ouvrir l'enseigne-ment sur la vie: v. Ponteil, *Histoire de l'enseignement*, pp. 248 et 263, et Gerbod, *La condition universitaire*, pp. 443 et 451–2.

[3] Ce qui le distingue d'autres élèves de Michelet comme Wallon, qui s'oriente d'abord vers la recherche, ou Ravaisson, qui se tourne très tôt vers la haute administration universitaire.

[4] Gerbod, *La condition universitaire*, p. 400 (citant un article de la *Revue de l'Instruction publique*).

[5] Les troisième et quatrième tomes de l'*Histoire des Romains* étaient prêts en 1850, 'mais Duruy y plaidait la cause de l'empire et il ne voulut pas les publier avant 1872' (Lavisse, *Un ministre, Victor Duruy*, p. 22).

C'est Charles Nisard qui, au nom de l'orthodoxie universitaire,[1] mena l'attaque dans le très officiel *Journal de l'Instruction publique.*[2] Partisan inconditionnel de Sparte, 'ce gouvernement fort et tout d'une pièce qui assure à l'aristocratie dorienne sa supériorité morale' et qui seul sait 'créer des choses durables',[3] Nisard reproche à Duruy de manifester pour Athènes une 'admiration juvénile' et, avec condescendance, il énumère les multiples tares que l'érudition réactionnaire se plaisait en 1851, et se plaît encore de nos jours, à trouver dans la démocratie athénienne.[4] Le fin mot de cette querelle a été lâché dès le début: dépourvu de toute 'hauteur de vues', Duruy n'est qu'un professeur de collège; il en a le langage et les idées. Comprenons que l'Université reste indéfectiblement spartiate. Est-ce à dire, comme le suggère Nisard, que l'enseignement secondaire serait désormais acquis à Athènes? Pour avoir consulté des manuels officiels où l'éloge de Cimon et de Phocion voisine avec la critique de l'"ambition insatiable' des Athéniens,[5] nous en sommes un peu moins sûrs; il est vrai que, sous la monarchie de Juillet, un mouve-

---

[1] 'En l'année 1851, il y avait une histoire officielle et orthodoxe...Il n'était pas permis... de ne point admirer absolument et sans réserve les Spartiates...La grandeur morale de Lacédémone était un des ornements du palais de carton doré que l'université offrait à l'admiration de ses élèves' (Lavisse, *ibid.*).

[2] Compte rendu de l'*Histoire grecque* par M. Victor Duruy, professeur d'histoire au Lycée Saint-Louis, *Journal général de l'Instruction publique et des cultes* (1851), pp. 557–60; réponse de Duruy, pp. 606–7. Frère du célèbre universitaire Désiré Nisard – que Victor Hugo qualifiait, dans *Toute la lyre* (VIII. 25), de 'bourgeois authentique / Ane en littérature et lièvre en politique' – Charles Nisard est spécialiste de littérature populaire française et rédacteur de nombreux articles dans des revues gouvernementales: v. la notice de la *Biographie Firmin-Didot*, ainsi que Gerbod, *La condition universitaire*, pp. 390 et 397, et la thèse de J. Malavie, *Un bourgeois de Louis-Philippe: Désiré Nisard dans la crise de 1848* (Lille, 1972), p. 18.

[3] La démonstration est délicate, s'agissant de Sparte: aussi Nisard appelle-t-il à l'aide deux 'oligarchies' qui furent durables, Rome et Venise; la conclusion est simple: la démocratie athénienne au contraire 'mourut épuisée après quatre-vingts ans de gloire'!

[4] Essentiellement le règne des ambitieux comme Alcibiade ou, ce qui est pire encore, des 'oisifs, des besogneux' – entendons: du peuple – 'des brouillons et des démagogues'. Nisard n'a de sympathie que pour la 'démocratie' de Solon, d'indulgence que pour la démocratie restaurée d'après 403.

[5] Dans le très officiel *Précis de l'histoire ancienne* de Poirson et Cayx (Paris, 1827), on apprend que le peuple 'compromet le salut de l'État par ses décisions furieuses' (p. 76), que la constitution de Solon est le principe de la 'courte...grandeur' d'Athènes (p. 77). V. aussi pp. 148 (Cimon, le plus grand des Athéniens), 149 (ambition athénienne), 154 (Périclès dégrade à jamais la constitution de Solon), 178 (Socrate partisan d'une 'aristocratie modérée'), 238 (Phocion). Dans l'*Histoire ancienne* de T. Burette (Paris, 1835, Cahiers d'histoire universelle à l'usage des collèges...sous la direction de MM. Dumont, Gaillardin, Wallon et Duruy – déjà!) on trouve un éloge de Lycurgue qui 'formula ces principes sous l'influence du génie dorien' (4e cahier, p. 13), un éloge de Cimon (5e cahier, p. 79) et les habituelles remarques sur les démagogues et le tempérament capricieux des Athéniens (5e cahier, pp. 69 et 80).

ment s'esquissa vers la condamnation de Sparte et de sa 'terrible politique'.[1] Mais entre Athènes et Sparte, le procès n'est pas encore gagné, ainsi que l'observe Duruy dans la réponse qu'il fit à Nisard. Réponse intéressante à bien des égards. Parce que, assumant fièrement l'"humble condition de professeur', Duruy y revendique le droit de 'faire un livre pour ceux qui doivent le lire'. Parce que surtout la distinction qu'il y établit entre Athènes et son régime ('Ce n'est pas la démocratie qui m'attire mais les grandes choses qu'elle a faites') ne doit pas être mise au compte de la seule prudence. Laissons-lui la parole: 'Mes préférences dans le passé ne sont pas politiques, mais philosophiques... [Je suis], en Grèce, *du côté d'Athènes qui a produit*, contre Sparte qui a été stérile.' Ainsi cette polémique dessine nettement les positions antagonistes qui, désormais, s'affronteront: Sparte ou la réaction,[2] Athènes ou la production.

L'histoire à la Duruy se veut édifiante; des faits, elle entend bien tirer des leçons[3] et, distribuant bons et mauvais points, risque fort de rater des phénomènes essentiels: ainsi, les lamentations y sont de rigueur sur 'l'insurmontable instinct d'isolement municipal né du morcellement du sol et qui s'oppose à la formation d'un grand État hellénique';[4] mais, dans ce schéma, la cité-état fait tout au plus figure d'incident regrettable. Autant dire que l'antiquité y est plus que jamais éclairée par le présent. Duruy historien de Rome lit le droit romain à travers la *Déclaration des Droits de l'Homme*[5] et, derrière l'historien de la Grèce qui décrit avec enthousiasme la 'politique sociale' de Périclès, perce le ministre qui, introduisant en 1863 l'histoire contemporaine dans les lycées, mettra au centre des études la défaite du socialisme, 'vaincu par les constants efforts du Gouvernement... pour donner satisfaction... aux intérêts populaires'.[6]

[1] Burette, *Histoire ancienne*, 6e cahier, p. 76. La 10e édition du Poirson et Cayx (1846) est également beaucoup plus mesurée dans la critique d'Athènes.

[2] Duruy écrit: 'Voilà, Monsieur, pourquoi je suis hautement, dans le siècle qui suit les guerres médiques, pour la démocratie athénienne dont l'heure était venue, contre l'oligarchie dont l'heure était passée' (*Histoire grecque*, p. 607).

[3] *Ibid*. Préface, p. xiv.
Ibid.

[5] Les 'erreurs' de Duruy ont été relevées par C. Lescœur, 'Le droit privé des Romains dans l'*Histoire* de M. Duruy', *Bulletin de l'Institut catholique de Paris* (1895), pp. 3–30. Duruy veut atténuer le fossé qui sépare l'esclave de l'homme libre (*Histoire grecque*, pp. 6, 10, 13, 22) et la femme de l'homme (*ibid*. pp. 19–20), et prend le *jus commercii* pour le droit de faire du commerce (*ibid*. p. 11).

[6] Le programme d'Histoire contemporaine de la classe de Philosophie (24 septembre 1863) a été rédigé par Duruy; on en trouvera des extraits chez Rohr, *Victor Duruy*, pp. 181–4.

Certes il est, pour toute forme de société, un temps, une heure,[1] et le temps de la Grèce est à jamais révolu. Mais cette distance n'exclut pas que dans l'antiquité grecque un bourgeois libéral se sente en pays de connaissance. Car la Grèce est du bon côté. Du côté du commerce, de la colonisation, en un mot de la civilisation, parce que son destin géographique lui a donné 'la mer pour domaine'.[2] Du côté de l'Occident face à 'l'immobile Orient': n'a-t-elle pas inventé la morale privée et la liberté civile, portant pour la première fois 'le flambeau qui éclaire encore l'Europe et que l'Europe à son tour porte au Nouveau Monde, depuis trois siècles à peine découvert, et dans ce vieil Orient qu'elle vient de retrouver'?[3] Du côté de la liberté politique enfin, puisqu'une évolution nécessaire a conduit les Grecs de la royauté à 'la cité se gouvernant elle-même'.[4] Schéma encombrant, dont les historiens de la Grèce ont encore bien du mal à se débarrasser...Un pas de plus et la Grèce, à en croire Duruy, inventait le régime représentatif. Lisons la page xvii de la Préface, elle en vaut la peine: 'La Grèce a tout vu, tout pratiqué. Elle finissait par le seul système qui eût pu la sauver: par une démocratie modérée qui donnait satisfaction à ses instincts invétérés de liberté et par *un gouvernement presque représentatif* qui rendait l'union possible.' Entendons que 'la formation d'un grand État hellénique eût sauvé la Grèce' par l'unité et 'les conditions égales offertes à tous'.[5] La fiction serait-elle la pointe la plus avancée de l'histoire? De fait, lorsque Duruy renonce à rêver la Grèce, il se prend au contraire à regretter amèrement la subordination grecque de l'individu à l'État, les dangers qui pesaient sur la propriété, les guerres civiles, l'esclavage qui empêcha la formation d'une 'classe moyenne assez forte pour imposer la paix aux partis'.[6]

Mais si malgré tout la Grèce antique est 'l'école du monde', c'est à Athènes qu'elle le doit, et prise entre l'éloge et le blâme, l'*Histoire grecque* s'ordonne autour de l'opposition de Sparte et d'Athènes. Pôle très négatif, Sparte, symbole de l'aliénation à l'État, n'est qu'une 'machine de guerre incapable de produire' et de participer au

---

[1] Réponse à C. Nisard, *Histoire grecque*, p. 607.

[2] *Histoire grecque*, pp. 5–7, 46, 67, 83; v. aussi l'*Histoire de la Grèce ancienne* (1862), pp. 2–4 et 9.

[3] *Histoire grecque*, Préface, p. xvi; sur l'opposition de l'Orient et de l'Occident, v. *ibid.* pp. 28, 37, 236, 302, etc.   [4] *Ibid.* Préface, p. viii.

[5] Duruy fait allusion à l'histoire de la ligue achéenne entre 272 et 221; v. *Histoire grecque*, pp. 609–31, et les développements de l'*Histoire des Romains*, t. i (Paris, 1843), pp. 478–81.

[6] *Histoire grecque*, Préface, pp. xvii–xviii; dans l'*Histoire des Romains*, t. ii (Paris, 1870), p. 40, Duruy affirme que la classe moyenne faisait la force de Rome.

'labeur commun' de l'humanité.[1] Pôle presque entièrement positif, Athènes est douce à l'esclave, ouverte à l'étranger, maternelle pour les orphelins de guerre.[2] Dotée des 'institutions les plus humaines, les plus vraiment libérales que l'Antiquité ait eues', cette Athènes mérite que l'historien avoue la 'sympathique affection' qu'il éprouve pour elle.[3] L'État – nous laissons bien entendu à Duruy la responsabilité de cette dénomination anachronique – y use de ses richesses pour aider les citoyens en une sorte d'assistance sociale généralisée; la propriété, la famille et le travail y sont protégés par Athéna, 'divinité ouvrière qui créa l'olivier, inventa les arts utiles et enseigna à l'épouse les vertus domestiques'.[4] Le commerce et l'impérialisme s'y épaulent mutuellement, pour le plus grand profit de la civilisation, de la prospérité et de l'équilibre social,[5] et Duruy n'a que louanges pour l'*archè* athénienne qui 'livrait au génie du commerce et des arts ces mers pacifiées'.[6] Mieux encore: commerce et liberté politique vont désormais la main dans la main[7] et, en déplaçant sur la Pnyx la tribune aux harangues, Thémistocle a voulu 'que les orateurs pussent de là montrer sans cesse au peuple la mer qui [s'étend] à ses pieds comme son domaine'.[8] Il ne s'agit plus, dès lors, de critiquer la démocratie, et Duruy prend parti, pour Périclès bien sûr, mais aussi, pour la première fois peut-être dans l'historiographie française de la Grèce, pour Éphialte, 'le vertueux Éphialte' dont le seul crime est d'avoir 'fait boire à longs traits aux Athéniens la coupe de la liberté',[9] et pour l'armée de Samos en guerre ouverte avec les oligarques de la *polis*, 'car Athènes n'était plus dans Athènes mais sur la flotte'.[10]

Nous arrêterons ici notre voyage à travers l'imaginaire bourgeois puisque, aussi bien, le paradigme d'Athènes y est définitivement constitué. Ce qui ne signifie pas que dans cette Athènes nous voyions

[1] *Histoire grecque*, Préface, p. xii et pp. 58–9, 63, 65–7.
[2] *Ibid.* Préface, p. x. Dans l'édition de 1862 Duruy renvoie au *Ménexène* (249 a–b), sans se soucier de l'écart entre son Athènes 'maternelle' et celle de Platon qui, face aux orphelins, assume le rôle du *père*. Écart significatif: il faut à toute force assurer la promotion de la femme à Athènes!   [3] *Ibid.* Préface, p. x.
[4] *Histoire grecque*, Préface de l'édition de 1862, p. x; v. *Histoire grecque*, pp. 437 et 474 (Duruy contre Platon) et, dans l'édition de 1862, une étrange addition (t. II, p. 138) sur Socrate défenseur de 'la sainteté de la famille et du travail' (?).
[5] *Ibid.* pp. 204, 242–3, 246–7, 272, 284, 293, 400.
[6] *Ibid.* p. 281; Préface, p. ix ('Cette domination qui assure la sécurité des mers, qui excite l'industrie et le commerce, qui sème le bien-être et provoque l'intelligence, est le moment le plus heureux de la Grèce, et le plus brillant de la vie de l'humanité').
[7] *Ibid.* p. 394, à propos des Trente.   [8] *Ibid.* p. 246; même idée p. 293.
[9] *Ibid.* p. 258.
[10] *Ibid.* p. 379. Pour une prise de position en faveur d'Athènes, v. encore pp. 271–2, 285, 296.

une conquête, un progrès réel ou le terme d'une irrésistible évolution : les silences et les contradictions de l'histoire à la Duruy pèseront lourd sur les questions que désormais les historiens vont poser à l'antiquité. Ainsi la terre, ce modèle grec de la richesse, ce critère grec de citoyenneté, est systématiquement occultée par Duruy au profit 'du commerce, de l'industrie, de la banque',[1] la crise agraire du VIIe siècle est inconnue ou ignorée, indigne en tout cas de figurer parmi les causes de la colonisation,[2] Solon n'est crédité que d'une réforme monétaire, et la fortune des Pentacosiomédimnes s'évalue en drachmes, avant d'être convertie en francs.[3] Quant à la démocratie, Duruy ne s'en accommode qu'en la tirant du côté des régimes censitaires, voire représentatifs. Non sans contradictions. A quelques pages de distance, il loue Athènes d'avoir fait de ses citoyens une aristocratie par rapport à laquelle esclaves, métèques et étrangers sont le peuple[4] et regrette que Périclès ait limité la citoyenneté à 'une imperceptible minorité de quatorze mille citoyens', bien incapable de 'tenir asservies' les multitudes qui constituent l'empire.[5] Il peut encore écrire ceci : 'L'assemblée générale..., placée à la tête de l'empire, n'était qu'une *chambre de représentants* plus nombreuse que la nôtre'[6] – l'empire est celui d'Athènes, l'assemblée générale est l'*ekklésia* : faut-il insister sur l'énormité du contre-sens? – et, quelques pages plus loin : 'Le citoyen, même le plus obscur, se sent un personnage important car il a sa voix dans une assemblée populaire où rarement plus de cinq mille personnes assistent.'[7]

Athènes ou l'histoire bourgeoise. Athènes ou la bourgeoisie face à ses propres hésitations : République ou empire? Empire autoritaire? Empire libéral? Athènes assume simultanément toutes ces figures...

Voilà : nous avons tenté d'esquisser ici comment s'est constitué en France le visage de l'Athènes bourgeoise. Il en est bien d'autres, en d'autres pays de l'Europe et du monde. Aussi notre tentative ne prendra-t-elle son intérêt que dans la mesure où il sera possible un jour de confronter les multiples figures de ces multiples Athènes.

---

[1] *Ibid.* p. 280, où Duruy recouvre bien vite la richesse agraire sous la fortune mobilière. Duruy sait pourtant reconnaître l'importance de la terre lorsqu'il s'agit de Rome : 'Au Moyen Age, avoir de la terre, c'était prendre rang parmi les nobles; à Rome, c'était devenir véritablement citoyen, c'était avoir la vraie richesse;...la seule d'ailleurs que Rome, sans industrie, sans commerce, connût et respectât' (*Histoire des Romains*, t. I, p. 170). On en déduira que, pour Duruy, la richesse agraire disparaît avec l'industrie et le commerce!

[2] *Histoire grecque*, p. 141; v. encore l'ajout de 1862 (I, p. 255).   [3] *Ibid.* pp. 181–3.
[4] *Ibid.* p. 265.   [5] *Ibid.* p. 275.   [6] *Ibid.* p. 285.   [7] *Ibid.* p. 293.

10

EIGHTEENTH-CENTURY AMERICAN POLITICAL THOUGHT

MEYER REINHOLD

'How strangely is antiquity treated!' wrote Thomas Paine in 1792, repudiating the doctrine of precedents. 'To answer some purposes, it is spoken of as the times of darkness and ignorance, and to answer others, it is put for the light of the world.'[1] In eighteenth-century America during the formative time of the new nation (c. 1750–90) reading of the classics and uses of knowledge of antiquity were indeed grossly selective, complacently antiquarian, instrumental.[2] The prize of knowledge for the leaders of the revolutionary generation – politicians, pamphleteers, patriots – was not systematic learning and the truth but freedom from the mother country and establishment and management of a stable and durable multi-state republic, with the guidance of what John Adams called 'the divine science of politics'.

Typical of the centrality of political thought for the Founding Fathers is Josiah Quincy's provision in his will (1774): 'I give to my son, when he shall arrive at the age of fifteen years, Algernon Sidney's works, – John Locke's works, – Lord Bacon's works, – Gordon's Tacitus, – and Cato's Letters. May the Spirit of Liberty rest upon him!'[3] The almost reverential appeal to classical political theory and

---

[1] *The Rights of Man*, in *The Complete Writings of Thomas Paine*, ed. Philip S. Foner (New York, 1945), vol. I, p. 387. Cf. Howard M. Jones, *Revolution & Romanticism* (Cambridge, Mass., 1974), pp. 151–87.

[2] Louis B. Wright, 'The purposeful reading of our colonial ancestors', *Journal of English Literary History*, IV (1937), 85–111; Charles F. Mullett, 'Classical influences in the American Revolution', *Classical Journal*, XXXV (1939–40), 92–104; Bernard Bailyn, *Education in the Forming of American Society* (Chapel Hill, 1960), pp. 33–6; Meyer Reinhold, *The Classick Pages. Classical Reading of Eighteenth-Century Americans* (University Park, Pennsylvania, 1975), pp. 10–18; *idem*, 'The quest for "useful knowledge" in eighteenth-century America', *Proceedings of the American Philosophical Society*, CXIX (1975), 108–32. The absence of systematic classical scholarship in America's first two centuries is documented by the silence of John E. Sandys, *A History of Classical Scholarship* (1908; reprinted New York, 1967), vol. III, pp. 450–2; Rudolf Pfeiffer, *History of Classical Scholarship from 1300–1850* (Oxford, 1976).

[3] Josiah Quincy, *Memoir of the Life of Josiah Quincy Jun.* (Boston, 1825), p. 350. Cf. Rev. Jonathan Mayhew in 1776 in his thanksgiving sermon on the repeal of the Stamp Act: 'Having been initiated, in youth, in the doctrines of civil liberty, as they were taught by such men as Plato, Demosthenes, and Cicero, and other renowned persons among the

practice as the absolute standard for inspiration, guidance and testing of governmental innovation through comparative process was endemic. This leap into the classical past for political precedents gleaned from the 'perfect Models of Antiquity'[1] is in full view, for example, in the grandiloquent flourish of the remarkable Hugh Henry Brackenridge, in 1779, in a *Letter to the Poets, Philosophers, Orators, Statesmen and Heroes of Antiquity*:

It is indeed high time [for you] to abandon [the British] and to turn your attention to the free people of America. Here your correspondence will be much courted, and your observations very generally attended to...History and politics...will be more to the taste of the present times; and for that reason I am particularly anxious to interest in our behalf those great legislators [of antiquity]...The sentiments of these great men upon Government, will be of great service at the present day...It would much oblige us, if Solon and some others, of your best politicians would send up a few observations on the nature of Government in general, which we may use as a compass to steer our opinions in this wide waste of argument.[2]

The late Hannah Arendt concluded that 'without the classical example...none of the men of the revolutions on either side of the Atlantic would have possessed the courage for what then turned out to be unprecedented action'. American classicists would like to agree with her; few American intellectual historians do.[3]

No-one may doubt, however, that there occurred in the Revolutionary Age – the golden age of the classical tradition in America – the greatest outpouring of lessons from antiquity in the public arena that America was ever again to witness. The Founding Fathers ransacked the ancient world as a usable past for guide-lines, parallels, analogies to present political problems, and indeed for partisan politics. They frequently scoured ancient history and political theory and institutions as 'the lamp of experience' in search of authoritative precedents to legitimate and validate conclusions already arrived at

ancients, and such as Sidney, Milton, Locke and Hoadley among the moderns; I liked them; they seemed rational' (*The Snare Broken* (Boston, 1766), p. 43).

[1] Richard Peters, *A Sermon on Education, Wherein Some Account is Given of the Academy Established in the City of Philadelphia* (Philadelphia, 1751).

[2] *United States Magazine* (January 1779), pp. 11–14; or Hugh Henry Brackenridge, *Gazette Publications* (Carlisle, Pennsylvania, 1806), pp. 221–3. Cf. James Madison in letter to Jefferson, 30 June 1789: 'We are in a wilderness without a single footstep to guide us. Our successors will have an easier task...' (*Papers of Thomas Jefferson*, ed. Julian P. Boyd (Princeton, 1950–), vol. xv, pp. 224–5).

[3] *On Revolution* (New York, 1963), p. 197. For Arendt on the classical sources and the impact of ancient political theory on the American Revolution see also pp. 13–14, 20, 119, 139–215. Clinton Rossiter, e.g., *Seedtime of the Republic* (New York, 1953), p. 357, held that the ancient authors taught the Founding Fathers nothing new.

through wide reading in contemporary literature and through the exercise of reason.[1] For the Founding Fathers instinctively associated liberty and republicanism with the ancient commonwealths, 'those free Governments of old, whose History we so much admire, and whose Example we think it an Honour to imitate'.[2] And it was preeminently the Roman republic that was their exemplar, serving as a timeless model in which the civic virtues as well as corrupting vices stood out with classical clarity. In their quest for good government many among the Revolutionary generation were inspired by this comparative method, this almost ritualistic communion with ancient thought, with high optimism and confidence in the viability of a *novus ordo saeclorum*.

Yet for the most part this aggregation of classical knowledge was extracted not from the original texts but from such 'short cuts' as traitorous translations, modern histories of the ancient world, handbooks of antiquities and encyclopaedias.[3] Ezra Stiles, president of Yale College, could write to Jefferson in 1790 in response to a scholarly inquiry:

> We too much content ourselves with perusing the modern and inaccurate and injudicious Retailers of ancient History neglecting the original Historians, whether in the original Languages or their Translations...[Students] read only the modern Writers or Compilers of antient History...[4]

More significantly, the understanding of ancient republicanism and of classical political theory that reached the Founding Fathers was a filtered and refracted one, derived from the works of selected contemporary transatlantic political theorists and publicists assiduously read by early Americans.[5] And it was especially from the

---

[1] This is why Bernard Bailyn concluded that the classics were 'illustrative, not determinative of thought'. See *The Ideological Origins of the American Revolution* (Cambridge, Mass., 1967), pp. 23–6.

[2] William Livingston in *The Independent Reflector*, by William Livingston and Others (1753), ed. Milton M. Klein (Cambridge, Mass., 1963), p. 279.

[3] Reinhold, *The Classick Pages, passim*; H. Trevor Colbourn, *The Lamp of Experience. Whig History and the Intellectual Origins of the American Revolution* (Chapel Hill, 1965), Appendix II, pp. 199–232, for popular books on ancient history and politics in numerous eighteenth-century American libraries.

[4] Letter to Jefferson, 27 August 1790, in *Papers of Thomas Jefferson*, vol. XVII, p. 443.

[5] See, e.g., James W. Johnson, *The Formation of English Neo-Classical Thought* (Princeton, 1967), pp. 31–105; Charles F. Mullett, 'Ancient historians and "enlightened" reviewers', *The Review of Politics*, XXI (1959), 550–65; Michael Kraus, 'Literary relations between Europe and America in the eighteenth century', *William and Mary Quarterly*, 3rd ser., I (1944), 210–34; R. N. Stromberg, 'History in the eighteenth century', *Journal of the History of Ideas*, XII (1951), 295–304; Zera S. Fink, *The Classical Republicans. An Essay in the Recovery of a Pattern of Thought in Seventeenth Century England* (Evanston,

ideology of the English radical Whigs that Americans imported and naturalised their model of antiquity. Throughout the eighteenth century the *Independent Whig* and *Cato's Letters* of John Trenchard and Thomas Gordon, as well as Gordon's political discourses prefixed to his 'best seller' translations of Tacitus and Sallust were 'required reading' for American libertarians. These disquisitions equipped them with an ideological code, with classical political vocabulary and with political models. Gordon taught Americans that the Roman republic especially was 'the standard and Pattern...and useful Instruction..., an Example to us'. In line with the prevailing deterministic 'uniformitarian' theory of history, the ancient prototypes were deemed highly instructive because

Mankind will always be the same, will always act within one Circle; and when we know what they did a Thousand Years ago in any Circumstance, we shall know what they will do a Thousand Years hence in the same. This is what is called Experience...[1]

As early as 1765 John Adams outlined, in part, the blend of 'experience' that was to guide the Founding Fathers:

Let us study the law of nature; search into the spirit of the British Constitution; read the histories of the ancient ages; contemplate the great examples of Greece and Rome; set before us the conduct of our British ancestors, who have defended for us the inherent rights of mankind against foreign and domestic tyrants and usurpers...Let every sluice of knowledge be opened and set a-flowing.[2]

Indeed the classical doctrine of *ius naturale* enjoyed immense prestige in eighteenth-century America, as counter-claim overriding repugnant enactments of the crown and Parliament. But though the classical roots of the American appeal to 'inalienable rights' and the 'higher law' were known and cited (Aristotle, the Stoics, notably Cicero *De Legibus* III.4.10), Americans ardently espoused this concept less from direct knowledge of the ancient sources than from the

1945); Caroline Robbins, *The Eighteenth-Century Commonwealthman* (Cambridge, Mass., 1959); Gerald Stourzh, *Alexander Hamilton and the Idea of Republican Government* (Stanford, 1970), ch. II; Edwin A. Miles, 'The young American nation and the classical world', *Journal of the History of Ideas*, xxxv (1974), 259–74.
[1] From *Cato's Letters*, no. 18 (25 February 1720), in David L. Jacobson, *The English Libertarian Heritage* (Indianapolis, 1965), pp. 57–61. Cf. Colbourn, *The Lamp of Experience*; Gordon S. Wood, *The Creation of the American Republic 1776–1787* (Chapel Hill, 1969), pp. 45–53 ('The appeal of antiquity'). Pope mocked Gordon's 'Whigizing' of Tacitus: 'There's honest Tacitus once talked as big, / But is he now an independent Whig?' (unpublished MS. reading after verse 26 in 'Epilogue to the Satires', Dialogue I).
[2] *Dissertation on the Canon Law and Feudal Law* (1765), in *The Works of John Adams* (Boston, 1850–6), vol. III, p. 462.

English heritage of law and government, especially as mediated through Milton, Coke, Algernon Sidney and Locke, and from the continental jurists de Vattel, Pufendorf and Burlamaqui.[1] These sources were superficially summarised by John Adams in 1774, when he asserted that American revolutionary rights were founded on 'the principles of Aristotle and Plato, of Livy and Cicero, and Sidney, Harrington and Locke; the principles of nature and eternal reason'.[2]

Now the models of antiquity which Americans perceived, and were content with, were largely simplistic stereotypes, and these tended to fall into polarised patterns. For example, in the 1760s James Otis formulated the prevailing American view that Greece was a better mother of colonies than Rome, which dominated hers overbearingly and brutally.[3] The founders of the first modern republic, on the crest of utopian aspirations and from a need for both 'instant history' and historical legitimation, tended to idealise extravagantly the ancient republics. John Adams, while acknowledging the general progress of mankind, maintained that 'the knowledge of the principles and construction of free governments... have remained at a full stand for two or three thousand years'. Hence he turned his political sights to 'the ancient seats of liberty, the republics of Greece and Rome'; and in 1782 he wrote to Lafayette:

I [am]...a republican on principle...Almost every thing that is estimable in civil life has originated under such governments. Two republican powers, Athens

---

[1] Carl Becker, *The Declaration of Independence. A Study in the History of Political Ideas* (New York, 1922), pp. 24–79; Edward S. Corwin, *The 'Higher Law' Background of American Constitutional Law* (Ithaca, 1955); or *Harvard Law Review* XLII (1928–9), pp. 149–85, 365–409; Charles G. Haines, *The Revival of Natural Law Concepts* (Cambridge, Mass., 1930); Benjamin F. Wright, *American Interpretations of Natural Law* (Cambridge, Mass., 1931); Cornelia G. LeBoutillier, *American Democracy and Natural Law* (New York, 1950); H. Trevor Colbourn, 'Thomas Jefferson's use of the past', *William and Mary Quarterly*, 3rd ser., XV (1958), 56–70; Stourzh, *Alexander Hamilton*, pp. 1–37; Paul K. Conkin, *Self-Evident Truths* (Bloomington, 1974).

[2] *Novanglus*, in *Works*, vol. IV, p. 15. Similarly, Jefferson recalled in 1825 (in letter to Henry Lee) that the Declaration of Independence 'was intended to be an expression of the American mind...All its authority rests then on the harmonizing sentiments of the day, whether expressed in conversation, in letters, in printed essays, or in the elementary books of public right, as Aristotle, Cicero, Locke, Sidney, etc.' (*Writings of Thomas Jefferson*. Memorial Edition (Washington, D.C., 1905), vol. XVI, pp. 118–19.

[3] Cf. Richard M. Gummere, *The American Colonial Mind and the Classical Tradition. Essays in Comparative Culture* (Cambridge, Mass., 1963), pp. 97–119. Jefferson, for example, excerpted passages from Stanyan's *Grecian History* based on Thucydides that dealt with how Greek colonies freed themselves from mother countries: *The Commonplace Book of Thomas Jefferson. A Repertory of his Ideas of Government*, ed. Gilbert Chinard (Baltimore, 1926), pp. 181–5.

and Rome, have done more honor to our species than all the rest of it. A new country can be planted only by such a government.[1]

Yet among the Greek states it was not Athens, suspect because of its turbulent history, direct democracy, factionalism and demagogues, that was venerated by Americans,[2] but rather Sparta. From Plutarch's *Lycurgus* and contemporary European celebration of Sparta, notably by Montesquieu, American leaders judged Sparta to be a model of freedom and order, a stable, long-lived commonwealth, its people distinguished by virtue, simple life-style, patriotism, vigour. As 'brave and as free a people as ever existed' John Dickinson called the Spartans.[3] While the republic of Carthage was also studied as model because of its longevity, it was above all Rome that Americans turned to as republican archetype. This appeal of the Roman republic to Americans lay in its pluralistic culture, its perdurability, flexibility in policy, balanced constitution, agricultural economy, religious toleration, the vaunted purity of its great men and its 'Roman virtues' (especially patriotism, self-sacrifice, frugality).[4] For Alexander Hamilton Rome was 'the nurse of freedom'; and 'the Roman republic attained to the utmost height of human greatness'.[5] John Adams was unrestrained: 'The Roman

---

[1] *On the Canon Law and Feudal Law*, in *Works*, vol. III, p. 454; vol. IV, p. 284; vol. VII, p. 593. On classical models of republicanism in America see, e.g., Edward McNall Burns, 'The philosophy of history of the Founding Fathers', *The Historian*, XVI (1954), 143–7, 162–3; Miles, 'The young American nation'; Gordon S. Wood, 'Republicanism as a revolutionary ideology', *The Role of Ideology in the American Revolution*, ed. John H. Howe Jr (New York, 1970), pp. 83–97.

[2] See the criticism of Greek factionalism, for example by John Adams in his *Defence of the Constitutions of Government of the United States of America* (1787/8), in *Works*, vol. IV, p. 287: 'In the name of human and divine benevolence, is such a system as this to be recommended to Americans, in this age of the world?'; by Alexander Hamilton, 'The Continentalist no. I' (July 1781), *Papers of Alexander Hamilton*, ed. Harold C. Syrett (New York, 1961), vol. II, p. 657: 'No friend to order or to rational liberty, can read without pain and disgust the history of the commonwealths of Greece'; by Fisher Ames of Massachusetts, in *Debates in the Several Conventions on the Adoption of the Federal Constitution* (Philadelphia, 1891), vol. II, p. 8: 'Such were the paltry democracies of Greece and Asia Minor, so much extolled, and so often proposed as a model for our imitation.'

[3] *Letters from a Farmer in Pennsylvania*, letter III, 1767/8 (New York, 1903), p. 30. Charles Pinckney of South Carolina rejected the militarism of Sparta (*Records of the Federal Convention of 1787*, ed. Max Farrand, rev. ed. (4 vols., New Haven, 1937; reprinted 1966), vol. I, p. 401; Hamilton ridiculed Sparta's severe lifestyle (*Papers*, vol. III, p. 102). Elizabeth Rawson's comment in *The Spartan Tradition in European Thought* (Oxford, 1969), p. 368 ('Note on the United States'), that Sparta was generally thought irrelevant to the United States is incorrect for the Revolutionary Age.

[4] Documentation in Johnson, *Formation of English Neo-Classical Thought*; Fink, *Classical Republicans*; Robbins, *Eighteenth-Century Commonwealthman*.

[5] In *A Full Vindication of the Measures of Congress . . .* (1774), in *Papers*, vol. I, p. 53; 'Federalist', no. 34, *The Federalist*, by Alexander Hamilton, James Madison and John Jay, ed. Benjamin F. Wright (Cambridge, Mass., 1961), p. 249.

constitution formed the noblest people and the greatest power that has ever existed.'[1]

As counterthrust to the image of a decadent and corrupt England exported to America mostly by the radical Whigs, Americans envisaged the New World as the land of virtue *par excellence*. The 'incantation of virtue' swelled to a crescendo in eighteenth-century America,[2] taking secular form about 1730, and then being redirected into politico-ethical channels in the crisis atmosphere of the Revolutionary Age. True, this American cult of virtue at its height – civic virtue as public spirit for the public good – had its subterranean roots in the ancient preoccupation with virtue and moral knowledge and in the classical republics and heroes idealised by Americans. But the quest for republican virtue in America was fired to an intense glow by the teachings of the Whig tracts, Lord Bolingbroke's 'Letters on the study and use of history', published in 1752, and Montesquieu's *Esprit des Lois*.[3] A few examples from a virtual flood of exhortations to 'virtue' will illustrate. John Adams wrote in 1776, 'Politicks...is the Science of human Happiness and human Happiness is clearly best promoted by Virtue...'; and 'Public Virtue is the only Foundation of Republics. There must be a positive Passion for the public good, the public Interest....'[4] Robert Livingston of New York proclaimed, 'More virtue is expected from our People than any People ever had'; and an anonymous slogan said, 'No virtue, no commonwealth'.[5]

Among the numerous classical rôle models in America, mostly from Plutarch's republican saints and martyrs, pride of place was given above all to Cicero and hardly less to Cato Uticensis. Indeed, the Catonic model in America long served as a clarion call to

---

[1] *Works*, vol. IV, p. 439.

[2] Norman S. Fiering, 'President Samuel Johnson and the circle of knowledge', *William and Mary Quarterly*, 3rd ser., XXVIII (1971), 233–4.

[3] Lawrence M. Levin, *The Political Doctrine of Montesquieu's 'Esprit des Lois': Its Classical Background* (New York, 1936), pp. 68–70; Paul M. Spurlin, *Montesquieu in America, 1760–1801* (Baton Rouge, 1940); Stourzh, *Alexander Hamilton*, pp. 63–75 ('Virtue as the principle of republican government'); Henry F. May, *The American Enlightenment* (New York, 1976), pp. 155–6; Kenneth Silverman, *A Cultural History of the American Revolution* (New York, 1976), pp. 505–6; Eric Foner, *Tom Paine and Revolutionary America* (New York, 1976), pp. 158–60; Meyer Reinhold, 'The classics and the quest for virtue in eighteenth-century America', *The Usefulness of Classical Learning in the Eighteenth-Century* (University Park, Pennsylvania, 1977), pp. 6–26.

[4] *Warren-Adams Letters* (2 vols., Boston, 1917–25, reprinted New York, 1972), vol. I, pp. 202, 222 (both in 1776).

[5] Livingston, cited by Wood, *Creation of the American Republic*, p. 95; Anon. cited by Silverman, *Cultural History of the American Revolution*, p. 505.

dedication to virtue, civic duty and freedom. The high popularity of
Addison's tragedy *Cato* in eighteenth-century America – there were
numerous performances from New Hampshire to South Carolina
and at least eight American editions before 1800 – is proof enough.[1]
Particularly cultivated also was the cautionary model of Cincinnatus,
who epitomised the early American deprecation of lengthy holds on
the reins of power. Among the many Americans who imitated or
recalled Cincinnatus were Washington, John Adams, Jefferson,
Israel Putnam, John Jay, and even the suspect Order of the
Cincinnati, the association of retired army officers of the Revolutionary army founded immediately after the peace with Britain, in
1783. In that year too, long before Washington was elected first
president of the United States, Charles Wilson Peale's victory arch
depicted him as Cincinnatus, and he was greeted in Philadelphia on
8 December 1783 with the following lines:

> So HE who Rome's proud legions sway'd,
> Return'd and sought his native shade.[2]

This paradigmatic return to the plough, to the ancestral estate in
America was more than a symbolic gesture; it was a response to a mix
of impulses: the gentleman's 'Sabine Farm' ideal of the eighteenth
century, English country ideology, the value of frugality espoused by
the British commonwealthmen, the moral exaltation of agriculture
in the eighteenth century, the devaluation of trades as banausic, and
of cities and commerce as corruptive, encouraging luxury and
political ambition, traditional American 'primitivism' (up to 1800
about 90 per cent of the American people were engaged in some
form of agriculture) and the legacy of classical political theory of a
free agricultural commonwealth composed of self-sufficient,
economically independent farmer–soldier–citizens.[3] American
agrarianism was, like its classical antecedents, politico-ethical in
nature: an agricultural base for the republic with availability of

---

[1] Reinhold, *The Classick Pages*, pp. 147–51; Frederic M. Litto, 'Addison's *Cato* in the
colonies', *William and Mary Quarterly*, 3rd ser., XXIII (1966), 431–49. On Cato as symbol
of republicanism in the eighteenth century see Johnson, *Formation of English Neo-Classical
Thought*, pp. 95–105.

[2] Silverman, *Cultural History of the American Revolution*, pp. 425, 434.

[3] St John Crèvecoeur, *Letters from An American Farmer*, 1782 (Garden City, s.d.); Douglass
G. Adair, 'The intellectual origins of Jeffersonian democracy: republicanism, the class
struggle, and the virtuous farmer' (dissertation, Yale, 1943), pp. i–ii, 27–30, 65–95,
272–95; A. Whitney Griswold, *Farming and Democracy* (New York, 1948), pp. 18–46;
J. G. A. Pocock, 'Civic humanism and its role in Anglo-American thought', *Il Pensiero
Politico*, I (1968), 18–46, or *Politics, Language and Time. Essays on Political Thought* (New
York, 1971), pp. 80–103.

freehold land was deemed by most of the Founding Fathers to be
a prime safeguard for liberty and stability. The virtuous farmer, the
purity and simplicity of his life, were widely invoked, a model
conjured up from a classical past simpler than the English and
French present. The American poet of the Revolution Philip
Freneau wrote in 1775 in his 'American liberty, a poem':

> like the ancient Romans, you
> At once are soldiers, and are farmers too.[1]

While invoking classical republican models, the Founding Fathers
were fully aware of the classical cyclical theory of political change
with its admonition of the impermanence of political systems, the
decay and death of states, and rotation of governments. The classical
component, however, was but one of the many streams that flowed
into American political thought: English, continental, American
colonial. In addition to the theory of cycles, the doctrine of mixed
government, separation of powers, country ideology, natural law,
these were all vigorously debated in England in the late seventeenth/
early eighteenth centuries. Notably, regarding the doctrine of
balanced government, there was already a vast literature in England
during the constitutional discussions preceding the civil wars of the
seventeenth century, and this literature was available to Americans
in the Revolutionary Age, as was Montesquieu's *Esprit des Lois*,
whose roots reach back to Machiavelli. Moreover, separation of
powers in America (among colonial governor, council and colonial
assembly) was already in practice as far back as the Virginia Charter
of 1624, so that Americans were receptive to such a principle from
their own institutional history in colonial times.[2]

Why then, it may be asked, did the Americans in the Revolutionary Age so often have recourse to the 'pure fountains' of antiquity?

---

[1] *The Poems of Philip Freneau*, ed. Fred L. Pattee (2 vols., Princeton, 1902), vol. I, p. 150.
[2] The principal classical sources Americans knew, analysed, and cited are: Thucydides
III.81–3; Plato, *Republic* VIII; Aristotle, *Politics* V; Polybius, VI. 3–9; Sallust, *Catilina* 5.9,
9–10; Livy I (*Praefatio*); Tacitus, *Annales* III.26–8. On the mix of American political
theory see: Benjamin F. Wright, 'The origins of separation of powers in America',
Economica, XIII (1933), 169–85; Stanley Pargellis, 'The theory of balanced government',
The Constitution Reconsidered, ed. Conyers Read (New York, 1938), pp. 37–49; Stow
Persons, 'The cyclical theory of history in eighteenth century America', *American
Quarterly*, VI (1954), 147–63; Edward M. Burns, 'The philosophy of history of the
Founding Fathers', *The Historian*, XVI (1954), 142–68; Stanley N. Katz, 'The origins of
American constitutional thought', *Perspectives in American History*, III (1969), 474–90;
Bernard Bailyn, *The Origins of American Politics* (New York, 1968); John Ellis, 'Habits of
mind and an American enlightenment', *American Quarterly*, XXVIII (1976), 164.

Since the only precedents for republican government were to be found in the ancient states, 'They were *obliged* to study Greece and Rome, if they would gain "experimental" wisdom in the dangers and potentialities of the republican form.'[1] Moreover, there were no precedents in English history for a league of states. Thus ancient political theory and experience served Americans as an empirical laboratory for exploring and testing the political options. And, deeply troubled by the fact that the republics of antiquity were all in the graveyard of history, Americans were also practising what a contemporary called 'political pathology', performing, as it were, autopsies on the dead republics with a view to discovering how to retard the process of inevitable decay through proper safeguards for the first modern republic.[2]

The prime safeguard was deemed to be the balance inherent in the 'mixed constitution' of classical derivation, with its blending of monarchic, aristocratic and democratic elements. The ideal of balance was indeed one of the dominant metaphors of the Revolutionary Age, responsive to a highly pluralistic society with many opposing interests in thirteen colonies and numerous sub-cultures. As early as 1772 John Adams declared that 'The best Governments of the world have been mixed. The Republics of Greece, Rome, Carthage were all mixed Governments.'[3] In his massive *Defence of the Constitutions of Government of the United States of America* (1787/8), he applauded Cicero's advocacy of the mixed constitution of three elements as 'founded on a reason that is unchangeable'.[4] The constitutional practices of Sparta, Carthage and Rome were thus carefully studied by the Founding Fathers, and the ancient sources for balanced government (Plato, *Laws* III; Aristotle, *Politics*, e.g., 1265b, 1269a–b, 1294b, 1316a–b; Cicero; Polybius VI; Plutarch, *Lycurgus*) were ransacked as unimpeachable authorities. Adams was fully aware of the mortality of ancient republics despite their balanced constitutions, and of Tacitus' gloomy hindsight comment

---

[1] Douglass G. Adair, 'Experience must be our only guide: history, democratic theory, and the United States Constitution', *Reinterpretation of the American Revolution 1763–1789*, ed. Jack P. Greene (New York, 1968), p. 405, or *Fame and the Founding Fathers. Essays by Douglass Adair*, ed. Trevor Colbourn (Williamsburg, 1974).

[2] See, e.g., Wood, 'Republicanism as a revolutionary ideology'.

[3] John Adams, *Diary and Autobiography*, ed. L. H. Butterfield (4 vols., Cambridge, Mass., 1962), vol. II, p. 58. Note Adams' rejection of Athens in his *Defence*: 'We shall learn to prize the checks and balances of a free government,...if we recollect the miseries of Greece, which arose from its ignorance of them' (*Works*, vol. IV, p. 285).

[4] *Works*, vol. IV, pp. 294–5.

(*Ann.* IV.33.1) on the impossibility or evanescent character of a balanced constitution.[1] Yet he argued that

A Balance, with all its difficulty, must be preserved, or liberty is lost forever. Perhaps a perfect balance, if it ever existed, has not been long maintained in its perfection; yet, such a balance as has been sufficient to liberty, has been supported in some nations for many centuries together...[2]

Despite this, he could not refrain from such rhetoric as 'The institutions now made in America will not wholly wear out for thousands of years.'[3]

The paramount model for the Founding Fathers of a constitution structured to retard political decay and assure at the same time freedom and stability was the constitution of Rome of the end of the third/early second centuries B.C. – as analysed by Polybius in book VI, the vaunted prototype of a commonwealth since the Renaissance, the favourite source for classical republicanism in the seventeenth and eighteenth centuries. John Adams[4] was aware that the blessings of the Roman constitution did not long survive Polybius' analysis, and proceeded to assess the weaknesses of the Roman government, attributing the fall of the republic – with the advantages of hindsight – to imperfect, 'ineffectual balance', and prescribing stronger negative votes, separated powers and checks and counter-checks. As it turned out, indeed, rather than a 'melting pot' of a 'mixed constitution', the Constitution of the United States, put together in Philadelphia in 1787, was a document of numerous compromises, based on the principles of a broadly pluralistic balance and separation of powers, despite the confidence placed by the Founding Fathers in the Polybian mixed constitution of Rome. It is not uninstructive for an understanding of the eighteenth-century uncritical use of antiquity to compare their reliance on Polybius with our own view of his treatment of Rome's constitution as a tendentious and theoretical analysis of Roman government prepared in support of the Roman nobility. Moreover, Polybius' method is vitiated by his schematic application of Greek political categories and vocabulary to Rome, and his treatment is highly selective and glosses over the actual

---

[1] In *Defence*, in *Works*, vol. IV, pp. 294, 297–8.
[2] *Discourses on Davila* (1790), in *Works*, vol. VI, p. 399. On Adams' excerpts from Polybius VI and his comments on the 'balanced constitution' of Rome see *Works*, vol. IV, pp. 435–43, 540–1.
[3] *Defence*, in *Works*, vol. IV, p. 298.
[4] *Ibid.* vol. IV, pp. 540–1.

domination of the Senate and the Roman nobility.[1] We may add other cautions regarding the American appeal to the ancient mixed constitutions and to Polybius: Carthage, Sparta and Rome were imperial states striving for internal balance so as to present a posture of strength toward their subjects and foreign states; that such categories as monarchic, aristocratic, democratic were unsuitable for America; and that the Greek political theory of the *mikte* identified ideal balance with unchangeable, immobile perfection, a goal incompatible with the dynamism of America.

It was at the Constitutional Convention of 1787, at the various state ratifying conventions, and in the pamphlet literature and political tracts spun off in great numbers to influence the structure of the new government, that the appeal to classical political theory and practice reached its peak. John Adams, in Europe at the time as American representative, in writing his *Defence* ransacked ancient sources and modern works for classical constitutions and leagues.[2] Many of the delegates to the Convention in Philadelphia did their classical homework diligently, especially Madison, Hamilton and James Wilson. William Pierce (delegate from Georgia) said of Madison, for example, that he 'ran through the whole Scheme of the Government, – pointed out the beauties and defects of ancient Republics; compared their situation with ours wherever it appeared to bear any analogy'.[3] It is clear that the precedents, analogies and lessons Madison and others quarried from antiquity were not mere window dressing or 'pedantry in politics', but solemn exercises in

---

[1] On Polybius' methods, the nature and weakness of his analysis of the Roman constitution, and the American preoccupation with 'mixed government' and appeal to classical sources, see: Adair, 'Intellectual origins of Jeffersonian democracy', pp. 152–86; Kurt von Fritz, *The Theory of the Mixed Constitution in Antiquity* (New York, 1954); F. W. Walbank, *A Historical Commentary on Polybius* (Oxford, 1954), vol. I, pp. 635–746; Paul Pédech, *La méthode historique de Polybe* (Paris, 1964), pp. 303–30; Thomas Cole, 'The sources and composition of Polybius VI', *Historia*, XIII (1964), 478–82; Frank W. Walbank, 'Polybius and the Roman state', *Greek, Roman and Byzantine Studies*, V (1964), 239–60; E. Graeber, *Die Lehre von der Mischverfassung bei Polybius* (Bonn, 1968); Frank W. Walbank, *Polybius* (Sather Classical Lectures, vol. XLII, Berkeley, 1972), pp. 130–56; Arnaldo Momigliano, 'Polybius' Reappearance in Western Europe', *Polybe* (Fondation Hardt, Entretiens, vol. XX (Vandœuvres and Genève, 1973), pp. 345–72; Claude Nicolet, 'Polybe et les institutions romaines', *ibid.* pp. 209–58.

[2] *Works*, vols. IV–VI.

[3] *Records of the Federal Convention*, vol. I, p. 110. See also William Pierce's comments on the classical knowledge of other delegates to the Convention, *ibid.* vol. III, pp. 87–97. For example Luther Martin, from the small state of Maryland, cited Rollin's *Ancient History*, chapter and verse, in support of two senators from each state on the grounds that in the Amphictyonic Council there were two representatives from each of the Greek cities 'who were nothwithstanding the disposition of the Towns equal' (*ibid.* vol. I, p. 459).

comparative political institutions and history. The records of the Federal Convention, and the 'Federalist' papers, written by Madison, Hamilton and John Jay (notably nos. 6, 9, 18, 38, 63, 70) are dotted with classical parallels and lessons. It is discernible that some of these were extracted from translations of Plato, Aristotle, Demosthenes, Polybius, Livy, Cicero, Sallust, Strabo, Tacitus and Plutarch, but most were from contemporary works on ancient political theory and history, such as Rollin, Vertot, Edward Montagu, Adam Ferguson, Walter Moyle, Conyers Middleton, Mably, Millot, Mitford and Gillies.[1]

One of the prime lessons adduced from antiquity by the Founding Fathers was the unsuitability of 'direct assembly government' because of the instances known of instability and capriciousness of decisions in ancient republics. Further, such direct participation of citizens was incompatible with a republic possessing a large territory. Hence the Founding Fathers introduced into the Constitution the principle of representative government, repeatedly proclaiming that 'the secret of representation' was invented by them, and that this innovation constituted a major advance over the governments of the ancient republics.[2] But, aside from the term 'senate', it is to be noted

[1] Richard M. Gummere, 'John Adams, Togatus', *Philological Quarterly*, xiii (1934), 203–10; *Records of the Federal Convention, passim*; R. A. Ames and H. C. Montgomery, 'The influence of Rome on the American Constitution', *Classical Journal*, xxx (1934–5), 19–27; Mullett, 'Classical influences'; Gilbert Chinard, 'Polybius and the American Constitution', *Journal of the History of Ideas*, i (1940), 38–58; Adair, 'Intellectual origins of Jeffersonian democracy', pp. 24–5, 82, 113; *idem*, 'Experience must be our only guide', pp. 129–32; Dorothy M. Robathan, 'John Adams and the classics', *New England Quarterly*, xix (1946), pp. 91–8; Epaminondas P. Panagopoulos, 'Classicism and the framers of the Constitution' (dissertation, Chicago, 1952); Raoul S. Naroll, 'Clio and the Constitution. The influence of the study of history on the Federal Convention of 1787' (Dissertation, Univ. of California, Los Angeles, 1953), pp. 11–21, 14–16, 35–6; Burns, 'Philosophy of history of the Founding Fathers', pp. 143–7, 162–5; Richard M. Gummere, 'The classical politics of John Adams', *Boston Public Library Quarterly*, ix (1957), 167–82; Winton U. Solberg, *The Federal Convention and the Union of American States* (New York, 1958), pp. xix–xxiii; *Notes of Debates in the Federal Convention of 1787*, Reported by James Madison (Athens, Ohio, 1966), *passim*; Richard M. Gummere, 'The classical ancestry of the United States Constitution', *American Quarterly*, xiv (1961), pp. 3–18; *idem*, *The American Colonial Mind and the Classical Tradition*, pp. 173–90; *The Federalist*; William Gribbin, 'Rollin's histories and American republicanism', *William and Mary Quarterly*, 3rd ser., xxix (1972), pp. 611–22; George Kennedy, 'Classical influences on *The Federalist*', *Classical Traditions in Early America*, ed. John W. Eadie (Ann Arbor, 1976), pp. 119–38.

[2] E.g., Alexander Hamilton, *Debates in the Several State Conventions on the Adoption of the Federal Constitution*, ed. Jonathan Elliott (Philadelphia, 1891), vol. ii, pp. 352–3; James Wilson, *Works*, ed. Robert G. McCloskey (2 vols., Cambridge, Mass., 1967), vol. i, p. 763; David Ramsay of South Carolina, speech on 4 July 1778, in *Chronicles of the American Revolution*, ed. Alden T. Vaughan (New York, 1965), p. 321. Cf. W. Neil

that not a single direct adaptation from ancient institutions was incorporated into the Constitution;[1] and that the principle and practice of separation of powers already existed in both colonial governments and in state constitutions before 1787.[2]

Great attention was directed at the time of the Convention to the theoretical and practical aspects of federalism, and in this connection the debates and polemical literature analysed the merits and failures of Greek leagues. Of all classical political models ancient federalism was the most extensively studied because there were no precedents in the English experience or in colonial America.[3] The best informed about Greek leagues were Adams, Madison and James Wilson, yet their knowledge was limited; for the most part they repeated similar information on Greek leagues found in secondary works.[4] The confederation most frequently cited by the Founding Fathers was the Amphictyonic Council, because it was the one most commonly instanced in handbooks and histories. For example, in the frequently used work of Abbé Mably on Greek institutions they found the Amphictyonic Council elevated to 'une république fédérative', and 'les états généraux de la Grèce'.[5] James Wilson's vacillation is instructive. In 1790/1, in support of the United States Constitution, he lectured that the Amphictyonic Council was 'the Congress of the United States of Greece'; that 'the general intention and invariable aim of all its modellers and directers was, to form a complete representation of all Greece'; and that 'the establishment of the

Franklin, 'Some aspects of representation in the American colonies', *North Carolina Historical Review*, vi (1929), 38–68; Gordon S. Wood, *Representation in the American Revolution* (Charlottesville, 1969).

[1] E.g., Madison, 'Federalist', no. 63, *The Federalist*, pp. 414–17; Wilson, *Works*, vol. i, p. 186.

[2] E.g., Adair, 'Intellectual origins of Jeffersonian democracy', pp. 82, 113; Panagopoulos, 'Classicism and the framers of the Constitution', pp. 176–97, 208–10; Benjamin F. Wright, 'The origins of separation of powers in America', pp. 169–85.

[3] Cf. Walter H. Bennett, *American Theories of Federalism* (University, Alabama, 1964), pp. 54, 68–9.

[4] See, e.g., Madison's sources on Greek leagues in *Letters and Other Writings of James Madison* (4 vols., Philadelphia, 1865), vol. i, pp. 293–8 ('Notes on ancient and modern confederacies preparatory to the federal Convention of 1787'). On the wide range of secondary works on ancient political institutions consulted by Madison see *The Mind of the Founder. Sources of the Political Thought of James Madison*, ed. Marvin Meyers (Indianapolis, 1973), pp. 69–73; on those used by John Adams see Alfred Iacuzzi, *John Adams, Scholar* (New York, 1952). Americans were, of course, ignorant of epigraphic evidence and critical research on Greek leagues. For the present state of this knowledge see Jakob A. O. Larsen, *Representative Government in Greek and Roman History* (Sather Classical Lectures, vol. xxviii, Berkeley, 1955); *idem*, *Greek Federal States* (Oxford, 1968); *idem*, 'Amphictionies', *OCD*, 2nd ed. (Oxford, 1970), p. 54.

[5] *Observations sur l'histoire de la Grèce* (Paris, 1766), pp. 9–10.

Amphictyons should be admired, as a great master-piece in human politicks'.[1] But earlier at the Constitutional Convention Wilson had said:

If a proper model were not to be found in other Confederacies it is not to be wondered at. The number of them was small and the duration of some at least short. The Amphyctionic and Achaean were formed in the infancy of political science; and appear by their History & fate, to have contained radical defects... They soon fell victims to the inefficacy of their organization... There is no reason to adopt their Example...[2]

We may ourselves object to their adducing of the Amphictyonic Council as a flawed analogy, for it was neither a political body nor a federative league, but a religious organisation of twelve tribal groupings. In general, the lessons drawn from the Greek leagues were the deficiencies of the Amphictyonic, Achaean, Aetolian and Lycian leagues: their short duration, the tyranny of the larger states over the smaller, and the destruction of the ancient leagues by foreign intervention (Macedon, Rome).[3] The Lycian Confederacy was especially admired by some, for Montesquieu's endorsement of it as the 'model of an excellent confederate republic' carried great weight because it embodied the principle of proportional representation. Madison went so far as to call the Achaean League 'the last hope of ancient liberty'.[4]

Yet the Founding Fathers were not unaware of the limitations and slipperiness of their knowledge of Greek leagues and of the unsuitability of such precedents for the United States. As early as 1776 Stephen Hopkins of Rhode Island, best known as signer of the Declaration of Independence, cautioned that 'too little is known of the antient confederations to say what was their practice'.[5] James Madison, who spoke and wrote most on the Greek leagues (especially in 'Federalist', no. 18) acknowledged reliance on 'imperfect

[1] 'Of Man, as a member of a confederation', *Works*, vol. I, pp. 247–8.
Notes of Debates in the Federal Convention, p. 161; *Records of the Federal Convention*, vol. I, p. 350.
[3] Hamilton, *Papers*, vol. II, pp. 655–6 (from 'The Continentalist no. II', July 1781); *Records of the Federal Convention*, vol. I, pp. 143, 343, 348, 350, 473 (by James Wilson); vol. I, pp. 317–20, 326 (by Madison), 285, 296 (by Hamilton), 441, 454 (by Luther Martin); Madison, 'Federalist', no. 18, *The Federalist*, pp. 171–6; *Debates in the Several State Conventions*, vol. III, pp. 129–30; *The Writings of James Madison*, ed. Gaillard Hunt (New York, 1904), vol. V, pp. 139–40 (at Virginia Ratifying Convention); James Wilson, 'Of man, as a member of a confederation', *Works*, vol. I, pp. 249–50, 265–6.
[4] 'Federalist', no. 18, *The Federalist*, p. 176.
[5] *Journals of the Continental Congress, 1774–1789* (Washington, D.C., 1906), vol. VI, p. 1105 (August 1776).

monuments', a 'very imperfect account'.[1] James Wilson pointed out at the Pennsylvania Ratifying Convention how defective their knowledge of the ancient leagues was:

Ancient history discloses, and barely discloses to our view, confederate republicks – the Achaean league, the Lycian confederacy, and the Amphictyonick council... Besides, the situation and dimensions of these confederacies, and the state of society, manners, and habits in them, were so different from those of the United States, that the most correct description could have supplied but a very small fund of applicable remarks.[2]

Wilson also reported that he had endeavoured to learn more about the Lycian League, with little success.[3] In short, the Founding Fathers' knowledge of Greek leagues was superficial and refracted at best, their application of lessons therefrom generally partisan and opportunistic. Edward Freeman, Larsen's great predecessor in the study of federal government in antiquity, summed this up as follows: the American Founding Fathers 'instinctively saw the intrinsic interest and practical importance of the history of Federal Greece, and they made what use they could of the little light they enjoyed on the subject'. But, Freeman reminds us, the founders of the American union were not scholars, but practical politicians.[4]

The constant appeal to historical examples ('the lamp of experience', Patrick Henry; 'Experience must be our only guide', John Dickinson at the Convention arguing that 'reason may mislead us') clashed with the uneasiness on the part of many that history might mislead, and that ultimately reason must be the guide.[5] Madison leaned more and more to the latter view, advising 'quitting the dim light of historical research, attaching ourselves purely to the dictates of reason and good sense'; and he concluded that 'As far as antiquity can instruct us on this subject, its examples support the reasoning we have employed.'[6] And it was Madison who neatly summed up the prevailing compromise between ancient thought,

---

[1] *The Federalist*, p. 174; *Notes of Debates in the Federal Convention*, p. 3.

[2] *Works*, vol. II, p. 762.

[3] *Debates in the Several State Conventions*, vol. II, p. 483: 'I have endeavored, in all the books that I have access to, to acquire some information relative to the *Lycian republic*; but its history is not to be found; the few facts that relate to it are mentioned only by Strabo; and however excellent the model it might present, we are reduced to the necessity of working without it.'

[4] Edward A. Freeman, *History of Federal Government in Greece and Italy*, 2nd ed. by J. B. Bury (London, 1893), pp. 95–111, 243–51, esp. 250.

[5] *Notes of Debates in the Federal Convention*, p. 447.

[6] *The Federalist*, pp. 419, 453.

reason and present needs, the operative mix of empiricism and rationalism:

Is it not the glory of the people of America that, whilst they have paid a decent regard to the opinions of former times and other nations, they have not suffered a blind veneration for antiquity...to overrule the suggestions of their good sense... and the lessons of their own experience.[1]

The aged Benjamin Franklin at the Convention unequivocally deplored the appeal to ancient models:

We indeed seem to feel our own want of political wisdom, since we have been running about in search of it. We have gone back to ancient history for models of government and examined the different forms of those Republics which having been formed with the seeds of their own destruction now no longer exist.[2]

Some, like the pragmatic Gouverneur Morris, deplored the hunt for classical precedents as an academic futility improper in the practical science of government, and as productive of 'the same pedantry with our young scholars just fresh from the university who would fain bring everything to a Roman standard'.[3]

Still others urged emancipation from the ancient models on the grounds of the great advances made in political knowledge since antiquity. Hamilton, for example, declared: 'The science of politics..., like most other sciences, has received great improvement. The efficacy of various principles is now well understood, which were either not known at all, or imperfectly known to the ancients.'[4] Dissociation from ancient political models was also urged because of their unsuitability for American national character and the uniqueness of the American experience. Hamilton wrote: 'There is a total dissimulation in the circumstances, as well as the manners, of society among us; and it is as ridiculous to seek models in the simple ages of Greece and Rome, as it would be to go in quest of them among the Hottentots and Laplanders'; and 'Neither the manners nor the genius of Rome are suited to the republic or the age we live in. All her maxims and habits were military, her government was constituted for war. Ours is unfit for it, and our Situation still less than our constitution, invites us to emulate the conduct of Rome...'[5]

Similarly, Thomas Paine uncompromisingly rejected 'the complimentary references' to antiquity. 'The wisdom, civil governments,

---

[1] 'Federalist', no. 14, *The Federalist*, p. 154.
[2] *Records of the Federal Convention*, vol. I, p. 457.
[3] *Diary and Letters of Gouverneur Morris*, ed. Anne C. Morris (New York, 1888), vol. I, p. 114.
[4] 'Federalist', no. 9, *The Federalist*, p. 125.
[5] 'The Continentalist no. VI' (July 1782), in *Papers*, vol. III, p. 103; vol. IV, p. 140 (1787).

and sense of honor of the states of Greece and Rome, are frequently held up as objects of excellence and imitation.' But why, he wrote, do we need to go 'two or three thousand years back for lessons and examples'.

We do great injustice to ourselves by placing them in a superior line...I have no notion of yielding the palm of the United States to any Grecians or Romans that were ever born. We have equalled the bravest in times of danger, and excelled the wisest in construction of civil governments.[1]

At the Constitutional Convention the thoughts of Charles Pinckney of South Carolina raised the most serious doubts about analogies from antiquity:

The people of this country are not only very different from the inhabitants of any state we are acquainted with in the modern world; but I assert that their situation is distinct...from the people of Greece or Rome, or of any state we are acquainted with among the antients...Can we copy from Greece or Rome? Can this apply to the free yeomanry of America? We surely differ from the whole. Our situation is unexampled...[2]

More important, this breaking away from the comparative historico-political method and the concept of 'uniformitarianism' was accompanied by critical analysis and rejection of analogy in constitution making and governmental practice. Though Madison acknowledged that 'there are many points of similitude which render these examples not unworthy of our attention', he recommended caution: 'I am not unaware of the circumstances which distinguish the American from other popular governments, as well ancient as modern; and which render extreme circumspection necessary, in reasoning from one case to the other.'[3] James Wilson was even more circumspect:

I know that much and pleasing ingenuity has been exerted, in modern times, in drawing entertaining parallels between some of the ancient constitutions and some of the mixed governments that have since existed in Europe. But I suspect that on strict examination, the instances of resemblance will be found to be few and weak ...and not to be drawn immediately from the ancient constitutions themselves, as they were intended and understood by those who framed them.[4]

[1] *Complete Writings*, vol. i, pp. 123–4 (*The Crisis*, no. v (1778)).
[2] *Secret Proceedings and Debates of the Convention* (Richmond, 1839), p. 175; cf. *Records of the Federal Convention, loc. cit.*, vol. i, p. 401; *Notes of Debates in the Federal Convention*, p. 185.
[3] 'Federalist', no. 63, *The Federalist*, p. 416.
[4] *Works*, vol. ii, pp. 762–3 (1790/1). Cf. pp. 774 (4 July 1788) for an instance of the growing pejorative assessment of antiquity: 'You have heard of Sparta, of Athens, and of Rome; you have heard of their admired constitutions, and of their high-prized freedom', but they were inferior to Americans because their constitutions were imposed by lawgivers without the consent of the people.

The most incisive critique of the use of analogies for the American government from ancient political theory and practice was made in 1785 by a young Marylander William Vans Murray, then a law student in London. In a brilliant essay Murray assailed the idealisation of antiquity as unhistorical, rejecting the excessive use of classical parallels to America, which he considered to be a unique society. He also explicitly rejected Montesquieu's doctrine that civic virtue combined with frugality was essential to sustain republics. All classically based views, Murray declared, are 'Arguements derived from the falsely imagined character of antiquity'. He wrote:

It is impossible to say that ancient republics were models...the picture of ancient governments, except freedom, could furnish but a slight resemblance to the American democracies...From such precedents Americans can learn little more than the contagion of enthusiasm. From antiquity they could gain little.

In sum, such comparisons were to Murray 'fancied analogy', misguided admiration, 'phantasms of scientifical superstition'.[1]

In this connection the debate between John Adams and John Taylor of Virginia (planter, lawyer, political leader, friend of Jefferson and Madison) is particularly significant. Though Taylor's *Inquiry into the Principles and Policy of the Government of the United States* appeared in 1814, it was twenty years in the writing and reflects eighteenth-century polemics in transition to the nineteenth century. Taylor sharply criticised Adams' political philosophy in the *Defence* for 'following the analysis of antiquity' and for his reliance on three generic constitutional forms – monarchic, aristocratic, democratic. The United States, maintained Taylor, was something new and unique. Taylor rejected Adams' praise of Sparta's mixed constitution and its longevity; Sparta, Taylor argued, had no democratic balance, its government was in the hands of a minority, and 'duration [is not] evidence of political perfection'. Greek governments were based on fraud; in the Roman republic the aristocracy ruled by fraud to preserve its power. Therefore, searching 'among the relicks of antiquity' is irrelevant to America. 'Instead of diving after wisdom into the gloom of antiquity', we must start from the knowledge that in America 'human character has undergone a moral change'.

The history of ancient times is hardly more weighty, when opposed to living evidence, than the wanderings of fancy; it is invariably treacherous in some degree,

[1] William Vans Murray, *Political Sketches* (London, 1787), published also in *American Museum*, II (September 1787), 228–35. Cf. Alexander de Conde, 'William Vans Murray's *Political Sketches*: a defence of the American experiment', *Mississippi Valley Historical Review*, XLI (1954–5), 623–40.

and comes, like an oracle, from a place into which light cannot penetrate. We are to determine, whether we will be intimidated by apparitions of departed time... to shut our eyes, lest we should see the superiority of our policy, not in theory, but in practice, not in history, but in sight.[1]

Adams' reply was the timeworn formula: there is one eternal, unchangeable truth – that all men are the same everywhere, and that therefore antiquity is relevant to modern problems.[2]

Henry Steele Commager has given us a provocative analysis of the tension between the old and the new, between antiquity and the young republic in Revolutionary America. The classical world to which the Founding Fathers had appealed for guidance was a stereotype, an abstraction, a rational model outside historical time. But America was in fact a unique, dynamic, revolutionary, pluralistic, progressive nation, and could not be forced into the classical mould.[3] Indeed, after peace with Britain in 1783 there rapidly emerged a sense of national pride, self-confidence in government and resultant conviction of superiority over the ancient republics, rampant materialism, growth of democratic forms, anti-intellectualism, deterioriation of the quality of and respect for the traditional classical education, as well as rampant luxury, factionalism and abuses of power. Belief in a morally better society after the classical pattern, which had no deep roots in America, began to wither rapidly after 1789.[4] The classical models and classical political theory had served useful purposes in the crisis of the independence movement and the forging of the Constitution. They were now to be jettisoned. The retreat from antiquity and disenchantment with the ancient guide-lines were in full swing in the early national period. The ancient world was losing its bloom as absolute standard for testing modern political innovations.

There can be no more decisive evidence of the loss of reverence for

---

[1] *An Inquiry into the Principles and Policy of the Government of the United States*, ed. Leon Baritz (Indianapolis, 1969), esp. pp. 11–13, 19–25, 121–2, 171–2, 345.

[2] *Works*, vol. VI, pp. 443–522, esp. letters VIII, XIII, XVIII.

[3] 'The American enlightenment and the ancient world: a study in paradox', *Proceedings of the Massachusetts Historical Society*, LXXXIII (1971), pp. 3–15, or *Jefferson, Nationalism, and the Enlightenment* (New York, 1975), pp. 125–39. Cf. J. G. A. Pocock, 'On the non-revolutionary character of paradigms', *Politics, Language and Time. Essays on Political Thought and History* (New York, 1971), pp. 273–91.

[4] D. H. Meyer, *The Instructed Conscience. The Shaping of the American National Ethic* (Philadelphia, 1972), p. 142; Miles, 'The young American nation'; Henry F. May, *The Enlightenment in America* (New York, 1976), pp. 223, 359; Meyer Reinhold, 'The Silver Age of classical studies in America, 1790–1830', *Ancient and Modern. Studies in Honor of Gerald O. Else* (Ann Arbor, 1977), pp. 181–213.

the ancient republics and classical political theory than the profound revisionism in the thinking of Jefferson and Adams, both long advocates of the classical tradition, both now retired from the educative rigours of the American presidency. In 1816 Jefferson wrote to Isaac Tiffany:

But so different was the style of society then, and with those people, from what it is now and with us, that I think little edification can be obtained from their writings on the subject of government...The introduction of this new principle of representative democracy has rendered useless almost everything written before on the structure of government; and, in a great measure, relieves our regret, if the political writings of Aristotle, or of any other ancient, have been lost, or are unfaithfully rendered or explained to us.[1]

A few years later, in an exchange with Adams in 1819, Jefferson wrote:

When the enthusiasm...subsides into cool reflection, I ask myself, what was that government which the virtues of Cicero were so zealous to restore, and the ambitions of Caesar to subvert?...they never had [good government], from the rape of the Sabines to the ravages of the Caesars...Steeped in corruption, vice and venality, as the whole nation was..., what could even Cicero, Cato, Brutus have done, had it been referred to them, to establish a good government for their country?[2]

Adams' reply shortly after was: 'I never could discover that [the Romans] possessed much virtue, or real liberty...'[3]

Most Americans would now have agreed with Jefferson when he said in 1816: 'I like the dreams of the future better than the history of the past.'[4] Two decades later Alexis de Tocqueville came to one of his solemn, quotable conclusions:

Comparing the republics of America to those of Greece and Rome..., when one comes to thinking of all the efforts made to judge the latter in the light of the former, and by studying what happened two thousand years ago to predict what will occur nowadays, I am tempted to burn my books in order to apply none but new ideas to such a new social state.[5]

[1] *Writings of Thomas Jefferson*, vol. xv, pp. 65–6.
[2] *Ibid.* vol. xv, p. 233.
[3] *Ibid.* p. 237.
[4] *Ibid.* p. 59.
[5] *Democracy in America*, ed. J. P. Mayer and Max Lerner (first pub. 1835–40; New York, 1966), p. 278.

PART III

ANTIQUITY AS
A SOURCE OF FACTS

11

VICO AND ANCIENT RHETORIC*

G. COSTA

Any study on Vico's attitude towards ancient rhetoric must necessarily start with a careful analysis of the *Institutiones oratoriae*, a minor work composed by the Italian philosopher for a practical purpose. During the academic year 1699–1700, when Vico began his career as a professor of Latin Eloquence at the University of Naples, he wrote the first draft of the *Institutiones* as a teaching aid for his lectures. He revised and enriched this work in the following years. Thus two different versions of the *Institutiones* are extant: one preserved in the National Library of Naples, ascribed to the year 1711, and the other, belonging to Benedetto Croce's Vichian collection, written at a later time, that is in 1738. Since not only the author of the *New Science*, but also his son Gennaro, who first substituted and then succeeded him as a Professor of Latin Eloquence, based their lectures on the *Institutiones*, the relevance of this work from the standpoint of intellectual history is beyond any question. Fausto Nicolini rightly claimed that the *Institutiones* should be regarded as 'the official text of rhetoric studied in Naples for more than a century'.[1]

Yet the *Institutiones* were considered for a long time a mere compilation, void of intrinsic merit. Andrea Sorrentino, in a book published some fifty years ago, tried to give a fair appraisal of the influence of ancient rhetoric on Vichian thought, and called the attention of scholars to various sources: Aristotle (*Rhetoric, Topics*, and *Analytics*); Cicero (*Orator, De oratore, Topica, De inventione, De partitione oratoria, Brutus*, and *Academicae quaestiones*); the pseudo-Ciceronian *Rhetorica ad Herennium*; Quintilian (*Institutio oratoria*).[2] For instance, the Italian philosopher identifies rhetoric with eloquence, and defines it as 'the capability of speaking properly in order to persuade' ('Rhetorica sive eloquentia est facultas dicendi apposite ad persuadendum') in a passage which Sorrentino has convincingly

---

* This paper reflects my research on the rôle of the Longinian sublime in Italian literature, on which I am presently working as a J. S. Guggenheim Fellow.

[1] G. B. Vico, *Versi d'occasione e scritti di scuola*, ed. F. Nicolini (Bari, 1941), p. 223. Cf. B. Croce and F. Nicolini, *Bibliografia vichiana* (Naples, 1947–8), vol. I, pp. 111–12.

[2] A. Sorrentino, *La retorica e la poetica di Vico, ossia la prima concezione estetica del linguaggio* (Turin, 1927), p. 112 and *passim*.

compared with Aristotle's *Rhetoric* 1.1355b, Cicero's *Orator* xix.61, and Quintilian's *Institutio oratoria* 1.15.[1] It is evident that Sorrentino did not share his contemporaries' disregard for rhetoric which was forced on Italian culture by the tremendous success of Croce's aesthetic ideas. But he was aware of the idealistic climate that dominated Italian intellectual circles, and adopted a kind of compromise between the new trend and the old one. In fact, he tended to underrate the influence of classical sources, while emphasising the rôle played by baroque poetics in the development of Vichian thought. This position did not appear unorthodox and anachronistic, since Croce himself had pointed out the relevance of baroque writers such as Matteo Pellegrini and Sforza Pallavicino from the standpoint of the history of aesthetics.[2]

Contemporary studies on the relationship between rhetoric and philosophy make Sorrentino's strategy obsolete. An Italian follower of Perelman's new rhetoric, Alessandro Giuliani, was able to break new ground by contributing to Vichian scholarship an essay intended to be 'a first attempt to identify the relationship between Vico and the contemporary revival of rhetoric'.[3] Giuliani sharply criticises Croce and his followers for having neglected the *Institutiones*, and laments the fact that this work is still buried under 'the heavy judgment of idealistic historiography'.[4] He observes that 'Perelman is one of the few contemporary scholars who shows awareness of Vico's *Institutiones* by using them extensively in his *Traité de l'argumentation* (1958).'[5] Giuliani shows that Vichian thought is moulded after the classical theory of controversy (*status*), and stresses the importance of the Greek and Latin sources of the *Institutiones*, while completely ignoring Sorrentino's suggestions about the essential rôle of baroque rhetoric in Vichian philosophy. He also insists on Vico's debt to the Byzantine and humanistic commentaries on the rhetorical treatise of Hermogenes of Tarsus.[6] Giuliani's essay, full of refreshing and

---

[1] G. B. Vico, *Opere*, ed. F. S. Pomodoro (Napoli, 1858–69), vol. vii, p. 33 (*Institutiones oratoriae, De natura rhetoricae*); *idem*, *Versi d'occasione*, p. 159. Cf. Sorrentino, *La retorica*, pp. 51–2.

[2] *Ibid.* p. 112 and *passim*.

[3] A. Giuliani, 'Vico's rhetorical philosophy and the new rhetoric', *Giambattista Vico's, Science of Humanity*, ed. by G. Tagliacozzo and D. P. Verene (Baltimore and London, 1976), p. 31. The original version of Giuliani's study, entitled 'La filosofia retorica di Vico e la nuova retorica', appeared in *Società Nazionale di Scienze, Lettere ed Arti in Napoli, Atti dell'Accademia di Scienze Morali e Politiche*, lxxxv (1974), 142–60.

[4] Giuliani, 'Vico's rhetorical philosophy', p. 31.

[5] *Ibid.* p. 44.   [6] *Ibid.* pp. 43–4.

stimulating ideas, has the great merit of demonstrating clearly that rhetoric is a basic component of Vico's thought. This is indeed a far cry from Sorrentino's timid and compromising attitude.

However, the familiarity that Vico had with ancient rhetoric went beyond the boundaries set by Sorrentino and Giuliani. Let us look at a passage of the older extant draft of the *Institutiones* (1711), which, in my opinion, deserves a close examination: 'From all these rules concerning elocution one can produce three basic kinds or types of expression, covering, as their genera, all possible styles. They are the sublime, the humble, and the moderate.'[1] Sorrentino explains this Vichian statement on the basis of the *Rhetorica ad Herennium* iv.viii,[2] and we find such reference correct inasmuch as the latter work affords 'the first extant division of the styles into three'.[3] But it must also be noted that the terminology used in the *Rhetorica* is quite different from the one used by Vico: 'There are...three kinds of style, called types, to which discourse, if faultless, confines itself: the first we call the Grand; the second the Middle; the third, the Simple.'[4] It is evident, therefore, that the highest kind of expression is *sublime* (*sublimis*) according to Vico, while it is *grand* (*gravis*) according to the author of the *Rhetorica*. In view of such discrepancy in terminology, we can postulate, in addition to the source pointed out by Sorrentino, another one which also escaped Giuliani's attention, notwithstanding the fact that it is a masterpiece of ancient rhetoric. I am alluding, of course, to the anonymous treatise *On the sublime* (Περὶ ὕψους), falsely attributed to Longinus and considered by George Kennedy as 'the most sensitive piece of literary criticism surviving from antiquity'.[5]

In fact, the grand style mentioned in the *Rhetorica ad Herennium* precisely corresponds to the one called ἁδρόν by the Greeks,[6] while

---

[1] Vico, *Opere*, vol. vii, p. 130 (*Institutiones oratoriae, De formis dicendi*); *idem, Versi d'occasione*, p. 195.

[2] Sorrentino, *La retorica*, pp. 66–7.

[3] [Cicero], *Ad C. Herennium, De ratione dicendi* (*Rhetorica ad Herennium*), with an English translation by H. Caplan (London and Cambridge, Mass., 1954), p. 252, n. c.

[4] *Ibid.* p. 253.

[5] G. Kennedy, *The Art of Rhetoric in the Roman World, 300 B.C.–A.D. 300* (Princeton, N.J., 1972), p. 369. On the problem of Vico's attitude towards 'Longinus' cf. G. Costa, 'G. B. Vico e lo pseudo-Longino', *Giornale critico della filosofia italiana*, xlvii (1968), 502–28. Andrea Battistini has made some scanty remarks in his interesting book on Vico (A. Battistini, *La degnità della retorica, Studi su G. B. Vico* (Pisa, 1975), pp. 11, 43, 156n., 199 and 219). The same scholar has acknowledged in a recent review-article that my paper has demonstrated the Longinian component of Vichian philosophy (A. Battistini, 'Rassegna vichiana, 1968–1975', *Lettere italiane*, xxviii (1976), 80).

[6] [Cicero], *Ad C. Herennium*, p. 252, n. c.

Vico's sublime style presupposes the ὕψος of the Longinian treatise, although his terminology is not consistent, since the sublime mode of expression is also referred to in the *Institutiones* as the magnificent one (*magnifica forma*): 'The opposite of the magnificent form is the tumid one (*tumida forma*), which is also sometimes frigid.'[1] However this remark about the faulty style corresponding to the sublime or magnificent one echoes not only the *Rhetorica ad Herennium* IV.x.15, warning against the swollen form (*sufflata figura*), but also 'Longinus', quoted by Harry Caplan in his commentary on the *Rhetorica*.[2] Indeed the author of the treatise *On the Sublime*, III.4, is very explicit on this subject: 'Altogether, tumidity seems particularly hard to avoid... But evil are the swellings, both in the body and in diction, which are inflated and unreal, and threaten us with the reverse of our aim.'[3]

The Longinian component of the *Institutiones* appears the more likely, if we consider Vico's attitude towards the book *On the Sublime* in some other works of his, composed before and after 1711. Right at the beginning of the eighteenth century, the Italian philosopher demonstrated that he was acquainted with the Longinian treatise. In fact, a reference to 'the most judicious Longinus' can be found in Vico's third inaugural oration, held at the University of Naples in 1701 or 1702. The passage in question sternly reprimands an unidentified scholar who 'does not include Virgil in the category of heroic poets, because the most judicious Longinus made a comparison between Cicero and Demosthenes, but did not make any between Virgil and Homer'.[4] It is not easy to identify the target of this attack. Antonio Corsano has suggested that the person censured by Vico may be Pierre Bayle who was the object of hostile criticism in various works of the Italian philosopher.[5] But Corsano's proposal

---

[1] Vico, *Opere*, vol. VII, p. 131; *idem*, *Versi d'occasione*, p. 195. It should be noted that a confusion of terminology was favoured by the *princeps*, edited by Francesco Robortello under the following title: Διονυσίου Λογγίνου ῥήτορος περὶ ὕψους βιβλίον. *Dionysii Longini rhetoris praestantissimi liber de grandi sive de sublimi orationis genere* (Basel, 1554). The term *sublime* does not appear either in the first Latin version, that may have preceded the *princeps* ('Dionysii Longini de altitudine et granditate orationis, MS. Vat. Lat. 3441, fols. 12–31) or in the first vernacular translation, founded on the *princeps* ('Libro della altezza del dire di Dionysio Longino rhetore, tradotto dalla greca nella toscana lingua da Giovannj di Niccolò da Falgano Fiorentino, in Fiorenza, l'anno D.N.S. MDLXXV', MS. Biblioteca Nazionale, Florence, Magl. VI, 33). Cf. D. St Marin, *Bibliography of the 'Essay on the Sublime'* (Περὶ ὕψους) (printed privately for the author, 1967), pp. 7–9.

[2] [Cicero], *Ad C. Herennium*, p. 264, n. a.

[3] Longinus, *On the Sublime*, ed. W. Rhys Roberts (Cambridge, 1899), pp. 47–9.

[4] G. B. Vico, *Le orazioni inaugurali, il De Italorum sapientia e le polemiche*, ed. G. Gentile and F. Nicolini (Bari, 1914), p. 29 ('Oratio' III).

[5] A. Corsano, *Giambattista Vico* (Bari, 1956), p. 37.

does not seem convincing, since the Vichian passage implies that the unknown scholar was a detractor of Virgil and a partisan of Homer, which certainly cannot be said of Bayle.[1] We will therefore leave aside this difficult problem of identification, and turn our attention to Vico's classical source, *On the Sublime* XII.4–5, where the prince of Greek eloquence is praised at the expense of his Roman counterpart:

Cicero differs from Demosthenes in elevated passages. For the latter is characterised by sublimity which is for the most part rugged, Cicero by profusion... the great opportunity of Demosthenes' high-pitched elevation comes where intense utterance and vehement passion are in question, and in passages in which the audience is to be utterly enthralled.[2]

Vico, who shared with his contemporaries the erroneous belief that the Longinian treatise was composed in the third century A.D., may well have wondered why it contained no allusion at all to Virgil's *Aeneid*, although it dealt with Homer, who was often compared to the Roman poet. Through this omission, which appeared to him the result of a critical evaluation, Vico might have been led to feel that Virgil, according to 'Longinus', had nothing to do with the sublime. More important than this kind of guesswork is the unquestionable fact that Vico's interest in the book *On the Sublime* was far from cursory, as appears from his essay 'On the ancient wisdom of the Italians' ('De antiquissima Italorum sapientia'), published in 1710, just one year before the earlier extant draft of the *Institutiones oratoriae*. The 'Ancient wisdom' contains a devastating attack against the rationalistic brand of rhetoric advocated by the French Jesuit Dominique Bouhours on the basis of Cartesian philosophy. Vico contends that the geometric method of Cartesianism cannot be applied to real life, the domain of caprice, unpredictability and chance. In view of this, whoever intends to compose an oration after a geometric pattern, is obliged to strip eloquence of all witticism and to address his audience in the way, not of an orator, but of a school-teacher. Yet the French rationalists professed a great admiration for Demosthenes. This means, according to Vico, that they did not realise that the Greek writer's style had no connection with the geometric method, but was rather 'a sequence of inversions (*hyperbata*), as was pointed out by Dionysius Longinus, the most acute among rhetoricians'.[3]

---

[1] G. Finsler, *Homer in der Neuzeit von Dante bis Goethe, Italien, Frankreich, England, Deutschland* (Leipzig, 1912), pp. 198–9.

[2] Longinus, *On the Sublime*, pp. 77–9.

[3] Vico, *Le orazioni inaugurali*, p. 181 ('De antiquissima' VII, v).

Indeed the author of the treatise *On the Sublime*, XXII.1, had insisted on inversions, which are 'departures in the order of expressions or ideas from the natural sequence; and they bear, it may be said, the very stamp and impress of vehement emotion'.[1] Moreover 'Longinus' had stressed how frequently Demosthenes made use of inversion in a memorable page that could not escape Vico's inquisitive mind:

> Demosthenes is not so masterful as Thucydides, but of all writers he most abounds in this kind of figure, and through his use of *hyperbata* makes a great impression of vehemence, yes and of unpremeditated speech, and moreover draws his hearers with him into all the perils of his long inversions. For he will often leave in suspense the thought which he has begun to express...and then unexpectedly, after a long interval, he adds the long-awaited conclusion at the right place, namely the end, and produces a far greater effect by this very use, so bold and hazardous, of *hyperbaton*.[2]

This effective characterisation of Demosthenes' style is faithfully echoed by Vico in the 'Ancient wisdom', where it becomes a polemic argument against the introduction of the geometric method into rhetorical matters:

> he begins by announcing the subject of his speech; then, as if he wanted to divert the attention of his audience, he enters deeply into a digression that seems to have nothing to do with the announced subject; finally he demonstrates the link existing between the substance of the digression and the subject announced at the beginning: thanks to this technique, the lightnings of his eloquence strike the more terrifying, the less they are expected.[3]

Another significant reference to 'Longinus' is to be found in the 'Ancient wisdom' where Vico analyses the Latin word *numen* in connection with the *verum/factum* doctrine, a pillar of his thought:

> The Latins called the divine will *numen*, as if their best and greatest God manifested his will through fact itself, and did so with the same facility and rapidity which can be found in the wink of an eye. Thus it seems clear that they said with just one word both of the things admired in Moses by Dionysius Longinus, who, speaking about divine omnipotence, used the dignified and grand expression: *Dixit et facta sunt*.[4]

The Longinian rhetoric of the sublime compenetrates Vico's thought at this early but important stage of its development. It is also interesting to note that the Italian philosopher did not hesitate to quote *On*

---

[1] Longinus, *On the Sublime*, p. 103.
[2] *Ibid.* pp. 105-7 (XXII.3-4).
[3] Vico, *Le orazioni inaugurali*, p. 181.
[4] *Ibid.* p. 188 ('De antiquissima' VIII, II). For a stimulating treatment of the *verum/factum* principle cf. I. Berlin, *Vico and Herder, Two Studies in the History of Ideas* (London, 1976), pp. 99-142.

the Sublime IX.9, containing a famous reference to Genesis 1.3 and 9, which was the bone of contention between Boileau and Huet: 'the legislator of the Jews, no ordinary man, having formed and expressed a worthy conception of the might of the Godhead, writes at the very beginning of his Laws, "God said" – what? "Let there be light, and there was light; let there be land, and there was land."'[1]

But Vico's reference to the Longinian remark on the Bible appears to be even more relevant, in view of the fact that the same passage was quoted by many contemporaries of the Italian philosopher, including Giuseppe Valletta, a great bibliophile who exerted a deep influence on Neapolitan culture at the beginning of the eighteenth century, and had in his rich library a trilingual edition of *On the Sublime*.[2] There is no doubt that Vico's increasing interest in 'Longinus', as attested by the 'Ancient wisdom', reflects a general trend of European as well as Italian contemporary culture. In fact, Longinian quotations are conspicuous in the documents of the Franco-Italian dispute going on at that time. I am alluding, of course, to the so-called Bouhours–Orsi controversy, involving the best representatives of early eighteenth-century Italian intellectual life.

It is not my intention to deal at length with this complex episode in the cultural relations between France and Italy which was credited by a British scholar, John G. Robertson, with laying the foundation of a new conception of poetry and literature.[3] I just want to call your attention to the indisputable fact that the Bouhours–Orsi controversy greatly contributed to the fortune of the treatise *On the Sublime* on the Italian scene, proof of which are the numerous quotations from 'Longinus' in Orsi's *Remarks on a Famous French Book Entitled 'La manière de bien penser dans les ouvrages d'esprit'*, published in 1703.[4] Vico's link with the Franco-Italian dispute, pointed out by scholars such as Croce, Sorrentino and Mario Fubini,[5] is corroborated by

---

[1] Longinus, *On the Sublime*, p. 65. Cf. S. H. Monk, *The Sublime, A Study of Critical Theories in XVIII-Century England* (New York, 1935), pp. 33–5.

[2] G. Valletta, *Opere filosofiche*, ed. M. Rak (Florence, 1975), pp. 256–7, 281 and 575.

[3] According to Robertson, 'the movement that was ushered in by the Bouhours–Orsi controversy was of very real importance for the literary evolution, not only of Italy herself, but also of Spain, France, and even of England and Germany' (J. G. Robertson, *Studies in the Genesis of Romantic Theory in the Eighteenth Century* (Cambridge, 1923), p. 16).

[4] G. G. Orsi, *Considerazioni sopra un famoso libro franzese intitolato 'La manière de bien penser dans les ouvrages d'esprit,' cioè 'La maniera di ben pensare ne' componimenti,' divise in sette dialoghi* (Bologna, 1703), pp. 266, 308–14, 317 and *passim*.

[5] On Croce and Fubini cf. Croce and Nicolini, *Bibliografia vichiana*, pp. 747 and 867; M. Fubini, 'Vico e Bouhours', *Stile e umanità di Giambattista Vico*, 2nd ed. (Milano and

a coincidence that cannot be a matter of chance: both passages from
On the Sublime mentioned in the 'Ancient Wisdom' (i.e. the comparison between Demosthenes and Cicero as well as the allusion to
Genesis 1.3 and 9) had already been quoted by Father Bouhours in
his *Manière de bien penser*.[1] This fact speaks for itself, and reveals the
origin of Vico's admiration for 'Longinus'. Even Bouhours' adversary, Orsi, had discussed at length the Longinian remark on the
Bible: the Italian critic, through a free interpretation of the *brevis
oratio* (βραχὺς λόγος) formulated in the so-called *Rhetorica ad
Alexandrum*, XXII.3, had fused together the viewpoint expressed by the
author of *On the Sublime* and the ideas on Laconism developed in an
influential seventeenth-century work, *The Aristotelic Telescope*, by
Emanuele Tesauro.[2] Besides, Orsi had called attention to the
Longinian position on the Bible by refuting Bishop Huet's assertion
that the author of *On the Sublime* wrongly considered Genesis 1.3 and 9
as a piece of sublime style.[3] Moreover, Orsi had quoted *On the
Sublime* XXII.1, in order to substantiate his idea that 'the apparent
confusion of inversion sometimes produces an excellent effect in the
sublime form',[4] and, in addition, he referred to the description of
Demosthenes' oratorical gift to be found in *On the Sublime* XII.4.[5] In
view of these indications, we can safely reach the conclusion that
Vico inherited from the Franco-Italian controversy not only a new
sensitivity to literary and linguistic problems, but also a typically
Longinian brand of rhetoric which became an essential component
of his anti-rationalistic thought.

The active rôle that 'Longinus' had in the Bouhours–Orsi dispute
is further reflected in the Vichian treatise *On the Study Methods of Our*

Napoli, 1965), pp. 135–46; *idem*, 'Muratori e Gravina', *Atti del Congresso internazionale di
studi muratoriani, Modena, 1972* (Florence, 1975), vol. I, *L. A. Muratori e la cultura con-
temporanea*, p. 52. Sorrentino's substantial contribution has been acknowledged neither
by Croce–Nicolini nor by Fubini. Yet the fourth chapter of his book is very instructive
(Sorrentino, *La retorica*, pp. 85–105).

[1] D. Bouhours, *La manière de bien penser dans les ouvrages d'esprit, Dialogues*, 3rd ed. (Amsterdam, 1705), pp. 131 and 138 ('Dialogue' II).

[2] Orsi, *Considerazioni*, pp. 350–5. Cf. Ἀριστοτέλης. *Aristotelis opera omnia; Graece et Latine*
(Paris, 1874–87), vol. I, p. 435 (*Rhetorica ad Alexandrum* XXII.3); E. Tesauro, *Il cannoc-
chiale aristotelico, o sia idea dell'arguta et ingeniosa elocutione*, 4th ed. (Rome, 1664), pp. 508–16
(ch. VII, 'Treatise on metaphor'). A Latin translation of Tesauro's work appeared in
Cologne in the year 1714. Cf. *British Museum, General Catalogue of Printed Books*, vol.
CCXXXVI (1964), col. 481; *Catalogue général des livres imprimés de la Bibliothèque Nationale,
Auteurs*, vol. CLXXXIV (1957), col. 732.

[3] Orsi, *Considerazioni*, pp. 351–3. Cf. P.-D. Huet, *Demonstratio evangelica ad Serenissimum
Delphinum*, 3rd ed. (Paris, 1690), pp. 65–6.

[4] Orsi, *Considerazioni*, p. 350. [5] *Ibid.* p. 425.

Time, published in the same year 1710. In this work, the Italian philosopher, following in the footsteps of Orsi, Ludovico Antonio Muratori and Eustachio Manfredi, claims that the French language is unsuited to the sublime style, because it is too rich in abstract terms:

But though the French language cannot rise to any great sublimity or splendor, it is admirably suited to the subtle style. Rich in substantives, especially those denoting what the Scholastics call abstract essences, the French language can always condense into a small compass the essentials of things. Since arts and sciences are mostly concerned with general notions, French is therefore splendidly suited to the didactic genre.[1]

The relevance of this remark did not escape the reviewer of the *Giornale de' letterati d'Italia*, a periodical deeply involved in the Franco-Italian controversy: 'as far as eloquence is concerned, what he says about the French language should not be ignored; that is, that such a language is not appropriate to the sublime and ornate manner of speaking, but only to the familiar one'.[2] Indeed Vico's characterisation of French, founded on the Longinian treatise, was a significant step in the direction of a new, negative attitude towards French classicism which marked a radical change in European taste. This can be easily proved by comparing the Vichian position with the following statement coming from Edmund Burke's *A Philosophical Enquiry into the Origin of Our Ideas of the Sublime and Beautiful* (1757): 'It may be observed that very polished languages, and such as are praised for their superior clearness and perspicuity, are generally deficient in strength. The French language has that perfection, and that defect.'[3]

To Vico, 'Longinus' continued to be a source of inspiration, as it appears from a *lapsus* he made in the second Part of the *Universal Law*, entitled *De constantia iurisprudentis* (1721), by wrongly attributing to

[1] G. B. Vico, *On the Study Methods of Our Time*, trans. E. Gianturco (Indianapolis, New York and Kansas City, 1965), p. 40 (VII). Cf. M. Fubini, *Dal Muratori al Baretti, Studi sulla critica e sulla cultura del Settecento*, 3rd ed. (Bari, 1968), pp. 133–4; *idem*, 'Vico e Bouhours', pp. 140–4.

[2] *Giornale de' letterati d'Italia*, I (1710), 325–6; Vico, *Le orazioni inaugurali*, p. 283.

[3] E. Burke, *A Philosophical Enquiry into the Origin of Our Ideas of the Sublime and Beautiful*, ed. J. T. Boulton (London and New York, 1958), p. 176 (Part V, § VII). Cf. my review of this edition in *Giornale critico della filosofia italiana*, XXXVIII (1959), 413–16. The possibility of Vico's influence on Burke appears the more likely in consideration of the fact that *On the Study Methods of Our Time* was publicised in England by the *Memoirs of Literature* (1710), as I have demonstrated in my note on 'Vico e Michel de La Roche', *Bollettino del Centro di Studi Vichiani*, II (1972), pp. 63–5). On Vico's anticipation of Burke's opposition to Cartesianism cf. Berlin, *Vico and Herder*, p. 72.

the author of *On the Sublime* a remark on Homer's use of onomatopoeia: 'the same sound of burning flesh, σίζ-, extolled by Dionysius
Longinus in Homer as a sublime expression, because it renders the
hiss emitted by Polyphemus' eye while it was scorched, is also made
by our children'.[1] The obvious reference is *Odyssey* IX.394: 'ὡς τοῦ σίζ'
ὀφθαλμὸς ἐλαϊνέῳ περὶ μοχλῷ' (or, in A. T. Murray's translation:
'even so did his eye hiss round the stake of olive-wood').[2] As to the
remark itself, it appears, not in *On the Sublime*, but in Demetrius'
On Style (Περὶ ἑρμηνείας) II.94–5, containing also a reference to *Iliad*
XVI.161: 'Our authorities define "onomatopoeic" words as those
which are uttered in imitation of an emotion or an action, as "hissed"
and "lapping".'[3] In fact, Demetrius stresses Homer's exceptional
capacity for creating new, onomatopoeic words: 'Homer impresses
his readers greatly by his employment of words resembling inarticu-
late sounds, and by their novelty above all...As a word-maker,
Homer seems, in fact, to resemble those who first gave things their
names.'[4] However, Vico's wrong quotation is symptomatic insofar as
it reveals his predilection for 'Longinus'. It also shows that the Italian
philosopher was fully aware of the similarities existing between
On the Sublime and *On Style*. Thus Vico would probably subscribe to
W. Rhys Roberts' view according to which the Longinian ὕψος
'corresponds closely to the χαρακτὴρ μεγαλοπρεπής of Demetrius'.[5]

The Italian writer did not hesitate about extending to Dante's
Divine Comedy the favourable judgement that Demetrius had passed
on Homer's use of onomatopoeia: 'Dante created the word "cric"
[*Inferno* XXXII.30], similar to the σίζ- coined by Homer, in order to
express the sound of breaking glass, which is also laughed at as
childish.'[6] Of course, Vico did not share this negative attitude, since
he had reached a primitivistic concept of poetry, founded on two

---

[1] G. B. Vico, *Il diritto universale*, ed. F. Nicolini (Bari, 1936), Part II, p. 368 (*De constantia iurisprudentis* II, XII, IX).

[2] Homer, *The Odyssey*, with an English translation by A. T. Murray (Loeb, London and New York, 1919), vol. I, pp. 330–1.

[3] Demetrius, *On Style*, with an English translation by W. Rhys Roberts, in Aristotle, *The Poetics*, 'Longinus', *On the Sublime*, Demetrius, *On Style* (Loeb, London and New York, 1927), p. 363. Cf. Homer, *The Iliad*, with an English translation by A. T. Murray (Loeb, London and New York, 1924–5), vol. II, pp. 176–7.

[4] Demetrius, *On Style*, p. 363.

[5] *Ibid.* p. 283.

[6] Vico, *Il diritto universale*, Part III, *Notae, dissertationes*, p. 621 (*Notae in librum alterum* 21). Cf. Dante Alighieri, *La Commedia secondo l'antica vulgata*, ed. G. Petrocchi (Verona, 1966–7), vol. II, *Inferno*, p. 547; M. Fubini, 'Il mito della poesia primitiva e la critica dantesca di G. B. Vico', *Stile e umanità*, pp. 147–74.

essential components: the Longinian sublime and Locke's epoch-making contribution to the history of psychology, the highly influential *Essay Concerning Human Understanding* (1689), where special attention is paid to the development of our psyche in its earlier stage. Since I have already insisted elsewhere on the impact of Locke's philosophy and psychology on Vico's thought,[1] I will just summarise my viewpoint on this subject. It is indeed an anomaly of Vichian scholarship to have ignored the Lockean frame of Vico's thought, that is to say, the European source of his original philosophy, in order to confine its roots to the late seventeenth- and early eighteenth-century Neapolitan culture. This line of research, cultivated by scholars such as Nicolini, Corsano and Badaloni,[2] has produced excellent works that have shed new light on the Neapolitan and Italian culture in Vico's time. But they tend to over-estimate the intellectual rôle of some minor local scientists and philosophers, without paying enough attention to the great suggestive force exerted on Vico's mind by Locke's *Essay*, available not only in a French, but also in a Latin translation. In fact, the Italian philosopher transferred the Lockean pattern of human psychological development from the individual to society at large, that is to say, from individual psychology to ethno-psychology. In so doing, he was led to attribute a prominent position to primitive poetry and primitive society, not only through Locke's penetrating analysis of the child's intellectual development, but also through the Longinian sublime, viewed in the perspective of the Franco-Italian controversy and of the more comprehensive quarrel between the Ancients and the Moderns, that famous Battle of the Books which marked the rise of the modern idea of progress.[3]

The Longinian inspiration is perfectly fused with the Lockean psychology in a primitivistic passage of *De constantia* where Vico asserts that poets are similar to children and women, who were considered on the same footing by the Italian philosopher, notoriously married to an illiterate person, because they are both close to nature. In other words, children and women are primitive beings coexisting with civilised men, and, for this reason, they are able to attain the sublime, as 'Longinus notes that Sappho excelled in the

---

[1] G. Costa, 'Vico e Locke', *Giornale critico della filosofia italiana*, XLXI (1970), 344–61; *idem* 'Vico e il Settecento', *Forum Italicum*, x (1976), 10–30.

[2] Berlin, *Vico and Herder*, pp. 118–23.

[3] G. Highet, *The Classical Tradition, Greek and Roman Influences on Western Literature* (Oxford, 1949), pp. 261–88.

ode translated by Catullus.'[1] Here Vico appears to have in mind not only chapter x.1–3, but also chapter viii.1–4 of the Longinian treatise, where one of the five sources of the sublime is identified with 'vehement and inspired passion' ('τὸ σφοδρὸν καὶ ἐνθουσιαστικὸν πάθος') and the following principle is accordingly stated: 'there is no tone so lofty as that of genuine passion, in its right place, when it bursts out in a wild gust of mad enthusiasm and as it were fills the speaker's words with frenzy.'[2]

The Longinian influence on Vico was so strong that in the same work he made another blunder, similar to the one I have pointed out above, by attributing to 'Longinus' a remark that is to be found in Demetrius' On Style. This second lapsus is even more instructive than the first one, inasmuch as it reveals, in addition to Vico's partiality for the treatise On the Sublime, the source of his Longinianism, that is to say, Orsi's Remarks, as well as his capacity for giving a personal interpretation to cultural sollicitations. In fact, in a section of De constantia dedicated to poetic metamorphoses, Vico mentions the folk tales that had been collected by a great Neapolitan writer, Giambattista Basile (a precursor of Perrault and the brothers Grimm), and makes an interesting comparison of ancient, mediaeval and modern popular traditions. Among ancient folk tales, the Italian philosopher includes 'that fable in which Longinus finds the best of the Homeric sublime: the huge boulder hurled against Acis by Polyphemus, on which there were forests and pastures, as well as shepherds roaming with their herds, or the great pine-trunk handled as a staff by the same giant, when he was guiding his animals'.[3] It is evident that Vico erroneously ascribes to 'Longinus' the following passage of Demetrius' On Style, ii.115: 'Frigidity, like elevation, arises at three points. One of these is the thought itself, as when a writer once said, in describing how Homer's Cyclops cast a boulder after the ship of Odysseus: "when the boulder was in mid career goats were browsing on it." The words are frigid because the conceit is extravagant and impossible.'[4]

---

[1] Vico, Il diritto universale, Part ii, p. 369 (De constantia iurisprudentis ii, xii, xiii).

[2] Longinus, On the Sublime, pp. 57–9.

[3] Vico, Il diritto universale, Part ii, p. 373 (De constantia iurisprudentis ii, xii, xvii). I consider 'Aeacis' a misprint for 'Acis', although Vico did not correct it in the original edition of the Universal Law that he sent to the Casanatense Library in Rome. Cf. Joh. Baptistae Vici de universi juris uno principio et fine uno liber unus, vol. ii, Liber alter qui est de constantia jurisprudentis (Naples, 1721) (Casanatense, H xiii 13), p. 73. On this copy of the Universal Law with autograph marginalia cf. Vico, Il diritto universale, Part iii, p. 791.

[4] Demetrius, On Style, pp. 373–5.

Demetrius did not refer to Homer, but Vico was induced to believe that he did by Orsi's *Remarks*, where the same passage is quoted in Pietro Vettori's Latin version, and is wrongly considered a censure aimed at the author of the *Odyssey*.[1] Along with Demetrius' *On Style*, Orsi quoted Francesco Panigarola's comment on the same passage, and discussed at length the frigidity due to a misuse of hyperbole.[2] Later he recognised his blunder, and apologised for it in his 'Fourth Letter' addressed to Madame Dacier, which appeared in the years 1705 and 1707.[3] But Vico either did not read Orsi's 'Fourth Letter', or had only a superficial knowledge of it, since he not only interpreted the passage quoted above in connection with Homer's *Odyssey*, as Orsi did, but even attributed it mistakenly to 'Longinus', which the author of the *Remarks* did not do. Our philosopher also made another apparent blunder: he mentioned Acis in the place of Odysseus, whose name appears in Demetrius' original remark and in Orsi's variations on it. By replacing the legend of Odysseus with the legend of Acis, the lover of Galatea, slain by the jealous Polyphemus and changed to a river god, Vico implicitly extends the quality of the Homeric sublime from the *Odyssey* to Ovid's *Metamorphoses*, where the legend of Acis is dealt with in an episode containing also a reference to the pine-trunk used by the Cyclops as a staff ('pinus, baculi quae praebuit usum').[4] But what is even more striking, is the transvaluation that Demetrius' remark undergoes in Vico's mind: the blame put upon an unknown epigone of Homer becomes the approval of a part

---

[1] Orsi, *Considerazioni*, pp. 325–6. Cf. G. degli Aromatari, *Degli autori del ben parlare per secolari e religiosi opere diverse* (Venice, 1643), Part III, 'Degli stili et eloquenza', I, 'Demetrii Phalerei de elocutione cum Petri Victorii Florentini Latina interpretatione', pp. 56–7 (ch. cxv). Demetrius' passage was frequently quoted in the manuals of rhetoric: see, for instance, Bernardo Pinelli, 'Rhetorica ecclesiastica, seu ars bene concionandi, Genuae, Domi S. Syri, Anno 1625', University Library, Padua, MS. 985, fol. 111r. On Pinelli cf. A. Oldoini, *Athenaeum Ligusticum, seu syllabus scriptorum Ligurum* (Perugia, 1680), pp. 114–15.

[2] Orsi, *Considerazioni*, pp. 325–30. Cf. Aromatari, *Degli autori del ben parlare*, Part III, ii, 'Il Predicatore di Monsignor Panicarola, o vero Demetrio Falereo dell'elocutione con le parafrasi, comenti e discorsi di Monsignor Panicarola', pp. 340–2 (particella LXIV). On Panigarola cf. G. Tiraboschi, *Storia della letteratura italiana* (Roma, 1782–5), vol. VII, Part III, pp. 424–9.

[3] *Quarta lettera indirizzata alla dottissima e chiarissima Dama Franzese, Madame Anne La Feure Dacier, dal marchese Giovan Gioseffo Orsi in proposito del suo libro intitolato 'Considerazioni sopra la maniera di ben pensare'* (Bologna, 1705), in *Lettere di diversi autori in proposito delle Considerazioni del marchese Giovan Gioseffo Orsi sopra il famoso libro franzese intitolato 'La manière de bien penser dans les ouvrages d'esprit'* (Bologna, 1707), pp. 178–9.

[4] Ovid, *Metamorphoses*, with an English translation by F. J. Miller (Loeb, London and Cambridge, Mass., 1951), II, pp. 282–3 (XIII.782). For the full account of Acis' legend cf. *ibid.* II, pp. 280–91 (XIII.750–897).

of Ovid's poem, in which Vico finds the same 'Homeric sublime' that 'Longinus' had implicitly found in 'the story of the Cyclops', which he had considered exceptional in the *Odyssey*, witnessing 'the ebb and flow of greatness, and a fancy roving in the fabulous and incredible, as though the ocean were withdrawing into itself and was being laid bare within its own confines.'[1]

This kaleidoscope of blunders and misinterpretations shows beyond any doubt that Vico's creative power is at work. In his own way, by dint of an apparently easy-going scholarship, the Italian philosopher makes use of the Longinian view he has perfectly assimilated. Now he has acquired a new tool of interpretation that offers great possibilities to his inquisitive mind. Vico will make the best of it in the three editions of his major work, the *New Science*, which appeared in the years 1725, 1730 and 1744. In all of these, Vico asserts the original idea that the Longinian sublime is to be found above all in the highly emotional creations of primitive poetry, identified with mythology. This free interpretation of 'Longinus' sounds as follows in the final edition of the *New Science*:

In such fashion the first men of the gentile nations, children of nascent mankind, created things according to their own ideas. But this creation was infinitely different from that of God. For God, in his purest intelligence, knows things, and, by knowing them, creates them; but they, in their robust ignorance, did it by virtue of a wholly corporeal imagination. And because it was quite corporeal, they did it with marvellous sublimity; a sublimity such and so great that it excessively perturbed the very persons who by imagining did the creating, for which they were called 'poets,' which is Greek for 'creators'.[2]

Here the fusion of the Longinian sublime with Locke's empiricism has attained its perfection. In fact, the British philosopher's penetrating analysis of the development of human mind from childhood to maturity, founded on the rejection of innate ideas, is the historical premiss of Vico's position. But the Italian philosopher shows a great deal of originality by transferring the same process of development from individual man to human civilisation, and by emphasising the poetic relevance of the origins.

It is not a mere chance that Vico defines such poetic relevance by the rhetorical category of the sublime: 'Now this is the threefold labour of great poetry: (1) to invent sublime fables suited to the

---

[1] Longinus, *On the Sublime*, p. 67 (ix.13–14).

[2] *The New Science of Giambattista Vico*, trans. T. G. Bergin and M. H. Fisch (Ithaca and London, 1970), p. 75. Cf. G. B. Vico, *La Scienza nuova prima*, ed. F. Nicolini (Bari, 1931), pp. 148–9 (iii, iv, 258); *Cinque libri di Giambattista Vico de' principj d'una scienza nuova d'intorno alla comune natura delle nazioni* (Napoli, 1730), p. 192.

popular understanding, (2) to perturb to excess, with a view to the end proposed: (3) to teach the vulgar to act virtuously, as the poets have taught themselves.'[1] This Longinian definition of 'great poetry' perfectly fits the first fable created by the theological poets under the impact of fear, when faced with a thunderbolt: 'In this fashion the first theological poets created the first divine fable, the greatest they ever created: that of Jove, king and father of men and gods, in the act of hurling the lightning bolt; an image so popular, disturbing, and instructive that its creators themselves believed in it, and feared, and worshipped it in fearful religions.'[2] It is interesting to note that Vico implicitly considers terror as a basic ingredient of the sublime, and, in view of this, he appears to be very close to some British interpreters of 'Longinus', such as John Dennis and Edmund Burke.[3]

This is a far cry from Vico's attitude in the first draft of the *Institutiones oratoriae* (1711), where the sublime appears associated not with the origins, but with the maturity of human civilization. In the section 'On the ages of the Latin language' Vico maintains that the life of that language went through the same stages as human life: infancy, adolescence, maturity, old age and decrepitude. The sublime does not belong to the earlier stages (infancy and adolescence), but to the middle one (maturity), corresponding to the historical period dominated by the great personalities of Julius Caesar and Octavian Augustus. In fact, the word 'sublime' is used only in reference to Virgil.[4] But Vico was perfectly aware of the progress he had made on this matter in subsequent years, as it appears from the second extant version of the *Institutiones* (1738), where, in dealing again with the infancy of the Latin language, he referred his students to his *New Science*, containing a thorough analysis of the origins of languages and literatures.[5] Yet, in spite of this, his account of the history of the Latin language does not present any radical change in the later version of the *Institutiones*. Was it so because the *Institutiones* had only the practical purpose of giving Vico and his son Gennaro an outline for their courses? This explanation, suggested by Nicolini,[6] does not seem to be completely satisfactory.

In my opinion, Vico did not make any substantial change in his history of Roman culture because it contained an idea that he cherished very much and was reluctant to abandon: the idea that the

---

[1] *The New Science*, p. 75.   [2] *Ibid.* p. 76.
[3] Monk, *The Sublime*, pp. 51–4 and 92–3.
[4] Vico, *Opere*, vol. VII, p. 77 (*Institutio Oratoria, De Latinae linguae aetatibus*).
[5] Vico, *Versi d'occasione*, pp. 201–2.   [6] *Ibid.* pp. 203 and 221–2.

decline of eloquence is a direct consequence of the loss of liberty. In fact, he attributed the involution of the Latin language to the tyranny of Tiberius, who obliged the Romans to hide their real feelings and to adopt, out of adulation and fear, 'an improper and obscure style'.[1] It is a view deeply rooted in the discussions on the decline of eloquence, that took place in the first and second centuries A.D.[2] The same view was considered in Vico's time an essential part of the treatise *On the Sublime*, wrongly attributed to the staunch adversary of the Emperor Aurelian, Cassius Longinus, who was put to death by the Romans, upon their conquest of Palmyra. In fact, the edition of 'Longinus' in Valletta's library, presumably used by Vico, is the one published in Utrecht by Jacob Tollius in the year 1694, which warranted this interpretation, supported in the foot-notes by various authorities, including the first editor of the treatise, Francesco Robortello, who synthesised the Longinian attitude in the formula: 'Libertas alumna et mater eloquentiae.'[3] In consideration of this, Vico's reluctance to change the section of the *Institutiones oratoriae* entitled 'On the ages of the Latin language' may well be a consequence of his respect for 'Longinus' and for a rhetorical tradition that identified political liberty with literary creativity. This explanation appears to be fully justified on the basis of Vico's political attitude, which was open to the suggestions of British political thought, as I have demonstrated in a paper read at the conference on 'Vico and contemporary thought', held in New York City in January 1976.[4]

---

[1] Vico, *Opere*, vol. VII, p. 77.   [2] Kennedy, *The Art of Rhetoric*, pp. 446–64.

[3] Διονυσίου Λογγίνου περὶ ὕψους καὶ τἆλλα εὑρισκόμενα. *Dionysii Longini de sublimitate commentarius, ceteraque quae reperiri potuere. In usum Serenissimi Principis Electoralis Branden-burgici. Jacobus Tollius e quinque codicibus MSS. emendavit, et Fr. Robortelli, Fr. Porti, Gabrielis de Petra, Ger. Langbaenii et Tanaquilli Fabri notis integris suas subjecit, novamque versionem suam Latinam et Gallicam Boilavii, cum ejusdem ac Dacierii suisque notis Gallicis addidit* (Utrecht, 1694), pp. 229–30n. Cf. Valletta, *Opere filosofiche*, p. 575. Vico does not give any precise reference, but quotes Gerard Langbain's preface to 'Longinus' (*Cinque libri*, p. 375; G. B. Vico, *La Scienza nuova giusta l'edizione del 1744*, ed. F. Nicolini (Bari, 1928), vol. II, p. 29), which is reproduced in the introductory part of Jacob Tollius' edition under the title 'Gerardi Langbaenii προθεωρία ubi in auctoris prosapiam et patriam inquiritur' (there is no pagination). A copy of the same edition with marginalia in the hand of the Florentine scholar Anton Maria Salvini is preserved in the Vatican Library (Ferraioli III 1494). Salvini encouraged Anton Francesco Gori to make an Italian translation of *On the Sublime* which was highly influential in the eighteenth century (D. St Marin, *Bibliography*, pp. 12–13). As to Robortello's position, cf. the *princeps* (Basel, 1554), p. 68. On the political component of the Longinian treatise cf. C. P. Segal, "Ύψος and the problem of cultural decline in the *De sublimitate*', *Harvard Studies in Classical Philology*, LXIV (1959), 121–46.

[4] G. Costa, 'Un convegno vichiano a New York', *Bollettino del Centro di Studi Vichiani*, VI (1976), 202–7; *idem*, 'Vico's political thought in his time and ours', *Social Research*, XLIII, no. 3 (Autumn 1976), pp. 612–24.

12

ADAM SMITH'S THEORY OF LAW
AND SOCIETY

PETER G. STEIN

Adam Smith was a Professor of Moral Philosophy and his economic ideas grew out of his professional interest in ethics. His first book was *The Theory of Moral Sentiments*, published in 1759, which he himself considered to be his most important work. It dealt in a systematic way with how man as an individual should behave to his fellow men according to the principles of morality. The *Wealth of Nations*, which appeared in 1776, dealt with the economic factors which affected man's relations with the society in which he lived. Smith hoped to complete his study of man in society with an account of 'the general principles of law and government, and of the different revolutions they have undergone in the different ages and periods of society, not only in what concerns justice, but in what concerns police, revenue, and arms and whatever else is the object of law.'[1]

He never published this last part of his study, but we can obtain a good idea of its main themes, and the manner in which he tackled them, from two reports, based on students' notes, of lectures which he gave as part of the moral philosophy course in the University of Glasgow.[2] The present study is based on the fuller version, which is derived from his course in the academic year 1762-3.

The Theory of Moral Sentiments had looked at conduct from the point of view of the individual; jurisprudence considered it from the point of view of the statesman. 'Jurisprudence is the theory of the rules by which civil governments ought to be directed...The first and chief design of every system of government is to maintain justice; to prevent the members of a society from incroaching on one another's property.'[3] 'Justice is violated whenever one is deprived of what he

---

[1] *The Theory of Moral Sentiments*, ed. D. D. Raphael and A. L. Macfie (Glasgow Edition of the Works and Correspondence of Adam Smith, vol. I, Oxford, 1976), p. 342.

[2] The shorter report was published as *Lectures on Police, Justice, Revenue and Arms by Adam Smith*, ed. E. Cannan (Oxford, 1896). The longer report is published for the first time, and the shorter republished with it, in Adam Smith, *Lectures on Jurisprudence*, ed. R. L. Meek, D. D. Raphael and P. G. Stein (Glasgow Edition, vol. V, Oxford, 1978). All quotations from the lectures are from this edition.   [3] *Lectures*, p. 5.

had a right to and could justly demand from others, or rather, when we do him any injury or hurt without a cause.'[1] So justice is defined in terms of rights.

Smith based his discussion of rights on the work of the classical natural rights theorists, Grotius, Pufendorf and, in particular, his own teacher and predecessor in the Glasgow Chair, Francis Hutcheson.

Hutcheson's scheme, which Smith followed, was based on the different rights which a man has, first, as an individual, secondly, as a member of a family and, thirdly, as a citizen of a state. The injury which he suffers, and consequently the right which he enjoys, is in each case peculiar to the quality in which he is considered. Smith distinguishes sharply between legal rights, which he calls perfect rights, on the one hand, and moral rights, which are imperfect, on the other. He is critical of the natural rights theorists for blurring this distinction and makes it clear that he is only concerned with perfect rights, that is, rights relating to what we have a title to demand and to compel another to perform within the limits of the legal process.

The rights which a man enjoys as a man are natural in the sense that they arise independently of any human action. They are reducible to three, his rights to his person, to his reputation and to his estate. Estate includes both rights to property and personal rights arising from contract or delinquency. So far, Smith adheres to the standard natural rights scheme. It is when he proceeds to consider the various ways in which property arises that he begins to diverge from his predecessors. They treated natural rights as applicable in any society. Smith observes that the rules concerning the acquisition of property are far from universally applicable. They vary considerably according to the state that the society in question has reached. He then introduces the four stages through which societies pass as they develop: hunters, shepherds, agriculture and commerce.[2]

In the first stage, that of hunters, there is almost no private property, so that theft is unimportant, few laws are needed, and penalties are not severe. In the second stage, when there are flocks and herds, property becomes more important, more laws are required and theft is punished with greater rigour. In the third stage, that of agriculture, there are fewer opportunities for open robbery than in

---

[1] *Ibid.* p. 7.
[2] *Ibid.* pp. 14ff.; cf. R. L. Meek, *Social Science and the Ignoble Savage* (Cambridge, 1976), *passim.*

the pastoral stage, but 'many ways added in which property may be interrupted as the subjects of it are considerably extended'.[1] In this stage the laws will be more complex, but the punishment for their breach will be less severe. A still further extension of laws is required in the stage of commerce.

Although, like Locke before him, Smith identifies justice with the maintenance of property, he shows clearly that property means something quite different according to the stage of development achieved by the society in question. It is no good talking in general terms about preserving property; we have to know what stage the society we are discussing has reached.

Smith does recognise a general framework of legal notions which are found universally in any society: property, contract, punishment for injury, marriage, succession and so on. These ideas are part of the nature of man, whatever the state of society he is living in. But the extent of these notions, their content, what can be obtained by way of protection and reparation through the legal process, depend on how strong the community is, how far it can force the individual to do things he does not want to do and particularly how wealthy it is.

Considerations like these affect people's attitudes and expectations of what the law should do to the individual. The rules by which disputes in a society are settled should be defined by reference to what engages the sympathy of the 'impartial spectator' in that society.[2] To justify his view that legal rules are governed by what the impartial spectator in the society would approve, Smith has to offer empirical evidence of actual societies in different stages of development.

It was here that his wide knowledge of classical literature, gained no doubt during the seven years he spent at Balliol College, Oxford, was indispensable. In the first place, classical writers provided detailed evidence about primitive societies and their characteristic customs. The Greeks, as described by Homer, were in an early stage of development, and Smith treated Homer almost as a text of social anthropology. Tacitus' *Germania*, with its details of the life-style of the German tribes with whom the Romans of the first century A.D. came into contact, was another obvious source. Smith had a gift for isolating the material facts from the most discursive accounts, and he

[1] *Lectures*, p. 16.
[2] *Ibid.* p. 17. The impartial spectator had been introduced in *The Theory of Moral Sentiments*; cf. T. D. Campbell, *Adam Smith's Science of Morals* (London, 1971), pp. 127ff.; D. D. Raphael, 'The impartial spectator', *Proceedings of the British Academy*, LVIII (1972), 335–54.

readily saw similarities in the habits and attitudes of the early peoples of antiquity and those of the North American Indians or the Tartars of the Asian steppes, as described by the eighteenth-century travel writers. He had studied the works of Charlevoix[1] and Lafitau[2] on the habits of the North American Indians.

These contemporary writings alone could not have provided a sufficiently convincing basis for his ideas. They were in general too much devoted to the curious and the fanciful. The classics provided more than just factual data. They showed how people thought about things. Homer shows us not only the way in which the Greeks lived at the time of the Trojan War, but also how they thought, what their attitudes were and what were the views of an impartial Greek spectator of Agamemnon and his contemporaries. Smith points out that the geographical and other circumstances favoured the improvement of arts and sciences in Greece in comparison with other areas.

The lands would be divided and well improved and the country would acquire considerable wealth. And as a nation in this way would be vastly more wealthy than their neighbours, having more of what Homer calls κειμήλια, that is goods stored up, they would be very apt to be attacked and plundered by their neighbouring nations, who would often set out on piraticall expeditions from their country. We find that at the time of the Trojan War such expeditions were frequently undertaken, nor were pirates then looked on as any way dishonourable.[3]

Odysseus, when asked whether he was a merchant or a pirate, says he was a pirate.

This was a much more honourable character than that of a merchant, which was always looked on with great contempt by them. A pirate is a military man who acquires his livelihood by warlike exploits, whereas a merchant is a peaceable one who has no occasion for military skill and would not be much esteemed in a nation consisting of warriors chiefly.[4]

In the area of legal institutions, however, Roman law was pre-eminent among the classical sources used by Smith. The importance of the Roman legal sources for lawyers lay in the sophistication of the reasoning of the jurists, excerpted in Justinian's *Digest*. Smith appreciated this aspect of Roman law,[5] but more relevant to his purpose was the fact the Roman legal sources showed the develop-

---

[1] F.-X. de Charlevoix, *Histoire et description générale de la Nouvelle France, avec le Journal historique d'un voyage...dans l'Amérique septentrionale* (Paris, 1744).

[2] J. F. Lafitau, *Mœurs des sauvages amériquains, comparées aux mœurs des premiers temps* (Paris, 1724).

[3] *Lectures*, p. 224.　　　　　　　　　　　　[4] *Ibid.*

[5] For example in his discussion of acquisition of property by accession (*ibid.* pp. 29–32).

ment of the system from the Twelve Tables at the very beginning of the Roman republic to the legislation of the later empire. Furthermore, non-legal Latin literature showed the social context in which these laws evolved. Only English law could offer a similarly detailed documentation of the way in which legal rules appropriate for a primitive society were changed to fit the development of that society, or, in some cases, were not changed when they should have been, for some quite fortuitous reason.

The fact that Smith was a Scotsman was significant in this regard. Scots were much more conscious than were Englishmen of legal systems other than their own. Scots law was itself based on Roman law, but the land law, being feudal in origin, was similar to English law. Since the Union of 1707, English influence on Scots law had been increasing. Smith therefore was at home in both Roman law and English law as well as in Scots law and could draw parallels from their respective evolution.

As an example of Smith's use of his sources to reach a conclusion different from that of the natural lawyers, his account of the nature of contractual obligation may be considered. The traditional explanation of Grotius and Pufendorf was that what made a contract binding was the promisor's declaration of his will which bound him to keep his word.[1] Smith argued that it was rather the expectation which the promisor's declaration created in the promisee.[2] An impartial spectator would not always consider that every declaration of intent should be relied on by the promisee.

Thus primitive societies make light of breaches of contract and do not always hold contracts binding. Smith observes that Nicolas of Damascus, as quoted by Stobaeus, has many passages 'very useful with regard to the state of society in the first periods of it'. According to Nicolas, among eastern nations 'no contract was binding, not even that of restoring a *depositum*, that in which the obligation seems to be strongest as the injury in the breach of it is most glaring'.[3] It was only with the advance of commerce that contracts became frequent. Only then is there a need for credit to be given and so an informal promise might reasonably create in the promisee a ground of expectation, which would be disappointed if the promise were not fulfilled.

---

[1] Grotius, *De iure belli ac pacis* II.11.2ff.; Pufendorf, *De iure naturae et gentium* III.5.5ff.
[2] *Lectures*, pp. 87ff. This criticism had been anticipated by Hutcheson and Hume.
[3] *Ibid.* p. 88.

When he comes to deal with crime and punishment, Smith again disagrees with Grotius and other natural law writers. They argued that the origin of punishment for crime was consideration of the public good.[1] The real source, said Smith, must be the resentment of the injured party and so the measure of punishment is the point at which the view of the impartial spectator concurs with the victim of the crime in the manner of his revenge.[2]

In early societies it was left to the victim to get his own satisfaction for crimes.

In the description of the shield of Achilles, in one of the compartments the story represented is the friends of a slain man receiving presents from the slayer. The government did not then intermeddle in those affairs; and we find that the stranger who comes on board the ship of Telemachus tells us he fled from the friends of a man whom he had slain, and not from the officers of justice.[3]

Some of the ground covered by Smith and some of the examples cited by him had been discussed earlier by Montesquieu in his *L'esprit des lois*, published in 1748. Montesquieu certainly recognised the connection between law and the circumstances of society. But his method of treatment was fragmentary rather than systematic; he failed to order his observations around an organising principle. In the words of Lord Kames, the Scottish judge and littérateur, whose influence Smith acknowledged, Montesquieu 'abounds with observations no less pleasing than solid. But a sprightly genius, prone to novelty and refinement, has betrayed him into manifold errors.'[4]

Smith takes issue with Montesquieu on the origin of the distinction between *furtum manifestum* and *nec manifestum* in Rome. Montesquieu had suggested that the law which made the thief caught in the act liable for fourfold, but the thief not caught in the act liable only for double, had been borrowed from Sparta.[5] There, he held, young men were encouraged to steal provided they could get away with it. Smith shows that Montesquieu has misunderstood the relevant passage from Plutarch,[6] and furthermore had no justification for assuming that the Romans had taken it over. The real reason for the distinction was that 'the resentment of a person against a thief when

[1] Grotius II.20.7ff.; Pufendorf VIII.3.9ff.
[2] *Lectures*, p. 104.
[3] *Ibid.* p. 108; the references are to *Iliad* XVIII.500 and *Odyssey* XV.271.
[4] H. Home, Lord Kames, *Elucidations Respecting the Law of Scotland* (Edinburgh, 1777), p. xii; cf. P. Stein, 'Law and society in eighteenth-century Scottish thought', *Scotland in the Age of Improvement*, ed. N. Phillipson and R. L. Mitchison (Edinburgh, 1970), pp. 148ff.
[5] *De l' esprit des lois*, XXIX.13.   [6] *Life of Lycurgus* 17–18

he is caught in the fact [is greater] than when he is only discovered afterwards and the theft must be proved against him which gives the person's resentment time to cool. The satisfaction he requires is much greater in the former than in the latter case.'[1]

After man as an individual comes man as a member of a family. Under this head, Smith considers three relationships: husband and wife; father and son; and master and servant. His treatment of marriage draws heavily on the history of the marriage laws of Rome. In the earliest times the wife was absolutely in the power of her husband. At this period, Smith explains, the fortune a woman could bring to her husband on marriage was very small and insufficient to entitle her to bargain with him; her only option was to submit to his power. However, as the wealth of the community increased, rich heiresses became not uncommon and, in their favour, a new kind of marriage was introduced. By the *instrumenta dotalia* the terms on which the husband was to enjoy the wife's property were settled, and she no longer entered his power. This new sort of marriage 'tho' it had none of the old solemnities, was found by the lawyers to save the lady's honour and legitimate the children'.[2] It was created by consent and could be dissolved by the will of either party. Since this new form of marriage was found to be much more convenient and adapted to the licentiousness of the times, the old forms were abandoned. Smith enjoyed showing that this new form of free marriage was itself 'productive of the worst consequences'.

It tended plainly to corrupt the moralls of the women. The wives often passed thro' 4 or 5 different husbands, which tended to give them but very loose notions of chastity and good behaviour. And as this was frequently practised by women of the highest stations and most conspicuous rank in the whole state, the corruption could meet with no opposition...female chastity was rarely to be met with. For tho' the anecdotes and annalls of the private life of the Romans at that time have come down to us in a very imperfect manner, yet there is hardly a great man in the end of the Republick who is not a cuckold upon record. Cicero, Caesar, Pompey, Marc Antony, Dollabella etc. are all reckorded in this character.[3]

The eastern emperors restricted this licence of divorce, and in the western empire it was abolished because the savage nations which overran the west of Europe were in an earlier stage of development, in which the wife was still under the subjection of her husband.

Later, as a result of the influence of the Christian clergy, marriage

[1] *Lectures*, p. 129; cf. Smith's criticism of Montesquieu's discussion of polygamy (*ibid.* pp. 154–5).   [2] *Ibid.* p. 144.   [3] *Ibid.* p. 145.

came to be almost indissoluble. Smith makes some curious comments on the change which he considers this indissolubility of marriage produced in the character of 'the passion of love'.

This passion was formerly esteemed to be a very silly and ridiculous one...There is no poem of a serious nature grounded on that subject either amongst the Greeks or Romans. There is no ancient tragedy, except Phaedra, the plot of which turns on a love story, tho' there are many on all other passions, as anger, hatred, revenge, ambition etc.[1]

The story of Dido in the *Aeneid* is in no sense a love story, nor is the *Iliad*.

The cause of the Trojan War was the rape of Helen etc. but what sort of a love story is it? Why, the Greek chiefs combine to bring back Helen to her husband; but he never expresses the least indignation against her for her infidelity. It is all against Paris who carried away his wife along with his goods...The reason why this passion made so little figure then in comparison of what it now does is plainly this. The passion itself is of nature rather ludicrous; the frequency and easieness of divorce made the gratification of it of no great moment...The choice of the person was of no very great importance, as the union might be dissolved at any time. This was the case both amongst the Greeks and Romans. But when marriage became indissoluble, the matter was greatly altered. The choice of the object of this passion, which is commonly the forerunner of marriage, became a matter of the greatest importance. The union was perpetuall and consequently the choice of the person was a matter which would have a great influence on the future happiness of the parties. From that time therefore we find that love makes the subject of all our tragedies and romances.[2]

(Smith himself was a life-long bachelor.)

The development of Roman law also provided a model for the second family relationship, that of father and children. At first the power of the father was altogether absolute, but gradually it was limited.

The Twelve Tables gave the father the power of sale but Smith makes the interesting suggestion that this extended only to those sons who were unmarried, for when a man takes a wife from another family he becomes bound to her for his labour and his work.[3] She and the children claim his attention so that it would be very hard that the son should be separated from her and sold to be the slave of another man. In practice the father's power over his sons would be curbed by pressure from other members of the family and by public opinion.

[1] *Ibid.* p. 149.   [2] *Ibid.* pp. 149–50.   [3] *Ibid.* p. 173.

Smith cites in this regard the story of Lucius Manlius, who

was called before the praetors for sending [his son] out to the country to work with the slaves and not giving him proper education, as the story is told in Cicero's *Offices*. When therefore the publick took cognizance of so small an offence against the parentall duty, it is not probable it would pass by the arbitrary punishment of crimes which were not liable to a publick correction.[1]

We must look behind the legal rule at what actually happened. When we consider the gradual recognition of the right of the son to have property of his own independently of his father, we will see that 'the power of the fathers, tho' very considerable, does not appear to have been so unbounded as we are apt to imagine.'[2]

In the case of the third family relationship, master and servant, Smith shows a deep understanding of how slavery operated in antiquity and draws important parallels with its working in his own time. He insisted on the point that slavery was the norm in the world and that its abolition in the small corner of the world, which was western Europe, was exceptional. He shows in detail that slavery was inferior to free labour on economic grounds but he recognises that the condition of the slave, though legally the same in all societies which tolerate it, is 'a much more tollerable one in a poor and barbarous people than in a rich and polished one'.[3]

In a poor country, the number of slaves in relation to the number of freemen is small, they are a valuable asset and they represent no threat. In a rich country their numbers are great, they considerably outnumber the freemen and so constitute a formidable body who must be kept down. Horace shows that no-one who aspired to be a gentleman in the Rome of Augustus would have less than ten slaves,[4] and there are many illustrations of the barbarity with which Romans of that period treated their slaves. The Germans of the same period, however, as Tacitus shows, treated their slaves with great humanity.[5]

Smith then draws a similar contrast between the contemporary treatment of slaves in the colonies of continental North America and that in the West Indian sugar islands. In the former their masters cannot afford to keep a great number and they are 'treated with great humanity and used in a very gentle manner'. In the sugar islands, on the other hand, the planters can afford to keep a multitude

---

[1] *Ibid.* p. 174; the reference is to *De officiis* iii.112 (Smith misremembers Manlius as Valerius Corvus).

[2] *Lectures*, p. 175. [3] *Ibid.* p. 182.

[4] *Satires* 1.2.3ff.; 1.3.11ff. [5] *Germania* xxv.

of slaves, and are in continual dread of an insurrection, so that 'the greatest rigour and severity is consequently exercised upon them.'[1]

Smith had a comprehensive knowledge of the contents of classical writers and he showed a magisterial power of selection in the use he made of it. What interested him was the evidence which the classics produced on how the impartial spectator in different stages of society looked on legal institutions. From these data he inferred a scheme of legal development. He did not say that this scheme would always be followed. The general course which society would naturally take was laid down by the invisible hand of an all-wise author of Nature. But human action could and did prevent particular societies from taking that course.[2] Smith paid little attention to the views of ancient writers on justice or government. He looked on them as rational men trying to make society better, but their theories were of little interest to him. However, he was impressed to be told by ancient writers that the two sources of all seditions at both Athens and Rome were popular demands for an agrarian law and for an abolition of debts.[3]

The classics provided a quarry from which he extracted the insights on the nature of civil society which served his purposes. Others like Montesquieu and Hume had made similar extractions. Smith differed from them in three respects.

First, he was more disciplined and systematic in the use of the material. He saw that sometimes the evidence of antiquity confirmed contemporary data, as in the case of the effects of slavery on a society, and sometimes it provided a contrast with modern society or it illustrated a stage which modern society had already passed through, as in the case of marriage. He had the ability to work out useful typologies, such as his classification of the four types of marriage: polygamy, monogamy where both parties can divorce at will, monogamy where only the husband can divorce and monogamy where only the state can allow a divorce.[4]

Secondly, Smith was historical, and saw legal institutions as continuously changing in reaction to new social situations. The view of the natural lawyers that intestate succession was based on the presumed will of the testator could not be correct, because it implies that testamentary succession preceded intestate succession. According to this view, the testator expressed his actual intentions in a will

---

[1] *Lectures*, p. 183.
[2] Campbell, *Adam Smith's Science of Morals*, pp. 6off.
[3] *Lectures*, p. 197.   [4] *Ibid.* pp. 159–60.

and, if he failed to make one, the law distributed his estate as he was presumed to have intended. This is unhistorical, for in all societies, intestate succession precedes testamentary. The latter is 'one of the greatest extentions of property we can conceive' and presupposes an advanced state of social development.[1]

Thirdly, Smith brought a robust commonsense to his explanations. He preferred down-to-earth explanations to subtle ones. The rule found in many systems that a husband can divorce his wife for her adultery but she has no corresponding right is not designed, as was usually claimed, to prevent spurious offspring being imposed on the husband. 'The real reason is that it is men who make the laws with respect to this; they generally will be inclined to curb the women as much as possible and give themselves the more indulgence.'[2]

It was the combination of this no-nonsense approach and an extensive knowledge of the contents of classical literature that enabled Smith to set legal institutions squarely in their social and historical context. After that it was not so big a step to isolate the data which thirteen years later formed the basis of the *Wealth of Nations*.

[1] *Ibid.* p. 38.   [2] *Ibid.* p. 147.

13

THE EARLY HUMAN FAMILY:
SOME VIEWS 1770–1870

S. G. PEMBROKE

There being obvious limits to what can be attempted either in the space of thirty minutes or within the erratic competence of the speaker, I am proposing to confine myself to one aspect of theories of early human society mooted during the last hundred years with which this conference is concerned, namely the organisation of the human family, the variety of its forms and their successive evolution. I propose therefore to start with the Scottish Enlightenment; to pose the question why (at least in this field) what have subsequently been seen as anticipations, by Adam Ferguson and more notably by John Millar of Glasgow, of the deluge of evolutionary theories unloosed in the sixties of the following century remained so largely without influence before this time; and to draw attention to one further such schema dating from the first half of the nineteenth century, what John Burrow has called 'the missing half-century in the history of social anthropology',[1] a theory which I believe may have exerted a fairly decisive influence in the second half.

The second part of Adam Ferguson's *Essay on the History of Civil Society*, published in 1767, is devoted to 'the History of Rude Nations'. This is unusually explicit about the use of ancient sources. Ferguson is cautious about putting mythical traditions (what he calls 'the domestic antiquities of nations') to historical use, but he does regard them as having a sort of social or collective value. 'When traditionary fables are rehearsed by the vulgar,' he states, 'they bear the marks of a national character', whereas 'in the management of mere antiquaries...they become even unfit to amuse the fancy, or to serve any purpose whatsoever'. In the same way the Homeric poems, although their content is not of historical value as a narrative, 'may', he says, 'with great justice, be cited to ascertain what were the conceptions and sentiments of the age in which they were composed...The Greek fable accordingly, conveying a character of its authors, throws light on an age of which no other

---

[1] J. W. Burrow, *Evolution and Society* (Cambridge, 1966), pp. 17–18.

record remains.'[1] It is however for the Greek and Roman historians that he reserves his highest praise, and though he clearly has Caesar and Tacitus in view when he refers to 'the most authentic and instructive representations of the tribes from whom we descend', it is characteristic of his subject-matter that the writer whom he singles out in this context should be Greek and not Roman.

Thucydides, notwithstanding the prejudice of his country against the name of *Barbarian*, understood that it was in the customs of barbarous nations he was to study the more ancient manners of Greece.

The Romans might have found an image of their own ancestors, in the representations they have given of ours: and if ever an Arab clan shall become a civilized nation, or any American tribe escape the poison which it is administered by our traders of Europe, it may be from the relations of the present times, and the descriptions which are now given by travellers, that such a people, in after ages, may best collect the accounts of their origin. It is in their present condition, that we are to behold, as in a mirrour, the features of our own progenitors; and from thence we are to draw our conclusions with respect to the influence of situations, in which, we have reason to believe, our fathers were placed.

What should distinguish a German or a Briton, in the habits of his mind or his body, in his manners or apprehensions, from an American, who like him, with his bow and his dart, is left to traverse the forest; and in a like severe or variable climate, is obliged to subsist by the chace?[2]

The method is of course precisely that by which Thucydides came to align the backward parts of Greece with the non-Greek world, and to identify as barbarian the Mycenaean or Geometric tombs excavated in his own time on the island of Delos.[3] It is perhaps worth adding, in view of the importance of his predecessor as a source for the theories to which this approach was to give rise in the century after Ferguson, that Herodotus also believed that the Greek people had come into being by a process of differentiation from a non-Greek, 'Pelasgic' substratum, the transformation being accompanied by one of language and resulting in the Greeks' being less prone to silly foolishness than were their neighbours.[4] For Ferguson himself, however, the immediate impetus towards extending his purview from the continent of Europe to that of America was provided by Charlevoix's *Journal historique d'un voyage fait par ordre du roi dans*

[1] 1767 ed., pp. 116–17 = ed. Duncan Forbes (Edinburgh, 1966), p. 77.
[2] *Ibid.* pp. 121–2; ed. Forbes, p. 80.
[3] Thucydides 1.10.1; cf. R. M. Cook, in *Annual of the British School at Athens*, L (1955), 267–70; Charlotte R. Long, *American Journal of Archaeology*, LXII (1958), 297–306.
[4] Herodotus 1.57–8; cf. also 60.3.

l'Amérique septentrionale,[1] published in 1744, and the description of the Algonquin, Huron and Iroquois tribes given twenty years earlier by Joseph François Lafitau, of which an important study has recently been made by Vidal-Naquet.[2]

The full title of Lafitau's work is *Les mœurs des sauvages amériquains, comparées aux mœurs des premiers temps*, and the comparative element is at least as important as the purely descriptive passages on Iroquois institutions, though these were hardly to be bettered until the publication of Lewis H. Morgan's *League of the Iroquois* in 1858. The book is intended to demonstrate that the New World was populated from the Old – not by the routes suggested by Grotius, via Greenland to the northern continent and from Africa via the Magellan Straits to South America, but across Asia.[3] In support of this thesis Lafitau marshalled a staggering command not only of ancient literature and ethnography but also of the writings of contemporary travellers since the Renaissance. His contention was that the similarity between customs reported from the New World and those which had been recorded on the fringes of the ancient one was so striking, and the customs themselves so distinctive, that they could only be explained in terms of a common origin, their persistence in the continent of America being due to the power of religion as a conservative force. Thus the transvestism of certain individuals among the Sioux and other tribes was clearly the same as, and derived from, that of the worshippers of Cybele and Aphrodite in ancient Asia Minor.[4] The Illinois preserved a funeral custom which Apollonius Rhodius mentioned when his Argonauts sailed past the Caucasus: burying their womenfolk but sewing the bodies of males in skins and suspending them from trees.[5] The *couvade*, the practice of men taking to bed

---

[1] F.-X. de Charlevoix, *Histoire et description générale de la Nouvelle France*, 3 vols. in 4⁰ (in vol. III) = 6 vols. in 12⁰ (in vols. V and VI). The journal takes the form of a series of letters dating from 1720 to 1723.

[2] P. Vidal-Naquet, 'Les jeunes: le cru, l'enfant grec et le cuit', *Faire de l'histoire*, ed. J. Le Goff and P. Nora, vol. III (Paris, 1974), pp. 136–40; cf. Michèle Duchet, 'Discours ethnologique et discours historique: le texte de Lafitau', *Studies on Voltaire and the Eighteenth Century*, CLI–CLV (1976), 607–26.

[3] Vol. I (2 vols. in 4⁰) (Paris, 1724), pp. 33–41.

[4] *Ibid.* pp. 52–3 (Polybius XXI.37.6; Diodorus Siculus XXVI.13.1; Dionysius of Halicarnassus II.19.5).

[5] *Ibid.* vol. II, pp. 402–7. Cf. Apollonius Rhodius III.200–9 and scholia; Stobaeus IV.55.15 (Nicolas of Damascus 90 F 121); Aelian, *Varia historia* IV.1; Silius Italicus XIII.486–7; G. Ferrand, ed., 'Le *Tuhfāt al-albāb* de Abū Hāmid al-Andalusī al-Garnātī' (1162), *Journal asiatique*, CCVII (1925), 84–5 (German trans. in G. Dorn, *Mélanges asiatiques* (St Petersburg), VI (1873), 701); G. Interiano, 'Della vita de Zychi, chiamati i Ciarcassi'

and simulating childbirth at the time their wives were due to be delivered of a real child – a practice which in the second half of the nineteenth century was to be seized on as evidence of the desperate lengths to which husbands had had to go in order to establish the paternity of their children – had been widespread in the ancient Mediterranean, from the Iberians in the west to the Tibareni on the south coast of the Black Sea, and was still taking place not only among the Caribs and Galibi of South America but in Japan and on the French side of the Pyrenees, from which the word itself had been taken.[1] Lafitau was reluctant to accept reports of people with eyes on their chests and no heads either from the ancient world or from the Iroquois informant of the Jesuit missionary who was his chief source, but even here the latter did something to corroborate ancient testimony, and the suggestion advanced was that the head was not totally absent, merely set very low on the shoulders so as to be concealed by the hair (the illustration in the quarto edition is in fact hairless).[2] Lafitau explained this and other more common physical characteristics, such as skin colour and face structure, by the theory known in the nineteenth century as that of 'maternal impressions', the belief (which has biblical as well as classical antecedents) that the imagination of expectant mothers could be affected by anything they happened to see while the child was in the womb and that this spectacle could modify or even determine the child's appearance, and he concluded that a standing predilection for, and association with, people of the same general appearance assured the perpetuation of the same features from one generation to another.[3] Charlevoix was more sceptical on all these points and unusual in rejecting all criteria for the determination of American origins other than language.[4]

(1502), in G. B. Ramusio, *Secondo volume delle Navigationi et Viaggi* (Venice, 1559), fol. 142C.

[1] Lafitau, *Mœurs des sauvages amériquains*, vol. I, pp. 49–50; cf. *ibid.* pp. 256–9 (Apollonius Rhodius II.1011–14; Diodorus Siculus v.14.2; Strabo III.4.17, p. 165); E. B. Tylor, *Researches into the Early History of Mankind*, 2nd ed. (London, 1870), pp. 293–304; also now P. G. Rivière, in *Journal of the Royal Anthropological Institute*, n.s. IX (1974), 423–35.

[2] *Mœurs des sauvages amériquains*, vol. I, pp. 64–7 and Pl. III, 2 (p. 105).

[3] *Ibid.* pp. 68–9 quoting Genesis xxx.38–9. Cf. Empedocles in [Plutarch], *Placita Philosophorum* v.12.2 (31 A 81 Diels–Kranz); Dionysius of Halicarnassus, *De imitatione* VI.31; Pliny, *Historia naturalis* VII.52; Galen, *De theriaca ad Pisonem* 11 (XIV.253 Kühn); Soranus, *Gynaecia* I.39.1; Heliodorus, *Aethiopica* IV.8; Oppian, *Cynegetica* I.328–67; Isidore, *Origines* XII.1.58–9.

[4] 'Dissertation préliminaire sur l'origine des Amériquains', *Histoire et description générale*, vol. III, in 4⁰, pp. 36–8, 43 = vol. V, in 12⁰, pp. 53–7, 63–4. On the background to this debate see R. H. Popkin in *Classical Influences on European Culture, A.D. 1500–1700*, ed. R. R. Bolgar (Cambridge, 1976), pp. 271–80.

Among the more distinctive or at least novel institutions on which Lafitau based his identification was of course matrilineal descent; and he gave a detailed description of the workings of the system among the Iroquois, for which he assembled a large number of ancient parallels, notably the statement of Herodotus that the Lycians of Asia Minor traced their descent through their mothers and not, like all other peoples, through their fathers, and that it was the mother's status, not that of the father, which determined the status of the child. To this he was able to add a wide range of other reports of gynaecocracy and *l'empire des femmes* from ancient writers, so wide in fact that it would not in his view have constituted a single and sufficient proof of his general conclusion that the Iroquois and the Hurons were actually descended from the Lycians.[1] He did, however, present a sufficiently clear picture of the workings of the system to enable Adam Ferguson firstly to attribute it to the age prior to the establishment of property, and secondly to distinguish the vesting of the household in women and its transmission through them (at a time when the sole objects of ownership were 'the food of to-morrow' and the tools by which this was to be obtained) from any suggestion that this entailed the women's having, as he put it, 'acquired an ascendant' over the males. On the contrary, he wrote, 'it is the care and trouble with which the warrior does not choose to be embarrassed. It is a servitude, and a continual toil, where no honours are won; and they whose province it is, are in fact the slaves and the helots of their country.' Against this, however, he put the view that the contempt in which males at this stage held 'sordid and mercenary arts' had the effect of deferring 'the cruel establishment of slavery' in a more literal sense and that, to this extent, the custom was preferable to much that succeeded it.[2]

A somewhat different view was taken by John Millar in his *Observations Concerning the Distinction of Ranks in Society*, published in 1771, revised in 1773 and finally reissued and extensively rewritten under the title *The Origin of the Distinction of Ranks* in 1779.[3] The opening chapter of this work was, in all three versions, devoted to 'the rank and condition of women in different ages' and emphasised the extent to which, prior to the successive refinement of the passions

[1] *Mœurs des sauvages amériquains*, vol. i, pp. 69–90; cf. *ibid.* pp. 535–90 (Herodotus 1.173. 4–5).
[2] *Essay*, 1767 ed., pp. 125–6 = ed. Forbes, p. 83.
[3] Also reprinted in William C. Lehmann, *John Millar of Glasgow (1735–1801)* (Cambridge, 1960), pp. 173–322.

in the pastoral ages and later through the introduction of agriculture, women are 'degraded below the other sex, and reduced under an authority, which, in early periods, is...exerted with a degree of harshness and severity suited to the dispositions of the people'.[1] In support of this, Millar adduces an extensive range of ancient and contemporary evidence, the latter by no means restricted, even primarily, to the continent of America and its use justified in the following terms:

Our information...with regard to the state of mankind in the rude parts of the world is chiefly derived from the relations of travellers, whose character and situation in life, neither set them above the suspicion of being easily deceived, nor of endeavouring to misrepresent the facts which they have related. From the number, however, and the variety of those relations, they acquire, in many cases, a degree of authority, upon which we may depend with security, and to which the narration of any single person, how respectable soever, can have no pretension. When illiterate men, ignorant of the writings of each other, and who, unless on religious subjects, had no speculative systems to warp their opinions, have, in distant ages and countries, described the manner of people in similar circumstances, the reader has an opportunity of comparing their several descriptions, and from their agreement or disagreement is enabled to ascertain the credit that is due to them...In proportion to the singularity of any event, it is the more improbable that different persons, who design to impose upon the world, but who have no concert with each other, should agree in relating it.[2]

Widening his scope in this way, Millar used sources both ancient and modern to illustrate the effects of poverty and barbarism on the condition of women. These were in antiquity clear enough in the promiscuous or collective marriages attributed to Eastern Iran by the Greek ethnographic tradition, in the institution of wife-lending at Sparta and elsewhere, and in the enforced prostitution reported by Herodotus and Strabo in Asia Minor.[3] More recent writers, some contemporary, showed the lending of wives to guests to be a world-wide practice; in Africa and South America alike, women were forbidden to eat at table with their husbands, while the purchase of wives, so far from being confined to the Old Testament, was normal in all savage nations, whether in Asia, Africa or America.[4] Millar did however include a separate section on 'the influence acquired by the mother of a family, before marriage is completely established', since

[1] *The Origin of the Distinction of Ranks* (1779), p. 42 = ed. Lehmann, p. 193.
[2] *Ibid.* pp. 15–16 = ed. Lehmann, p. 193.
[3] *Ibid.* pp. 28–9 = ed. Lehmann, pp. 187–8 (Plutarch, *Lycurgus*, 15.11ff., Herodotus 1. 94.1, 199, 216.1, Strabo XI.13.11 p. 526, 14.16 pp. 532–3).
[4] *Ibid.* pp. 32–3, 49–51 = ed. Lehmann, pp. 188–9, 195–6.

while marriage was 'a very early institution', it was not necessarily a primordial one, and there were several nations in which it was either unknown or took place 'in a very imperfect and limited manner'.

To a people who are little acquainted with that institution it will appear that children have much more connexion with their mother. If a woman has no notion of attachment or fidelity to any particular person, if notwithstanding her occasional intercourse with different individuals she continues to live by herself, or with her own relations, the child which she has borne, and which she maintains under her own inspection, must be regarded as a member of her own family, and the father, who lives at a distance, can have no opportunity of establishing an authority over it.[1]

In this connection, Millar referred not only to the Lycians but to the ancient tradition that marriage had been invented by the Athenian King Cecrops and that children had previously taken their mother's name.[2] These ancient testimonies were corroborated by the system of succession among the North American tribes described by Charlevoix, and also by 'an unusual form of polygamy' (usually known as polyandry) on the coast of Malabar in India, one wife being married to several husbands, an institution to which a chapter had already been devoted by Montesquieu but which was now shown to confirm Caesar's description of ancient Britain.[3]

Like Charlevoix, Millar emphasised that the dignity and influence of women in North American society and their participation in public assemblies were only attained in middle age. He is however torn between this view and one suggesting a greater degree of emancipation. The Preface indicates that references given are often selective, 'from an apprehension of being tedious', but there are signs that in some cases, as when he describes husbands in Peru and Formosa taking up residence with the families of their wives, he has been content to put his faith in a single Jesuit missionary. Since these references are in turn largely suppressed in the most recent edition, it may be worth setting out a brief passage from Le Gobien's account of the Mariana Islands on the subject of male infidelity.

[1] *Ibid.* pp. 57–8 = ed. Lehmann, p. 199.
[2] *Ibid.* pp. 58–9. For Cecrops, Millar refers to A. Y. Goguet, *De l'origine des loix, des arts, et des sciences* (Paris, 1758), vol. II (p. 33), citing the English translation published at Edinburgh in 1761 (vol. II, pp. 17–18).
[3] *Origin*, pp. 60–7 = ed. Lehmann, pp. 200–3; Charlevoix, *Histoire et description générale*, vol. III, in 4°, pp. 268, 269, 287–8 = vol. v, in 12°, pp. 395, 397, 423–5; Caesar, *Bellum Gallicum* v. 14.4–5, cf. Montesquieu, *De l'esprit des lois* xvi.5.

Quand une femme est convaincuë que son époux a des attachemens, dont elle n'a pas sujet d'estre contente, elle le fait sçavoir à toutes les femmes du village, qui se donnent un rendez vous. Elles s'y trouvent la lance à la main, & le chapeau de leurs maris sur la teste. Dans cet équipage guerrier, elles s'avancent en corps de bataille vers la maison du mari, dont on se plaint. Elles commencent par désoler ses terres, fouler & arracher ses grains, dépouïller ses arbres de leurs fruits, & faire par tout un dégast épouvantable. Elles fondent ensuite toutes ensemble sur la maison; & si ce malheureux mari n'a pas pris la précaution de se retirer & de se mettre à couvert, elles l'y attaquent, & le poursuivent jusqu'à ce qu'elles l'en aïent chassé.[1]

It was perhaps at least partly with this description in mind that Millar concluded that 'the celebrated traditions of the Amazons', although they are 'evidently mixed with fable, and appear to contain much exaggeration', cannot have been 'entirely destitute of real foundation'.[2]

Almost a century was to elapse before problems of this kind again received widespread attention, though a fourth edition of *The Origin of Ranks* appeared in 1806 and it had also been translated into both French and German. The cultural and historical factors which may have contributed to this period of neglect cannot be surveyed here. It would in any case be hard to link these with the growing preoccupations which in the 1850s led Bachofen to abandon his work in the sphere of orthodox historical Roman jurisprudence and turn to the pursuit of origins, proposing to Savigny a history in which Romulus would be featured as a very modern figure and not the Adam of Italy, though in the event it was based far more on Greek evidence than that of Roman writers.[3] *Das Mutterrecht* was published in 1861, but its main thesis had been outlined under the title 'Über das Weiberrecht' at a conference of German philologists and

---

[1] C. Le Gobien, *Histoire des isles Marianes* (Paris, 1700), pp. 60-1 (also noticed by Christoph Meiners, *Geschichte des weiblichen Geschlechts*, vol. 1 (Hanover, 1788), pp. 105-6). The fine speech placed by Le Gobien in the mouth of a dissident native called Hurao (*Histoire des isles Marianes*, pp. 140-4, cf. p. 183) was reproduced by Charles de Brosses, *Histoire des navigations aux terres australes*, vol. 11 (Paris, 1756), p. 497, and as he indicates is a classic portrayal of the noble savage.

[2] *Origin*, pp. 67-8 = ed. Lehmann, pp. 202-3; cf. already *Observations Concerning the Distinction of Ranks in Society* (1771), p. 17 = 1773 ed., p. 21.

[3] J. J. Bachofen, 'Eine Selbstbiographie', *Zeitschrift für vergleichende Rechtswissenschaft*, XXXIV (1916), 363-4, 377 = ed. A. Bäumler (Halle, 1927), pp. 33-4, 45 (September 1854); to be reissued in vol. IX of the *Gesammelte Werke*. Bachofen had already pointed to the importance of the law of inheritance in his inaugural lecture of 1841 (*Gesammelte Werke*, vol. 1 (Basel, 1943), p. 14) and wrote his study of the Lex Voconia (published 1843) in the summer of the same year; cf. Karl Meuli, 'Nachwort', in Bachofen, *Gesammelte Werke*, vol. III (1948), pp. 1011-128.

Orientalists in Stuttgart five years previously.[1] This earlier paper might, given better publicity, have found a wider readership than the longer work, through which few but the most diligent of non-specialists were able to make their way without being deterred by the lengthy mid-sentence notes which continued to interrupt the text, until finally relegated to their rightful place at the foot of the page in Karl Meuli's meticulous edition of 1948. For Bachofen, comparative evidence was at this stage at most of secondary importance, although it begins to play a larger part in the closing pages of *Mutterrecht* and was later to claim his attention undivided.[2] The book itself was for students of antiquity to some extent anticipated by an article on gynaecocracy in Asia Minor – the threefold empire of women in the rôles of queens, priestesses and Amazons – published by Baron d'Eckstein in the *Revue archéologique* for 1858.[3] A more remarkable anticipation is to be found in one section of *La politique universelle: decrets de l'avenir*, published in 1852 by the prolific Émile de Girardin and reissued separately two years later under the more informative title *La liberté dans le mariage par l'égalité des enfants devant la mère.*[4] This took as its starting-point the extremely high proportion of illegitimate births in contemporary Europe and the underprivileged status of the children in question. De Girardin proposed that this should be instantly rectified by the introduction of a system whereby children would take their mother's name and property would be transmitted in the female line, reverting, in the case of those fathers not willing to make a free gift of their property to their wives or children during their own lifetime, to ascendants in the female line.[5] He adds an

[1] *Verhandlungen der 16ten Versammlung deutscher Philologen, Schulmänner und Orientalisten in Stuttgart vom 23. bis 26. September 1856*, pp. 40–63.
[2] *Gesammelte Werke*, ed. K. Meuli, vol. II (1948), pp. 306, 497–501, 521–3; vol. III, pp. 837, 983–95. In 1870 Bachofen announced his intention of making a world-wide survey of contemporary survivals of the institution, culminating in his *Antiquarische Briefe* of 1880–5 (*Gesammelte Werke*, vol. VIII (1966), pp. 9–414), of which some 10,000 pages remain unpublished. See letter to Meyer-Ochsner, *Gesammelte Werke*, vol. X (1967), pp. 449–50, no. 276; J. Dörmann, *ibid.* vol. VIII, pp. 523–602 and, more briefly, K. Meuli, 'J. J. Bachofens Alterswerk', in his own *Gesammelte Schriften*, vol. II (Basle, 1975), pp. 1124–38.
[3] 'Les Cares ou Cariens de l'antiquité,' *Revue archéologique*, XIV (1857), 321–37, 381–402; XV (1858), 445–74, 509–30. Bachofen is likely to have known Emil Rückert, *Troja's Ursprung, Blüthe, Untergang und Wiedergeburt in Latium* (Hamburg and Gotha, 1846), pp. 44–9, in which the story of the Amazons is seen as the mythological expression of uterine descent, Lycia connected with Locri Epizephyrii and an apparent survival of the custom in nineteenth-century Lesbos mentioned, for which cf. Bachofen, *Gesammelte Werke*, vol. II, p. 306.
[4] The latter version was known to Bachofen (*Gesammelte Werke*, vol. III, p. 927, n. 2).
[5] 1852 ed., pp. 205–47; slightly expanded 1854 ed., pp. 1–72.

anthology of marriage customs, uses and abuses, both ancient and modern, which includes matrilineal descent and which is itself something of a phenomenon in view of the author's output and the range of his other activities.[1] It was, however, barely noticed at the time, and at this stage it may be appropriate to revert from the Continent and consider another Scot, J. F. McLennan, who published *Primitive Marriage: An Inquiry into the Origin of the Form of Capture* at Edinburgh in 1865.

McLennan's intellectual career is well-documented in the *Dictionary of National Biography* and has more recently been re-examined by John Burrow.[2] His first major undertaking, in between freelance writing, was the article 'Law' in the eighth edition of the *Encyclopaedia Britannica* (1857). In this he quotes from Comte and refers to Adam Smith, but there is nothing which anticipates the startling thesis he was to expound in *Primitive Marriage*, namely that the oldest system of kinship was through females only; that the oldest form of marriage was polyandry of the Nayar kind, a single woman being married to a number of men; that this form was in turn replaced by the Tibetan or 'fraternal' form of polyandry, whereby a woman's husbands are all one another's brothers, and finally that by this roundabout means the principle of kinship through males came gradually to be recognised alongside, and eventually to replace, that through females.

McLennan did not read Bachofen until the following year (1866). On doing so he fully acknowledged that he had been anticipated by the classical scholar in the discovery of kinship through mothers and that the honour for this should be assigned, 'without stint or qualification', to Bachofen.[3] It is however more surprising to learn that McLennan did not come across Millar's *Origin of Ranks* until 1871, a hundred years after its first publication, though there are no grounds for rejecting this statement, and the one item of ancient evidence which is strikingly common to both, the story of Cecrops introducing marriage in Athens, of which McLennan made use in a separate article on 'Kinship in Ancient Greece' published in the *Fortnightly Review* the year after *Primitive Marriage*, is most likely to

[1] 1852 ed., pp. 249–72, cf. esp. 250–2; completely rewritten 1854 ed., pp. 76–82.
[2] Burrow, *Evolution and Society*, pp. 230–4.
[3] J. F. McLennan, 'Bachofen's "*Das Mutterrecht*"', *Studies in Ancient History*, 2nd ed. (London, 1886), pp. 319–25, cf. also 'Kinship in Ancient Greece' (*Fortnightly Review*, IV (1866), 569–88, 682–91, reissued in *Studies in Ancient History*, pp. 195–246), p. 582, n. 1.

have been taken from a common source.[1] What may perhaps be worth drawing attention to is a near-contemporary source which McLennan does acknowledge and from which some indirect light may be gained on the eclipse of Millar in the nineteenth century.

One of the most striking things about *Primitive Marriage* is the up-to-date look of its testimonies: reports of travellers from the Caucasus, Afghanistan and Siberia, some as recent as 1864. He also knows Lewis H. Morgan's circular letter and questionnaire of 1859 about kinship terms.[2] There is however one work cited more than once as a secondary source, the *Descriptive Ethnology* of R. G. Latham, published in 1859, and this work may well have been what set McLennan on the track of more first-hand information, since almost all the main phenomena he made it his task to explain and bring into relation with one another are given a more or less substantive treatment by Latham: notably, first, 'polyandria', which he admitted to be widespread, but was reluctant to regard as having so general a character that it could be termed an institution; secondly, the phenomenon of groups within which marriage could not take place – what McLennan was to term exogamy; and finally, and most striking of all, the practice of female infanticide, which McLennan felt no reluctance in regarding as general and to which he attributed the imbalance of males and females necessitating group marriages between one woman and a number of men.[3]

Robert Gordon Latham was made a Fellow of this College in 1832, at the age of twenty. Seven years later, he was appointed to the Chair of English at University College, London. Shortly thereafter, he also took up medicine and for a while combined his philological and ethnological activities with acting as Assistant Physician at University College Hospital. By 1849 he had resigned from both positions and in 1852 became Director of the Ethnological Department at Crystal Palace. His distinction in all these fields left him uniquely qualified to

---

[1] McLennan, *Studies in Ancient History*, p. 324, n. 1. McLennan had already cited Goguet (*De l'origine des lois*) for this tradition in *Primitive Marriage* (1865), p. 220 (1886, p. 121), adding to Goguet's reference (Varro in Augustine, *Civitas dei* XVIII.9) the *Suda* entry for Prometheus. He now added Justin II.6.7 and compared the Boeotian story in Strabo IX.2.4, p. 402 (Ephorus 70 F 119), *Studies in Ancient History*, p. 236, n. 1 (1866, pp. 685–6)).

[2] *Primitive Marriage* (1865), p. 122 n. (*Studies in Ancient History* (1886), p.66 n. 1). Morgan's circular, published in *Smithsonian Miscellaneous Collections*, vol. II (1862), art. 10, was also printed by the editors of the *Cambrian Journal*, 2nd series, II (1860), 143–58, under 'Correspondence', with the schedule completed for the Welsh nation by the Reverend J. Williams ab Ithel.

[3] *Descriptive Ethnology* (London, 1859), vol. I, pp. 44–6, 80; vol. II, pp. 445–6, 462–4.

carry on the work of James Cowles Prichard in maintaining the unity of mankind against a succession of challengers of whom the most influential was Lord Kames.[1] Kames' *Sketches of the History of Man* (1774, second edition 1788) was explicitly intended as a popular work, with English translations subjoined, 'chiefly with a view to the female sex', and prefaced by a 'Discourse concerning the origin of men and language' which rejected Buffon's definition of a species in favour of the view that the varieties of Man were as distinct as those of dogs and that the confusion of Babel had 'necessarily to be admitted' as a 'real history' and not allegorical since it alone could reconcile sacred history with this profane but in his view self-evident fact.[2]

It is worth bearing this background in mind when one comes to examine Kames' 'Sketch of the progress of the female sex', since here too the effect and evident intention is to place the emphasis on diversity and to discredit the efforts of his contemporaries to find uniformity in social evolution. His view of the respective rôles of the sexes is stated at the outset: 'the man, bold and vigorous, is qualified for being a protector: the woman, delicate and timid, requires protection. The man, as a protector, is directed by nature to govern: the woman, conscious of inferiority, is disposed to obey'.[3] He then poses the question whether matrimony is 'an appointment of nature, or only of municipal law', and proceeds to demolish the mainly ancient evidence for a primitive state of promiscuity. To do this, he sees he must 'remove the bias of great names' by terming Herodotus 'grossly credulous' and pointing to the headless men with eyes on their chests to be found in the vicinity of the promiscuous Garamantes of Pliny. There is, he states, no such custom as promiscuity in the East Indies of his own time, and these were so little known to the Greeks 'that their authors cannot be much relied on, in the accounts which they give of that distant region'. Promiscuity being ruled out, he is left with no alternative but to accept matrimony as an appointment of nature. He accepts that this may include polygamy, but that is due to 'the low condition of the female sex among savages' and

[1] See further Randolph Quirk, *The Study of the Mother-Tongue (An Inaugural Lecture)* (London: University College, 1961), pp. 7–17 and references. Latham edited Prichard's posthumous *Eastern Origin of the Celtic Nations* (1857), and was unambiguous in rejecting the term 'race' in his own *Natural History of the Varieties of Man* (London, 1850), p. 564.

[2] Vol. 1 (1788), pp. 3–84. For some contemporary reactions cf. Ian Simpson Ross, *Lord Kames and the Scotland of his day* (Oxford, 1972), pp. 344–8.

[3] Kames, *Sketches*, vol. ii, p. 3.

'intimately connected with the custom of purchasing wives'.[1] What he calls female succession, that is, inheritance by the sister's son as reported in America and known to Ferguson and Millar, is represented as something confined to royal families: 'female succession', he states blandly, 'depends in some degree on the nature of the government'.[2] And finally a further wedge is driven between the two continents which Ferguson and Millar had attempted to link. 'The northern nations of Europe, as appears from the foregoing sketch, must be excepted from these conclusions. Among them, women were from the beginning courted and honoured, nor was polygamy ever known among them.'[3] In the two generations after Kames, his opponents had more than enough to cope with in combating his view of the diversity of mankind, while at the same time keeping up with a growing and increasingly complex body of physical, linguistic, and ethnographic data, without also pinning their flags to the mast of uniform social evolution.[4]

It is however possible to end on a less gloomy note. I have mentioned one group of Pacific islands, the Marianas, in which as Millar put it 'the wife is absolute mistress of the house, and the husband is not at liberty to dispose of anything without her permission'.[5] But the most notorious such island discovered in the eighteenth century was undoubtedly Tahiti. On 27 June 1767, just over a week after H.M.S. *Dolphin*, commanded by Captain Samuel Wallis, put in at the island, the natives brought a party of young girls to one of the boats and made signs inviting the crew to take on board any of these they chose. The officer in the boat refused to allow this, but the ship's master, George Robertson, entered the crew's reaction in his journal.

When our boats returned to the ship, all the sailors swore they neaver saw handsomer made women in their lives, and declard they would all to a man, live on two thirds allowance, rather nor lose so fine an opportunity of geting a Girl apiece – this piece of news made all our men madly fond of the shore, even the sick which had been on the Doctors list for some weeks before, now declared they

[1] *Ibid.* vol. II, pp. 8–9, 29, 42; cf. vol. I, pp. 70–1. The Cecrops story is interpreted as a prohibition of polygamy (vol. II, pp. 7–8).

[2] *Ibid.* vol. II, p. 68.

[3] *Ibid.* pp. 69–70. In the first edition (1774, vol. I, p. 206) this conclusion was at least partly based on Ossian (*ibid.* pp. 281–308; later omitted).

[4] Cf. in general George W. Stocking, Jr., ed., *James Cowles Prichard, Researches into the Physical History of Man (1813)* (Chicago, 1973), pp. vii–cx. A full-scale intellectual biography of Prichard based on primary material is being undertaken by Mr John Crump.

[5] *Origin*, pp. 61–2 = ed. Lehmann, p. 200.

would be happy if they were permitted to go ashore, at same time said a Young Girl would make an Excelent Nurse, and they were Certain of recovering faster under a Young Girls care nor all the Doctor would do for them.[1]

This was no more than a prelude to the revelations of what was seen as an almost wholly permissive society which were to be conveyed to Europe as a result of the subsequent voyages of Bougainville and Cook, and though the latter left little doubt of his revulsion at some of the practices he witnessed, the most abiding impression of Tahiti in the 1770s was that of an earthly paradise.[2] Philibert Commerson, the French naturalist who accompanied Bougainville, went so far, in a letter he wrote to a number of his friends, as to make this the formal expression of a religion of love.

Nés sous le plus beau ciel, nourris des fruits d'vne terre feconde sans culture, regis par des peres de famille plutot que par des rois, ils ne reconnoissent d'autre dieu que l'amour. Tous les jours lui sont consacrés, toute l'isle est son temple, toutes les femmes en sont les autels, tous les hommes les sacrificateurs...L'acte de creer son semblable est un acte de religion; les preludes en sont encouragés par les voeux et les chants de tout le peuple assemblé et la fin celebrée par des applaudissemens universels; tout etranger est admis a participer a ces heureux misteres; c'est même un des devoirs de l'hospitalité que de les inviter, de sorte que le bon Vtopien joüit sans cesse ou du sentiment de ses propres plaisirs ou du spectacle de ceux des autres.

Commerson himself apparently intended this letter for private circulation, but an earlier version was published in 1769 and the above text was reissued on two subsequent occasions, in 1798 and 1853, when copies of the original were discovered.[3] There is a strong probability that the first of these was noticed by Charles Fourier, who was consistent in dating his own *découverte* to 1799 and saw in Tahiti at the time of its discovery the sole surviving instance of free love, '*phanérogamie simple*', the initial stage in his schema of social evolution,

[1] George Robertson, *The Discovery of Tahiti* (London: Hakluyt Society, 1948), p. 167, cf. pp. 188–90.

[2] Cf. in general J. C. Beaglehole, 'A note on Polynesian history', *The Journals of Captain James Cook*, vol. i (Cambridge, 1955), pp. clxxxvi–cxc.

[3] P. Crassous, 'Lettres de Commerson', *La décade philosophique* (an VI), 4 (vol. xviii [1798]), pp. 133–4, repeated without acknowledgement in A. M. Sané, *Tableau historique, typographique et moral des peuples des quatre parties du monde*, vol. ii (Paris, an IX [1801]), pp. 493–4. The letter is dated 17 April 1769 and therefore a revision of that addressed to Lalande, dated 25 February and published later the same year in the November issue of the *Mercure de France*, p. 198 (cf. Beaglehole, *Journals of Captain Cook*, vol. i, p. clxxiii, n. 1). The revisions are retained in a further undated copy addressed to Dr Dumolin and published in *Annales de l'Académie de Macon*, ii (1853), 330, whose orthography is adopted here.

which among the many other aspects of his complex and all-embracing thought has been largely neglected and receives almost no space in the classic study by Hubert Bourgin.[1] What led to the downfall of this original state elsewhere was an excess of population, resulting in poverty, and this in turn led first to the establishment of private property and then to that of marriage, 'the child of poverty' which Fourier likened to the invention of a third sex determined to condemn the other two to boredom.[2] With marriage, the state of savagery was inaugurated, to be succeeded by the rise of patriarchal power, 'composite falsity', which was tyrannical in nature and could be exercised only in circumstances of unnatural isolation, such as those in which the Old Testament depicted Abraham sending Agar and Ishmael out into the desert to starve, simply because he had no further use for them.[3] It only remained for patriarchal families to be united once more, and the result was barbarism, leading finally to civilisation, a worse outcome than any state which had preceded it.[4]

[1] For a brief outline cf. Nicholas V. Riasanovsky, *The Teaching of Charles Fourier* (Berkeley and Los Angeles, 1969), pp. 139–48. Fourier was aware of infanticide on Tahiti, a practice reported by Cook and hence also by F. Babié de Bercenay, ed., *Voyages chez les peuples sauvages*, vol. II (Paris, an IX [1801]), pp. 140–371. He was however about this time a regular reader of *La décade philosophique* and the *Mercure de France*, from which (along with the *Gazette Nationale* (*Le Moniteur*)) much can be learnt about his early reading; cf. H. Bourgin, *Fourier* (Paris, 1905), pp. 62–3, 124–6.

[2] *Théorie des quatre mouvements*, 2nd ed. (Paris, 1841), p. 164 = *Œuvres*, vol. I, 3rd ed. (Paris, 1846, reprinted Anthropos, 1967), p. 112.

[3] The charge of anti-Semitism (Riasanovsky, *Teaching of Charles Fourier*, p. 253) is sufficiently met by *Les trois nœuds* (below, n. 4), pp. 453–4: 'ce n'est pas aux Juifs qu'il faut imputer la faute, c'est au Patriarchat...ils redeviendroient les plus braves des peuples s'ils formaient un État régulier adonné à la guerre'. Fourier's view of race characteristically emphasises the positive aspects of variety, cf. *Théorie des quatre mouvements*, 2nd ed. (Paris, 1841) (*Œuvres*, vol. I (1967)), p. 52, n. I: 'Dieu établit dans tous les genres de ses productions des nuances distinguées en Séries ascendante et descendante, et pourquoi se serait-il écarté, en créant l'espèce humaine, d'un ordre qu'il suit dans toutes les œuvres créées, depuis les astres jusqu'aux insectes?' Again characteristically, this is quite the opposite of a warrant for human dissociation, cf. the proposal for the creation of a new race (combining such distinctive features as resistance to extremes of temperature with night vision) through inter-marriage (*Les trois nœuds*, pp. 416–18). The emphasis placed on albinos and the elsewhere discredited Patagonian giants show that the main source is the revised version of Buffon's *Histoire naturelle de l'espèce humaine*; cf. *Œuvres*, ed. Sonnini, vol. XX (Paris, an VIII [1800]), pp. 341–77, 385–405; J. J. Virey, *Histoire naturelle du genre humain*, 1st ed. (Paris, an IX [1800]), vol. I, pp. 175, n. 2, 200; vol. II, p. 247, and more briefly G. Cuvier, *Tableau élémentaire de l'histoire naturelle des animaux* (Paris, an VI), pp. 71–6.

[4] 'Des lymbes obscures', *La Phalange*, IX (1849), 5–38, 97–103; 'Les trois nœuds du mouvement', *ibid.* pp. 111–69 = *Œuvres*, vol. XII (Paris, 1968), pp. 415–73. As was observed by the first editors, this latter version (11e pièce, cote suppl., Archives Nationales 10 AS 13.1) is among the earliest of Fourier's manuscripts and bears a marginal note (p. 466) of the *Gazette nationale* with the Republican date '16 pluviose'. 'Des lymbes obscures' (p. 6) refers to an event of 1800 and it is probably the huge profit made by

Each of these main stages was further divided into four successive phases, while transitional or mixed societies provided a framework into which specific ethnographic data could be fitted, such as polyandry in Nepal or the system of matrimonial exchanges reported from the Canary Islands.[1]

Fourier's scathing denunciation of civilisation goes well beyond the scope of this paper, but it is well known how soon it caught the attention of Marx and Engels. Already in 1843 the latter was recommending it to his English readers as 'scientific research, cool, unbiassed, systematic thought', from which more was to be derived than from Saint-Simonism.[2] The fullest exposition of Fourier's theory of social evolution is that given in two manuscripts published posthumously in 1849, and though three years before this Engels is found expressing some impatience at the mainly cosmogonic contents of other manuscripts published in the same series, the dearth of extant correspondence for the year 1849 makes it uncertain how far he persisted with these.[3] As late as 1870, however, Marx uses Fourier's

---

Ouvrard in supplying the French army in Italy, reported in the same year (an VI, no. 25, p. 542 [5 February]), to which this alludes, the author cited being not a contributor to the newspaper but the preacher Jean-Baptiste Massillon (1663–1742), one of whose sermons Fourier is here modifying in summary, *Grand-Carême*, no. 49 (*Œuvres*, vol. 1 (Paris, 1870), p. 374).

[1] 'Des lymbes obscures', p. 36. For the Canary Islands the source must be P. Boutier and J. Le Verrier, *Histoire de la premiere descouuerte et conqueste des Canaries* (Paris, 1630), p. 134, repeated in J. B. G. M. Bory de Saint-Vincent, *Essai sur les isles fortunées* (Paris, an XI [1803]), p. 100; cf. P. B. Webb and S. Berthelot, *Histoire naturelle des îles canaries*, vol. 1, 1 (Paris, 1842), p. 101. Another transitional phenomenon is *Javanisme*, nowhere in his published writings defined by Fourier but sometimes placed half way between *sauvagerie* and *Otahitisme*, 'Échelle parallèle des attractions', *La Phalange* VI (1847), 307; *Théorie de l'unité universelle*, vol. IV, 2nd ed. (Paris, 1841), p. 550 = *Œuvres*, vol. V (1966). Java is elsewhere more than once cited for *mœurs phanérogames*, and the reference is probably to the custom reported from Java by A. Pigafetta, *Premier voyage autour du monde (1519–22)* (Paris, an IX [1801]), p. 217), where it is stated that the young men had only to fasten bells to their persons and ring these to obtain the girls' favours; see further Donald F. Lach, *Asia in the Making of Europe*, vol. 1, 2 (Chicago, 1965), p. 553, n. 298 and Virey, *Histoire naturelle*, vol. II, p. 35, n. 1.

[2] 'Progress of social reform on the continent, no. 1: France', *The New Moral World (and Gazette of the Rational Society)*, V, 3rd series (4 November 1843), no. 19, p. 145 = *Marx–Engels Gesamtausgabe*, vol. 1, 2 (Berlin, 1930), p. 437.

[3] 'Die Phalange enthält nichts als Unsinn. Die Mittheilungen aus Fouriers Nachlass beschränken sich alle auf das mouvement aromal und die Begattung der Planeten, die plus ou moins von hinten zu geschehen scheint', Engels to Marx, 19 August 1846. Attention has been drawn to the importance of Kepler's *Harmonice mundi* (1519), of which Fourier owned a copy, in shaping his cosmogony, S. Debout Oleskiewicz, *Revue internationale de philosophie*, 16e année, no. 60 (1962), pp. 195–9; and on Kepler's use of sexual analogies see also D. P. Walker, 'Kepler's celestial music', *Journal of the Warburg and Courtauld Institutes*, XXX (1967), p. 243, n. 76. Similar ideas are expressed in Restif de la Bretonne's *Philosophie de Monsieur Nicolas*, vol. II (Paris, 1796), pp. 33–82, but the most

term *Phanérogamie* to characterise early Welsh society, and finally (to step beyond this deadline) in the winter of 1880 he is to be seen excerpting Lewis H. Morgan's *Ancient Society* and suddenly inserting the statement that Fourier characterised the epoch of civilisation by monogamy and private property in land.[1] It is hard to avoid the conclusion that the single most important contribution to the history of the human family made in the first half of the nineteenth century was that which challenged most radically both the desirability and the finality of its outcome.

likely source for this aspect of Fourier's thinking is the sexual system of Linnaeus, whose terminology (*unigynes, digynes*, etc.) he adopts wholesale for his *clavier puissanciel des caractères*, simply transferring it from plants to mankind, *La Phalange*, VI (1847), 5–47; cf. *Le nouveau monde amoureux, passim* = *Œuvres*, vol. VII (Paris, 1967). The term *phanérogamie* is itself Linnaean.

[1] 'Fouriers Phantasie mise en pratique', Marx to Engels, 10 May 1870; Engels to Marx (and reply), 11 May 1870; Lawrence Krader, ed., *The Ethnological Notebooks of Karl Marx* (Assen: Van Gorcum, 1972), p. 120.

PART IV

THE NINETEENTH
CENTURY

14

THE ENGLISH UTILITARIANS AND ATHENIAN DEMOCRACY

H. O. PAPPÉ

The English utilitarians, or Benthamites, have not generally been considered as exponents of Greek thought. Matthew Arnold 'was delivered from the bondage of Bentham', when he read in the *Deontology* that 'Socrates and Plato were talking nonsense under the pretence of talking wisdom and morality'.[1] Carlyle's 'Signs of the Times' is the *locus classicus* of British anti-utilitarianism.[2] He claimed that Locke, Hume, Adam Smith, Delolme and Bentham had subverted the classical pursuit of the Beautiful and Good and of inner perfection, and had replaced it by the calculation of the Profitable, by Experience and Utility; they had treated the body-politic as a machine. A great fellow of this College, John Maynard Keynes, held the Benthamite neglect of the Platonic tradition and the concomitant over-evaluation of the economic criterion responsible for the present moral decay.[3] The list of such condemnations can be extended *ad libitum*, especially if continental 'physicians of culture' are taken into account.

As these views are widely accepted propositions, they call for a

[1] Matthew Arnold, *Culture and Anarchy* (1869), ed. J. Dover Wilson (Cambridge, 1961), p. 67.
[2] Thomas Carlyle, 'Signs of the times', *Edinburgh Review*, XLIX (1829), 439–59. On the other hand, Thomas de Quincey, Carlyle's contemporary and fellow prose-poet, and, like him, an interpreter of German idealism, extolled the Benthamite economics of Ricardo as a rejection of Adam Smith's empiricism and a return to Aristotelian philosophy; one of de Quincey's two considerable contributions to the literature of political economy was *Dialogues of Three Templars on Political Economy* (1824), in *The Collected Works*, ed. D. Masson, vol. IX (Edinburgh, 1890), written in the form of a Platonic dialogue with Phaedrus, Philebus and XXZ (the author) as the speakers. Wilhelm Roscher, the founder of the first German Historical School of Political Economy, owed the inspiration for his historical-comparative and sociological method equally to Thucydides and Adam Smith; his aim was to develop political economy in the way, 'den schon die Sokratiker gebahnt, den A. Smith und Malthus mit grossem historischen Sinn betreten haben' (1840), quoted by Gottfried Eisermann, *Die Grundlagen des Historismus in der deutschen Nationalökonomie* (Stuttgart, 1956), p. 130 and *passim*.
[3] John Maynard Keynes, *Two Memoirs* (London, 1949), pp. 96–7. His strictures on Benthamite thought did not protect him, though, from similar attacks on 'the Benthams and Keyneses of this world' in a recent polemic against *Bentham* by D. J. Manning (London, 1968), p. 110.

dialectical investigation with a view to proving them to be belief rather than knowledge.

As regards Bentham, I shall be very short. In his peculiar version of the principle of utility he was indebted only marginally to Greek philosophy; the thinkers who had inspired him in this respect were Fénelon in the first place, Hume, Beccaria and Helvétius. However, his quest for certainty drew him towards Aristotle to whom he returned repeatedly all through his life. He was not interested in Aristotle's *Politics*; if the *Constitution of Athens* had been accessible in his time, it might have been another matter. He did not look to Athenian democracy for an example. It had never been, he said, government by the people, as nine-tenths of the population, women, dependants, metics and slaves, were excluded from participation; nor had there been sufficient safeguards against the abuse of power by administrators.[1] What attracted Bentham was Aristotle's syllogistic logic of the understanding which he undertook to supplement by an equally precise deontic logic of the will or of imperation, a monumental achievement of intrinsic and not yet exhausted significance.[2] But it does not make him an Aristotelian, though perhaps an Aristotle of the art of legislation.

On the other hand, James Mill and John Stuart Mill were Platonists. Both contributed to Plato scholarship; both followed in his footsteps in thought and action; both were philosopher-kings of sorts as they played an eminent rôle in the administration of British India; they were concerned with the theory as well as the practice of politics. The history of modern Platonism, as far as I can see, has taken no notice of James Mill, and little of John Mill. According to Professor Manasse's recent account in the *Dictionary of the History of Ideas*,[3] modern Platonism started with Schleiermacher and did not reach England until Jowett, influenced by German scholarship, published his *Dialogues of Plato* in 1870; the earlier English translation

[1] Jeremy Bentham, *Fragment on Government* (London, 1776), ch. II, § 34, including n. 2; *Introduction to the Principles of Morals and Legislation* (London, 1789) ch. XVI, § 44, n. 1.

[2] *Ibid.* Preface, paras. 35–6; *Logic* (1816), in *The Works of Jeremy Bentham* (Edinburgh, 1843–59), ed. J. Bowring, vol. VIII, pp. 215–93, with its motto (p. 241): 'Logic, say the Aristotelians, is the art by which the mind of man is conducted to the tabernacle of knowledge. Let us now add – in its road to the temple of happiness.' See the relevant commentaries by Charles W. Everett, Elie Halévy, C. K. Ogden, David Baumgardt, Mary Mack, and, most recently, David Lyons, *In the Interest of the Governed* (Oxford, 1973) and Bhikhu Parekh, *Bentham's Political Thought* (London, 1973).

[3] E. M. Manasse, 'Platonism since the Enlightenment', *Dictionary of the History of Ideas* ed. Philip P. Wiener (New York, 1973), vol. III, pp. 515–25 (especially p. 522).

by Thomas Taylor in 1804 had been generally ignored by English scholars, though it had left its mark on Shelley and Blake's mystical poetry and on American transcendentalists. George Grote is mentioned only marginally, though honourably, as having founded modern English Plato scholarship almost simultaneously with Jowett; 'in his magisterial work on Plato' (published in 1865), Mr Manasse reminds us, 'he tried to separate the dialectic critic Plato from the dogmatic metaphysician'. Jowett himself, however, expressed his pre-eminent indebtedness to Grote, 'my father Parmenides', though he pictured Plato as the father of Idealism in contrast to Grote's utilitarian interpretation.[1] Grote, whose contributions to Greek scholarship date in fact back to 1826, was a disciple of James Mill.

As regards John Mill, the only Plato scholar who appears to have taken notice of him, was Paul Shorey who was well versed in continental and Anglo-American Platonism. In about 1930 he described Mill as 'perhaps the greatest of nineteenth-century Platonists'. He stated that he discovered traces of Plato in most of Mill's work, and that Mill's review of Grote's *Plato*, an essay of over a hundred pages, 'remains to this day the best available general introduction to the study of Plato'.[2] Mill's distinguished biographers and commentators have on the whole attributed only minor significance to his Platonism.

James Mill's Hellenism may have been sparked off by his education at Montrose Academy. This school had been the first in Scotland to take up the teaching of Greek in the sixteenth century; during Mill's residence, Montrose was the first Scottish place to have a Unitarian church; it was the time of the French Revolution, and the small shipping centre was astir with political debate and sedition trials.[3] When Mill went up to Edinburgh to read theology, he was

---

[1] B. Jowett, *The Dialogues of Plato* (1870), 3rd ed. (Oxford, 1892), vol. I, Preface, pp. x–xii. Grote in turn called James Mill his 'master Parmenides' in 1868, when he dissented from the last two chapters of Mill's *Analysis of the Phenomena of the Human Mind* (Mrs Grote, *The Personal Life of George Grote* (London, 1873), p. 296). Grote's *History of Greece*, apart from Niebuhr, had been inspired by James Mill's regard for myth, religion, law, art and crafts as relevant constituents of historical understanding; Grote said that 'we know of no work which surpasses [Mill's] *History of British India* in the main excellencies attainable by historical writers' (Alexander Bain, *James Mill. A Biography* (London, 1882), p. 458). Regarding Grote's work see M. L. Clarke, *George Grote. A Biography* (London, 1962); Arnaldo Momigliano, 'George Grote and the study of Greek history', *Studies in Historiography* (London, 1966), pp. 56–74; Wilhelm Dilthey, 'George Grote' (1877), *Gesammelte Schriften*, vol. xv (Göttingen, 1970), pp. 251–8.

[2] Paul Shorey, *Platonism Ancient and Modern* (Berkeley, 1938), pp. 231–2.

[3] For details see A. L. Lazenby, 'James Mill: the formation of a Scottish émigré writer', unpublished doctoral dissertation (University of Sussex, 1972), fols. 356–61, and

admitted to the second-year class in Greek. He attended Greek courses throughout his studies; there was not a term in which he did not take out Plato's works from the General Library. Apart from his wide reading in English, Latin and French, his favourite Greek writers over the years included Aristotle, Thucydides, Herodotus, Demosthenes, Isocrates, Lucian, Xenophon, Dionysius of Halicarnassus, Aristophanes, and Euripides. Alexander Bain thought it probable that Mill's 'Greek studies imbued him with the democratic ideal of Government, but this supposes an independent bias on his part; for few have ever been made liberal politicians by classical authors alone'.[1] Thirty years after Mill's death George Grote wrote that 'of all persons whom we have known [Mill] was the one who stood least remote from the lofty Platonic ideal of Dialectic – τοῦ διδόναι καὶ δέχεσθαι λόγον..., competent alike to examine others, or to be examined by them...'.[2] We know from John Mill that 'there is no author to whom my father thought himself more indebted for his own mental culture than Plato'.[3]

Thomas Taylor's *Works of Plato* appeared in 1804. James Mill published two major review articles, the first in the *Literary Journal* in 1804, the second in the *Edinburgh Review* in 1809.[4] He welcomed an English version of Plato at a time when even original texts were not readily accessible. But he condemned Taylor's pseudo-archaic style and pointed out large numbers of mistranslated passages. Taylor, he said, was faithful neither to the letter nor to the spirit of Plato. He was a Plotinist rather than a Platonist; he arbitrarily imputed views to Plato which were those of the adversaries of Socrates, while interspersing his notes with attacks on the inductive philosophy of Bacon and Newton, whom he believed to be perverters of reason and misleaders of mankind. Mill, professing his admiration, 'bordering on enthusiasm', for Plato, called for a return to the teachings of the master himself rather than the metaphysics of the Alexandrian School championed by Taylor or excessive attention to matters of style and prosody.

In his own interpretation of Plato, Mill took his motto from

Alexander Bain's masterly biography. Much recent literature on James Mill as a political philosopher and historian has been acrimonious and uninformed, though justice has been done to his achievements as an economist and administrator.

[1] Bain, *James Mill*, p. 35.
[2] *Ibid.* p. 459.
[3] *Autobiography*, ed. H. Laski (World's Classics, Oxford, 1924), p. 18.
[4] *Literary Journal*, III (1804), 449–61 and 577–89; *Edinburgh Review*, XIV (1809), 187–211.

Cicero: 'In Platonis libris nihil affirmatur.' He distinguished between the negative and the inquiring aspects of Plato. His negative object was 'to expose some false impressions which are most likely to be held to prevail'. The inquiring dialogues were meant 'to give specimens of investigation, to let in rays of light, to analyse particular points...to encourage speculation rather than lay down and establish any system of opinions'. Mill thus broke with the traditional conception of Plato as the moral teacher in contrast to Aristotle, the systematic philosopher. At the same time as Schleiermacher, he emphasised that the Socratic dialectic was a method of scientific inquiry as well as a practical instrument of education and inspiration. Grote was later to take up James Mill's interpretation. But while equally eschewing the ulterior affirmatives of the *arcana coelestia*, which Proclus and Ficino had imputed to Plato, Grote drew a firm line between the Socratic Plato, who professed ignorance, and the late works which revealed 'the peremptory, dictatorial affirmative of Lykurgus'. Mill expressed no such misgivings. Did the Plato of the *Republic* appeal to a dictatorial streak in his own character? He explained his conception of the *Republic* twenty-five years later in the course of his controversy with Macaulay and Sir James Mackintosh.

On the assumption that all those in power were actuated by self-interest, Mill had expressed himself in favour of an extended suffrage for all male citizens over forty as a means of achieving the identity of interests between governors and governed on which the stability of the state depends. He assumed that the lower classes, once educated, would accept and follow the lead of the middle rank who excelled in science, art and legislation.[1] Macaulay attacked Mill's position as scholastic and purely verbal. He said that Mill had deduced his political propositions from the premiss of a dogmatic and narrow conception of human nature; he had neglected the inductive investigation of historical and social experience.[2] Mill's reply, in the *Fragment on Mackintosh*, was that he had merely applied Plato's insights into the political process together with Hume's theory of

---

[1] James Mill's essay on 'Government' was first published in 1821 in the supplement to the fifth edition of the *Encyclopaedia Britannica*, and in book form in 1828, together with his essays on Jurisprudence, Liberty of the Press, Prisons and Prison Discipline, Colonies, Law of Nations and Education.

[2] Macaulay's articles attacking Mill's utilitarian logic and politics were in response to the book mentioned above, n. 1; they appeared in the *Edinburgh Review*, XLIX (1829), 159–89, 273–300; L (1829), 99–125; reprinted posthumously, against the author's wishes, in *The Miscellaneous Essays of Lord Macaulay*. Most recent accounts of the debate have failed to take Mill's crucial *Fragment on Mackintosh* into account.

government.[1] Quoting passages from books III and v, Mill claimed that

> the whole of Plato's *Republic* may be regarded as a development of the principle applied by Mr. Mill: that identity of interests between the governors and the governed affords the only security for government...Plato bent the whole force of his penetrating mind to discover the means of such identification; but being ignorant, as all the ancients were, of the divine principle of representation, found himself obliged to have recourse to extraordinary methods.

Plato, Mill said, had been the subject of ignorant ridicule, but, given the circumstances of his time, it would not have been easy to find another combination of means better adapted to the end.

As for James Mill's own position, his theory of government was in fact not a geometric deduction from a one-sided interpretation of human nature, as Macaulay, backed by John Stuart Mill, believed. Nor did he ignore what he called the immense variety of historical facts, passions, habits, opinions, prejudices and thought; he was after all a great historian himself. His science of government was a hypothetical science, postulating *homo politicus*, in the same way as political economy derived its principles from a hypothetical *homo oeconomicus*. In this respect Mill followed Hume, whose political science was based upon 'the maxim that, in contriving any system of government and fixing the several checks and controls of the constitution, every man ought to be supposed a *Knave* and to have no other end in all his actions than private interest...a maxim true in politics though false in life'.[2] As J. S. Mill later observed, this theory was merely a science of government, not a comprehensive political science which must take account of all determining variables as well as perturbing causes.[3] James Mill's science of government was a logical consequence of Bentham's dichotomy of private and public ethics,[4] which itself was a response to the separation of state and society which made the eighteenth century so deeply different in its structure and mentality from the Greek *politeia*. Like Plato's, but

---

[1] Mill's *Fragment on Mackintosh* (London, 1835), predominantly concerned with Sir James Mackintosh's *Dissertation on the Progress of Ethical Philosophy* (Edinburgh, 1830, also published in vol. 1 of the 7th ed. of the *Encyclopaedia Britannica*), contains the definitive exposition of Benthamite utilitarianism and political philosophy. See esp. pp. 279–94, 356–7.

[2] David Hume, 'On the independency of parliament', *Essays Moral, Political, and Literary*, ed. T. H. Green and T. H. Grose (London, 1875), Part I, Essay VI, pp. 117–19.

[3] J. S. Mill, *Logic*, book VI, ch. VIII, § 3, penultimate para. See also Mill's article 'The rationale of political representation', *London Review* (July 1835), 341–2.

[4] Bentham, *Principles of Morals and Legislation*, ch. XVII.

unlike the Athenian citizen, Mill's citizen did not participate in politics except at election time or, in particular cases, as a juror or a political writer. In terms of the ancient conception of liberty he was therefore not free, as Rousseau had in fact pointed out with regard to the British constitution.[1] However, a new type of liberty had developed by the eighteenth century, the negative liberty which prevents the state from meddling in the citizen's private, ethical and aesthetic life or in his commerce. It was in this social and cultural sphere that he was expected to participate and exercise and develop his abilities. The political sphere was not concerned with human nature and culture except in protecting it from inroads on the part of the government or offenders. Some contemporaries, like Adam Ferguson, regretted this development; many recognised its drawbacks, but the utilitarians welcomed the severe demarcation of the limitations of the state.[2]

Accordingly, James Mill's conception of democracy was basically different from Plato's despite his professed Platonism. Plato's rulers were all-powerful; Mill's were to be restrained by all possible devices. Plato expected the *Demos* to conform; Mill's profession of democracy was qualified by his desire to preserve the unshackled initiative of the individual citizen. Mill's image of the middle class was less puritan, though more élitist, than Plato's, nor did he share Plato's notion of justice as an individual rather than a social quality. Unlike Plato's insight into the impermanence of forms of government, Mill pronounced his preferred constitution, representative government, to be the definitive solution of the problem of order and progress. In the last resort, however, he attributed little significance to the form of constitutions as long as there were sufficient safeguards to restrict the power of government. Though he professed an overriding concern for the stability of the state, it must not be forgotten that his equally strong zeal for reform was, as Dicey expressed it, 'big with revolution'.[3]

And so to John Stuart Mill. I start with four quotations:

The battle of Marathon, even as an event in English history, is more important than the battle of Hastings.[4]

[1] Jean-Jacques Rousseau, *Contrat social*, book III, ch. xv.
[2] See my forthcoming 'Sismondi's system of liberty', to be published in the *Journal of the History of Ideas*.
[3] A. V. Dicey, *Law and Public Opinion in England* (London, 1905; 2nd ed., 1914), p. 305.
[4] 'Early Grecian history and legend', *Edinburgh Review*, LXXXIV (1846), 343; reprinted in *Dissertations and Discussions*, vol. II (1862), p. 283.

It may be better to be a John Knox than an Alcibiades, but, it is better to be a Pericles than either.[1]

On Athenian democracy:

Notwithstanding the defects of the social system and moral ideas of antiquity, the practice of the dicastery and the ecclesia raised the intellectual standard of the average Athenian citizen far beyond anything, of which there is an example in any other mass of men, ancient or modern.[2]

And on doctrinaire democracy:

No government produces all possible beneficial effects – all are attended by inconveniences which cannot be combated by means drawn from the very causes which produce them...[It is often better to turn to practical arrangements which do not follow from the general principle of the government.] Under a government of legitimacy, the presumption is rather in favour of institutions of popular origin; and in a democracy, in favour of arrangements tending to check the impetus of the popular will.[3]

The history of John Mill's education at the hands of his father, Bentham, John Austin and George Grote has been the subject of ample comment and argument. I may just recall that he started his Greek studies at the age of three, and that by the age of seven, he had read Aesop's *Fables*, Xenophon's *Anabasis*, *Cyropaedia* and *Memorabilia*, Diogenes Laertius, part of Lucian, Isocrates and six of Plato's dialogues, including the *Theaetetus* which of course he was unable to understand. (However, later on he was to prove his independent understanding of this dialogue by disagreeing with Grote's interpretation of the Protagorean *homo mensura* doctrine.) Between the ages of eight and twelve, Mill's Greek reading included Thucydides (twice), Polybius, Demosthenes, Aeschines, Pindar, Anacreon, the *Iliad* and the *Odyssey*, Theocritus, Sophocles' *Electra*, *Ajax* and *Philoctetes*, Euripides' *Phoenician Women* and *Medea*, Aristophanes' *Plutus*, the *Clouds* and the *Frogs*, as well as Aristotle's *Rhetoric* and the first four books of the *Organon*; he made synoptic tables of both these works. He was thirteen when he read the *Gorgias*, the *Protagoras* and the *Republic*, of which he made an abstract. Nearly forty years later Mill said of the Platonic dialogues and dialectics: 'all this even at that age took such hold of me that it became part of my own mind; and I have ever felt myself, beyond any modern that I know of except my father, and perhaps even beyond him, a pupil of Plato, and cast in the

[1] *On Liberty*, ed. R. B. McCallum (Oxford, 1946), p. 55.
[2] *Representative Government*, ed. R. B. McCallum (Oxford, 1946), p. 150.
[3] *Logic*, book VI, ch. II, § 4.

mould of his dialectics'.[1] In fact, nearly all his works reveal a dialectical architecture in his way of unfolding an argument or depicting his own intellectual, moral and aesthetic development.

Mill had read widely in logic, ethics and jurisprudence before he took up Bentham's *Introduction to the Principles of Morals and Legislation* and Dumont's version of the *Traité de législation* at the age of sixteen or seventeen. Despite his later reservations he admired Bentham's inventive genius and his ability to impart to morals and politics those habits of thought and modes of investigation which are essential to the idea of science, and which Bacon had imparted to physics.[2] What enraptured Mill, was Bentham's exhaustive method of detail, his systematic questioning of every seemingly self-evident truth, his interminable classifications and elaborate demonstrations, his way of analysing situations and unmasking moral, political and legal fictions and fallacies. However, if Mill felt at home with Bentham, it was because Plato had smoothed the way for him. He tells us that he was able to appreciate Bentham's achievement because his own study of 'logic and the dialectics of Plato, which had formed so large a part of my previous training, had given me a strong relish for accurate classification'.[3] True, Bentham had ignored Plato's significance, but, as Mill put it, 'Plato had anticipated him in the process to which he declared that he owed everything.'[4]

For Mill there were no basic contradictions in the development of conventional logic from Socrates and Aristotle to Bacon and his own conception which, in Karl Britton's words, 'found logic deductive and...left it both inductive and deductive'.[5] According to Mill every syllogism with a factual conclusion must rest upon the inductive inference contained in the major premiss. This proposition, George Grote concluded from his examination of the *Prior Analytics* and the *Metaphysics*, was in agreement with 'Aristotle's main doctrine – of Induction as a process antithetical to and separate from Deduction, yet as an essential preliminary thereto'.[6] Besides,

---

[1] *The Early Draft of John Stuart Mill's Autobiography*, ed. Jack Stillinger (Urbana, 1961), p. 48. The main sources regarding Mill's early reading are his *Autobiography* and Alexander Bain's *John Stuart Mill. A Criticism* (London, 1882).
[2] 'Bentham' (1838), *Essays on Ethics, Religion and Society*, in *Collected Works*, ed. J. M. Robson, vol. x (Toronto, 1969), p. 83.
[3] *Autobiography*, p. 55.
[4] 'Bentham', p. 88.
[5] Karl Britton, *John Stuart Mill* (London, 1953), p. 147.
[6] George Grote, *Aristotle*, ed. A. Bain and C. Croom-Robertson (1876; 2nd ed., London, 1880), pp. 198–201.

there is good biographical evidence to relate Mill's logic to that of the Socratic Plato.

It is usually recognised that the immediate occasion for Mill's decision to write a treatise on logic was Archbishop Whately's *Logic*, which he read and discussed with some friends, including George Grote, after its publication in 1826, and Macaulay's attack on his father James Mill's theory of government. However, at the same time Mill was busily engaged in writing abstracts in his own translation together with annotations of nine of Plato's dialogues. Some, though still extant in manuscript, have remained unpublished (*Parmenides, Lysis, Euthyphron, Charmides, Laches*). But the *Protagoras*, the *Phaedrus*, the *Gorgias* and the *Apology*, as well as certain passages from the *Parmenides* and other dialogues, were finally published in 1834 in W. J. Fox's brilliant periodical, the *Monthly Repository*. We owe it to Mrs Ruth Borchardt that they were republished in 1946 under the title *Four Dialogues of Plato*. Mill's annotations foreshadowed most of his later preoccupations and works. As regards logic, Mill extolled Plato's method in his comments on the *Phaedrus*, 'this twofold process of analysis and synthesis... the grand instrument of Plato's philosophizing'.[1] Apart from his father's tuition, Mill, by this time, had read Schleiermacher's essay on the 'Worth of Socrates as a philosopher' in Connop Thirlwall's translation.[2] Schleiermacher, who drew a separating line between Socrates and Plato, portrayed Socrates, not so much as a moral teacher, but as the founder of scientific method and the art of dialectics, which aimed at distinguishing true knowledge from mere opinion by a combination of induction and deduction. Mill found his own view confirmed by Schleiermacher's understanding of Socrates, although he never shared Schleiermacher's monolithic interpretation of Plato as an artist-philosopher. Like Grote he appreciated different facets of Plato, the dialectic critic, the artist, the dogmatic philosopher and the religious mystic, without wishing to force these qualities into full harmony with each other.

Why were the Mills and George Grote so deeply interested in the

---

[1] *Four Dialogues of Plato. Translations and Notes by John Stuart Mill*, ed. Ruth Borchardt (London, 1946), p. 103.

[2] *Ibid.* pp. 42–3. Thirlwall's translation of Schleiermacher's essay (1815) was first published in the *Philological Museum* (Cambridge), and later in book form, together with Diogenes Laertius' *Life of Socrates*, ed. G. F. Wiggers (London, 1840). Mill is likely to have discussed the essay with George Grote who received Schleiermacher as a visitor in his house in 1828. Mrs Grote, *Personal Life*, p. 48.

dialectical method? Were they not Utopians in adopting and developing a formal procedure which they expected to help unravel true and false as well as scrutinising and illuminating moral and political questions? In the present climate of opinion, which favours intuition or reconstructive imagination while rejecting experiment and ratiocination, even judicious attempts at developing a methodology of the social sciences have become suspect. It is, however, not only the apostles of continental Romanticism who reject the idea of an objective social science. The question became very much a Cambridge and family debate in the wake of John Stuart Mill's *Logic* and *Utilitarianism*, with John Grote, George's brother, attacking the utilitarian position, and Neville Keynes, John Maynard's father, siding with Mill;[1] it was indeed a debate largely carried on in terms of the right understanding of Platonic philosophy. For John Grote political and moral notions like justice were a matter of intuition engendered by feelings of sympathy and moral imagination. Mill, while equally taking imagination and affections into account, was aware of the practical need to reconcile the diverging intuitions of contending parties by arguments and insights derived from a neutral and critical procedure such as the Platonic *elenchus* had first introduced. He did not regard the inductive–deductive method as a tool for discovering new truths nor as a ritual facilitating pure speculation. He conceived of it as a formal method for putting opinions and hypotheses to the test by pinpointing and eliminating traditional prejudices and verbal or logical fallacies.[2] Any victim of summary justice or political arbitrariness will understand the need for formal safeguards as an integral part of the democratic process, insofar as it serves the interests of the individual no less than those of the state or society.

Unlike his father, John Mill wished to proceed from a mere

---

[1] John Grote, *A Treatise on the Moral Ideals*, ed. J. B. Mayor (Cambridge, 1876); 'A discussion between Prof. Henry Sidgwick and the late Prof. John Grote on the utilitarian basis of Plato's Republic', *Classical Review*, III (1889), 97–102, quoted by L. D. Macdonald, *John Grote* (The Hague, 1966), pp. 210–15; John Neville Keynes, *The Scope and Method of Political Economy* (London, 1891); W. E. Johnson, *Logic*, 3 Parts (Cambridge, 1921–4), esp. Part II and Part I, Preface. See J. L. Mackie, 'Mill's methods of induction', *Encyclopedia of Philosophy*, ed. Paul Edwards (New York, 1967), vol. v, pp. 324–32.

[2] Mill's philosophy is of course complex, its validity a matter of controversy which cannot be treated here. Of great scientists, Justus von Liebig described his *Organic Chemistry* as an application of ideas found in Mill's *Logic* while Sir Peter Medawar rejects Mill's methodology as unrealistic. On all counts, however, book VI of the *Logic* is a fundamental contribution to the logic of the social sciences.

hypothetical science of *government* to a comprehensive ('concrete' and 'inverse' deductive) science and art of *politics* which took account of history, individual dispositions and general civilisation.[1] His political, social and economic analysis was more searching, and he asked deeper questions, perhaps deeper than we are fitted to answer. Unlike Bentham and James Mill, he relied, not merely on institutions, checks and controls, but also on the aspirations and qualities of individual citizens. He returned to the ancient democratic ideal. 'The worth of a State, in the long run, is the worth of the individuals composing it...a State which dwarfs its men...even for beneficial purposes – will find...that the perfection of machinery will in the end avail nothing.'[2] Mill feared that representative democracy would eventually turn into bureaucracy. Bureaucratic government would have the advantage of accumulated experience, but would succumb to its occupational disease, routine; it would lead to a pedantocracy and a society of place-hunters.[3]

His unbounded admiration for Socrates caused Mill to exaggerate the value of dissent: 'improvement in human affairs is wholly the work of the uncontented characters'.[4] Mill's ideas concerning the middle class and the stationary state, that is the need for education and the ideal of a non-acquisitive society, were in keeping with, and probably influenced by, Plato and Aristotle. His clear insight into the class struggle, much clearer than his father's, and prior to Marx's, must have been sharpened by his Greek mentors, though, of course, they were not the only influence in this regard. Mill cherished the ideals of an egalitarian, even socialist, democracy; at the same time, he was keenly aware of the dangers inherent in ignorance and in the possession of power; it corrupted man as well as classes of men. 'One of the greatest dangers, therefore, of democracy, as of all other forms of government...is the danger of class legislation' by any 'class of men; the Demos, or any other'.[5] Like Plato and Bentham, but unlike his father, Mill was of course the champion of the equality of women.

---

[1] *Logic*, book VI, esp. chs. VI, IX, X, XI.
[2] *On Liberty*, p. 104.
[3] *Ibid.* pp. 99ff., also pp. 54, 60, 62, 104; *Representative Government*, pp. 159, 179, 187, 189, 193.
[4] *Representative Government*, p. 145. 'Uncontented' is not equivalent to 'discontented', although leading social reformers today do not appear to make this distinction. Mill's extolling of the autonomous character, like many of his ideas, anticipates Max Weber, while diverging from Hume's judicious rejection of extravagance in political and social life (*A Dialogue*, concluding paras.).
[5] *Ibid.* pp. 186–7.

Going beyond Greek models, he argued in favour of dissenting minorities, proportional representation as a means towards that end, and the right of workers to combine in trade unions; he was ambiguous as regards picketing and the closed shop.[1] Following Sismondi and his disciples, Mill championed industrial democracy, workers' participation and profit sharing as well as land reform in favour of the peasantry. In the Scots tradition he advocated cultural democracy, the widening of educational opportunity, intellectual, moral, and aesthetic, for as he put it, 'Modern nations will have to learn the lesson that the well-being of a people must exist by means of justice and self-government, the δικαιοσύνη and σωφροσύνη of the individual citizen'.[2] He may have been too optimistic here, but, again, he formulated his thought with an idealised Athens in mind.

May I finally say that, given the limited time at my disposal, I have not attempted to present an exhaustive account of Hellenic influences on the work of the English utilitarians.

[1] 'Thornton on labour and its claims' (1869), *Essays on Economics and Society*, in *Collected Works*, vol. IV, Part II (Toronto, 1967), 631–68.
[2] *Principles of Political Economy*, book IV, ch. VII, § 2.

15

DIE BEDEUTUNG DER KLASSISCHEN VORBILDER BEIM ALTEN GOETHE

THOMAS GELZER

Goethes und seiner meisten deutschen Zeitgenossen Interesse am Altertum unterscheidet sich wesentlich von demjenigen etwa in den angelsächsischen Ländern, oder auch in Frankreich und in der Schweiz, durch den weitgehenden Ausschluss alles dessen, was den Staat und die Politik betrifft. Es konzentriert sich dagegen fast ausschliesslich auf die Domäne von Kunst, Literatur und Philosophie, dessen also, was man im Deutschen, im wesentlichen seit und wegen Goethe, als 'Bildung' oder spezifischer als 'Geistesbildung' zu bezeichnen gewohnt ist.[1]

In allen Perioden seines Lebens hat Goethe den Vorbildern des klassischen Altertums in dieser Hinsicht ihre bestimmte Bedeutung zugemessen, und zwar in zweierlei Richtung: einerseits zur Bildung des Geschmacks für die Beurteilung geschaffener Kunstwerke, und anderseits als Muster für die eigene schöpferische Gestaltung. Aber seine Beurteilung der Bedeutung dieser Vorbilder war durch die verschiedenen Zeiten hin Wandlungen unterworfen, und Goethe war sich dessen, besonders in seinen späteren Jahren, als er sich selber zum Gegenstand der Geschichte geworden war, auch durchaus bewusst. Aus diesem Problemkreis möchte ich hier einen Aspekt herausgreifen: wie sich nämlich Goethes Einschätzung des klassischen Altertums als Vorbild[2] in seinem Alter, der Zeit als er etwa von seinem 75. Altersjahr an den zweiten Teil des *Faust* gestaltete, unterscheidet von derjenigen seiner hochklassizistischen Periode um 1800. Seine Auffassungen in dieser späteren Zeit haben sich namentlich auch deutlich entfernt von denjenigen Wilhelm von Humboldts,

---

[1] Zu 'Bildung', in diesem Wortgebrauch wohl zuerst bei Moses Mendelssohn, durch Goethe 'in den gemeindeutschen Wortschatz übergegangen', s. F. Kluge und A. Götze, *Etymologisches Wörterbuch der deutschen Sprache*, 13nte. Aufl. (Berlin, 1943), s.v.

[2] Die Belege zu Goethes Beschäftigung mit dem Altertum und seinen Autoren sind verzeichnet von E. Grumach, *Goethe und die Antike, Eine Sammlung* (2 Bde., Berlin, 1949); Goethes eigene Äusserungen zum *Faust* von H. G. Gräf, *Goethe über seine Dichtungen*, Teil II, Bd. II (Frankfurt a.M., 1904), dazu weitere Sammlungen verzeichnet von H. Henning, *Faust-Bibliographie*, Teil II, *Goethes Faust*, Bd. II, *Sekundärliteratur zu Goethes Faust, 1. Halbband* (Berlin und Weimar, 1970), S. 5ff.

die dann über die von seinen Ideen wesentlich mitbestimmten Institutionen der Universität und des Gymnasiums ihre unmittelbare Wirkung auf die Bildung der Deutschen im neunzehnten Jahrhundert ausgeübt haben. Während etwa Humboldt in einem Brief an F. G. Welcker 1823 betont, dass er auch die Werke anderer alter Literaturen wie etwa das *Mahabharata*, das *Ramayana* und das *Nibelungenlied*, in der Ursprache zu lesen und zu beurteilen imstande sei, und doch 'alle Einmischung und allen Parallelismus' mit dem dagegen unvergleichlich viel höher bewerteten Homer and überhaupt mit der griechischen Literatur ausschliesst,[1] sind bei Goethe in derselben Zeit andere Einflüsse hinzugekommen, die ihn zu einem wesentlich differenzierteren Verhältnis zum klassischen Altertum gebracht haben.

I

Da wir hier nicht die Fülle der Dokumentation ausbreiten können,[2] wollen wir diesen Gegensatz an einem konkreten Beispiel illustrieren, der 'Helena' nämlich, deren dichterische Gestaltung Goethe in diesen beiden Lebensabschnitten beschäftigt hat. Der Konzeption des zweiten Teils des *Faust* lag von Anfang an die Absicht einer Wirkung auf die Bildung seiner Zeitgenossen zugrunde. Darüber hat sich Goethe immer wieder geäussert, besonders eingehend etwa gegenüber dem Bremer Schriftsteller und Übersetzer K. J. L. Iken (1789–1841), der ihm am 25. August 1827 begeistert und mit

---

[1] 'Ich bin nicht günstiger gestimmt gegen die Einmischung des Indischen und Ägyptischen. Denn was man auch von der Schönheit und Erhabenheit des Ramayana, Mahabharat, der Nibelungen sagen mag, um nur das zu nennen, was ich doch nun, so gut als ein anderer, in grossen Stücken in der Urschrift gelesen habe, so fehlt immer gerade das Eine, in dem der ganze Zauber des Griechischen liegt, was man mit keinem Worte ganz aussprechen kann, aber was man tief und menschlich fühlt, was machen würde, dass in jeder ernsthaftesten und heitersten, glücklichsten und wehmütigsten Katastrophe des Lebens, ja im Momente des Todes, einige Verse des Homer, und, ich möchte sagen, wenn sie aus dem Schiffskatalogus wären, mir mehr das Gefühl des Überschwankens der Menschheit in die Gottheit (was doch die Summe alles menschlichen Fühlens und alles irdischen Trostes ist) geben würden, als irgend etwas von einem anderen Volke...' (*W. v. Humboldts Briefe an F. G. Welcker*, hsg. R. Haym (Berlin, 1859), S. 101f.; hier zitiert nach M. Wegner, *Altertumskunde* (Freiburg und München, 1951), S. 161f.; vgl. unten, S. 318, Anm. 1.

[2] Sammlung der Sekundärliteratur zu Goethe und die Antike bei Grumach, *Goethe und die Antike*, S. 1053–74; zur Fülle dieser Arbeiten vgl. die einleitenden Bemerkungen zu Goethe und die Antike in *Goethe-Bibliographie*, begründet v. H. Pyritz...fortgeführt v. H. Nicolai, G. Burkhardt und K. Schröder (Heidelberg, 1965), S. 385f. (zur Literatur bis 1954) und dass. Bd. II (Heidelberg, 1968), S. 98f. (zur Literatur 1955–64). Eine Diskussion der äusserst umfangreichen Sekundärliteratur ist hier unmöglich. Im folgenden werden nur einzelne Nachweise zu Autoren gegeben, deren Arbeiten mir zur Vorbereitung dieses Kurzreferats von besonderem Nutzen waren.

einfühlendem Verständnis über die eben erschienene 'Helena'
geschrieben hatte. Ihm antwortete er am 27. September mit
erklärenden Ausführungen, die uns eine Reihe von höchst aufschluss-
reichen Stichworten zu unserem Gegenstand liefern:[1]

Bei der hohen Kultur der Bessern unsres Vaterlandes konnte ich zwar ein solches
beifälliges Ergreifen gar wohl erwarten... Ich zweifelte niemals, dass die Leser,
für die ich eigentlich schrieb, den Hauptsinn dieser Darstellung sogleich erfassen
würden. Es ist Zeit, dass der leidenschaftliche Zwiespalt zwischen Klassikern und
Romantikern sich endlich versöhne. Dass wir uns bilden ist die Hauptforderung;
woher wir uns bilden wäre gleichgültig, wenn wir uns nicht an falschen Mustern
zu verbilden fürchten müssten. Ist es doch eine weitere und reinere Umsicht in
und über griechische und römische Literatur, der wir die Befreiung aus mönchischer Barbarei zwischen dem 15. und 16. Jahrhundert verdanken! Lernen wir
nicht auf dieser hohen Stelle alles in seinem wahren ethisch-aesthetischen Werte
schätzen, das Älteste wie das Neuste!... Von einer Seite wird dem Philologen
nichts Geheimes bleiben, er wird sich vielmehr an dem wiederbelebten Altertum,
das er schon kennt, ergötzen; von der andern Seite wird ein Fühlender dasjenige
durchdringen, was gemütlich hie und da versteckt liegt...

Auf den ersten Blick sieht dieses Bekenntnis zur Bildung an den
Mustern der griechischen und römischen Literatur recht ähnlich aus
wie das, was der Maler und nachmals berühmte Archäologe und
Ausgräber von Pompeii, Wilhelm Zahn (1800–71), berichtet über
die Äusserungen Goethes, als er ihm zehn Tage früher, am 17.
September 1827, die eben aus Italien zurückgebrachten farbigen
Durchzeichnungen neu entdeckter pompeianischer Wandmalereien
vorlegen durfte.[2] Bei deren Betrachtung sei Goethe in stille Andacht
versunken und dann in die Worte ausgebrochen: 'Ja, die Alten sind
auf jedem Gebiete der heiligen Kunst unerreichbar. – Sehen Sie,
meine Herren, ich glaube auch etwas geleistet zu haben, aber gegen
einen der grossen attischen Dichter, wie Aeschylos und Sophokles,
bin ich doch gar nichts.' Zahn lässt hier Goethe allerdings grade
jenen Tragiker nicht erwähnen, den er sich für die 'Helena'
besonders zum Vorbild genommen hatte, Euripides. Dieser hatte
Goethe zu allen Zeiten besonders zur schöpferischen Auseinandersetzung angeregt, für die Iphigenie nicht weniger als zur Zeit, als er
mit Schiller seinen Aufsatz 'Über epische und dramatische Dichtung'
von 1797 diskutierte, und dann besonders wieder, als er sich von 1821

[1] Der Brief hier zitiert nach J. W. Goethe, *Briefe der Jahre 1814–1832*, hsg. C. Beutler
(Artemis-Gedenkausgabe, Bd. xxi, Zürich, 1951), S. 761–4; Gräf, *Goethe über seine
Dichtungen*, Nr. 1531, lag nur das Briefkonzept vom 23. September 1827 vor.
[2] Hier zitiert nach *Goethes Gespräche*, nach Biedermann ergänzt und hsg. W. Herwig,
Bd. iii, Teil ii (Zürich, 1972), Nr. 6056, S. 198–204 ('O. Glagau, Ein Künstlerbesuch
beim Altmeister Goethe' nach dem Bericht von W. Zahn, 1864).

an an den Versuch einer Wiederherstellung des *Phaethon* anhand der von Gottfried Hermann publizierten Bruchstücke und an die Übersetzung einer Szene seines Lieblingsstücks, der *Bachantinnen* (1244–98) machte. Bei beiden unterstützten ihn die Philologen Göttling und Riemer, denen er auch die 'Helena' zum Revidieren übergab, beide publizierte er in seiner Hauszeitschrift *Über Kunst und Altertum*, und mit beiden beschäftigte er sich gerade 1825 und 1826, zur Zeit der Ausarbeitung der 'Helena', wieder besonders intensiv. Euripides hat man also im konkretesten Wortsinn zu jenen 'klassischen Mustern' zu rechnen, an denen sich Goethe für sein in der 'Helena' wiederbelebtes Altertum gebildet hat, und an denen die Philologen sich ergötzen konnten. In dieser Hinsicht setzte er damals nur fort, was er 1800 begonnen, dann aber unvollendet hatte liegen lassen.

II

An Humboldt schrieb er am 22. Oktober 1826, um sein Interesse auf das bevorstehende Erscheinen der 'Helena' hinzulenken: 'Erinnern Sie sich wohl noch, mein Teuerster, einer dramatischen "Helena", die im zweiten Teile des "Faust" erscheinen sollte? Aus Schillers Briefen vom Anfang des Jahrhunderts sehe ich, dass ich ihm den Anfang vorzeigte, auch dass er mich zur Fortsetzung treulich ermahnte.' Die, auch Humboldt damals vorgelesene, Fassung des Anfangs von 1800, auf die er damit verweist, ist uns als Fragment von 265 Versen erhalten, und Goethe hat bekanntlich diese Versreihe in der endgültigen Fassung mit unbedeutenden Abweichungen, aber mit einigen Erweiterungen (namentlich um drei Interventionen des Chors und ganz wenige Verse der Helena selber) wiederverwendet.[1] Sie besteht aus einem Monolog der Helena bis zu ihrem Eintritt in den Palast (jetzt 8489–515, 8524–59, 8569–90), ihrem Dialog mit der Chorführerin, nachdem sie drinnen der bedrohlichen Schreckgestalt am Herd begegnet ist (8638–96), dem Chorlied nach dem Erscheinen der Phorkyas, die ihr gefolgt ist (8697–753), und dem ersten Redentausch zwischen der Phorkyas und Helena (8754–802). Grade weil die Verse dieses nach dem Muster des Euripides gestalteten Stücks in der ersten Fassung von 1800 und in der

---

[1] *Werke*, hsg. Erich Schmidt (Weimarer Ausgabe), Bd. xv, Abt. 2, S. 72–81; über die Umarbeitung und den Stilwandel zwischen der ersten und der zweiten Verwendung dieser Verse vgl. z. B. E. Trunz, *Goethes Werke* (Hamburger Ausgabe), Bd. III, 6te. Aufl. (Hamburg, 1962), S. 579ff. nach R. Alewyn, 'Goethe und die Antike', *Das humanistische Gymnasium*, XLIII (1932), 114–24.

endgültigen von 1826 sozusagen identisch sind, ist es so faszinierend zu beobachten, wie verschieden die Funktion ist, die diese selben Verse im Zusammenhang der damals geplanten und der zuletzt ausgeführten Version zu erfüllen haben, und wie sich daran eben auch die Veränderung der Bedeutung dieses selben antiken Vorbilds von der einen zur andern ablesen lässt. Die entscheidenden Aufklärungen über jene erste Periode erhalten wir eben aus dem Briefwechsel mit Schiller und aus einem Bericht Friedrich Schlegels, mit dem Goethe sich damals darüber unterhalten hat.

Am 12. September 1800 meldet Goethe erstmals an Schiller: 'Meine Helena ist aufgetreten.' Sie erscheint, wie dem Philologen nicht verborgen bleibt,[1] in einer Situation, die dem Prolog des euripideischen *Orestes* (53ff.) nachgebildet ist, von Menelaos bei der Rückkehr von Troia in die Stadt vorausgesandt (8524ff.). Schiller hält die Wirkung fest, die ihre Prologrede auf ihn ausgeübt hat (23. September 1800): 'Ihre neuliche Vorlesung hat mich mit einem grossen und vornehmen Eindruck hinterlassen, der edle hohe Geist der alten Tragödie weht aus dem Monolog einem entgegen und macht den gehörigen Effekt, indem er ruhig mächtig das Tiefste aufregt...', ja, Schiller ist von ihrer Form so beeindruckt, dass er selber sich das ungewohnte klassische Versmass anzueignen beabsichtigt (27. September 1800):

Wenn Sie mir den Hermann von den griechischen Silbenmassen[2] zu lesen verschaffen könnten, so wäre mir's sehr lieb; Ihre neuliche Vorlesung hat mich auf die Trimeters aufmerksam gemacht, und ich wünschte in die Sache mehr einzudringen. Auch habe ich grosse Lust mich in Nebenstunden etwas mit dem Griechischen zu beschäftigen, nur um so weit zu kommen, dass ich in die griechische Metrik eine Einsicht erhalte.

Friedrich Schlegel folgerte nach mehreren Unterhaltungen mit Goethe (an A. W. Schlegel): 'dass ein gewaltiges griechisches Trauerspiel von ihm zu erwarten ist in Trimetern und chorähnlichen Chören...' Die Vorstellung, die in Goethes Unterhaltungen und durch die Vorlesungen der Trimeter und Chorlieder geweckt worden war, ist also diejenige von einer antikisierenden Tragödie, und die davon ausgehende Anregung wirkt weiter. Schiller teilt

---

[1] Die Nachweise z. B. bei Dorothea Lohmeyer, *Faust und die Welt, Der zweite Teil der Dichtung, Eine Anleitung zum Lesen des Textes*, 2te. Aufl. (München, 1975), 'Die Euripideischen Motive', S. 292–4.

[2] Gottfried Hermann, *De metris poetarum Graecorum et Latinorum* (1796); die Nachweise Anm. S. 313, 1. S. 319, 2. S. 320, 2 bei Grumach, *Goethe und die Antike*, S. 251ff.

schon am 13. Mai 1801 Körner mit:[1] 'Ich habe grosse Lust, mich nunmehr in der einfachen Tragödie nach der strengsten griechischen Form zu versuchen.' Sein 'Sujet' ist die *Braut von Messina*. 'Es besteht, den Chor mit gerechnet, nur aus 20 Szenen und fünf Personen. Goethe billigt den Plan ganz...'

Aber Goethe gerät mit seiner eigenen 'Helena' in Schwierigkeiten, wie er die klassische antike Heroine nach ihrem Monolog mit dem Teufelswerk des Mephisto verbinden soll (an Schiller 12. September 1800): 'Nun zieht mich aber das Schöne in der Lage meiner Heldin so sehr an, dass es mich betrübt, wenn ich es zunächst in eine Fratze verwandeln soll. Wirklich fühle ich nicht geringe Lust, eine ernsthafte Tragödie auf das Angefangene zu gründen.' Aufschlussreich sind die Ausdrücke, die Schiller in seinem Kommentar zu diesen Bedenken für die klassische Komponente dieser Verbindung und für das ihr Entgegengesetzte verwendet (13. September 1800):

Lassen Sie sich aber ja nicht durch den Gedanken stören, wenn die schönen Gestalten und Situationen kommen, dass es schade sei, sie zu verbarbarieren... Das Barbarische der Behandlung, das Ihnen durch den Geist des Ganzen auferlegt wird, kann den höheren Gehalt nicht zerstören und das Schöne nicht aufheben, nur es anders spezifizieren... Eben das Höhere und Vornehmere in den Motiven wird dem Werk einen eigenen Reiz geben, und Helena ist in diesem Stück ein Symbol für alle die schönen Gestalten, die sich hinein verirren werden.

Und Goethe bestätigt (16. September 1800): 'Der Trost,... dass durch die Verbindung des Reinen und des Abenteuerlichen ein nicht ganz verwerfliches Ungeheuer entstehen könne, hat sich durch die Erfahrung schon an mir bestätigt, indem aus dieser Amalgamation seltsame Erscheinungen, an denen ich selber einiges Gefallen habe, hervortreten.' Die Lösung folgt wieder Euripides: in einer ebenfalls vom *Orestes* (1005ff.) angeregten Situation – dort versuchen Orest und Pylades Helena im eigenen Palast zu ermorden – lässt er die Phorkyas, als vorgebliche alte Schaffnerin, Helena in ihrem Palast drohend entgegentreten (8653ff.). Damit ist ihm ein weiterer Schritt in der Richtung der intendierten klassischen Tragödie gelungen (an Schiller 23. September 1800): 'Die Hauptmomente des Plans sind in Ordnung, und... das sehe ich schon, dass von diesem Gipfel aus, sich erst die rechte Ansicht über das Ganze zeigen wird.' Und wieder ermutigt Schiller (23. September 1800): 'Gelingt Ihnen diese Synthese des Edlen mit dem Barba-

---

[1] Zitiert nach F. Schiller, *Sämtliche Werke*, Bd. II, *Dramen II*, hsg. G. Fricke, G. Göpfert und H. Stubenrauch, 4te. Aufl. (München, 1965), S. 1277.

rischen,...so wird auch der Schlüssel zu dem übrigen Teil des Ganzen gefunden sein...'

Die Leitbegriffe, in denen die Intentionen bei diesem Experiment einer klassischen Tragödie in Trimetern nach Euripides qualifiziert werden, sind also: 'das Schöne in der Lage meiner Heldin', 'die schönen Gestalten und Situationen', 'das Höhere und Vornehmere', 'der grosse und vornehme Eindruck', 'das Edle', 'das Reine', 'das Symbol für alle schönen Gestalten', 'dieser Gipfel', 'der edle hohe Geist der alten Tragödie' – und dem steht gegenüber das, was nicht klassisch griechisch ist: 'das Barbarische', 'das Abenteuerliche'; die Verbindung damit könnte das Klassische 'verbarbarieren', würde zum 'Ungeheuer'.

Das Bild von einer hochklassizistischen Tragödie, das sich in dieser Terminologie für den Plan von 1800 erkennen lässt, tritt noch markanter heraus, wenn man die Funktion mit berücksichtigt, die dieser Teil in der damals vorgesehenen Anlage des ganzen *Faust II* zu erfüllen gehabt hätte: 'Es ist eine meiner ältesten Konzeptionen', fährt Goethe in dem zitierten Brief an Humboldt (22. Oktober 1826) fort. 'Sie ruht auf der Puppenspiel-Überlieferung, dass Faust den Mephistopheles genötigt, ihm die Helena zum Beilager heranzuschaffen.' Dieser Überlieferung entsprechend hätte sich, nach der 'Skizze der Urgestalt',[1] die Goethe 1816 für das 18. Buch von *Dichtung und Wahrheit* diktierte, dieses klassizistische Drama der 'Helena' nicht in Griechenland, sondern in einem alten Schloss in Deutschland abspielen sollen: 'Sie glaubt soeben von Troia zu kommen und in Sparta einzutreffen.' Der Gegensatz des Klassischen und des Barbarischen kommt in diesem Plan noch recht handfest zum Ausdruck: 'Faust tritt auf und steht als deutscher Ritter sehr wunderlich gegen die antike Heldengestalt. Sie findet ihn abscheulich, allein, da er zu schmeicheln weiss, so findet sie sich nach und nach in ihn, und er wird der Nachfolger so mancher Heroen und Halbgötter.' Die Verschmelzung der verschiedenen Elemente zu einer ernsthaften Tragödie war auf dieser Stufe der Erfindung noch nicht gelungen, und das Fragment wurde abgelegt unter dem ebenfalls bezeichnenden Titel: 'Helena im Mittelalter. Satyr-Drama'.

[1] So bezeichnet von Erich Schmidt, 'Paralipomenon 63', *Werke* (Weimarer Ausgabe), Bd. xv, Abt. 2, S. 173–7.

In der Fassung von 1826 sind dann dieselben Verse erstens in einer veränderten dramatischen Situation verwendet. Helena glaubt jetzt nicht mehr nur in Sparta einzutreffen, sondern, wie es Goethe in der Ankündigung für *Kunst und Altertum* ausdrückt: 'Gegenwärtig ist genug, wenn man zugibt, dass die wahre Helena auf antik-tragischem Kothurn vor ihrer Urwohnung in Sparta auftreten könne.' Zweitens tritt aber damit das klassische Stück ein in ein völlig verändertes Bezugssystem. Im selben Brief an Humboldt schreibt er dazu:

Ich habe von Zeit zu Zeit daran gearbeitet; aber abgeschlossen konnte das Stück nicht werden, als in der Fülle der Zeiten, da es denn jetzt seine volle 3000 Jahre spielt, von Troias Untergang bis zur Einnahme von Missolunghi. Dies kann man also auch für eine Zeiteinheit nehmen, im höheren Sinne. Die Einheit des Orts und der Handlung sind aber auch im gewöhnlichen Sinne auf's genaueste beobachtet.

Nicht nur die Zeiten, sondern auch die Literaturen des Altertums und der Neuzeit, von Homer bis Byron, sind damit in einer Einheit im höheren Sinne verbunden. Damit wird nun auch das Klassische nicht mehr dem Barbarischen gegenübergestellt, sondern, wie Goethe an Iken erklärte, ist jetzt der 'Hauptsinn dieser Darstellung – dass der leidenschaftliche Zwiespalt zwischen Klassikern und Romantikern sich endlich versöhne.' Auch dieses Gegensatzpaar führt übrigens Goethe 1830 auf die Zeit und die Umstände zurück, in denen jene erste Konzeption der *Helena* entstanden war (Eckermann, 21. März 1830):

Der Begriff von klassischer und romantischer Poesie, der jetzt...so viel Streit und Spannungen verursacht, ist ursprünglich von mir und Schiller ausgegangen... Die Schlegel ergriffen die Idee und trieben sie weiter, sodass sie sich denn jetzt über die ganze Welt ausgedehnt hat und nun jedermann von Klassizismus und Romantizismus redet, woran vor fünfzig Jahren niemand dachte.

Die *Helena* hat damit in dieser neuen Konzeption eine in mehreren Hinsichten veränderte Funktion erhalten.

Was bedeutet das nun für die klassischen Vorbilder? Bei der endgültigen Ausarbeitung der 'Helena' hat Goethe für diesen ersten, klassischen Teil weitere euripideische Motive verwendet: für die Drohung mit der Opferung der Helena auf Befehl des Menelaos (8920ff.) den entsprechenden Befehl ihres Mannes in den *Troerinnen* (876ff.), und dann für den Abschluss durch eine Entrückung in die mittelalterliche Burg (9113ff., 9142ff.) die Entrückung der Helena durch Apoll am Ende des *Orestes* (1692ff.). Mit der ganzen 'Helena' haben aber auch diese klassischen Vorbilder im weiteren Zusammenhang der neuen Konzeption ihre Funktion verändert.

Die Stichwörter, die er in seiner Erklärung an Iken gibt, lassen die Richtung erkennen, in der sich Goethes Verhältnis zu ihnen entwickelt hat: 'Dass wir uns bilden, ist die Hauptforderung' – und eben für diese Bildung haben die Vorbilder ihre Bedeutung; aber welche? 'Woher wir uns bilden wäre gleichgültig, wenn wir uns nicht an falschen Mustern zu verbilden fürchten müssen.' Gleichgültig – die klassischen Vorbilder sind also nicht die einzig möglichen Muster. Und doch behalten sie ihre Bedeutung, jetzt aber mit einer spezifischen Begründung: 'Ist es doch eine weitere und reinere Umsicht in und über griechische und römische Literatur, der wir die Befreiung aus mönchischer Barbarei zwischen dem 15. und 16. Jahrhundert verdanken!' Die klassischen Vorbilder stehen am Beginn unserer eigenen europäischen Literatur der Neuzeit. Weil die klassische antike Literatur neue Wertmassstäbe setzte, öffnete sie den Weg zu neuen Entwicklungen, die damals zur Überwindung einer ganz spezifischen 'Barbarei' führten. Heute aber haben sie ihre Bedeutung in einem viel weiteren Rahmen: 'Lernen wir nicht auf dieser hohen Stelle alles in seinem wahren ethisch–aesthetischen Werte schätzen, das Älteste wie das Neuste?' Also: 'alles', nicht nur historische Meisterwerke unserer Kultur, auch nicht etwa nur das Klassische oder das Romantische, sondern besonders auch 'das Neuste' kann richtig geschätzt werden, gemessen an diesem Qualitätsmasstab. Nicht zufällig richtet Goethe diese Erklärung an Iken, den Übersetzer persischer und neugriechischer Literatur, dessen Schriften er kurz darauf (1828) selber im Rahmen seines Bildungsprogramms der 'Weltliteratur'[1] in *Kunst und Altertum* bespricht.

IV

Was war geschehen mit den klassischen Vorbildern seit 1800, und was war die Voraussetzung dafür, dass Goethe nun sogar sagen konnte, dass es 'gleichgültig' wäre, 'woher wir uns bilden'? Goethe selber hatte seit jener Zeit seine eigene Bildung, angeregt von der

---

[1] Goethes eigene Äusserungen zum Thema 'Weltliteratur' sind bequem zusammengestellt und hsg. von Fritz Strich in J. W. Goethe, *Schriften zur Literatur* (Artemis-Gedenkausgabe, Bd. XIV, Zürich, 1950), diejenigen zur Antike, S. 601–716, zum Orient, S. 717–25, zur europäischen Literatur, S. 726–968, mit ausgezeichneten Bemerkungen zur Bedeutung der Antike innerhalb dieses Konzepts in der 'Einführung', S. 1030ff.

romantischen philologischen und historischen Wissenschaft, in neue, ihm bisher kaum bekannte Gebiete ausgeweitet, die ihn in schöpferischer Auseinandersetzung mit 'Mustern' ganz anderer Herkunft zu neuen eigenen Gestaltungen geführt hatten. Grade die persische Dichtung gehörte dazu. Auch sie wurde ihm 'musterhaft', mit der ganzen Poesie des alten Orients,[1] der persischen und arabischen, die er sich in entschiedener Zuwendung seit 1808 immer gründlicher aneignete bis zum Studium der originalen Sprachdenkmäler. 'Die sämtlichen Gedichte Hafis in der von Hammerschen Übersetzung', die er ein Jahr zuvor kennengelernt hatte, übten dann jene überwältigende Wirkung auf ihn aus, die er in den *Tag- und Jahresheften* (zu 1815) schildert: 'Wenn ich früher den hier und da in Zeitschriften übersetzt mitgeteilten einzelnen Stücken dieses herrlichen Poeten nichts abgewinnen konnte, so wirkten sie doch jetzt zusammen desto lebhafter auf mich ein, und ich musste mich dagegen produktiv verhalten, weil ich sonst vor der mächtigen Erscheinung nicht hätte bestehen können.' Sie war mit dem Erscheinen des *West-östlichen Divans* (1819), der Frucht dieser Anregungen, keineswegs beendet. Eben zur Zeit der Arbeit an der 'Helena', im März 1826, bekannte er erneut:

> So der Westen wie der Osten
> Geben Reines Dir zu kosten.

Der *Divan*, das Werk des damals 70-jährigen, ist nur ein Beispiel, wenn auch das grossartigste, für die Wirkungen dieser neuen Öffnung auf den alten Goethe. Hier ist nicht der Ort, auf den unmittelbaren Niederschlag einzutreten, den die ununterbrochene Beschäftigung mit dem Orient auch im zweiten Teil des *Faust* gefunden hat,[2] noch auch auf jene anderen Gebiete, der Naturwissenschaft und der Kunst, der Literatur vom deutschen und europäischen Mittelalter

---

[1] Über die Gefahr der falschen 'Vergleichung' spricht sich Goethe, im Gegensatz zu Humboldt (1823, also nach dem Erscheinen des *Divan*, s. S. 310, Anm. 1), aus in den *Noten und Abhandlungen zu besserem Verständnis des West-östlichen Divans*, im Abschnitt 'Warnung': 'Wir wissen die Dichtkunst der Orientalen zu schätzen...aber man vergleiche sie mit sich selbst, man ehre sie in ihrem eigenen Kreise, und vergesse doch dabei, dass es Griechen und Römer gegeben. Niemandem verarge man, welchem Horaz bei Hafis einfällt...Was wir aber inständig bitten, ist, dass man Ferdusi nicht mit Homer vergleiche, weil er in jedem Sinne, dem Stoff, der Form, der Behandlung nach, verlieren muss...Haben wir Deutsche nicht unsern herrlichen "Nibelungen" durch solche Vergleichung den grössten Schaden getan?' Und über seine eigene Aneignung im Abschnitt 'Übersetzungen', *ibid.*; s. dazu z. B. Goethe, *Schriften zur Literatur*, hsg. Strich, S. 986ff.

[2] Dazu J. C. Bürgel, 'Goethe und Hafis', *Drei Hafis-Studien* (Bern und Frankfurt a.M., 1975), S. 6f. mit neuster Sekundärliteratur zu Goethes Gebrauch des Orients.

bis zu den fernsten aussereuropäischen Völkern, die sich Goethe zur selben Zeit mit ungeheurer Intensität neu erschlossen hat.[1]

In diesem Kosmos sind die klassischen Vorbilder zwar nicht die einzigen möglichen Muster der Bildung; aber sie erhalten deshalb für Goethe nicht eine verminderte, wohl aber eine veränderte, und im weiteren Zusammenhang eher noch wesentlichere Bedeutung. 'Je mehr man durchdrungen ist von dem Werte der Bildung, die wir den alten Schriftstellern verdanken', schreibt er am 22. Juli 1821 an J. H. Voss Sohn, 'desto mehr lernt man nach und nach einsehen, dass ein ganzes Leben dazu gehört, sie recht zu verstehen und also gründlich zu nutzen.' Die philologische und historische Wissenschaft der Romantik, der er den Zugang zu so vielen neuen Gebieten verdankte, eröffnete ihm nicht weniger auch neue Einsichten in das Wesen und den Wert der alten Schriftsteller selber, die ihn dazu führten, sie in einer neuen Weise 'recht zu verstehen'. Die Arbeiten der Philologen, die er mit grösstem Interesse verfolgte, regten ihn auch gerade zu jener erneuten schöpferischen Auseinandersetzung mit Euripides an, dessen Faszination ihn bis in sein letztes Lebensjahr nicht mehr losliess. 'Die von Herrn Professor und Ritter Hermann 1821 freundlichst mitgeteilten Fragmente[2] wirkten wie alles, was von diesem edlen Geist- und Zeitverwandten jemals zu mir gelangt, auf mein Innerstes kräftig und entschieden', bekannte er schon 1823 bei der ersten Präsentation des restaurierten *Phaethon*, auf den er wieder 1827 in *Kunst und Altertum* zurückkam.

Den 1826 neugestalteten 'Helena-Akt' stellte er mit der Ausarbeitung des ganzen *Faust II* nach und nach in seinen neuen, weiteren Zusammenhang hinein. Ihm liess er 1830 unmittelbar ein Stück vorausgehen, von dem ebenfalls in jener ersten Skizze von 1816 noch nicht die Rede war, die 'Klassische Walpurgisnacht'. Der Freiheit, mit der er jetzt als Dichter über die mythologischen Gestalten des Altertums verfügt, gibt er darin sowohl durch die Darstellung selber wie besonders auch durch mehr oder weniger offen ausgesprochene Erklärungen Ausdruck. Zumal in jenen berüchtigten 'Piquen' (Eckermann, 21. März 1830) lässt er sein neues geschichtliches

---

[1] Ausser den *Schriften zur Literatur* vgl. dazu J. W. Goethe, *Übertragungen*, zusammengestellt und hsg. (mit Nachwort 'Goethe als Übersetzer' und Anmerkungen) F. Ernst (Artemis-Gedenkausgabe, Bd. xv, Zürich, 1953) mit, u. a., Poesie und Prosa aus dem Orient, dem Neugriechischen, von europäischer, amerikanischer, chinesischer und sonstiger asiatischer Herkunft.

[2] G. Hermann, *Euripidis fragmenta duo Phaethontis e cod. Claromontano edita* (Leipzig, 1821), oder *Opuscula*, Bd. iii (1828), S. 3–21.

Verständnis zur Sprache kommen, das er sich als angeregt Anteil nehmender Beobachter der gelehrten Diskussionen der Zoëga, Creuzer, Daube, Schelling, Hermann, Voss, Lobeck u. a. um die romantische Deutung der antiken und orientalischen Mythen und Mysterien erworben hatte.[1] Unter ihnen findet sich auch jener ironische Hinweis zum Verständnis des freien Gebrauchs, den er sich von der Gestalt der Helena zu machen erlaubt. Faust, der sich über das jugendliche Alter – 'erst zehen Jahr' – wundern muss, in dem Helena zum ersten Mal 'umfreit' worden war (7426ff.), wird von Chiron belehrt:

> Ich seh', die Philologen,
> Sie haben dich so wie sich selbst belogen.
> Ganz eigen ist's mit mythologischer Frau,
> Der Dichter bringt sie, wie er's braucht, zur Schau.

Umgekehrt müsste sie ja in seiner 'Helena', wollte man nachrechnen, schon recht bejahrt sein; aber eben: 'den Poeten bindet keine Zeit' (7433) – auch darin nicht, dass er sie jetzt im 'Helena-Akt' gleichzeitig im Altertum vor dem Palast des Menelas in Sparta, mit Faust im Mittelalter und mit Euphorion–Byron zusammen in der Neuzeit auftreten lassen kann, 'volle 3000 Jahre', in jener 'Zeiteinheit...im höheren Sinne'. Die vergleichende Beschäftigung mit den *Philokteten* des Aeschylus, Sophokles und Euripides, zu der ihn eben 1826 ebenfalls ein Aufsatz Hermanns anregte,[2] bestätigte ihn in der Bewunderung dieser Freiheit im Umgang mit dem Mythus: 'Darin waren nun wieder die Griechen so gross, dass sie weniger auf die Treue eines historischen Faktums gingen, als darauf, wie es der Dichter behandelte' (Eckermann, 31. Januar 1827). Anlässlich des *Phaethon* stellte er auch fest, dass die Griechen sich nicht starr an die drei Einheiten banden, namentlich nicht an die des Ortes, 'und man sieht also, dass die gute Darstellung ihres Gegenstandes ihnen mehr galt als der blinde Respekt vor einem Gesetz, das an sich nie viel zu bedeuten hatte' (Eckermann, 24. Februar 1825).

Anderseits wendet er sich wiederholt in kräftigen Worten gegen die herablassende Kritik, die 'schwache Personagen' – gemeint ist namentlich A. W. Schlegel – unter den Kritikern und Kunstrichtern der neuesten Zeit an Euripides übten (Eckermann, 28. März 1827;

---

[1] S. dazu K. Reinhardt, 'Die Klassische Walpurgisnacht, Entstehung und Bedeutung', *Von Werken und Formen* (Godesberg, 1948), S. 348–405, dort besonders zu 'Goethes Verhältnis zur wissenschaftlichen Mythologie der deutschen Romantik', S. 378ff.

[2] G. Hermann, *De Aeschyli Philocteta dissertatio* (Leipzig, 1826), oder *Opuscula*, III (1828), S. 113–29.

13. Februar 1831).[1] Nicht zufällig hält er also daran fest, unter den alten Schriftstellern besonders grade sein Vorbild mit dieser Freiheit 'gründlich zu nutzen' für diese neugestaltete 'Helena'. In dieser Dichtung 'in der Fülle der Zeiten' liefert es also die Masstäbe dafür, 'alles in seinem wahren ethisch-aesthetischen Werte schätzen' zu lernen, den Bezugspunkt des Schönen, von dem aus alle jene anderen Hervorbringungen des menschlischen Geistes beurteilt, die richtigen von den 'falschen Mustern' unterschieden werden können, an denen wir uns 'zu verbilden fürchten müssten'.

V

Hatte Schiller 1800 die klassische 'Helena...in diesem Stück' im Gegensatz zum 'Barbarischen' verstanden als 'ein Symbol für alle die schönen Gestalten, die sich hinein verirren werden', so macht Goethe im neuen Bezugsrahmen der endgültigen Fassung des *Faust II* ihre Schönheit dazu auch einer Symbolik ganz anderer Art dienstbar. Ihren Hintergrund bildet ein ebenfalls unmittelbar aus Texten des Altertums erworbenes und in schöpferischer Auseinandersetzung zu seinem eigenen Gebrauch umgebildetes Lehrgebäude, das als geistiges System der Welterklärung in der Bildung des alten Goethe eine zentrale Stellung einnimmt, der Neuplatonismus.[2]

1811 hat er sich, am Ende des achten Buches von *Dichtung und Wahrheit* ausgesprochen über 'seine eigene Religion'. Diese bildete er sich 'mit grosser Behaglichkeit. Der neue Platonismus lag zum Grunde; das Hermetische, Kabbalistische gab auch seinen Beitrag her.' Darauf schildert er die dreifältige Gottheit der 'Elohim', die Schöpfung durch Luzifer und seinen Abfall, bis die Gottheit die Verbindung mit der Schöpfung durch den Menschen wieder herstellt. Mit dem Menschen 'ward jener Abfall zum zweiten Mal eminent, obgleich die ganze Schöpfung nichts ist und nichts war als ein Abfallen und Zurückkehren zum Ursprünglichen'.

Der weitere Zusammenhang, in dessen Mitte nun die Verbindung des Faust mit 'der schönsten Frau' (7398) im 'Helena-Akt' steht, ist

---

[1] Vgl. z. B. auch *Tagebücher* 13.–23. November 1831; *Gespräch* mit Göttling am 3. März 1832.

[2] Zu Goethes Kenntnis des Neuplatonismus und zu dessen Verwendung im *Faust* können hier keine detaillierten Nachweise gegeben werden; dazu demnächst mehr in *Wege der Forschung: Faust II*, hsg. Werner Keller; vorläufig s. vom Verf., 'Antike Hintergründe in den letzten Szenen des *Faust*', *Neue Zürcher Zeitung* (3. September 1966); von älterer Literatur besonders ergiebig: Max Wundt, 'Plotin und die Romantik', *Neue Jahrbb. f.d. klass. Altertum...* xxxv/xxxvi (1915), 649–72 und 'Noch einmal Goethe und Plotin', *ibid.* xli (1918), 140f.

zuletzt und zuinnerst durch den geheimnisvollen Sinn jenes 'offenbaren Rätsels' konstituiert, zu dessen Auflösung Goethe den Leser des Faust in Gesprächen und Briefen ständig herausfordert und anleitet. Erst in der allerletzten Arbeitsperiode, in den Jahren 1830 und 1831, gelang es ihm, nach mehreren später wieder aufgegebenen Ansätzen und Versuchen, durch eine Reihe entscheidender neuer Erfindungen diese innere symbolische Verbindung zwischen den äusserlich-dramatisch beinahe unverbunden nebeneinander stehenden Akten herzustellen. Eben dieses 'Abfallen und Zurückkehren zum Ursprünglichen' hat er in den damals geschaffenen mythischen Bildern als neuplatonische Seelenbiographie des Faust dargestellt. Damit erhielt nun nicht nur die 'Helena' einen neuen, erst jetzt ganz deutlich hervortretenden Sinn, sondern alle die mythologischen Bilder, in die er dieses höhere Geheimnis einkleidete, wurden damit zu einem Zweck verwendet, der ihre Bedeutung nochmals tiefgreifend veränderte.

Auch zu den originalen Zeugnissen des Neuplatonismus vermittelte ihm den Zugang die romantische Philologie. Die Kenntnisse über den geschichtlichen Zusammenhang jener hermetischen und kabbalistischen Schriften, die er seit seiner Jugend kannte, mit dem antiken Neuplatonismus, erwarb er sich besonders 1809 mit den ausgedehnten philosophiegeschichtlichen Studien zur *Geschichte der Farbenlehre*.[1] Angeregt von Creuzer hatte er nach Schillers Tod 1805 in der Einsamkeit von Lauchstädt, zunächst in der lateinischen Übersetzung des Ficino, dann mit Wolfs Unterstützung im Original den Plotin gelesen. Das erste Kapitel der Schrift *Von der geistigen Schönheit* (5,8,1), dessen Übersetzung er sogleich an Zelter und Wolf schickte, mit dem er sich später immer wieder beschäftigte und das er schliesslich 1829 in verbesserter Fassung 'Makariens Archiv' in den *Wanderjahren* einfügte, beginnt mit den Worten:

Da wir überzeugt sind, dass derjenige, der die intellektuelle Welt beschaut und des wahrhaften Intellekts Schönheit gewahr wird, auch wohl ihren Vater, der über allen Sinn erhaben ist, bemerken könne, so versuchen wir nach Kräften einzusehen, und für uns selbst auszudrücken – insofern sich dergleichen machen lässt – auf welche Weise wir die Schönheit des Geistes und der Welt anzuschauen vermögen.

Der Zusammenhang der neuplatonischen Seelenbiographie, den

---

[1] Nachweise s. *Goethes Werke* (Hamburger Ausgabe), Bd. ix, 7te. Aufl. (München, 1974), *Autobiographische Schriften*, Bd. i, hsg. L. Blumenthal, kommentiert von Erich Trunz, S. 718ff., 724ff.

Goethe in dieser letzten Arbeitsphase im *Faust II* geschaffen hat, kann hier nur im Umriss angedeutet und in neuplatonisch abstrakter, also ganz ungoethischer Begrifflichkeit bezeichnet werden. Das 'Abfallen' symbolisiert er als Schau des Schönen in einer abfallenden Stufenfolge. Das 'Ursprüngliche' lässt er Faust schauen bei den 'Müttern' (6213ff.), 'im Grenzenlosen' (6428ff.), das heisst beim 'Verweilen' am ausserkosmischen, überhimmlischen Ort, der μονή. Von dort bringt Faust als erinnertes Bild des Geistes 'tief im Sinn' (6487ff.) das Abbild der ursprünglichen Schönheit (6483ff.), Helena, bei der Beschwörung im 'Rittersaal' (6421ff.) mit hinunter in den Kosmos (6434ff.) zur 'ersten Geburt', der ἀπογέννησις. Er darf es nicht berühren, bis es den ganzen Abstieg durch alle Stufen bis in die Materie vollendet hat. Darum paralysiert ihn (6566ff.) der voreilige Versuch. Auf der Stufe der Seele, im sublunaren Raum der Geister in der 'Klassischen Walpurgisnacht', hilft ihm die Erinnerung in der Vision am unteren Peneios (7271ff.) bei der λῆξις, der 'Erlosung' oder 'Wahl' des richtigen Lebens für den 'Vorgang', die πρόοδος, zur 'Geburt' in die Materie (7489ff.). Dorthin, in die γένεσις, kann er dank seinem Enthusiasmus für die Schönheit 'ins Leben ziehn die einzigste Gestalt' (7439), sodass er sie dann als körperliches Wesen, Helena, berühren darf (9586ff.). Diese Vereinigung währt nur kurz (9939ff.). Im vierten Akt erlebt er dann eine Vision, die seine Seele wieder hinanzieht bis zur frühesten Liebe (10042ff.), das heisst eine 'Rückwendung', ἐπιστροφή, während seines Erdenlebens. Im fünften folgt schliesslich das 'Zurückkehren zum Ursprung', mit der Trennung seines 'Unsterblichen' nacheinander vom Leibe (11612ff.), von der Seele (11954ff.), schliesslich vom Geist (12088ff.), bis vor jene selber wieder nicht mehr darstellbare 'über allen Sinn erhabene' erneute Schau des Ursprünglichen, Unbeschreiblichen, Unzulänglichen (*inaccessibile*) (12104ff.), das heisst die 'Wiedereinsetzung in den ursprünglichen Zustand', ἀποκατάστασις.

Diese Verwendung der mythischen Gestalten als Bilder des Geistes zur symbolischen Darstellung der 'intellektuellen Welt' des Neuplatonismus eröffnet der Freiheit bei ihrem Gebrauch von einer anderen Seite her einen viel weiteren Spielraum. Die symbolische Vereinigung Helenas mit Faust (9574–694) wird, dem Publikum ebenfalls unsichtbar, zwar erst im ganz neuen, romantischen 'Teile der Oper' (Eckermann, 25. Januar 1827) des 'Helena-Aktes' ausgeführt. Im ersten, klassischen Teil (8489–9126), der am Beginn auch die alten Verse von 1800 umfasst, wird zwar erst vorbereitend ihre Schönheit der Hässlichkeit der Phorkyas gegenübergestellt (8736ff.). Aber der Hauptsinn des Ganzen ist ja, den Zwiespalt des Klassischen und Romantischen zu versöhnen, und Goethe weist durch die im zweiten Teil schon vor der Vereinigung wiederholte Deutung eben dieser Schönheit (9218ff.) und dieser Hässlichkeit (9438ff.) mit allem Nachdruck darauf hin, dass dieser 'mit reiner, altertümlicher Liebe' verfasste 'Quasi-Prolog' (an S. Boisserée, 10. Dezember 1826) als deren Grundlage mit der folgenden Handlung des zweiten Teils, 'der Axe, auf der das ganze Stück dreht' (an S. Boisserée, 19. Januar 1827), innig verbunden ist. Auch der nach dem klassischen Vorbild des Euripides gestaltete erste Teil der 'Helena' ist damit unmittelbar einbezogen in jene Symbolik der neuplatonischen Schau des Schönen.

Mit diesem Gebrauch der Mythen verlagert sich das Gewicht ihrer Bedeutung von ihrem Bezug auf die Vorbilder als *sujet* der Darstellung auf ihre Verwendbarkeit zur bildlichen Darstellung höherer 'intellektueller' Inhalte. Eine Folge davon ist, dass derselbe Inhalt durch verschiedene Bilder dargestellt werden kann und somit die Mythen austauschbar werden. Damit er die Identität des dargestellten Inhalts nicht verkenne, weist Goethe seinen Leser ausdrücklich darauf hin bei der Vision auf dem 'Hochgebirg' zu Beginn des vierten Aktes. Nun wandelt sich das Bild der Schönheit, 'Junonen ähnlich, Leda'n, Helenen' (10050), und zuletzt 'steigert sich die holde Form' (10064) zu jener ersten Jugendliebe, die dann im letzten Akt wieder erscheint in der Gestalt von 'Una Poenitentium, sonst Gretchen genannt' (12069ff.). Sind für die Stufen der Schönheit beim 'Abfallen' mythische Bilder aus dem Altertum verwendet, die auf Helena hinführen, so stammen die Bilder beim 'Zurückkehren zum Ursprünglichen' in den letzten Szenen, die das erhöhte Gretchen mit sich bringen, aus jenen Bereichen des Mittelalters, die sich der alte Goethe neu erschlossen hatte. Dazu erklärt er Eckermann (6. Juni 1831), 'dass ich bei so übersinnlichen, kaum zu ahnenden Dingen mich sehr leicht im Vagen hätte verlieren können, wenn ich nicht meinen poetischen Intentionen durch die scharf umrissenen christlich-kirchlichen Figuren und Vorstellungen eine wohltätig beschränkende Form und Festigkeit gegeben hätte.' Als literarisches Vorbild wählt er diesmal das *Paradiso* des Dante, mit dem er sich eben nach dem Abschluss der 'Helena', im August und September 1826, angeregt durch die Übersetzung von Karl Streckfuss auf seine Weise schöpferisch auseinanderzusetzen begonnen hatte.[1] Als christliche symbolische Form umhüllt also nun Gretchen beim Zurückkehren denselben Gedankeninhalt wie vorher beim Abfallen Helena, und am Schluss die 'Ohnegleiche' (12070), die da schwebt 'zu Höhen der ewigen Reiche' (12032f.) als 'Jungfrau, Mutter, Königin, Göttin' (12102f.) denselben wie am Anfang die von Plutarch inspirierten 'Mütter' (Eckermann, 18. Januar 1830) zu denen Faust zuerst 'in der Gebilde losgebundne Reiche' (6277) gegangen war. Im symbolischen Gebrauche dieser allerletzten Schaffensperiode sind also jene anderen Vorbilder in eine reale Konkurrenz mit den klassischen Mustern getreten.

VI

Der Wandel in Goethes Verhältnis zu den klassischen Vorbildern zwischen der Zeit um 1800 und seinem Alterswerk ist so deutlich wie die neue Funktion, die damit die antiken 'Muster' in einem neuen, weiteren Zusammenhang erhalten haben. Ebenso deutlich sind Goethes Absicht und sein Wunsch, nach ihrer Anleitung auf die Bildung seiner Zeitgenossen einzuwirken – im Alter noch eindeutiger und ausgesprochener als in der Periode des Hochklassizismus.[2] Schon zu seinen Lebzeiten, und besonders in seinem höheren Alter hat er in der Tat eine ausserordentlich starke Wirkung auf die deutsche wie auf die europäische Bildung ausgeübt. Zur Zeit, als er am zweiten Teil des *Faust* arbeitete, wurden seine Werke schon ins Französische, Englische, Russische und in andere Sprachen übersetzt. Er konnte auch selber schon berichten über die Aufnahme seiner Helena gleich nach ihrem Erscheinen in Kritiken weit über Deutschland hinaus:[3] 'Hier strebt nun der Schotte, das Werk zu durchdringen, der Franzose, es zu verstehen, der Russe, sich es anzueignen. Und so hätten die Herren Carlyle, Ampère und Schewireff, ganz ohne Verabredung, die sämtlichen Kategorien der möglichen Teilnahme an einem Kunst- und Naturprodukt vollständig durchgeführt.' Im Vertrauen auf dieses Interesse an seinem Werk und auf jene hohe

---

[1] Die schöpferische Auseinandersetzung führt auch hier sogleich zu einer aesthetischen Würdigung, eigener Übersetzung, einem Gedicht an Zelter; s. dazu und zu dem in den neueren Faust-Kommentaren etwas vergessenen Gebrauch Dantes (und anderer Literatur über die himmlische Hierarchie), Erich Schmidt, 'Danteskes im "Faust"', *Archiv f. d. Studium der neueren Sprachen und Literaturen*, CVII (1901), 241–52.

[2] 'Möge das Studium der griechischen und römischen Literatur immerfort die Basis der höheren Bildung bleiben', setzt er noch 1829 unter die Maximen *Aus Makariens Archiv*, in den *Wanderjahren*.

[3] 'Helena in Edinburgh, Paris und Moskau', in *Über Kunst und Altertum*, Bd. VI, H. 2 (1828).

Kultur der Bessern seines Vaterlandes konnte er also auch erwarten, dass die Leser, für die er eigentlich schrieb, den Sinn seiner Darstellung sogleich erfassen würden. Immerhin hielt er doch den vollendeten *Faust II* bis zu seinem Tode zurück. Er wurde erst aus seinem Nachlass herausgegeben durch Riemer und Eckermann, der ihm 1836 und 1848 seine *Gespräche* nachschickte, nicht zuletzt um das schwierige Alterswerk zu erklären.

So ist es, aus der Rückscheu betrachtet, umso bemerkenswerter, wie zögernd sich dieser Wandel noch zu Goethes Lebzeiten und nach dem Erscheinen seines literarischen Nachlasses gleich nach seinem Tode in der Wirkung auf seine Zeitgenossen Geltung verschaffte. Ihr Interesse galt mehr der Person des berühmten alten Dichters, dessen Bild aber festgelegt blieb auf die Werke und den Stil, denen er seinen Ruhm verdankte und die seinen Lesern leichter verständlich waren, auf 'Sturm und Drang' und 'Weimarer Klassik'. Nach seinem Tode dauerte es lange, bis eine ernsthafte Auseinandersetzung mit seinem Alterswerk, mit dem zweiten Teil des *Faust* und den *Wanderjahren* überhaupt einsetzte. Der *West-östliche Divan* blieb bis zum Beginn unseres Jahrhunderts sozusagen ganz vergessen. Das Publikum war befremdet von dieser mit so viel Reflexion und Symbolik befrachteten Dichtung. Dass Goethe sich selber weiter entwickelt hatte und seine späteren Jahre ganz der Aufgabe widmete, seine lebendige neue Erfahrung für die Bildung seiner Zeitgenossen zu gestalten, wurde ausserhalb des engeren Kreises seiner Freunde kaum wahrgenommen. Man zog es vor, ihn sich so vorzustellen, wie man es gewohnt war und wie man ihn haben wollte. Für *Goethe in der Epoche seiner Vollendung* prägte Otto Harnack 1887 das deutsche Wort 'Klassik'.[1] So ist es wohl auch zu verstehen, dass etwa ein Wilhelm Zahn,[2] der Goethe erst 1827 persönlich kennen gelernt hatte, 1864 in der Wiedergabe jenes ersten Gesprächs, das er damals mit ihm geführt hatte, auch den 78-jährigen alten Herrn noch zu dem bedingungslosen Klassizisten machte, für den er ihn glaubte halten zu müssen.

[1] S. dazu René Wellek, 'Das Wort und der Begriff "Klassizismus" in der Literaturgeschichte', *Schweizer Monatshefte*, XLV (1965/6), 154–73, dort 163.

[2] Was davon auf das Konto des Redaktors dieses Berichtes, Otto Glagau, geht (s. oben S. 311, Anm. 2), ist allerdings nicht auszumachen, spielt aber für die allgemeine Tendenz auch keine Rolle.

16

CLASSICAL ELEMENTS IN THE SOCIAL, POLITICAL AND EDUCATIONAL THOUGHT OF THOMAS AND MATTHEW ARNOLD

R. R. BOLGAR

When Matthew Arnold's *Culture and Anarchy* first appeared, it contained a notorious passage which later editions tactfully omitted:

> I remember my father in one of his unpublished letters written more than forty years ago, when the political and social state of the country was gloomy and troubled, and there were riots in many places, goes on after strongly insisting on the badness and foolishness of the government, and on the harm and dangerousness of our feudal and aristocratic constitution of society, and ends thus: 'As for the rioting, the old Roman way of dealing with *that* is always the right one; flog the rank and file, and fling the ringleaders from the Tarpeian Rock'. And this opinion we can never forsake, however our Liberal friends may think a little rioting, and what they call popular demonstrations, useful sometimes to their own interests and to the interests of the valuable practical operations they have in hand...[1]

What does this diatribe, which was suppressed on second thoughts, tell us about the Arnolds? It makes us see that Thomas, the great headmaster, had no love for the aristocracy; that his son Matthew felt only a modified enthusiasm for Liberal reforms; and that they both hated sedition. They were neither rebels, nor reactionaries, which explains why posterity has labelled them moderates. But that label, though very convenient, is also very uninformative. If all extremists resemble each other, must we not admit – adapting Tolstoy's dictum – that every moderate is moderate in his own way, and that if we are to understand the Arnolds, the precise nature of their moderation needs to be described?

Thomas was born into a family that had been trying for some generations to establish itself in the more prosperous section of the professional middle class.[2] The Arnolds like their contemporaries the

---

[1] Matthew Arnold, *Culture and Anarchy*, ed. J. Dover Wilson (Cambridge, 1971, p. 203. This passage which appeared in the first (1869) edition was cut out of the second in 1875.

[2] The Arnolds were a modestly prosperous family of Suffolk farmers. Thomas' grandfather became an officer in the Excise. His father was collector of customs for the Isle of

Austens, whose circumstances were similar to theirs, were respectably and energetically dedicated to the great nineteenth-century aim of social advancement. They believed in hard work, honesty and the regular performance of their duties; and what was perhaps even more important, they were deeply religious, inspired by that fashionable evangelical fervour whose workings we see reflected in the pages of *Mansfield Park*; and their earnest piety, as well as their belief in honest effort, was transmitted to the young Thomas.

Hundreds of children must have had this sort of family background at the beginning of the nineteenth century, and the characteristics that were to make Thomas an exceptional person must be traced in part at least to other influences. They derived from his experiences in boyhood and adolescence and from the particular quality of his mind. When he was six years old, his father died. The family was left in financial difficulties, and although his mother managed to send him to Winchester and Oxford, there was very little money to spare for his personal expenditure. He had the experience, mortifying for a boy who was anxious to shine, of passing his formative years among companions whose purses were for the most part longer than his own; and he came to nourish a resentment against unearned, undeserved wealth, which was to last all his days.

Resentments rooted in envy are powerful emotions, and they can find expression in a variety of ways. Thomas was a young man for whom ideas mattered. He chose to rationalise his feelings, to elaborate them into an intellectual system. Unfortunately, his mind, though vigorous, was also rather narrow, unsubtle and insufficiently troubled by hesitations and second thoughts, so that the rationalisations he favoured had all the vices of simplicity. His Christian principles were used to justify a radicalism that led him at times to champion the French Revolution in a way which shocked his contemporaries. Since Christ ordered us to love one another, the exploitation of the poor by the idle rich was plainly indefensible.

The experiences of Thomas' maturity shaped and diversified but did not fundamentally alter these beliefs which had been rough-hewn by the circumstances of his youth. We find him dissatisfied with the England of his day. The church was disunited and neglectful of its social duties. The rich were greedy and selfish, the poor greedy and ignorant, without any defence against those popular demagogues

Wight and the supervisor of its postal service (Norman Wymer, *Dr. Arnold of Rugby* (London, 1953), pp. 10–11).

who appealed to the worst elements among them and to the worst impulses of the remainder. He was convinced that the world was moving inevitably towards an epoch of democratic rule, which he defined as the possession of power by the masses; and the only task left for men of good will was to ensure that democracy when it came took on a healthy form. Thomas' projected Utopia was a society of independent property owners, frugal, industrious and sufficiently educated to recognise their common good, a society consisting exclusively of Christians under the leadership of a unified, regenerated church. He was an advocate of reform without to any extent believing in 'the people'. Their sufferings engaged his interest, but he had no confidence in their political ability, no trust in their intelligence.

This was a combination of ideas typical of the early nineteenth century. Thomas' evangelical faith was responsible for his choosing the church to be the official guardian of values in his ideal community and for his feeling charitable towards the poor. It guaranteed his sympathy for them, but it also determined the limits he set on that sympathy, since it taught him that there was a clear difference between good and bad, and that the salvation of mankind depended on those who opted for goodness. He was no egalitarian. The notion that everyone – foolish and prudent, idle and hard-working, irresponsible and conscientious – deserved equal consideration was not one he could swallow.

From the ideology of his own times, Thomas derived his belief in progress, which made him inclined to consider change as not only inevitable, but also as desirable, since viewed on a broad enough scale it appeared to have been generally for the better. He was always ready to condemn politicians who supported the established order. 'No excesses of popular wickedness', he wrote to his friend the Chevalier Bunsen in 1833, 'shall ever make me forget the wickedness of Toryism.'[1] But was change necessarily beneficial? He could not make up his mind. He had read, he had admired, Coleridge, and he was not without fear for the future. The sufferings of the poor stirred his charity. The neglect of their interests by the rich outraged his sense of justice. He attacked 'the high rents and the game laws and the carelessness which keeps the poor ignorant and wonders that they are brutal';[2] but he had no confidence in the political ability of 'the

---

[1] Arthur Penrhyn Stanley, *The Life and Correspondence of Thomas Arnold D.D.*, 9th ed. (London, 1875), vol. I, p. 292.   [2] *Ibid.* p. 234.

people'. He wondered if they could ever learn to exercise political power, even if efforts were made to educate them, so long as they were tied to a life of dreary work.

They who by circumstances are confined to a limited sphere, who see little variety, who have never associated with highly cultivated minds, and above all with minds cultivated under different circumstances of rank, profession, and country, must labour under disadvantages that no mere book instruction can remove.[1]

Christian tradition and late-eighteenth-century thought can be seen therefore to have provided Thomas Arnold with some important general concepts. Now we must consider another source from which he drew intellectual sustenance. We must turn to the classical literatures which are the proper subject of this paper; for we shall meet there subtle echoes of many of the concepts we have already discussed.

Let us take, for example, Thomas' plan to treat the church as the moral representative of the state. The idea that the state has a moral aspect, which distinguishes it from a random collection of individuals, can be found in Aristotle.[2] The further notion that religion might embody this moral aspect is certainly suggested by the cults that grew up in ancient times to honour divinities who like Athena at Athens were particularly associated with a city. The rôle Thomas envisaged for the church went beyond the idea, prevalent in Rome for instance, that the well-being of the state demanded the proper performance of certain rites; but we can see how the latter might have suggested the former.

Or again take the expectation that power was bound to pass to the people, which caused Thomas so much anxiety. The idea of classifying constitutions as monarchical, aristocratic and democratic had originated with the Greeks. It was thanks to them that these categories became a permanent feature of our political thinking, though they were over-simplified, as Aristotle had been the first to point out. Ancient historians had described a great number of bloody struggles between kings and nobles, and many that were even more bloody between the nobility and the common people, while Athens, the best known of Greek cities, was put on record as having passed from monarchical to aristocratic, and then to popular, rule. This example of Athens was perhaps the one that proved decisive. The idea grew

---

[1] *Thomas Arnold on Education*, ed. T. W. Bamford (Cambridge, 1970), p. 60.
[2] Geoffrey E. R. Lloyd, *Aristotle, the Growth and Structure of his Thought* (Cambridge, 1968), pp. 249–51.

up that the three traditional types of constitution were likely to appear in a fixed sequence with power passing to progressively larger groups; and when in the eighteenth century this sequence came to be regarded as an obvious instance of progress, the stage was set for the emergence of a belief in the inevitability of democracy.

Closely connected with these political concepts, was the notion, widely asserted by the ancients, that there was a natural difference between rulers and ruled, between those born to be masters and those born to be slaves. This theory of natural slavery together with its corollary, the Aristotelian principle that Justice consists in each man getting what he deserves, so that those superior in virtue were entitled to greater rewards, was likely to make a strong impression on a classical scholar like Thomas, who was worried about the political competence of the labouring classes.[1] It counteracted his radicalism and strengthened his support of the existing social hierarchy.

It is possible to look upon Thomas Arnold as a man whose radical impulses were smothered by a middle-class upbringing and the pressures of a middle-class career. It is equally possible to regard him as the exponent of a humane compromise between a desire for stability and a zeal for reform. The facts are evident; and how we judge them depends merely on our prejudices. Matthew presents a more difficult problem. Growing up in his father's shadow, rebelling while he admired, he developed precisely those character traits that his father had neglected.

When Thomas visited France in 1825, he wrote: 'It is my delight to see the feudal castles in ruins; never, I trust, to be rebuilt or reoccupied.'[2] Matthew, had he been present, would have deplored the loss. He was responsive to beauty, charmed by elegance. His taste was catholic, embracing most forms of art, and the range of his reading in the major literatures of Europe strikes the student of his notebooks with awe. Unlike Thomas whose attention was fixed remorselessly on the world of affairs, he was fascinated by his own sensations, his own sentiments, and his mind was exceptionally subtle. Thomas had revelled in arguing from simple principles to clear-cut conclusions. Matthew's ideas move obliquely to their goal. He hesitates and qualifies, preferring the strategy of an indirect approach.

The Christianity of his early years retained its power to stir his

[1] On the working class and its need for leadership: *Thomas Arnold on Education*, p. 67.
[2] Stanley, *Life of Thomas Arnold*, vol. i, p. 63.

emotions. But there were contemporary arguments for agnosticism that had great force, and that he found convincing. He could not accept his father's simple faith in the New Testament as an infallible guide through life's difficulties, and when he came to formulate his social programme in *Culture and Anarchy*, it was to a sort of Idealist Philosophy that he turned for support.

Man's purpose in life was 'to ascertain what perfection is and to make it prevail'. But our fates are interdependent. 'We are members of one great whole', so that 'perfection is not possible while the individual remains isolated'.[1] Society as a whole had to improve; and until perfection was attained (which was not likely to happen on this earth), social institutions would always be in need of amendment. A readiness to accept reforms was therefore a pre-condition of successful living.

Thomas had disliked the rich and powerful. Matthew enjoyed their company and found their attentions flattering. He copied into his notebook Menander's maxim: 'choose equality and flee greed', but he was delighted when Disraeli drew him aside at Lady Ainslie's to 'the poet's sofa' and complimented him on being the only English writer to become a classic in his lifetime. 'You have coined phrases', Dizzy murmured, 'that have passed into common usage.' One suspects, alas, that he had 'barbarians and philistines' in mind, or the infelicitous 'sweetness and light'. We feel – and Matthew may have felt – that he was being praised for the wrong reasons. But the letter he wrote to his sister subsequently describing every detail of the incident betrays his very obvious pleasure.[2] His dislike was reserved for lower-middle-class Nonconformity.

Thomas' way of life had not been one that brought him into contact with the poor. All the same, he had felt it his duty to visit the sick and unfortunate and had financed a dispensary for them at Rugby out of his own pocket.[3] Matthew as an inspector of schools saw a great many working-class children. He wrote indignantly of their miserable state, but it was in general terms.[4] His correspondence does not suggest that he ever felt any personal interest in the young creatures who passed before him. This remoteness of his is unattrac-

---

[1] Matthew Arnold, *Culture and Anarchy*, pp. 47–8.
[2] *Letters of Matthew Arnold 1848–88*, ed. George W. E. Russell (London, 1895), vol. II, p. 168.
[3] Wymer, *Dr. Arnold of Rugby*, pp. 143–4.
[4] See for example his attack on overpopulation (Matthew Arnold, *Culture and Anarchy*, pp. 194–5).

tive when one takes into account the warm interest he could show in his social equals; and one is driven to find excuses for him. The urban poor he met with in east London and elsewhere must have been more wretched and more brutalised than the country-folk his parents comforted in Rugby. He may have had good reasons for despair. But when he writes about the labouring classes he does tend to emphasise their ignorance, their tendency to violence and their irresponsibility. It is hard to escape the impression that he saw them, not as individuals who hoped and suffered, but as creatures less than human. His conviction that it was his duty to help the advance of democracy was a triumph of principle over natural inclination.

The social analysis that meets us in Matthew's writings is more detailed than anything Thomas produced, but it follows the pattern laid down by Thomas, a pattern that owes a good deal to classical modes of thought. We hear about the unity of the state based on a respect for law, the traditional three types of constitution, the traditionally accepted sequence of political change. We also find traces of the notion that some may be naturally fitted to rule, others to be ruled. The major difference between the systems proposed by the father and the son is that Thomas wanted to entrust the social training of the citizen body to the church, while Matthew favoured the state; but as they both regarded the church as an aspect of the state, this amounted to little more than a difference of emphasis.

On first looking at the Arnolds, one is struck by the many rôles each of them played: Thomas was a scholar, a teacher, a reforming headmaster and a leading figure in the ecclesiastical controversies of his day; Matthew was a poet, a literary critic and an educationist. It takes one some time to realise the unity behind this variety. The rôles they filled with such distinction were marginal to their real purpose. We should see them as opportunities for self-expression taken because they were the ones chance offered. What Thomas wanted, what Matthew wanted – and to some extent achieved – was to attain the dignity of a sage. They wanted the contemporary world to look to them for a solution of its problems, and their social and political ideas were consequently central to their achievement.

This does not mean however that we can afford to disregard the specialised activities to which they owed their reputations.

His more recent biographers have taken the view that what Thomas did at Rugby was to add a moral dimension to public school life; and if we are concerned with his influence on a national scale, that is certainly true. He did however attempt a number of other reforms, which are not without interest. He encouraged games and sports of every kind, and although the fame of Rugby football dates from after his time, he seems to have laid the foundations for its development. He introduced modern history into the curriculum. The boys were made to read Russell's *Modern Europe*, stopping discreetly short before the last chapter that described the French Revolution; and Thomas' own lessons on Thucydides were enriched by references to more recent events. He is also supposed to have placed great emphasis on translating Greek or Latin into good English at sight. His pupils had to learn to think on their feet.

A healthy body – high moral standards – a knowledge of affairs – skill in speaking: ancient education had set itself these goals. It is true that it had not pursued all four at the same time. The Greeks had been the people who made a fetish of physical training, while the *vir bonus dicendi peritus*, well-informed on a great number of topics, was Cicero's ideal orator. Thomas was unhistorical perhaps in combining the two traditions. But here as elsewhere we can see that he was influenced by the practice of antiquity.

Matthew's essential contribution to educational thought – other than his championing of state intervention – will be found in two essays: one called 'On the modern element in literature', the other 'Literature and science'.[1] He begins with the premiss that what matters in life is a man's attitude to his fellows, his responsiveness to knowledge and beauty, and the understanding of the world that this responsiveness brings. Literature is the best instrument of education, because it informs us broadly (if not always accurately) about life and acquaints us at first hand with beauty. On all these counts, it is superior to the natural sciences, which T. H. Huxley wanted to make the keystone of the school curriculum. Science deals with the physical world, which comprises only a sector of our experience, and the habits of accurate observation and analysis that it inculcates, though immensely useful, are not the only habits we require.

We are persuaded to put our trust in literature; but that still leaves the question of which literatures we are to study. Matthew had read the best six languages could offer and had benefited from it, but

---

[1] 'On the modern element in literature', Arnold's inaugural lecture as Professor of Poetry at Oxford (1857) was published posthumously in *Essays in Criticism* (3rd series, Boston, 1910). 'Literature and science', originally the Rede Lecture at Cambridge, was published in *The Nineteenth Century* (August 1882) and was included in *Discourses in America* (London, 1885).

a class of school-children could not be expected to follow his example. Education is a field where choices have to be made. Much that is excellent, much that we love dearly, has to be discarded; and so Matthew formulates his concept of 'intellectual deliverance', which can help us to decide what we ought to retain.

He reminds us that we are confronted in our daily lives by a multitude of facts, which come to us tumbled and unco-ordinated, and which we wish and need to comprehend. Intellectually, our keenest desire is to be delivered from confusion. Our most urgent problem in view of the chaos around us is to discover a point of view that will make comprehension easy. Consequently, the literatures that can help us most are those whose authors solved this problem for their own times; and among these, the literature of Athens of the fifth and fourth centuries B.C. is surely pre-eminent. Since it can show us how order is imposed upon experience, it deserves to form the centrepiece of our education.

The argument is impressive. It is almost convincing. But there remains a doubt. Does the evidence justify Matthew's claims? It is true that Plato gave shape to philosophy, that Aristotle summarised the learning of his time, and Thucydides transformed historiography. But eminent as they were, their achievements were fragmentary, and their methods, which we have inherited, do not solve our problems. Matthew must have had something else in mind when he talked of the Greeks mastering chaos. Where the Greeks were supreme, where their triumphs inspire us and can fairly serve us for models was in the sphere of poetry and art. Better than any other culture, the Greek managed to accord proper weight to aesthetic satisfaction and to dignity of moral sentiment; and it was this achievement that Matthew plainly had in mind. His educational aims depend on the values he established as a critic.

Like Senancour, who was one of his favourite authors, Matthew as a young man hankered after some high purpose in life – and found none. We can recognise in his experience the common malaise of his period: the disenchantment that was due to the successive collapse of two optimistic dreams, the Enlightenment's illusion that a benevolent God has provided us with a universe geared to our needs, and the Revolutionary illusion that Reason acting on the principle of the greatest good of the greatest number could inaugurate an era of lasting happiness. The young Matthew saw himself placed in a deterministic world, hostile to man's purposes, where every creature strove blindly for self-preservation. The beauties and marvels that he as a poet valued were chance products whose existence was measured in moments.

Painting this pessimistic picture of the universe, he moulded his poems round figures drawn from Greek legend: Circe, Mycerinus, Empedocles; and it is easy to find Greek parallels for much of what he says. We recognise in his work the Greeks' sadness at the swift passing of beauty and the horror they felt in the face of a universe that was indifferent to man. Only the bitter longing for some sort of spiritual order that runs through many of these poems strikes us as essentially modern.

Later Matthew's ideas underwent a change. A notebook compiled during his middle years records Goethe's dictum: 'das Schöne ist eine Manifestation geheimer Naturgesetze'.[1] He came to attribute an objective reality to beauty and even to moral grandeur; and it seemed to him that the joyful celebration of this beauty and grandeur was poetry's proper task. Goethe's notion, which lends a mystical importance to our aesthetic responses, came to play a dominant rôle in his educational thinking. Poetry organises our experience in an aesthetically satisfying manner. It creates beauty, which is an expression of the deepest roots of our being. Therefore a good knowledge of literature is vitally important for the conduct of our daily lives; and Greek literature, the most beautiful we possess, will be our best instrument for training the young.

Matthew, we are sometimes told, gave an English voice to German Hellenism, and the pattern of his indebtedness is interesting. The theory that literature can teach us about life, because beauty is an essential ingredient of both, was novel, a product of nineteenth-century speculation. But there was a simpler form of it that was traditional. The Greeks and Romans had believed that literature instructed men in the art of living though they failed to specify how this occurred. And we are led to suspect that Matthew, the classical scholar, was drawn to Goethe's formulation because it contained this familiar element.

The next step in Matthew's argument is also interesting. Goethe's plea for a literary basis to education had not made out a case for Greek literature in particular. What he said in support of literature applied as much to Dante as to Homer, to Shakespeare as to

---

[1] *The Notebooks of Matthew Arnold*, ed. H. Lowry, K. Young, W. M. Dunn (New York and Oxford, 1952), p. 131.

Sophocles. When Matthew wrote: 'the instinct for beauty is served by Greek literature and art as it is served by no other literature and art'[1] he was interpreting Goethe's programme in terms of an older tradition. He was harking back to the ancient belief in the superiority of the Greek genius which had existed already in the third century B.C. when we find the Roman Senate commissioning Livius Andronicus to produce Latin versions of Athenian plays. He was construing a nineteenth-century idea in terms suggested by his classical training.

It is evident that we have here a pattern of development similar to the one we observed in the case of Thomas Arnold. Thomas had linked the eighteenth-century notion of progress with the sequence of constitutional changes that had carried Athens and other ancient states from monarchy to democracy. He had identified the class divisions of his day with the ones that had existed in antiquity, and so mixing old and new conceptions had arrived at the conclusion that power in England was bound to pass to the masses.

Minds shaped by the reading of Greek and Roman literature, as Thomas' was at Winchester and Matthew's at Rugby, were ready to welcome the new ideas that the nineteenth century produced. They did not consciously cling to the past. But if we want to form a more accurate picture of the way such classically trained minds functioned, we shall do well to remember that England in the nineteenth century (unlike the England we know today) still had much in common with ancient Rome. It had an empire to whose inhabitants the empire-builder could feel superior. Ownership of land and success in trade were still the main avenues to wealth; and wealth mattered. It established divisions between social groups that affected men's competence and characters as well as their spending power. The poor were ignorant, crude in their responses and prone to violence, and there were rivalries within the ruling class that recalled the struggles between the *Optimates* and the *Populares*. Education had a practical value. It could lift a man out of the ranks of those doomed to a servile existence; and the education that counted was still of a general sort – literacy, some knowledge of the world, the ability to handle ideas. Outstanding talent, as well as luck, could take a man up the social ladder, and when he started with some advantage of wealth, as Cicero did or Disraeli, it could take him very far.

A nineteenth-century Englishman could ignore the differences

---

[1] 'Literature and science', *Poetry and Prose*, ed. J. Bryson (London, 1954), p. 655.

produced by time and could interpret his society in Roman terms. He could look for Cicero's virtues in his legislators and see the faults of Spartacus in Feargus O'Connor. He could regard India as a province, the North-West Frontier as Hadrian's Wall and hope that the subjugation of the Zulus would be followed by the civilising effort that justified the defeat of Boadicea.

The classically educated thought along these lines, and this had an effect on their response to the original ideas that emerged during the nineteenth century. We can see, for example, that the new notions they accepted most readily were those that could fit into the Graeco-Roman picture of the world. Liberty interested them more than equality; and when they adopted a modern concept such as the eighteenth-century idea of progress, they worked out its implications within the framework of ancient experience. Progress was envisaged as the kind of change that had occurred frequently in antiquity.

The Renaissance had used classical knowledge as a springboard for new achievements. The Arnolds' classical learning functioned rather as a limiting factor that confined their ideas within certain traditionally recognised grooves. Goethe who distanced himself from Greece after a struggle and came to see the ancient view of the universe as only one possibility among many, which a man could use without submitting to its domination, remained an exceptional case in his century. Matthew, although he had Goethe's example before him, never became fully conscious of the hold exercised over him by the classical past and so never escaped its spell. It is not surprising that he should at times have felt that he was

> Wandering between two worlds, one dead,
> The other powerless to be born.

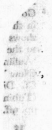

17

NIETZSCHE'S DEBT TO HERACLITUS

U. HÖLSCHER

We cannot talk of a Heraclitean tradition in the way we talk of the Platonic tradition. References to Heraclitus – outside of scholarly histories of philosophy[1] – are isolated and sporadic and are mostly restricted to the commonplace notion of the weeping philosopher who deplored eternal change.[2]

One would on the face of it expect to find references of a more substantial character from the Renaissance onwards: in Nicholas of Cusa for example or in Giordano Bruno, since it was Cusanus who coined the formula *coincidentia oppositorum*,[3] which we associate with the doctrine of Heraclitus, and since there is much in Bruno to remind us of the Heraclitean idea of the unity of the many (ἓν πάντα).[4] But such pre-Socratic concepts reached the Renaissance through stoicism and Neoplatonism. They were not borrowed directly. Their function at this time was to articulate a new idea of the universe, they indicate the transformation of the Neoplatonist system into a cosmology and a monistic philosophy of immanence.

Spinoza and later on Shaftesbury belonged to this tradition; and that is important since there is an obvious connection between the two of them and the 'Heraclitism' of the late eighteenth century as we find it in Goethe[5] and Hölderlin. Hölderlin seems to have been the first to study Heraclitus directly; and it was from him that Hegel derived the inspiration for his philosophical system.[6] The Heraclitean

---

[1] E.g. Ralph Cudworth, *Systema intellectuale huius mundi* (1680) or Jacob Brucker, *Historia critica philosophiae* (1742).

[2] The source of this tradition is Lucian, 'Vitarum auctio', Op. 14, *Works*, vol. II, ed. and trans. A. M. Harmon (London, 1960).

[3] Cusanus, *Docta ignorantia* 1.4.

[4] Heraclitus, fr. 50, *Fragmente der Vorsokratiker*, ed. Diels–Kranz, vol. I; cf. Giordano Bruno, *De la causa, principio et uno*.

[5] ...oethe's 'Heraclitism' presents a special problem. Besides some explicit references – as ... e poem 'Dauer im Wechsel' – his view on nature and on the way of knowledge ... a general affinity with Heraclitus, from the Goethe-inspired fragment 'Die Natur' ... scientific and poetical works of later years; cf. my chapter on Heraclitus in ... gliches Fragen' (reprinted in English in *The Pre-Socratics*, ed. A. Mourelatos ... York, 1974), pp. 229ff.).

[6] ...ieter Henrich, 'Hölderlin über Urteil und Sein', *Hölderlin-Jahrbuch 1965/6* ... gen), pp. 73ff.; *idem*, 'Hegel im Kontext', pp. 9ff., *Hegel und Hölderlin* (1971),

maxim in Hölderlin's *Hyperion*: τὸ ἓν διαφέρον ἑαυτῷ,[1] became the formula for Hegel's dialectical philosophy of history: 'The One, distinguished from itself, unites with itself.'[2]

I think Nietzsche too belongs to this tradition that saw the transformation of Platonic metaphysics into a cosmology, a process to which Heraclitus stood as sponsor. Nietzsche was always keen to find himself precursors in spite of his wish to promote 'a revaluation of all values'. In a late fragment he talks of 'my ancestors Heraclitus, Empedocles, Spinoza, Goethe',[3] and in *Ecce homo*, written shortly before his breakdown, he singles out Heraclitus from other Greek philosophers: 'in dessen Nähe überhaupt mir wärmer, mir wohler wird als irgendwo sonst'. In Heraclitus' thought, he says, 'muss ich unter allen Umständen das mir Verwandteste anerkennen, was bisher gedacht worden ist'.[4]

In Nietzsche's work one can discern three stages. 1. His early writings, *The Birth of Tragedy* and the *Untimely Meditations*, show him still under the sway of Schopenhauer's metaphysics, of the dualism of 'die Welt als Wille und Vorstellung'. Nietzsche uses this dualism to develop his aesthetics that contrasted the 'Dionysian' with the 'Apollonian'. 2. The middle period, beginning with *Human All too Human*, marks a turning away from metaphysics towards a preoccupation with moral phenomena. It finds expression in various forms of enlightenment and free-thought: materialism, positivism, sensualism, relativism, scepticism. 3. The third stage is reached with the poetical work *Also sprach Zarathustra*. All Nietzsche's late writings, *Beyond Good and Evil*, the *Genealogy of Morals*, the *Twilight of the Idols*, can be regarded as extensions of *Zarathustra*.

At the end of the first period, which coincides with his tenure of his Basle Professorship of Classical Philology, comes the unfinished treatise *Philosophy in the Tragic Epoch of the Greeks* (1873)[5] (which I will abbreviate as the *Philosophers Treatise*). I shall be speaking principally

---

[1] *Hyperion* I.2 (last letter), in *Sämtliche Werke*, ed. Friedr. Beissner, Kleine Stuttgarter Ausgabe (1958), vol. III, p. 85.

[2] Hegel, *Geschichte der Philosophie* I.1: 'Heraklit' (Jubiläumsausgabe (Stuttgart 1928), vol. XVII, p. 352). It is interesting that Hegel cites Heraclitus according to the old collection of fragments by Henricus Stephanus, *Poesis philosophica* (1573), the same collection which Hölderlin seems to have used in the Stifts Library at Tübingen; cf. U. Hölscher, *Empedokles und Hölderlin* (Frankfurt-am-Main, 1965), pp. 8f.

[3] F. Nietzsche, *Werke*, Kröner Grossoktavausgabe (20 vols., Leipzig, 1921–6), vol. XIV, p. 263 (11).

[4] *Ibid.* vol. xv, p. 65.   [5] *Ibid.* x, pp. 5–92.

about this treatise and will make only brief references to the rest of his work.

The *Philosophers Treatise* was conceived as a support for the *Birth of Tragedy*: 'die Bestätigung aus der Philosophie ihrer Zeitgenossen'.[1] Its title shows that he takes the teachings of the pre-Socratics as a tragic philosophy, and that accounts for his interest in these philosophers as 'Persönlichkeiten'.[2] He appears to have distributed his interest evenly among them, but a noticeable warmth creeps into his tones when he comes to talk of Heraclitus.[3] He speaks of that 'sensation of solitude which possessed the Ephesian hermit of the temple of Artemis, a sensation whose nature could be surmised only by one who found himself awestruck in the most savagely wild of mountain wildernesses'. He speaks too of Heraclitus' 'pride' and 'his lack of compassionate feelings': 'Sein Auge, lodernd nach innen gerichtet, blickt erstorben und eisig, wie zum Scheine nur, nach aussen',[4] and quotes his ἐδιζησάμην ἐμεωυτόν (I explored myself),[5] concluding: 'In einem abgelegenen Heiligtum, neben kalter, ruhig-erhabener Architektur mag so ein Wesen begreiflicher erscheinen. Unter Menschen war Heraklit, als Mensch, ungläublich.'[6] It is obvious that Nietzsche was painting himself largely in this portrait, and motifs from it recur, with philosophical significance, in his later writings, where we meet again the wilderness, the mountains, the solitude, the self-exploration and even the temple.

Nietzsche's interpretation of Heraclitus depends to a great extent on the philological learning of his time. He regards Heraclitus as the exponent of an Eternal Becoming, of the periodic destruction of the world and the struggle of opposites. His originality lies in his treatment of Heraclitus as the successor of Anaximander, taking his philosophy to have been an answer to Anaximander's problems. He presents Anaximander as the first 'metaphysician'[7] who behind the world of multiplicity, of the Finite, of coming-to-be and passing-away, looked for a One that was eternal, infinite and divine, by which and out of which all finite things came to be. Heraclitus, in opposition to Anaximander, 'leugnete die Zweiheit ganz diverser Welten; er schied nicht mehr eine physische Welt von einer

---

[1] *Ibid.* p. 101. [2] *Ibid.* p. 6. [3] *Ibid.* pp. 30–47, chs. 5–8.
[4] *Ibid.* p. 45. [5] Heraclitus, fr. 101, *Fragmente der Vorsokratiker*, ed. Diels.
[6] Nietzsche, *Werke*, vol. x, p. 46.
[7] *Ibid.* vol. x, p. 28.

metaphysischen',[1] and then ventured on another, 'still more audacious step':

er leugnete überhaupt das Sein. Denn diese eine Welt, die er übrig behielt,... zeigt nirgends ein Verharren ...Lauter als Anaximander rief Heraklit es aus: Ich sehe nichts als Werden...Ihr gebraucht Namen der Dinge, als ob sie eine starre Dauer hätten: aber selbst der Strom, in den ihr zum zweiten Male steigt, ist nicht derselbe wie bei dem ersten Male![2]

Nietzsche takes over the Platonic–Sophistic interpretation of Heraclitus.[3] But his later destruction of the ontology of the Thing and the Concept is already prefigured here. There is no Being! Being is just a creation of the human Will, impressed upon Becoming. In *Zarathustra*, he will use the Heraclitean metaphor: 'Euren Willen und eure Werte setztet ihr auf den Strom des Werdens.'[4]

Nietzsche calls this doctrine of 'eternal and universal Becoming' a 'terrible and paralysing conception' and compares it to an earth-quake which makes one 'lose confidence in the solid ground'.[5] Here he is already describing that loss of all firm concepts and values, which under the title of 'European nihilism'[6] he himself is to complete at a later stage and then tries to transcend. But he sees its transcendence foreshadowed in Heraclitus: 'Es gehörte eine erstaunliche Kraft dazu, diese Wirkung in das Entgegengesetzte, in das Erhabne und das beglückte Erstaunen zu übertragen.'[7] In making this transcendence, Heraclitus depended on his intuition of the cosmos, contemplating the whole of its coming-to-be and passing-away as a struggle of polarities. In the Heraclitean idea of 'polemos' Nietzsche anticipates to some degree his own later concept of the Will to Power. Already here in his interpretation of Heraclitus it has two aspects. First, there is no Justice (δίκη) that would stand superior to the struggle, for 'the struggle of the Many is itself pure Justice! and indeed, the One is the Many!'[8] We recognise here Heraclitus' δίκην ἔριν and ἐν πάντα.[9] Thus the bitterness of the pain which accompanies the process of Becoming is cancelled out in the tragic

[1] *Ibid.* vol. x, p. 31. [2] *Ibid.* pp. 31–2.
[3] Today, we distinguish the 'Fluss-Lehre' of the 'pretended' Heracliteans (Aristotle, *Met.* 1010 a 11) from the true doctrine of Heraclitus.
[4] *Also sprach Zarathustra*, Part 2: 'Von der Selbstüberwindung', Nietzsche, *Werke*, vol. v p. 165.
[5] *Ibid.* vol. x, p. 34.
[6] *Zur Genealogie der Moral*, Part III, no. 27, *ibid.* vol. VII, p. 480.
[7] *Ibid.* vol. x, p. 34. [8] *Ibid.* p. 36.
[9] Heraclitus, frs. 80 and 50, *Fragmente der Vorsokratiker*, ed. Diels.

realisation that it is the immanent principle of Life. Secondly, 'Die Dinge selbst haben garkeine eigentliche Existenz, sie sind das Erblitzen und der Funkenschlag gezückter Schwerter, sie sind das Aufglänzen des Sieges im Kampf der entgegengesetzten Qualitäten.'[1] The motif of *Aufglänzen* (flashing up) has no equivalent in Heraclitus. Nietzsche introduces it in order to suggest that Being is just a phantom, that Reality is pure phenomenality. In doing this he follows the Platonic–Protagorean interpretation of Heraclitus. His aim is the ontological rehabilitation of Seeming. Later, in the *Twilight of the Idols*, he will call Heraclitus as a witness to this: 'Ich nehme, mit hoher Ehrerbietung, den Namen Heraklits beiseite...Damit wird Heraklit ewig Recht behalten, dass das Sein eine leere Fiktion ist. Die scheinbare Welt ist die einzige, die "wahre Welt" ist nur hinzugelogen.'[2] What he fathers on Heraclitus, already in the *Philosophers Treatise*, is the overthrow of metaphysics – metaphysics regarded as a two-world doctrine.

At this point in the *Philosophers Treatise* Nietzsche invents a fictitious moment of doubt for Heraclitus, where the latter is shown questioning his own conclusions. If we – he lets Heraclitus say – look at Becoming as the struggle of opposites, and at 'things' as sparks struck off in the course of the struggle, need we not then assume, behind these appearances and this Becoming, the existence of a world of eternal, ungenerated and indestructible essences? 'Ist Heraklit', Nietzsche asks, 'auf einem Umwege vielleicht doch wieder in die doppelte Weltordnung (Anaximanders) hineingeraten?'[3] But then he dismisses these doubts as 'unheraclitean evasions and wrong turnings' and makes Heraclitus cut them short with a repeated affirmation: 'The One *is* the Many. The Opposites are neither eternal essences, nor phantoms of our senses', but – and now he quotes Heraclitus' astonishing solution, 'Die Welt ist das Spiel des Zeus, oder physikalischer ausgedrückt, des Feuers mit sich selbst, das Eine ist nur in diesem Sinne zugleich das Viele.'[4]

We possess a preliminary draft of Nietzsche's *Philosophers Treatise* in the manuscript of his lecture on the Pre-Socratic philosophers,[5] where the genesis of these meditations becomes clearer. There too we

---

[1] Nietzsche, *Werke*, vol. x, p. 35.
[2] Section 3: 'Die "Vernunft" in der Philosophie', ch. 2, *ibid*. vol. viii, p. 77.
[3] *Ibid*. vol. x, p. 37.   [4] *Ibid*. pp. 37–8.
[5] 'Philologica iii,' *ibid*. vol. xix, pp. 125–234.

find the same reference to a 'wrong-turning' and its rectification; but this time it is presented not as a doubt that tempts Heraclitus, but as Nietzsche's own reasoning.

He takes as his starting-point Jacob Bernays' interpretation of Heraclitus which presents the history of the world as a recurring cycle of birth and destruction by fire, rebirth and fresh destruction, according to the law of *hybris* and punishment.[1] Nietzsche tenders this, it is true, as a conception of Anaximander's that Heraclitus has not yet quite thrown off;[2] for it was Anaximander – the meta-physician! – who had explained all coming-to-be and passing-away as guilt and retribution. Heraclitus is shown as taking a similar view: 'Der Weltprozess ist ein ungeheurer Bestrafungsakt...So endlich gewinnen wir den düstern Gesamtausdruck der Heraklitischen Züge: derentwegen ihn die Spätern als den "weinenden Philosophen" bezeichnen.' But at this point Nietzsche suddenly changes course: 'Diese ganze Annahme ist zu verwerfen: aber ihre Besprechung führt in das Herz der heraklitischen Anschauung.'[3] It is not philology, but a philosophical intuition, that makes him reject Bernays' interpretation and replace it by another, which, we can say today, will prove even philologically a better one.[4]

It is at this turning-point in the lecture's argument that we become aware of a change in Nietzsche's own philosophical thinking. We have here a renunciation of metaphysics, which in the completed treatise he will present as Heraclitus' own conclusion. From a biographical point of view, this renunciation constitutes a critical moment in Nietzsche's philosophical development. He breaks with the metaphysical Schopenhauerian ideas that inspired the *Birth of Tragedy* and the *Untimely Meditations* and opens the way for the formation of his own philosophy; and it is interesting that this move is made under the auspices of Heraclitus.

Nietzsche's new outlook finds its first expression in a new interpretation of Heraclitus, which starts from Heraclitus' statement about the identity of opposites: 'For the god, all things are beautiful and good and just.'[5] He claims for Heraclitus the view which he will later

---

[1] *Die Heraklitischen Briefe* (1869), p. 13.
[2] Nietzsche, *Werke*, vol. XIX, p. 183.   [3] *Ibid.* p. 184.
[4] Most modern interpreters regard the ecpyrosis doctrine as a stoic misinterpretation of Heraclitus; cf. K. Reinhardt, 'Heraklits Lehre vom Feuer', *Vermächtnis der Antike*, pp. 41ff., and G. S. Kirk, *Heraclitus, The Cosmic Fragments* (Cambridge, 1954), pp. 319ff.
[5] Heraclitus, fr. 102, *Fragmente der Vorsokratiker*.

unfold in *Beyond Good and Evil*. The maxim 'All is good' implies for him saying 'Yes' to all negative phenomena. Heraclitus is represented as the first great *Ja-sager*, the first in the line that runs through Spinoza and Goethe to Zarathustra's *Ja-und-Amen-Lied*. This is what Nietzsche has in mind when he talks about his 'line of ancestors'.

The new interpretation centres on Heraclitus' cosmic simile of the playing child: 'Time is a child playing at draughts.'[1] 'Hier ist Unschuld und doch Entstehenlassen und Zerstören. Es soll kein Tropfen von ἀδικία in der Welt zurückbleiben.'[2] The idea of Chance and Necessity and of the 'Innocence of Becoming'[3] is formulated for the first time here in connection with Heraclitus; and whenever the 'play' metaphor occurs in his later works, Nietzsche is treading in the footsteps of Heraclitus, though with his concept of creating and destroying he diverges from the strictly Heraclitean meaning of the simile. This concept will later characterise his idea of the 'Dionysian' – a transmutation of the old demiourgos motif into the Amoral.

The phrase 'no drop of injustice...' points to the theme of 'justification' which runs through the whole of Nietzsche's work: 'justification of the world', 'justification of life', 'justification of transience, of suffering, of Becoming, of history.'[4] This is a theme that springs ultimately from a theological source, from a deep-rooted Protestant Christianity.

In the succeeding anti-metaphysical period of Nietzsche's development references to Heraclitus become at first less frequent. But it is noteworthy that the River metaphor is now used to denote Man's Becoming.[5] Becoming is History. In the Untimely Meditation 'On the use and disadvantage of History' he had been still sharply critical of the modern 'historical sense' and the practice of thinking in terms of 'processes',[6] but now he says: 'We need History', and philosophers are blamed for their 'lack of an historical sense'.[7]

The interpretation of Heraclitean Becoming in the sense of Evolution radically alters Nietzsche's attitude to History, and will lead later to his conception of a genealogy of morals and a genealogy of

---

[1] Heraclitus, fr. 52, *ibid.*
[2] Nietzsche, *Werke*, vol. xix, p. 184.
[3] *Ibid.* vol. xii, pp. 393, 396; vol. xiii, pp. 127, 128; vol. xiv, p. 307.
[4] *Ibid.* vol. i, p. 45; vol. vi, pp. 14, 125; vol. xvi, pp. 391, 167, 362; vol. xv, p. 192.
[5] *Menschliches-Allzumenschliches*, vol. ii, § 1, aph. 223, in *ibid.* vol. iii, p. 121; cf. aph. 185.
[6] *Ibid.* vol. i, p. 366, *passim.*
[7] *Götzen-Dämmerung*: 'Die "Vernunft" in der Philosophie', aph. 1, in *ibid.* vol. viii, p. 76.

cognition.[1] That Man – his morals *and* his cognitive power – had developed gradually was a possibility that Kant had not considered. Nietzsche's new view of History pointed the way towards surmounting Kantian transcendentalism.

With *Zarathustra* references to Heraclitus suddenly multiply. Even the Zarathustra figure, the choice of which appears unmotivated, can be shown to have been a substitute for Heraclitus. It is true that in the *Philosophers Treatise* Nietzsche had explicitly refused to connect Heraclitus with the Persian Zoroaster and adopted the view of Jacob Bernays who, in his *Rheinisches Museum* article, sharply rejected the philological thesis that there was some relation between Heraclitean and Zoroastrian teachings other than 'die Beziehung der tiefstgreifenden Opposition'.[2] But it was this very idea of an 'opposition' to the old dualistic system attached to the name of the historical Zarathustra, the inversion of dualism into its opposite, that prompted (he claims in *Ecce homo*) his choice of name for his new Zarathustra.[3] We can trace a threefold identification here: he identifies himself first with Heraclitus, then with the Zarathustra figure,[4] and finally Heraclitus is linked with the new Zarathustra. For the omnipresence of Heraclitus in *Zarathustra*, for the intimate equation between the two of them, we have the evidence of a passage where Zarathustra almost refers to Heraclitus by name. It comes where he points to the ruins of an old temple: 'Wahrlich, wer hier einst seine Gedanken in Stein nach oben türmte, um das Geheimnis alles Lebens wusste er gleich dem Weisesten.'[5] The temple represents the philosophy of Heraclitus, the principle of strife and the harmony of opposites.

Of the Heraclitean reminiscences in *Zarathustra* I want to mention only the theory of the Eternal Recurrence. This had been long familiar to Nietzsche as part of the stoic interpretation of Heraclitus where it features in connection with the Great Year, the μέγας ἐνιαυτός in the doxography of the philosopher.[6] Nietzsche writes in

---

[1] *Ibid.* vol. xii, p. 33 (no. 62); vol. xiii, p. 23; vol. xvi, pp. 29, 47, 61f., 69, 111, *passim*.
[2] *Rheinisches Museum*, vii (1850), 94.
[3] *Ecce homo*: 'Warum ich ein Schicksal bin', aph. 3, Nietzsche, *Werke*, vol. xv, p. 118.
[4] E.g.:

> Da, plötzlich, Freundin! wurde Eins zu Zwei –
> – Und Zarathustra ging an mir vorbei...

> (*Fröhliche Wissenschaft*: Lieder des Prinzen Vogelfrei, 'Sils-Maria', in *ibid.* vol. v, p. 360; cf. *Jenseits von Gut und Böse*, Nachgesang, in *ibid.* vol. vii, p. 279).

[5] *Also sprach Zarathustra*, Part i: 'Von den Taranteln', in *ibid.* vol. vi, p. 147.
[6] Aëtius ii.31, 2–4, see H. Diels, *Doxographi graeci* (Berlin, 1879), p. 363f.

Ecce homo: 'diese Lehre Zarathustras *könnte* zuletzt auch schon von Heraklit gelehrt worden sein';[1] and Zarathustra's animals, the eagle and the snake, speak to their master thus: 'Oh Zarathustra,...du bist der Lehrer der Ewigen Wiederkunft...Du lehrst, dass es ein Grosses Jahr des Werdens gibt, ein Ungeheuer von grossem Jahr: das muss sich, einer Sanduhr gleich, immer wieder von neuem umdrehen, damit es von neuem ablaufe.'[2] But about this idea of time as a circle one would have to speak, no longer as a philologist, but in philosophical terms. What it implies is that linear time, as the Kantian form of perception, is transcended so that we arrive at an intuition of the essence of Time, which is no longer an infinite line but simultaneity – comparable perhaps to the concept of Space in modern physics, which instead of infinite Space reckons with the circular bending of a finite Space.

Nietzsche, in his last works, aims at an understanding of the world as a whole along lines that had been laid down in his early interpretation of Heraclitus. He wants to regain a cosmological standpoint which lies beyond traditional metaphysics and beyond the transcendentalist subjectivism of modern times.

To show this, I shall end by quoting an aphorism from the *opus postumum*[3] in which he explains what he thinks 'the world' means to him – and you will hear the Heraclitean reminiscences transformed into modern physics in this new and vitalistic Heraclitus:

Diese Welt: ein Ungeheuer von Kraft, ohne Anfang, ohne Ende, eine feste, eherne Grösse von Kraft, welche nicht grösser, nicht kleiner wird, die sich nicht verbraucht, sondern nur verwandelt...als Spiel von Kräften und Kraftwellen zugleich Eines und Vieles...ein Meer in sich selber stürmender und flutender Kräfte, ewig sich wandelnd, ewig zurücklaufend, mit ungeheuren Jahren der Wiederkehr, mit einer Ebbe und Flut seiner Gestaltungen, aus den einfachsten in die vielfältigsten hinaustreibend, aus dem Stillsten, Starrsten, Kältesten hinaus in das Glühendste, Wildeste, Sich-selber-Widersprechendste, und dann wieder aus der Fülle heimkehrend zum Einfachen, aus dem Spiel der Widersprüche zurück bis zur Lust des Einklangs, sich selber bejahend noch in dieser Gleichheit seiner Bahnen, sich selber segnend als das, was ewig wiederkommen muss, als ein Werden, das kein Sattwerden, keinen Überdruss, keine Müdigkeit kennt...

It is this turn to cosmology that Nietzsche calls the 'regaining of the

---

[1] *Ecce homo*: 'Die Geburt der Tragödie', in *ibid.* vol. xv, p. 65.
[2] *Also sprach Zarathustra*, Part III: 'Der Genesende', in Nietzsche, *Werke*, vol. VI, p. 321.
[3] *Ibid.* vol. XVI, p. 401.

ancient ground':[1] in it he recognises 'the actual worth and dignity of German philosophy':

fortzufahren in der Entdeckung des Altertums, in der Aufgrabung der antiken Philosophie, vor allem der Vorsokratiker – der bestverschütteten aller griechischen Tempel! Vielleicht, dass man einige Jahrhunderte später urteilen wird, dass alles deutsche Philosophieren darin seine eigentliche Würde habe, ein schrittweises Wiedergewinnen des antiken Bodens zu sein... Wir nähern uns heute allen jenen grundsätzlichen Formen der Weltauslegung wieder, welche der griechische Geist, in Anaximander, Heraklit, Parmenides, Empedokles, Demokrit und Anaxagoras, erfunden hat, – wir werden von Tag zu Tag griechischer.

[1] *Ibid.* vol. xv, p. 445.

18

RENAN ET LA PHILOLOGIE
CLASSIQUE*

JEAN SEZNEC

La notion de philologie tient une place centrale dans la pensée de Renan; elle a joué un rôle décisif dans sa carrière, et dans sa vie.

Sa vocation lui a été révélée au Grand Séminaire de Saint-Sulpice en 1843; il avait alors vingt ans. Rappelons ce qu'avaient été jusque là ses études. Il les avait commencées en 1832 en Bretagne, au petit collège de Tréguier, où il avait pour condisciples de petits paysans travaillant – la plupart – pour être prêtres. Il a donc appris le latin, et solidement, comme on l'apprenait alors. Il a obtenu les prix de version et de narration latines; et le latin, comme nous le verrons, restera à ses yeux l'une des bases de toute éducation.

Mais, dans ses *Souvenirs d'enfance et de jeunesse*, il note l'effet singulier de cet enseignement sur des écoliers bretons. 'Le latin produisait sur ces natures frustes et fortes des effets comparables aux réactions des Germains à l'époque carlovingienne: c'était le contact des barbares avec la civilisation. L'état d'esprit d'un Saxo Grammaticus, d'un Rabanus Maurus, sont des choses très claires pour moi: nous étions, nous aussi, comme des mastodontes faisant leurs humanités. Nous nous communiquions sur Salluste, sur Tite-Live, des réflexions qui devaient fort ressembler à celles qu'échangeaient entre eux les disciples de Saint Gall ou de Saint Colomban apprenant le latin. Ce que j'ai vu à Tréguier m'a donné une grande aptitude pour comprendre les phénomènes historiques.'[1] Le voici maintenant à Paris, où il doit continuer sa préparation à la carrière ecclésiastique au Petit Séminaire de Saint-Nicolas du Chardonnet. C'est là qu'il fait, en 1840 et 1841, sa rhétorique; et nous avons, de cette période, un cahier intitulé: 'Recueil de mes lectures', où il notait, dit-il, 'tout ce que mes lectures m'ont fait découvrir dans les auteurs grecs et

---

* Les vues générales de Renan sur la philologie se trouvent dans les articles et comptes rendus suivants: 'Histoire de la philologie dans l'antiquité' (1848); 'Les congrès philologiques en Allemagne' (1848); 'Les Grammairiens grecs' (1854). Ces textes ont été recueillis dans les *Mélanges d'histoire et de voyages* (1878); de larges extraits en ont été incorporés dans *L'avenir de la science* (1890).

[1] *Souvenirs*, éd. Garnier-Flammarion (Paris, 1973), p. 108.

349

latins de plus remarquable soit comme pensée, soit comme expression'.

Que lui fait-on lire? Les *Odes* d'Horace, le *Pro Archia* de Cicéron; Virgile, Tacite. Pour le grec, le troisième chant de l'*Iliade*, le *Prométhée* d'Eschyle, l'*Apologie de Socrate*. Il sera bon helléniste comme il avait été bon latiniste; et dès ce temps-là sa prédilection pour la Grèce commence à se dessiner. Il ne cessera pas d'approfondir sa familiarité avec les classiques.[1] Cependant, il lui reste à découvrir l'Orient. Or il passe, à l'automne de 1843, au Grand Séminaire de Saint-Sulpice où il va faire sa classe de théologie. De là date sa rencontre avec l'hébreu, rencontre capitale, et dramatique, puisque, deux ans plus tard, Renan quitte le séminaire, et renonce à la prêtrise.

Il avait commencé l'hébreu sous un maître admirable, M. Le Hir; il fit des progrès si extraordinaires qu'on lui confia bientôt le cours de grammaire hébraïque. Cette circonstance, écrit-il, fixa ma vie; je découvris que j'étais philologue d'instinct. L'obligation de clarifier et de systématiser mes idées en vue des leçons faites à mes condisciples décida ma vocation.[2]

Renan avait simplement découvert la critique des textes, dont la philologie est l'indispensable instrument.

Les nécessités de l'exégèse biblique l'obligent à examiner le livre sacré; or, ce livre, il le lit désormais dans l'original. Et qu'y découvre-t-il? Des erreurs, des contradictions, des impossibilités historiques et des inconséquences grammaticales. Bref, il relève partout, dans ce texte prétendu *révélé*, les traces d'une composition tout humaine.[3]

Ses *Cahiers de jeunesse* de 1845 et de 1846 fourmillent d'observations de ce genre: 'Il n'est plus possible de prétendre que le second livre d'Isaïe a été écrit par Isaïe...Le livre de Daniel, qui est supposé appartenir à la période de la Captivité, est un apocryphe composé vers 170 avant Jésus-Christ. Celui de Judith est historiquement inacceptable.' Dans la Genèse, dans les Nombres, dans le Pentateuque, on détecte des altérations, des interpolations. Le passage des Nombres généralement utilisé pour prouver que Moïse écrivit le Pentateuque est plutôt la preuve du contraire. Et que dire de la traduction des Septante, et de la Vulgate? Les traducteurs grecs

---

[1] H. Tronchon, *Ernest Renan et l'étranger* (Paris, 1928), ch. 1: 'Renan et l'Antiquité', pp. 40–4.
[2] *Souvenirs*, p. 176.　　　　　　　　　　[3] *Ibid.* p. 177.

emploient des termes ambigus, Saint Jérôme des termes faux; il prend un nom pour un adjectif, commet des erreurs de ponctuation, etc.

Ce qui frappe, c'est le ton péremptoire de ces observations, de la part d'un jeune homme qui a commencé l'hébreu il y a seulement quelques mois; c'est aussi le fait qu'elles portent sur des points de détail, des minuties; mais tel est, justement, le processus de la philologie: elle part d'une remarque insignifiante en apparence, qui conduit à mettre en question des matières d'une immense importance – et, finalement, à mettre en doute des croyances traditionnelles, acceptées sans contrôle. C'est précisément l'expérience de Renan; et ce sera sa démarche constante.

'Mes raisons pour quitter le séminaire', conclut-il, 'furent toutes de l'ordre philologique et critique; elles ne furent nullement de l'ordre métaphysique, de l'ordre politique, ni de l'ordre moral.'[1] Moins encore de l'ordre sentimental. Quand un jeune prêtre se défroque (Renan n'était pas prêtre encore, mais il avait franchi les premiers degrés du sacerdoce, pris les ordres mineurs) le public ne manque pas de dire: 'Où est la femme?' C'est, dit Renan, l'éternel lieu commun par lequel les laïcs croient expliquer les cas de ce genre. Ils n'auraient pas manqué de l'invoquer si on avait pu prétendre que j'avais quitté le séminaire pour d'autres raisons que celles de la philologie.

Mais, après tout, la philologie n'est-elle pas femme aussi, et femme séduisante? Elle fut épousée par Mercure, s'il faut en croire Martianus Capella.

Sorti du séminaire, Renan va devoir affronter le monde, et d'abord gagner sa vie; pour cela, il lui faut des diplômes. Il les conquiert l'un après l'autre, ce qui le ramène aux classiques. Tout en continuant à étudier les langues orientales au Collège de France, il prépare sa licence ès lettres, et passe brillamment l'examen, loué par ses examinateurs pour l'aisance et la correction de sa dissertation latine, et son thème grec irréprochable. Mais il s'impatiente de la nature des épreuves, artificielles à son gré. Ainsi la licence comporte une épreuve de *vers* latins. 'Bonté du ciel! 's'écrie Renan, 'se peut-il qu'on nous impose encore ces chaînes?' Tout cela, c'est encore l'humanisme superficiel de l'ancienne rhétorique; ce sont des puérilités.

Ce qui l'intéresse, ici encore, ce sont les textes eux-mêmes: il les lit

[1] *Ibid.* p. 179.

du même œil critique avec lequel il avait lu la Bible. Il discutait sur les variantes des textes de Saint Paul et de Saint Clément; il corrige à présent une lecture fautive de Suétone, et une lettre d'Hadrien. Au reste, il découvre, chez les glossateurs et les interprètes de la littérature gréco-romaine, les mêmes faiblesses qu'il avait dénoncées chez les exégètes – et les mêmes ridicules.[1]

Un exemple amusant est celui des cigales, chantées par Anacréon dans son Ode 43. C'est le passage qui a été traduit en latin par Joshua Barnes, Professeur de grec à Cambridge à la fin du XVIIe siècle.

> Beatam praedicamus te, o cicada
> Quod arboribus in summis
> Exiguo rore potato
> Rex veluti, cantillas.

Ce même passage a été traduit en anglais par Thomas Moore:

> O thou, of all creations blest,
> Sweet insect! that delight'st to rest
> Upon the wild wood's leafy tops,
> To drink the dew that morning drops...

Les cigales *boivent* la rosée; mais un commentateur cite des textes où il est dit qu'elles *mangent*. Terrible problème! dit Renan, qui propose ironiquement la solution: elles boivent *et* elles mangent.

'Je commence à croire', ajoute-t-il, 'que les folies et l'ἀκρισία que j'attribuais en propre aux commentateurs des livres sacrés appartiennent à *tous* les commentateurs, à toute cette race de suceurs qui s'attachent aux grandes œuvres, et veulent de force en extraire un jus qui souvent n'y est pas.'

Voyez l'histoire des cigales, buveuses *et* mangeuses de rosée. C'est le principe que dans les contradictions apparentes il faut affirmer les deux *simultanément*, absolument comme on affirme simultanément les deux généalogies de Jésus-Christ. 'On peut noblement commenter,' conclut Renan; 'mais il faut avouer qu'un petit esprit qui s'en mêle tombe dans d'étranges petitesses. *Ces sottises me tuent.*'

Réduire la philologie à ces chicanes enfantines, c'est ne rien comprendre à sa nature, ni à son rôle – le rôle capital qu'elle a joué depuis la Renaissance et celui, plus essentiel encore, qu'elle doit continuer à jouer dans le présent, et qu'elle est appelée à jouer dans l'avenir.

Car – Renan le dit et le répète – 'Les vrais fondateurs de l'esprit

[1] J. Pommier, 'Le jeune Renan et les commentateurs', *Dialogues avec le passé* (Paris, 1967) p. 14. L'exemple des cigales vient de notes prises à divers cours.

moderne sont les philologues de la Renaissance. Ce qui avait manqué au Moyen-Age, ce n'était pas la curiosité du passé, ni la persévérance du travail. Il lui manquait d'avoir appris le grec et d'avoir lu *dans le texte* Aristote et Platon.'[1] (C'est ici le lieu de rappeler que Renan soumit à l'Institut en 1848 un Mémoire sur 'L'histoire de la langue grecque en Occident depuis la fin du Ve siècle jusqu'à la fin du XIVe'.)

Certes, 'les érudits de la Renaissance n'avaient pas la sévère méthode de notre siècle, mais ne pourrions-nous pas aussi leur envier leur puissant amour, et leur désintéressement? Quel est le philologue de nos jours qui apporte dans ses recherches l'ivresse des premiers humanistes, Pétrarque, Boccace, Le Pogge, Traversari – ces hommes possédés par l'ardeur du savoir, portant jusqu'à la mysticité le culte des études nouvelles?'

Or, ces études alors nouvelles sont en passe de devenir, aux yeux de Renan, la science par excellence. Le XIXe siècle est celui de la Critique, qui soumet à l'examen les vieilles autorités. Et quel est l'instrument de cet examen, sinon la philologie? C'est elle qui passe au crible les anciennes croyances; c'est elle qui est la sauvegarde contre le retour des superstitions. 'Le jour où elle périrait, la critique périrait avec elle, la barbarie renaîtrait, la crédulité serait de nouveau maîtresse du monde.'[2]

Le XIXe siècle est celui de l'Histoire; et la philologie, qui possède désormais des moyens inconnus aux âges précédents, va permettre de constituer l'histoire ou mieux, l'embryogénie de l'esprit humain.

Telle est en effet la fin suprême des études philologiques, et leur ultime résultat. Et c'est pourquoi, dans son *Avenir de la Science*, Renan salue la philologie comme la science de l'avenir.

L'avenir de la Science ne parut qu'en 1890; mais Renan avait conçu cette œuvre à vingt-cinq ans, sitôt après son abandon du sacerdoce, et au lendemain de la révolution de 1848. 'Je me trouvai alors', dit-il, 'en face de moi-même. J'éprouvai le besoin de résumer la *foi nouvelle* qui avait remplacé chez moi le catholicisme ruiné'; mais son problème personnel, sa crise morale, se confondaient avec ceux du peuple, dont les anciennes croyances avaient été ébranlées ou détruites, elles aussi, par la révolution. Par quoi remplacer ces croyances? Sur quels soutiens appuyer, désormais, l'ordre social? Et comment rebâtir, sans les vieux rêves, la base d'une existence heureuse et noble?[3]

[1] *L'avenir de la science*, dans *Œuvres complètes*, éd. Calmann-Lévy, t. III, p. 839.
[2] *Ibid.* pp. 844–5.　　　　　　[3] *Ibid.* pp. 727, 752 et *passim*.

Dorénavant, affirme le jeune Renan, la science seule peut fournir à l'homme ces vérités sans lesquelles la vie serait intolérable, et la société impossible. La science seule peut résoudre pour l'homme les questions dont sa nature réclame impérieusement la réponse. 'Je veux dire', répète-t-il, 'le sens que j'attache à la science, comment elle est à mes yeux inséparable de la philosophie qu'elle renferme, comment elle est *une religion*, sacrée au même titre qu'elle, puisque seule elle peut résoudre le grand problème des choses.'

La science sera donc une religion de rechange – la religion de demain. La science – mais quelle science? Eh bien, celle-là même qui l'a détourné de l'église: la philologie. C'est elle qu'il propose à ses contemporains – non, dit-il, comme une Californie à exploiter, mais comme une voie de salut, comme un chemin à suivre pour retrouver celui du ciel.

Cette prétention paraît démesurée. On est tenté d'y voir le cas du spécialiste enivré de son sujet; on peut y soupçonner aussi un orgueil de caste, un orgueil quasi-sacerdotal. 'Renan', remarque un de ses critiques, 'appartenait à cette catégorie de savants qui sont insolemment remplis de leur importance. Pourquoi la philologie les gonfle-t-elle ainsi? Est-ce parce qu'elle leur donne une certitude qui leur paraît égale à celle des mathématiques, et parce qu'ils croient pénétrer, par elle, jusqu'aux origines de la société et des religions?'[1]

Renan n'est pas exempt de cet orgueil; mais il s'efforce de légitimer les ambitions qu'il revendique pour la philologie. Si ces ambitions paraissent extravagantes, c'est qu'on méconnaît son objet, et son pouvoir.

D'abord, 'à une époque où l'on demande avant tout au savant à quoi il s'occupe, et à quel résultat il arrive, le philologue trouve peu de faveur. On comprend le physicien, le chimiste, l'astronome; on ne comprend pas le philologue.'[2]

Pour commencer, il y a un malentendu sur son nom: on s'imagine qu'il ne travaille que sur des mots – et quoi de plus frivole? C'est qu'on ne sait pas distinguer, comme le faisait Zénon, le philologue du logophile.

Une autre cause de malentendu, c'est que le domaine du philologue n'est pas défini. Il est aussi vague que celui de la philosophie, ou de la poésie. Au premier coup d'œil, la philologie semble ne présenter qu'un ensemble d'études sans unité scientifique. Elle est

---

[1] A. Bellessort, *Les intellectuels et l'avènement de la Troisième République* (Paris, 1931), p. 133.
[2] *Mélanges d'histoire et de voyages*, p. 391.

moins une science spéciale qu'un aspect sous lequel on envisage les choses de l'esprit. Le vrai philologue doit être à la fois linguiste, historien, archéologue, etc. Ces recherches diverses, renfermées sous le même nom, font croire volontiers au public que le philologue n'est qu'un *amateur* – ou pis encore une sorte de taupe. Il explore le passé, çà et là, à peu près comme certaines espèces d'animaux fouisseurs creusant des mines souterraines pour le plaisir d'en faire.[1]

Mais ce qui contribue surtout à le déconsidérer, ou même à le ridiculiser, c'est l'*humilité* des moyens qu'il emploie. N'est-il pas un homme qui passe sa vie à déchiffrer de vieux marbres, à interpréter et à commenter des textes qui, aux yeux de l'ignorance, ne sont que bizarres, ou absurdes?

Ici encore, le vulgaire se trompe, faute de percevoir les résultats derniers, les vérités générales auxquels conduisent ces investigations en apparence futiles. On se moque d'un grammairien comme on se moque du naturaliste disséquant des limaçons; mais d'où viennent tant de vues nouvelles sur la marche des littératures, sur la poésie spontanée, sur les âges primitifs, si ce n'est de l'étude patiente des plus arides détails? Vico, Wolff, Niebuhr, Strauss, auraient-ils enrichi la pensée de tant d'aperçus nouveaux sans la plus minutieuse érudition?[2]

Le plus grave, c'est que même les partisans et les admirateurs de la philologie la défendent avec de mauvais arguments.

Au congrès des philologues allemands à Bonn en 1841, Welcker fit une communication: 'Über die Bedeutung der Philologie'. Il prit le mot dans le sens restreint: la science des littératures classiques, c'est-à-dire des littératures *modèles*, qui exercent une influence heureuse sur les lettres et l'éducation esthétique des nations modernes. Les anciens, autrement dit, sont pour Welcker beaucoup plus des objets d'admiration que des objets de science: il n'envisage la philologie que du point de vue de l'humaniste, et non du point de vue du savant.

Pour Renan, cette attitude est inacceptable: elle a pour effet de rétrécir le domaine de la philologie, et sa portée. 'Si on ne cultive les littératures anciennes,' répond-il à Welcker, 'que pour y chercher des modèles, à quoi bon cultiver celles qui – tout en ayant leurs beautés originales – ne sont point *imitables* pour nous? Il faudrait donc se borner à l'antiquité grecque et latine – et même, dans ces limites, l'étude des chefs d'œuvre seule aurait du prix'.[3]

Or, 'les littératures de l'Orient, que M. Welcker traite avec beaucoup de mépris, et les œuvres de second ordre des littératures

[1] *Ibid.*   [2] *Ibid.* p. 416; cf. *Avenir*, p. 837.   [3] *Avenir*, p. 890; *Mélanges*, p. 425.

classiques, si elles servent moins à former le goût, offrent quelquefois plus d'intérêt philosophique, et nous en apprennent plus *sur l'histoire de l'esprit humain* que les monuments accomplis des époques de perfection'. De toutes les branches des études philologiques, répète l'orientaliste Renan, l'Orient peut offrir *pour l'histoire de l'esprit humain* les plus précieuses données.

D'une manière générale, Renan rejette comme détestable un autre argument invoqué en faveur de la philologie, à savoir qu'elle est un moyen d'éducation, et qu'elle se confond, en fait, avec l'enseignement.

Cette confusion commune entre la science et l'école, l'érudit et le professeur, provoque son exaspération. 'Supposer', dit Renan, 'que la philologie ne vaut quelque chose que parce qu'elle sert à l'enseignement, c'est lui enlever sa dignité; c'est la réduire à la pédagogie; c'est la pire des humiliations. Il faut chercher le prix du savoir en lui-même, et non dans l'usage qu'on en peut faire pour l'instruction de l'enfance.'

Malheureusement, c'est là le préjugé français. 'Les Français confondent la science avec l'instruction publique, comme si les recherches sérieuses n'avaient de valeur qu'en tant qu'elles servent à l'enseignement. De là l'idée que, l'éducation finie, on n'a point à s'en occuper, et que ces matières ne concernent que les professeurs. Il est difficile de trouver, en France, un philologue qui n'appartienne en quelque manière au corps enseignant, et un livre philologique qui ne se rapporte à un but universitaire. Étrange cercle vicieux!' s'écrie Renan. 'Car si ces choses ne sont bonnes qu'à être professées, si ceux-là seuls les étudient qui doivent les enseigner, à quoi bon les enseigner?' La vérité, c'est qu'aux Français les études classiques rappellent le collège; or les Français ont peur de tout ce qui sent l'école. C'est la raison profonde de leur répugnance à l'égard de la philologie et de l'érudition en général. Ils ont peur, en les prenant au sérieux, de passer pour *pédants*.

'Notre susceptibilité sur ce point', explique Renan, 'est peut-être une des causes pour lesquelles la philologie, bien que représentée en France par des noms illustres, est toujours retenue par je ne sais quelle pudeur, et n'ose s'avouer franchement elle-même. Nous sommes si timides contre le ridicule que tout ce qui peut y prêter devient suspect: toute recherche savante passe pour pédantisme et devient un épouvantail pour des esprits légers.'[1]

---

[1] *Mélanges*, pp. 414 et 419.

Les Allemands, eux, n'ont pas ces pudeurs, ni ces craintes; au contraire.

Dans leurs congrès philologiques revit le pédantisme naïf et pesant des humanistes de la Renaissance. Discours pompeux, compliments emphatiques, adresses en style lapidaire – tout cela, chez nos voisins, a encore le privilège de ne pas faire sourire. Chaque congrès finit d'ordinaire par un banquet relevé de vers latins, d'acrostiches, de jeux littéraires. La joie même est classique chez ces respectables érudits: on joue avec des citations de Virgile et d'Homère; et on boit en pensant à Horace.[1]

Il existe bien aussi un pédantisme français; mais c'est selon l'expression de Madame de Staël, que cite Renan, le pédantisme de la légèreté.

Mais quelle est l'attitude *personnelle* de Renan vis-à-vis des langues classiques, et de leur rôle dans les temps modernes? Avec quels arguments fait-il, lui, leur apologie? et comment justifie-t-il, lui, leur place dans l'éducation?

Je voudrais essayer de vous montrer maintenant que son plaidoyer pour la philologie classique marque un retour de Renan l'orientaliste à la tradition de l'Occident.

En ce qui concerne l'éducation, ses déclarations sont catégoriques: 'l'étude de nos langues classiques, inséparables l'une de l'autre, sera toujours chez nous, *par la force des choses*, la base de l'éducation'. Il entend par 'la force des choses' la nécessité de maintenir le contact avec nos origines: seule cette continuité nous rend intelligibles à nous-mêmes.

'Notre civilisation, nos institutions, nos langues, sont construites avec des éléments grecs et latins: *donc* le grec et le latin nous sont imposés *par les faits*. Ne pas les savoir ce serait renier nos origines et rompre avec nos pères. Il nous faut ce commerce direct avec nos ancêtres. L'éducation philologique ne saurait consister à apprendre les langues modernes, l'éducation morale à se nourrir exclusivement des idées et des institutions actuelles. Il faut remonter à la source, et se mettre d'abord sur la voie du passé pour arriver, *par la même route que l'humanité*, à l'intelligence du présent.

'Les langues classiques sont le livre sacré des modernes. Là sont les racines de la nation, ses titres, la raison de ses mots et par conséquent de ses institutions. Chaque idée moderne est entée sur une tige antique.'[2] Telle est la véritable justification des études classiques. Cela ne signifie pas qu'on doive leur consacrer une existence entière.

[1] *Ibid.* p. 413.　　　　　[2] *Ibid.* pp. 386–8.

Renan parle avec dédain de 'ce pauvre Havet [l'éminent latiniste] qui ne songeait qu'à bien faire toute sa vie son cours de version latine à la Sorbonne'. Cela signifie, simplement, que le latin et le grec sont les fondations. Et c'est à ce titre, d'abord, qu'ils sont essentiels à l'éducation.

Mais la connaissance précise des langues classiques n'est pas moins essentielle pour l'intelligence et la juste appréciation des littératures antiques.

Ces littératures sont des objets d'admiration; mais cette admiration n'est légitime que si elle repose sur la connaissance des textes originaux – des textes, et des contextes, c'est-à-dire du milieu qui les a produits.

C'est un point sur lequel Renan revient inlassablement: l'admiration, pour n'être pas vaine, doit être historique, c'est-à-dire érudite. Le savant seul a le droit d'admirer.[1] L'erreur des modernes a été de s'imaginer que l'on pouvait se passer du contact *direct* avec les œuvres antiques; bien mieux – ou bien pis – qu'un ignorant, incapable de les lire, était d'autant plus sensible à leur beauté.

De cette *sotte* admiration, comme il l'appelle, Renan donne des exemples divertissants.

Écoutez, dit-il, Joseph de Maistre: 'Pour sentir les beautés de la Vulgate, conseille de Maistre, faites choix d'un ami *qui ne soit pas* hébraïsant, et vous verrez comment une syllabe, un mot, et je ne sais quelle aile légère donnée à la phrase feront jaillir sous vos yeux des beautés de premier ordre.'

'Avec ce système-là,' dit Renan, 'et surtout avec le secours d'un ami *qui ne soit pas* helléniste, je me charge de trouver des beautés de premier ordre dans la plus mauvaise traduction d'Homère ou de Pindare, indépendamment de celles qui y sont.' Comment, en effet, comprendre les beautés d'Homère sans être savant, sans connaître l'antique, sans avoir le sens du primitif?[2]

Autre exemple: Chateaubriand. 'L'admiration de Chateaubriand pour les anciens n'est si souvent défectueuse que parce que le sens esthétique éminent dont il était doué ne reposait pas sur une solide instruction. Il admire, par exemple, la simplicité d'Homère ne décrivant la grotte de Calypso que par une simple épithète: *tapissée de lilas*. Or, voici le passage: ἐν σπέεσι γλαφυροῖσι, λιλαιομένη πόσιν εἶναι (Calypso brûlait du désir d'avoir Ulysse pour époux).' 'Je crois, Dieu me pardonne!' s'écrie Renan, 'que Chateaubriand a vu

---

[1] *Avenir*, p. 882.   [2] *Ibid.* p. 1142, n. 132.

des lilas dans λιλαιομένη. C'est que Chateaubriand n'était pas helléniste.'[1]

Latin et grec sont inséparables, Renan le répète; mais il ne les place pas au même rang. La langue, la littérature latines sont d'emprunt, et de reflet. Elles sont issues de la Grèce; et le mérite de Rome a été précisément de les transmettre. 'Quel fait immense dans l'histoire de l'humanité que l'initiation du monde latin à la culture grecque!' Rome, grâce à sa vocation impériale, est devenue l'intermédiaire, l'agent de diffusion. Elle n'avait pour elle que la force. Cette force, heureusement, a servi à propager l'œuvre grecque, c'est-à-dire la civilisation.

Il y a eu, d'ailleurs, un moment dans l'histoire où les deux génies classiques se sont fondus en une personne unique. Marc-Aurèle, philosophe grec et empereur romain, résume ce double génie: il reste le représentant idéal de ce monde antique qui périt avec lui.

Cependant il est clair que Renan *préfère* la Grèce à Rome; et cette préférence va jusqu'à la partialité. Il se plaît, par exemple, à noter que les Grecs, conquis par les Romains, n'ont jamais cessé de se considérer supérieurs par l'esprit. Ils ont refusé de se laisser influencer par la culture latine, et même ils l'ont systématiquement dédaignée. 'Rome, après avoir enlevé à la Grèce son indépendance, n'a pas su peser d'un atome sur sa direction intellectuelle, philosophique, religieuse, ni obtenir d'elle un moment d'attention. A part quelques Grecs sans caractère ralliés à leurs vainqueurs, jamais Hellène digne de ce nom n'a fait à la littérature latine l'honneur de s'en occuper. Sous les Antonins, justement, un grammairien grec comme Apollonius d'Alexandrie ne nomme ni Cicéron, ni Virgile, non plus que s'ils n'avaient jamais existé'.[2] Certes, Renan dénonce l'orgueil des philologues grecs qui se persuadaient que les dieux parlaient leur langue, et pour qui tout ce qui n'est pas grec est barbare, et ne mérite pas l'attention; mais, philologue lui-même, il reconnaît, et il rappelle, que c'est la grammaire grecque, transmise par les Latins, qui s'enseigne encore dans nos écoles: c'est elle qui fournit à chacun de nous les catégories du langage, c'est-à-dire l'élément le plus essentiel de la pensée.[3]

'Il n'est rien que nous ne tenions de la Grèce.' Renan n'est jamais las d'affirmer cette dette. Dès 1857, quand il commence son *Averroès*,

---

[1] *Ibid.* n. 133. Renan commet ici une confusion, et son ironie est injustifiée, comme l'a prouvé (après d'autres critiques) R. Lebègue dans: 'Chateaubriand et Renan', *Revue d'histoire littéraire de la France*, LIX (1959), 43.

[2] *Mélanges*, pp. 435–6.   [3] *Ibid.* pp. 428–9.

il proclame, 'Tout ce que l'Orient sémitique, tout ce que le Moyen âge ont eu de philosophie proprement dite, ils le doivent à la Grèce. Si donc il s'agissait de choisir dans le passé une autorité, la Grèce seule aurait le droit de nous donner des leçons.'

'Non pas, ajoute-t-il, cette Grèce d'Égypte et de Syrie, altérée par le mélange d'idées barbares, mais la Grèce originale dans son expression pure et classique.'[1]

Cette remarque sur la Grèce impure des Syriens, nous la retrouverons à propos de Saint Paul, dans la *Prière sur l'Acropole*. Te souviens-tu, dit Renan à Pallas Athéné, du jour où un laid petit juif, parlant le grec des Syriens, vint ici, parcourut tes parvis sans te comprendre, et lut tes inscriptions tout de travers?

En fait, et de bonne heure, Renan a préludé à cette *Prière*, qui est un hymne d'adoration envers la Grèce. Ce texte célèbre ne parut qu'en 1876; mais tous ses thèmes avaient été, de longue date, ébauchés. Voici quelques-uns de ces préludes, dont le ton devient de plus en plus fervent.

'La supériorité de la Grèce sur le reste de l'humanité, *en particulier sur ce qu'ont fait les Latins*, ce principe fondamental que la Grèce est la source de tout art, de toute science, de toute noblesse, voilà le dogme capital...Oui, l'étude de la Grèce doit être le fond de toute éducation libérale – on admire trop Rome...

'C'est la Grèce, cette divine feuille de mûrier jetée au milieu des mers, la Grèce, cette mère glorieuse de toute civilisation, qui a tracé le contour vrai de l'esprit humain.'

Cet éloge exalté finit par prendre un accent religieux. 'Rêver de la Grèce, vivre en Grèce par l'esprit, est pour l'homme cultivé ce qu'est pour le chrétien vivre dans le royaume de Dieu'; mais Athènes est le *seul* point du monde où le parfait existe; elle devrait être l'universel pèlerinage.

Ce pèlerinage, Renan l'avait fait en 1865: c'est la vue du Parthénon qui lui avait révélé la perfection.

Pourtant, ce n'est point d'Athènes que nous est venue notre religion: c'est de Jérusalem. Et Renan a consacré quelque trente années de sa vie à écrire les dix-sept volumes des *Origines du Christianisme*, et de l'*Histoire du peuple d'Israël*.

Mais, parvenu à la fin de sa tâche, il exprime un regret, et un vœu, significatifs. Il avait cru trouver dans la destinée du peuple juif, aboutissant à Jésus et au Christianisme, non seulement l'événement

[1] *Ibid.* p. 150.

capital de l'histoire du monde, mais la seule révélation qui se rapprochât de l'absolu. Le Parthénon, 'cet idéal cristallisé en marbre pentélique', lui a apporté une seconde manifestation du divin. Du coup, la perspective a changé. 'Voici,' explique-t-il dans le préambule de sa *Prière*, 'qu'à côté du miracle juif venait se placer pour moi le miracle grec – une chose qui n'a existé qu'une fois, qui ne s'était jamais vue, qui ne se reverra plus, mais dont l'effet durera éternellement, je veux dire un type de beauté éternelle, sans aucune tache locale ou nationale.'[1] Oui, 'le plus grand des miracles de l'histoire, c'est la Grèce. Heureux qui écrira cette histoire avec amour. Si je pouvais mener une seconde vie, certainement je la consacrerais à l'histoire grecque.'

Permettez-moi, en manière de conclusion, de citer quelques fragments de la *Prière* où Renan récapitule sa vie: ses origines, son éducation, et l'itinéraire intellectuel qui l'a finalement conduit aux pieds de Pallas – bien tard, il y insiste:

'O noblesse! ô beauté simple et vraie! déesse dont le culte signifie raison et sagesse, toi dont le temple est une leçon éternelle de conscience et de sincérité, j'arrive tard au seuil de tes mystères... Tard je t'ai connue, beauté parfaite...'

Trop tard peut-être; car il se croit, il se veut à présent converti à la Raison pure; il déclare: 'J'oublierai toute discipline, hormis la tienne...Je n'aimerai que toi. Je vais apprendre ta langue, désapprendre tout le reste...'[2] Mais, au fond de lui-même, il reste tourmenté par la nostalgie de l'irrationel et le charme des souvenirs de son enfance chrétienne, qu'il n'a pu arracher de son cœur.

Voici l'évocation de sa Bretagne natale:

Je suis né, déesse aux yeux bleus, de parents barbares, chez les Cimmériens bons et vertueux qui habitent au bord d'une mer sombre, hérissée de rochers, toujours battue par les orages. On y connaît à peine le soleil; les fleurs sont les mousses marines, les algues et les coquillages qu'on trouve au fond des baies solitaires. Les nuages y paraissent sans couleur, et la joie même y est un peu triste; mais des fontaines d'eau froide y sortent du rocher, et les yeux des jeunes filles y sont comme ces vertes fontaines où, sur des fonds d'algues ondulées, se mire le ciel.[3]

Telle est la Bretagne, et Renan est resté – incurablement – breton. A côté de la *Prière sur l'Acropole*, il a composé une autre prière, où il invoque non plus Pallas Athéné, mais ses propres ancêtres dont il a hérité ce trait essentiel, caractéristique des races celtiques: l'idéalisme. Et il se proclame non seulement leur héritier, mais leur

---

[1] *Souvenirs*, p. 74.   [2] *Ibid.* p. 79.   [3] *Ibid.* p. 75.

interprète; car c'est par lui, Renan, que ces 'pères de la tribu obscure au foyer de laquelle il puisa la foi à l'invisible' arrivent à la vie, et à la voix.[1]

Et voici, à présent, le souvenir de son éducation:

Des prêtres d'un culte étranger, venus des Syriens de Palestine, prirent soin de m'élever. Ces prêtres étaient sages et saints...Leurs temples sont trois fois hauts comme le tien, ô Eurythmie, et semblables à des forêts; seulement ils ne sont pas solides; ils tombent en ruine au bout de cinq à six cents ans; ce sont des fantaisies de barbares, qui s'imaginent qu'on peut faire quelque chose de bien en dehors des règles que tu as tracées à tes inspirés, ô Raison. Mais ces temples me plaisaient; je n'avais pas étudié ton art divin; j'y trouvais Dieu. On y chantait des cantiques dont je me souviens encore: 'Salut, étoile de la mer...reine de ceux qui gémissent en cette vallée de larmes' ou bien: 'Rose mystique, Tour d'ivoire, Maison d'or, étoile du matin...' Tiens, déesse, quand je me rappelle ces chants, mon cœur se fond, je deviens presque apostat. Pardonne-moi ce ridicule; tu ne peux te figurer le charme que les magiciens barbares ont mis dans ces vers, et combien il m'en coûte de suivre la raison toute nue.[2]

La *Prière sur l'Acropole* – et de là vient sa résonance pathétique – est aussi une confession.

---

[1] Préface aux *Essais de morale et de critique* (1860). Un de ces essais est consacré à 'La poésie des races celtiques'.

[2] *Souvenirs*, p. 78.

INDEX

Names in this index are cited in the form used in their country of origin with a few obvious exceptions such as Aesop or Livy. Where this might lead to difficulties of identification, cross-references have been provided. Figures in bold type indicate that the subject of the entry is discussed at some length. Figures in italics indicate that a reference is given. Where such a reference is to a modern work (a secondary authority), the name of the author follows in brackets. Where more authorities are mentioned than can be listed conveniently, the brackets carry the words 'with bibliography'. Full titles with place and date of publication are given for the most part only where a work is mentioned for the first time, but such mentions can be traced by looking up the italicised entries under the modern author's name. The dates shown are A.D. unless otherwise indicated.

375